MASTERWORKS OF ECONOMICS

MASTERWORKS OF Economics

DIGESTS OF 10 GREAT CLASSICS

Edited by

Leonard Dalton Abbott

DOUBLEDAY & COMPANY, INC., GARDEN CITY, N. Y., 1946

PRINTED IN THE UNITED STATES
AT
THE COUNTRY LIFE PRESS, GARDEN CITY, N. Y.

CONTENTS

PREFACE BY THE EDITORS

THIS VOLUME is one of a series of books which will make available to the modern reader the key classics in each of the principal fields of knowledge.

The plan of this series is to devote one volume to each subject, such as Philosophy, Economics, Science, History, Government, and Autobiography, and to have each volume represent its field by authoritative condensations of ten to twelve famous books universally recognized as masterworks of human thought and knowledge. The names of the authors and the books have long been household words, but the books themselves are not generally known, and many of them are quite inaccessible to the public. With respect to each subject represented, one may say that seldom before have so many original documents of vital importance been brought together in a single volume. Many readers will welcome the opportunity of coming to know these masterworks at first hand through these comprehensive and carefully prepared condensations, which include the most significant and influential portion of each book—in the author's own words. Furthermore, the bringing together in one volume of the great classics in individual fields of knowledge will give the reader a broad view and a historical perspective of each subject.

Each volume of this series has a general introduction to the field with which it deals, and in addition each of the classics is preceded by a biographical introduction.

The plan and scope of the Masterworks Series are indicated by the classics selected for the present volume, "Masterworks of Economics," and for these five volumes which will follow:

MASTERWORKS OF PHILOSOPHY

Plato—*Dialogues*
Aristotle—*Nicomachean Ethics*
Bacon—*Novum Organum*
Descartes—*Principles of Philosophy*

Spinoza—*Ethics*
Locke—*Concerning Human Understanding*
Kant—*Critique of Pure Reason*
Schopenhauer—*The World as Will and Idea*
Nietzsche—*Beyond Good and Evil*
William James—*Pragmatism*
Henri Bergson—*Creative Evolution*

MASTERWORKS OF AUTOBIOGRAPHY

St. Augustine—*Confessions*
Benvenuto Cellini—*Autobiography*
Pepys—*Diary*
Benjamin Franklin—*Autobiography*
Rousseau—*Confessions*
Goethe—*Truth and Poetry*
Hans Christian Andersen—*The True Story of My Life*
Newman—*Apologia pro Vita Sua*
Tolstoy—*Childhood, Boyhood, Youth*
Henry Adams—*The Education of Henry Adams*

MASTERWORKS OF SCIENCE

Euclid—*Elements*
Archimedes—*Of Floating Bodies, and Other Propositions*
Copernicus—*On the Revolutions of the Heavenly Spheres*
Galileo—*Dialogues Concerning Two New Sciences*
Newton—*Principia*
Dalton—*The Atomic Theory*
Lyell—*Principles of Geology*
Darwin—*The Origin of Species*
Faraday—*Experimental Researches in Electricity*
Mendel—*Experiments in Plant Hybridization*
Mendeleyev—*The Periodic Law*
Curie—*Radioactivity*
Einstein—*Relativity: The Special and General Theory*

MASTERWORKS OF GOVERNMENT

Plato—*The Republic*
Aristotle—*Politics*
Machiavelli—*The Prince*
Grotius—*The Rights of War and Peace*
Hobbes—*Leviathan*

Locke—*Of Civil Government*
Montesquieu—*The Spirit of Laws*
Rousseau—*The Social Contract*
Hamilton—from *The Federalist*
Jefferson—on *Democracy*
Kropotkin—*The State: Its Historic Role*
Lenin—*The State and Revolution*
Wilson—on *The League of Nations*

MASTERWORKS OF HISTORY

Herodotus—*History*
Thucydides—*The Peloponnesian War*
Caesar—*The Gallic Wars*
Tacitus—*The Annals*
Bede—*Ecclesiastical History of the English People*
Gibbon—*The Decline and Fall of the Roman Empire*
Symonds—*Renaissance in Italy*
Macaulay—*The History of England*
Carlyle—*The French Revolution*
George Bancroft—*The History of the United States*
Charles A. and Mary R. Beard—*The Rise of American Civilization*

All these books have had a profound effect upon the thinking and activities of mankind. To know them is to partake of the world's great heritage of wisdom and achievement. Here, in the Masterworks Series, epoch-making ideas of past and present stand forth freshly and vividly—a modern presentation of the classics to the modern reader.

ALVIN JOHNSON, LL.D.
President Emeritus, The New School for Social Research
ROBERT ANDREWS MILLIKAN, SC.D.
Chairman of the Executive Council, California Institute of Technology
ALEXANDER MACLAREN WITHERSPOON, PH.D.
Associate Professor of English, Yale University

ACKNOWLEDGMENT

The editor wishes to thank the Viking Press, Inc., for permission to include the condensation of Veblen's "The Theory of the Leisure Class" in this volume. The pages of this condensation are from *The Theory of the Leisure Class* by Thorstein Veblen, by permission of the Viking Press, Inc., New York.

L. D. A.

ACKNOWLEDGMENT

The Editor wishes to thank the Viking Press, Inc., for permission to include the condensation of Veblen's "The Theory of the Leisure Class" in this volume. The pages of this condensation are from *The Theory of the Leisure Class* by Thorstein Veblen, by permission of the Viking Press, Inc., New York.

L. D. A.

MASTERWORKS OF ECONOMICS

INTRODUCTION

THE PURPOSE of this volume is to make some of the masterpieces of economic literature easily accessible. The works presented are worthy of anyone's concentrated study. Viewed as efforts to analyze and to interpret the increasingly complex forms which economic life has assumed since the early seventeenth century, they are fascinating. Regarded as signposts pointing the way to the social future, they are perhaps even more intriguing. In each case the books are offered in digest form.

The word "economics" came into general usage about fifty years ago; the subject suggests an essentially modern department of learning. Some three hundred years ago, when scholars were investigating the production, distribution, and consumption of wealth, they began to use the term "political economy." This term goes back to ancient Greece, but the ancient world had only fitful foreshadowings of economic science.

In 1615 Antoine de Montchrétien, French dramatist, poet, and hardware manufacturer, published his *Treatise on Political Economy,* the first attempt in modern times to evaluate economic principles. It is little more than a mercantilistic pamphlet, and it was dedicated to Louis XIII and the queen mother Marie de Médicis. The period in which Montchrétien lived marked a time when medieval conditions were rapidly giving way to those of modern life. Nationalism was the order of the day. Each country was trying, by means of tariffs and strict regulations, to promote its own prosperity. The rise of chartered companies and the opening up of world markets had made it possible for manufacturers and traders to amass great fortunes. These fortunes were concentrated in bullion, or "treasure," and the notion was widespread that the precious metals, gold and silver, were the sole repositories of wealth.

Mercantilism, a national policy before it was an economic doctrine, gave formal expression to this idea and carried with it, as a kind of corollary, a "balance of trade" theory according to which each country endeavored to export more than it imported and to receive payment in bullion. Among the first writers on mercantilism was Edward Misselden, a prominent English merchant of the early seventeenth century. One of its ablest exponents was another outstanding merchant, Thomas Mun, author of *England's Treasure by Foreign Trade,* published in 1664.

A powerful reaction against the tenets of mercantilism appeared in France among the physiocrats, or *économistes,* of the eighteenth century. In place of a nationalistic bias these French thinkers offered a cosmopolitan doctrine based on free trade and on competition. Against the mercantilistic conception of commerce they set the idea of agriculture. They taught that nature is the only source of wealth and that manufacturers, artificers, and merchants are "unproductive." They advocated a single tax on the net product (*produit net*) of land and proposed that industry and commerce be exempted from taxation.

The leading exponent of the physiocratic school was François Quesnay, court physician during the reign of Louis XV. His *Tableau économique,* published in 1768, attempts to show, by means of arithmetical formulas, how the products of agriculture would be distributed among the several classes of the community in a state of perfect liberty. To Quesnay's associate, Vincent de Gournay, is attributed the now proverbial phrase: *Laissez faire, laissez passer.* A third physiocratic writer, Turgot, finance minister of Louis XVI, wrote a book, *Reflections on the Formation and Distribution of Wealth,* published in 1766, in which he anticipated many of the doctrines that Adam Smith, a Scotsman, was to formulate in the *Wealth of Nations.*

Adam Smith's *Wealth of Nations* appeared in 1776. In a section of his book devoted to the analysis of systems of political economy, Smith takes up, first, the "principle of the mercantile system." He asserts that gold and silver "are to be bought for a certain price like all other commodities," and are therefore no more important than any other form of wealth. He goes on to pay a tribute to the "agricultural system" of M. Quesnay, whom he had met during a visit to France and whom he describes as "ingenious and profound." One feature in the physiocratic system he says he cannot accept—namely, the afore-mentioned doctrine that artificers, manufacturers, and merchants are unproductive. Apart from this feature he regards the system as "perhaps the nearest approximation to the truth that has yet been published upon the subject of political economy."

Like the physiocrats, with whom he had so much in common, Adam Smith was concerned with the "natural" laws of wealth. He believed in the beneficence of nature and he taught that all would be well with men if they knew how to grasp and to follow nature's laws. He recognized "an invisible hand" operating in human affairs, and he thought of this in terms of natural law. Few, if any, declarations of economic principle in any age have had more influence than Adam Smith's enunciation of the idea that every man, so long as he does not violate the laws of justice, should be "left perfectly free to pursue his own interest in his own way, and to bring both his industry and capital into competition with those of any other man, or order of men."

This attitude made a strong appeal to the manufacturers and merchants of the time; it almost seemed to be giving to their acquisitive ambitions and activities a kind of sanctity. The weak point in Adam Smith's philosophy, according to his critics, lay in its failure to allow sufficiently for the selfish and predatory instincts of humanity. Smith himself drew up a bill of exceptions to the beneficent workings of natural liberty. He gave his approval to the act of navigation instituted by Oliver Cromwell, on the ground that it was necessary for the defense of the country. He also approved of the imposition of duties on imported produce to counterbalance taxes levied at home on domestic produce of the same kind. Smith stood on the threshold of an industrial revolution occasioned by the use of steam and the invention of machinery. A rapidly expanding capitalistic economy was soon to decree the exploitation of large numbers of men, women, and children, who were compelled to work for long hours under insanitary conditions. The question has arisen: Would Smith have favored social legislation mitigating the hardships introduced by the factory system? A strong vein of sympathy with the working class runs through the *Wealth of Nations*. "No society," says Smith, "can surely be flourishing and happy, of which the far greater part of the members are poor and miserable. It is but equity, besides, that they who feed, clothe, and lodge the whole body of the people, should have such a share of the produce of their own labour as to be themselves well fed, clothed, and lodged."

Adam Smith was optimistic in his outlook, but his optimism was not shared by Malthus, Ricardo, and others of the so-called classical school of economists who followed him. Malthus, indeed, prefaces his *Essay on the Principle of Population,* published in 1798, with the statement that his view of human life "has a melancholy hue"; and Ricardo expressed his fear that the "progressive" state of society in which he lived might degenerate into a "stationary" state in which population would no longer increase and capital would no longer accumulate.

It has not been sufficiently recognized, perhaps, that Malthus' attitude left little, if any, room for progress. His apprehensions regarding the growth of population darkened his entire horizon. According to Malthus, the relationships existing in his time between landlord and tenant, employer and employee, master and servant, would not be substantially changed. For the "lower classes," as he put it, there was little hope for improvement other than that afforded by a diminishing birth rate. Some persons, Malthus clearly states, have a better right to existence than others; and the tendency of population is constantly to bring into the world human beings for whom nature refuses to provide, and who consequently "have not the slightest right to any share in the existing store of the necessaries of life"; whom she tells as interlopers to be gone, "and does not hesitate to extort by force obedience to her mandates," employing for that purpose "hunger and pestilence, war and crime, mortality and neglect of infantine life, prostitution, and syphilis."

Ricardo's tone is entirely different, but can hardly be described as cheerful. There was something almost inhuman in his detachment. Yet although, like Malthus, he took a somber view of human affairs, his doctrines were destined to open the way to dynamic social philosophies aiming at economic improvement. His *Principles of Political Economy and Taxation,* published in 1817, starts with a chapter in which he lays down the proposition: "The value of a commodity, or the quantity of any other commodity for which it will exchange, depends on the relative quantity of labour which is necessary for its production." This conception of value as embodied labor was later to be turned to revolutionary ends by Karl Marx and other socialistic thinkers. In the second chapter of Ricardo's *Principles* we get the "differential" theory of rent which carried his name to the ends of the earth and which has been discussed in hundreds of books and essays. This is, in effect, that the rent of land is determined by the excess of its produce over that which the same application can secure from the least productive land in use. Or, to put it in another way, the differences between production costs on soil of maximum fertility and those on less fertile soil give rise to a differential income in favor of the owners of the more fertile soil. The Ricardian theory, which easily fits into a concept of "unearned increment," was used by Henry George to support his arguments in behalf of the single tax.

Five years before the publication of Adam Smith's *Wealth of Nations* a man was born in Wales who was destined to exert a strong influence on both the practical and theoretical sides of economic development. His name was Robert Owen. Like Mun and Turgot, he played a prominent part in practical affairs. He succeeded not only in making money in his cotton mills but also in establishing model working and living conditions for the men, women, and children whom he employed. Unlike Smith, Owen saw an unrestrained, laissez-faire economy bringing poverty and disease to thousands.

It was not until he became a crusader that Owen tasted defeat, first in an effort to persuade the British Parliament to pass the kind of legislation that he wanted, and, secondly, in the management of his communistic colony in New Harmony, Indiana. He discovered that human nature is stubborn and that social progress is slow.

Owen's economic philosophy found its most complete expression in *A New View of Society* (1813). The word socialism was first used by

Owen and his followers. He was later called a "utopian" socialist by Karl Marx. It was Owen's hope that "villages of co-operation" might be instituted by the state or the poor law authorities or, in default of state action, by philanthropic subscription. When his communistic experiments failed, he turned to trade-unionism, to labor exchanges, and to consumers' co-operation. These movements, however, appealed to him not as ends in themselves but as steps toward the building of a co-operative order of society.

The ideas of Robert Owen, Saint-Simon, Fourier, and other so-called utopian socialists on the possibilities of co-operation in economic life influenced the thinking of John Stuart Mill to the extent that he injected large humanitarian considerations into his economic analyses. He believed in using governmental powers to bring about a wider diffusion of property. One of the fiscal reforms that he favored was taxation and regulation of inheritances and bequests in such a way as to break up large fortunes. Another was a plan for appropriating the unearned increment of land. But Mill, also influenced by Ricardo, was ever trying to reconcile the seemingly opposite doctrines of competition, in which he believed, and of co-operation, which he also held to be necessary. He looked forward to a marked improvement in the condition of wageworkers, and he believed that the working class was destined to play an increasingly important role in the development of society. It is as a connecting link between Adam Smith, Malthus, and Ricardo, on the one hand, and Karl Marx and Henry George, on the other, that John Stuart Mill is chiefly significant.

In the five books and seventy-three chapters of Mill's own *Principles of Political Economy,* published in 1848, we can see a mind divided. Mill radically modified the older and fatalistic conception of "economic man" molded by his environment, and put in its place a conception of man creating the world anew. Where Adam Smith had seen only a sequence of events in nature, Mill saw the living human will operating.

Emphasis on what Mill called the "probable futurity of the working classes" found militant expression in Karl Marx's *Capital,* published in 1867. No two thinkers could have been more unlike, temperamentally, than John Stuart Mill and Karl Marx, yet both made important contributions to the collectivist trend.

It is interesting to note that Marx, in his intense reaction from "utopianism," chose to align himself with Adam Smith and Ricardo rather than with his socialistic predecessors Owen, Saint-Simon, and Fourier. He knew, of course, that Smith and Ricardo were individualists, committed in large degree to a philosophy of "laissez faire." But, in Marx's view, their penetrating analyses of what he regarded as the evolving capitalistic order of society were indispensable to the further development of economic science. A third thinker, the German philosopher Hegel, whom Marx had studied in his youth, furnished the idea of "dialectic," another indispensable element in Marx's philosophy.

The word dialectic comes from a Greek word meaning the art of disputation and the discrimination of truth from error. In Hegel's philosophy, which was rooted, like Charles Darwin's biological philosophy, in the idea of development, thesis and antithesis are succeeded by synthesis. The underlying conception of both Hegel's and Marx's dialectic is that one-sided tendencies correct one another—that truth is born of the conflict of ideas, and that justice is born of the conflict of forces in actual life. Marx applied this conception to the "class struggle" of capitalists and wage-workers. He believed that the capitalist system is based on exploitation and that its irreconcilable conflicts will lead to its dissolution. Just as slavery passed into serfdom, and as feudalism passed into capitalism, so, according to Marx, capitalism in its turn will pass into socialism. Hegel was a philosophical idealist and Marx was a philosophical materialist, but this fact does not interfere with Marx's acknowledgment of his intellectual debt to Hegel. "The mystification which dialectic suffers in Hegel's hands," says Marx in his preface to the second German edition of *Capital,* "by no means prevents him from being the first to present its general form of working in a comprehensive and conscious manner. With him it is standing on its head. It must be turned right side up again, if you would discover the rational kernel within the mystical shell."

Capital is nothing if it is not a fighting book. Marx admires Adam Smith and Ricardo up to certain points, but he emphasizes what he regards as their limitations. He accuses Malthus of "shameless plagiarism"; he says that John Stuart Mill represents "a shallow syncretism"; and he characterizes Jeremy Bentham as "that insipid, pedantic, leather-tongued oracle of the ordinary bourgeois intelligence of the nineteenth century."

Implicit in *Capital* are Marx's economic interpretation of history, his theory of economic crises, and his confidence in the ultimate triumph of the working class. Some of his prophecies have not been fulfilled and some of his theorems are not demonstrable, but his mental energy and his passionate championship of the rights of workingmen are still a vital force in human affairs. At the core of his doctrine is the idea of surplus value, which he may or may not have exaggerated. According to his collaborator Frederick Engels, the originality of Marx lies in his discovery not of the labor theory of value or of the conception of surplus value—these he took from the school of Ricardo—but of the fact that "the transformation of money into capital is based on the purchase and sale of labor power."

Henry George's *Progress and Poverty,* published in 1879, marked a shift of emphasis from the capital-labor relationship to land. George interprets labor and capital in terms of partnership rather than of antagonism, and he draws on Ricardo's differential theory of rent rather than on his theory of value. The Malthusian theory he scorns. He says: "The reason why, in spite of the increase of productive power, wages constantly tend to a minimum which will give but a bare living, is that, with increase in productive power, rent tends to even greater increase, thus producing a constant tendency to the forcing down of wages."

The single tax on land values which Henry George proposed may appropriately be viewed as a reversion, in a later generation and in a different setting, to the *impôt unique* of the French physiocrats. It was also an effort to return to "natural liberty" and to check the advance of socialism.

After Henry George, the economic doctrines of Thorstein Veblen, author of *The Theory of the Leisure Class* (1899) and *The Engineers and the Price System* (1921), exhibited new and startling tendencies. Veblen had no respect for modern civilization. He saw in social development a culture struggle rather than a class struggle. Man's vanity, as well as his economic interest, is involved. According to Veblen, the production of goods under capitalism is motivated by the desire to get money, and in the last resort goods are subordinated to money. The acquisitive instinct, the habits of the merchant, vested interests, absentee ownership, are making, he said, the industrial system more and more unworkable. Technological inventions are throwing multitudes out of work. Periods of prosperity are followed by periods of depression. Industrial friction within nations and between nations inevitably leads to wars.

There is no clear alternative, in Veblen's writings, to the present economic system. He was not an enthusiast or a propagandist. All he would say was that the present grows out of the past and that the future will grow out of the present. Some form of "technocracy" seemed to be the logic of his attitude, and by technocracy he meant a system in which the engineers (conceived of in an immensely extended sense) would dominate production and distribution.

For more than three centuries—from 1615, the year of the publication of Antoine de Montchrétien's *Treatise on Political Economy,* to 1921, the year of the publication of Thorstein Veblen's *Engineers and the Price System*—the economic pendulum has been swinging between liberty and legislation, between competition and co-operation, between capitalism and some form of collectivism. The debate is still going on. While neither side in innumerable disputes can be said to have won complete victories, we are bound to recognize that, during the period covered by this book, society, in America as well as in most of the European countries, has been moving towards economic democracy and the extension of government functions. Ideas that would once have seemed revolutionary are now regarded as commonplace. Labor unions have been legalized; factory laws and employers' liability acts have been passed; social-security legislation has been enacted; old-age pensions are granted.

Economic science may be still in its infancy, but its masterworks, as presented in these pages, have inspired, and are still inspiring, the policies of nations. With the groundwork already established, it is reasonable to predict that political economy will achieve a greater and greater clarity, and will contribute, in an increasing degree, to human welfare.

ENGLAND'S TREASURE BY FOREIGN TRADE

by

THOMAS MUN

CONTENTS

England's Treasure by Foreign Trade

THOMAS MUN

1571–1641

THOMAS MUN was the son of a London merchant of Queen Elizabeth's time. He enjoyed the advantages of wealth and education and was early engaged in mercantile affairs in the Mediterranean region, especially in Italy and the Levant. In his *England's Treasure by Foreign Trade* (or *England's Treasure by Forraign Trade,* as the title is spelled in Mun's archaic English) he describes the growth of the port of Leghorn as he personally observed it, and tells how Ferdinand I, grand duke of Tuscany, lent him forty thousand crowns, free of interest, for transmission to Turkey, where he was about to obtain merchandise for Italy. In 1615, as a well-known merchant, he was elected a member of the East India Company. From that time on he was active in promoting the interests of the company.

In 1621 Mun published a book entitled *A Discourse of Trade, from England unto the East-Indies; answering to diverse Objections which are usually made against the same.* The purpose of this book was to meet the growing criticism of methods employed by the East India Company and, in particular, to defend the right of the company to export bullion.

The period was one in which the "bullionists" held full sway. The reigning economic doctrine was that money, if not the chief form of wealth, was at least its chief embodiment, and that the wealth of a country was best represented by the amount of coin and bullion within its borders. In support of this doctrine the English government had legally prohibited the exportation of specie and had attempted to control not only international exchange but also the individual transactions of merchants in their commerce with foreign nations. The entire issue had been dramatized when, in 1613, one of the ships of the East India Company, carrying a large amount of bullion, had been shipwrecked.

It was Thomas Mun's contention that the government policy was based on false premises. The East India trade, he argued, was profitable to England because it brought into the country necessary and useful commodities which could be purchased elsewhere only at a higher cost. He maintained that a large proportion of these goods were re-exported at a profit, so that the net result was an inflow rather than an outflow of bullion.

The ensuing debate—the first important economic controversy in England—involved Gerard de Malynes, an assay master at the English mint, and Edward Misselden, a prominent member of the rich and powerful merchandising company known as the Merchants Adventurers. Malynes, a bullionist, attacked Mun's argument, while Misselden defended it along lines which anticipated Mun's subsequent position.

Mun's second and best-known book, *England's Treasure by Foreign Trade, or, the Balance of our Foreign Trade Is the Rule of our Treasure,* was written about 1630 but was not published until after his death. It broke definitely with bullionist doctrines and laid the foundations for what was coming to be known as the mercantilist position.

The mercantilists were nationalists in an era in which the emergence of nations was all-important. They were called mercantilists because they held that England's prosperity was bound up in the possibilities of foreign commerce or merchandising. What they sought to achieve was a system of industrial protection that would develop to the utmost the national resources. For Mun, as for every mercantilist, the index of prosperity was to be found not in a "balance of bargain" (based on the regulation of individual transactions) but in a "balance of trade" which would encourage exports in the mass and restrict imports in the mass.

Mun declares in *England's Treasure* that the object of national policy should be "to sell more to strangers yearly than we consume of theirs in value." He compares the prudence of a kingdom with that of a private person, and argues that just as an individual can get rich only by spending less than his income, so also a nation can get rich only if it spends (imports) less than it sells (exports).

In a series of clear admonitions he advises England to cultivate its wastelands, to reduce consumption of foreign wares and avoid frivolous changes of fashion, to be clever in selling to foreign nations, and to ship only in English bottoms. He recommends that taxes be removed from raw materials used in manufacturing of later exports, and is confident that this advice, if followed, "will turn to the profit of the kingdom in the balance of trade, and thereby also enable the King to lay up the more treasure." Mun recognizes that non-commodity items affect the direction and amount of the balance of trade paid in bullion, and specifically lists "the expences of travelers, the gifts to Ambassadors and Strangers, the fraud of some rich goods not entered into the Custom-house, the gain which is made here by Strangers by change and re-change, Interest of money, insurance upon Englishmen's goods and their lives."

In reproducing Mun's treatise, which follows, the editor has taken the liberty of modernizing the spelling of such words as might be confusing to the reader. However, the original spelling and capitalization have been retained where there can be no question of the meaning.

ENGLAND'S TREASURE BY FOREIGN TRADE

1. The means to enrich this Kingdom, and to increase our Treasure

ALTHOUGH a Kingdom may be enriched by gifts received, or by purchase taken from some other Nations, yet these are things uncertain and of small consideration when they happen. The ordinary means therefore to increase our wealth and treasure is by *Foreign Trade,* wherein we must ever observe this rule; to sell more to strangers yearly than we consume of theirs in value. For suppose that when this Kingdom is plentifully served with the Cloth, Lead, Tin, Iron, Fish and other native commodities, we do yearly export the overplus to foreign Countries to the value of twenty two hundred thousand pounds; by which means we are enabled beyond the Seas to buy and bring in foreign wares for our use and Consumptions, to the value of twenty hundred thousand pounds; By this order duly kept in our trading, we may rest assured that the Kingdom shall be enriched yearly two hundred thousand pounds, which must be brought to us in so much Treasure; because that part of our stock which is not returned to us in wares must necessarily be brought home in treasure.

For in this case it cometh to pass in the stock of a Kingdom, as in the estate of a private man; who is supposed to have one thousand pounds yearly revenue and two thousand pounds of ready money in his Chest: If such a man through excess shall spend one thousand five hundred pounds *per annum,* all his ready money will be gone in four years; and in the like time his said money will be doubled if he take a Frugal course to spend but five hundred pounds *per annum;* which rule never faileth likewise in the Commonwealth, but in some cases (of no great moment) which I will hereafter declare, when I shall show by whom and in what manner this balance of the Kingdom's account ought to be drawn up yearly, or so often as it shall please the State to discover how much we gain or lose by trade with foreign Nations. But first I will say something concerning those ways and means which will increase our exportations and diminish our importations of wares; which being done,

I will then set down some other arguments both affirmative and negative to strengthen that which is here declared, and thereby to show that all the other means which are commonly supposed to enrich the Kingdom with Treasure are altogether insufficient and mere fallacies.

2. *The particular ways and means to increase the exportation of our commodities, and to decrease our Consumption of foreign wares*

The revenue or stock of a Kingdom by which it is provided of foreign wares is either *Natural* or *Artificial*. The Natural wealth is so much only as can be spared from our own use and necessities to be exported unto strangers. The Artificial consists in our manufactures and industrious trading with foreign commodities, concerning which I will set down such particulars as may serve for the cause we have in hand.

1. First, although this Realm be already exceeding rich by nature, yet might it be much increased by laying the waste grounds (which are infinite) into such employments as should no way hinder the present revenues of other manured lands, but hereby to supply our selves and prevent the importations of Hemp, Flax, Cordage, Tobacco, and divers other things which now we fetch from strangers to our great impoverishing.

2. We may likewise diminish our importations, if we would soberly refrain from excessive consumption of foreign wares in our diet and raiment, with such often change of fashions as is used, so much the more to increase the waste and charge; which vices at this present are more notorious amongst us than in former ages. Yet might they easily be amended by enforcing the observation of such good laws as are strictly practised in other Countries against the said excesses; where likewise by commanding their own manufactures to be used, they prevent the coming in of others, without prohibition, or offence to strangers in their mutual commerce.

3. In our exportations we must not only regard our own superfluities, but also we must consider our neighbours' necessities, that so upon the wares which they cannot want, nor yet be furnished thereof elsewhere, we may (besides the vent of the Materials) gain so much of the manufacture as we can, and also endeavour to sell them dear, so far forth as the high price cause not a less vent in the quantity. But the superfluity of our commodities which strangers use, and may also have the same from other Nations, or may abate their vent by the use of some such like wares from other places, and with little inconvenience; we must in this case strive to sell as cheap as possible we can, rather than to lose the utterance of such wares. For we have found of late years by good experience, that

being able to sell our Cloth cheap in Turkey, we have greatly increased the vent thereof, and the *Venetians* have lost as much in the utterance of theirs in those Countries, because it is dearer. And on the other side a few years past, when by the excessive price of Wools our Cloth was exceeding dear, we lost at the least half our clothing for foreign parts, which since is no otherwise (well near) recovered again than by the great fall of price for Wools and Cloth. We find that twenty five in the hundred less in the price of these and some other Wares, to the loss of private men's revenues, may raise above fifty upon the hundred in the quantity vented to the benefit of the public. For when Cloth is dear, other Nations do presently practise clothing, and we know they want neither art nor materials to this performance. But when by cheapness we drive them from this employment, and so in time obtain our dear price again, then do they also use their former remedy. So that by these alterations we learn, that it is in vain to expect a greater revenue of our wares than their condition will afford, but rather it concerns us to apply our endeavours to the times with care and diligence to help our selves the best we may, by making our cloth and other manufactures without deceit, which will increase their estimation and use.

4. The value of our exportations likewise may be much advanced when we perform it our selves in our own Ships, for then we get only not the price of our wares as they are worth here, but also the Merchants' gains, the charges of insurance, and freight to carry them beyond the seas. As for example, if the *Italian* Merchants should come hither in their own shipping to fetch our Corn, our red Herrings or the like, in this case the Kingdom should have ordinarily but 25s. for a quarter of Wheat, and 20s. for a barrel of red herrings, whereas if we carry these wares our selves into *Italy* upon the said rates, it is likely that we shall obtain fifty shillings for the first, and forty shillings for the last, which is a great difference in the utterance or vent of the Kingdom's stock. And although it is true that the commerce ought to be free to strangers to bring in and carry out at their pleasure, yet nevertheless in many places the exportation of victuals and munition are either prohibited, or at least limited to be done only by the people and Shipping of those places where they abound.

5. The frugal expending likewise of our own natural wealth might advance much yearly to be exported unto strangers; and if in our raiment we will be prodigal, yet let this be done with our own materials and manufactures, as Cloth, Lace, Embroideries, Cutworks and the like, where the excess of the rich may be the employment of the poor, whose labours notwithstanding of this kind, would be more profitable for the Commonwealth, if they were done to the use of strangers.

6. The Fishing in his Majesty's seas of *England, Scotland* and *Ireland* is our natural wealth, and would cost nothing but labour, which the

Dutch bestow willingly, and thereby draw yearly a very great profit to themselves by serving many places of Christendom with our Fish, for which they return and supply their wants both of foreign Wares and Money, besides the multitude of Mariners and Shipping, which hereby are maintain'd, whereof a long discourse might be made to show the particular manage of this important business. Our Fishing plantation likewise in *New-England, Virginia, Greenland,* the *Summer Islands* and the *New-found-land,* are of the like nature, affording much wealth and employments to maintain a great number of poor, and to increase our decaying trade.

7. A Staple or Magazine for foreign Corn, Indigo, Spices, Raw-silks, Cotton wool or any other commodity whatsoever, to be imported will increase Shipping, Trade, Treasure, and the King's customs, by exporting them again where need shall require, which course of Trading, hath been the chief means to raise *Venice, Genoa,* the *low-Countries,* with some others; and for such a purpose *England* stands most commodiously, wanting nothing to this performance but our own diligence and endeavour.

8. Also we ought to esteem and cherish those trades which we have in remote or far Countries, for besides the increase of Shipping and Mariners thereby, the wares also sent thither and receiv'd from thence are far more profitable unto the kingdom than by our trades near at hand; As for example; suppose Pepper to be worth here two Shillings the pound constantly, if then it be brought from the *Dutch* at *Amsterdam,* the Merchant may give there twenty pence the pound, and gain well by the bargain; but if he fetch this Pepper from the *East-indies,* he must not give above three pence the pound at the most, which is a mighty advantage, not only in that part which serveth for our own use, but also for that great quantity which (from hence) we transport yearly unto divers other Nations to be sold at a higher price: whereby it is plain, that we make a far greater stock by gain upon these *Indian* Commodities, than those Nations do where they grow, and to whom they properly appertain, being the natural wealth of their Countries. But for the better understanding of this particular, we must ever distinguish between the gain of the Kingdom, and the profit of the Merchant; for although the Kingdom payeth no more for this Pepper than is before supposed, nor for any other commodity bought in foreign parts more than the stranger receiveth from us for the same, yet the Merchant payeth not only that price, but also the freight, insurance, customs and other charges which are exceeding great in these long voyages; but yet all these in the Kingdom's account are but commutations among ourselves, and no Privation of the Kingdom's stock, which being duly considered, together with the support also of our other trades in our best Shipping to *Italy, France, Turkey,* the *East Countries* and other places, by transporting and venting the wares which

we bring yearly from the *East Indies;* It may well stir up our utmost endeavours to maintain and enlarge this great and noble business, so much importing the Public wealth, Strength, and Happiness. Neither is there less honour and judgment by growing rich (in this manner) upon the stock of other Nations, than by an industrious increase of our own means, especially when this latter is advanced by the benefit of the former, as we have found in the *East Indies* by sale of much of our Tin, Cloth, Lead and other Commodities, the vent whereof doth daily increase in those Countries which formerly had no use of our wares.

9. It would be very beneficial to export money as well as wares, being done in trade only, it would increase our Treasure; but of this I write more largely in the next Chapter to prove it plainly.

10. It were policy and profit for the State to suffer manufactures made of foreign Materials to be exported custom-free, as Velvets and all other wrought Silks, Fustians, thrown Silks and the like, it would employ very many poor people, and much increase the value of our stock yearly issued into other Countries, and it would (for this purpose) cause the more foreign Materials to be brought in, to the improvement of His Majesty's Customs. I will here remember a notable increase in our manufacture of winding and twisting only of foreign raw Silk, which within 35 years to my knowledge did not employ more than 300 people in the City and suburbs of London, where at this present time it doth set on work above fourteen thousand souls, as upon diligent enquiry hath been credibly reported unto His Majesty's Commissioners for Trade. And it is certain, that if the said foreign Commodities might be exported from hence, free of custom, this manufacture would yet increase very much, and decrease as fast in *Italy* and in the *Netherlands.* But if any man allege the *Dutch* proverb, *Live and let others live;* I answer, that the Dutchmen notwithstanding their own Proverb, do not only in these Kingdoms, encroach upon our livings, but also in other foreign parts of our trade (where they have power) they do hinder and destroy us in our lawful course of living, hereby taking the bread out of our mouth, which we shall never prevent by plucking the pot from their nose, as of late years too many of us do practise to the great hurt and dishonour of this famous Nation; We ought rather to imitate former times in taking sober and worthy courses more pleasing to God and suitable to our ancient reputation.

11. It is needful also not to charge the native commodities with too great customs, lest by endearing them to the stranger's use, it hinder their vent. And especially foreign wares brought in to be transported again should be favoured, for otherwise that manner of trading (so much importing the good of the Commonwealth) cannot prosper nor subsist. But the Consumption of such foreign wares in the Realm may be the

more charged, which will turn to the profit of the kingdom in the *Balance of the Trade,* and thereby also enable the King to lay up the more Treasure out of his yearly incomes.

12. Lastly, in all things we must endeavour to make the most we can of our own, whether it be *Natural* or *Artificial;* And forasmuch as the people which live by the Arts are far more in number than they who are masters of the fruits, we ought the more carefully to maintain those endeavours of the multitude, in whom doth consist the greatest strength and riches both of King and Kingdom: for where the people are many, and the arts good, there the traffic must be great, and the Country rich. The *Italians* employ a greater number of people, and get more money by their industry and manufactures of the raw Silks of the Kingdom of *Cicilia,* than the King of *Spain* and his Subjects have by the revenue of this rich commodity. But what need we fetch the example so far, when we know that our own natural wares do not yield us so much profit as our industry? For Iron ore in the Mines is of no great worth, when it is compared with the employment and advantage it yields being digged, tried, transported, bought, sold, cast into Ordnance, Muskets, and many other instruments of war for offence and defence, wrought into Anchors, bolts, spikes, nails and the like, for the use of Ships, Houses, Carts, Coaches, Ploughs, and other instruments for Tillage. Compare our Fleece-wools with our Cloth, which requires shearing, washing, carding, spinning, Weaving, fulling, dying, dressing and other trimmings, and we shall find these Arts more profitable than the natural wealth, whereof I might instance other examples, but I will not be more tedious, for if I would amplify upon this and the other particulars before written, I might find matter sufficient to make a large volume, but my desire in all is only to prove what I propound with brevity and plainness.

3. *The Exportation of our Moneys in Trade of Merchandize is a means to increase our Treasure*

This Position is so contrary to the common opinion, that it will require many and strong arguments to prove it before it can be accepted of the Multitude, who bitterly exclaim when they see any monies carried out of the Realm; affirming thereupon that we have absolutely lost so much Treasure, and that this is an act directly against the long continued laws made and confirmed by the wisdom of this Kingdom in the High Court of Parliament, and that many places, nay *Spain* it self which is the Fountain of Money, forbids the exportation thereof, some cases only excepted. To all which I might answer, that *Venice, Florence, Genoa,* the *Low Countries* and divers other places permit it, their people applaud it, and find great benefit by it; but all this makes a noise and proves nothing, we must therefore come to those reasons which concern the business in question.

First, I will take that for granted which no man of judgment will deny, that we have no other means to get Treasure but by foreign trade, for Mines we have none which do afford it, and how this money is gotten in the managing of our said Trade I have already showed, that it is done by making our commodities which are exported yearly to over balance in value the foreign wares which we consume; so that it resteth only to show how our moneys may be added to our commodities, and being jointly exported may so much the more increase our Treasure.

We have already supposed our yearly consumptions of foreign wares to be for the value of twenty hundred thousand pounds, and our exportations to exceed that two hundred thousand pounds, which sum we have thereupon affirmed is brought to us in treasure to balance the account. But now if we add three hundred thousand pounds more in ready money unto our former exportations in wares, what profit can we have (will some men say) although by this means we should bring in so much ready money more than we did before, seeing that we have carried out the like value.

To this the answer is, that when we have prepared our exportations of wares, and sent out as much of every thing as we can spare or vent abroad: It is not therefore said that then we should add our money thereunto to fetch in the more money immediately, but rather first to enlarge our trade by enabling us to bring in more foreign wares, which being sent out again will in due time much increase our Treasure.

For although in this manner we do yearly multiply our importations to the maintenance of more Shipping and Mariners, improvement of His Majesty's Customs and other benefits: yet our consumption of those foreign wares is no more than it was before; so that all the said increase of commodities brought in by the means of our ready money sent out as is afore written, doth in the end become an exportation unto us of a far greater value than our said moneys were, which is proved by three several examples following.

1. For I suppose that 100000. *l.* being sent in our Shipping to the East Countries, will buy there one hundred thousand quarters of wheat clear aboard the Ships, which being after brought into *England* and housed, to export the same at the best time for vent thereof in *Spain* or *Italy,* it cannot yield less in those parts than two hundred thousand pounds to make the Merchant but a saver, yet by this reckoning we see the Kingdom hath doubled that Treasure.

2. Again this profit will be far greater when we trade thus in remote Countries, as for example, if we send one hundred thousand pounds into

the *East-Indies* to buy Pepper there, and bring it hither, and from hence send it for *Italy* or *Turkey,* it must yield seven hundred thousand pounds at least in those places, in regard of the excessive charge which the Merchant disburseth in those long voyages in Shipping, Wages, Victuals, Insurance, Interest, Customs, Imposts, and the like, all which notwithstanding the King and the Kingdom gets.

3. But where the voyages are short & the wares rich, which therefore will not employ much Shipping, the profit will be far less. As when another hundred thousand pounds shall be employed in *Turkey* in raw Silks, and brought hither to be after transported from hence into *France,* the *Low Countries,* or *Germany,* the Merchant shall have good gain, although he sell it there but for one hundred and fifty thousand pounds: and thus take the voyages altogether in their *Medium,* the moneys exported will be returned unto us more than Trebled. But if any man will yet object, that these returns come to us in wares, and not really in money as they were issued out,

The answer is (keeping our first ground) that if our consumption of foreign wares be no more yearly than is already supposed, and that our exportations be so mightily increased by this manner of Trading with ready money as is before declared: It is not then possible but that all the over-balance or difference should return either in money or in such wares as we must export again, which, as is already plainly showed will be still a greater means to increase our Treasure.

For it is in the stock of the Kingdom as in the estates of private men, who having store of wares, do not therefore say that they will not venture out or trade with their money (for this were ridiculous) but do also turn that into wares, whereby they multiply their Money, and so by a continual and orderly change of one into the other grow rich, and when they please turn all their estates into Treasure; for they that have Wares cannot want money.

Neither is it said that Money is the Life of Trade, as if it could not subsist without the same; for we know that there was great trading by way of commutation or barter when there was little money stirring in the world. The *Italians* and some other Nations have such remedies against this want, that it can neither decay nor hinder their trade, for they transfer bills of debt, and have Banks both public and private, wherein they do assign their credits from one to another daily for very great sums with ease and satisfaction by writings only, whilst in the mean time the Mass of Treasure which gave foundation to these credits is employed in Foreign Trade as a Merchandize, and by the said means they have little other use of money in those countries more than for their ordinary expences. It is not therefore the keeping of our money in the Kingdom, but the necessity and use of our wares in foreign Countries, and our want of their commodities that causeth the vent and consumption on all sides, which makes a quick and ample Trade. If we were once poor, and now having gained some store of money by trade with resolution to keep it still in the Realm; shall this cause other Nations to spend more of our commodities than formerly they have done, whereby we might say that our trade is Quickened and Enlarged? no verily, it will produce no such good effect: but rather according to the alteration of times by their true causes we may expect the contrary; for all men do consent that plenty of money in a Kingdom doth make the native commodities dearer, which as it is to the profit of some private men in their revenues, so is it directly against the benefit of the Public in the quantity of the trade; for as plenty of money makes wares dearer, so dear wares decline their use and consumption, as hath been already plainly showed in the last Chapter upon that particular of our cloth; And although this is a very hard lesson for some great landed men to learn, yet I am sure it is a true lesson for all the land to observe, lest when we have gained some store of money by trade, we lose it again by not trading with our money. I knew a Prince in *Italy* (of famous memory) *Ferdinando the first,* great Duke of *Tuscanie,* who being very rich in Treasure, endeavoured therewith to enlarge his trade by issuing out to his Merchants great sums of money for very small profit; I my self had forty thousand crowns of him *gratis* for a whole year, although he knew that I would presently send it away in *Specie* for the parts of *Turkey* to be employed in wares for his Countries, he being well assured that in this course of trade it would return again (according to the old saying) with a Duck in the mouth: This noble and industrious Prince by his care and diligence to countenance and favour Merchants in their affairs, did so increase the practice thereof, but there is scarce a Nobleman or Gentleman in all his dominions that doth not Merchandize either by himself or in partnership with others, whereby within these thirty years the trade to his port of *Leghorn* is so much increased, that of a poor little town (as I my self knew it) it is now become a fair and strong City, being one of the most famous places for trade in all Christendom. And yet it is worthy our observation, that the multitude of Ships and wares which come thither from *England,* the *Low Countries,* and other places have little or no means to make their returns from thence but only in ready money, which they may and do carry away freely at all times, to the incredible advantage of the said great Duke of *Tuscanie* and his subjects, who are much enriched by the continual great concourse of Merchants from all the States of the neighbour Princes, bringing them plenty of money daily to supply their wants of the said wares. And thus we see that the current of Merchandize which carries away their Treasure, becomes a flowing stream to fill them again in a greater measure with money.

There is yet an objection or two as weak as all the rest: that is, if we trade with our Money we shall issue out the less wares; as if a man should say, those Countries which heretofore had occasion to consume our Cloth, Lead, Tin, Iron, Fish, and the like, shall now make use of our monies in the place of those necessaries, which were most absurd to affirm, or that the Merchant had not rather carry out wares by which there is ever some gains expected, than to export money which is still but the same without any increase.

But on the contrary there are many Countries which may yield us very profitable trade for our money, which otherwise afford us no trade at all, because they have no use of our wares, as namely the *East-Indies* for one in the first beginning thereof, although since by industry in our commerce with those Nations we have brought them into the use of much of our Lead, Cloth, Tin, and other things, which is a good addition to the former vent of our commodities.

Again, some men have alleged that those Countries which permit money to be carried out, do it because they have few or no wares to trade withal: but we have great store of commodities, and therefore their action ought not to be our example.

To this the answer is briefly, that if we have such a quantity of wares as doth fully provide us of all things needful from beyond the seas: why should we then doubt that our moneys sent out in trade, must not necessarily come back again in treasure; together with the great gains which it may procure in such manner as is before set down? And on the other side, if those Nations which send out their monies do it because they have but few wares of their own, how come they then to have so much Treasure as we ever see in those places which suffer it freely to be exported at all times and by whomsoever? I answer, *Even by trading with their Moneys;* for by what other means can they get it, having no Mines of Gold or Silver?

Thus may we plainly see, that when this weighty business is duly considered in his end. as all our humane actions ought well to be weighed, it is found much contrary to that which most men esteem thereof, because they search no further than the beginning of the work, which misinforms their judgments, and leads them into error: For if we only behold the actions of the husbandman in the seed-time when he casteth away much good corn into the ground, we will rather account him a mad man than a husbandman: but when we consider his labours in the harvest which is the end of his endeavours, we find the worth and plentiful increase of his actions.

4. *Foreign Trade is the only means to improve the price of our Lands*

It is a common saying, that plenty or scarcity of money makes all things dear or good or cheap; and this money is either gotten or lost in foreign trade by the over or under-balancing of the same, as I have already showed. It resteth now that I distinguish the seeming plenties of money from that which is only substantial and able to perform the work: For there are divers ways and means whereby to procure plenty of money into a Kingdom, which do not enrich but rather impoverish the same by the several inconveniences which ever accompany such alterations.

As first, if we melt down our plate into Coin (which suits not with the Majesty of so great a Kingdom, except in cases of great extremity) it would cause Plenty of money for a time, yet should we be nothing the richer, but rather this treasure being thus altered is made the more apt to be carried out of the Kingdom, if we exceed our means by excess in foreign wares, or maintain a war by Sea or Land, where we do not feed and clothe the Soldier and supply the armies with our own native provisions, by which disorders our treasure will soon be exhausted.

Again, if we think to bring in store of money by suffering foreign Coins to pass current at higher rates than their intrinsic value compared with our Standard, or by debasing or by enhancing our own moneys, all these have their several inconveniences and difficulties, but admitting that by this means plenty of money might be brought into the Realm, yet should we be nothing the richer, neither can such treasure so gotten long remain with us. For if the stranger or the English Merchants bring in this money, it must be done upon a valuable consideration, either for wares carried out already, or after to be exported, which helps us nothing except the evil occasions of excess or war aforenamed be removed which do exhaust our treasure: for otherwise, what one man bringeth for gain, another man shall be forced to carry out for necessity; because there shall ever be a necessity to balance our Accounts with strangers, although it should be done with loss upon the rate of the money, and Confiscation also if it be intercepted by the Law.

The conclusion of this business is briefly thus. That as the treasure which is brought into the Realm by the balance of our foreign trade is that money which only doth abide with us, and by which we are enriched: so by this plenty of money thus gotten (and no otherwise) do our Lands improve. For when the Merchant hath a good dispatch beyond the Seas for his Cloth and other wares, he doth presently return to buy up the greater quantity, which raiseth the price of our Wools and other commodities, and consequently doth improve the Landlords' Rents as the Leases expire daily: And also by this means money being gained, and brought more abundantly into the Kingdom, it doth enable many men to buy Lands, which will make them the dearer. But if our foreign trade come to a stop or declination by neglect at home or injuries abroad, whereby the Merchants are impoverished, and thereby the wares of the Realm less issued, then do all the said benefits cease, and our Lands fall of price daily.

5. *The diversity of gain by Foreign Trade*

In the course of foreign trade there are three sorts of gain, the first is that of the Commonwealth, which may be done when the Merchant (who is the principal Agent therein) shall lose. The second is the gain of the Merchant, which he doth sometimes justly and worthily effect, although the Commonwealth be a loser. The third is the gain of the King, whereof he is ever certain, even when the Commonwealth and the Merchant shall be both losers.

Concerning the first of these, we have already sufficiently showed the ways and means whereby a Commonwealth may be enriched in the course of trade, whereof it is needless here to make any repetition, only I do in this place affirm, that such happiness may be in the Commonwealth, when the Merchant in his particular shall have no occasion to rejoice. As for example, suppose the *East-India* Company send out one hundred thousand pounds into the *East Indies,* and receive home for the same the full value of three hundred thousand pounds; Hereby it is evident that this part of the Commonwealth is trebled, and yet I may boldly say that which I can well prove, that the said Company of Merchants shall lose at least fifty thousand pounds by such an adventure if the returns be made in *Spice, Indigo, Calicoes, Benjamin, refined Saltpeter,* and such other bulky wares in their several proportions according to their vent and use in these parts of *Europe*. For the freight of Shipping, the insurance of the adventure, the charges of Factors abroad and Officers at home, the forbearance of the Stock, His Majesty's Customs and Imposts, with other petty charges incident, cannot be less than two hundred and fifty thousand pounds, which being added to the principal produceth the said loss. And thus we see, that not only the Kingdom but also the King by his Customs and Imposts may get notoriously, even when the Merchant notwithstanding shall lose grievously; which giveth us good occasion here to consider, how much more the Realm is enriched by this noble Trade, when all things pass so happily that the Merchant is a gainer also with the King and Kingdom.

In the next place I affirm, that a Merchant by his laudable endeavours may both carry out and bring in wares to his advantage by selling them and buying them to good profit, which is the end of his labours; when nevertheless the Commonwealth shall decline and grow poor by a disorder in the people, when through Pride and other Excesses they do consume more foreign wares in value than the wealth of the Kingdom can satisfy and pay by the exportation of our own commodities, which is the very quality of an unthrift who spends beyond his means.

Lastly, the King is ever sure to get by trade, when both the Commonwealth and Merchant shall lose severally as afore-written, or jointly, as it may and doth sometimes happen, when at one and the same time our Commodities are over-balanced by foreign wares consumed, and that the Merchants success prove no better than is before declared.

But here we must not take the King's gain in this large sense, for so we might say that His Majesty should get, although half the trade of the Kingdom were lost; we will rather suppose that whereas the whole trade of the Realm for Exportations and Importations is now found for to be about the yearly value of four millions and a half pounds; it may be yet increased two hundred thousand pounds *per annum* more by the importation and consumption of foreign wares. By this means we know that the King shall be a gainer near twenty thousand pounds, but the Commonwealth shall lose the whole two hundred thousand pounds thus spent in excess. And the Merchant may be a loser also when the trade shall in this manner be increased to the profit of the King; who notwithstanding shall be sure in the end to have the greatest loss, if he prevent not such unthrifty courses as do impoverish his Subjects.

6. *The observation of the Statute of Employments to be made by strangers, cannot increase, nor yet preserve our Treasure*

To keep our money in the Kingdom is a work of no less skill and difficulty than to augment our Treasure: for the causes of their preservation and production are the same in nature. The statute for employment of stranger's wares into our commodities seemeth at the first to be a good and a lawful way leading to those ends; but upon th' examination of the particulars, we shall find that it cannot produce such good effects.

For as the use of foreign trade is alike unto all Nations, so may we easily perceive what will be done therein by strangers, when we do but observe our own proceedings in this weighty business, by which we do not only seek with the vent of our own commodities to supply our wants of foreign wares, but also to enrich ourselves with treasure: all which is done by a different manner of trading according to our own occasions and the nature of the places whereunto we do trade; as namely in some Countries we sell our commodities and bring away their wares, or part in money; in other Countries we sell our goods and take their money, because they have little or no wares that fits our turns: again in some places we have need of their commodities, but they have little use of ours; so they take our money which we get in other Countries: And thus by a course of traffic (which changeth according to the occurrence of time) the particular members do accommodate each other, and all accomplish the whole body of the trade, which will ever languish if the harmony of her health be distempered by the diseases of excess at home, violence abroad, charges and restrictions at home or abroad: but in this place I have occasion to speak only of restriction, which I will perform briefly.

There are three ways by which a Merchant may make the returns of his wares from beyond the Seas, that is to say in money, in commodities, or by Exchange. But the Statute of employment doth not only restrain money (in which there is a seeming providence and Justice) but also the use of the Exchange by bills, which doth violate the Law of Commerce, and is indeed an Act without example in any place of the world where we have trade, and therefore to be considered, that whatsoever (in this kind) we shall impose upon strangers here, will presently be made a Law for us in their Countries, especially where we have our greatest trade with our vigilant neighbours, who omit no care nor occasion to support their traffic in equal privileges with other Nations. And thus in the first place we should be deprived of that freedom and means which now we have to bring Treasure into the Kingdom, and therewith likewise we should lose the vent of much wares which we carry to divers places, whereby our trade and our Treasure would decay together.

Secondly, if by the said Statute we thrust the exportation of our wares (more than ordinary) upon the stranger, we must then take it from the *English,* which were injurious to our Merchants, Mariners and Shipping, besides the hurt to the Commonwealth in venting the Kingdom's stock to the stranger at far lower rates here than we must do if we sold it to them in their own Countries.

Thirdly, whereas we have already sufficiently showed, that if our commodities be over balanced in value by foreign wares, our money must be carried out. How is it possible to prevent this by tying the Stranger's hands, and leaving the English loose? shall not the same reasons and advantage cause that to be done by them now, that was done by the other before? or if we will make a statute (without example) to prevent both alike, shall we not then overthrow all at once? the King in his customs and the Kingdom in her profits; for such a restriction must of necessity destroy much trade, because the diversity of occasions and places which make an ample trade require that some men should both export and import wares; some export only, others import, some deliver out their monies by exchange, others take it up; some carry out money, others bring it in, and this in a greater or lesser quantity according to the good husbandry or excess in the Kingdom, over which only if we keep a strict law, it will rule all the rest, and without this all other Statutes are no rules either to keep or procure us Treasure.

Lastly, to leave no Objection unanswered, if it should be said that a Statute comprehending the English as well as the stranger must needs keep our money in the Kingdom. What shall we get by this, if it hinder the coming in of money by the decay of that ample Trade which we enjoyed in the freedom thereof? is not the Remedy far worse than the Disease? shall we not live more like Irishmen than Englishmen, when the King's revenues, our Merchants, Mariners, Shipping, Arts, Lands, Riches, and all decay together with our Trade?

Yea but, say some men, we have better hopes than so; for th' intent of the Statute is, that as all the foreign wares which are brought in shall be employed in our commodities, thereby to keep our money in the Kingdom: So we doubt not but to send out a sufficient quantity of our own wares over and above to bring in the value thereof in ready money.

Although this is absolutely denied by the reasons afore written, yet now we will grant it, because we desire to end the dispute: For if this be true, that other Nations will vent more of our commodities than we consume of theirs in value, then I affirm that the overplus must necessarily return unto us in treasure without the use of the Statute, which is therefore not only fruitless but hurtful, as some other like restrictions are found to be when they are fully discovered.

7. *It will not increase our treasure to enjoin the Merchant that exporteth Fish, Corn or Munition; to return all or part of the value in Money*

Victuals and Munition for war are so precious in a Commonwealth, that either it seemeth necessary to restrain the exportation altogether, or (if the plenty permits it) to require the return thereof in so much treasure; which appeareth to be reasonable and without difficulty, because *Spain* and other Countries do willingly part with their money for such wares, although in other occasions of trade they straightly prohibit the exportation thereof: all which I grant to be true, yet notwithstanding we must consider that all the ways and means which (in course of trade) force treasure into the Kingdom, do not therefore make it ours: for this can be done only by a lawful gain, and this gain is no way to be accomplished but by the overbalance of our trade, and this overbalance is made less by restrictions: therefore such restrictions do hinder the increase of our treasure. The Argument is plain, and needs no other reasons to strengthen it, except any man be so vain to think that restrictions would not cause the less wares to be exported. But if this likewise should be granted, yet to enjoin the Merchant to bring in money for Victuals and Munition carried out, will not cause us to have one penny the more in the Kingdom at the year's end; for whatsoever is forced in one way must out again another way: because only so much will remain and abide with us as is gained and incorporated into the estate of the Kingdom by the overbalance of the trade.

This may be made plain by an example taken from an Englishman, who had occasion to buy and consume the wares of divers strangers for the value of six hundred pounds, and having wares of his own for the value of one thousand pounds, he sold them to the said strangers, and presently forced all the money from them into his own power; yet upon clearing of the reckoning between them there remained only four hundred pounds to the said Englishman for overbalance of the wares bought and sold; so the rest which he had received was returned back from whence he forced it. And this shall suffice to show that whatsoever courses we take to force money into the Kingdom, yet so much only will remain with us as we shall gain by the balance of our trade.

8. The undervaluing of our Money which is delivered or received by Bills of Exchange here or beyond the Seas, cannot decrease our treasure

The Merchants Exchange by Bills is a means and practice whereby they that have money in one Country may deliver the same to receive it again in another Country at certain times and rates agreed upon, whereby the lender and the borrower are accommodated without transporting of treasure from State to State.

These Exchanges thus made between man and man, are not contracted at the equal value of the moneys, according to their respective weights and fineness: First, because he that delivereth his money doth respect the venture of the debt, and the time of forbearance; but that which causeth an under or overvaluing of moneys by Exchange, is the plenty or scarcity thereof in those places where the Exchanges are made. For example, when here is plenty of money to be delivered for *Amsterdam,* then shall our money be undervalued in Exchange, because they who take up the money, seeing it so plentifully thrust upon them, do thereby make advantage to themselves in taking the same at an undervalue.

And contrariwise, when here is scarcity of money to be delivered for *Amsterdam,* the deliverer will make the same advantage by overvaluing our money which he delivereth. And thus we see that as plenty or scarcity of money in a Common-wealth doth make all things dear or good cheap: so in the course of exchange it hath ever a contrary working; wherefore in the next place it is fit to set down the true causes of this effect.

As plenty or scarcity of money do make the price of the exchange high or low, so the over or under balance of our trade doth effectually cause the plenty or scarcity of money. And here we must understand, that the balance of our trade is either General or Particular. The General is, when all our yearly traffic is jointly valued, as I have formerly showed; the particular is when our trade to *Italy, France, Turkey, Spain,* and other Countries are severally considered: and by this latter course we shall perfectly find out the places where our money is under or overvalued in Exchange: For although our general exportations of wares may be yearly more in value than that which is imported: whereby the difference is made good to us in so much treasure; nevertheless the particular trades do work diversely. For peradventure the *Low Countries* may bring us more in value than we sell them, which if it be so, then do the *Low Country* Merchants not only carry away our treasure to balance the account between us, but also by this means money being plentiful here to be delivered by exchange, it is therefore undervalued by the takers, as I have before declared; And contrariwise if we carry more wares to *Spain,* and other places than we consume of theirs, then do we bring away their treasure, and likewise in the Merchants exchange we overvalue our own money.

Yet still there are some who will seem to make this plain by Demonstration, that the undervaluing of our money by Exchange doth carry it out of the Kingdom: for, say they, we see daily great store of our English Coins carried over, which pass current in the Low-Countries, and there is great advantage to carry them thither, to save the loss which the Low-Countrymen have in the Exchange; for if one hundred pounds sterling delivered here, is so much undervalued, that ninety pounds of the same sterling money carried over *in specie* shall be sufficient to make repayment and full satisfaction of the said hundred pounds at *Amsterdam:* Is it not then (say they) the undervaluing of our Money which causeth it to be carried out of the Realm?

To this Objection I will make a full and plain Answer, showing that it is not the undervaluing of our money in exchange, but the overbalancing of our trade that carrieth away our treasure. For suppose that our whole trade with the Low-Countries for wares brought into this Realm be performed only by the Dutch for the value of five hundred thousand pounds yearly; and that all our commodities transported into the said Low-Countries be performed only by the English for four hundred thousand pounds yearly: Is it not then manifest, that the Dutch can exchange only four hundred thousand pounds with the English upon the *Par pro*

Pari or equal value of the respective Standards? So the other hundred thousand pounds which is the overbalance of the trade, they must of necessity carry that away in money. And the self same loss of treasure must happen if there were no exchange at all permitted: for the *Dutch* carrying away our money for their wares, and we bringing in their foreign Coins for their [our] commodities, there will be still one hundred thousand pounds loss.

Now let us add another example grounded upon the aforesaid proportion of trade between us and the *Low Countries*. The *Dutch* (as aforewritten) may exchange with the *English* for four hundred thousand pounds and no more upon the equal value of the monies, because the *English* have no further means to satisfy. But now suppose that in respect of the plenty of money, which in this case will be here in the hands of the *Dutch* to deliver by exchange, our money (according to that which hath been already said) be undervalued ten *per cent.* then is it manifest that the *Dutch* must deliver four hundred and forty thousand pounds to have the Englishman's four hundred thousand pounds in the *Low Countries:* so that there will then remain but 60000 pounds for the *Dutch* to carry out of the Realm to balance the account between them and us. Whereby we may plainly perceive that the undervaluing of our money in exchange, will not carry it out of the Kingdom, as some men have supposed, but rather is a means to make a less quantity thereof to be exported, than would be done at the *Par pro pari*.

Further let us suppose that the English Merchant carrieth out as much wares in value as the Dutch Merchant bringeth in, whereby the means is equal between them to make their returns by exchange without carrying away of any money to the prejudice of either State. And yet notwithstanding the Dutch Merchant for his occasions or advantage will forsake this course of exchange, and will venture to send part of his returns in ready money.

To this the answer is, that hereupon it must follow of necessity, that the Dutch shall want just so much means in exchange with the English, who therefore shall be forced to bring in the like sum of money from beyond the Seas, as the *Dutch* carried out of this Realm; so that we may plainly perceive that the monies which are carried from us within the balance of our trade are not considerable, for they do return to us again: and we lose those monies only which are made of the over-balance of our general trade, that is to say, That which we spend more in value in foreign wares, than we utter of our own commodities. And the contrary of this is the only means by which we get our treasure. In vain therefore hath *Gerard Malines* laboured so long, and in so many printed books to make the world believe that the undervaluing of our money in exchange doth exhaust our treasure, which is a mere fallacy of the cause, attributing that to a Secondary means, whose effects are wrought by another Principal Efficient, and would also come to pass although the said Secondary means were not at all. As vainly also hath he propounded a remedy by keeping the price of Exchange by Bills at the *par pro pari* by public Authority, which were a new-found Office without example in any part of the world, being not only fruitless but also hurtful, as hath been sufficiently proved in this Chapter, and therefore I will proceed to the next.

9. *The order and means whereby we may draw up the balance of our Foreign Trade*

Now, that we have sufficiently proved the Balance of our Foreign Trade to be the true rule of our Treasure; It resteth that we show by whom and in what manner the said balance may be drawn up at all times, when it shall please the State to discover how we prosper or decline in this great and weighty business, wherein the Officers of his Majesty's Customs are the only Agents to be employed, because they have the accounts of all the wares which are issued out or brought into the Kingdom; and although (it is true) they cannot exactly set down the cost and charges of other men's goods bought here or beyond the seas; yet nevertheless, if they ground themselves upon the book of Rates, they shall be able to make such an estimate as may well satisfy this enquiry: for it is not expected that such an account can possibly be drawn up to a just balance, it will suffice only that the difference be not over great.

First therefore, concerning our Exportations, when we have valued their first cost, we must add twenty-five *per cent.* thereunto for the charges here, for freight of Ships, insurance of the *Adventure,* and the *Merchant's* Gains; and for our Fishing Trades, which pay no Custom to his Majesty, the value of such Exportations may be easily esteem'd by good observations which have been made, and may continually be made, according to the increase or decrease of those affairs, the present estate of this commodity being valued at one hundred and forty thousand pounds issued yearly. Also we must add to our Exportations all the moneys which are carried out in Trade by license from his Majesty.

Secondly, for our Importations of Foreign Wares, the Custom-books serve only to direct us concerning the quantity, for we must not value them as they are rated here, but as they cost us with all charges laden into our Ships beyond the Seas, in the respective places where they are bought: for the Merchant's gain, the charges of Insurance, Freight of Ships, Customs, Imposts, and other Duties here, which do greatly endear them unto our use and consumption, are notwithstanding but Commutations amongst our selves, for the Stranger hath no part thereof: wherefore our said Importations ought to be valued at twenty five *per cent.* less than they are rated to be worth here. And although this may seem to be too great allowance upon many rich Commodities, which come but from the *Low Countries* and other places near hand, yet will it be found reasonable, when we consider it in gross Commodities, and upon Wares laden in remote Countries, as our Pepper, which cost us, with charges, but four pence the pound in the *East Indies,* and it is here rated at twenty pence the pound: so that when all is brought into a *medium,* the valuation ought to be made as afore-written. And therefore, the order which hath been used to multiply the full rates upon wares inwards by twenty, would produce a very great error in the Balance, for in this manner the ten thousand bags of Pepper, which this year we have brought hither from the *East Indies,* should be valued at very near two hundred and fifty thousand pounds, whereas all this Pepper in the Kingdom's account, cost not above fifty thousand pounds, because the Indians have had no more of us, although we paid them extraordinary dear prices for the same. All the other charges (as I have said before) is but a change of effects amongst our selves, and from the Subject to the King, which cannot impoverish the Common-wealth. But it is true, that whereas nine thousand bags of the said Pepper are already shipped out for divers foreign parts; These and all other Wares, foreign or domestic, which are thus transported Outwards, ought to be cast up by the rates of his Majesty's Custom-money, multiplied by twenty, or rather by twenty five (as I conceive) which will come nearer the reckoning, when we consider all our Trades to bring them into a *medium.*

Thirdly, we must remember, that all Wares exported or imported by Strangers (in their shipping) be esteemed by themselves, for what they carry out, the Kingdom hath only the first cost and the custom: And what they bring in, we must rate it as it is worth here, the Custom, Impost, and petty charges only deducted.

Lastly, there must be good notice taken of all the great losses which we receive at Sea in our Shipping either outward or homeward bound: for the value of the one is to be deducted from our Exportations, and the value of the other is to be added to our Importations: for to lose and to consume doth produce one and the same reckoning. Likewise if it happen that His Majesty doth make over any great sums of money by Exchange to maintain a foreign war, where we do not feed and clothe the Soldiers, and Provide the armies, we must deduct all this charge out of our Exportations or add it to our Importations; for this expence doth either carry out or hinder the coming in of so much Treasure. And here we must remember the great collections of money which are supposed to be made throughout the Realm yearly from our Recusants by Priests and Jesuits, who secretly convey the same unto their Colleges, Cloisters and Nunneries beyond the Seas, from whence it never returns to us again in any kind; therefore if this mischief cannot be prevented, yet it must be esteemed and set down as a clear loss to the Kingdom, except (to balance this) we will imagine that as great a value may perhaps come in from foreign Princes to their Pensioners here for Favours or Intelligence, which some States account good Policy, to purchase with great Liberality; the receipt whereof notwithstanding is plain Treachery.

There are yet some other petty things which seem to have reference to this Balance, of which the said Officers of His Majesty's Customs can take no notice, to bring them into the account. As namely, the expences of travelers, the gifts to Ambassadors and Strangers, the fraud of some rich goods not entered into the Custom-house, the gain which is made here by Strangers by change and re-change, Interest of money, insurance upon English men's goods and their lives: which can be little when the charges of their living here is deducted; besides that the very like advantages are as amply ministered unto the English in foreign Countries, which doth counterpoize all these things, and therefore they are not considerable in the drawing up of the said Balance.

10. *The conclusion upon all that hath been said, concerning the Exportation or Importation of Treasure*

The sum of all that hath been spoken, concerning the enriching of the Kingdom, and th' increase of our treasure by commerce with strangers, is briefly thus. That it is a certain rule in our foreign trade, in those places where our commodities exported are overbalanced in value by foreign wares brought into this Realm, there our money is undervalued in exchange; and where the contrary of this is performed, there our money is overvalued. But let the Merchants exchange be at a high rate, or at a low rate, or at the *Par pro pari,* or put down altogether; Let Foreign Princes enhance their Coins, or debase their Standards, and let His Majesty do the like, or keep them constant as they now stand; Let foreign Coins pass current here in all payments at higher rates than they are worth at the Mint; Let the Statute for employments by Strangers stand in force or be repealed; Let the mere Exchanger do his worst; Let Princes oppress, Lawyers extort, Usurers bite, Prodigals waste, and lastly let Merchants carry out what money they shall have occasion to use in traffic. Yet all these actions can work no other effects in the course of trade than is declared in this discourse. For so much Treasure only will be brought in or carried out of a Commonwealth, as the ForeignTrade doth over or under balance in value. And this must come to pass by a Necessity beyond all resistance.

So that all other courses (which tend not to this end) howsoever they may seem to force money into a Kingdom for a time, yet are they (in the end) not only fruitless but also hurtful: they are like to violent floods which bear down their banks, and suddenly remain dry again for want of waters.

Behold then the true form and worth of foreign Trade, which is, *The great Revenue of the King, the honour of the Kingdom, The Noble profession of the Merchant, The School of our Arts, The supply of our wants, The employment of our poor, The improvement of our Lands, The Nursery of our Mariners, The walls of the Kingdoms, The Means of our Treasure, The Sinews of our wars, The terror of our Enemies.* For all which great and weighty reasons, do so many well governed States highly countenance the profession, and carefully cherish the action, not only with policy to increase it, but also with power to protect it from all foreign energies: because they know it is a Principal in Reason of State to maintain and defend which doth Support them and their estates.

REFLECTIONS ON THE FORMATION AND DISTRIBUTION OF WEALTH

by

ANNE ROBERT JACQUES TURGOT

CONTENTS

Reflections on the Formation and Distribution of Wealth

ANNE ROBERT JACQUES TURGOT

1727–1781

ANNE ROBERT JACQUES TURGOT, French statesman and economist of the physiocratic school, was born in Paris in 1727 and came from a Norman family which for generations had been supplying administrative officers to the state. He studied theology and at the age of twenty-two was elected prior of the Sorbonne. In that capacity he delivered in 1750 an address "On the Benefits which the Christian Religion has Conferred on Mankind," and in the same year an account of "The Historical Progress of the Human Mind" in which he predicted as inevitable the separation of the American colonies from the mother country. A year later he turned from theological to legal studies and decided to enter the administrative and judicial service. He held successively the posts of deputy counselor to the *procureur général,* counselor to the Parlement de Paris, and *maître des requêtes.* In 1755 and 1756 he accompanied his friend Vincent de Gournay, then a minister of commerce under Louis XV, on tours of inspection through rural France.

It may have been Gournay who first awakened Turgot's interest in physiocratic doctrine. The favorite maxim of Gournay was *laisser faire, laisser passer.* Another of Turgot's intimate friends was François Quesnay, court physician and physiocratic enthusiast. Of French economic writers Quesnay was the first to use the word "physiocracy," interpreted to mean "the rule of nature." The physiocrats were generally known in their own time as *économistes.*

The physiocratic doctrine was a reaction against mercantilism. The mercantile policy, with its emphasis on nationalism and protection of industry, had tended to centralize manufacture and to sacrifice the country to the towns. The new doctrine was the very antithesis of the old one. It looked with favor on internationalism and free trade, and it placed agriculture at the very center of its system. Only the land, according to the physiocratic argument, was productive. Manufacturers and "artificers" were unproductive. The physiocrats proposed a tax on the "net produce" of land—a "single tax" that anticipated the doctrine of Henry George more than a hundred years later.

In 1761 Turgot was appointed administrator of the district of Limoges, which included some of the poorest and most overtaxed parts of France. He held this office for thirteen years, and tried to apply in a practical way some of his economic principles. He improved the system of tax collection, constructed new roads, increased facilities for grain trading, established a system of poor relief, and strengthened the schools. During this period Turgot was writing articles for the great liberal French Encyclopedia and was corresponding with Voltaire and Benjamin Franklin. A congenial group in Paris in the winter of 1765–66 included David Hume (then secretary of the British Embassy) and Adam Smith, who was traveling with the Duke of Buccleuch. In the quickening of minds to which Turgot contributed when he visited Paris, the physiocratic system was beginning to take literary form.

Ten years before the appearance of the *Wealth of Nations* Turgot wrote his *Reflections on the Formation and Distribution of Wealth,* which, according to Condorcet, French *philosophe* and political theorist, contained in germ the larger work. This brief treatise was first published in Dupont de Nemours' periodical, the *Ephémérides du Citoyen.* One of its purposes had been to enlighten two Chinese students who had been brought to France and educated by Jesuits and then sent back to their native land with a royal annuity and the understanding that they were to keep their European patrons informed regarding the state of literature and science in their country. Turgot had drawn up a list of questions for these students to answer, and prepared the *Reflections* in order to give them a better understanding of his interrogations. Among the fundamental themes which the treatise covers are: division of labor, the origin and use of money, the improvement of agriculture, the nature of capital and the different modes of its employment, the legitimacy of interest and loans, and the revenue from land.

In 1774, on the accession of Louis XVI, Turgot was appointed minister of marine. Later in the same year he became controller of finance. The country was in a desperate financial situation, and Turgot's first act was to submit to the King his guiding principles: "No bankruptcy, no increase of taxation, no borrowing." He proceeded to attempt to carry out on a national scale the reforms which he had initiated in the Limoges district. In six famous edicts he proposed to abolish the system of unpaid labor (the *corvées*) then prevailing throughout the country; to suppress various taxes and tolls upon corn, cattle, et cetera, in Paris; and also to suppress the trade guilds, or corporations, which were raising the prices of commodities beyond reasonable limits. It had been Turgot's hope that revolution might be averted by timely reforms; but his program was not accepted, and in 1776, as a result of the opposition of Parliament and of exasperated privileged groups, he was dismissed from office. Jacques Necker, the father of Madame de Staël, took his place in a France that was rapidly approaching the revolutionary abyss. It is worth recording that the legislatures of the French Revolution re-enacted the measures which Louis XVI and his ministers had rejected.

Turgot represented a rare combination of statesman and theorist. In the world of practical affairs he pointed the way to progressive legislation. In the domain of economic theory he helped to expose fallacies and opened the path to a new period signalized by the publication of Adam Smith's *Wealth of Nations*.

REFLECTIONS ON THE FORMATION AND DISTRIBUTION OF WEALTH

1. Impossibility of Commerce upon the supposition of an equal division of lands, wherein every man should possess only what was necessary for his own support

IF THE LAND were so distributed among all the inhabitants of a country that each of them had precisely the quantity of it necessary for his support and nothing more, it is evident that, all being equal, no one would be willing to work for others. No one, besides, would possess anything with which to pay for the labour of another; for each, having only as much land as he needed to produce his subsistence, would consume all that he had gathered, and would have nothing that he could exchange for the labour of the others.

2. The above hypothesis has never existed, & could not have continued. The diversity of soils & the multiplicity of wants lead to the exchange of the products of the land for other products

This hypothesis can never have existed, because the lands have been cultivated before they have been divided; that very cultivation having been the sole motive for division and for the law which assures to each his property. Now the first who have cultivated have probably cultivated as much ground as their forces permitted, and consequently more than was necessary for their support.

Even if this state could have existed, it could not possibly have been durable; each man, as he got from his field nothing but his subsistence, and had nothing wherewith to pay the labour of the others, could only supply his other wants in the way of shelter, clothing, etc., by his own labour; and this would be almost impossible; *every piece of land by no means producing everything.*

He whose land was only fit for grain and would produce neither cotton nor hemp would be without cloth wherewith to clothe himself. Another would have a piece of land fit for cotton which would not produce grain. A third would be without wood wherewith to warm himself, while a fourth would be without grain wherewith to feed himself. Experience would soon teach each what was the kind of product for which his land would be best adapted, and he would limit himself to the cultivation of that particular crop, in order to procure for himself the things he was devoid of by means of exchange with his neighbours; and these, having in their turn made the same reflections, would have cultivated the crop best suited to their field and abandoned the cultivation of all the others.

3. *The products of the land require preparations long & difficult, in order to render them fit to satisfy the wants of man*

The crops which the land produces to satisfy the different wants of man cannot serve that purpose, for the most part, in the state in which nature gives them; they must undergo various changes and be prepared by art. Wheat must be converted into flour and then into bread; hides must be tanned or dressed; wool and cotton must be spun; silk must be drawn from the cocoons; hemp and flax must be soaked, peeled, and spun; next, different textures must be made from them; and then they must be cut and sewn into garments, footgear, etc. If the man who causes his land to produce all these different things and uses them to supply his wants were himself obliged to put them through all these intermediate stages, it is certain that he would succeed very badly. The greater part of these preparations demand an amount of care, of attention, of long experience, such as are only to be acquired by working continuously and on a great quantity of materials. Take for example the preparation of hides; what labourer could attend to all the details necessary in this operation, which lasts several months and sometimes several years? If he could, would he be able to, for a single hide? What loss of time, of space, of material, which might have served either at the same time or successively to tan a great quantity of hides! But even should he succeed in tanning a single hide, he only needs one pair of shoes; what shall he do with the rest? Shall he kill an ox to have this pair of shoes? Shall he cut down a tree to make himself a pair of sabots? One might say the same thing concerning all the other wants of each man, who, if he were reduced to his own field and his own labour, would consume much time and trouble to be very badly equipped in every respect, and would cultivate his land very badly.

4. *The necessity of these preparations brings about the exchange of produce for labour*

The same motive which has established the exchange of crop for crop between the Cultivators of different kinds of soil must, then, have necessarily brought about the exchange of crop for labour between the Cultivators and another part of the society, which shall have preferred the occupation of preparing and working up the produce of the land to that of growing it. Everyone profited by this arrangement, for each by devoting himself to a single kind of work succeeded much better in it. The Husbandman obtained from his field the greatest amount of produce possible, and procured for himself much more easily all the other things he needed by the exchange of his surplus than he would have done by his own labour. The Shoemaker, by making shoes for the Husbandman, obtained for himself a part of the latter's harvest. Each workman laboured to satisfy the wants of the workmen of all the other kinds, who, on their side, all laboured for him.

5. *Pre-eminence of the Husbandman who produces over the Artisan who works up materials. The Husbandman is the first mover in the circulation of labours; it is he who causes the land to produce the wages of all the Artisans*

It must however be observed that the Husbandman, furnishing all with the most important and most considerable article of their consumption, (I mean their food and also the materials of almost every industry) has the advantage of a greater independence. His labour, in the sequence of the labours divided among the different members of the society, retains the same primacy, the same pre-eminence, as the labour which provided his own food had among the different kinds of labour which, when he worked alone, he was obliged to devote to his different kinds of wants. We have here neither a primacy of honour nor of dignity; it is one of *physical necessity.* The Husbandman, we may say in general terms, can get on without the labour of the other workmen, but no workman can labour if the Husbandman does not enable him to live. In this circulation, which, by the reciprocal exchange of wants, renders men necessary to one another and forms the bond of the society, it is, then, the labour of the Husbandman which imparts the first impulse. What his labour causes the land to produce beyond his personal wants is the only fund for the wages which all the other members of the society receive in exchange for their labour. The latter, in making use of the price of this exchange to buy in their turn the products of the Husbandman, only return to him exactly what they have received from him. We have here a very essential difference between these two kinds of labours, upon which it is necessary to lay stress in order to be well assured of the evidence on which it rests, before we accept the innumerable consequences which flow from it.

6. *The wages of the Workman are limited to his subsistence by the competition among the Workmen. He gets only his livelihood*

The mere Workman, who has only his arms and his industry, has nothing except in so far as he succeeds in selling his toil to others. He sells it more or less dear; but this price, more or less high as it may be, does not depend upon himself alone: it results from the agreement which he makes with him who pays his labour. The latter pays him as little as he can; as he has the choice among a great number of Workmen, he prefers the one who works cheapest. The Workmen are therefore obliged to lower the price, in competition with one another. In every kind of work it cannot fail to happen, and as a matter of fact it does happen, that the wages of the workman are limited to what is necessary to procure him his subsistence.

7. *The Husbandman is the only person whose labour produces something over and above the wages of the labour. He is therefore the sole source of all wealth*

The position of the Husbandman is very different. The land pays him directly the price of his labour, independently of any other man or any agreement. Nature does not bargain with him to oblige him to content himself with what is absolutely necessary. What she grants is proportioned neither to his wants, nor to a contractual valuation of the price of his days of labour. It is the physical result of the fertility of the soil, and of the wisdom, far more than of the laboriousness, of the means which he has employed to render it fertile. As soon as the labour of the Husbandman produces more than his wants, he can, with this superfluity that nature accords him as a pure gift, over and above the wages of his toil, buy the labour of the other members of the society. The latter, in selling to him, gain only their livelihood; but the Husbandman gathers, beyond his subsistence, a wealth which is independent and disposable, which he has not bought and which he sells. He is, therefore, the sole source of the riches, which, by their circulation, animate all the labours of the society; because he is the only one whose labour produces over and above the wages of the labour.

8. *First division of the society into two classes: the one* productive, *or that of the Cultivators; the second* stipendiary, *or that of the Artisans*

Here then we have the whole society divided, by a necessity founded on the nature of things, into two classes: equally industrious. But one of these by its labour produces, or rather draws from the land, riches which are continually springing up afresh, and which supply the whole society with its subsistence and with the materials for all its needs. The other, occupied in giving to materials thus produced the preparations and the forms which render them suitable for the use of men, sells its labour to the first class, and receives in exchange its subsistence. The first may be called the ***productive*** class, and the second the ***stipendiary*** class.

9. *In the first ages the Proprietor cannot have been distinguished from the Cultivator*

Up to this point we have not yet distinguished the Husbandman from the Proprietor of the lands; and in fact they were not originally distinct. It is by the labour of those who have been the first to till the fields, and who have enclosed them, in order to secure to themselves the harvest, that all the lands have ceased to be common to all, and that landed properties have been established. Until the societies have been consolidated, and the public force, or law, now become superior to individual force, has been able to guarantee to each man the tranquil possession of his property against all invasion from without, a man could retain the ownership of a field only in the way he had acquired it and by continuing to cultivate it. It would not have been safe to get his field cultivated by somebody else, who, having taken all the trouble, would have had difficulty in understanding that the whole harvest did not belong to him. Moreover, in this early time, as every industrious man would find as much land as he wished, he could not be tempted to till the soil for others. It was necessary that every proprietor should cultivate his field himself, or give it up altogether.

10. *Progress of the society; all the lands have a master*

But the land filled up, and was more and more cleared. The best lands at length came to be all occupied. There remained for the last comers only the sterile soils rejected by the first. But in the end all land found its master, and those who could not have properties had at first no other resource than that of exchanging the labour of their arms, in the employments of the *stipendiary* class, for the superfluous portion of the crops of the cultivating Proprietor.

11. The Proprietors begin to be able to throw the labour of cultivation upon hired Cultivators

But since the land returned, to the master who cultivated it, not only his subsistence, not only that wherewith to procure for himself by way of exchange the other things he needed, but also a considerable superfluity, he could, with this superfluity, pay men to cultivate his land; and for men who live on wages, it was as good to earn them in this business as in any other. Thus ownership could be separated from the labour of cultivation; and soon it was.

12. Inequality in the division of properties: causes which render that inevitable

The original Proprietors at first occupied, as has been already said, as much of the ground as their forces permitted them to cultivate with their family. A man of greater strength, more industrious, more anxious about the future, took more of it than a man of a contrary character. He whose family was more numerous, as he had more needs and more hands at his disposal, extended his possessions further: here was already a first inequality. All pieces of ground are not equally fertile: two men, with the same extent of ground and the same labour, could obtain a very different produce from it: second source of inequality. Properties, in passing from fathers to children, are divided into portions more or less small, according as the families are more or less numerous; as generations succeed one another, sometimes the inheritances are still further subdivided, sometimes they are reunited again by the extinction of some of the branches: third source of inequality. The contrast between the intelligence, the activity, and, above all, the economy of some and the indolence, inaction and dissipation of others, was a fourth principle of inequality and the most powerful of all. The negligent and improvident Proprietor, who cultivates badly, who, in abundant years, consumes the whole of his superfluity in frivolities, finds himself reduced, on the least accident, to request assistance from his neighbour who has been more prudent, and to live by borrowing. If, by new accidents, or through a continuance of his neglect, he finds himself not in a condition to repay, if he is obliged to have recourse to new loans, he will at last have no other resource than to abandon a part or even the whole of his estate to his creditor, who will take it as an equivalent; or to assign it to another, in exchange for other values wherewith he will discharge his obligation to his creditor.

13. Consequence of this inequality: the Cultivator distinguished from the Proprietor

Here, then, we have landed properties as objects of commerce, and bought and sold. The portion of the extravagant or unfortunate Proprietor serves for the increase of that of the Proprietor who has been more fortunate or more prudent; and, in this infinitely varied inequality of possessions, it is impossible but that many Proprietors should have more than they can cultivate. Besides, it is natural enough that a rich man should wish to enjoy his wealth in tranquillity, and that instead of employing his whole time in toilsome labours, he should prefer to give a part of his superfluity to people who will work for him.

14. Division of the produce between the Cultivator & the Proprietor. Net produce *or revenue*

By this new arrangement the produce of the land is divided into two parts. The one includes the subsistence and the profits of the Husbandman, which are the reward of his labour and the condition upon which he undertakes to cultivate the field of the Proprietor. What remains is that independent and disposable part which the land gives as a pure gift to him who cultivates it, over and above his advances and the wages of his trouble; and this is the portion of the Proprietor, or the *revenue* with which the latter can live without labour and which he carries where he will.

15. New division of the Society into three classes, of Cultivators, of Artisans & of Proprietors; or the productive *class, the* stipendiary *class and the* disposable *class*

Here then we have the Society divided into three classes; the class of Husbandmen, for which we may keep the name of *productive class;* the class of Artisans and others who *receive stipends* from the produce of the land; and the class of Proprietors, the only one which, not being bound by the need of subsistence to a particular labour, can be employed for the general needs of the Society, such as war and the administration of justice, either by a personal service, or by the payment of a part of their revenue with which the State or the Society may engage men to discharge these functions. The name which, for this reason, suits it the best is that of *disposable class*.

16. Resemblance between the two working or non-disposable classes

The two classes of the Cultivators and the Artisans resemble each other in many respects, and above all in this, that those who compose them possess no revenue and live equally on wages, which are paid them out of the produce of the land. Both have also this in common, that they get nothing but the price of their labour and of their advances, and this price is nearly the same in the two classes; the Proprietor bargaining with those who cultivate the land to yield to them as small a part of the produce as possible, in the same way as he chaffers with his Shoemaker to buy his shoes as cheaply as possible. In a word, the Cultivator and the Artisan receive, neither of them, more than the recompense of their labour.

17. Essential difference between the two working classes

But there is this difference between the two kinds of labours, that the labour of the Cultivator produces his own wages, and, in addition, the revenue which serves to pay the whole class of Artisans and other stipendiaries; while the Artisans receive simply their wages; that is to say their part of the produce of the land in exchange for their labour, and do not produce any revenue. The Proprietor has nothing except through the labour of the Cultivator; he receives from him his subsistence, and that wherewith he pays the labours of the other stipendiaries. He has need of the Cultivator through the necessity of the physical order, in virtue of which the land produces nothing without labour; but the Cultivator has need of the Proprietor only by virtue of the human conventions and the civil laws which have been obliged to guarantee to the first Cultivators and to their heirs the ownership of the grounds which they have occupied even after they ceased to cultivate them. But these laws could guarantee to the man who took no part in the work himself only that portion of the produce which the land gives over and above the recompense due to the Cultivators. The Proprietor is obliged to give up this latter, on pain of losing the whole. The Cultivator, confined though he is to the recompense of his labour, thus preserves that natural and physical primacy which renders him the first mover of the whole machine of the Society and which causes his own subsistence as well as the wealth of the Proprietor and the wages of all the other labours to depend upon his labour alone. The Artisan, on the contrary, receives his wages, whether it be from the Proprietor or from the Cultivator, and gives them, in exchange for his labour, only the equivalent of these wages and nothing more.

Thus, although neither the Cultivator nor the Artisan gains more than the recompense of his labour, the Cultivator causes, over and above that recompense, the revenue of the Proprietor to come into existence; and the Artisan causes no revenue to come into existence either for himself or for others.

18. *This difference justifies their being distinguished as* productive & barren *class respectively*

We can then distinguish the two non-disposable classes as the *productive class,* which is that of the Cultivators, and the *barren class,* which includes all the other stipendiary members of the Society.

19. *Of capitals in general, & of the revenue of money*

There is another way of being rich, without labouring and without possessing lands, of which I have not yet spoken. It is necessary to explain its origin and its connection with the rest of the system of the distribution of riches in the society, of which I have just drawn the outline. This way consists in living upon what is called the revenue of one's money, or upon the interest one draws from money placed on loan.

20. *Birth of Commerce. Principle of the valuation of commercial things*

Reciprocal want has led to the exchange of what people have for what they have not. People exchange one kind of produce for another, or produce for labour. In these exchanges it is necessary that the two parties should agree both as to the quality and the quantity of each of the things exchanged. In this agreement it is natural that each should wish to receive as much and give as little as he can; and both being equally masters of what they have to give in the exchange, each has to balance the attachment he has for the commodity he gives against the desire he has for the commodity he wishes to receive, and to fix in accordance therewith the quantity of each of the things exchanged. If the parties are not in accord, it will be necessary that they should approach one another by yielding a little on one side and a little on the other, offering more and contenting themselves with less. I will suppose that one has need of corn, and the other of wine, and that they agree to exchange *one bushel of corn* for *six pints of wine*. It is evident that by each of them *one bushel of corn* and *six pints of wine* are looked upon as exactly equivalent, and that in this particular exchange the price of *a bushel* of corn is *six pints* of wine, and the price of *six pints* of wine is *a bushel* of corn. But in another exchange between other men this price will be different, according as one of them happens to have a more or less pressing need of the commodity belonging to the other; and *a bushel* of corn may possibly be exchanged for *eight pints* of wine, while *another bushel* will be exchanged for only *four pints*. Now it is evident that no one of these three prices can be regarded as the true price of a bushel of corn rather than the others; for with each of the contracting parties the wine he has received was the equivalent of the corn he has given: in a word, so long as we consider each exchange as isolated and standing by itself, the value of each of the things exchanged has no other measure than the need or the desire and the means of the contracting parties, balanced one against the other, and it is fixed by nothing but the agreement of their will.

21. *How the current value establishes itself in the exchange of commodities*

However, it happens sometimes that several Individuals have wine to offer to the man who has corn: if one is not willing to give more than *four pints* for *a bushel,* the Proprietor of the corn will not give him his corn, when he comes to learn that someone else will give him *six* or *eight pints* for the same *bushel*. If the former wishes to have corn, he will be obliged to raise the price to the level of him who offers more. The Sellers of wine profit on their side by the competition among the Sellers of corn: no one makes up his mind to part with his commodity until he has compared the different offers that are made to him of the commodity he is in need of, and he gives the preference to the highest offer. The value of corn and of wine is no longer debated between two isolated Individuals in relation to their relative wants and abilities; it is fixed by the balance of the wants and abilities of the whole body of the Sellers of corn with those of the whole body of the Sellers of wine. For he who would willingly give *eight pints* of wine for *a bushel* of corn will only give *four* when he learns that a Proprietor of corn consents to give *two bushels* of corn for *eight pints*. The price midway between the different offers and the different demands will become the current price, whereto all the Buyers and Sellers will conform in their exchanges; and it will be true to say that *six pints* of wine are the equivalent of *a bushel* of corn for everyone if that is the *mean* price, until a diminution of the offer on the one side or of the demand on the other causes this valuation to change.

22. *Commerce gives to each article of commerce a current value, with respect to every other article; whence it follows that every article of commerce is the equivalent of a certain quantity of every other article, & can be regarded as a pledge which represents it*

Corn is exchanged not only for wine, but for all other articles which the proprietors of corn may need; for wood, leather, wool, cotton, etc.: it is the same with wine and with every other kind of produce. If *one bushel* of corn is the equivalent of *six pints* of wine, and *one sheep* is the equivalent of *three bushels* of corn this same *sheep* will be the equivalent of *eighteen pints* of wine. He who having corn needs wine can, without inconvenience, exchange his corn for a sheep, in order afterward to exchange this sheep for the wine he stands in need of.

23. *Each article of commerce can serve as the scale or common measure wherewith to compare the value of all others*

It follows from this that in a country where Commerce is very brisk, where there is much production and much consumption, where there are many offers and demands for all kinds of commodities, each kind will have a current price relatively to each other kind; that is to say, a certain quantity of one will be equivalent to a certain quantity of each of the others. Thus the same quantity of corn that will be worth eighteen pints of wine will be worth also one sheep, one piece of dressed leather, a certain quantity of iron: and all those things will have in commerce an equal value. To express and make known the value of any particular thing, it is evident that it is sufficient to declare the quantity of any other known commodity which may be regarded as its equivalent. Thus, in order to make known the value of a piece of leather of a certain size, we may say indifferently that it is worth *three bushels of corn* or *eighteen pints of wine*. We may in the same way express the value of a certain quantity of wine by the number of sheep or bushels of corn that it is worth in Commerce.

We see by this that all the kinds of commodities that can be the object of Commerce measure one another, so to speak; that each may serve as a common measure or a scale of comparison to which to refer the values of all the others; and in like manner each commodity becomes in the hands of its possessor a means to procure all the others: a sort of universal pledge.

24. *Different articles have been able to serve & have served as ordinary money*

Many Nations have adopted as a common measure of value in their language and in their Commerce different substances more or less precious; there are even today certain Barbarous Peoples who employ a kind of little shell called *Caurits*. I remember to have seen at College apricot stones exchanged and passed as a kind of money among the Scholars, who made use of them to play at different games. I have already spoken of the reckoning by head of cattle. One finds traces of it in the Laws of the ancient German Nations who destroyed the Roman Empire. The early Romans, or at least the Latins their ancestors, also made use of it. It is said that the first coin struck in copper represented the value of a sheep, and bore the imprint of that animal, and that it is from this that the word *pecunia* has come, from *pecus*. This conjecture has a good deal of probability.

25. *The Metals, and especially gold and silver, are more fit for this purpose than any other substance; & why*

We have thus come to the introduction of the precious metals into Commerce. All the metals, as one after the other they have been discovered, have been admitted into the exchanges in proportion to their real utility. Their brilliancy has caused them to be sought for to serve as ornament; their ductility and solidity have rendered them fit to make vessels more durable and lighter than those of clay. But these substances could not be in Commerce without becoming almost immediately the universal Money; a piece of any metal, whatever it may be, has exactly the same qualities as another piece of the same metal, provided it is equally pure: moreover the facility with which a metal can, by various operations of Chemistry, be separated from others with which it may be alloyed, makes it possible always to reduce them to the degree of purity, or, as they call it, to *the title,* that one desires: and then the value of the metal can only vary according to its weight. In expressing, then, the value of each commodity by the weight of the metal one gives in exchange we have the clearest, the most convenient, and the most exact expression of all the values; and henceforth it is impossible that it should not in practice be preferred to every other. Nor are the metals less suitable than other commodities to become the universal pledge of all the values they can measure: as they are susceptible of all imaginable divisions, there is no article of Commerce whose value, great or small, cannot be exactly paid for by a certain quantity of metal. To this advantage of lending themselves to every kind of division, they add that of being unalterable: and those that are rare, like gold and silver, have a very great value in a very inconsiderable weight and bulk.

These two metals are, then, of all merchandise the most easy to verify as to their quality, to divide as to their quantity, to keep forever without alteration, and to transport to all places at the least expense. Everyone who has a surplus commodity, and has not at the moment any need of another commodity for use, will hasten to exchange it for money; with which he is more sure, than with anything else, to be able to procure the commodity he shall wish for at the moment he is in want of it.

26. *Gold & Silver are constituted, by the nature of things, money, & universal money; independently of all convention & of all law*

Thus, then, we come to the constitution of gold and silver as money and universal money, and that without any arbitrary convention among men, without the intervention of any law, but by the nature of things. They are not, as many people have imagined, signs of values; they have themselves a value. If they are susceptible of being the measure and the pledge of other values, they have this property in common with all the other articles that have a value in Commerce. They differ only because being at once more divisible, more unalterable, and more easy to transport than the other commodities, it is more convenient to employ them to measure and represent the values.

27. *All economic undertakings, particularly those of manufacture & commerce, could not fail to be extremely limited before the introduction of gold & silver in commerce*

It is hardly necessary to remark that undertakings of all kinds, but especially those of manufacture and still more those of commerce, must needs have been greatly limited before the introduction of gold and silver in commerce; since it was almost impossible to accumulate considerable capitals, and still more difficult to multiply and divide payments, as much as is necessary to facilitate and multiply exchanges to the extent which is demanded by a thriving commerce and circulation. Agriculture alone could maintain itself a little, because cattle are the principal object of the advances it requires; moreover, it is probable that there was then no other agricultural undertaker but the proprietor. As to crafts of all kinds, they must have languished greatly before the introduction of money. They were limited to the roughest kinds of occupations, for which the Proprietors furnished the advances by feeding the Workmen and by providing them with materials, or which they caused to be carried on at home by their Domestics.

28. *Capitals being as necessary to all undertakings as labour and industry, the industrious man is ready to share the profits of his undertaking with the Capitalist who furnishes him with the funds of which he has need*

Since capitals are the indispensable foundation of every undertaking, since also money is a principal means for economising from small gains, amassing profits, and growing rich, those who, though they have industry and the love of labour, have no capitals or not enough for the undertakings they wish to embark in, have no difficulty in making up their minds to give up to the Possessors of capitals or money, who are willing to trust them with it, a portion of the profits they expect to gain over and above the return of their advances.

29. *The loan upon interest. Nature of the loan*

The Possessors of money balance the risk their capital may run if the enterprise does not succeed, with the advantage of enjoying a definite profit without labour; and they are influenced thereby to demand more or less profit or interest for their money, or to consent to lend it in return for the interest the Borrower offers them. Here, then, is another outlet open to the Possessor of money,—lending on interest, or the trade in money. For one must not make a mistake; lending on interest is nothing in the world but a commercial transaction in which the Lender is a man who sells the use of his money and the Borrower a man who buys it; precisely as the Proprietor of an estate and his Farmer sell and buy respectively the use of a piece of land which is let out. This is what is perfectly expressed by the name the Latins gave to the interest of money placed on loan,—*usura pecuniæ,* a word the French Rendering of which has become hateful in consequence of the false ideas which have been formed as to the interest of money.

30. *Errors of the Schoolmen refuted*

It is for want of having looked at lending on interest in its true light that certain moralists, more rigid than enlightened, have endeavoured to make us regard it as a crime. The Scholastic theologians have concluded from the fact that money produces nothing by itself that it was unjust to demand interest for money placed on loan. Full of their prejudices, they have believed their doctrine was sanctioned by this passage of the Gospel: *Mutuum date, nihil inde sperantes.* Those theologians who have adopted more reasonable principles on the subject of interest have had to endure the harshest reproaches from writers of the opposite party.

Nevertheless it needs but little reflection to realise the frivolity of the pretexts which have been made use of to condemn the taking of interest. A loan is a reciprocal contract, free between the two parties, which they make only because it is advantageous to them. It is evident that, if the Lender finds it to his advantage to receive something as the hire of his money, the Borrower is equally interested in finding the money of which he stands in need; as is shown by his making up his mind to borrow and to pay the hire of the money: but on what principle can one imagine a crime in a contract which is advantageous to the two parties, with which both are content and which certainly does not injure anyone else. To say that the Lender takes advantage of the Borrower's need of money to demand interest for it is to talk as absurdly as if one should say that a Baker who demands money for the bread he sells takes advantage of the Purchaser's need of bread. If, in the latter case, the money is the equivalent of the bread the Purchaser receives, the money which the Borrower receives today is equally the equivalent of the capital and of the interest which he promises to return at the expiration of a certain time; for, in short, it is an advantage for the Borrower to have during this interval the money he stands in need of, and it is a disadvantage to the Lender to be deprived of it. This disadvantage is capable of being estimated, and it is estimated; the interest is the price of it. This price ought to be higher if the Lender runs a risk of losing his capital by the insolvency of the Borrower. The bargain, therefore, is perfectly equal on both sides, and consequently fair. Money considered as a physical substance, as a mass of metal, does not produce anything; but money employed in advances for enterprises in Agriculture, Manufacture, and Commerce procures a definite profit. With money one can purchase an estate, and thereby procure a revenue. The person, therefore, who lends his money does not merely give up the barren possession of that money; he deprives himself of the profit or of the revenue which he would have been able to procure by it; and the interest which indemnifies him for this privation cannot be regarded as unjust.

31. True foundation of the interest of money

A man, then, may let his money as properly as he may sell it; and the possessor of money may do either one or the other, not only because the money is the equivalent of a revenue and a means to procure a revenue, not only because the lender loses during the time of the loan the revenue he might have secured by it, not only because he risks his capital, not only because the borrower may employ it in advantageous purchases or in undertakings from which he will draw large profits: the Proprietor of money may properly draw the interest of it in accordance with a more general and more decisive principle. Even if all the foregoing were not the case, he would none the less have a right to require the interest of the loan, simply because his money is his own. Since it is his own, he is free to keep it; nothing makes it his duty to lend: if, then, he does lend, he may attach to his loan such a condition as he chooses. In this he does no wrong to the borrower, since the latter acquiesces in the condition, and has no sort of right to the sum lent. The profit that a man may obtain by the use of the money is doubtless one of the commonest motives influencing the borrower to borrow on interest; it is one of the sources of the ease he finds in paying this interest; but this is by no means what gives a right to the lender to require it; it is enough for him that his money is his own, and this right is inseparable from that of property.

32. There exists no truly disposable revenue in a State except the net produce of lands

We see, by what has been said, that the interest of money placed on loan is taken either from the revenue of lands or from the profits of undertakings in agriculture, industry or commerce. But as to these profits themselves, we have already shown that they were only a part of the produce of lands; that the produce of lands falls into two parts; that the one was set aside for the wages of the cultivator, for his profits, and for the return of his advances and the interest upon them: and that the other was the share of the proprietor, that is to say, the revenue the proprietor expended at his pleasure, and from which he contributed to the general expenses of the State. We have shown that all that the other classes of the Society receive is merely the wages and the profits that are paid either by the proprietor from his revenue, or by the agents of the productive class from the part which is set aside to satisfy their needs, for which they are obliged to purchase commodities from the industrial class. Whether these profits be distributed in wages to workmen, in profits to undertakers, or in interest upon advances, they do not change their nature, and do not increase the sum of the revenue produced by the productive class over and above the price of its labour,—in which sum the industrial class participates only to the extent of the price of its labour.

The proposition, then, remains unshaken that there is no revenue save the net produce of lands, and that all other annual profit is either paid by the revenue, or forms part of the expenditure which serves to produce the revenue.

33. *The land has also furnished the whole amount of moveable riches, or capitals, in existence, & these are formed only by part of its produce being saved every year*

Not only does there not exist nor can there exist any other revenue than the net produce of lands, but it is also the land which has furnished all the capitals which make up the sum of all the advances of agriculture and commerce. It was that which offered without tillage the first rude advances which were indispensable for the earliest labours; all the rest is the accumulated fruit of the economy of the centuries that have followed one another since man began to cultivate the earth. This economizing has doubtless taken place not only out of the revenues of the proprietors, but also out of the profits of all the members of the working classes. It is even generally true that, although the proprietors have a greater superfluity, they save less because as they have more leisure, they have more desires and more passions; they regard themselves as more assured of their fortunes; they think more about enjoying it agreeably than about increasing it: luxury is their inheritance. The wage-receivers, and especially the undertakers of the other classes, who receive profits proportionate to their advances, to their talent and to their activity, although they have no revenue properly so called, have yet a superfluity beyond their subsistence; and almost all of them, devoted as they are to their undertakings, occupied in increasing their fortunes, removed by their labour from expensive amusements and passions, save all their superfluity to invest it again in their business and so increase it. Most of the undertakers in agriculture borrow little, and scarcely any of them seek to make a profitable employment of anything but their own funds. The undertakers in other employments, who wish to make their fortunes stable, also try to get into the same position; and, unless they have great ability, those who carry on their enterprises upon borrowed funds run great risk of failing. But, although capitals are partly formed by saving from the profits of the working classes, yet, as these profits always come from the earth,—inasmuch as they are all paid, either from the revenue, or as part of the expenditure which serves to produce the revenue,—it is evident that capitals come from the land just as much as the revenue does; or, rather, that they are nothing but the accumulation of the part of the values produced by the land that the proprietors of the revenue, or those who share it with them, can lay by every year without using it for the satisfaction of their wants.

34. Although money is the immediate subject of saving, and is, so to speak, the first material of capitals when they are being formed, specie forms but an almost inappreciable part of the sum total of capitals

We have seen that money plays scarcely any part in the sum total of existing capitals; but it plays a great part in the formation of capitals. In fact, almost all savings are made in nothing but money; it is in money that the revenues come to the proprietors, that the advances and the profits return to undertakers of every kind; it is, therefore, from money that they save, and the annual increase of capitals takes place in money: but none of the undertakers make any other use of it than to convert it *immediately* into the different kinds of effects upon which their undertaking depends; and thus this money returns to circulation, and the greater part of capitals exists only in effects of different kinds, as we have already explained above.

AN INQUIRY INTO THE NATURE AND CAUSES OF THE WEALTH OF NATIONS

by

ADAM SMITH

CONTENTS

The Wealth of Nations

ADAM SMITH

1723–1790

ADAM SMITH, author of what is often described as the greatest book on economics ever written, was born at the small seaport town of Kirkcaldy, Scotland, in 1723. His father was a controller of customs. He studied moral philosophy at the University of Glasgow under Francis Hutcheson, whom he called the "never-to-be-forgotten Hutcheson" and from whom he learned, he said, to esteem "natural liberty." In 1748 he lectured in Edinburgh on rhetoric and belles-lettres. At this time began his lifelong friendship with David Hume, Scottish philosopher, historian, and political economist. Adam Smith became successively professor of logic and professor of moral philosophy in the University of Glasgow from 1751 to 1763. His first book, *The Theory of Moral Sentiments,* which argues that sympathy, rather than utility or self-interest, is the basis of morals, was published in 1759. It brought him fame and led to his selection as tutor to the young Duke of Buccleuch, with whom he traveled on the continent of Europe. In France he met and highly esteemed François Quesnay and others of the French *"économistes,"* or physiocrats. Smith lived in France, chiefly in Paris and Toulouse, until the year 1766. Meanwhile, the ideas which he embodied in *The Wealth of Nations* were ripening in his mind. It was not until ten years later, however, that the book was actually published. There is no doubt that Smith was strongly influenced by David Hume, as well as by the French physiocrats, and the appearance of the book was greeted by Hume in an enthusiastic letter in which he said: "It has depth and solidity and acuteness, and is so much illustrated by curious facts that it must at last attract the public attention."

During the years that followed the publication of his magnum opus, Adam Smith was feted and courted. He was appointed one of the commissioners of customs for Scotland in 1778, and lived in Edinburgh with his mother and a maiden cousin. Benjamin Franklin had visited him, and when Smith went to London he entered the charmed circle of Samuel Johnson's friends. In 1787 he was elected Lord Rector of the University of Glasgow. *The Wealth of Nations* appeared in five editions during Smith's lifetime and has been published in scores of editions since his death in 1790. It has been translated into all the chief European languages. The full title of this famous work is actually *An Inquiry into the Nature and Causes of the Wealth of Nations,* but it is almost universally spoken of as *The Wealth of Nations.*

The fact that *The Wealth of Nations* and the American Declaration of Independence were promulgated in the same year is much more than a coincidence. Adam Smith may appropriately be regarded as the patron saint of the capitalist system in the sense in which Thomas Jefferson was the formulator of the political ideals on which this country is based. Both Smith and Jefferson expressed, in memorable fashion, the spirit of the times, and both pointed to the opening of a new era.

The originality of Adam Smith's point of view lies in the fact that, in contradistinction to both the mercantilists and the physiocrats, he finds the real source of a country's wealth in its annual labor. On the first page of *The Wealth of Nations* he says: "The annual labour of every nation is the fund which originally supplies it with all the necessaries and conveniences of life which it annually consumes, and which consist always either in the immediate produce of that labour, or in what is purchased with that produce from other nations."

Growing out of this attitude are the ideas of division of labor and exchange value. Smith calls attention, at the outset of his book, to the immense importance of division of labor (as illustrated in the complexities of pinmaking). Then he says that man is the only animal that trucks, barters, and exchanges one thing for another. He saw that the idea of exchange value furnished a suitable central and unifying principle for economic discussion.

The system of Adam Smith is mainly a theory of production, and it has been properly called an "industrial system," for human industry is its efficient principle; but it is based on manufacture industry in the original sense of the word manufacture, and was formulated before the industrial revolution had, to any great extent, substituted machine industry for handwork. Viewing everything from the standpoint of production, Adam Smith reached the conclusion that "natural" value belongs to whatever embodies labor; that labor is the cause of value—the real "price" of things.

Distribution he also interpreted as a "natural" function, accounting for the shares meted out to each by construing them in terms of the "necessary" equivalence of effort and effect in production. Nature, he contended, makes no mistakes and is not wasteful. Therefore, under conditions of natural competition, effect must be proportioned to effort, and vice versa.

Adam Smith believed in free trade, and his arguments in this connection were quoted in the British Parliament and influenced the younger Pitt, King George the Third's prime minister, in negotiating a reciprocal treaty of commerce with France.

AN INQUIRY INTO THE NATURE AND CAUSES OF THE WEALTH OF NATIONS

Introduction and Plan of Work

THE annual labour of every nation is the fund which originally supplies it with all the necessaries and conveniences of life which it annually consumes, and which consist always either in the immediate produce of that labour, or in what is purchased with that produce from other nations.

According therefore, as this produce, or what is purchased with it, bears a greater or smaller proportion to the number of those who are to consume it, the nation will be better or worse supplied with all the necessaries and conveniences for which it has occasion.

But this proportion must in every nation be regulated by two different circumstances; first, by the skill, dexterity, and judgment with which its labour is generally applied; and, secondly, by the proportion between the number of those who are employed in useful labour, and that of those who are not so employed. Whatever be the soil, climate, or extent of territory of any particular nation, the abundance or scantiness of its annual supply must, in that particular situation, depend upon those two circumstances.

The abundance or scantiness of this supply too seems to depend more upon the former of those two circumstances than upon the latter. Among the savage nations of hunters and fishers, every individual who is able to work, is more or less employed in useful labour, and endeavours to provide, as well as he can, the necessaries and conveniences of life, for himself, or such of his family or tribe as are either too old, or too young, or too infirm to go a hunting and fishing. Such nations, however, are so miserably poor, that from mere want, they are frequently reduced, or, at least, think themselves reduced, to the necessity sometimes of directly destroying, and sometimes of abandoning their infants, their old people, and those afflicted with lingering diseases, to perish with hunger, or to be devoured by wild beasts. Among civilized and thriving nations, on the contrary, though a great number of people do not labour at all, many of whom consume the produce of ten times, frequently of a hundred times more labour than the greater part of those who work; yet the produce of the whole labour of the society is so great, that all are often abundantly supplied, and a workman, even of the lowest and poorest order, if he is frugal and industrious, may enjoy a greater share of the necessaries and conveniences of life than it is possible for any savage to acquire.

The causes of this improvement, in the productive powers of labour, and the order, according to which its produce is naturally distributed among the different ranks and conditions of men in the society, make the subject of the First Book of this Inquiry.

Whatever be the actual state of the skill, dexterity, and judgment with which labour is applied in any nation, the abundance or scantiness of its annual supply must depend, during the continuance of that state, upon the proportion between the number of those who are annually employed in useful labour, and that of those who are not so employed. The number of useful and productive labourers, it will hereafter appear, is every where in proportion to the quantity of capital stock which is employed in setting them to work, and to the particular way in which it is so employed. The Second Book, therefore, treats of the nature of capital stock, of the manner in which it is gradually accumulated, and of the different quantities of labour which it puts into motion, according to the different ways in which it is employed.

Nations tolerably well advanced as to skill, dexterity, and judgment, in the application of labour, have followed very different plans in the general conduct or direction of it; and those plans have not all been equally favourable to the greatness of its produce. The policy of some nations has given extraordinary encouragement to the industry of the country; that of others to the industry of towns. Scarce any nation has dealt equally and impartially with every sort of industry. Since the downfall of the Roman empire, the policy of Europe has been more favourable to arts, manufactures, and commerce, the industry of towns; than to agriculture, the industry of the country. The circumstances which seem to have introduced and established this policy are explained in the Third Book.

Though those different plans were, perhaps, first introduced by the private interests and prejudices of particular orders of men, without any regard to, or foresight of, their consequences upon the general welfare of the society; yet they have given occasion to very different theories of political economy; of which some magnify the importance of that industry which is carried on in towns, others of that which is carried on in the country. Those theories have had a considerable influence, not only upon the opinions of men of learning, but upon the public conduct of princes and sovereign states. I have endeavoured, in the Fourth Book, to explain, as fully and distinctly as I can, those different theories, and the principal effects which they have produced in different ages and nations.

To explain in what has consisted the revenue of the great body of the people, or what has been the nature of those funds, which, in different ages and nations, have supplied their annual consumption, is the object of these Four first Books. The Fifth and last Book treats of the revenue of the sovereign, or commonwealth.

Book One: Of the Causes of Improvement in the productive Powers of Labour, and of the Order according to which its Produce is naturally distributed among the different Ranks of the People.

I. Of the Division of Labour

The greatest improvement in the productive powers of labour, and the greater part of the skill, dexterity, and judgment with which it is any where directed, or applied, seem to have been the effects of the division of labour.

The effects of the division of labour, in the general business of society, will be more easily understood, by considering in what manner it operates in some particular manufactures. It is commonly supposed to be carried furthest in some very trifling ones; not perhaps that it really is carried further in them than in others of more importance: but in those trifling manufactures which are destined to supply the small wants of but a small number of people, the whole number of workmen must necessarily be small; and those employed in every different branch of the work can often be collected into the same workhouse, and placed at once under the view of the spectator. In those great manufactures, on the contrary, which are destined to supply the great wants of the great body of the people, every different branch of the work employs so great a number of workmen, that it is impossible to collect them all into the same workhouse. We can seldom see more, at one time, than those employed in one single branch. Though in such manufactures, therefore, the work may really be divided into a much greater number of parts, than in those of a more trifling nature, the division is not near so obvious, and has accordingly been much less observed.

To take an example, therefore, from a very trifling manufacture; but one in which the division of labour has been very often taken notice of, the trade of the pinmaker; a workman not educated to this business (which the division of labour has rendered a distinct trade), nor acquainted with the use of the machinery employed in it (to the invention of which the same division of labour has probably given occasion), could scarce, perhaps, with his utmost industry, make one pin in a day, and certainly could not make twenty. But in the way in which this business is now carried on, not only the whole work is a peculiar trade, but it is divided into a number of branches, of which the greater part are likewise peculiar trades. One man draws out the wire, another straights it, a third cuts it, a fourth points it, a fifth grinds it at the top for receiving the head; to make the head requires two or three distinct operations; to put it on, is a peculiar business, to whiten the pins is another; it is even a trade by itself to put them into the paper; and the important business of making a pin is, in this manner, divided into about eighteen distinct operations, which, in some manufactories, are all performed by distinct hands, though in others the same man will sometimes perform two or three of them. I have seen a small manufactory of this kind where ten men only were employed, and where some of them consequently performed two or three distinct operations. But though they were very poor, and therefore but indifferently accommodated with the necessary machinery, they could, when they exerted themselves, make among them about twelve pounds of pins in a day. There are in a pound upwards of four thousand pins of a middling size. Those ten persons, therefore, could make among them upwards of forty-eight thousand pins in a day. Each person, therefore, making a tenth part of forty-eight thousand pins, might be considered as making four thousand eight hundred pins in a day. But if they had all wrought separately and independently, and without any of them having been educated to this peculiar business, they certainly could not each of them have made twenty, perhaps not one pin in a day; that is, certainly, not the two hundred and fortieth, perhaps not the four thousand eight hundredth part of what they are at present capable of performing, in consequence of a proper division and combination of their different operations.

In every other art and manufacture, the effects of the division of labour are similar to what they are in this very trifling one; though, in many of them, the labour can neither be so much subdivided, nor reduced to so great a simplicity of operation. The division of labour, however, so far as it can be introduced, occasions, in every art, a proportionable increase of the productive powers of labour. The separation of different trades and employments from one another, seems to have taken place, in consequence of this advantage. This separation too is generally carried furthest in those countries which enjoy the highest degree of industry and improvement; what is the work of one man in a rude state of society, being generally that of several in an improved one. In every improved society, the farmer is generally nothing but a farmer; the manufacturer, nothing but a manufacturer. The labour too which is necessary to produce any one complete manufacture, is almost always divided among a great number of hands. How many different trades are employed in each branch of the linen and woollen manufactures, from the growers of the flax and the wool, to the bleachers and smoothers of the linen, or to the dyers and dressers of the cloth! The nature of agriculture, indeed, does not admit of so many subdivisions of labour, nor of so complete a separation of one business from another, as manufactures. It is impossible to separate so entirely, the business of the grazier from that of the corn farmer, as the trade of the carpenter is commonly separated from that of the smith. The spinner is almost always a distinct person from the weaver; but the ploughman, the harrower, the sower of the seed, and the reaper of the corn, are often the same. The occasions for those different sorts of labour returning with the different seasons of the year, it is impossible that one man should be constantly employed in any one of them. This impossibility of making so complete and entire a separation of all the different branches of labour employed in agriculture, is perhaps the reason why the improvement of the productive powers of labour in this art, does not always keep pace with their improvement in manufactures. The most opulent nations, indeed, generally excel all their neighbours in agriculture as well as in manufactures; but they are commonly more distinguished by their superiority in the latter than in the former. Their lands are in general better cultivated, and having more labour and expence bestowed upon them, produce more in proportion to the extent and natural fertility of the ground. But this superiority of produce is seldom much more than in proportion to the superiority of labour and expence. In agriculture, the labour of the rich country is not always much more productive than that of the poor; or, at least, it is never so much more productive, as it commonly is in manufactures. The corn of the rich country, therefore, will not always, in the same degree of goodness, come cheaper to market than that of the poor. The corn of Poland, in the same degree of goodness, is as cheap as that of France, notwithstanding the superior opulence and improvement of the latter country. The corn of France is, in the corn provinces, fully as good, and in most years nearly about the same price with the corn of England, though, in opulence and improvement, France is perhaps inferior to England. The cornlands of England, however, are better cultivated than those of France, and the cornlands of France are said to be much better cultivated than those of Poland. But though the poor country, notwithstanding the inferiority of its cultivation, can, in some measure, rival the rich in the cheapness and goodness of its corn, it can pretend to no such competition in its manufactures; at least if those manufactures suit the soil, climate, and situation of the rich country. The silks of France are better and cheaper than those of England, because the silk manufacture, at least under the present high duties upon the importation of raw silk, does not so well suit the climate of England as that of France. But the hardware and the coarse woollens of England are beyond all comparison superior to those of France, and much cheaper too in the same degree of goodness. In Poland there are said to be scarce any manufactures of any kind, a few of those coarser household manufactures excepted, without which no country can well subsist.

This great increase of the quantity of work, which, in consequence of the division of labour, the same number of people are capable of performing, is owing to three different circumstances; first, to the increase of dexterity in every particular workman; secondly, to the saving of the time which is commonly lost in passing from one species of work to another; and lastly, to the invention of a great number of machines which facilitate and abridge labour, and enable one man to do the work of many.

First, the improvement of the dexterity of the workman necessarily increases the quantity of the work he can perform; and the division of labour, by reducing every man's business to some one simple operation, and by making this operation the sole employment of his life, necessarily increases very much the dexterity of the workman. A common smith, who, though accustomed to handle the hammer, has never been used to make nails, if upon some particular occasion he is obliged to attempt it, will scarce, I am assured, be able to make above two or three hundred nails in a day, and those too very bad ones. A smith who has been accustomed to make nails, but whose sole or principal business has not been that of a nailer, can seldom with his utmost diligence make more than eight hundred or a thousand nails in a day. I have seen several boys under twenty years of age who had never exercised any other trade but that of making nails, and who, when they exerted themselves, could make, each of them, upwards of two thousand three hundred nails in a day. The making of a nail, however, is by no means one of the simplest operations. The same person blows the bellows, stirs or mends the fire as there is occasion, heats the iron, and forges every part of the nail: In forging the head too he is obliged to change his tools. The different operations into which the making of a pin, or of a metal button, is subdivided, are all of them much more simple, and the dexterity of the person, of whose life it has been the sole business to perform them, is usually much greater. The rapidity with which some of the operations of those manufactures are performed, exceeds what the human hand could, by those who had never seen them, be supposed capable of acquiring.

Secondly, the advantage which is gained by saving the time commonly lost in passing from one sort of work to another, is much greater than we should at first view be apt to imagine it. It is impossible to pass very quickly from one kind of work to another, that is carried on in a different place, and with quite different tools. A country weaver, who cultivates a small farm, must lose a good deal of time in passing from his loom to the field, and from the field to his loom. When the two trades can be carried on in the same workhouse, the loss of time is no doubt much less. It is even in this case, however, very considerable. A man commonly saunters a little in turning his hand from one sort of employment to another. When he first begins the new work he is seldom very keen and hearty; his mind, as they say, does not go to it, and for some time he rather trifles than applies to good purpose. The habit of sauntering and of indolent careless application, which is naturally, or rather necessarily acquired by every country workman who is obliged to change his work and his tools every half hour, and to apply his hand in twenty different ways almost every day of his life; renders him almost always slothful and lazy, and incapable of any vigorous application even on the most pressing occasions. Independent, therefore, of his deficiency in point of dexterity, this cause alone must always reduce considerably the quantity of work which he is capable of performing.

Thirdly, and lastly, every body must be sensible how much labour is facilitated and abridged by the application of proper machinery. It is unnecessary to give any example. I shall only observe, therefore, that the invention of all those machines by which labour is so much facilitated and abridged, seems to have been originally owing to the division of labour. Men are much more likely to discover easier and readier methods of attaining any object, when the whole attention of their minds is directed towards that single object, than when it is dissipated among a great variety of things. But in consequence of the division of labour, the whole of every man's attention comes naturally to be directed towards some one very simple object. It is naturally to be expected, therefore, that some one or other of those who are employed in each particular branch of labour should soon find out easier and readier methods of performing their own particular work, wherever the nature of it admits of such improvement. A great part of the machines made use of in those manufactures in which labour is most subdivided, were originally the inventions of common workmen, who, being each of them employed in some very simple operation, naturally turned their thoughts towards finding out easier and readier methods of performing it. Whoever has been much accustomed to visit such manufactures, must frequently have been shewn very pretty machines, which were the inventions of such workmen, in order to facilitate and quicken their own particular part of the work. In the first fire engines, a boy was constantly employed to open and shut alternately the communication between the boiler and the cylinder, according as the piston either ascended or descended. One of those boys, who loved to play with his companions, observed that, by tying a string from the handle of the valve which opened this communication to another part of the machine, the valve would open and shut without his assistance, and leave him at liberty to divert himself with his playfellows. One of the greatest improvements that has been made upon this machine, since it was first invented, was in this manner the discovery of a boy who wanted to save his own labour.

All the improvements in machinery, however, have by no means been the inventions of those who had occasion to use the machines. Many improvements have been made by the ingenuity of the makers of the machines, when to make them became the business of a peculiar trade; and some by that of those who are called philosophers or men of speculation, whose trade it is not to do any thing, but to observe every thing; and who, upon that account, are often capable of combining together the powers of the most distant and dissimilar objects. In the progress of society, philosophy or speculation becomes, like every other employment, the principal or sole trade and occupation of a particular class of citizens. Like every other employment too, it is subdivided into a great number of different branches, each of which affords occupation to a peculiar tribe or class of philosophers; and this subdivision of employment in philosophy, as well as in every other business, improves dexterity, and saves time. Each individual becomes more expert in his own peculiar branch, more work is done upon the whole, and the quantity of science is considerably increased by it.

It is the great multiplication of the productions of all the different arts, in consequence of the division of labour, which occasions, in a well-governed society, that universal opulence which extends itself to the lowest ranks of the people. Every workman has a great quantity of his own work to dispose of beyond what he himself has occasion for; and every other workman being exactly in the same situation, he is enabled to exchange a great quantity of his own goods for a great quantity, or, what comes to the same thing, for the price of a great quantity of theirs. He supplies them abundantly with what they have occasion for, and they accommodate him as amply with what he has occasion for, and a general plenty diffuses itself through all the different ranks of the society.

Observe the accommodation of the most common artificer or day labourer in a civilized and thriving country, and you will perceive that the number of people of whose industry a part, though but a small part, has been employed in procuring him this accommodation, exceeds all computation. The woollen coat, for example, which covers the day labourer, as coarse and rough as it may appear, is the produce of the joint labour of a great multitude of workmen. The shepherd, the sorter of the wool, the wool comber or carder, the dyer, the scribbler, the spinner, the weaver, the fuller, the dresser, with many others, must all join their different arts in order to complete even this homely production. How many merchants and carriers, besides, must have been employed in transporting the materials from some of those workmen to others who often live in a very distant part of the country! How much commerce and navigation in particular, how many shipbuilders, sailors, sailmakers, ropemakers, must have been employed in order to bring together the different drugs made use of by the dyer, which often come from the remotest corners of the world! What a variety of labour too is necessary in order to produce the tools of the meanest of those workmen! To say nothing of such complicated machines as the ship of the sailor, the mill of the fuller, or even the loom of the weaver, let us consider only what a variety of labour is requisite in order to form that very simple machine, the shears with which the shepherd clips the wool. The miner, the builder of the furnace for smelting the ore, the feller of the timber, the burner of the charcoal to be made use of in the smelting house, the brickmaker, the bricklayer, the workmen who attend the furnace, the millwright, the forger, the smith, must all of them join their different arts in order to produce them. Were we to examine, in the same manner, all the different parts of his dress and household furniture, the coarse linen shirt which he wears next his skin, the shoes which cover his feet, the bed which he lies on, and all the different parts which compose it, the kitchen grate at which he prepares his victuals, the coals which he makes use of for that purpose, dug from the bowels of the earth, and brought to him perhaps by a long sea and a long land carriage, all the other utensils of his kitchen, all the furniture of his table, the knives and forks, the earthen or pewter plates upon which he serves up and divides his victuals, the different hands employed in preparing his bread and his beer, the glass window which lets in the heat and the light, and keeps out the wind and the rain, with all the knowledge and art requisite for preparing that beautiful and happy invention, without which these northern parts of the world could scarce have afforded a very comfortable habitation, together with the tools of all the different workmen employed in producing those different conveniences; if we examine, I say, all these things, and consider what a variety of labour is employed about each of them, we shall be sensible that without the assistance and co-operation of many thousands, the very meanest person in a civilised country could not be provided, even according to, what we very falsely imagine, the easy and simple manner in which he is commonly accommodated. Compared, indeed, with the more extravagant luxury of the great, his accommodation must no doubt appear extremely simple and easy; and yet it may be true, perhaps, that the accommodation of an European prince does not always so much exceed that of an industrious and frugal peasant, as the accommodation of the latter exceeds that of many an African king, the absolute master of the lives and liberties of ten thousand naked savages.

II. Of the Principle Which Gives Occasion to the Division of Labour

This division of labour, from which so many advantages are derived, is not originally the effect of any human wisdom, which foresees and intends that general opulence to which it gives occasion. It is the necessary, though very slow and gradual, consequence of a certain propensity in human nature which has in view no such extensive utility; the propensity to truck, barter, and exchange one thing for another.

Whether this propensity be one of those original principles in human nature, of which no further account can be given; or whether, as seems more probable, it be the necessary consequence of the faculties of reason and speech, it belongs not to our present subject to enquire. It is common to all men, and to be found in no other race of animals, which seem to know neither this nor any other species of contracts. Two greyhounds, in running down the same hare, have sometimes the appearance of acting in some sort of concert. Each turns her towards his companion, or endeavours to intercept her when his companion turns her towards himself. This, however, is not the effect of any contract, but of the accidental concurrence of their passions in the same object at that particular time. Nobody ever saw a dog make a fair and deliberate exchange of one bone for another with another dog. Nobody ever saw one animal by its gestures and natural cries signify to another, this is mine, that yours; I am willing to give this for that. When an animal wants to obtain something either of a man or of another animal, it has no other means of persuasion but to gain the favour of those whose service it requires. A puppy fawns upon its dam, and a spaniel endeavours by a thousand attractions to engage the attention of its master who is at dinner, when it wants to be fed by him. Man sometimes uses the same arts with his brethren, and when he has no other means of engaging them to act according to his inclinations, endeavours by every servile and fawning attention to obtain their good will. He has not time, however, to do this upon every occasion. In civilized society he stands at all times in need of the co-operation and assistance of great multitudes, while his whole life is scarce sufficient to gain the friendship of a few persons. In almost every other race of animals each individual, when it is grown up to maturity, is entirely independent, and in its natural state has occasion for the assistance of no other living creature. But man has almost constant occasion for the help of his brethren, and it is in vain for him to expect it from their benevolence only. He will be more likely to prevail if he can interest their self-love in his favour, and shew them that it is for their own advantage to do for him what he requires of them. Whoever offers to another a bargain of any kind, proposes to do this. Give me that which I want, and you shall have this which you want, is the meaning of every such offer; and it is in this manner that we obtain from one another the far greater part of those good offices which we stand in need of. It is not from the benevolence of the butcher, the brewer, or the baker, that we expect our dinner, but from their regard to their own interest. We address ourselves, not to their humanity but to their self-love, and never talk to them of our own necessities but of their advantages. Nobody but a beggar chooses to depend chiefly upon the benevolence of his fellow citizens. Even a beggar does not depend upon it entirely. The charity of well-disposed people, indeed, supplies him with the whole fund of his subsistence. But though this principle ultimately provides him with all the necessaries of life which he has occasion for, it neither does nor can provide him with them as he has occasion for them. The greater part of his occasional wants are supplied in the same manner as those of other people, by treaty, by barter, and by purchase. With the money which one man gives him he purchases food. The old clothes which another bestows upon him he exchanges for other old clothes which suit him better, or for lodging, or for food, or for money, with which he can buy either food, clothes, or lodging, as he has occasion.

As it is by treaty, by barter, and by purchase, that we obtain from one another the greater part of those mutual good offices which we stand in need of, so it is this same trucking disposition which originally gives occasion to the division of labour. In a tribe of hunters or shepherds a particular person makes bows and arrows, for example, with more readiness and dexterity than any other. He frequently exchanges them for cattle or for venison with his companions; and he finds at last that he can in this manner get more cattle and venison, than if he himself went to the field to catch them. From a regard to his own interest, therefore, the making of bows and arrows grows to be his chief business, and he becomes a sort of armourer. Another excels in making the frames and covers of their little huts or moveable houses. He is accustomed to be of use in this way to his neighbours, who reward him in the same manner with cattle and with venison, till at last he finds it his interest to dedicate himself entirely to this employment, and to become a sort of house carpenter. In the same manner a third becomes a smith or a brazier; a fourth a tanner or dresser of hides or skins, the principal part of the clothing of savages. And thus the certainty of being able to exchange all that surplus part of the produce of his own labour, which is over and above his own consumption, for such parts of the produce of other men's labour as he may have occasion for, encourages every man to apply himself to a particular occupation, and to cultivate and bring to perfection whatever talent or genius he may possess for that particular species of business.

The difference of natural talents in different men is, in reality, much less than we are aware of; and the very different genius which appears to distinguish men of different professions, when grown up to maturity, is not upon many occasions so much the cause, as the effect of the division of labour. The difference between the most dissimilar characters, between a philosopher and a common street porter, for example, seems to arise not so much from nature, as from habit, custom, and education. When they came into the world, and for the first six or eight years of their existence, they were, perhaps, very much alike, and neither their parents nor playfellows could perceive any remarkable difference. About that age, or soon after, they come to be employed in very different occupations. The difference of talents comes then to be taken notice of, and widens by degrees, till at last the vanity of the philosopher is willing to acknowledge scarce any resemblance. But without the disposition to truck, barter, and exchange, every man must have procured to himself every necessary and conveniency of life which he wanted. All must have had the same duties to perform, and the same work to do, and there could have been no such difference of employment as could alone give occasion to any great difference of talents.

As it is this disposition which forms that difference of talents, so remarkable among men of different professions, so it is this same disposition which renders that difference useful. Many tribes of animals acknowledged to be all of the same species, derive from nature a much more remarkable distinction of genius, than what, antecedent to custom and education, appears to take place among men. By nature a philosopher is not in genius and disposition half so different from a street porter, as a mastiff is from a greyhound, or a greyhound from a spaniel, or this last from a shepherd's dog. Those different tribes of animals, however, though all of the same species, are of scarce any use to one another. The strength of the mastiff is not in the least supported either by the swiftness of the greyhound, or by the sagacity of the spaniel, or by the docility of the shepherd's dog. The effects of those different geniuses and talents, for want of the power or disposition to barter and exchange, cannot be brought into a common stock, and do not in the least contribute to the better accommodation and conveniency of the species. Each animal is still obliged to support and defend itself, separately and independently, and derives no sort of advantage from that variety of talents with which nature has distinguished its fellows. Among men, on the contrary, the most dissimilar geniuses are of use to one another; the different produces of their respective talents, by the general disposition to truck, barter, and exchange, being brought, as it were, into a common stock, where every man may purchase whatever part of the produce of other men's talents he has occasion for.

III. That the Division of Labour Is Limited by the Extent of the Market

As it is the power of exchanging that gives occasion to the division of labour, so the extent of this division must always be limited by the extent of that power, or, in other words, by the extent of the market. When the market is very small, no person can have any encouragement to dedicate himself entirely to one employment, for want of the power to exchange all that surplus part of the produce of his own labour, which is over and above his own consumption, for such parts of the produce of other men's labour as he has occasion for.

There are some sorts of industry, even of the lowest kind, which can be carried on no where but in a great town. A porter, for example, can find employment and subsistence in no other place. A village is by much too narrow a sphere for him; even an ordinary market town is scarce large enough to afford him constant occupation. In the lone houses and very small villages which are scattered about in so desert a country as the Highlands of Scotland, every farmer must be butcher, baker, and brewer for his own family. In such situations we can scarce expect to find even a smith, a carpenter, or a mason, within less than twenty miles of another of the same trade. The scattered families that live at eight or ten miles distance from the nearest of them, must learn to perform themselves a great number of little pieces of work, for which, in more populous countries, they would call in the assistance of those workmen. Country workmen are almost every where obliged to apply themselves to all the different branches of industry that have so much affinity to one another as to be employed about the same sort of materials. A country carpenter deals in every sort of work that is made of wood: a country smith in every sort of work that is made of iron. The former is not only a carpenter, but a joiner, a cabinet maker, and even a carver in wood, as well as a wheelwright, a ploughwright, a cart and waggon maker.

As by means of water carriage a more extensive market is opened to every sort of industry than what land carriage alone can afford it, so it is upon the seacoast, and along the banks of navigable rivers, that industry of every kind naturally begins to subdivide and improve itself, and it is frequently not till a long time after that those improvements extend themselves to the inland parts of the country. The extent of their market, therefore, must for a long time be in proportion to the riches and populousness of that country, and consequently their improvement must always be posterior to the improvement of that country. In our North American colonies the plantations have constantly followed either the seacoast or the banks of navigable rivers, and have scarce any where extended themselves to any considerable distance from both.

The nations that, according to the best authenticated history, appear to have been first civilized, were those that dwelt round the coast of the Mediterranean Sea. That sea, by far the greatest inlet that is known in the world, having no tides, nor consequently any waves except such as are caused by the wind only, was, by the smoothness of its surface, as well as by the multitude of its islands, and the proximity of its neighbouring shores, extremely favourable to the infant navigation of the world; when, from their ignorance of the compass, men were afraid to quit the view of the coast, and from the imperfection of the art of shipbuilding, to abandon themselves to the boisterous waves of the ocean.

IV. Of the Origin and Use of Money

When the division of labour has been once thoroughly established, it is but a very small part of a man's wants which the produce of his own labour can supply. He supplies the far greater part of them by exchanging that surplus part of the produce of his own labour, which is over and above his own consumption, for such parts of the produce of other men's labour as he has occasion for. Every man thus lives by exchanging, or becomes in some measure a merchant, and the society itself grows to be what is properly a commercial society.

But when the division of labour first began to take place, this power of exchanging must frequently have been very much clogged and embarrassed in its operations. One man, we shall suppose, has more of a certain commodity than he himself has occasion for, while another has less. The former consequently would be glad to dispose of, and the latter to purchase, a part of this superfluity. But if this latter should chance to have nothing that the former stands in need of, no exchange can be made between them. The butcher has more meat in his shop than he himself can consume, and the brewer and the baker would each of them be willing to purchase a part of it. But they have nothing to offer in exchange, except the different productions of their respective trades, and the butcher is already provided with all the bread and beer which he has immediate occasion for. No exchange can, in this case, be made between them. He cannot be their merchant, nor they his customers; and they are all of them thus mutually less serviceable to one another. In order to avoid the inconveniency of such situations, every prudent man in every period of society, after the first establishment of the division of labour, must naturally have endeavoured to manage his affairs in such a manner, as to have at all times by him, besides the peculiar produce of his own industry, a certain quantity of some one commodity or other, such as he imagined few people would be likely to refuse in exchange for the produce of their industry.

Many different commodities, it is probable, were successively both thought of and employed for this purpose. In the rude ages of society, cattle are said to have been the common instrument of commerce; and, though they must have been a most inconvenient one, yet in old times we find things were frequently valued according to the number of cattle which had been given in exchange for them. The armour of Diomede, says Homer, cost only nine oxen; but that of Glaucus cost an hundred oxen. Salt is said to be the common instrument of commerce and exchanges in Abyssinia; a species of shells in some parts of the coast of India; dried cod at Newfoundland; tobacco in Virginia; sugar in some of our West India colonies; hides or dressed leather in some other countries; and there is at this day a village in Scotland where it is not uncommon, I am told, for a workman to carry nails instead of money to the baker's shop or the alehouse.

In all countries, however, men seem at last to have been determined by irresistible reasons to give the preference, for this employment, to metals above every other commodity. Metals can not only be kept with as little loss as any other commodity, scarce any thing being less perishable than they are, but they can likewise, without any loss, be divided into any number of parts, as by fusion those parts can easily be reunited again; a quality which no other equally durable commodities possess, and which more than any other quality renders them fit to be the instruments of commerce and circulation. The man who wanted to buy salt, for example, and had nothing but cattle to give in exchange for it, must have been obliged to buy salt to the value of a whole ox, or a whole sheep, at a time. He could seldom buy less than this, because what he was to give for it could seldom be divided without loss; and if he had a mind to buy more, he must, for the same reasons, have been obliged to buy double or triple the quantity, the value, to wit, of two or three oxen, or of two or three sheep. If, on the contrary, instead of sheep or oxen, he had metals to give in exchange for it, he could easily proportion the quantity of the metal to the precise quantity of the commodity which he had immediate occasion for.

Different metals have been made use of by different nations for this purpose. Iron was the common instrument of commerce among the ancient Spartans; copper among the ancient Romans; and gold and silver among all rich and commercial nations.

Those metals seem originally to have been made use of for this purpose in rude bars, without any stamp or coinage. Thus we are told by Pliny, upon the authority of Timæus, an ancient historian, that, till the time of Servius Tullius, the Romans had no coined money, but made use of unstamped bars of copper, to purchase whatever they had occasion for. These rude bars, therefore, performed at this time the function of money.

The use of metals in this rude state was attended with two very considerable inconveniencies; first with the trouble of weighing; and, secondly, with that of assaying them. In the precious metals, where a small difference in the quantity makes a great difference in the value, even the business of weighing, with proper exactness, requires at least very accurate weights and scales. The weighing of gold in particular is an operation of some nicety. In the coarser metals, indeed, where a small error would be of little consequence, less accuracy would, no doubt, be necessary. Yet we should find it excessively troublesome, if every time a poor man had occasion either to buy or sell a farthing's worth of goods, he was obliged to weigh the farthing. The operation of assaying is still more difficult, still more tedious, and, unless a part of the metal is fairly melted in the crucible, with proper dissolvents, any conclusion that can be drawn from it, is extremely uncertain. Before the institution of coined money, however, unless they went through this tedious and difficult operation, people must always have been liable to the grossest frauds and impositions, and instead of a pound weight of pure silver, or pure copper, might receive in exchange for their goods, an adulterated composition of the coarsest and cheapest materials, which had, however, in their outward appearance, been made to resemble those metals. To prevent such abuses, to facilitate exchanges, and thereby to encourage all sorts of industry and commerce, it had been found necessary, in all countries that have made any considerable advances towards improvement, to affix a public stamp upon certain quantities of such particular metals, as were in those countries commonly made use of to purchase goods. Hence the origin of coined money, and of those public offices called mints; institutions exactly of the same nature with those of the aulnegers and stampmasters of woollen and linen cloth. All of them are equally meant to ascertain, by means of a public stamp, the quantity and uniform goodness of those different commodities when brought to market.

The first public stamps of this kind that were affixed to the current metals, seem in many cases to have been intended to ascertain, what it was both most difficult and most important to ascertain, the goodness or fineness of the metal, and to have resembled the sterling mark which is at present affixed to plate and bars of silver, or the Spanish mark which is sometimes affixed to ingots of gold, and which being struck only upon one side of the piece, and not covering the whole surface, ascertains the fineness, but not the weight of the metal. Abraham weighs to Ephron the four hundred shekels of silver which he had agreed to pay for the field of Machpelah. They are said however to be the current money of the merchant, and yet are received by weight and not by tale, in the same manner as ingots of gold and bars of silver are at present. The revenues of the ancient Saxon kings of England are said to have been paid, not in money but in kind, that is, in victuals and provisions of all sorts. William the Conqueror introduced the custom of paying them in money. This money, however, was, for a long time, received at the exchequer, by weight and not by tale.

The inconveniency and difficulty of weighing those metals with exactness gave occasion to the institution of coins, of which the stamp, covering entirely both sides of the piece and sometimes the edges too, was supposed to ascertain not only the fineness, but the weight of the metal. Such coins, therefore, were received by tale as at present, without the trouble of weighing.

It is in this manner that money has become in all civilized nations the universal instrument of commerce, by the intervention of which goods of all kinds are bought and sold, or exchanged for one another.

What are the rules which men naturally observe in exchanging them either for money or for one another, I shall now proceed to examine. These rules determine what may be called the relative or exchangeable value of goods.

The word VALUE, it is to be observed, has two different meanings, and sometimes expresses the utility of some particular object, and sometimes the power of purchasing other goods which the possession of that object conveys. The one may be called "value in use"; the other, "value in exchange." The things which have the greatest value in use have frequently little or no value in exchange; and on the contrary, those which have the greatest value in exchange have frequently little or no value in use. Nothing is more useful than water: but it will purchase scarce any thing; scarce any thing can be had in exchange for it. A diamond, on the contrary, has scarce any value in use; but a very great quantity of other goods may frequently be had in exchange for it.

In order to investigate the principles which regulate the exchangeable value of commodities, I shall endeavour to show,

First, what is the real measure of this exchangeable value; or, wherein consists the real price of all commodities.

Secondly, what are the different parts of which this real price is composed or made up.

And, lastly, what are the different circumstances which sometimes raise some or all of these different parts of price above, and sometimes sink them below their natural or ordinary rate; or, what are the causes which sometimes hinder the market price, that is, the actual price of commodities, from coinciding exactly with what may be called their natural price.

I shall endeavour to explain, as fully and distinctly as I can, those three subjects in the three following chapters.

V. Of the Real and Nominal Price of Commodities, or of Their Price in Labour, and Their Price in Money

Every man is rich or poor according to the degree in which he can afford to enjoy the necessaries, conveniencies, and amusements of human life. But after the division of labour has once thoroughly taken place, it is but a very small part of these with which a man's own labour can supply him. The far greater part of them he must derive from the labour of other people, and he must be rich or poor according to the quantity of that labour which he can command, or which he can afford to purchase. The value of any commodity, therefore, to the person who possesses it, and who means not to use or consume it himself, but to exchange it for other commodities, is equal to the quantity of labour which it enables him to purchase or command. Labour, therefore, is the real measure of the exchangeable value of all commodities.

The real price of every thing, what every thing really costs to the man who wants to acquire it, is the toil and trouble of acquiring it. What every thing is really worth to the man who has acquired it, and who wants to dispose of it or exchange it for something else, is the toil and trouble which it can save to himself, and which it can impose upon other people. What is bought with money or with goods is purchased by labour, as much as what we acquire by the toil of our own body. That money or those goods indeed save us this toil. They contain the value of a certain quantity of labour which we exchange for what is supposed at the time to contain the value of an equal quantity. Labour was the first price, the original purchase-money that was paid for all things. It was not by gold or by silver, but by labour, that all the wealth of the world was originally purchased; and its value, to those who possess it, and who want to exchange it for some new productions, is precisely equal to the quantity of labour which it can enable them to purchase or command.

Wealth, as Mr. Hobbes says, is power. But the person who either acquires, or succeeds to a great fortune, does not necessarily acquire or succeed to any political power, either civil or military. His fortune may, perhaps, afford him the means of acquiring both, but the mere possession of that fortune does not necessarily convey to him either. The power which that possession immediately and directly conveys to him, is the power of purchasing; a certain command over all the labour, or over all the produce of labour which is then in the market. His fortune is greater or less, precisely in proportion to the extent of this power; or to the quantity either of other men's labour, or, what is the same thing, of the produce of other men's labour, which it enables him to purchase or command. The exchangeable value of every thing must always be precisely equal to the extent of this power which it conveys to its owner.

But though labour be the real measure of the exchangeable value of all commodities, it is not that by which their value is commonly estimated. It is often difficult to ascertain the proportion between two different quantities of labour. The time spent in two different sorts of work will not always alone determine this proportion. The different degrees of hardship endured, and of ingenuity exercised, must likewise be taken into account. There may be more labour in an hour's hard work than in two hours' easy business; or in an hour's application to a trade which it cost ten years' labour to learn, than in a month's industry at an ordinary and obvious employment. But it is not easy to find any accurate measure either of hardship or ingenuity. In exchanging indeed the different productions of different sorts of labour for one another, some allowance is commonly made for both. It is adjusted, however, not by any accurate measure, but by the higgling and bargaining of the market, according to that sort of rough equality which, though not exact, is sufficient for carrying on the business of common life.

Every commodity besides, is more frequently exchanged for, and thereby compared with, other commodities than with labour. It is more natural therefore, to estimate its exchangeable value by the quantity of some other commodity than by that of the labour which it can purchase. The greater part of people too understand better what is meant by a quantity of a particular commodity, than by a quantity of labour. The one is a plain palpable object; the other an abstract notion, which, though it can be made sufficiently intelligible, is not altogether so natural and obvious.

But when barter ceases, and money has become the common instrument of commerce, every particular commodity is more frequently exchanged for money than for any other commodity. The butcher seldom carries his beef or his mutton to the baker, or the brewer, in order to exchange them for bread or for beer; but he carries them to the market, where he exchanges them for money, and afterwards exchanges that money for bread and for beer. The quantity of money which he gets for them regulates too the quantity of bread and beer which he can afterwards purchase. It is more natural and obvious to him, therefore, to estimate their value by the quantity of money, the commodity for which he immediately exchanges them, than by that of bread and beer, the commodities for which he can exchange them only by the intervention of another commodity; and rather to say that his butcher's meat is worth threepence or fourpence a pound, than that it is worth three or four pounds of bread, or three or four quarts of small beer. Hence it comes to pass, that the exchangeable value of every commodity is more frequently estimated by the quantity of money, than by the quantity either of labour or of any other commodity which can be had in exchange for it.

Gold and silver, however, like every other commodity, vary in their value, are sometimes cheaper and sometimes dearer, sometimes of easier and sometimes of more difficult purchase. The quantity of labour which any particular quantity of them can purchase or command, or the quantity of other goods which it will exchange for, depends always upon the fertility or barrenness of the mines which happen to be known about the time when such exchanges are made. The discovery of the abundant mines of America reduced, in the sixteenth century, the value of gold and silver in Europe to about a third of what it had been before. As it cost less labour to bring those metals from the mine to the market, so when they were brought thither they could purchase or command less labour; and this revolution in their value, though perhaps the greatest, is by no means the only one of which history gives some account. But as a measure of quantity, such as the natural foot, fathom, or handful, which is continually varying in its own quantity, can never be an accurate measure of the quantity of other things; so a commodity which is itself continually varying in its own value, can never be an accurate measure of the value of other commodities. Equal quantities of labour, at all times and places, may be said to be of equal value to the labourer. In his ordinary state of health, strength and spirits; in the ordinary degree of his skill and dexterity, he must always lay down the same portion of his ease, his liberty, and his happiness. The price which he pays must always be the same, whatever may be the quantity of goods which he receives in return for it. Of these, indeed, it may sometimes purchase a greater and sometimes a smaller quantity; but it is their value which varies, not that of the labour which purchases them. At all times and places that is dear which it is difficult to come at, or which it costs much labour to acquire; and that cheap which is to be had easily, or with very little labour. Labour alone, therefore, never varying in its own value, is alone the ultimate and real standard by which the value of all commodities can at all times and places be estimated and compared. It is their real price; money is their nominal price only.

But though equal quantities of labour are always of equal value to the labourer, yet to the person who employs him they appear sometimes to be of greater and sometimes of smaller value. He purchases them sometimes with a greater and sometimes with a smaller quantity of goods, and to him the price of labour seems to vary like that of all other things. It appears to him dear in the one case, and cheap in the other. In reality, however, it is the goods which are cheap in the one case, and dear in the other.

In this popular sense, therefore, labour, like commodities, may be said to have a real and a nominal price. Its real price may be said to consist in the quantity of the necessaries and conveniencies of life which are given for it; its nominal price, in the quantity of money. The labourer is rich or poor, is well or ill rewarded, in proportion to the real, not to the nominal price of his labour.

The distinction between the real and the nominal price of commodities and labour, is not a matter of mere speculation, but may sometimes be of considerable use in practice. The same real price is always of the same value; but on account of the variations in the value of gold and silver, the same nominal price is sometimes of very different values. When a landed estate, therefore, is sold with a reservation of a perpetual rent, if it is intended that this rent should always be of the same value, it is of importance to the family in whose favour it is reserved, that it should not consist in a particular sum of money. Its value would in this case be liable to variations of two different kinds; first, to those which arise from the different quantities of gold and silver which are contained at different times in coin of the same denomination; and, secondly, to those which arise from the different values of equal quantities of gold and silver at different times.

Princes and sovereign states have frequently fancied that they had a temporary interest to diminish the quantity of pure metal contained in their coins; but they seldom have fancied that they had any to augment it. The quantity of metal contained in the coins, I believe of all nations, has, accordingly, been almost continually diminishing, and hardly ever augmenting. Such variations therefore tend almost always to diminish the value of a money rent.

The discovery of the mines of America diminished the value of gold and silver in Europe. This diminution, it is commonly supposed, though I apprehend without any certain proof, is still going on gradually, and is likely to continue to do so for a long time. Upon this supposition, therefore, such variations are more likely to diminish, than to augment the value of a money rent, even though it should be stipulated to be paid, not in such a quantity of coined money of such a denomination (in so many pounds sterling, for example), but in so many ounces either of pure silver, or of silver of a certain standard.

The rents which have been reserved in corn have preserved their value much better than those which have been reserved in money, even where the denomination of the coin has not been altered. By the 18th of Elizabeth it was enacted, That a third of the rent of all college leases should be reserved in corn, to be paid, either in kind, or according to the current prices at the nearest public market. The money arising from this corn rent, though originally but a third of the whole, is in the present times, according to Doctor Blackstone, commonly near double of what arises from the other two thirds. The old money rents of colleges must, according to this account, have sunk almost to a fourth part of their ancient value; or are worth little more than a fourth part of the corn which they were formerly worth. But since the reign of Philip and Mary the denomination of the English coin has undergone little or no alteration, and the same number of pounds, shillings, and pence have contained very nearly the same quantity of pure silver. This degradation, therefore, in the value of the money rents of colleges, has arisen altogether from the degradation in the value of silver.

When the degradation in the value of silver is combined with the diminution of the quantity of it contained in the coin of the same denomination, the loss is frequently still greater. In Scotland, where the denomination of the coin has undergone much greater alterations than it ever did in England, and in France, where it has undergone still greater than it ever did in Scotland, some ancient rents, originally of considerable value, have in this manner been reduced almost to nothing.

Equal quantities of labour will at distant times be purchased more nearly with equal quantities of corn, the subsistence of the labourer, than with equal quantities of gold and silver, or perhaps of any other commodity. Equal quantities of corn, therefore, will, at distant times, be more nearly of the same real value, or enable the possessor to purchase or command more nearly the same quantity of the labour of other people. They will do this, I say, more nearly than equal quantities of almost any other commodity; for even equal quantities of corn will not do it exactly. The subsistence of the labourer, or the real price of labour, as I shall endeavour to show hereafter, is very different upon different occasions; more liberal in a society advancing to opulence, than in one that is standing still; and in one that is standing still, than in one that is going backwards. Every other commodity, however, will at any particular time purchase a greater or smaller quantity of labour in proportion to the quantity of subsistence which it can purchase at that time. A rent therefore reserved in corn is liable only to the variations in the quantity of labour which a certain quantity of corn can purchase. But a rent reserved in any other commodity is liable, not only to the variations in the quantity of labour which any particular quantity of corn can purchase, but to the variations in the quantity of corn which can be purchased by any particular quantity of that commodity.

Though the real value of a corn rent, it is to be observed however, varies much less from century to century than that of a money rent, it varies much more from year to year. The money price of labour, as I shall endeavour to show hereafter, does not fluctuate from year to year with the money price of corn, but seems to be every where accommodated, not to the temporary or occasional, but to the average or ordinary price of that necessary of life. The average or ordinary price of corn again is regulated, as I shall likewise endeavour to show hereafter, by the value of silver, by the richness or barrenness of the mines which supply the market with that metal, or by the quantity of labour which must be employed, and consequently of corn which must be consumed, in order to bring any particular quantity of silver from the mine to the market. But the value of silver, though it sometimes varies greatly from century to century, seldom varies much from year to year, but frequently continues the same, or very nearly the same, for half a century or a century together. The ordinary or average money price of corn, therefore, may, during so long a period, continue the same or very nearly the same too, and along with it the money price of labour, provided, at least, the society continues, in other respects, in the same or nearly in the same condition. In the mean time the temporary and occasional price of corn may frequently be double, one year, of what it had been the year before, or fluctuate, for example, from five and twenty to fifty shillings the quarter. But when corn is at the latter price, not only the nominal, but the real value of a corn rent will be double of what it is when at the former, or will command double the quantity either of labour or of the greater part of other commodities; the money price of labour, and along with it that of most other things, continuing the same during all these fluctuations.

Labour, therefore, it appears evidently, is the only universal, as well as the only accurate measure of value, or the only standard by which we can compare the values of different commodities at all times and at all places. We cannot estimate, it is allowed, the real value of different commodities from century to century by the quantities of silver which were given for them. We cannot estimate it from year to year by the quantities of corn. By the quantities of labour we can, with the greatest accuracy, estimate it both from century to century and from year to year. From century to century, corn is a better measure than silver, because from century to century, equal quantities of corn will command the same quantity of labour more nearly than equal quantities of silver. From year to year, on the contrary, silver is a better measure than corn, because equal quantities of it will more nearly command the same quantity of labour.

But though in establishing perpetual rents, or even in letting very long leases, it may be of use to distinguish between real and nominal price; it is of none in buying and selling, the more common and ordinary transactions of human life.

At the same time and place the real and the nominal price of all commodities are exactly in proportion to one another. The more or less money you get for any commodity, in the London market, for example, the more or less labour it will at that time and place enable you to purchase or command. At the same time and place, therefore, money is the exact measure of the real exchangeable value of all commodities. It is so, however, at the same time and place only.

Though at distant places, there is no regular proportion between the real and the money price of commodities, yet the merchant who carries goods from the one to the other has nothing to consider but their money price, or the difference between the quantity of silver for which he buys them, and that for which he is likely to sell them. Half an ounce of silver at Canton in China may command a greater quantity both of labour and of the necessaries and conveniencies of life, than an ounce at London. A commodity, therefore, which sells for half an ounce of silver at Canton may there be really dearer, of more real importance to the man who possesses it there, than a commodity which sells for an ounce at London is to the man who possesses it at London. If a London merchant, however, can buy at Canton for half an ounce of silver, a commodity which he can afterwards sell at London for an ounce, he gains a hundred per cent. by the bargain, just as much as if an ounce of silver was at London exactly of the same value as at Canton. It is of no importance to him that half an ounce of silver at Canton would have given him the command of more labour and of a greater quantity of the necessaries and conveniencies of life than an ounce can do at London. An ounce at London will always give him the command of double the quantity of all these, which half an ounce could have done there, and this is precisely what he wants.

As it is the nominal or money price of goods, therefore, which finally determines the prudence or imprudence of all purchases and sales, and thereby regulates almost the whole business of common life in which price is concerned, we cannot wonder that it should have been so much more attended to than the real price.

VI. Of the Component Parts of the Price of Commodities

In that early and rude state of society which precedes both the accumulation of stock and the appropriation of land, the proportion between the quantities of labour necessary for acquiring different objects seems to be the only circumstance which can afford any rule for exchanging them for one another. If among a nation of hunters, for example, it usually costs twice the labour to kill a beaver which it does to kill a deer, one beaver should naturally exchange for or be worth two deer. It is natural that what is usually the produce of two days' or two hours' labour, should be worth double of what is usually the produce of one day's or one hour's labour.

If the one species of labour should be more severe than the other, some allowance will naturally be made for this superior hardship; and the produce of one hour's labour in the one way may frequently exchange for that of two hours' labour in the other.

Or if the one species of labour requires an uncommon degree of dexterity and ingenuity, the esteem which men have for such talents, will naturally give a value to their produce, superior to what would be due to the time employed about it. Such talents can seldom be acquired but in consequence of long application, and the superior value of their produce may frequently be no more than a reasonable compensation for the time and labour which must be spent in acquiring them. In the advanced state of society, allowances of this kind, for superior hardship and superior skill, are commonly made in the wages of labour; and something of the same kind must probably have taken place in its earliest and rudest period.

In this state of things, the whole produce of labour belongs to the labourer; and the quantity of labour commonly employed in acquiring or producing any commodity, is the only circumstance which can regulate the quantity of labour which it ought commonly to purchase, command, or exchange for.

As soon as stock has accumulated in the hands of particular persons, some of them will naturally employ it in setting to work industrious people, whom they will supply with materials and subsistence, in order to make a profit by the sale of their work, or by what their labour adds to the value of the materials. In exchanging the complete manufacture either for money, for labour, or for other goods, over and above what may be sufficient to pay the price of the materials, and the wages of the workmen, something must be given for the profits of the undertaker of the work who hazards his stock in this adventure. The value which the workmen add to the materials, therefore, resolves itself in this case into two parts, of which the one pays their wages, the other the profits of their employer upon the whole stock of materials and wages which he advanced. He could have no interest to employ them, unless he expected from the sale of their work something more than what was sufficient to replace his stock to him; and he could have no interest to employ a great stock rather than a small one, unless his profits were to bear some proportion to the extent of his stock.

The profits of stock, it may perhaps be thought, are only a different name for the wages of a particular sort of labour, the labour of inspection and direction. They are, however, altogether different, are regulated by quite sufficient principles, and bear no proportion to the quantity, the hardship, or the ingenuity of this supposed labour of inspection and direction. They are regulated altogether by the value of the stock employed, and are greater or smaller in proportion to the extent of this stock. Let us suppose, for example, that in some particular place, where the common annual profits of manufacturing stock are ten per cent. there are two different manufactures, in each of which twenty workmen are employed at the rate of fifteen pounds a year each, or at the expence of three hundred a year in each manufactory. Let us suppose too, that the coarse materials annually wrought up in the one cost only seven hundred pounds, while the finer materials in the other cost seven thousand. The capital annually employed in the one will in this case amount only to one thousand pounds; whereas that employed in the other will amount to seven thousand three hundred pounds. At the rate of ten per cent. therefore, the undertaker of the one will expect an yearly profit of about one hundred pounds only; while that of the other will expect about seven hundred and thirty pounds. But though their profits are so very different, their labour of inspection and direction may be either altogether or very nearly the same. In many great works, almost the whole labour of this kind is committed to some principal clerk. His wages properly express the value of this labour of inspection and direction. Though in settling them some regard is had commonly, not only to his labour and skill, but to the trust which is reposed in him, yet they never bear any regular proportion to the capital of which he oversees the management; and the owner of this capital, though he is thus discharged of almost all labour, still expects that his profits should bear a regular proportion to his capital. In the price of commodities, therefore, the profits of stock constitute a component part altogether different from the wages of labour, and regulated by quite different principles.

In this state of things, the whole produce of labour does not always belong to the labourer. He must in most cases share it with the owner of the stock which employs him. Neither is the quantity of labour commonly employed in acquiring or producing any commodity, the only circumstance which can regulate the quantity which it ought commonly to purchase, command, or exchange for. An additional quantity, it is evident, must be due for the profits of the stock which advanced the wages and furnished the materials of that labour.

As soon as the land of any country has all become private property, the landlords, like all other men, love to reap where they never sowed, and demand a rent even for its natural produce. The wood of the forest, the grass of the field, and all the natural fruits of the earth, which, when land was in common, cost the labourer only the trouble of gathering them, come, even to him, to have an additional price fixed upon them. He must give up to the landlord a portion of what his labour either collects or produces. This portion, or, what comes to the same thing, the price of this portion, constitutes the rent of land, and in the price of the greater part of commodities makes a third component part.

The real value of all the different component parts of price, it must be observed, is measured by the quantity of labour which they can, each of them, purchase or command. Labour measures the value not only of that part of price which resolves itself into labour, but of that which resolves itself into rent, and of that which resolves itself into profit.

In every society the price of every commodity finally resolves itself into some one or other, or all of those three parts; and in every improved society, all the three enter more or less, as component parts, into the price of the far greater part of commodities.

In the price of corn, for example, one part pays the rent of the landlord, another pays the wages or maintenance of the labourers and labouring cattle employed in producing it, and the third pays the profit of the farmer. These three parts seem either immediately or ultimately to make up the whole price of corn. A fourth part, it may perhaps be thought, is necessary for replacing the stock of the farmer, or for compensating the wear and tear of his labouring cattle, and other instruments of husbandry. But it must be considered that the price of any instrument of husbandry, such as a labouring horse, is itself made up of the same three parts; the rent of the land upon which he is reared, the labour of tending and rearing him, and the profits of the farmer who advances both the rent of this land, and the wages of this labour. Though the price of the corn, therefore, may pay the price as well as the maintenance of the horse, the whole price still resolves itself either immediately or ultimately into the same three parts of rent, labour, and profit.

VII. Of the Natural and Market Price of Commodities

There is in every society or neighbourhood an ordinary or average rate both of wages and profit in every different employment of labour and stock. This rate is naturally regulated, as I shall show hereafter, partly by the general circumstances of the society, their riches or poverty, their advancing, stationary, or declining condition; and partly by the particular nature of each employment.

There is likewise in every society or neighbourhood an ordinary or average rate of rent, which is regulated too, as I shall show hereafter, partly by the general circumstances of the society or neighbourhood in which the land is situated, and partly by the natural or improved fertility of the land.

These ordinary or average rates may be called the natural rates of wages, profit, and rent, at the time and place in which they commonly prevail.

When the price of any commodity is neither more nor less than what is sufficient to pay the rent of the land, the wages of the labour, and the profits of the stock employed in raising, preparing, and bringing it to market, according to their natural rates, the commodity is then sold for what may be called its natural price.

The commodity is then sold precisely for what it is worth, or for what it really costs the person who brings it to market; for though in common language what is called the prime cost of any commodity does not comprehend the profit of the person who is to sell it again, yet if he sells it at a price which does not allow him the ordinary rate of profit in his neighbourhood, he is evidently a loser by the trade; since by employing his stock in some other way he might have made that profit. His profit, besides, is his revenue, the proper fund of his subsistence. As, while he is preparing and bringing the goods to market, he advances to his workmen their wages, or their subsistence; so he advances to himself, in the same manner, his own subsistence, which is generally suitable to the profit which he may reasonably expect from the sale of his goods. Unless they yield him this profit, therefore, they do not repay him what they may very properly be said to have really cost him.

Though the price, therefore, which leaves him this profit, is not always the lowest at which a dealer may sometimes sell his goods, it is the lowest at which he is likely to sell them for any considerable time; at least where there is perfect liberty, or where he may change his trade as often as he pleases.

The actual price at which any commodity is commonly sold is called its market price. It may either be above, or below, or exactly the same with its natural price.

The market price of every particular commodity is regulated by the proportion between the quantity which is actually brought to market, and the demand of those who are willing to pay the natural price of the commodity, or the whole value of the rent, labour, and profit, which must be paid in order to bring it thither. Such people may be called the effectual demanders, and their demand the effectual demand; since it may be sufficient to effectuate the bringing of the commodity to market. It is different from the absolute demand. A very poor man may be said in some sense to have a demand for a coach and six; he might like to have it; but his demand is not an effectual demand, as the commodity can never be brought to market in order to satisfy it.

When the quantity of any commodity which is brought to market falls short of the effectual demand, all those who are willing to pay the whole value of the rent, wages, and profit, which must be paid in order to bring it thither, cannot be supplied with the quantity which they want. Rather than want it altogether, some of them will be willing to give more. A competition will immediately begin among them, and the market price will rise more or less above the natural price, according as either the greatness of the deficiency, or the wealth and wanton luxury of the competitors, happen to animate more or less the eagerness of the competition. Among competitors of equal wealth and luxury the same deficiency will generally occasion a more or less eager competition, according as the acquisition of the commodity happens to be of more or less importance to them. Hence the exorbitant price of the necessaries of life during the blockade of a town or in a famine.

When the quantity brought to market exceeds the effectual demand, it cannot be all sold to those who are willing to pay the whole value of the rent, wages and profit, which must be paid in order to bring it thither. Some part must be sold to those who are willing to pay less, and the low price which they give for it must reduce the price of the whole. The market price will sink more or less below the natural price, according as the greatness of the excess increases more or less the competition of the sellers, or according as it happens to be more or less important to them to get immediately rid of the commodity. The same excess in the importation of perishable, will occasion a much greater competition than in that of durable commodities; in the importation of oranges, for example, than in that of old iron.

When the quantity brought to market is just sufficient to supply the effectual demand and no more, the market price naturally comes to be either exactly, or as nearly as can be judged of, the same with the natural price. The whole quantity upon hand can be disposed of for this price, and cannot be disposed of for more. The competition of the different dealers obliges them all to accept of this price, but does not oblige them to accept of less.

The quantity of every commodity brought to market naturally suits itself to the effectual demand. It is the interest of all those who employ their land, labour, or stock, in bringing any commodity to market, that the quantity never should exceed the effectual demand; and it is the interest of all other people that it never should fall short of that demand.

If at any time it exceeds the effectual demand, some of the component parts of its price must be paid below their natural rate. If it is rent, the interest of the landlords will immediately prompt them to withdraw a part of their land; and if it is wages or profit, the interest of the labourers in the one case, and of their employers in the other, will prompt them to withdraw a part of their labour or stock from this employment. The quantity brought to market will soon be no more than sufficient to supply the effectual demand. All the different parts of its price will rise to their natural rate, and the whole price to its natural price.

If, on the contrary, the quantity brought to market should at any time fall short of the effectual demand, some of the component parts of its price must rise above their natural rate. If it is rent, the interest of all other landlords will naturally prompt them to prepare more land for the raising of this commodity; if it is wages or profit, the interest of all other labourers and dealers will soon prompt them to employ more labour and stock in preparing and bringing it to market. The quantity brought thither will soon be sufficient to supply the effectual demand. All the different parts of its price will soon sink to their natural rate, and the whole price to its natural price.

The natural price, therefore, is, as it were, the central price, to which the prices of all commodities are continually gravitating. Different accidents may sometimes keep them suspended a good deal above it, and sometimes force them down even somewhat below it. But whatever may be the obstacles which hinder them from settling in this center of repose and continuance, they are constantly tending towards it.

But though the market price of every particular commodity is in this manner continually gravitating, if one may say so, towards the natural price, yet sometimes particular accidents, sometimes natural causes, and sometimes particular regulations of police, may, in many commodities, keep up the market price, for a long time together, a good deal above the natural price.

VIII. Of the Wages of Labour

The produce of labour constitutes the natural recompence or wages of labour.

In that original state of things, which precedes both the appropriation of land and the accumulation of stock, the whole produce of labour belongs to the labourer. He has neither landlord nor master to share with him.

Had this state continued, the wages of labour would have augmented with all those improvements in its productive powers, to which the division of labour gives occasion. All things would gradually have become cheaper. They would have been produced by a smaller quantity of labour; and as the commodities produced by equal quantities of labour would naturally in this state of things be exchanged for one another, they would have been purchased likewise with the produce of a smaller quantity.

But this original state of things, in which the labourer enjoyed the whole produce of his own labour, could not last beyond the first introduction of the appropriation of land and the accumulation of stock. It was at an end, therefore, long before the most considerable improvements were made in the productive powers of labour, and it would be to no purpose to trace further what might have been its effect upon the recompence or wages of labour. As soon as land becomes private property, the landlord demands a share of almost all the produce which the labourer can either raise, or collect from it. His rent makes the first deduction from the produce of the labour which is employed upon land.

It seldom happens that the person who tills the ground has wherewithal to maintain himself till he reaps the harvest. His maintenance is generally advanced to him from the stock of a master, the farmer who employs him, and who would have no interest to employ him, unless he was to share in the produce of his labour, or unless his stock was to be replaced to him with a profit. This profit makes a second deduction from the produce of the labour which is employed upon land.

The produce of almost all other labour is liable to the like deduction of profit. In all arts and manufactures the greater part of the workmen stand in need of a master to advance them the materials of their work, and their wages and maintenance till it be completed. He shares in the produce of their labour, or in the value which it adds to the materials upon which it is bestowed; and in this share consists his profit.

It sometimes happens, indeed, that a single independent workman has stock sufficient both to purchase the materials of his work, and to maintain himself till it be completed. He is both master and workman, and enjoys the whole produce of his own labour, or the whole value which it adds to the materials upon which it is bestowed. It includes what are usually two distinct revenues, belonging to two distinct persons, the profits of stock, and the wages of labour.

Such cases, however, are not very frequent, and in every part of Europe, twenty workmen serve under a master for one that is independent; and the wages of labour are every where understood to be, what they usually are, when the labourer is one person, and the owner of the stock which employs him another.

What are the common wages of labour, depends every where upon the contract usually made between those two parties, whose interests are by no means the same. The workmen desire to get as much, the masters to give as little as possible. The former are disposed to combine in order to raise, the latter in order to lower the wages of labour.

It is not, however, difficult to foresee which of the two parties must, upon all ordinary occasions, have the advantage in the dispute, and force the other into a compliance with their terms. The masters, being fewer in number, can combine much more easily; and the law, besides, authorises, or at least does not prohibit their combinations, while it prohibits those of the workmen. We have no acts of parliament against combining to lower the price of work; but many against combining to raise it. In all such disputes the masters can hold out much longer. A landlord, a farmer, a master manufacturer, or merchant, though they did not employ a single workman, could generally live a year or two upon the stocks which they have already acquired. Many workmen could not subsist a week, few could subsist a month, and scarce any a year without employment. In the long run the workman may be as necessary to his master as his master is to him, but the necessity is not so immediate.

We rarely hear, it has been said, of the combinations of masters, though frequently of those of workmen. But whoever imagines, upon this account, that masters rarely combine, is as ignorant of the world as of the subject. Masters are always and every where in a sort of tacit, but constant and uniform combination, not to raise the wages of labour above their actual rate. To violate this combination is every where a most unpopular action, and a sort of reproach to a master among his neighbours and equals. We seldom, indeed, hear of this combination, because it is the usual, and one may say, the natural state of things which nobody ever hears of. Masters too sometimes enter into particular combinations to sink the wages of labour even below this rate. These are always conducted with the utmost silence and secrecy, till the moment of execution, and when the workmen yield, as they sometimes do, without resistance, though severely felt by them, they are never heard of by other people. Such combinations, however, are frequently resisted by a contrary defensive combination of the workmen; who sometimes too, without any provocation of this kind, combine of their own accord to raise the price of their labour. Their usual pretences are, sometimes the high price of provisions; sometimes the great profit which their masters make by their work. But whether their combinations be offensive or defensive, they are always abundantly heard of. In order to bring the point to a speedy decision, they have always recourse to the loudest clamour, and sometimes to the most shocking violence and outrage. They are desperate, and act with the folly and extravagance of desperate men, who must either starve, or frighten their masters into an immediate compliance with their demands. The masters upon these occasions are just as clamorous upon the other side, and never cease to call aloud for the assistance of the civil magistrate, and the rigorous execution of those laws which have been enacted with so much severity against the combinations of servants, labourers, and journeymen. The workmen, accordingly, very seldom derive any advantage from the violence of those tumultuous combinations, which, partly from the interposition of the civil magistrate, partly from the superior steadiness of the masters, partly from the necessity which the greater part of the workmen are under of submitting for the sake of present subsistence, generally end in nothing, but the punishment or ruin of the ringleaders.

But though in disputes with their workmen, masters must generally have the advantage, there is however a certain rate below which it seems impossible to reduce, for any considerable time, the ordinary wages even of the lowest species of labour.

A man must always live by his work, and his wages must at least be sufficient to maintain him. They must even upon most occasions be somewhat more; otherwise it would be impossible for him to bring up a family, and the race of such workmen could not last beyond the first generation. Mr. Cantillon seems, upon this account, to suppose that the lowest species of common labourers must every where earn at least double their own maintenance, in order that one with another they may be enabled to bring up two children; the labour of the wife, on account of her necessary attendance on the children, being supposed no more than sufficient to provide for herself. But one half the children born, it is computed, die before the age of manhood. The poorest labourers, therefore, according to this account, must, one with another, attempt to rear at least four children, in order that two may have an equal chance of living to that age. But the necessary maintenance of four children, it is supposed, may be nearly equal to that of one man. The labour of an able-bodied slave, the same author adds, is computed to be worth double his maintenance; and that of the meanest labourer, he thinks, cannot be worth less than that of an able-bodied slave. Thus far at least seems certain, that, in order to bring up a family, the labour of the husband and wife together must, even in the lowest species of common labour, be able to earn something more than what is precisely necessary for their own maintenance; but in what proportion, whether in that above mentioned, or in any other, I shall not take upon me to determine.

There are certain circumstances, however, which sometimes give the labourers an advantage, and enable them to raise their wages considerably above this rate; evidently the lowest which is consistent with common humanity.

When in any country the demand for those who live by wages; labourers, journeymen, servants of every kind, is continually increasing;

when every year furnishes employment for a greater number than had been employed the year before, the workmen have no occasion to combine in order to raise their wages. The scarcity of hands occasions a competition among masters, who bid against one another, in order to get workmen, and thus voluntarily break through the natural combination of masters not to raise wages.

The demand for those who live by wages, it is evident, cannot increase but in proportion to the increase of the funds which are destined for the payment of wages. These funds are of two kinds; first, the revenue which is over and above what is necessary for the maintenance; and, secondly, the stock which is over and above what is necessary for the employment of their masters.

When the landlord, annuitant, or monied man, has a greater revenue than what he judges sufficient to maintain his own family, he employs either the whole or a part of the surplus in maintaining one or more menial servants. Increase this surplus, and he will naturally increase the number of those servants.

When an independent workman, such as a weaver or shoemaker, has got more stock than what is sufficient to purchase the materials of his own work, and to maintain himself till he can dispose of it, he naturally employs one or more journeymen with the surplus, in order to make a profit by their work. Increase this surplus, and he will naturally increase the number of his journeymen.

The demand for those who live by wages, therefore, necessarily increases with the increase of the revenue and stock of every country, and cannot possibly increase without it. The increase of revenue and stock is the increase of national wealth. The demand for those who live by wages, therefore, naturally increases with the increase of national wealth, and cannot possibly increase without it.

It is not the actual greatness of national wealth, but its continual increase, which occasions a rise in the wages of labour. It is not, accordingly, in the richest countries, but in the most thriving, or in those which are growing rich the fastest, that the wages of labour are highest. England is certainly, in the present times, a much richer country than any part of North America. The wages of labour, however, are much higher in North America than in any part of England.

Though North America is not yet so rich as England, it is much more thriving, and advancing with much greater rapidity to the further acquisition of riches. The most decisive mark of the prosperity of any country is the increase of the number of its inhabitants. In Great Britain, and most other European countries, they are not supposed to double in less than five hundred years. In the British colonies in North America, it has been found, that they double in twenty or five-and-twenty years. Nor in the present times is this increase principally owing to the continual importation of new inhabitants, but to the great multiplication of the species. Those who live to old age, it is said, frequently see there from fifty to a hundred, and sometimes many more, descendants from their own body. Labour is there so well rewarded that a numerous family of children, instead of being a burthen is a source of opulence and prosperity to the parents. The labour of each child, before it can leave their house, is computed to be worth a hundred pounds clear gain to them. A young widow with four or five young children, who, among the middling or inferior ranks of people in Europe, would have so little chance for a second husband, is there frequently courted as a sort of fortune. The value of children is the greatest of all encouragements to marriage. We cannot, therefore, wonder that the people in North America should generally marry very young. Notwithstanding the great increase occasioned by such early marriages, there is a continual complaint of the scarcity of hands in North America. The demand for labourers, the funds destined for maintaining them, increase, it seems, still faster than they can find labourers to employ.

Though the wealth of a country should be very great, yet if it has been long stationary, we must not expect to find the wages of labour very high in it. The funds destined for the payment of wages, the revenue and stock of its inhabitants, may be of the greatest extent; but if they have continued for several centuries of the same, or very nearly of the same extent, the number of labourers employed every year could easily supply, and even more than supply, the number wanted the following year. There could seldom be any scarcity of hands, nor could the masters be obliged to bid against one another in order to get them. The hands, on the contrary, would, in this case, naturally multiply beyond their employment. There would be a constant scarcity of employment, and the labourers would be obliged to bid against one another in order to get it. If in such a country the wages of labour had ever been more than sufficient to maintain the labourer, and to enable him to bring up a family, the competition of the labourers and the interest of the masters would soon reduce them to this lowest rate which is consistent with common humanity. China has been long one of the richest, that is, one of the most fertile, best cultivated, most industrious, and most populous countries in the world. It seems, however, to have been long stationary. Marco Polo, who visited it more than five hundred years ago, describes its cultivation, industry, and populousness, almost in the same terms in which they are described by travellers in the present times. It had perhaps, even long before his time, acquired that full complement of riches which the nature of its laws and institutions permits it to acquire. The accounts of all travellers, inconsistent in many other respects, agree in the low wages of labour, and in the difficulty which a labourer finds in bringing up a family in China. If by digging the ground a whole day he can get what will purchase a small quantity of rice in the evening, he is contented. The condition of artificers is, if possible, still worse. Instead of waiting indolently in their workhouses, for the calls of their customers, as in Europe, they are continually running about the streets with the tools of their respective trades, offering their service, and as it were begging employment. The poverty of the lower ranks of people in China far surpasses that of the most beggarly nations in Europe. In the neighbourhood of Canton many hundred, it is commonly said, many thousand families have no habitation on the land, but live constantly in little fishing boats upon the rivers and canals. The subsistence which they find there is so scanty that they are eager to fish up the nastiest garbage thrown overboard from any European ship. Any carrion, the carcase of a dead dog or cat, for example, though half putrid and stinking, is as welcome to them as the most wholesome food to the people of other countries. Marriage is encouraged in China, not by the profitableness of children, but by the liberty of destroying them. In all great towns several are every night exposed in the street, or drowned like puppies in the water. The performance of this horrid office is even said to be the avowed business by which some people earn their subsistence.

China, however, though it may perhaps stand still, does not seem to go backwards. Its towns are nowhere deserted by their inhabitants. The lands which had once been cultivated are nowhere neglected. The same or very nearly the same annual labour must therefore continue to be performed, and the funds destined for maintaining it must not, consequently, be sensibly diminished. The lowest class of labourers, therefore, notwithstanding their scanty subsistence, must some way or another make shift to continue their race so far as to keep up their usual numbers.

But it would be otherwise in a country where the funds destined for the maintenance of labour were sensibly decaying. Every year the demand for servants and labourers would, in all the different classes of employments, be less than it had been the year before. Many who had been bred in the superior classes, not being able to find employment in their own business, would be glad to seek it in the lowest. The lowest class being not only overstocked with its own workmen, but with the overflowings of all the other classes, the competition for employment would be so great in it, as to reduce the wages of labour to the most miserable and scanty subsistence of the labourer. Many would not be able to find employment even upon these hard terms, but would either starve, or be driven to seek a subsistence either by begging, or by the perpetration perhaps of the greatest enormities. Want, famine, and mortality would immediately prevail in that class, and from thence extend themselves to all the superior classes, till the number of inhabitants in the country was reduced to what could easily be maintained by the revenue and stock which remained in it, and which had escaped either the tyranny or calamity which had destroyed the rest. This perhaps is nearly the present state of Bengal, and of some other of the English settlements in the East Indies. In a fertile country which had before been much depopulated, where subsistence, consequently, should not be very difficult, and where, notwithstanding, three or four hundred thousand people die of hunger in one year, we may be assured that the funds destined for the maintenance of the labouring poor are fast decaying. The difference between the genius of the British constitution which protects and governs North America, and that of the mercantile company which oppresses and domineers in the East Indies, cannot perhaps be better illustrated than by the different state of those countries.

The liberal reward of labour, therefore, as it is the necessary effect, so it is the natural symptom of increasing national wealth. The scanty maintenance of the labouring poor, on the other hand, is the natural symptom that things are at a stand, and their starving condition that they are going fast backwards.

In Great Britain the wages of labour seem, in the present times, to be evidently more than what is precisely necessary to enable the labourer to bring up a family. In order to satisfy ourselves upon this point it will not be necessary to enter into any tedious or doubtful calculation of what may be the lowest sum upon which it is possible to do this. There are many plain symptoms that the wages of labour are nowhere in this country regulated by this lowest rate which is consistent with common humanity.

First, in almost every part of Great Britain there is a distinction, even in the lowest species of labour, between summer and winter wages. Summer wages are always highest. But on account of the extraordinary expence of fuel, the maintenance of a family is most expensive in winter. Wages, therefore, being highest when this expence is lowest, it seems evident that they are not regulated by what is necessary for this expence; but by the quantity and supposed value of the work. A labourer, it may be said indeed, ought to save part of his summer wages in order to defray his winter expence; and that through the whole year they do not exceed what is necessary to maintain his family through the whole year. A slave, however, or one absolutely dependent on us for immediate subsistence, would not be treated in this manner. His daily subsistence would be proportioned to his daily necessities.

Secondly, the wages of labour do not in Great Britain fluctuate with the price of provisions. These vary everywhere from year to year, frequently from month to month. But in many places the money price of labour remains uniformly the same sometimes for half a century together. If in these places, therefore, the labouring poor can maintain their families in dear years, they must be at their ease in times of moderate plenty, and in affluence in those of extraordinary cheapness. The high price of provisions during these ten years past has not in many parts of the kingdom been accompanied with any sensible rise in the money price of labour. It has, indeed, in some; owing probably more to the increase of the demand for labour than to that of the price of provisions.

Thirdly, as the price of provisions varies more from year to year than the wages of labour, so, on the other hand, the wages of labour vary more from place to place than the price of provisions. The prices of bread and butcher's meat are generally the same or very nearly the same through the greater part of the united kingdom. These and most other things which are sold by retail, the way in which the labouring poor buy all things, are generally fully as cheap or cheaper in great towns than in the remoter parts of the country, for reasons which I shall have occasion to explain hereafter. But the wages of labour in a great town and its neighbourhood are frequently a fourth or a fifth part, twenty or five-and-twenty per cent. higher than at a few miles distance.

Fourthly, the variations in the price of labour not only do not correspond either in place or time with those in the price of provisions, but they are frequently quite opposite.

Grain, the food of the common people, is dearer in Scotland than in England, whence Scotland receives almost every year very large supplies. But English corn must be sold dearer in Scotland, the country to which it is brought, than in England, the country from which it comes; and in proportion to its quality it cannot be sold dearer in Scotland than the Scotch corn that comes to the same market in competition with it. The quality of grain depends chiefly upon the quantity of flour or meal which it yields at the mill, and in this respect English grain is so much superior to the Scotch, that, though often dearer in appearance, or in proportion to the measure of its bulk, it is generally cheaper in reality, or in proportion to its quality, or even to the measure of its weight. The price of labour, on the contrary, is dearer in England than in Scotland. If the labouring poor, therefore, can maintain their families in the one part of the united kingdom, they must be in affluence in the other. Oatmeal indeed supplies the common people in Scotland with the greatest and the best part of their food, which is in general much inferior to that of their neighbours of the same rank in England. This difference, however, in the mode of their subsistence is not the cause, but the effect, of the difference in their wages; though, by a strange misapprehension, I have frequently heard it represented as the cause. It is not because one man keeps a coach while his neighbour walks a-foot, that the one is rich and the other poor; but because the one is rich he keeps a coach, and because the other is poor he walks a-foot.

But though it is certain that in both parts of the united kingdom grain was somewhat dearer in the last century than in the present, it is equally certain that labour was much cheaper. If the labouring poor, therefore, could bring up their families then, they must be much more at their ease now. In England the improvements of agriculture, manufactures and commerce began much earlier than in Scotland. The demand for labour, and consequently its price, must necessarily have increased with those improvements. In the last century, accordingly, as well as in the present, the wages of labour were higher in England than in Scotland. They have risen too considerably since that time, though, on account of the greater variety of wages paid there in different places, it is more difficult to ascertain how much. The price of labour, it must be observed, cannot be ascertained very accurately any where, different prices being often paid at the same place and for the same sort of labour, not only according to the different abilities of the workmen, but according to the easiness or hardness of the masters. Where wages are not regulated by law, all that we can pretend to determine is what are the most usual; and experience seems to show that law can never regulate them properly, though it has often pretended to do so.

The real recompence of labour, the real quantity of the necessaries and conveniencies of life which it can procure to the labourer, has, during the course of the present century, increased perhaps in a still greater proportion than its money price. Not only grain has become somewhat cheaper, but many other things, from which the industrious poor derive an agreeable and wholesome variety of food, have become a great deal cheaper. Potatoes, for example, do not at present, through the greater part of the kingdom, cost half the price which they used to do thirty or forty years ago. The same thing may be said of turnips, carrots, cabbages; things which were formerly never raised but by the spade, but which are now commonly raised by the plough. All sort of garden stuff too has become cheaper. The greater part of the apples and even of the onions consumed in Great Britain were in the last century imported from Flanders. The great improvements in the coarser manufactures of both linen and woollen cloth furnish the labourers with cheaper and better clothing; and those in the manufactures of the coarser metals, with cheaper and better instruments of trade, as well as with many agreeable and convenient pieces of household furniture. Soap, salt, candles, leather, and fermented liquors, have, indeed, become a good deal dearer; chiefly from the taxes which have been laid upon them. The quantity of these, however, which the labouring poor are under any necessity of consuming, is so very small, that the increase in their price does not compensate the diminution in that of so many other things. The common complaint that luxury extends itself even to the lowest ranks of the people, and that the labouring poor will not now be contented with the same food, clothing and lodging which satisfied them in former times, may convince us that it is not the money price of labour only, but its real recompence, which has augmented.

Is this improvement in the circumstances of the lower ranks of the people to be regarded as an advantage or as an inconveniency to the society? The answer seems at first sight abundantly plain. Servants, labourers and workmen of different kinds, make up the far greater part of every great political society. But what improves the circumstances of the greater part can never be regarded as an inconveniency to the whole. No society can surely be flourishing and happy, of which the far greater part of the members are poor and miserable. It is but equity, besides, that they who feed, clothe and lodge the whole body of the people, should have such a share of the produce of their own labour as to be themselves tolerably well fed, clothed and lodged.

Poverty, though it no doubt discourages, does not always prevent marriage. It seems even to be favourable to generation. A half-starved Highland woman frequently bears more than twenty children, while a pampered fine lady is often incapable of bearing any, and is generally exhausted by two or three. Barrenness, so frequent among women of fashion, is very rare among those of inferior station. Luxury in the fair sex, while it inflames perhaps the passion for enjoyment, seems always to weaken, and frequently to destroy altogether, the powers of generation.

But poverty, though it does not prevent the generation, is extremely unfavourable to the rearing of children. The tender plant is produced, but in so cold a soil, and so severe a climate, soon withers and dies. It is not uncommon, I have been frequently told, in the Highlands of Scotland for a mother who has borne twenty children not to have two alive. Several officers of great experience have assured me, that so far from recruiting their regiment, they have never been able to supply it with drums and fifes from all the soldiers' children that were born in it. A greater number of fine children, however, is seldom seen any where than about a barrack of soldiers. Very few of them, it seems, arrive at the age of thirteen or fourteen. In some places one half the children born die before they are four years of age; in many places before they are seven; and in almost all places before they are nine or ten. This great mortality, however, will every where be found chiefly among the children of the common people, who cannot afford to tend them with the same care as those of better station. Though their marriages are generally more fruitful than those of people of fashion, a smaller proportion of their children arrive at maturity. In foundling hospitals, and among the children brought up by parish charities, the mortality is still greater than among those of the common people.

Every species of animals naturally multiplies in proportion to the means of their subsistence, and no species can ever multiply beyond it. But in civilized society it is only among the inferior ranks of people that the scantiness of subsistence can set limits to the further multiplication of the human species; and it can do so in no other way than by destroying a great part of the children which their fruitful marriages produce.

The liberal reward of labour, by enabling them to provide better for their children, and consequently to bring up a greater number, naturally tends to widen and extend those limits. It deserves to be remarked too, that it necessarily does this as nearly as possible in the proportion which the demand for labour requires. If this demand is continually increasing, the reward of labour must necessarily encourage in such a manner the marriage and multiplication of labourers, as may enable them to supply that continually increasing demand by a continually increasing population. If the reward should at any time be less than what was requisite for this purpose, the deficiency of hands would soon raise it; and if it should at any time be more, their excessive multiplication would soon lower it to this necessary rate. The market would be so much understocked with labour in the one case, and so much overstocked in the other, as would soon force back its price to that proper rate which the circumstances of the society required. It is in this manner that the demand for men, like that for any other commodity, necessarily regulates the production of men; quickens it when it goes on too slowly, and stops it when it advances too fast. It is this demand which regulates and determines the state of propagation in all the different countries of the world, in North America, in Europe, and in China; which renders it rapidly progressive in the first, slow and gradual in the second, and altogether stationary in the last.

The wear and tear of a slave, it has been said, is at the expence of his master; but that of a free servant is at his own expence. The wear and tear of the latter, however, is, in reality, as much at the expence of his master as that of the former. The wages paid to journeymen and servants of every kind must be such as may enable them, one with another, to continue the race of journeymen and servants, according as the increasing, diminishing, or stationary demand of the society may happen to require. But though the wear and tear of a free servant be equally at the expence of his master, it generally costs him much less than that of a slave. The fund destined for replacing or repairing, if I may say so, the wear and tear of the slave, is commonly managed by a negligent master or careless overseer. That destined for performing the same office with regard to the free man, is managed by the free man himself. The disorders which generally prevail in the economy of the rich, naturally introduce themselves into the management of the former: the strict frugality and parsimonious attention of the poor as naturally establish themselves in that of the latter. Under such different management, the same purpose must require very different degrees of expence to execute it. It appears, accordingly, from the experience of all ages and nations, I believe, that the work done by freemen comes cheaper in the end than that performed by slaves. It is found to do so even at Boston, New York, and Philadelphia, where the wages of common labour are so very high.

The liberal reward of labour, therefore, as it is the effect of increasing wealth, so it is the cause of increasing population. To complain of it, is to lament over the necessary effect and cause of the greatest public prosperity.

It deserves to be remarked, perhaps, that it is in the progressive state, while the society is advancing to the further acquisition, rather than when it has acquired its full complement of riches, that the condition of the labouring poor, of the great body of the people, seems to be the happiest and the most comfortable. It is hard in the stationary, and miserable in the declining state. The progressive state is in reality the cheerful and the hearty state to all the different orders of the society. The stationary is dull; the declining melancholy.

The liberal reward of labour, as it encourages the propagation, so it increases the industry of the common people. The wages of labour are the encouragement of industry, which, like every other human quality, improves in proportion to the encouragement it receives. A plentiful subsistence increases the bodily strength of the labourer, and the comfortable hope of bettering his condition, and of ending his days perhaps in ease and plenty, animates him to exert that strength to the utmost. Where wages are high, accordingly, we shall always find the workmen more active, diligent, and expeditious, than where they are low; in England, for example, than in Scotland; in the neighbourhood of great towns, than in remote country places.

The increase in the wages of labour necessarily increases the price of many commodities, by increasing that part of it which resolves itself into wages, and so far tends to diminish their consumption both at home and abroad. The same cause, however, which raises the wages of labour, the increase of stock, tends to increase its productive powers, and to make a smaller quantity of labour produce a greater quantity of work. The owner of the stock which employs a great number of labourers, necessarily endeavours, for his own advantage, to make such a proper division and distribution of employment, that they may be enabled to produce the greatest quantity of work possible. For the same reason, he endeavours to supply them with the best machinery which either he or they can think of. What takes place among the labourers in a particular workhouse, takes place, for the same reason, among those of a great society. The greater their number, the more they naturally divide themselves into different classes and subdivisions of employment. More heads are occupied in inventing the most proper machinery for executing the work of each, and it is, therefore, more likely to be invented. There are many commodities, therefore, which, in consequence of these improvements, come to be produced by so much less labour than before, that the increase of its price is more than compensated by the diminution of its quantity.

IX. Of the Profits of Stock

The rise and fall in the profits of stock depend upon the same causes with the rise and fall in the wages of labour, the increasing or declining state of the wealth of the society; but those causes affect the one and the other very differently.

The increase of stock, which raises wages, tends to lower profit. When the stocks of many rich merchants are turned into the same trade, their mutual competition naturally tends to lower its profit; and when there is a like increase of stock in all the different trades carried on in the same society, the same competition must produce the same effect in them all.

It is not easy, it has already been observed, to ascertain what are the average wages of labour even in a particular place, and at a particular time. We can, even in this case, seldom determine more than what are the most usual wages. But even this can seldom be done with regard to the profits of stock. Profit is so very fluctuating, that the person who carries on a particular trade cannot always tell you himself what is the average of his annual profit. It is affected, not only by every variation of price in the commodities which he deals in, but by the good or bad fortune both of his rivals and of his customers, and by a thousand other accidents to which goods when carried either by sea or by land, or even when stored in a warehouse, are liable. It varies, therefore, not only from year to year, but from day to day, and almost from hour to hour. To ascertain what is the average profit of all the different trades carried on in a great kingdom, must be much more difficult; and to judge of what it may have been formerly, or in remote periods of time, with any degree of precision, must be altogether impossible.

But though it may be impossible to determine with any degree of precision, what are or were the average profits of stock, either in the present, or in ancient times, some notion may be formed of them from the interest of money. It may be laid down as a maxim, that wherever a great deal can be made by the use of money, a great deal will commonly be given for the use of it; and that wherever little can be made by it, less will commonly be given for it. According, therefore, as the usual market rate of interest varies in any country, we may be assured that the ordinary profits of stock must vary with it, must sink as it sinks, and rise as it rises. The progress of interest, therefore, may lead us to form some notion of the progress of profit.

By the 37th of Henry VIII all interest above ten per cent. was declared unlawful. More, it seems, had sometimes been taken before that. In the reign of Edward VI religious zeal prohibited all interest. This prohibition, however, like all others of the same kind, is said to have produced no effect, and probably rather increased than diminished the evil of usury. The statute of Henry VIII was revived by the 13th of Elizabeth, cap. 8. and ten per cent. continued to be the legal rate of interest till the 21st of James I when it was restricted to eight per cent. It was reduced to six per cent. soon after the restoration, and by the 12th of Queen Anne, to five per cent. All these different statutory regulations seem to have been made with great propriety. They seem to have followed and not to have gone before the market rate of interest, or the rate at which people of good credit usually borrowed. Since the time of Queen Anne, five per cent. seems to have been rather above than below the market rate.

Since the time of Henry VIII the wealth and revenue of the country have been continually advancing, and, in the course of their progress, their pace seems rather to have been gradually accelerated than retarded. They seem, not only to have been going on, but to have been going on faster and faster. The wages of labour have been continually increasing during the same period, and in the greater part of the different branches of trade and manufactures the profits of stock have been diminishing.

It generally requires a greater stock to carry on any sort of trade in a great town than in a country village. The great stocks employed in every branch of trade, and the number of rich competitors, generally reduce the rate of profit in the former below what it is in the latter. But the wages of labour are generally higher in a great town than in a country village. In a thriving town the people who have great stocks to employ, frequently cannot get the number of workmen they want, and therefore bid against one another in order to get as many as they can, which raises the wages of labour, and lowers the profits of stock. In the remote parts of the country there is frequently not stock sufficient to employ all the people, who therefore bid against one another in order to get employment, which lowers the wages of labour, and raises the profits of stock.

In Scotland, though the legal rate of interest is the same as in England, the market rate is rather higher. There are few trades which cannot be carried on with a smaller stock in Scotland than in England. The common rate of profit, therefore, must be somewhat greater. The wages of labour, it has already been observed, are lower in Scotland than in England. The country too is not only much poorer, but the steps by which it advances to a better condition, for it is evidently advancing, seem to be much slower and more tardy.

France is perhaps in the present times not so rich a country as England; and though the legal rate of interest has in France frequently been lower than in England, the market rate has generally been higher; for there, as in other countries, they have several very safe and easy methods of evading the law. The profits of trade, I have been assured by British merchants who had traded in both countries, are higher in France than in England; and it is no doubt upon this account that many British subjects choose rather to employ their capitals in a country where trade is in disgrace, than in one where it is highly respected. The wages of labour are lower in France than in England. When you go from Scotland to England, the difference which you may remark between the dress and countenance of the common people in the one country and in the other, sufficiently indicates the difference in their condition. The contrast is still greater when you return from France. France, though no doubt a richer country than Scotland, seems not to be going forward so fast.

The province of Holland, on the other hand, in proportion to the extent of its territory and the number of its people, is a richer country than England. The government there borrows at two per cent., and private people of good credit at three. The wages of labour are said to be higher in Holland than in England, and the Dutch, it is well known, trade upon lower profits than any people in Europe. The trade of Holland, it has been pretended by some people, is decaying, and it may perhaps be true that some particular branches of it are so. But these symptoms seem to indicate sufficiently that there is no general decay. When profit diminishes, merchants are very apt to complain that trade decays; though the diminution of profits is the natural effect of its prosperity, or of a greater stock being employed in it than before.

In our North American and West Indian colonies, not only the wages of labour, but the interest of money, and consequently the profits of stock, are higher than in England. In the different colonies both the legal and the market rate of interest run from six to eight per cent. High wages of labour and high profits of stock, however, are things, perhaps, which scarce ever go together, except in the peculiar circumstances of new colonies. A new colony must always for some time be more understocked in proportion to the extent of its territory, and more underpeopled in proportion to the extent of its stock, than the greater part of other countries. They have more land than they have stock to cultivate. What they have, therefore, is applied to the cultivation only of what is most fertile and most favourably situated, the land near the seashore, and along the banks of navigable rivers. Such land too is frequently purchased at a price below the value even of its natural produce. Stock employed in the purchase and improvement of such lands must yield a very large profit, and consequently afford to pay a very large interest. Its rapid accumulation in so profitable an employment enables the planter to increase the number of his hands faster than he can find them in a new settlement. Those whom he can find, therefore, are very liberally rewarded. As the colony increases, the profits of stock gradually diminish. When the most fertile and best situated lands have been all occupied, less profit can be made by the cultivation of what is inferior both in soil and situation, and less interest can be afforded for the stock which is so employed. In the greater part of our colonies, accordingly, both the legal and the market rate of interest have been considerably reduced during the course of the present century. As riches, improvement, and population have increased, interest has declined. The wages of labour do not sink with the profits of stock. The demand for labour increases with the increase of stock whatever be its profits.

The acquisition of new territory, or of new branches of trade, may sometimes raise the profits of stock, and with them the interest of money, even in a country which is fast advancing in the acquisition of riches. The stock of the country not being sufficient for the whole accession of business, which such acquisitions present to the different people among whom it is divided, is applied to those particular branches only which afford the greatest profit. Part of what had before been employed in other trades, is necessarily withdrawn from them, and turned into some of the new and more profitable ones. In all those old trades, therefore, the competition comes to be less than before. The market comes to be less fully supplied with many different sorts of goods. Their price necessarily rises more or less, and yields a greater profit to those who deal in them, who can, therefore, afford to borrow at a higher interest.

The diminution of the capital stock of the society, or of the funds destined for the maintenance of industry, however, as it lowers the wages of labour, so it raises the profits of stock, and consequently the interest of money. By the wages of labour being lowered, the owners of what stock remains in the society can bring their goods at less expence to market than before, and less stock being employed in supplying the market than before, they can sell them dearer. Their goods cost them less, and they get more for them. Their profits, therefore, being augmented at both ends, can well afford a large interest. The great fortunes so suddenly and so easily acquired in Bengal and the other British settlements in the East Indies, may satisfy us that, as the wages of labour are very low, so the profits of stock are very high in those ruined countries. The interest of money is proportionably so. In Bengal, money is frequently lent to the farmers at forty, fifty, and sixty per cent. and the succeeding crop is mortgaged for the payment. As the profits which can afford such an interest must eat up almost the whole rent of the landlord, so such enormous usury must in its turn eat up the greater part of those profits. Before the fall of the Roman republic, a usury of the same kind seems to have been common in the provinces, under the ruinous administration of their proconsuls. The virtuous Brutus lent money in Cyprus at eight-and-forty per cent. as we learn from the letters of Cicero.

In a country which had acquired that full complement of riches which the nature of its soil and climate, and its situation with respect to other countries, allowed it to acquire; which could, therefore, advance no further, and which was not going backwards, both the wages of labour and the profits of stock would probably be very low. In a country fully peopled in proportion to what either its territory could maintain or its stock employ, the competition for employment would necessarily be so great as to reduce the wages of labour to what was barely sufficient to keep up the number of labourers, and, the country being already fully peopled, that number could never be augmented. In a country fully stocked in proportion to all the business it had to transact, as great a quantity of stock would be employed in every particular branch as the nature and extent of the trade would admit. The competition, therefore, would everywhere be as great, and consequently the ordinary profit as low as possible.

But perhaps no country has ever yet arrived at this degree of opulence. China seems to have been long stationary, and had probably long ago acquired that full complement of riches which is consistent with the nature of its laws and institutions. But this complement may be much inferior to what, with other laws and institutions, the nature of its soil, climate, and situation might admit of. A country which neglects or despises foreign commerce, and which admits the vessels of foreign nations into one or two of its ports only, cannot transact the same quantity of business which it might do with different laws and institutions. In a country too, where, though the rich or the owners of large capitals enjoy a good deal of security, the poor or the owners of small capitals enjoy scarce any, but are liable, under the pretence of justice, to be pillaged and plundered at any time by the inferior mandarines, the quantity of stock employed in all the different branches of business transacted within it, can never be equal to what the nature and extent of that business might admit. In every different branch, the oppression of the poor must establish the monopoly of the rich, who, by engrossing the whole trade to themselves, will be able to make very large profits. Twelve per cent. accordingly is said to be the common interest of money in China, and the ordinary profits of stock must be sufficient to afford this large interest.

A defect in the law may sometimes raise the rate of interest considerably above what the condition of the country, as to wealth or poverty, would require. When the law does not enforce the performance of contracts, it puts all borrowers nearly upon the same footing with bankrupts or people of doubtful credit in better regulated countries. The uncertainty of recovering his money makes the lender exact the same usurious interest which is usually required from bankrupts. Among the barbarous nations who overran the western provinces of the Roman empire, the performance of contracts was left for many ages to the faith of the contracting parties. The courts of justice of their kings seldom intermeddled in it. The high rate of interest which took place in those ancient times may perhaps be partly accounted for from this cause.

When the law prohibits interest altogether, it does not prevent it. Many people must borrow, and nobody will lend without such a consideration for the use of their money as is suitable, not only to what can be made by the use of it, but to the difficulty and danger of evading the law. The high rate of interest among all Mahometan nations is accounted for by Mr. Montesquieu, not from their poverty, but partly from this, and partly from the difficulty of recovering the money.

The lowest ordinary rate of profit must always be something more than what is sufficient to compensate the occasional losses to which every employment of stock is exposed. It is this surplus only which is neat or clear profit. What is called gross profit comprehends frequently, not only this surplus, but what is retained for compensating such extraordinary losses. The interest which the borrower can afford to pay is in proportion to the clear profit only.

The lowest ordinary rate of interest must, in the same manner, be something more than sufficient to compensate the occasional losses to which lending, even with tolerable prudence, is exposed. Were it not more, charity or friendship could be the only motives for lending.

In a country which had acquired its full complement of riches, where in every particular branch of business there was the greatest quantity of stock that could be employed in it, as the ordinary rate of clear profit would be very small, so the usual market rate of interest which could be afforded out of it, would be so low as to render it impossible for any but the very wealthiest people to live upon the interest of their money. All people of small or middling fortunes would be obliged to superintend themselves the employment of their own stocks. It would be necessary that almost every man should be a man of business, or engage in some sort of trade. The province of Holland seems to be approaching near to this state. It is there unfashionable not to be a man of business. Necessity makes it usual for almost every man to be so, and custom every where regulates fashion. As it is ridiculous not to dress, so is it, in some measure, not to be employed, like other people. As a man of a civil profession seems awkward in a camp or a garrison, and is even in some danger of being despised there, so does an idle man among men of business.

X. Of the Rent of Land

Rent, considered as the price paid for the use of land, is naturally the highest which the tenant can afford to pay in the actual circumstances of the land. In adjusting the terms of the lease, the landlord endeavours to leave him no greater share of the produce than what is sufficient to keep up the stock from which he furnishes the seed, pays the labour, and purchases and maintains the cattle and other instruments of husbandry, together with the ordinary profits of farming stock in the neighbourhood. This is evidently the smallest share with which the tenant can content himself without being a loser, and the landlord seldom means to leave him any more. Whatever part of the produce, or, what is the same thing, whatever part of its price, is over and above this share, he naturally endeavours to reserve to himself as the rent of his land, which is evidently the highest the tenant can afford to pay in the actual circumstances of the land. Sometimes, indeed, the liberality, more frequently the ignorance, of the landlord, makes him accept of somewhat less than this portion; and sometimes too, though more rarely, the ignorance of the tenant makes him undertake to pay somewhat more, or to content himself with somewhat less, than the ordinary profits of farming stock in the neighbourhood. This portion, however, may still be considered as the natural rent of land, or the rent for which it is naturally meant that land should for the most part be let.

The rent of land, it may be thought, is frequently no more than a reasonable profit or interest for the stock laid out by the landlord upon its improvement. This, no doubt, may be partly the case upon some occasions; for it can scarce ever be more than partly the case. The landlord demands a rent even for unimproved land, and the supposed interest or profit upon the expence of improvement is generally an addition to this original rent. Those improvements, besides, are not always made by the stock of the landlord, but sometimes by that of the tenant. When the lease comes to be renewed, however, the landlord commonly demands the same augmentation of rent, as if they had been all made by his own.

He sometimes demands rent for what is altogether incapable of human improvement. Kelp is a species of seaweed, which, when burnt, yields an alkaline salt, useful for making glass, soap, and for several other purposes. It grows in several parts of Great Britain, particularly in Scotland, upon such rocks only as lie within the high water mark, which are twice every day covered with the sea, and of which the produce, therefore, was never augmented by human industry. The landlord, however, whose estate is bounded by a kelp shore of this kind, demands a rent for it as much as for his corn fields.

The sea in the neighbourhood of the islands of Shetland is more than commonly abundant in fish, which make a great part of the subsistence of their inhabitants. But in order to profit by the produce of the water, they must have a habitation upon the neighbouring land. The rent of the landlord is in proportion, not to what the farmer can make by the land, but to what he can make both by the land and by the water. It is partly paid in sea fish; and one of the very few instances in which rent makes a part of the price of that commodity, is to be found in that country.

The rent of land, therefore, considered as the price paid for the use of the land, is naturally a monopoly price. It is not at all proportioned to what the landlord may have laid out upon the improvement of the land, or to what he can afford to take; but to what the farmer can afford to give.

Such parts only of the produce of land can commonly be brought to market of which the ordinary price is sufficient to replace the stock which must be employed in bringing them thither, together with its ordinary profits. If the ordinary price is more than this, the surplus part of it will naturally go to the rent of the land. If it is not more, though the commodity may be brought to market, it can afford no rent to the landlord. Whether the price is, or is not more, depends upon the demand.

There are some parts of the produce of land for which the demand must always be such as to afford a greater price than what is sufficient to bring them to market; and there are others for which it either may or may not be such as to afford this greater price. The former must always afford a rent to that landlord. The latter sometimes may, and sometimes may not, according to different circumstances.

Rent, it is to be observed, therefore, enters into the composition of the price of commodities in a different way from wages and profit. High or low wages and profit, are the causes of high or low price; high or low rent is the effect of it. It is because high or low wages and profit must be paid, in order to bring a particular commodity to market, that its price is high or low. But it is because its price is high or low; a great deal more, or very little more, or no more, than what is sufficient to pay those wages and profit, that it affords a high rent, or a low rent, or no rent at all.

The particular consideration, first, of those parts of the produce of land which always afford some rent; secondly, of those which sometimes may and sometimes may not afford rent; and, thirdly, of the variations which, in the different periods of improvement, naturally take place, in the relative value of those two different sorts of rude produce, when compared both with one another and with manufactured commodities, will divide this chapter into three parts.

PART ONE: Of the Produce of Land which always affords Rent

As men, like all other animals, naturally multiply in proportion to the means of their subsistence, food is always, more or less, in demand. It can always purchase or command a greater or smaller quantity of labour, and somebody can always be found who is willing to do something in order to obtain it. The quantity of labour, indeed, which it can purchase, is not always equal to what it could maintain, if managed in the most economical manner, on account of the high wages which are sometimes given to labour. But it can always purchase such a quantity of labour as it can maintain, according to the rate at which that sort of labour is commonly maintained in the neighbourhood.

But land, in almost any situation, produces a greater quantity of food than what is sufficient to maintain all the labour necessary for bringing it to market, in the most liberal way in which that labour is ever maintained. The surplus too is always more than sufficient to replace the stock which employed that labour, together with its profits. Something, therefore, always remains for a rent to the landlord.

The most desert moors in Norway and Scotland produce some sort of pasture for cattle, of which the milk and the increase are always more than sufficient, not only to maintain all the labour necessary for tending them, and to pay the ordinary profit to the farmer or owner of the herd or flock; but to afford some small rent to the landlord. The rent increases in proportion to the goodness of the pasture. The same extent of ground not only maintains a greater number of cattle, but as they are brought within a smaller compass, less labour becomes requisite to tend them, and to collect their produce. The landlord gains both ways; by the increase of the produce, and by the diminution of the labour which must be maintained out of it.

The rent of land not only varies with its fertility, whatever be its produce, but with its situation, whatever be its fertility. Land in the neighbourhood of a town gives a greater rent than land equally fertile in a distant part of the country. Though it may cost no more labour to cultivate the one than the other, it must always cost more to bring the produce of the distant land to market. A greater quantity of labour, therefore, must be maintained out of it; and the surplus, from which are drawn both the profit of the farmer and the rent of the landlord, must be diminished. But in remote parts of the country the rate of profits, as has already been shown, is generally higher than in the neighbourhood of a large town. A smaller proportion of this diminished surplus, therefore, must belong to the landlord.

Good roads, canals, and navigable rivers, by diminishing the expence of carriage, put the remote parts of the country more nearly upon a level with those in the neighbourhood of the town. They are upon that account the greatest of all improvements. They encourage the cultivation of the remote, which must always be the most extensive circle of the country. They are advantageous to the town, by breaking down the monopoly of the country in its neighbourhood. They are advantageous even to that part of the country. Though they introduce some rival commodities into the old market, they open many new markets to its produce. Monopoly, besides, is a great enemy to good management, which can never be universally established but in consequence of that free and universal competition which forces everybody to have recourse to it for the sake of self-defence.

PART TWO: Of the Produce of Land which sometimes does, and sometimes does not, afford Rent

Human food seems to be the only produce of land which always and necessarily affords some rent to the landlord. Other sorts of produce sometimes may and sometimes may not, according to different circumstances.

After food, clothing and lodging are the two great wants of mankind.

Land in its original rude state can afford the materials of clothing and lodging to a much greater number of people than it can feed. In its improved state it can sometimes feed a greater number of people than it can supply with those materials; at least in the way in which they require them, and are willing to pay for them. In the one state, therefore, there is always a superabundance of those materials, which are frequently, upon that account, of little or no value. In the other there is often a scarcity, which necessarily augments their value. In the one state a great part of them is thrown away as useless, and the price of what is used is considered as equal only to the labour and expence of fitting it for use, and can, therefore, afford no rent to the landlord. In the other they are all made use of, and there is frequently a demand for more than can be had. Somebody is always willing to give more for every part of them than what is sufficient to pay the expence of bringing them to market. Their price, therefore, can always afford some rent to the landlord.

The skins of the larger animals were the original materials of clothing. Among nations of hunters and shepherds, therefore, whose food consists chiefly in the flesh of those animals, every man, by providing himself with food, provides himself with the materials of more clothing than he can wear. If there was no foreign commerce, the greater part of them would be thrown away as things of no value. This was probably the case among the hunting nations of North America, before their country was discovered by the Europeans, with whom they now exchange their surplus peltry, for blankets, firearms, and brandy, which gives it some value. In the present commercial state of the known world, the most barbarous nations, I believe, among whom land property is established, have some foreign commerce of this kind, and find among their wealthier neighbours such a demand for all the materials of clothing, which their land produces, and which can neither be wrought up nor consumed at home, as raises their price above what it costs to send them to those wealthier neighbours. It affords, therefore, some rent to the landlord. When the greater part of the highland cattle were consumed on their own hills, the exportation of their hides made the most considerable article of the commerce of that country, and what they were exchanged for afforded some addition to the rent of the highland estates. The wool of England, which in old times could neither be consumed nor wrought up at home, found a market in the then wealthier and more industrious country of Flanders, and its price afforded something to the rent of the land which produced it. In countries not better cultivated than England was then, or than the highlands of Scotland are now, and which had no foreign commerce, the materials of clothing would evidently be so superabundant, that a great part of them would be thrown away as useless, and no part could afford any rent to the landlord.

The materials of lodging cannot always be transported to so great a distance as those of clothing, and do not so readily become an object of foreign commerce. When they are superabundant in the country which produces them, it frequently happens, even in the present commercial state of the world, that they are of no value to the landlord. A good stone quarry in the neighbourhood of London would afford a considerable rent. In many parts of Scotland and Wales it affords none. Barren timber for building is of great value in a populous and well-cultivated country, and the land which produces it affords a considerable rent. But in many parts of North America the landlord would be much obliged to any body who would carry away the greater part of his large trees. In some parts of the highlands of Scotland the bark is the only part of the wood which, for want of roads and water carriage, can be sent to market. The timber is left to rot upon the ground. When the materials of lodging are so superabundant, the part made use of is worth only the labour and expence of fitting it for that use. It affords no rent to the landlord, who generally grants the use of it to whoever takes the trouble of asking it. The demand of wealthier nations, however, sometimes enables him to get a rent for it. The paving of the streets of London has enabled the owners of some barren rocks on the coast of Scotland to draw a rent from what never afforded any before. The woods of Norway and of the coasts of the Baltic, find a market in many parts of Great Britain which they could not find at home, and thereby afford some rent to their proprietors.

Countries are populous, not in proportion to the number of people whom their produce can clothe and lodge, but in proportion to that of those whom it can feed. When food is provided, it is easy to find the necessary clothing and lodging. But though these are at hand, it may often be difficult to find food. In some parts even of the British dominions what is called A House, may be built by one day's labour of one man. The simplest species of clothing, the skins of animals, require somewhat more labour to dress and prepare them for use. They do not, however, require a great deal. Among savage and barbarous nations, a hundredth or little more than a hundredth part of the labour of the whole year, will be sufficient to provide them with such clothing and lodging as satisfy the greater part of the people. All the other ninety-nine parts are frequently no more than enough to provide them with food.

But when by the improvement and cultivation of land the labour of one family can provide food for two, the labour of half the society becomes sufficient to provide food for the whole. The other half, therefore, or at least the greater part of them, can be employed in providing other things, or in satisfying the other wants and fancies of mankind. Clothing and lodging, household furniture, and what is called Equipage, are the principal objects of the greater part of those wants and fancies. The rich man consumes no more food than his poor neighbour. In quality it may be very different, and to select and prepare it may require more labour and art; but in quantity it is very nearly the same. But compare the spacious palace and great wardrobe of the one, with the hovel and the few rags of the other, and you will be sensible that the difference between their clothing, lodging, and household furniture, is almost as great in quantity as it is in quality. The desire of food is limited in every man by the narrow capacity of the human stomach; but the desire of the conveniencies and ornaments of building, dress, equipage, and household furniture, seems to have no limit or certain boundary. Those, therefore, who have the command of more food than they themselves can consume, are always willing to exchange the surplus, or, what is the same thing, the price of it, for gratifications of this other kind. What is over and above satisfying the limited desire, is given for the amusement of those desires which cannot be satisfied, but seem to be altogether endless. The poor, in order to obtain food, exert themselves to gratify those fancies of the rich, and to obtain it more certainly, they vie with one another in the cheapness and perfection of their work.

Food is in this manner, not only the original source of rent, but every other part of the produce of land which afterwards affords rent, derives that part of its value from the improvement of the powers of labour in producing food by means of the improvement and cultivation of land.

PART THREE: Of the Variations in the Proportion between the respective Values of that Sort of Produce which always affords Rent, and of that which sometimes does and sometimes does not afford Rent

The increasing abundance of food, in consequence of increasing improvement and cultivation, must necessarily increase the demand for every part of the produce of land which is not food, and which can be applied either to use or to ornament. In the whole progress of improvement, it might therefore be expected, there should be only one variation in the comparative values of those two different sorts of produce. The value of that sort which sometimes does and sometimes does not afford rent, should constantly rise in proportion to that which always affords some rent. As art and industry advance, the materials of clothing and lodging, the useful fossils and minerals of the earth, the precious metals and the precious stones should gradually come to be more and more in demand, should gradually exchange for a greater and a greater quantity of food, or in other words, should gradually become dearer and dearer. This accordingly has been the case with most of these things upon most occasions, and would have been the case with all of them upon all occasions, if particular accidents had not upon some occasions increased the supply of some of them in a still greater proportion than the demand.

The value of a freestone quarry, for example, will necessarily increase with the increasing improvement and population of the country round about it; especially if it should be the only one in the neighbourhood. But the value of a silver mine, even though there should not be another within a thousand miles of it, will not necessarily increase with the improvement of the country in which it is situated. The market for the produce of a freestone quarry can seldom extend more than a few miles round about it, and the demand must generally be in proportion to the improvement and population of that small district. But the market for the produce of a silver mine may extend over the whole known world. Unless the world in general, therefore, be advancing in improvement and population, the demand for silver might not be at all increased by the improvement even of a large country in the neighbourhood of the mine.

Conclusion of the Chapter

I shall conclude this chapter with observing that every improvement in the circumstances of the society tends either directly or indirectly to raise the real rent of land, to increase the real wealth of the landlord, his power of purchasing the labour, or the produce of the labour of other people.

The extension of improvement and cultivation tends to raise it directly. The landlord's share of the produce necessarily increases with the increase of the produce.

That rise in the real price of those parts of the rude produce of land, which is first the effect of extended improvement and cultivation, and afterwards the cause of their being still further extended, the rise in the price of cattle, for example, tends too to raise the rent of land directly, and in a still greater proportion. The real value of the landlord's share, his real command of the labour of other people, not only rises with the real value of the produce, but the proportion of his share to the whole produce rises with it. That produce, after the rise in its real price, requires no more labour to collect it than before. A smaller proportion of it will, therefore, be sufficient to replace, with the ordinary profit, the stock which employs that labour. A greater proportion of it must, consequently, belong to the landlord.

The whole annual produce of the land and labour of every country, or what comes to the same thing, the whole price of that annual produce, naturally divides itself, it has already been observed, into three parts; the rent of land, the wages of labour, and the profits of stock; and constitutes a revenue to three different orders of people; to those who live by rent, to those who live by wages, and to those who live by profit. These are the three great, original and constituent orders of every civilized society, from whose revenue that of every other order is ultimately derived.

Book Two: Of the Nature, Accumulation, and Employment of Stock

Introduction

In that rude state of society in which there is no division of labour, in which exchanges are seldom made, and in which every man provides every thing for himself, it is not necessary that any stock should be accumulated or stored up beforehand, in order to carry on the business of the society. Every man endeavours to supply by his own industry his own occasional wants as they occur. When he is hungry, he goes to the forest to hunt; when his coat is worn out, he clothes himself with the skin of the first large animal he kills: and when his hut begins to go to ruin, he repairs it, as well as he can, with the trees and the turf that are nearest it.

But when the division of labour has once been thoroughly introduced, the produce of a man's own labour can supply but a very small part of his occasional wants. The far greater part of them are supplied by the produce of other men's labour, which he purchases with the produce, or what is the same thing, with the price of the produce of his own. But this purchase cannot be made till such time as the produce of his own labour has not only been completed, but sold. A stock of goods of different kinds, therefore, must be stored up somewhere sufficient to maintain him, and to supply him with the materials and tools of his work, till such time, at least, as both these events can be brought about. A weaver cannot apply himself entirely to his peculiar business, unless there is beforehand stored up somewhere, either in his own possession or in that of some other person, a stock sufficient to maintain him, and to supply him with the materials and tools of his work, till he has not only completed but sold his web. This accumulation must, evidently, be previous to his applying his industry for so long a time to such a peculiar business.

As the accumulation of stock must, in the nature of things, be previous to the division of labour, so labour can be more and more subdivided in proportion only as stock is previously more and more accumulated. The quantity of materials which the same number of people can work up, increases in a great proportion as labour comes to be more and more subdivided; and as the operations of each workman are gradually reduced to a greater degree of simplicity, a variety of new machines come to be invented for facilitating and abridging those operations. As the division of labour advances, therefore, in order to give constant employment to an equal number of workmen, an equal stock of provisions, and a greater stock of materials and tools than what would have been necessary in a ruder state of things, must be accumulated beforehand. But the number of workmen in every branch of business generally increases with the division of labour in that branch, or rather it is the increase of their number which enables them to class and subdivide themselves in this manner.

As the accumulation of stock is previously necessary for carrying on this great improvement in the productive powers of labour, so that accumulation naturally leads to this improvement. The person who employs his stock in maintaining labour, necessarily wishes to employ it in such a manner as to produce as great a quantity of work as possible. He endeavours, therefore, both to make among his workmen the most proper distribution of employment, and to furnish them with the best machines which he can either invent or afford to purchase. His abilities in both these respects are generally in proportion to the extent of his stock, or to the number of people whom it can employ. The quantity of industry, therefore, not only increases in every country with the increase of the stock which employs it, but, in consequence of that increase, the same quantity of industry produces a much greater quantity of work.

Such are in general the effects of the increase of stock upon industry and its productive powers.

In the following book I have endeavoured to explain the nature of stock, the effects of its accumulation into capitals of different kinds, and the effects of the different employments of those capitals.

I. Of the Division of Stock

When the stock which a man possesses is no more than sufficient to maintain him for a few days or a few weeks, he seldom thinks of deriving any revenue from it. He consumes it as sparingly as he can, and endeavours by his labour to acquire something which may supply its place before it be consumed altogether. His revenue is, in this case, derived from his labour only. This is the state of the greater part of the labouring poor in all countries.

But when he possesses stock sufficient to maintain him for months or years, he naturally endeavours to derive a revenue from the greater part of it; reserving only so much for his immediate consumption as may maintain him till this revenue begins to come in. His whole stock, therefore, is distinguished into two parts. That part which, he expects, is to afford him this revenue, is called his capital. The other is that which supplies his immediate consumption; and which consists either, first, in that portion of his whole stock which was originally reserved for this purpose; or, secondly, in his revenue, from whatever source derived, as it gradually comes in; or, thirdly, in such things as had been purchased by either of these in former years, and which are not yet entirely consumed; such as a stock of clothes, household furniture, and the like. In one, or other, or all of these three articles, consists the stock which men commonly reserve for their own immediate consumption.

There are two different ways in which a capital may be employed so as to yield a revenue or profit to its employer.

First, it may be employed in raising, manufacturing, or purchasing goods, and selling them again with a profit. The capital employed in this manner yields no revenue or profit to its employer, while it either remains in his possession, or continues in the same shape. The goods of the merchant yield him no revenue or profit till he sells them for money, and the money yields him as little till it is again exchanged for goods. His capital is continually going from him in one shape, and returning to him in another, and it is only by means of such circulation, or successive exchanges, that it can yield him any profit. Such capitals, therefore, may very properly be called circulating capitals.

Secondly, it may be employed in the improvement of land, in the purchase of useful machines and instruments of trade, or in such-like things as yield a revenue or profit without changing masters, or circulating any further. Such capitals, therefore, may very properly be called fixed capitals.

Different occupations require very different proportions between the fixed and circulating capitals employed in them.

The capital of a merchant, for example, is altogether a circulating capital. He has occasion for no machines or instruments of trade, unless his shop, or warehouse, be considered as such.

Some part of the capital of every master artificer or manufacturer must be fixed in the instruments of his trade. This part, however, is very small in some, and very great in others. A master tailor requires no other instruments of trade but a parcel of needles. Those of the master shoemaker are a little, though but a very little, more expensive. Those of the weaver rise a good deal above those of the shoemaker. The far greater part of the capital of all such master artificers, however, is circulated, either in the wages of their workmen, or in the price of their materials, and repaid with a profit by the price of the work.

In other works a much greater fixed capital is required. In a great ironwork, for example, the furnace for melting the ore, the forge, the slitt mill, are instruments of trade which cannot be erected without a very great expense. In coal works, and mines of every kind, the machinery necessary both for drawing out the water and for other purposes, is frequently still more expensive.

That part of the capital of the farmer which is employed in the instruments of agriculture is a fixed; that which is employed in the wages and maintenance of his labouring servants, is a circulating capital. He makes a profit of the one by keeping it in his own possession, and of the other by parting with it. The price or value of his labouring cattle is a fixed capital in the same manner as that of the instruments of husbandry: Their maintenance is a circulating capital in the same manner as that of the labouring servants. The farmer makes his profit by keeping the labouring cattle, and by parting with their maintenance. Both the price and the maintenance of the cattle which are bought in and fattened, not for labour, but for sale, are a circulating capital. The farmer makes his profit by parting with them. A flock of sheep or a herd of cattle that, in a breeding country, is bought in, neither for labour, nor for sale, but in order to make a profit by their wool, by their milk, and by their increase, is a fixed capital. The profit is made by keeping them. Their maintenance is a circulating capital. The profit is made by parting with it; and it comes back with both its own profit, and the profit upon the whole price of the cattle, in the price of the wool, the milk, and the increase. The whole value of the seed too is properly a fixed capital. Though it goes backwards and forwards between the ground and the granary, it never changes masters, and therefore does not properly circulate. The farmer makes his profit, not by its sale, but by its increase.

The general stock of any country or society is the same with that of all its inhabitants or members, and therefore naturally divides itself into the same three portions, each of which has a distinct function or office.

The First, is that portion which is reserved for immediate consumption, and of which the characteristic is that it affords no revenue or profit. It consists in the stock of food, clothes, household furniture, &c., which have been purchased by their proper consumers, but which are not yet entirely consumed. The whole stock of mere dwelling houses too subsisting at any one time in the country, make a part of this first portion. The stock that is laid out in a house, if it is to be the dwelling house of the proprietor, ceases from that moment to serve in the function of a capital, or to afford any revenue to its owner. A dwelling house, as such, contributes nothing to the revenue of its inhabitant; and though it is, no doubt, extremely useful to him, it is as his clothes and household furniture are useful to him, which, however, make a part of his expence, and not of his revenue. If it is to be let to a tenant for rent, as the house itself can produce nothing, the tenant must always pay the rent out of some other revenue which he derives either from labour, or stock, or land. Though a house, therefore, may yield a revenue to its proprietor, and thereby serve in the function of a capital to him, it cannot yield any to the public, nor serve in the function of a capital to it, and the revenue of the whole body of the people can never be in the smallest degree increased by it. Clothes, and household furniture, in the same manner, sometimes yield a revenue, and thereby serve in the function of a capital to particular persons. In countries where masquerades are common, it is a trade to let out masquerade dresses for a night. Upholsterers frequently let furniture by the month or by the year. Undertakers let the furniture of funerals by the day and by the week. Many people let furnished houses, and get a rent, not only for the use of the house, but for that of the furniture. The revenue, however, which is derived from such things, must always be ultimately drawn from some other source of revenue. Of all parts of the stock, either of an individual, or of a society, reserved for immediate consumption, what is laid out in houses is most slowly consumed. A stock of clothes may last several years: a stock of furniture half a century or a century: but a stock of houses, well built and properly taken care of, may last many centuries. Though the period of their total consumption, however, is more distant, they are still as really a stock reserved for immediate consumption as either clothes or household furniture.

The Second of the three portions into which the general stock of the society divides itself, is the fixed capital; of which the characteristic is, that it affords a revenue or profit without circulating or changing masters. It consists chiefly of the four following articles:

First, of all useful machines and instruments of trade which facilitate and abridge labour:

Secondly, of all those profitable buildings which are the means of procuring a revenue, not only to their proprietor who lets them for a rent, but to the person who possesses them and pays that rent for them; such as shops, warehouses, workhouses, farmhouses, with all their necessary buildings; stables, granaries, &c. These are very different from mere dwelling houses. They are a sort of instruments of trade, and may be considered in the same light:

Thirdly, of the improvements of land, of what has been profitably laid out in clearing, draining, enclosing, manuring, and reducing it into the condition most proper for tillage and culture. An improved farm may very justly be regarded in the same light as those useful machines which facilitate and abridge labour, and by means of which, an equal circulating capital can afford a much greater revenue to its employer. An improved farm is equally advantageous and more durable than any of those machines, frequently requiring no other repairs than the most profitable application of the farmer's capital employed in cultivating it:

Fourthly, of the acquired and useful abilities of all the inhabitants or members of the society. The acquisition of such talents, by the maintenance of the acquirer during his education, study, or apprenticeship, always costs a real expence, which is a capital fixed and realized, as it were, in his person. Those talents, as they make a part of his fortune, so do they likewise of that of the society to which he belongs. The improved dexterity of a workman may be considered in the same light as a machine or instrument of trade which facilitates and abridges labour, and which, though it costs a certain expence, repays that expence with a profit.

The Third and last of the three portions into which the general stock of the society naturally divides itself, is the circulating capital; of which the characteristic is, that it affords a revenue only by circulating or changing masters. It is composed likewise of four parts:

First, of the money by means of which all the other three are circulated and distributed to their proper consumers:

Secondly, of the stock of provisions which are in the possession of the butcher, the grazier, the farmer, the corn merchant, the brewer, &c. and from the sale of which they expect to derive a profit:

Thirdly, of the materials, whether altogether rude, or more or less manufactured, of clothes, furniture and building, which are not yet made up into any of those three shapes, but which remain in the hands of the growers, the manufacturers, the mercers, and drapers, the timber merchants, the carpenters and joiners, the brickmakers, &c.

Fourthly, and lastly, of the work which is made up and completed, but which is still in the hands of the merchant or manufacturer, and not yet disposed of or distributed to the proper consumers; such as the finished work which we frequently find ready-made in the shops of the smith, the cabinet maker, the goldsmith, the jeweller, the china merchant, &c. The circulating capital consists in this manner, of the provisions, materials, and finished work of all kinds that are in the hands of their respective dealers, and of the money that is necessary for circulating and distributing them to those who are finally to use, or to consume them.

Of these four parts three, provisions, materials, and finished work, are, either annually, or in a longer or shorter period, regularly withdrawn from it, and placed either in the fixed capital or in the stock reserved for immediate consumption.

Every fixed capital is both originally derived from, and requires to be continually supported by a circulating capital. All useful machines and instruments of trade are originally derived from a circulating capital, which furnishes the materials of which they are made, and the maintenance of the workmen who make them. They require too a capital of the same kind to keep them in constant repair.

No fixed capital can yield any revenue but by means of a circulating capital. The most useful machines and instruments of trade will produce nothing without the circulating capital which affords the materials they are employed upon, and the maintenance of the workmen who employ them. Land, however improved, will yield no revenue without a circulating capital, which maintains the labourers who cultivate and collect its produce.

To maintain and augment the stock which may be reserved for immediate consumption, is the sole end and purpose both of the fixed and circulating capitals. It is this stock which feeds, clothes, and lodges the people. Their riches or poverty depends upon the abundant or sparing supplies which those two capitals can afford to the stock reserved for immediate consumption.

II. Of the Accumulation of Capital, or of Productive and Unproductive Labour

There is one sort of labour which adds to the value of the subject upon which it is bestowed: there is another which has no such effect. The former, as it produces a value, may be called productive; the latter, unproductive labour. Thus the labour of a manufacturer adds, generally, to the value of the materials which he works upon, that of his own maintenance, and of his master's profit. The labour of a menial servant, on the contrary, adds to the value of nothing. Though the manufacturer has his wages advanced to him by his master, he, in reality, costs him no expence, the value of those wages being generally restored, together with a profit, in the improved value of the subject upon which his labour is bestowed. But the maintenance of a menial servant never is restored. A man grows rich by employing a multitude of manufacturers: he grows poor, by maintaining a multitude of menial servants. The labour of the latter, however, has its value, and deserves its reward as well as that of the former. But the labour of the manufacturer fixes and realizes itself in some particular subject or vendible commodity, which lasts for some time at least after that labour is past. It is, as it were, a certain quantity of labour stocked and stored up to be employed, if necessary, upon some other occasion. That subject, or what is the same thing, the price of that subject, can afterwards, if necessary, put into motion a quantity of labour equal to that which had originally produced it. The labour of the menial servant, on the contrary, does not fix or realize itself in any particular subject or vendible commodity. His services generally perish in the very instant of their performance, and seldom leave any trace or value behind them, for which an equal quantity of service could afterwards be procured.

The labour of some of the most respectable orders in the society is, like that of menial servants, unproductive of any value, and does not fix or realize itself in any permanent subject, or vendible commodity, which endures after that labour is past, and for which an equal quantity of labour could afterwards be procured. The sovereign, for example, with all the officers both of justice and war who serve under him, the whole army and navy, are unproductive labourers. They are the servants of the public, and are maintained by a part of the annual produce of the industry of other people. Their service, how honourable, how useful, or how necessary soever, produces nothing for which an equal quantity of service can afterwards be procured. The protection, security, and defence of the commonwealth, the effect of their labour this year, will not purchase its protection, security, and defence for the year to come. In the same class must be ranked, some both of the gravest and most important, and some of the most frivolous professions: churchmen, lawyers, physicians, men of letters of all kinds; players, buffoons, musicians, opera singers, opera dancers, &c. The labour of the meanest of these has a certain value, regulated by the very same principles which regulate that of every other sort of labour; and that of the noblest and most useful, produces nothing which could afterwards purchase or procure an equal quantity of labour. Like the declamation of the actor, the harangue of the orator, or the tune of the musician, the work of all of them perishes in the very instant of its production.

Both productive and unproductive labourers, and those who do not labour at all, are all equally maintained by the annual produce of the land and labour of the country. This produce, how great soever, can never be infinite, but must have certain limits. According, therefore, as a smaller or greater proportion of it is in any one year employed in maintaining unproductive hands, the more in the one case and the less in the other will remain for the productive, and the next year's produce will be greater or smaller accordingly; the whole annual produce, if we except the spontaneous productions of the earth, being the effect of productive labour.

Parsimony, and not industry, is the immediate cause of the increase of capital. Industry, indeed, provides the subject which parsimony accumulates. But whatever industry might acquire, if parsimony did not save and store up, the capital would never be the greater.

Parsimony, by increasing the fund which is destined for the maintenance of productive hands, tends to increase the number of those hands whose labour adds to the value of the subject upon which it is bestowed. It tends therefore to increase the exchangeable value of the annual produce of the land and labour of the country. It puts into motion an additional quantity of industry, which gives an additional value to the annual produce.

What is annually saved is as regularly consumed as what is annually spent, and nearly in the same time too; but it is consumed by a different set of people. That portion of his revenue which a rich man annually spends, is in most cases consumed by idle guests, and menial servants, who leave nothing behind them in return for their consumption. That portion which he annually saves, as for the sake of the profit it is immediately employed as a capital, is consumed in the same manner, and nearly in the same time too, but by a different set of people, by labourers, manufacturers, and artificers, who reproduce with a profit the value of their annual consumption. His revenue, we shall suppose, is paid him in money. Had he spent the whole, the food, clothing, and lodging, which the whole could have purchased, would have been distributed among the former set of people. By saving a part of it, as that part is for the sake of the profit immediately employed as a capital either by himself or by some other person, the food, clothing, and lodging, which may be purchased with it, are necessarily reserved for the latter. The consumption is the same, but the consumers are different.

By what a frugal man annually saves, he not only affords maintenance to an additional number of productive hands, for that or the ensuing year, but, like the founder of a public workhouse, he establishes as it were a perpetual fund for the maintenance of an equal number in all times to come. The perpetual allotment and destination of this fund, indeed, is not always guarded by any positive law, by any trust right or deed of mortmain. It is always guarded, however, by a very powerful principle, the plain and evident interest of every individual to whom any share of it shall ever belong. No part of it can ever afterwards be employed to maintain any but productive hands, without an evident loss to the person who thus perverts it from its proper destination.

The prodigal perverts it in this manner. By not confining his expence within his income, he encroaches upon his capital. Like him who perverts the revenues of some pious foundation to profane purposes, he pays the wages of idleness with those funds which the frugality of his forefathers had, as it were, consecrated to the maintenance of industry. By diminishing the funds destined for the employment of productive labour, he necessarily diminishes, so far as it depends upon him, the quantity of that labour which adds a value to the subject upon which it is bestowed, and, consequently, the value of the annual produce of the land and labour of the whole country, the real wealth and revenue of its inhabitants. If the prodigality of some was not compensated by the frugality of others, the conduct of every prodigal, by feeding the idle with the bread of the industrious, tends not only to beggar himself, but to impoverish his country.

The annual produce of the land and labour of any nation can be increased in its value by no other means, but by increasing either the number of its productive labourers, or the productive powers of those labourers who had before been employed. The number of its productive labourers, it is evident, can never be much increased, but in consequence of an increase of capital, or of the funds destined for maintaining them. The productive powers of the same number of labourers cannot be increased, but in consequence either of some addition and improvement to those machines and instruments which facilitate and abridge labour; or of a more proper division and distribution of employment. In either case an additional capital is almost always required. It is by means of an additional capital only, that the undertaker of any work can either provide his workmen with better machinery, or make a more proper distribution of employment among them. When the work to be done consists of a number of parts, to keep every man constantly employed in one way, requires a much greater capital than where every man is occasionally employed in every different part of the work. When we compare, therefore, the state of a nation at two different periods, and find, that the annual produce of its land and labour is evidently greater at the latter than at the former, that its lands are better cultivated, its manufactures more numerous and more flourishing, and its trade more extensive, we may be assured that its capital must have increased during the interval between those two periods, and that more must have been added to it by the good conduct of some, than had been taken from it either by the private misconduct of others, or by the public extravagance of government. But we shall find this to have been the case of almost all nations, in all tolerably quiet and peaceful times, even of those who have not enjoyed the most prudent and parsimonious governments. To form a right judgment of it, indeed, we must compare the state of the country at periods somewhat distant from one another. The progress is frequently so gradual, that, at near periods, the improvement is not only not sensible, but from the declension either of certain branches of industry, or of certain districts of the country, things which sometimes happen though the country in general be in great prosperity, there frequently arises a suspicion, that the riches and industry of the whole are decaying.

III. Of Stock Lent at Interest

The stock which is lent at interest is always considered as a capital by the lender. He expects that in due time it is to be restored to him, and that in the mean time the borrower is to pay him a certain annual rent for the use of it. The borrower may use it either as a capital, or as a stock reserved for immediate consumption. If he uses it as a capital, he employs it in the maintenance of productive labourers, who reproduce the value with a profit. He can, in this case, both restore the capital and pay the interest without alienating or encroaching upon any other source of revenue. If he uses it as a stock reserved for immediate consumption, he acts the part of a prodigal, and dissipates in the maintenance of the idle, what was destined for the support of the industrious. He can, in this case, neither restore the capital nor pay the interest, without either alienating or encroaching upon some other source of revenue, such as the property or the rent of land.

The stock which is lent at interest is, no doubt, occasionally employed in both these ways, but in the former much more frequently than in the latter. The man who borrows in order to spend will soon be ruined, and he who lends to him will generally have occasion to repent of his folly. To borrow or to lend for such a purpose, therefore, is in all cases, where gross usury is out of the question, contrary to the interest of both parties; and though it no doubt happens sometimes that people do both the one and the other; yet, from the regard that all men have for their own interest, we may be assured, that it cannot happen so very frequently as we are sometimes apt to imagine. Ask any rich man of common prudence, to which of the two sorts of people he has lent the greater part of his stock, to those who, he thinks, will employ it profitably, or to those who will spend it idly, and he will laugh at you for proposing the question. Even among borrowers, therefore, not the people in the world most famous for frugality, the number of the frugal and industrious surpasses considerably that of the prodigal and idle.

Almost all loans at interest are made in money, either of paper, or of gold and silver. But what the borrower really wants, and what the lender really supplies him with, is not the money, but the money's worth, or the goods which it can purchase. If he wants it as a stock for immediate consumption, it is those goods only which he can place in that stock. If he wants it as a capital for employing industry, it is from those goods only that the industrious can be furnished with the tools, materials, and maintenance, necessary for carrying on their work. By means of the loan, the lender, as it were, assigns to the borrower his right to a certain portion of the annual produce of the land and labour of the country, to be employed as the borrower pleases.

The quantity of stock, therefore, or, as it is commonly expressed, of money which can be lent at interest in any country, is not regulated by the value of the money, whether paper or coin, which serves as the instrument of the different loans made in that country, but by the value of that part of the annual produce which, as soon as it comes either from the ground, or from the hands of the productive labourers, is destined not only for replacing a capital, but such a capital as the owner does not care to be at the trouble of employing himself.

In some countries the interest of money has been prohibited by law. But as something can everywhere be made by the use of money, something ought everywhere to be paid for the use of it. This regulation, instead of preventing, has been found from experience to increase the evil of usury; the debtor being obliged to pay, not only for the use of the money, but for the risk which his creditor runs by accepting a compensation for that use. He is obliged, if one may say so, to insure his creditor from the penalties of usury.

In countries where interest is permitted, the law, in order to prevent the extortion of usury, generally fixes the highest rate which can be taken without incurring a penalty. This rate ought always to be somewhat above the lowest market price, or the price which is commonly paid for the use of money by those who can give the most undoubted security. If this legal rate should be fixed below the lowest market rate, the effects of this fixation must be nearly the same as those of a total prohibition of interest. The creditor will not lend his money for less than the use of it is worth, and the debtor must pay him for the risk which he runs by accepting the full value of that use. If it is fixed precisely at the lowest market price, it ruins with honest people, who respect the laws of their country, the credit of all those who cannot give the very best security, and obliges them to have recourse to exorbitant usurers. In a country, such as Great Britain, where money is lent to government at three per cent. and to private people upon good security at four, and four and a half, the present legal rate, five per cent., is perhaps, as proper as any.

IV. Of the Different Employment of Capitals

Though all capitals are destined for the maintenance of productive labour only, yet the quantity of that labour, which equal capitals are capable of putting into motion, varies extremely according to the diversity of their employment; as does likewise the value which that employment adds to the annual produce of the land and labour of the country.

A capital may be employed in four different ways: either, first, in procuring the rude produce annually required for the use and consumption of the society; or, secondly, in manufacturing and preparing that rude produce for immediate use and consumption; or, thirdly, in transporting either the rude or manufactured produce from the places where they abound to those where they are wanted; or, lastly, in dividing particular portions of either into such small parcels as suit the occasional demands of those who want them. In the first way are employed the capitals of all those who undertake the improvement or cultivation of lands, mines, or fisheries; in the second, those of all master manufacturers; in the third, those of all wholesale merchants; and in the fourth, those of all retailers. It is difficult to conceive that a capital should be employed in any way which may not be classed under some one or other of those four.

Each of those four methods of employing a capital is essentially necessary either to the existence or extension of the other three, or to the general conveniency of the society.

Unless a capital was employed in furnishing rude produce to a certain degree of abundance, neither manufactures nor trade of any kind could exist.

Unless a capital was employed in manufacturing that part of the rude produce which requires a good deal of preparation before it can be fit for use and consumption, it either would never be produced, because there could be no demand for it; or if it was produced spontaneously, it would be of no value in exchange, and could add nothing to the wealth of the society.

Unless a capital was employed in transporting, either the rude or manufactured produce, from the places where it abounds to those where it is wanted, no more of either could be produced than was necessary for the consumption of the neighbourhood. The capital of the merchant exchanges the surplus produce of one place for that of another, and thus encourages the industry and increases the enjoyments of both.

Unless a capital was employed in breaking and dividing certain portions either of the rude or manufactured produce, into such small parcels as suit the occasional demands of those who want them, every man would be obliged to purchase a greater quantity of the goods he wanted, than his immediate occasions required. If there was no such trade as a butcher, for example, every man would be obliged to purchase a whole ox or a whole sheep at a time. This would generally be inconvenient to the rich, and much more so to the poor. If a poor workman was obliged to purchase a month's or six months' provisions at a time, a great part of the stock which he employs as a capital in the instruments of his trade, or in the furniture of his shop, and which yields him a revenue, he would be forced to place in that part of his stock which is reserved for immediate consumption, and which yields him no revenue. Nothing can be more convenient for such a person than to be able to purchase his subsistence from day to day, or even from hour to hour, as he wants it. He is thereby enabled to employ almost his whole stock as a capital. He is thus enabled to furnish work to a greater value, and the profit, which he makes by it in this way, much more than compensates the additional price which the profit of the retailer imposes upon the goods. The prejudices of some political writers against shopkeepers and tradesmen, are altogether without foundation. So far is it from being necessary, either to tax them, or to restrict their numbers, that they can never be multiplied so as to hurt the publick, though they may so as to hurt one another. The quantity of grocery goods, for example, which can be sold in a particular town, is limited by the demand of that town and its neighbourhood. The capital, therefore, which can be employed in the grocery trade cannot exceed what is sufficient to purchase that quantity. If this capital is divided between two different grocers, their competition will tend to make both of them sell cheaper, than if it were in the hands of one only; and if it were divided among twenty, their competition would be just so much the greater, and the chance of their combining together, in order to raise the price, just so much the less. Their competition might perhaps ruin some of themselves; but to take care of this is the business of the parties concerned, and it may safely be trusted to their discretion. It can never hurt either the consumer, or the producer; on the contrary, it must tend to make the retailers both sell cheaper and buy dearer, than if the whole trade was monopolized by one or two persons.

The persons whose capitals are employed in any of those four ways are themselves productive labourers. Their labour, when properly directed, fixes and realizes itself in the subject or vendible commodity upon which it is bestowed, and generally adds to its price the value at least of their own maintenance and consumption. The profits of the farmer, of the manufacturer, of the merchant, and retailer, are all drawn from the price of the goods which the two first produce, and the two last buy and sell. Equal capitals, however, employed in each of those four different ways, will immediately put into motion very different quantities of productive labour, and augment too in very different proportions the value of the annual produce of the land and labour of the society to which they belong.

The capital of the retailer replaces, together with its profits, that of the merchant of whom he purchases goods, and thereby enables him to continue his business. The retailer himself is the only productive labourer whom it immediately employs. In his profits, consists the whole value which its employment adds to the annual produce of the land and labour of the society.

The capital of the wholesale merchant replaces, together with their profits, the capitals of the farmers and manufacturers of whom he purchases the rude and manufactured produce which he deals in, and thereby enables them to continue their respective trades. It is by this service chiefly that he contributes indirectly to support the productive labour of the society, and to increase the value of its annual produce. His capital employs too the sailors and carriers who transport his goods from one place to another, and it augments the price of those goods by the value, not only of his profits, but of their wages. This is all the productive labour which it immediately puts into motion, and all the value which it immediately adds to the annual produce. Its operation in both these respects is a good deal superior to that of the capital of the retailer.

Part of the capital of the master manufacturer is employed as a fixed capital in the instruments of his trade, and replaces, together with its profits, that of some other artificer of whom he purchases them. Part of his circulating capital is employed in purchasing materials, and replaces, with their profits, the capitals of the farmers and miners of whom he purchases them. But a great part of it is always, either annually, or in a much shorter period, distributed among the different workmen whom he employs. It augments the value of those materials by their wages, and by their masters profits upon the whole stock of wages, materials, and instruments of trade employed in the business. It puts immediately into motion, therefore, a much greater quantity of productive labour, and adds a much greater value to the annual produce of the land and labour of the society, than an equal capital in the hands of any wholesale merchant.

No equal capital puts into motion a greater quantity of productive labour than that of the farmer. Not only his labouring servants, but his labouring cattle, are productive labourers. In agriculture too nature labours along with man; and though her labour costs no expence, its produce has its value, as well as that of the most expensive workmen. The most important operations of agriculture seem intended, not so much to increase, though they do that too, as to direct the fertility of nature towards the production of the plants most profitable to man. A field overgrown with briars and brambles may frequently produce as great a quantity of vegetables as the best cultivated vineyard or cornfield. Planting and tillage frequently regulate more than they animate the active fertility of nature; and after all their labour, a great part of the work always remains to be done by her. The labourers and labouring cattle, therefore, employed in agriculture, not only occasion, like the workmen in manufactures, the reproduction of a value equal to their own consumption, or to the capital which employs them, together with its owners profits; but of a much greater value. Over and above the capital of the farmer and all its profits, they regularly occasion the reproduction of the rent of the landlord. This rent may be considered as the produce of those powers of nature, the use of which the landlord lends to the farmer. It is greater or smaller according to the supposed extent of those powers, or in other words, according to the supposed natural or improved fertility of the land. It is the work of nature which remains after deducting or compensating every thing which can be regarded as the work of man. It is seldom less than a fourth, and frequently more than a third of the whole produce. No equal quantity of productive labour employed in manufactures can ever occasion so great a reproduction. In them nature does nothing; man does all; and the reproduction must always be in proportion to the strength of the agents that occasion it. The capital employed in agriculture, therefore, not only puts into motion a greater quantity of productive labour than any equal capital employed in manufactures, but in proportion too to the quantity of productive labour which it employs, it adds a much greater value to the annual produce of the land and labour of the country, to the real wealth and revenue of its inhabitants. Of all the ways in which a capital can be employed, it is by far the most advantageous to the society.

It has been the principal cause of the rapid progress of our American colonies towards wealth and greatness, that almost their whole capitals have hitherto been employed in agriculture. They have no manufactures, those household and coarser manufactures excepted which necessarily accompany the progress of agriculture, and which are the work of the women and children in every private family. The greater part both of the exportation and coasting trade of America, is carried on by the capitals of merchants who reside in Great Britain. Even the stores and warehouses from which goods are retailed in some provinces, particularly in Virginia and Maryland, belong many of them to merchants who reside in the mother country, and afford one of the few instances of the retail trade of a society being carried on by the capitals of those who are not resident members of it. Were the Americans, either by combination or by any other sort of violence, to stop the importation of European manufactures, and, by thus giving a monopoly to such of their own countrymen as could manufacture the like goods, divert any considerable part of their capital into this employment, they would retard instead of accelerating the further increase in the value of their annual produce, and would obstruct instead of promoting the progress of their country towards real wealth and greatness. This would be still more the case, were they to attempt, in the same manner, to monopolize to themselves their whole exportation trade.

The consideration of his own private profit, is the sole motive which determines the owner of any capital to employ it either in agriculture, in manufactures, or in some particular branch of the wholesale or retail trade. The different quantities of productive labour which it may put into motion, and the different values which it may add to the annual produce of the land and labour of the society, according as it is employed in one or other of those different ways, never enter into his thoughts. In countries, therefore, where agriculture is the most profitable of all employments, and farming and improving the most direct roads to a splendid fortune, the capitals of individuals will naturally be employed in the manner most advantageous to the whole society. The profits of agriculture, however, seem to have no superiority over those of other employments in any part of Europe. Projectors, indeed, in every corner of it, have within these few years amused the public with most magnificent accounts of the profits to be made by the cultivation and improvement of land. Without entering into any particular discussion of their calculations, a very simple observation may satisfy us that the result of them must be false. We see every day the most splendid fortunes that have been acquired in the course of a single life by trade and manufactures, frequently from a very small capital, sometimes from no capital. A single instance of such a fortune acquired by agriculture in the same time, and from such a capital, has not, perhaps, occurred in Europe during the course of the present century. In all the great countries of Europe, however, much good land still remains uncultivated, and the greater part of what is cultivated, is far from being improved to the degree of which it is capable. Agriculture, therefore, is almost everywhere capable of absorbing a much greater capital than has ever yet been employed in it. What circumstances in the policy of Europe have given the trades which are carried on in towns so great an advantage over that which is carried on in the country, that private persons frequently find it more for their advantage to employ their capitals in the most distant carrying trades of Asia and America, than in the improvement and cultivation of the most fertile fields in their own neighbourhood, I shall endeavour to explain at full length in the two following books.

Book Three: Of the different Progress of Opulence in different Nations

Of the Natural Progress of Opulence

The great commerce of every civilized society, is that carried on between the inhabitants of the town and those of the country. It consists in the exchange of rude for manufactured produce, either immediately, or by the intervention of money, or of some sort of paper which represents money. The country supplies the town with the means of subsistence, and the materials of manufacture. The town repays this supply by sending back a part of the manufactured produce to the inhabitants of the country. The town, in which there neither is nor can be any reproduction of substances, may very properly be said to gain its whole wealth and subsistence from the country. We must not, however, upon this account, imagine that the gain of the town is the loss of the country. The gains of both are mutual and reciprocal, and the division of labour is in this, as in all other cases, advantageous to all the different persons employed in the various occupations into which it is subdivided. The inhabitants of the country purchase of the town a greater quantity of manufactured goods, with the produce of a much smaller quantity of their own labour, than they must have employed had they attempted to prepare them themselves. The town affords a market for the surplus produce of the country, or what is over and above the maintenance of the cultivators, and it is there that the inhabitants of the country exchange it for something else which is in demand among them. The greater the number and revenue of the inhabitants of the town, the more extensive is the market which it affords to those of the country; and the more extensive that market, it is always the more advantageous to a great number. The corn which grows within a mile of the town, sells there for the same price with that which comes from twenty miles distance. But the price of the latter must generally, not only pay the expence of raising and bringing it to market, but afford too the ordinary profits of agriculture to the farmer. The proprietors and cultivators of the country, therefore, which lies in the neighbourhood of the town, over and above the ordinary profits of agriculture, gain, in the price of what they sell, the whole value of the carriage of the like produce that is brought from more distant parts, and they save, besides, the whole value of this carriage in the price of what they buy. Compare the cultivation of the lands in the neighbourhood of any considerable town, with that of those which lie at some distance from it, and you will easily satisfy yourself how much the country is benefited by the commerce of the town. Among all the absurd speculations that have been propagated concerning the balance of trade, it has never been pretended that either the country loses by its commerce with the town, or the town by that with the country which maintains it.

As subsistence is, in the nature of things, prior to conveniency and luxury, so the industry which procures the former, must necessarily be prior to that which ministers to the latter. The cultivation and improvement of the country, therefore, which affords subsistence, must, necessarily, be prior to the increase of the town, which furnishes only the means of conveniency and luxury. It is the surplus produce of the country only, or what is over and above the maintenance of the cultivators, that constitutes the subsistence of the town, which can therefore increase only with the increase of this surplus produce. The town, indeed, may not always derive its whole subsistence from the country in its neighbourhood, or even from the territory to which it belongs, but from very distant countries; and this, though it forms no exception from the general rule, has occasioned considerable variations in the progress of opulence in different ages and nations.

That order of things which necessity imposes in general, though not in every particular country, is, in every particular country, promoted by the natural inclinations of man. If human institutions had never thwarted those natural inclinations, the towns could nowhere have increased beyond what the improvement and cultivation of the territory in which they were situated could support; till such time, at least, as the whole of that territory was completely cultivated and improved. Upon equal, or nearly equal profits, most men will choose to employ their capitals rather in the improvement and cultivation of land, than either in manufactures or in foreign trade. The man who employs his capital in land, has it more under his view and command, and his fortune is much less liable to accidents, than that of the trader, who is obliged frequently to commit it, not only to the winds and the waves, but to the more uncertain elements of human folly and injustice, by giving great credits in distant countries to men, with whose character and situation he can seldom be thoroughly acquainted. The capital of the landlord, on the contrary, which is fixed in the improvement of his land, seems to be as well secured as the nature of human affairs can admit of. The beauty of the country besides, the pleasures of a country life, the tranquillity of mind which it promises, and wherever the injustice of human laws does not disturb it, the independency which it really affords, have charms that more or less attract every body; and as to cultivate the ground was the original destination of man, so in every stage of his existence he seems to retain a predilection for this primitive employment.

Without the assistance of some artificers, indeed, the cultivation of land cannot be carried on, but with great inconveniency and continual interruption. Smiths, carpenters, wheelwrights, and ploughwrights, masons, and bricklayers, tanners, shoemakers, and tailors, are people, whose service the farmer has frequent occasion for. Such artificers too stand, occasionally, in need of the assistance of one another; and as their residence is not, like that of the farmer, necessarily tied down to a precise spot, they naturally settle in the neighbourhood of one another, and thus form a small town or village. The butcher, the brewer, and the baker, soon join them, together with many other artificers and retailers, necessary or useful for supplying their occasional wants, and who contribute still further to augment the town. The inhabitants of the town and those of the country are mutually the servants of one another. The town is a continual fair or market, to which the inhabitants of the country resort, in order to exchange their rude for manufactured produce. It is this commerce which supplies the inhabitants of the town both with the materials of their work, and the means of their subsistence. The quantity of the finished work which they sell to the inhabitants of the country, necessarily regulates the quantity of the materials and provisions which they buy. Neither their employment nor subsistence, therefore, can augment, but in proportion to the augmentation of the demand from the country for finished work; and this demand can augment only in proportion to the extension of improvement and cultivation. Had human institutions, therefore, never disturbed the natural course of things, the progressive wealth and increase of the towns would, in every political society, be consequential, and in proportion to the improvement and cultivation of the territory or country.

In our North American colonies, where uncultivated land is still to be had upon easy terms, no manufactures for distant sale have ever yet been established in any of their towns. When an artificer has acquired a little more stock than is necessary for carrying on his own business in supplying the neighbouring country, he does not, in North America, attempt to establish with it a manufacture for more distant sale, but employs it in the purchase and improvement of uncultivated land. From artificer he becomes planter, and neither the large wages nor the easy subsistence which that country affords to artificers, can bribe him rather to work for other people than for himself. He feels that an artificer is the servant of his customers, from whom he derives his subsistence; but that a planter who cultivates his own land, and derives his necessary subsistence from the labour of his own family, is really a master, and independent of all the world.

In countries, on the contrary, where there is either no uncultivated land, or none that can be had upon easy terms, every artificer who has acquired more stock than he can employ in the occasional jobs of the neighbourhood, endeavours to prepare work for more distant sale. The smith erects some sort of iron, the weaver some sort of linen or woollen manufactory. Those different manufactures come, in process of time, to be gradually subdivided, and thereby improved and refined in a great variety of ways, which may easily be conceived, and which it is therefore unnecessary to explain any further.

In seeking for employment to a capital, manufactures are, upon equal or nearly equal profits, naturally preferred to foreign commerce, for the same reason that agriculture is naturally preferred to manufactures. As the capital of the landlord or farmer is more secure than that of the manufacturer, so the capital of the manufacturer, being at all times more within his view and command, is more secure than that of the foreign merchant. In every period, indeed, of every society, the surplus part both of the rude and manufactured produce, or that for which there is no demand at home, must be sent abroad in order to be exchanged for something for which there is some demand at home. But whether the capital, which carries this surplus produce abroad, be a foreign or a domestic one, is of very little importance. If the society has not acquired sufficient capital both to cultivate all its lands, and to manufacture in the completest manner the whole of its rude produce, there is even a considerable advantage that that rude produce should be exported by a foreign capital, in order that the whole stock of the society may be employed in more useful purposes. The wealth of ancient Egypt, that of China and Indostan, sufficiently demonstrate that a nation may attain a very high degree of opulence, though the greater part of its exportation trade be carried on by foreigners. The progress of our North American and West Indian colonies would have been much less rapid, had not capital but what belonged to themselves been employed in exporting their surplus produce.

According to the natural course of things, therefore, the greater part of the capital of every growing society is, first, directed to agriculture, afterwards to manufactures, and last of all to foreign commerce. This order of things is so very natural, that in every society that had any territory, it has always, I believe, been in some degree observed. Some of their lands must have been cultivated before any considerable towns could be established, and some sort of coarse industry of the manufacturing kind must have been carried on in those towns, before they could well think of employing themselves in foreign commerce.

But though this natural order of things must have taken place in some degree in every such society, it has, in all the modern states of Europe, been, in many respects, entirely inverted. The foreign commerce of some of their cities has introduced all their finer manufactures, or such as were fit for distant sale; and manufactures and foreign commerce together, have given birth to the principal improvements of agriculture. The manners and customs which the nature of their original government introduced, and which remained after that government was greatly altered, necessarily forced them into this unnatural and retrograde order.

Book Four: Of Systems of political Economy

Introduction

Political economy, considered as a branch of the science of a statesman or legislator, proposes two distinct objects: first, to provide a plentiful revenue or subsistence for the people, or more properly to enable them to provide such a revenue or subsistence for themselves; and secondly, to supply the state or commonwealth with a revenue sufficient for the public services. It proposes to enrich both the people and the sovereign.

The different progress of opulence in different ages and nations, has given occasion to two different systems of political economy, with regard to enriching the people. The one may be called the system of commerce, the other that of agriculture. I shall endeavour to explain both as fully and distinctly as I can, and shall begin with the system of commerce. It is the modern system, and is best understood in our own country and in our own times.

I. Of the Principle of the Commercial or Mercantile System

That wealth consists in money, or in gold and silver, is a popular notion which naturally arises from the double function of money, as the instrument of commerce, and as the measure of value. In consequence of its being the instrument of commerce, when we have money we can more readily obtain whatever else we have occasion for, than by means of any other commodity. The great affair, we always find, is to get money. When that is obtained, there is no difficulty in making any subsequent purchase. In consequence of its being the measure of value, we estimate that of all other commodities by the quantity of money which they will exchange for. We say of a rich man that he is worth a great deal, and of a poor man that he is worth very little money. A frugal man, or a man eager to be rich, is said to love money; and a careless, a generous, or a profuse man, is said to be indifferent about it. To grow rich is to get money; and wealth and money, in short, are, in common language, considered as in every respect synonymous.

A rich country, in the same manner as a rich man, is supposed to be a country abounding in money; and to heap up gold and silver in any country is supposed to be the readiest way to enrich it. For some time after the discovery of America, the first enquiry of the Spaniards, when they arrived upon any unknown coast, used to be, if there was any gold or silver to be found in the neighbourhood? By the information which they received, they judged whether it was worth while to make a settlement there, or if the country was worth the conquering. Plano Carpino, a monk sent ambassador from the king of France to one of the sons of the famous Genghis Khan, says that the Tartars used frequently to ask him if there was plenty of sheep and oxen in the kingdom of France. Their enquiry had the same object with that of the Spaniards. They wanted to know if the country was rich enough to be worth the conquering. Among the Tartars, as among all other nations of shepherds, who are generally ignorant of the use of money, cattle are the instruments of commerce and the measures of value. Wealth, therefore, according to them, consisted in cattle, as according to the Spaniards it consisted in gold and silver. Of the two, the Tartar notion, perhaps, was the nearest to the truth.

Mr. Locke remarks a distinction between money and other moveable goods. All other moveable goods, he says, are of so consumable a nature that the wealth which consists in them cannot be much depended on, and a nation which abounds in them one year may, without any exportation, but merely by their own waste and extravagance, be in great want of them the next. Money, on the contrary, is a steady friend, which, though it may travel about from hand to hand, yet if it can be kept from going out of the country, is not very liable to be wasted and consumed. Gold and silver, therefore, are, according to him, the most solid and substantial part of the moveable wealth of a nation, and to multiply those metals ought, he thinks, upon that account, to be the great object of its political economy.

Others admit that if a nation could be separated from all the world, it would be of no consequence how much, or how little money circulated in it. The consumable goods which were circulated by means of this money, would only be exchanged for a greater or a smaller number of pieces; but the real wealth or poverty of the country, they allow, would depend altogether upon the abundance or scarcity of those consumable goods. But it is otherwise, they think, with countries which have connections with foreign nations, and which are obliged to carry on foreign wars, and to maintain fleets and armies in distant countries. This, they say, cannot be done, but by sending abroad money to pay them with; and a nation cannot send much money abroad, unless it has a good deal at home. Every such nation, therefore, must endeavour in time of peace to accumulate gold and silver, that, when occasion requires, it may have wherewithal to carry on foreign wars.

In consequence of these popular notions, all the different nations of Europe have studied, though to little purpose, every possible means of accumulating gold and silver in their respective countries. Spain and Portugal, the proprietors of the principal mines which supply Europe with those metals, have either prohibited their exportation under the severest penalties, or subjected it to a considerable duty. The like prohibition seems anciently to have made a part of the policy of most other European nations. It is even to be found, where we should least of all expect to find it, in some old Scotch acts of parliament, which forbid under heavy penalties the carrying gold or silver *forth of the kingdom*. The like policy anciently took place both in France and England.

When those countries became commercial, the merchants found this prohibition, upon many occasions, extremely inconvenient. They could frequently buy more advantageously with gold and silver than with any other commodity, the foreign goods which they wanted, either to import into their own, or to carry to some other foreign country. They remonstrated, therefore, against this prohibition as hurtful to trade.

They represented, first, that the exportation of gold and silver in order to purchase foreign goods, did not always diminish the quantity of those metals in the kingdom. That, on the contrary, it might frequently increase that quantity; because, if the consumption of foreign goods was not thereby increased in the country, those goods might be re-exported to foreign countries, and, being there sold for a large profit, might bring back much more treasure than was originally sent out to purchase them. Mr. Mun compares this operation of foreign trade to the seedtime and harvest of agriculture. "If we only behold," says he, "the actions of the husbandman in the seedtime, when he casteth away much good corn into the ground, we shall account him rather a madman than a husbandman. But when we consider his labours in the harvest, which is the end of his endeavours, we shall find the worth and plentiful increase of his actions."

They represented, secondly, that this prohibition could not hinder the exportation of gold and silver, which, on account of the smallness of their bulk in proportion to their value, could easily be smuggled abroad. That this exportation could only be prevented by a proper attention to, what they called, the balance of trade. That when the country exported to a greater value than it imported, a balance became due to it from foreign nations, which was necessarily paid to it in gold and silver, and thereby increased the quantity of those metals in the kingdom. But that when it imported to a greater value than it exported, a contrary balance became due to foreign nations, which was necessarily paid to them in the same manner, and thereby diminished that quantity. That in this case to prohibit the exportation of those metals could not prevent it, but only by making it more dangerous, render it more expensive. That the exchange was thereby turned more against the country which owed the balance, than it otherwise might have been; the merchant who purchased a bill upon the foreign country being obliged to pay the banker who sold it, not only for the natural risk, trouble and expence of sending the money thither, but for the extraordinary risk arising from the prohibition. But that the more the exchange was against any country, the more the balance of trade became necessarily against it; the money of that country becoming necessarily of so much less value, in comparison with that of the country to which the balance was due. That if the exchange between England and Holland, for example, was five per cent. against England, it would require a hundred and five ounces of silver in England to purchase a bill for a hundred ounces of silver in Holland: that a hundred and five ounces of silver in England, therefore, would be worth only a hundred ounces of silver in Holland, and would purchase only a proportionable quantity of Dutch goods: but that a hundred ounces of silver in Holland, on the contrary, would be worth a hundred and five ounces in England, and would purchase a proportionable quantity of English goods: that the English goods which were sold to Holland would be sold so much cheaper; and the Dutch goods which were sold to England, so much dearer, by the difference of the exchange; that the one would draw so much less Dutch money to England, and the other so much more English money to Holland, as this difference amounted to: and that the balance of trade, therefore, would necessarily be so much more against England, and would require a greater balance of gold and silver to be exported to Holland.

Those arguments were partly solid and partly sophistical. They were solid so far as they asserted that the exportation of gold and silver in trade might frequently be advantageous to the country. They were solid too, in asserting that no prohibition could prevent their exportation, when private people found any advantage in exporting them. But they were sophistical in supposing, that either to preserve or to augment the quantity of those metals required more the attention of government, than to preserve or to augment the quantity of any other useful commodities, which the freedom of trade, without any such attention, never fails to supply in the proper quantity. They were sophistical too, perhaps, in asserting that the high price of exchange necessarily increased, what they called, the unfavourable balance of trade, or occasioned the exportation of a greater quantity of gold and silver. That high price, indeed, was extremely disadvantageous to the merchants who had any money to pay in foreign countries. They paid so much dearer for the bills which their bankers granted them upon those countries. But though the risk arising from the prohibition might occasion some extraordinary expence to the bankers, it would not necessarily carry any more money out of the country. This expence would generally be all laid out in the country, in smuggling the money out of it, and could seldom occasion the exportation of a single sixpence beyond the precise sum drawn for. The high price of exchange too would naturally dispose the merchants to endeavour to make their exports nearly balance their imports, in order that they might have this high exchange to pay upon as small a sum as possible. The high price of exchange, besides, must necessarily have operated as a tax, in raising the price of foreign goods, and thereby diminishing their consumption. It would tend, therefore, not to increase, but to diminish, what they called, the unfavourable balance of trade, and consequently the exportation of gold and silver.

Such as they were, however, those arguments convinced the people to whom they were addressed. They were addressed by merchants to parliaments, and to the councils of princes, to nobles, and to country gentlemen; by those who were supposed to understand trade, to those who were conscious to themselves that they knew nothing about the matter. That foreign trade enriched the country, experience demonstrated to the nobles and country gentlemen, as well as to the merchants; but how, or in what manner, none of them well knew. The merchants knew perfectly in what manner it enriched themselves. It was their business to know it. But to know in what manner it enriched the country, was no part of their business. This subject never came into their consideration, but when they had occasion to apply to their country for some change in the laws relating to foreign trade. It then became necessary to say something about the beneficial effects of foreign trade, and the manner in which those effects were obstructed by the laws as they then stood. To the judges who were to decide the business, it appeared a most satisfactory account of the matter, when they were told that foreign trade brought money into the country, but that the laws in question hindered it from bringing so much as it otherwise would do. Those arguments therefore produced the wished-for effect. The prohibition of exporting gold and silver was in France and England confined to the coin of those respective countries. The exportation of foreign coin and of bullion was made free. In Holland, and in some other places, this liberty was extended even to the coin of the country. The attention of government was turned away from guarding against the exportation of gold and silver, to watch over the balance of trade, as the only cause which could occasion any augmentation or diminution of those metals. From one fruitless care it was turned away to another care much more intricate, much more embarrassing, and just equally fruitless. The title of Mun's book, *England's Treasure in [by] Foreign Trade,* became a fundamental maxim in the political economy, not of England only, but of all other commercial countries. The inland or home trade, the most important of all, the trade in which an equal capital affords the greatest revenue, and creates the greatest employment to the people of the country, was considered as subsidiary only to foreign trade. It neither brought money into the country, it was said, nor carried any out of it. The country therefore could never become either richer or poorer by means of it, except so far as its prosperity or decay might indirectly influence the state of foreign trade.

A country that has no mines of its own must undoubtedly draw its gold and silver from foreign countries, in the same manner as one that has no vineyards of its own must draw its wines. It does not seem necessary, however, that the attention of government should be more turned towards the one than towards the other object. A country that has wherewithal to buy wine, will always get the wine which it has occasion for; and a country that has wherewithal to buy gold and silver, will never be in want of those metals. They are to be bought for a certain price like all other commodities, and as they are the price of all other commodities, so all other commodities are the price of those metals. We trust with perfect security that the freedom of trade, without any attention of government, will always supply us with the wine which we have occasion for: and we may trust with equal security that it will always supply us with all the gold and silver which we can afford to purchase or to employ, either in circulating our commodities, or in other uses.

The quantity of every commodity which human industry can either purchase or produce, naturally regulates itself in every country according to the effectual demand, or according to the demand of those who are willing to pay the whole rent, labour and profits which must be paid in order to prepare and bring it to market. But no commodities regulate themselves more easily or more exactly according to this effectual demand than gold and silver; because, on account of the small bulk and great value of those metals, no commodities can be more easily transported from one place to another, from the places where they are cheap, to those where they are dear, from the places where they exceed, to those where they fall short of this effectual demand. If there were in England, for example, an effectual demand for an additional quantity of gold, a packet boat could bring from Lisbon, or from wherever else it was to be had, fifty tons of gold, which could be coined into more than five millions of guineas. But if there were an effectual demand for grain to the same value, to import it would require, at five guineas a ton, a million of tons of shipping, or a thousand ships of a thousand tons each. The navy of England would not be sufficient.

When the quantity of gold and silver imported into any country exceeds the effectual demand, no vigilance of government can prevent their exportation. All the sanguinary laws of Spain and Portugal are not able to keep their gold and silver at home. The continual importations from Peru and Brazil exceed the effectual demand of those countries, and sink the price of those metals there below that in the neighbouring countries. If, on the contrary, in any particular country their quantity fell short of the effectual demand, so as to raise their price above that of the neighbouring countries, the government would have no occasion to take any pains to import them. If it were even to take pains to prevent their importation, it would not be able to effectuate it. Those metals, when the Spartans had got wherewithal to purchase them, broke through all the barriers which the laws of Lycurgus opposed to their entrance into Lacedemon. All the sanguinary laws of the customs are not able to prevent the importation of the teas of the Dutch and Gottenburgh East India companies; because somewhat cheaper than those of the British company. A pound of tea, however, is about a hundred times the bulk of one of the highest prices, sixteen shillings, that is commonly paid for it in silver, and more than two thousand times the bulk of the same price in gold, and consequently just so many times more difficult to smuggle.

It is partly owing to the easy transportation of gold and silver from the places where they abound to those where they are wanted, that the price of those metals does not fluctuate continually like that of the greater part of other commodities, which are hindered by their bulk from shifting their situation, when the market happens to be either over- or under-stocked with them. The price of those metals, indeed, is not altogether exempted from variation, but the changes to which it is liable are generally slow, gradual, and uniform. In Europe, for example, it is supposed, without much foundation, perhaps, that, during the course of the present and preceding century, they have been constantly, but gradually, sinking in their value, on account of the continual importations from the Spanish West Indies. But to make any sudden change in the price of gold and silver, so as to raise or lower at once, sensibly and remarkably, the money price of all other commodities, requires such a revolution in commerce as that occasioned by the discovery of America.

If, notwithstanding all this, gold and silver should at any time fall short in a country which has wherewithal to purchase them, there are more expedients for supplying their place, than that of almost any other commodity. If the materials of manufacture are wanted, industry must stop. If provisions are wanted, the people must starve. But if money is wanted, barter will supply its place, though with a good deal of inconveniency. Buying and selling upon credit, and the different dealers compensating their credits with one another, once a month or once a year, will supply it with less inconveniency. A well-regulated paper money will supply it, not only without any inconveniency, but, in some cases, with some advantages. Upon every account, therefore, the attention of government never was so unnecessarily employed, as when directed to watch over the preservation or increase of the quantity of money in any country.

No complaint, however, is more common than that of a scarcity of money. Money, like wine, must always be scarce with those who have neither wherewithal to buy it, nor credit to borrow it. Those who have either, will seldom be in want either of the money, or of the wine which they have occasion for. This complaint, however, of the scarcity of money, is not always confined to improvident spendthrifts. It is sometimes general through a whole mercantile town, and the country in its neighbourhood. Overtrading is the common cause of it. Sober men, whose projects have been disproportioned to their capitals, are as likely to have neither wherewithal to buy money, nor credit to borrow it, as prodigals whose expence has been disproportioned to their revenue. Before their projects can be brought to bear, their stock is gone, and their credit with it. They run about everywhere to borrow money, and every body tells them that they have none to lend. Even such general complaints of the scarcity of money do not always prove that the usual number of gold and silver pieces are not circulating in the country, but that many people want those pieces who have nothing to give for them. When the profits of trade happen to be greater than ordinary, overtrading becomes a general error both among great and small dealers. They do not always send more money abroad than usual, but they buy upon credit both at home and abroad, an unusual quantity of goods, which they send to some distant market, in hopes that the returns will come in before the demand for payment. The demand comes before the returns, and they have nothing at hand, with which they can either purchase money, or give solid security for borrowing. It is not any scarcity of gold and silver, but the difficulty which such people find in borrowing, and which their creditors find in getting payment, that occasions the general complaint of the scarcity of money.

It would be too ridiculous to go about seriously to prove, that wealth does not consist in money, or in gold and silver; but in what money purchases, and is valuable only for purchasing. Money, no doubt, makes always a part of the national capital; but it has already been shown that it generally makes but a small part, and always the most unprofitable part of it.

It is not because wealth consists more essentially in money than in goods, that the merchant finds it generally more easy to buy goods with money, than to buy money with goods; but because money is the known and established instrument of commerce, for which every thing is readily given in exchange, but which is not always with equal readiness to be got in exchange for every thing. The greater part of goods besides are more perishable than money, and he may frequently sustain a much greater loss by keeping them. When his goods are upon hand too, he is more liable to such demands for money as he may not be able to answer, than when he has got their price in his coffers. Over and above all this, his profit arises more directly from selling than from buying, and he is upon all these accounts generally much more anxious to exchange his goods for money, than his money for goods. But though a particular merchant, with abundance of goods in his warehouse, may sometimes be ruined by not being able to sell them in time, a nation or country is not liable to the same accident. The whole capital of a merchant frequently consists in perishable goods destined for purchasing money. But it is but a very small part of the annual produce of the land and labour of a country which can ever be destined for purchasing gold and silver from their neighbours. The far greater part is circulated and consumed among themselves; and even of the surplus which is sent abroad, the greater part is generally destined for the purchase of other foreign goods. Though gold and silver, therefore, could not be had in exchange for the goods destined to purchase them, the nation would not be ruined. It might, indeed, suffer some loss and inconveniency, and be forced upon some of those expedients which are necessary for supplying the place of money. The annual produce of its land and labour, however, would be the same, or very nearly the same, as usual, because the same, or very nearly the same consumable capital would be employed in maintaining it. And though goods do not always draw money so readily as money draws goods, in the long run they draw it more necessarily than even it draws them. Goods can serve many other purposes besides purchasing money, but money can serve no other purpose besides purchasing goods. Money, therefore, necessarily runs after goods, but goods do not always or necessarily run after money.

It is not by the importation of gold and silver, that the discovery of America has enriched Europe. By the abundance of the American mines, those metals have become cheaper. A service of plate can now be purchased for about a third part of the corn, or a third part of the labour, which it would have cost in the fifteenth century. With the same annual expence of labour and commodities, Europe can annually purchase about three times the quantity of plate which it could have purchased at that time. But when a commodity comes to be sold for a third part of what had been its usual price, not only those who purchased it before can purchase three times their former quantity, but it is brought down to the level of a much greater number of purchasers, perhaps to more than ten, perhaps to more than twenty times the former number. So that there may be in Europe at present not only more than three times, but more than twenty or thirty times the quantity of plate which would have been in it, even in its present state of improvement, had the discovery of the American mines never been made. So far Europe has, no doubt, gained a real conveniency, though surely a very trifling one. The cheapness of gold and silver renders those metals rather less fit for the purposes of money than they were before. In order to make the same purchases, we must load ourselves with a greater quantity of them, and carry about a shilling in our pocket where a groat would have done before. It is difficult to say which is most trifling, this inconveniency, or the opposite conveniency. Neither the one nor the other could have made any very essential change in the state of Europe. The discovery of America, however, certainly made a most essential one. By opening a new and inexhaustible market to all the commodities of Europe, it gave occasion to new divisions of labour and improvements of art, which, in the narrow circle of the ancient commerce, could never have taken place for want of a market to take off the greater part of their produce. The productive powers of labour were improved, and its produce increased in all the different countries of Europe, and together with it the real revenue and wealth of the inhabitants. The commodities of Europe were almost all new to America, and many of those of America were new to Europe. A new set of exchanges, therefore, began to take place which had never been thought of before, and which should naturally have proved as advantageous to the new, as it certainly did to the old continent. The savage injustice of the Europeans rendered an event, which ought to have been beneficial to all, ruinous and destructive to several of those unfortunate countries.

The discovery of a passage to the East Indies, by the Cape of Good Hope, which happened much about the same time, opened, perhaps, a still more extensive range to foreign commerce than even that of America, notwithstanding the greater distance. There were but two nations in America, in any respect superior to savages, and these were destroyed almost as soon as discovered. The rest were mere savages. But the empires of China, Indostan, Japan, as well as several others in the East Indies, without having richer mines of gold or silver, were in every other respect much richer, better cultivated, and more advanced in all arts and manufactures than either Mexico or Peru, even though we should credit, what plainly deserves no credit, the exaggerated accounts of the Spanish writers, concerning the ancient state of those empires. But rich and civilized nations can always exchange to a much greater value with one another, than with savages and barbarians. Europe, however, has hitherto derived much less advantage from its commerce with the East Indies, than from that with America.

Money in common language, as I have already observed, frequently signifies wealth; and this ambiguity of expression has rendered this popular notion so familiar to us, that even they, who are convinced of its absurdity, are very apt to forget their own principles, and in the course of their reasonings to take it for granted as a certain and undeniable truth. Some of the best English writers upon commerce set out with observing, that the wealth of a country consists, not in its gold and silver only, but in its lands, houses, and consumable goods of all different kinds. In the course of their reasonings, however, the lands, houses, and consumable goods seem to slip out of their memory, and the strain of their argument frequently supposes that all wealth consists in gold and silver, and that to multiply those metals is the great object of national industry and commerce.

The two principles being established, however, that wealth consisted in gold and silver, and that those metals could be brought into a country which had no mines only by the balance of trade, or by exporting to a greater value than it imported; it necessarily became the great object of political economy to diminish as much as possible the importation of foreign goods for home consumption, and to increase as much as possible the exportation of the produce of domestic industry. Its two great engines for enriching the country, therefore, were restraints upon importation, and encouragements to exportation.

The restraints upon importation were of two kinds.

First, Restraints upon the importation of such foreign goods for home consumption as could be produced at home, from whatever country they were imported.

Secondly, Restraints upon the importation of goods of almost all kinds from those particular countries with which the balance of trade was supposed to be disadvantageous.

Those different restraints consisted sometimes in high duties, and sometimes in absolute prohibitions.

Exportation was encouraged sometimes by drawbacks, sometimes by bounties, sometimes by advantageous treaties of commerce with foreign states, and sometimes by the establishment of colonies in distant countries.

Drawbacks were given upon two different occasions. When the home manufactures were subject to any duty or excise, either the whole or a part of it was frequently drawn back upon their exportation; and when foreign goods liable to a duty were imported in order to be exported again, either the whole or a part of this duty was sometimes given back upon such exportation.

Bounties were given for the encouragement either of some beginning manufactures, or of such sorts of industry of other kinds as were supposed to deserve particular favour.

By advantageous treaties of commerce, particular privileges were procured in some foreign state for the goods and merchants of the country, beyond what were granted to those of other countries.

By the establishment of colonies in distant countries, not only particular privileges, but a monopoly was frequently procured for the goods and merchants of the country which established them.

The two sorts of restraints upon importation above-mentioned, together with these four encouragements to exportation, constitute the principal means by which the commercial system proposes to increase the quantity of gold and silver in any country by turning the balance of trade in its favour.

II. Of Restraints upon the Importation from Foreign Countries of Such Goods As Can Be Produced at Home

By restraining, either by high duties, or by absolute prohibitions, the importation of such goods from foreign countries as can be produced at home, the monopoly of the home market is more or less secured to the domestic industry employed in producing them. Thus the prohibition of importing either live cattle or salt provisions from foreign countries secures to the graziers of Great Britain the monopoly of the home market for butcher's meat. The high duties upon the importation of corn, which in times of moderate plenty amount to a prohibition, give a like advantage to the growers of that commodity. The prohibition of the importation of foreign woollens is equally favourable to the woollen manufacturers. The silk manufacture, though altogether employed upon foreign materials, has lately obtained the same advantage. The linen manufacture has not yet obtained it, but is making great strides towards it. Many other sorts of manufacturers have, in the same manner, obtained in Great Britain, either altogether, or very nearly a monopoly against their countrymen. The variety of goods of which the importation into Great Britain is prohibited, either absolutely, or under certain circumstances, greatly exceeds what can easily be suspected by those who are not well acquainted with the laws of the customs.

That this monopoly of the home market frequently gives great encouragement to that particular species of industry which enjoys it, and frequently turns towards that employment a greater share of both the labour and stock of the society than would otherwise have gone to it, cannot be doubted. But whether it tends either to increase the general industry of the society, or to give it the most advantageous direction, is not, perhaps, altogether so evident.

The general industry of the society never can exceed what the capital of the society can employ. As the number of workmen that can be kept in employment by any particular person must bear a certain proportion to his capital, so the number of those that can be continually employed by all the members of a great society, must bear a certain proportion to the whole capital of that society, and never can exceed that proportion. No regulation of commerce can increase the quantity of industry in any society beyond what its capital can maintain. It can only divert a part of it into a direction into which it might not otherwise have gone; and it is by no means certain that this artificial direction is likely to be more advantageous to the society than that into which it would have gone of its own accord.

Every individual is continually exerting himself to find out the most advantageous employment for whatever capital he can command. It is his own advantage, indeed, and not that of the society, which he has in view. But the study of his own advantage naturally, or rather necessarily leads him to prefer that employment which is most advantageous to the society.

First, every individual endeavours to employ his capital as near home as he can, and consequently as much as he can in the support of domestic industry; provided always that he can thereby obtain the ordinary, or not a great deal less than the ordinary profits of stock.

Thus, upon equal or nearly equal profits, every wholesale merchant naturally prefers the home trade to the foreign trade of consumption, and the foreign trade of consumption to the carrying trade. In the home trade his capital is never so long out of his sight as it frequently is in the foreign trade of consumption. He can know better the character and situation of the persons whom he trusts, and if he should happen to be deceived, he knows better the laws of the country from which he must seek redress. In the carrying trade, the capital of the merchant is, as it were, divided between two foreign countries, and no part of it is ever necessarily brought home, or placed under his own immediate view and command.

Secondly, every individual who employs his capital in the support of domestic industry, necessarily endeavours so to direct that industry, that its produce may be of the greatest possible value.

The produce of industry is what it adds to the subject or materials upon which it is employed. In proportion as the value of this produce is great or small, so will likewise be the profits of the employer. But it is only for the sake of profit that any man employs a capital in the support of industry; and he will always, therefore, endeavour to employ it in the support of that industry of which the produce is likely to be of the greatest value, or to exchange for the greatest quantity either of money or of other goods.

But the annual revenue of every society is always precisely equal to the exchangeable value of the whole annual produce of its industry, or rather is precisely the same thing with that exchangeable value. As every individual, therefore, endeavours as much as he can both to employ his capital in the support of domestic industry, and so to direct that industry that its produce may be of the greatest value; every individual necessarily labours to render the annual revenue of the society as great as he can. He generally, indeed, neither intends to promote the public interest, nor knows how much he is promoting it. By preferring the support of domestic to that of foreign industry, he intends only his own security; and by directing that industry in such a manner as its produce may be of the greatest value, he intends only his own gain, and he is in this, as in many other cases, led by an invisible hand to promote an end which was no part of his intention. Nor is it always the worse for the society that it was no part of it. By pursuing his own interest he frequently promotes that of the society more effectually than when he really intends to promote it. I have never known much good done by those who affected to trade for the public good. It is an affectation, indeed, not very common among merchants, and very few words need be employed in dissuading them from it.

It is the maxim of every prudent master of a family, never to attempt to make at home what it will cost him more to make than to buy. The tailor does not attempt to make his own shoes, but buys them of the shoemaker. The shoemaker does not attempt to make his own clothes, but employs a tailor. The farmer attempts to make neither the one nor the other, but employs those different artificers. All of them find it for their interest to employ their whole industry in a way in which they have some advantage over their neighbours, and to purchase with a part of its produce, or what is the same thing, with the price of a part of it, whatever else they have occasion for.

What is prudence in the conduct of every private family, can scarce be folly in that of a great kingdom. If a foreign country can supply us with a commodity cheaper than we ourselves can make it, better buy it of them with some part of the produce of our own industry, employed in a way in which we have some advantage. The general industry of the country, being always in proportion to the capital which employs it, will not thereby be diminished, no more than that of the above-mentioned artificers; but only left to find out the way in which it can be employed with the greatest advantage. It is certainly not employed to the greatest advantage, when it is thus directed towards an object which it can buy cheaper than it can make. The value of its annual produce is certainly more or less diminished, when it is thus turned away from producing commodities evidently of more value than the commodity which it is directed to produce. According to the supposition, that commodity could be purchased from foreign countries cheaper than it can be made at home. It could, therefore, have been purchased with a part only of the commodities, or, what is the same thing, with a part only of the price of the commodities, which the industry employed by an equal capital would have produced at home, had it been left to follow its natural course. The industry of the country, therefore, is thus turned away from a more, to a less advantageous employment, and the exchangeable value of its annual produce, instead of being increased, according to the intention of the lawgiver, must necessarily be diminished by every such regulation.

By means of such regulations, indeed, a particular manufacture may sometimes be acquired sooner than it could have been otherwise, and after a certain time may be made at home as cheap or cheaper than in the foreign country. But though the industry of the society may be thus carried with advantage into a particular channel sooner than it could have been otherwise, it will by no means follow that the sum total, either of its industry, or of its revenue, can ever be augmented by any such regulation. The industry of the society can augment only in proportion as its capital augments, and its capital can augment only in proportion to what can be gradually saved out of its revenue. But the immediate effect of every such regulation is to diminish its revenue, and what diminishes its revenue is certainly not very likely to augment its capital faster than it would have augmented of its own accord, had both capital and industry been left to find out their natural employments.

The natural advantages which one country has over another in producing particular commodities are sometimes so great, that it is acknowledged by all the world to be in vain to struggle with them. By means of glasses, hotbeds, and hotwalls, very good grapes can be raised in Scotland, and very good wine too can be made of them at about thirty times the expence for which at least equally good can be brought from foreign countries. Would it be a reasonable law to prohibit the importation of all foreign wines, merely to encourage the making of claret and burgundy in Scotland? But if there would be a manifest absurdity in turning towards any employment, thirty times more of the capital and industry of the country, than would be necessary to purchase from foreign countries an equal quantity of the commodities wanted, there must be an absurdity, though not altogether so glaring, yet exactly of the same kind, in turning towards any such employment a thirtieth, or even a three hundredth part more of either. Whether the advantages which one country has over another, be natural or acquired, is in this respect of no consequence. As long as the one country has those advantages, and the other wants them, it will always be more advantageous for the latter, rather to buy of the former than to make. It is an acquired advantage only, which one artificer has over his neighbour, who exercises another trade; and yet they both find it more advantageous to buy of one another, than to make what does not belong to their particular trades.

Merchants and manufacturers are the people who derive the greatest advantage from this monopoly of the home market. The prohibition of the importation of foreign cattle, and of salt provisions, together with the high duties upon foreign corn, which in times of moderate plenty amount to a prohibition, are not near so advantageous to the graziers and farmers of Great Britain, as other regulations of the same kind are to its merchants and manufacturers. Manufactures, those of the finer kind especially, are more easily transported from one country to another than corn or cattle. It is in the fetching and carrying manufactures, accordingly, that foreign trade is chiefly employed. In manufactures, a very small advantage will enable foreigners to undersell our own workmen, even in the home market. It will require a very great one to enable them to do so in the rude produce of the soil. If the free importation of foreign manufactures were permitted, several of the home manufactures would probably suffer, and some of them, perhaps, go to ruin altogether, and a considerable part of the stock and industry at present employed in them, would be forced to find out some other employment. But the freest importation of the rude produce of the soil could have no such effect upon the agriculture of the country.

If the importation of foreign cattle, for example, were made ever so free, so few could be imported, that the grazing trade of Great Britain could be little affected by it. Live cattle are, perhaps, the only commodity of which the transportation is more expensive by sea than by land. By land they carry themselves to market. By sea, not only the cattle, but their food and their water too, must be carried at no small expence and inconveniency. The short sea between Ireland and Great Britain, indeed, renders the importation of Irish cattle more easy. But though the free importation of them, which was lately permitted only for a limited time, were rendered perpetual, it could have no considerable effect upon the interest of the graziers of Great Britain.

The freest importation of salt provisions, in the same manner, could have as little effect upon the interest of the graziers of Great Britain as that of live cattle. Salt provisions are not only a very bulky commodity, but when compared with fresh meat, they are a commodity both of worse quality, and as they cost more labour and expence, of higher price. They could never, therefore, come into competition with the fresh meat, though they might with the salt provisions of the country. They might be used for victualling ships for distant voyages, and such like uses, but could never make any considerable part of the food of the people. The small quantity of salt provisions imported from Ireland since their importation was rendered free, is an experimental proof that our graziers have nothing to apprehend from it. It does not appear that the price of butcher's meat has ever been sensibly affected by it.

Even the free importation of foreign corn could very little affect the interest of the farmers of Great Britain. Corn is a much more bulky commodity than butcher's meat. A pound of wheat at a penny is as dear as a pound of butcher's meat at fourpence. The small quantity of foreign corn imported even in times of the greatest scarcity, may satisfy our farmers that they can have nothing to fear from the freest importation. The average quantity imported one year with another, amounts only, according to the very well informed author of the tracts upon the corn trade, to twenty-three thousand seven hundred and twenty-eight quarters of all sorts of grain, and does not exceed the five hundredth and seventy-one part of the annual consumption. But as the bounty upon corn occasions a greater exportation in years of plenty, so it must of consequence occasion a greater importation in years of scarcity, than in the actual state of tillage would otherwise take place. By means of it, the plenty of one year does not compensate the scarcity of another, and as the average quantity exported is necessarily augmented by it, so must likewise, in the actual state of tillage, the average quantity imported. If there were no bounty, as less corn would be exported, so it is probable that, one year with another, less would be imported than at present. The corn merchants, the fetchers and carriers of corn between Great Britain and foreign countries, would have much less employment, and might suffer considerably; but the country gentlemen and farmers could suffer very little. It is in the corn merchants accordingly, rather than in the country gentlemen and farmers, that I have observed the greatest anxiety for the renewal and continuation of the bounty.

Country gentlemen and farmers are, to their great honour, of all people, the least subject to the wretched spirit of monopoly. The undertaker of a great manufactory is sometimes alarmed if another work of the same kind is established within twenty miles of him. The Dutch undertaker of the woollen manufacture at Abbeville stipulated, that no work of the same kind should be established within thirty leagues of that city. Farmers and country gentlemen, on the contrary, are generally disposed rather to promote than to obstruct the cultivation and improvement of their neighbours farms and estates. They have no secrets, such as those of the greater part of manufacturers, but are generally rather fond of communicating to their neighbours, and of extending as far as possible any new practice which they have found to be advantageous.

To prohibit by a perpetual law the importation of foreign corn and cattle, is in reality to enact, that the population and industry of the country shall at no time exceed what the rude produce of its own soil can maintain.

There seem, however, to be two cases in which it will generally be advantageous to lay some burden upon foreign, for the encouragement of domestic industry.

The first is, when some particular sort of industry is necessary for the defence of the country. The defence of Great Britain, for example, depends very much upon the number of its sailors and shipping. The act of navigation, therefore, very properly endeavours to give the sailors and shipping of Great Britain the monopoly of the trade of their own country, in some cases, by absolute prohibitions, and in others by heavy burdens upon the shipping of foreign countries. The following are the principal dispositions of this act.

First, all ships, of which the owners, masters, and three fourths of the mariners are not British subjects, are prohibited, upon pain of forfeiting ship and cargo, from trading to the British settlements and plantations, or from being employed in the coasting trade of Great Britain.

Secondly, a great variety of the most bulky articles of importation can be brought into Great Britain only, either in such ships as are above described, or in ships of the country where those goods are produced, and of which the owners, masters, and three fourths of the mariners, are of that particular country; and when imported even in ships of this latter kind, they are subject to double aliens duty.

Thirdly, a great variety of the most bulky articles of importation are prohibited from being imported, even in British ships, from any country but that in which they are produced; under pain of forfeiting ship and cargo.

Fourthly, salt fish of all kinds, whale fins, whalebone, oil, and blubber, not caught by and cured on board British vessels, when imported into Great Britain, are subjected to double aliens duty.

When the act of navigation was made, though England and Holland were not actually at war, the most violent animosity subsisted between the two nations. It had begun during the government of the long parliament, which first framed this act, and it broke out soon after in the Dutch wars during that of the Protector and of Charles the Second. It is not impossible, therefore, that some of the regulations of this famous act may have proceeded from national animosity. They are as wise, however, as if they had all been dictated by the most deliberate wisdom. National animosity at that particular time aimed at the very same object which the most deliberate wisdom would have recommended, the diminution of the naval power of Holland, the only naval power which could endanger the security of England.

The act of navigation is not favourable to foreign commerce, or to the growth of that opulence which can arise from it. The interest of a nation in its commercial relations to foreign nations is, like that of a merchant with regard to the different people with whom he deals, to buy as cheap and to sell as dear as possible. But it will be most likely to buy cheap, when by the most perfect freedom of trade it encourages all nations to bring to it the goods which it has occasion to purchase; and, for the same reason, it will be most likely to sell dear, when its markets are thus filled with the greatest number of buyers. The act of navigation, it is true, lays no burden upon foreign ships that come to export the produce of British industry. Even the ancient aliens duty, which used to be paid upon all goods exported as well as imported, has, by several subsequent acts, been taken off from the greater part of the articles of exportation. But if foreigners, either by prohibitions or high duties, are hindered from coming to sell, they cannot always afford to come to buy; because coming without a cargo, they must lose the freight from their own country to Great Britain. By diminishing the number of sellers, therefore, we necessarily diminish that of buyers, and are thus likely not only to buy foreign goods dearer, but to sell our own cheaper, than if there was a more perfect freedom of trade. As defence, however, is of much more importance than opulence, the act of navigation is, perhaps, the wisest of all the commercial regulations of England.

The second case, in which it will generally be advantageous to lay some burden upon foreign for the encouragement of domestic industry, is, when some tax is imposed at home upon the produce of the latter. In this case, it seems reasonable that an equal tax should be imposed upon the like produce of the former. This would not give the monopoly of the home market to domestic industry, nor turn towards a particular employment a greater share of the stock and labour of the country, than what would naturally go to it. It would only hinder any part of what would naturally go to it from being turned away by the tax, into a less natural direction, and would leave the competition between foreign and domestic industry, after the tax, as nearly as possible upon the same footing as before it. In Great Britain, when any such tax is laid upon the produce of domestic industry, it is usual at the same time, in order to stop the clamorous complaints of our merchants and manufacturers, that they will be undersold at home, to lay a much heavier duty upon the importation of all foreign goods of the same kind.

This second limitation of the freedom of trade according to some people should, upon some occasions, be extended much farther than to the precise foreign commodities which could come into competition with those which had been taxed at home. When the necessaries of life have been taxed in any country, it becomes proper, they pretend, to tax not only the like necessaries of life imported from other countries, but all sorts of foreign goods which can come into competition with any thing that is the produce of domestic industry. Subsistence, they say, becomes necessarily dearer in consequence of such taxes; and the price of labour must always rise with the price of the labourers' subsistence. Every commodity, therefore, which is the produce of domestic industry, though not immediately taxed itself, becomes dearer in consequence of such taxes, because the labour which produces it becomes so. Such taxes, therefore, are really equivalent, they say, to a tax upon every particular commodity produced at home. In order to put domestic upon the same footing with foreign industry, therefore, it becomes necessary, they think, to lay some duty upon every foreign commodity, equal to this enhancement of the price of the home commodities with which it can come into competition.

Whether taxes upon the necessaries of life, such as those in Great Britain upon soap, salt, leather, candles, &c. necessarily raise the price of labour, and consequently that of all other commodities, I shall consider hereafter, when I come to treat of taxes. Supposing, however, in the mean time, that they have this effect, and they have it undoubtedly, this general enhancement of the price of all commodities, in consequence of that of labour, is a case which differs in the two following respects from that of a particular commodity, of which the price was enhanced by a particular tax immediately imposed upon it.

First, it might always be known with great exactness how far the price of such a commodity could be enhanced by such a tax: but how far the general enhancement of the price of labour might affect that of every different commodity about which labour was employed, could never be known with any tolerable exactness. It would be impossible, therefore, to proportion with any tolerable exactness the tax upon every foreign, to this enhancement of the price of every home commodity.

Secondly, taxes upon the necessaries of life have nearly the same effect upon the circumstances of the people as a poor soil and a bad climate. Provisions are thereby rendered dearer in the same manner as if it required extraordinary labour and expence to raise them. As in the natural scarcity arising from soil and climate, it would be absurd to direct the people in what manner they ought to employ their capitals and industry, so is it likewise in the artificial scarcity arising from such taxes. To be left to accommodate, as well as they could, their industry to their situation, and to find out those employments in which, notwithstanding their unfavourable circumstances, they might have some advantage either in the home or in the foreign market, is what in both cases would evidently be most for their advantage. To lay a new tax upon them, because they are already overburdened with taxes, and because they already pay too dear for the necessaries of life, to make them likewise pay too dear for the greater part of other commodities, is certainly a most absurd way of making amends.

Such taxes, when they have grown up to a certain height, are a curse equal to the barrenness of the earth and the inclemency of the heavens; and yet it is in the richest and most industrious countries that they have been most generally imposed. No other countries could support so great a disorder. As the strongest bodies only can live and enjoy health, under an unwholesome regimen; so the nations only, that in every sort of industry have the greatest natural and acquired advantages, can subsist and prosper under such taxes. Holland is the country in Europe in which they abound most, and which from peculiar circumstances continues to prosper, not by means of them, as has been most absurdly supposed, but in spite of them.

As there are two cases in which it will generally be advantageous to lay some burden upon foreign, for the encouragement of domestic industry; so there are two others in which it may sometimes be a matter of deliberation; in the one, how far it is proper to continue the free importation of certain foreign goods; and in the other, how far, or in what manner, it may be proper to restore that free importation after it has been for some time interrupted.

The case in which it may sometimes be a matter of deliberation how far it is proper to continue the free importation of certain foreign goods, is, when some foreign nation restrains by high duties or prohibitions the importation of some of our manufactures into their country. Revenge in this case naturally dictates retaliation, and that we should impose the like duties and prohibitions upon the importation of some or all of their manufactures into ours. Nations accordingly seldom fail to retaliate in this manner. The French have been particularly forward to favour their own manufactures by restraining the importation of such foreign goods as could come into competition with them. In this consisted a great part of the policy of Mr. Colbert, who, notwithstanding his great abilities, seems in this case to have been imposed upon by the sophistry of merchants and manufacturers, who are always demanding a monopoly against their countrymen. It is at present the opinion of the most intelligent men in France that his operations of this kind have not been beneficial to his country. That minister, by the tariff of 1667, imposed very high duties upon a great number of foreign manufactures. Upon his refusing to moderate them in favour of the Dutch, they in 1671 prohibited the importation of the wines, brandies and manufactures of France. The war of 1672 seems to have been in part occasioned by this commercial dispute. The peace of Nimeguen put an end to it in 1678, by moderating some of those duties in favour of the Dutch, who in consequence took off their prohibition. It was about the same time that the French and English began mutually to oppress each other's industry, by the like duties and prohibitions, of which the French, however, seem to have set the first example. The spirit of hostility which has subsisted between the two nations ever since, has hitherto hindered them from being moderated on either side. In 1697 the English prohibited the importation of bone lace, the manufacture of Flanders. The government of that country, at that time under the dominion of Spain, prohibited in return the importation of English woollens. In 1700, the prohibition of importing bone lace into England, was taken off upon condition that the importation of English woollens into Flanders should be put on the same footing as before.

There may be good policy in retaliations of this kind, when there is a probability that they will procure the repeal of the high duties or prohibitions complained of. The recovery of a great foreign market will generally more than compensate the transitory inconveniency of paying dearer during a short time for some sorts of goods. To judge whether such retaliations are likely to produce such an effect, does not, perhaps, belong so much to the science of a legislator, whose deliberations ought to be governed by general principles which are always the same, as to the skill of that insidious and crafty animal, vulgarly called a statesman or politician, whose councils are directed by the momentary fluctuations of affairs. When there is no probability that any such repeal can be procured, it seems a bad method of compensating the injury done to certain classes of our people, to do another injury ourselves, not only to those classes, but to almost all the other classes of them. When our neighbours prohibit some manufacture of ours, we generally prohibit, not only the same, for that alone would seldom affect them considerably, but some other manufacture of theirs. This may no doubt give encouragement to some particular class of workmen among ourselves, and by excluding some of their rivals, may enable them to raise their price in the home market. Those workmen, however, who suffered by our neighbours' prohibition will not be benefited by ours. On the contrary, they and almost all the other classes of our citizens will thereby be obliged to pay dearer than before for certain goods. Every such law, therefore, imposes a real tax upon the whole country, not in favour of that particular class of workmen who were injured by our neighbours' prohibition, but of some other class.

The case in which it may sometimes be a matter of deliberation, how far, or in what manner, it is proper to restore the free importation of foreign goods, after it has been for some time interrupted, is, when particular manufactures, by means of high duties or prohibitions upon all foreign goods which can come into competition with them, have been so far extended as to employ a great multitude of hands. Humanity may in this case require that the freedom of trade should be restored only by slow gradations, and with a good deal of reserve and circumspection. Were those high duties and prohibitions taken away all at once, cheaper foreign goods of the same kind might be poured so fast into the home market, as to deprive all at once many thousands of our people of their ordinary employment and means of subsistence. The disorder which this would occasion might no doubt be very considerable. It would in all probability, however, be much less than is commonly imagined, for the two following reasons:

First, all those manufactures, of which any part is commonly exported to other European countries without a bounty, could be very little affected by the freest importation of foreign goods. Such manufactures must be sold as cheap abroad as any other foreign goods of the same quality and kind, and consequently must be sold cheaper at home. They would still, therefore, keep possession of the home market, and though a capricious man of fashion might sometimes prefer foreign wares, merely because they were foreign, to cheaper and better goods of the same kind that were made at home, this folly could, from the nature of things, extend to so few, that it could make no sensible impression upon the general employment of the people.

Secondly, though a great number of people should, by thus restoring the freedom of trade, be thrown all at once out of their ordinary employment and common method of subsistence, it would by no means follow that they would thereby be deprived either of employment or subsistence. By the reduction of the army and navy at the end of the late war, more than a hundred thousand soldiers and seamen, a number equal to what is employed in the greatest manufactures, were all at once thrown out of their ordinary employment; but, though they no doubt suffered some inconveniency, they were not thereby deprived of all employment and subsistence. The greater part of the seamen, it is probable, gradually betook themselves to the merchant service as they could find occasion, and in the meantime both they and the soldiers were absorbed in the great mass of the people, and employed in a great variety of occupations.

To expect, indeed, that the freedom of trade should ever be entirely restored in Great Britain, is as absurd as to expect that an Occana or Utopia should ever be established in it. Not only the prejudices of the public, but what is much more unconquerable, the private interests of many individuals, irresistibly oppose it.

III. Conclusion of the Mercantile System

Consumption is the sole end and purpose of all production; and the interest of the producer ought to be attended to, only so far as it may be necessary for promoting that of the consumer. The maxim is so perfectly self-evident, that it would be absurd to attempt to prove it. But in the mercantile system, the interest of the consumer is almost constantly sacrificed to that of the producer; and it seems to consider production, and not consumption, as the ultimate end and object of all industry and commerce.

In the restraints upon the importation of all foreign commodities which can come into competition with those of our own growth, or manufacture, the interest of the home consumer is evidently sacrificed to that of the producer. It is altogether for the benefit of the latter, that the former is obliged to pay that enhancement of price which this monopoly almost always occasions.

It is altogether for the benefit of the producer that bounties are granted upon the exportation of some of his productions. The home consumer is obliged to pay, first, the tax which is necessary for paying the bounty, and secondly, the still greater tax which necessarily arises from the enhancement of the price of the commodity in the home market.

By the famous treaty of commerce with Portugal, the consumer is prevented by high duties from purchasing of a neighbouring country, a commodity which our own climate does not produce, but is obliged to purchase it of a distant country, though it is acknowledged, that the commodity of the distant country is of a worse quality than that of the near one. The home consumer is obliged to submit to this inconveniency, in order that the producer may import into the distant country some of his productions upon more advantageous terms than he would otherwise have been allowed to do. The consumer, too, is obliged to pay, whatever enhancement in the price of those very productions, this forced exportation may occasion in the home market.

But in the system of laws which has been established for the management of our American and West Indian colonies, the interest of the home consumer has been sacrificed to that of the producer with a more extravagant profusion than in all our other commercial regulations. A great empire has been established for the sole purpose of raising up a nation of customers who should be obliged to buy from the shops of our different producers, all the goods with which these could supply them. For the sake of that little enhancement of price which this monopoly might afford our producers, the home consumers have been burdened with the whole expence of maintaining and defending that empire. For this purpose, and for this purpose only, in the two last wars, more than two hundred millions have been spent, and a new debt of more than a hundred and seventy millions has been contracted over and above all that had been expended for the same purpose in former wars. The interest of this debt alone is not only greater than the whole extraordinary profit, which, it ever could be pretended, was made by the monopoly of the colony trade, but than the whole value of that trade, or than the whole value of the goods, which at an average have been annually exported to the colonies.

It cannot be very difficult to determine who have been the contrivers of this whole mercantile system; not the consumers, we may believe, whose interest has been entirely neglected; but the producers, whose interest has been so carefully attended to; and among this latter class our merchants and manufacturers have been by far the principal architects. In the mercantile regulations, which have been taken notice of in this chapter, the interest of our manufacturers has been most peculiarly attended to; and the interest, not so much of the consumers, as that of some other sets of producers, has been sacrificed to it.

IV. Of the Agricultural Systems, or of Those Systems of Political Economy Which Represent the Produce of Land as either the Sole or the Principal Source of the Revenue and Wealth of Every Country

The agricultural systems of political economy will not require so long an explanation as that which I have thought it necessary to bestow upon the mercantile or commercial system.

That system which represents the produce of land as the sole source of the revenue and wealth of every country has, so far as I know, never been adopted by any nation, and it at present exists only in the speculations of a few men of great learning and ingenuity in France. It would not, surely, be worth while to examine at great length the errors of a system which never has done, and probably never will do any harm in any part of the world. I shall endeavour to explain, however, as distinctly as I can, the great outlines of this very ingenious system.

Mr. Colbert, the famous minister of Lewis XIV, was a man of probity, of great industry and knowledge of detail; of great experience and acuteness in the examination of public accounts, and of abilities, in short, every way fitted for introducing method and good order into the collection and expenditure of the public revenue. That minister had unfortunately embraced all the prejudices of the mercantile system, in its nature and essence a system of restraint and regulation, and such as could scarce fail to be agreeable to a laborious and plodding man of business, who had been accustomed to regulate the different departments of public offices, and to establish the necessary checks and controls for confining each to its proper sphere. The industry and commerce of a great country he endeavoured to regulate upon the same model as the departments of a public office; and instead of allowing every man to pursue his own interest his own way, upon the liberal plan of equality, liberty and justice, he bestowed upon certain branches of industry extraordinary privileges, while he laid others under as extraordinary restraints. He was not only disposed, like other European ministers, to encourage more the industry of the towns than that of the country; but, in order to support the industry of the towns, he was willing even to depress and keep down that of the country. In order to render provisions cheap to the inhabitants of the towns, and thereby to encourage manufactures and foreign commerce, he prohibited altogether the exportation of corn, and thus excluded the inhabitants of the country from every foreign market for by far the most important part of the produce of their industry. This prohibition, joined to the restraints imposed by the ancient provincial laws of France upon the transportation of corn from one province to another, and to the arbitrary and degrading taxes which are levied upon the cultivators in almost all the provinces, discouraged and kept down the agriculture of that country very much below the state to which it would naturally have risen in so very fertile a soil and so very happy a climate. This state of discouragement and depression was felt more or less in every different part of the country, and many different inquiries were set on foot concerning the causes of it. One of those causes appeared to be the preference given, by the institutions of Mr. Colbert, to the industry of the towns above that of the country.

If the rod be bent too much one way, says the proverb, in order to make it straight you must bend it as much the other. The French philosophers, who have proposed the system which represents agriculture as the sole source of the revenue and wealth of every country, seem to have adopted this proverbial maxim; and as in the plan of Mr. Colbert the industry of the towns was certainly overvalued in comparison with that of the country; so in their system it seems to be as certainly undervalued.

The different orders of people who have ever been supposed to contribute in any respect towards the annual produce of the land and labour of the country, they divide into three classes. The first is the class of the proprietors of land. The second is the class of the cultivators, of farmers and country labourers, whom they honour with the peculiar appellation of the productive class. The third is the class of artificers, manufacturers, and merchants, whom they endeavour to degrade by the humiliating appellation of the barren or unproductive class.

According to this liberal and generous system, the most advantageous method in which a landed nation can raise up artificers, manufacturers, and merchants of its own, is to grant the most perfect freedom of trade to the artificers, manufacturers and merchants of all other nations. It thereby raises the value of the surplus produce of its own land, of which the continual increase gradually establishes a fund, which in due time necessarily raises up all the artificers, manufacturers and merchants whom it has occasion for.

When a landed nation, on the contrary, oppresses either by high duties or by prohibitions the trade of foreign nations, it necessarily hurts its own interest in two different ways. First, by raising the price of all foreign goods and of all sorts of manufactures, it necessarily sinks the real value of the surplus produce of its own land, with which, or, what comes to the same thing, with the price of which, it purchases those foreign goods and manufactures. Secondly, by giving a sort of monopoly of the home market to its own merchants, artificers, and manufacturers, it raises the rate of mercantile and manufacturing profit in proportion to that of agricultural profit, and consequently either draws from agriculture a part of the capital which had before been employed in it, or hinders from going to it a part of what would otherwise have gone to it. This policy, therefore, discourages agriculture in two different ways; first, by sinking the real value of its produce, and thereby lowering the rate of its profit; and, secondly, by raising the rate of profit in all other employments. Agriculture is rendered less advantageous, and trade and manufactures more advantageous than they otherwise would be; and every man is tempted by his own interest to turn, as much as he can, both his capital and his industry from the former to the latter employments.

Though, by this oppressive policy, a landed nation should be able to raise up artificers, manufacturers, and merchants of its own, somewhat sooner than it could do by the freedom of trade; a matter, however, which is not a little doubtful; yet it would raise them up, if one may say so, prematurely, and before it was perfectly ripe for them. By raising up too hastily one species of industry, it would depress another more valuable species of industry. By raising up too hastily a species of industry which only replaces the stock which employs it, together with the ordinary profit, it would depress a species of industry which, over and above replacing that stock with its profit, affords likewise a neat produce, a free rent to the landlord. It would depress productive labour, by encouraging too hastily that labour which is altogether barren and unproductive.

In what manner, according to this system, the sum total of the annual produce of the land is distributed among the three classes above mentioned, and in what manner the labour of the unproductive class does no more than replace the value of its own consumption, without increasing in any respect the value of that sum total, is represented by Mr. Quesnai, the very ingenious and profound author of this system, in some arithmetical formularies. The first of these formularies, which by way of eminence he peculiarly distinguishes by the name of the Economical Table, represents the manner in which he supposes this distribution takes place, in a state of the most perfect liberty, and therefore of the highest prosperity; in a state where the annual produce is such as to afford the greatest possible neat produce, and where each class enjoys its proper share of the whole annual produce. Some subsequent formularies represent the manner, in which, he supposes, this distribution is made in different states of restraint and regulation; in which, either the class of proprietors, or the barren and unproductive class, is more favoured than the class of cultivators, and in which, either the one or the other encroaches more or less upon the share which ought properly to belong to this productive class. Every such encroachment, every violation of that natural distribution, which the most perfect liberty would establish, must, according to this system, necessarily degrade more or less, from one year to another, the value and sum total of the annual produce, and must necessarily occasion a gradual declension in the real wealth and revenue of the society; a declension of which the progress must be quicker or slower, according to the degree of this encroachment, according as that natural distribution, which the most perfect liberty would establish, is more or less violated. Those subsequent formularies represent the different degrees of declension, which, according to this system, correspond to the different degrees in which this natural distribution of things is violated.

Some speculative physicians seem to have imagined that the health of the human body could be preserved only by a certain precise regimen of diet and exercise, of which every, the smallest, violation necessarily occasioned some degree of disease or disorder proportioned to the degree of the violation. Experience, however, would seem to show, that the human body frequently preserves, to all appearance at least, the most perfect state of health under a vast variety of different regimens; even under some which are generally believed to be very far from being perfectly wholesome. But the healthful state of the human body, it would seem, contains in itself some unknown principle of preservation, capable either of preventing or of correcting, in many respects, the bad effects even of a very faulty regimen. Mr. Quesnai, who was himself a physician, and a very speculative physician, seems to have entertained a notion of the same kind concerning the political body, and to have imagined that it would thrive and prosper only under a certain precise regimen, the exact regimen of perfect liberty and perfect justice. He seems not to have considered that in the political body, the natural effort which every man is continually making to better his own condition, is a principle of preservation capable of preventing and correcting, in many respects, the bad effects of a political economy, in some degree both partial and oppressive. Such a political economy, though it no doubt retards more or less, is not always capable of stopping altogether the natural progress of a nation towards wealth and prosperity, and still less of making it go backwards. If a nation could not prosper without the enjoyment of perfect liberty and perfect justice, there is not in the world a nation which could ever have prospered. In the political body, however, the wisdom of nature has fortunately made ample provision for remedying many of the bad effects of the folly and injustice of man; in the same manner as it has done in the natural body, for remedying those of his sloth and intemperance.

The capital error of this system, however, seems to lie in its representing the class of artificers, manufacturers, and merchants, as altogether barren and unproductive. The following observations may serve to show the impropriety of this representation.

First, this class, it is acknowledged, reproduces annually the value of its own annual consumption, and continues, at least, the existence of the stock or capital which maintains and employs it. But upon this account alone the denomination of barren or unproductive should seem to be very improperly applied to it. We should not call a marriage barren or unproductive, though it produced only a son and a daughter, to replace the father and mother, and though it did not increase the number of the human species, but only continued it as it was before. Farmers and country labourers, indeed, over and above the stock which maintains and employs them, reproduce annually a neat produce, a free rent to the landlord. As a marriage which affords three children is certainly more productive than one which affords only two; so the labour of farmers and country labourers is certainly more productive than that of merchants, artificers, and manufacturers. The superior produce of the one class, however, does not render the other barren or unproductive.

Secondly, it seems, upon this account, altogether improper to consider artificers, manufacturers, and merchants in the same light as menial servants. The labour of menial servants does not continue the existence of the fund which maintains and employs them. Their maintenance and employment is altogether at the expence of their masters, and the work which they perform is not of a nature to repay that expence. That work consists in services which perish generally in the very instant of their performance, and does not fix or realize itself in any vendible commodity which can replace the value of their wages and maintenance. The labour, on the contrary, of artificers, manufacturers and merchants, naturally does fix and realize itself in some such vendible commodity. It is upon this account that, in the chapter in which I treat of productive and unproductive labour, I have classed artificers, manufacturers, and merchants, among the productive labourers, and menial servants among the barren or unproductive.

Thirdly, it seems, upon every supposition, improper to say, that the labour of artificers, manufacturers, and merchants, does not increase the real revenue of the society. Though we should suppose, for example, as it seems to be supposed in this system, that the value of the daily, monthly, and yearly consumption of this class was exactly equal to that of its daily, monthly, and yearly production; yet it would not from thence follow that its labour added nothing to the real revenue, to the real value of the annual produce of the land and labour of the society. An artificer, for example, who, in the first six months after harvest, executes ten pounds' worth of work, though he should in the same time consume ten pounds' worth of corn and other necessaries, yet really adds the value of ten pounds to the annual produce of the land and labour of the society. While he has been consuming a half yearly revenue of ten pounds' worth of corn and other necessaries, he has produced an equal value of work capable of purchasing, either to himself or to some other person, an equal half yearly revenue. The value, therefore, of what has been consumed and produced during these six months is equal, not to ten, but to twenty pounds.

Fourthly, farmers and country labourers can no more augment, without parsimony, the real revenue, the annual produce of the land and labour of their society, than artificers, manufacturers, and merchants. The annual produce of the land and labour of any society can be augmented only in two ways; either, first, by some improvement in the productive powers of the useful labour actually maintained within it; or, secondly, by some increase in the quantity of that labour.

The improvement in the productive powers of useful labour depends, first, upon the improvement in the ability of the workman; and, secondly, upon that of the machinery with which he works. But the labour of artificers and manufacturers, as it is capable of being more subdivided, and the labour of each workman reduced to a greater simplicity of operation, than that of farmers and country labourers, so it is likewise capable of both these sorts of improvement in a much higher degree. In this respect, therefore, the class of cultivators can have no sort of advantage over that of artificers and manufacturers.

Fifthly and lastly, though the revenue of the inhabitants of every country was supposed to consist altogether, as this system seems to suppose, in the quantity of subsistence which their industry could procure to them; yet even upon this supposition, the revenue of a trading and manufacturing country must, other things being equal, always be much greater than that of one without trade or manufactures. By means of trade and manufactures, a greater quantity of subsistence can be annually imported into a particular country than what its own lands, in the actual state of their cultivation, could afford. The inhabitants of a town, though they frequently possess no lands of their own, yet draw to themselves by their industry such a quantity of the rude produce of the lands of other people as supplies them, not only with the materials of their work, but with the fund of their subsistence. What a town always is with regard to the country in its neighbourhood, one independent state or country may frequently be with regard to other independent states or countries. It is thus that Holland draws a great part of its subsistence from other countries: live cattle from Holstein and Jutland, and corn from almost all the different countries of Europe. A small quantity of manufactured produce purchases a great quantity of rude produce. A trading and manufacturing country, therefore, naturally purchases with a small part of its manufactured produce a great part of the rude produce of other countries; while, on the contrary, a country without trade and manufactures is generally obliged to purchase, at the expence of a great part of its rude produce, a very small part of the manufactured produce of other countries. The one exports what can subsist and accommodate but a very few, and imports the subsistence and accommodation of a great number. The other exports the accommodation and subsistence of a great number, and imports that of a very few only. The inhabitants of the one must always enjoy a much greater quantity of subsistence than what their own lands, in the actual state of their cultivation, could afford. The inhabitants of the other must always enjoy a much smaller quantity.

This system, however, with all its imperfections, is, perhaps, the nearest approximation to the truth that has yet been published upon the subject of political economy, and is upon that account well worth the consideration of every man who wishes to examine with attention the principles of that very important science. Though in representing the labour which is employed upon land as the only productive labour, the notions which it inculcates are perhaps too narrow and confined; yet in representing the wealth of nations as consisting, not in the unconsumable riches of money, but in the consumable goods annually reproduced by the labour of the society; and in representing perfect liberty as the only effectual expedient for rendering this annual reproduction the greatest possible, its doctrine seems to be in every respect as just as it is generous and liberal. Its followers are very numerous; and as men are fond of paradoxes, and of appearing to understand what surpasses the comprehension of ordinary people, the paradox which it maintains, concerning the unproductive nature of manufacturing labour, has not perhaps contributed a little to increase the number of its admirers. They have for some years past made a pretty considerable sect, distinguished in the French republic of letters by the name of, The Economists. Their works have certainly been of some service to their country; not only by bringing into general discussion, many subjects which had never been well examined before, but by influencing in some measure the public administration in favour of agriculture. It has been in consequence of their representations, accordingly, that the agriculture of France has been delivered from several of the oppressions which it before laboured under. The term during which such a lease can be granted, as will be valid against every future purchaser or proprietor of the land, has been prolonged from nine to twenty-seven years. The ancient provincial restraints upon the transportation of corn from one province of the kingdom to another, have been entirely taken away, and the liberty of exporting it to all foreign countries, has been established as the common law of the kingdom in all ordinary cases. This sect, in their works, which are very numerous, and which treat not only of what is properly called Political Economy, or of the nature and causes of the wealth of nations, but of every other branch of the system of civil government, all follow implicitly, and without any sensible variation, the doctrine of Mr. Quesnai. There is upon this account little variety in the greater part of their works. The most distinct and best connected account of this doctrine is to be found in a little book written by Mr. Mercier de la Riviere, sometime Intendant of Martinico, entitled, *The natural and essential Order of Political Societies*. The admiration of this whole sect for their master, who was himself a man of the greatest modesty and simplicity, is not inferior to that of any of the ancient philosophers for the founders of their respective systems. "There have been, since the world began," says a very diligent and respectable author, the Marquis de Mirabeau, "three great inventions which have principally given stability to political societies, independent of many other inventions which have enriched and adorned them. The first, is the invention of writing, which alone gives human nature the power of transmitting, without alteration, its laws, its contracts, its annals, and its discoveries. The second, is the invention of money, which binds together all the relations between civilized societies. The third, is the Economical Table, the result of the other two, which completes them both by perfecting their object; the great discovery of our age, but of which our posterity will reap the benefit."

As the political economy of the nations of modern Europe, has been more favourable to manufactures and foreign trade, the industry of the towns, than to agriculture, the industry of the country; so that of other nations has followed a different plan, and has been more favourable to agriculture than to manufactures and foreign trade.

The policy of China favours agriculture more than all other employments.

The policy of ancient Egypt too, and that of the Gentoo government of Indostan, seem to have favoured agriculture more than all other employments.

The sovereigns of China, of ancient Egypt, and of the different kingdoms into which Indostan has at different times been divided, have always derived the whole, or by far the most considerable part, of their revenue from some sort of land-tax or land-rent. This land-tax or land-rent, like the tithe in Europe, consisted in a certain proportion, a fifth, it is said, of the produce of the land, which was either delivered in kind, or paid in money, according to a certain valuation, and which therefore varied from year to year according to all the variations of the produce. It was natural therefore, that the sovereigns of those countries should be particularly attentive to the interests of agriculture, upon the prosperity or declension of which immediately depended the yearly increase or diminution of their own revenue.

The greatest and most important branch of the commerce of every nation, it has already been observed, is that which is carried on between the inhabitants of the town and those of the country. The inhabitants of the town draw from the country the rude produce which constitutes both the materials of their work and the fund of their subsistence; and they pay for this rude produce by sending back to the country a certain portion of it manufactured and prepared for immediate use. The trade which is carried on between those two different sets of people, consists ultimately in a certain quantity of rude produce exchanged for a certain quantity of manufactured produce. The dearer the latter, therefore, the cheaper the former; and whatever tends in any country to raise the price of manufactured produce, tends to lower that of the rude produce of the land, and thereby to discourage agriculture. The smaller the quantity of manufactured produce which any given quantity of rude produce, or, which comes to the same thing, which the price of any given quantity of rude produce is capable of purchasing, the smaller the exchangeable value of that given quantity of rude produce; the smaller the encouragement which either the landlord has to increase its quantity by improving, or the farmer by cultivating the land. Whatever, besides, tends to diminish in any country the number of artificers and manufacturers, tends to diminish the home market, the most important of all markets for the rude produce of the land, and thereby still further to discourage agriculture.

Those systems, therefore, which preferring agriculture to all other employments, in order to promote it, impose restraints upon manufactures and foreign trade, act contrary to the very end which they propose, and indirectly discourage that very species of industry which they mean to promote. They are so far, perhaps, more inconsistent than even the mercantile system. That system, by encouraging manufactures and foreign trade more than agriculture, turns a certain portion of the capital of the society from supporting a more advantageous, to support a less advantageous species of industry. But still it really and in the end encourages that species of industry which it means to promote. Those agricultural systems, on the contrary, really and in the end discourage their own favourite species of industry.

It is thus that every system which endeavours, either by extraordinary encouragements to draw towards a particular species of industry a greater share of the capital of the society than what would naturally go to it, or by extraordinary restraints to force from a particular species of industry some share of the capital which would otherwise be employed in it, is in reality subversive of the great purpose which it means to promote. It retards, instead of accelerating, the progress of the society towards real wealth and greatness, and diminishes, instead of increasing, the real value of the annual produce of its land and labour.

All systems either of preference or of restraint, therefore, being thus completely taken away, the obvious and simple system of natural liberty establishes itself of its own accord. Every man, as long as he does not violate the laws of justice, is left perfectly free to pursue his own interest his own way, and to bring both his industry and capital into competition with those of any other man or order of men. The sovereign is completely discharged from a duty in the attempting to perform which he must always be exposed to innumerable delusions, and for the proper performance of which no human wisdom or knowledge could ever be sufficient: the duty of superintending the industry of private people, and of directing it towards the employments most suitable to the interest of the society. According to the system of natural liberty, the sovereign has only three duties to attend to, three duties of great importance, indeed, but plain and intelligible to common understandings: first, the duty of protecting the society from the violence and invasion of other independent societies; secondly, the duty of protecting, as far as possible, every member of the society from the injustice or oppression of every other member of it, or the duty of establishing an exact administration of justice; and, thirdly, the duty of erecting and maintaining certain public works and certain public institutions, which it can never be for the interest of any individual or small number of individuals to erect and maintain, because the profit could never repay the expence to any individual or small number of individuals, though it may frequently do much more than repay it to a great society.

Book Five: Of the Revenue of the Sovereign or Commonwealth

I. Of the Expences of the Sovereign or Commonwealth

PART ONE: Of the Expence of Defence

The first duty of the sovereign, that of protecting the society from the violence and invasion of other independent societies, can be performed only by means of a military force. But the expence both of preparing this military force in time of peace, and of employing it in time of war, is very different in the different states of society, in the different periods of improvement.

The number of those who can go to war, in proportion to the whole number of the people, is necessarily much smaller in a civilized, than in a rude state of society. In a civilized society, as the soldiers are maintained altogether by the labour of those who are not soldiers, the number of the former can never exceed what the latter can maintain, over and above maintaining, in a manner suitable to their respective stations, both themselves and the other officers of government, and law, whom they are obliged to maintain. In the little agrarian states of ancient Greece, a fourth or a fifth part of the whole body of the people considered themselves as soldiers, and would sometimes, it is said, take the field. Among the civilized nations of modern Europe, it is commonly computed, that not more than one hundredth part of the inhabitants of any country can be employed as soldiers, without ruin to the country which pays the expence of their service.

The art of war, as it is certainly the noblest of all arts, so in the progress of improvement it necessarily becomes one of the most complicated among them. The state of the mechanical, as well as of some other arts, with which it is necessarily connected, determines the degree of perfection to which it is capable of being carried at any particular time. But in order to carry it to this degree of perfection, it is necessary that it should become the sole or principal occupation of a particular class of citizens, and the division of labour is as necessary for the improvement of this, as of every other art.

In these circumstances, there seem to be but two methods, by which the state can make any tolerable provision for the public defence.

It may either, first, by means of a very rigorous police, and in spite of the whole bent of the interest, genius and inclinations of the people, enforce the practice of military exercises, and oblige either all the citizens of the military age, or a certain number of them, to join in some measure the trade of a soldier to whatever other trade or profession they may happen to carry on.

Or secondly, by maintaining and employing a certain number of citizens in the constant practice of military exercises, it may render the trade of a soldier a particular trade, separate and distinct from all others.

If the state has recourse to the first of those two expedients, its military force is said to consist in a militia; if to the second, it is said to consist in a standing army. The practice of military exercises is the sole or principal occupation of the soldiers of a standing army, and the maintenance or pay which the state affords them is the principal and ordinary fund of their subsistence. The practice of military exercises is only the occasional occupation of the soldiers of a militia, and they derive the principal and ordinary fund of their subsistence from some other occupation. In a militia, the character of the labourer, artificer, or tradesman, predominates over that of the soldier: in a standing army, that of the soldier predominates over every other character; and in this distinction seems to consist the essential difference between those two different species of military force.

The first duty of the sovereign, that of defending the society from the violence and injustice of other independent societies, grows gradually more and more expensive, as the society advances in civilization. The military force of the society, which originally cost the sovereign no expence either in time of peace or in time of war, must, in the progress of improvement, first be maintained by him in time of war, and afterwards even in time of peace.

In modern war the great expence of firearms gives an evident advantage to the nation which can best afford that expence; and consequently, to an opulent and civilized, over a poor and barbarous nation. In ancient times the opulent and civilized found it difficult to defend themselves against the poor and barbarous nations. In modern times the poor and barbarous find it difficult to defend themselves against the opulent and civilized. The invention of firearms, an invention which at first sight appears to be so pernicious, is certainly favourable both to the permanency and to the extension of civilization.

PART TWO: Of the Expence of Justice

The second duty of the sovereign, that of protecting, as far as possible, every member of the society from the injustice or oppression of every other member of it, or the duty of establishing an exact administration of justice requires two very different degrees of expence in the different periods of society.

Among nations of hunters, as there is scarce any property, or at least none that exceeds the value of two or three days' labour; so there is seldom any established magistrate or any regular administration of justice. Men who have no property can injure one another only in their persons or reputations. But when one man kills, wounds, beats, or defames another, though he to whom the injury is done suffers, he who does it receives no benefit. It is otherwise with the injuries to property. The benefit of the person who does the injury is often equal to the loss of him who suffers it. Envy, malice, or resentment, are the only passions which can prompt one man to injure another in his person or reputation. But the greater part of men are not very frequently under the influence of those passions; and the very worst men are so only occasionally. As their gratification too, how agreeable soever it may be to certain characters, is not attended with any real or permanent advantage, it is in the greater part of men commonly restrained by prudential considerations. Men may live together in society with some tolerable degree of security, though there is no civil magistrate to protect them from the injustice of those passions. But avarice and ambition in the rich, in the poor the hatred of labour and the love of present ease and enjoyment, are the passions which prompt to invade property, passions much more steady in their operation, and much more universal in their influence. Wherever there is great property, there is great inequality. For one very rich man, there must be at least five hundred poor, and the affluence of the few supposes the indigence of the many. The affluence of the rich excites the indignation of the poor, who are often both driven by want, and prompted by envy, to invade his possessions. It is only under the shelter of the civil magistrate that the owner of that valuable property, which is acquired by the labour of many years, or perhaps of many successive generations, can sleep a single night in security. The acquisition of valuable and extensive property, therefore, necessarily requires the establishment of civil government.

It is in the age of shepherds, in the second period of society, that the inequality of fortune first begins to take place, and introduces among men a degree of authority and subordination which could not possibly exist before. The inferior shepherds and herdsmen feel that the security of their own herds and flocks depends upon the security of those of the great shepherd or herdsman; that the maintenance of their lesser authority depends upon that of his greater authority, and that upon their subordination to him depends his power of keeping their inferiors in subordination to them. They constitute a sort of little nobility, who feel themselves interested to defend the property and to support the authority of their own little sovereign, in order that he may be able to defend their property and to support their authority. Civil government, so far as it is instituted for the security of property, is in reality instituted for the defence of the rich against the poor, or of those who have some property against those who have none at all.

The judicial authority of such a sovereign, however, far from being a cause of expence, was for a long time a source of revenue to him. The persons who applied to him for justice were always willing to pay for it, and a present never failed to accompany a petition.

The office of judge is in itself so very honourable, that men are willing to accept of it, though accompanied with very small emoluments. The inferior office of justice of peace, though attended with a good deal of trouble, and in most cases with no emoluments at all, is an object of ambition to the greater part of our country gentlemen. The salaries of all the different judges, high and low, together with the whole expence of the administration and execution of justice, even where it is not managed with very good economy, makes, in any civilized country, but a very inconsiderable part of the whole expence of government.

The whole expence of justice too might easily be defrayed by the fees of court; and, without exposing the administration of justice to any real hazard of corruption, the public revenue might thus be entirely discharged from a certain, though, perhaps, but a small incumbrance.

The separation of the judicial from the executive power seems originally to have arisen from the increasing business of the society, in consequence of its increasing improvement. The administration of justice became so laborious and so complicated a duty as to require the undivided attention of the persons to whom it was entrusted. The person entrusted with the executive power, not having leisure to attend to the decision of private causes himself, a deputy was appointed to decide them in his stead. In the progress of the Roman greatness, the consul was too much occupied with the political affairs of the state, to attend to the administration of justice. A prætor, therefore, was appointed to administer it in his stead. In the progress of the European monarchies which were founded upon the ruins of the Roman empire, the sovereigns and the great lords came universally to consider the administration of justice as an office, both too laborious and too ignoble for them to execute in their own persons. They universally, therefore, discharged themselves of it by appointing a deputy, bailiff, or judge.

When the judicial is united to the executive power, it is scarce possible that justice should not frequently be sacrificed to, what is vulgarly called, politics. The persons entrusted with the great interests of the state may, even without any corrupt views, sometimes imagine it necessary to sacrifice to those interests the rights of a private man. But upon the impartial administration of justice depends the liberty of every individual, the sense which he has of his own security. In order to make every individual feel himself perfectly secure in the possession of every right which belongs to him, it is not only necessary that the judicial should be separated from the executive power, but that it should be rendered as much as possible independent of that power. The judge should not be liable to be removed from his office according to the caprice of that power. The regular payment of his salary should not depend upon the good will, or even upon the good economy of that power.

PART THREE: Of the Expence of public Works and public Institutions

The third and last duty of the sovereign or commonwealth is that of erecting and maintaining those public institutions and those public works, which, though they may be in the highest degree advantageous to a great society, are, however, of such a nature, that the profit could never repay the expence to any individual or small number of individuals, and which it therefore cannot be expected that any individual or small number of individuals should erect or maintain. The performance of this duty requires too very different degrees of expence in the different periods of society.

After the public institutions and public works necessary for the defence of the society, and for the administration of justice, both of which have already been mentioned, the other works and institutions of this kind are chiefly those for facilitating the commerce of the society, and those for promoting the instruction of the people. The institutions for instruction are of two kinds; those for the education of the youth, and those for the instruction of people of all ages. The consideration of the manner in which the expence of those different sorts of public works and institutions may be most properly defrayed, will divide this third part of the present chapter into three different articles.

Article I

OF THE PUBLIC WORKS AND INSTITUTIONS FOR FACILITATING THE COMMERCE OF THE SOCIETY

AND, FIRST, OF THOSE WHICH ARE NECESSARY FOR FACILITATING COMMERCE IN GENERAL

That the erection and maintenance of the public works which facilitate the commerce of any country, such as good roads, bridges, navigable canals, harbours, &c. must require very different degrees of expence in the different periods of society, is evident without any proof. The expence of making and maintaining the public roads of any country must evidently increase with the annual produce of the land and labour of that country, or with the quantity and weight of the goods which it becomes necessary to fetch and carry upon those roads. The strength of a bridge must be suited to the number and weight of the carriages, which are likely to pass over it. The depth and the supply of water for a navigable canal must be proportioned to the number and tonnage of the lighters, which are likely to carry goods upon it; the extent of a harbour to the number of the shipping which are likely to take shelter in it.

It does not seem necessary that the expence of those public works should be defrayed from that public revenue, as it is commonly called, of which the collection and application are in most countries assigned to the executive power. The greater part of such public works may easily be so managed, as to afford a particular revenue sufficient for defraying their own expence, without bringing any burden upon the general revenue of the society.

A highway, a bridge, a navigable canal, for example, may in most cases be both made and maintained by a small toll upon the carriages which make use of them: a harbour, by a moderate port duty upon the tonnage of the shipping which load or unload in it. The coinage, another institution for facilitating commerce, in many countries, not only defrays its own expence, but affords a small revenue or seignorage to the sovereign. The post office, another institution for the same purpose, over and above defraying its own expence, affords in almost all countries a very considerable revenue to the sovereign.

OF THE PUBLIC WORKS AND INSTITUTIONS WHICH ARE NECESSARY FOR FACILITATING PARTICULAR BRANCHES OF COMMERCE

The object of the public works and institutions above mentioned is to facilitate commerce in general. But in order to facilitate some particular branches of it, particular institutions are necessary, which again require a particular and extraordinary expence.

Some particular branches of commerce, which are carried on with barbarous and uncivilized nations, require extraordinary protection. An ordinary store or countinghouse could give little security to the goods of the merchants who trade to the western coast of Africa. To defend them from the barbarous natives, it is necessary that the place where they are deposited, should be, in some measure, fortified. The disorders in the government of Indostan have been supposed to render a like precaution necessary even among that mild and gentle people; and it was under pretence of securing their persons and property from violence, that both the English and French East India Companies were allowed to erect the first forts which they possessed in that country. Among other nations, whose vigorous government will suffer no strangers to possess any fortified place within their territory, it may be necessary to maintain some ambassador, minister, or consul, who may both decide, according to their own customs, the differences arising among his own countrymen; and, in their disputes with the natives, may, by means of his public character, interfere with more authority, and afford them a more powerful protection, than they could expect from any private man. The interests of commerce have frequently made it necessary to maintain ministers in foreign countries, where the purposes, either of war or alliance, would not have required any. The commerce of the Turkey Company first occasioned the establishment of an ordinary ambassador at Constantinople. The first English embassies to Russia arose altogether from commercial interests. The constant interference which those interests necessarily occasioned between the subjects of the different states of Europe, has probably introduced the custom of keeping, in all neighbouring countries, ambassadors or ministers constantly resident even in the time of peace. This custom, unknown to ancient times, seems not to be older than the end of the fifteenth or beginning of the sixteenth century; that is, than the time when commerce first began to extend itself to the greater part of the nations of Europe, and when they first began to attend to its interests.

The protection of trade in general has always been considered as essential to the defence of the commonwealth, and, upon that account, a necessary part of the duty of the executive power. The collection and application of the general duties of customs, therefore, have always been left to that power. But the protection of any particular branch of trade is a part of the general protection of trade; a part, therefore, of the duty of that power; and if nations always acted consistently, the particular duties levied for the purposes of such particular protection, should always have been left equally to its disposal. But in this respect, as well as in many others, nations have not always acted consistently; and in the greater part of the commercial states of Europe, particular companies of merchants have had the address to persuade the legislature to entrust to them the performance of this part of the duty of the sovereign, together with all the powers which are necessarily connected with it.

These companies, though they may, perhaps, have been useful for the first introduction of some branches of commerce, by making, at their own expence, an experiment which the state might not think it prudent to make, have in the long run proved, universally, either burdensome or useless, and have either mismanaged or confined the trade.

Article II

OF THE EXPENCE OF THE INSTITUTIONS FOR THE EDUCATION OF YOUTH

The institutions for the education of the youth may furnish a revenue sufficient for defraying their own expence. The fee or honorary which the scholar pays to the master naturally constitutes a revenue of this kind.

Even where the reward of the master does not arise altogether from this natural revenue, it still is not necessary that it should be derived from that general revenue of the society, of which the collection and application are, in most countries, assigned to the executive power. Through the greater part of Europe, accordingly, the endowment of schools and colleges makes either no charge upon that general revenue, or but a very small one. It every where arises chiefly from some local or provincial revenue, from the rent of some landed estate, or from the interest of some sum of money allotted and put under the management of trustees for this particular purpose, sometimes by the sovereign himself, and sometimes by some private donor.

The education of the common people requires, perhaps, in a civilized and commercial society, the attention of the public more than that of people of some rank and fortune. People of some rank and fortune are generally eighteen or nineteen years of age before they enter upon that particular business, profession, or trade, by which they propose to distinguish themselves in the world. They have before that full time to acquire, or at least to fit themselves for afterwards acquiring, every accomplishment which can recommend them to the public esteem, or render them worthy of it. Their parents or guardians are generally sufficiently anxious that they should be so accomplished, and are, in most cases, willing enough to lay out the expence which is necessary for that purpose. If they are not always properly educated, it is seldom from the want of expence laid out upon their education; but from the improper application of that expence.

It is otherwise with the common people. They have little time to spare for education. Their parents can scarce afford to maintain them even in infancy. As soon as they are able to work, they must apply to some trade by which they can earn their subsistence. That trade too is generally so simple and uniform as to give little exercise to the understanding; while, at the same time, their labour is both so constant and so severe, that it leaves them little leisure and less inclination to apply to, or even to think of anything else.

But though the common people cannot, in any civilized society, be so well instructed as people of some rank and fortune, the most essential parts of education, however, to read, write, and account, can be acquired at so early a period of life, that the greater part even of those who are to be bred to the lowest occupations, have time to acquire them before they can be employed in those occupations. For a very small expence the public can facilitate, can encourage, and can even impose upon almost the whole body of the people, the necessity of acquiring those most essential parts of education.

The public can facilitate this acquisition by establishing in every parish or district a little school, where children may be taught for a reward so moderate, that even a common labourer may afford it; the master being partly, but not wholly paid by the public; because, if he was wholly, or even principally paid by it, he would soon learn to neglect his business. In Scotland the establishment of such parish schools has taught almost the whole common people to read, and a very great proportion of them to write and account. In England the establishment of charity schools has had an effect of the same kind, though not so universally, because the establishment is not so universal. If in those little schools the books, by which the children are taught to read, were a little more instructive than they commonly are; and if, instead of a little smattering of Latin, which the children of the common people are sometimes taught there, and which can scarce ever be of any use to them; they were instructed in the elementary parts of geometry and mechanics, the literary education of this rank of people would perhaps be as complete as it can be. There is scarce a common trade which does not afford some opportunities of applying to it the principles of geometry and mechanics, and which would not therefore gradually exercise and improve the common people in those principles, the necessary introduction to the most sublime as well as to the most useful sciences.

The public can encourage the acquisition of those most essential parts of education by giving small premiums, and little badges of distinction, to the children of the common people who excel in them.

The public can impose upon almost the whole body of the people the necessity of acquiring those most essential parts of education, by obliging every man to undergo an examination or probation in them before he can obtain the freedom in any corporation, or be allowed to set up any trade either in a village or town corporate.

Article III

OF THE EXPENCE OF THE INSTITUTIONS FOR THE INSTRUCTION OF PEOPLE OF ALL AGES

The institutions for the instruction of people of all ages are chiefly those for religious instruction. This is a species of instruction of which the object is not so much to render the people good citizens in this world, as to prepare them for another and a better world in a life to come. The teachers of the doctrine which contains this instruction, in the same manner as other teachers, may either depend altogether for their subsistence upon the voluntary contributions of their hearers; or they may derive it from some other fund to which the law of their country may entitle them; such as a landed estate, a tythe or land tax, an established salary or stipend.

PART FOUR: Of the Expence of supporting the Dignity of the Sovereign

Over and above the expence necessary for enabling the sovereign to perform his several duties, a certain expence is requisite for the support of his dignity. This expence varies both with the different periods of improvement, and with the different forms of government.

In an opulent and improved society, where all the different orders of people are growing every day more expensive in their houses, in their furniture, in their tables, in their dress, and in their equipage; it cannot well be expected that the sovereign should alone hold out against the fashion. He naturally, therefore, or rather necessarily becomes more expensive in all those different articles too. His dignity even seems to require that he should become so.

As in point of dignity, a monarch is more raised above his subjects than the chief magistrate of any republic is ever supposed to be above his fellow citizens; so a greater expence is necessary for supporting that higher dignity. We naturally expect more splendor in the court of a king, than in the mansion house of a doge or burgomaster.

II. Of the Sources of the General or Public Revenue of the Society

The revenue which must defray, not only the expence of defending the society and of supporting the dignity of the chief magistrate, but all the other necessary expences of government, for which the constitution of the state has not provided any particular revenue, may be drawn, either, first, from some fund which peculiarly belongs to the sovereign or commonwealth, and which is independent of the revenue of the people; or, secondly, from the revenue of the people.

I. The subjects of every state ought to contribute towards the support of the government, as nearly as possible, in proportion to their respective abilities; that is, in proportion to the revenue which they respectively enjoy under the protection of the state. The expence of government to the individuals of a great nation, is like the expence of management to the joint tenants of a great estate, who are all obliged to contribute in proportion to their respective interests in the estate. In the observation or neglect of this maxim consists, what is called the equality or inequality of taxation.

II. The tax which each individual is bound to pay ought to be certain, and not arbitrary. The time of payment, the manner of payment, the quantity to be paid, ought all to be clear and plain to the contributor, and to every other person. Where it is otherwise, every person subject to the tax is put more or less in the power of the taxgatherer, who can either aggravate the tax upon any obnoxious contributor, or extort, by the terror of such aggravation, some present or perquisite to himself.

III. Every tax ought to be levied at the time, or in the manner, in which it is most likely to be convenient for the contributor to pay it. A tax upon the rent of land or of houses, payable at the same term at which such rents are usually paid, is levied at the time when it is most likely to be convenient for the contributor to pay; or, when he is most likely to have wherewithal to pay. Taxes upon such consumable goods as are articles of luxury, are all finally paid by the consumer, and generally in a manner that is very convenient for him. He pays them by little and little, as he has occasion to buy the goods. As he is at liberty too, either to buy, or not to buy, as he pleases, it must be his own fault if he ever suffers any considerable inconveniency from such taxes.

IV. Every tax ought to be so contrived as both to take out and to keep out of the pockets of the people as little as possible, over and above what it brings into the public treasury of the state. A tax may either take out or keep out of the pockets of the people a great deal more than it brings into the public treasury, in the four following ways. First, the levying of it may require a great number of officers, whose salaries may eat up the greater part of the produce of the tax, and whose perquisites may impose another additional tax upon the people. Secondly, it may obstruct the industry of the people, and discourage them from applying to certain branches of business which might give maintenance and employment to great multitudes. While it obliges the people to pay, it may thus diminish, or perhaps destroy, some of the funds which might enable them more easily to do so. Thirdly, by the forfeitures and other penalties which those unfortunate individuals incur who attempt unsuccessfully to evade the tax, it may frequently ruin them, and thereby put an end to the benefit which the community might have received from the employment of their capitals. An injudicious tax offers a great temptation to smuggling. But the penalties of smuggling must rise in proportion to the temptation. The law, contrary to all the ordinary principles of justice, first creates the temptation, and then punishes those who yield to it; and it commonly enhances the punishment too in proportion to the very circumstance which ought certainly to alleviate it, the temptation to commit the crime. Fourthly, by subjecting the people to the frequent visits and the odious examination of the taxgatherers, it may expose them to much unnecessary trouble, vexation, and oppression; and though vexation is not, strictly speaking, expence, it is certainly equivalent to the expence at which every man would be willing to redeem himself from it. It is in some one or other of these four different ways that taxes are frequently so much more burdensome to the people than they are beneficial to the sovereign.

AN ESSAY ON THE PRINCIPLE OF POPULATION

by

THOMAS ROBERT MALTHUS

CONTENTS

An Essay on the Principle of Population

THOMAS ROBERT MALTHUS

1766–1834

THOMAS ROBERT MALTHUS, author of *An Essay on the Principle of Population,* was the son of Daniel Malthus, a country gentleman living near Guildford, Surrey, England. He was born in 1766 and was instructed by his father as well as in private schools. At the age of nineteen he went to Cambridge University, where he distinguished himself as a scholar and took holy orders. For several months he held a curacy at Albury, Surrey. His chief interest, however, was not in the ministry but in social problems.

Daniel Malthus was a friend of David Hume, Scottish historian and philosopher, and of Jean-Jacques Rousseau, world-famous French writer and theorist. The times were stormy, and the spirit of revolution was in the air. The Marquis de Condorcet was propounding in France extravagantly optimistic theories regarding human perfectibility, and William Godwin in England was writing a book, *An Enquiry Concerning Political Justice,* which was soon not only to startle the world by reason of its anarchistic implications but was also to stimulate the younger Malthus to express his own views.

At first in his family circle and in conversation with his father and friends, young Malthus discussed the arguments used by Godwin and Condorcet. He could not doubt their talent as writers. What gave him pause, he said, was their seeming unwillingness to face the difficulties that made the realization of their ideals impossible. These difficulties, according to Malthus, were based on an inexorable law of nature—namely, that population tends to outstrip the means of subsistence.

Daniel Malthus was so impressed by his son's reasoning powers that he prevailed upon him to publish his views. The first *Essay on the Principle of Population* appeared anonymously in 1798.

The root idea underlying the *Essay* is clearly stated at its outset. "I think," says Malthus, "I may fairly make two postulata. First, that food is necessary to the existence of man. Secondly, that the passion between the sexes is necessary, and will remain nearly in its present state."

Implicit in Malthus's view are belief in the beneficent rule of God, a new conception of "vice" and "misery" as agents which tend to reduce population, and a plea for the abolition of Poor Laws, which, in his opinion, undermine a sense of responsibility in the needy and encourage overpopulation. An unforgettable turn is given to his arguments by his statement that "population, when unchecked, increases in a geometrical ratio," while "subsistence only increases in an arithmetical ratio."

Publication of the *Essay* led to an animated controversy. Prime Minister William Pitt and Archdeacon William Paley, England's famous theologian, both admitted that they were favorably impressed by Malthus's arguments, but other publicists attacked his position. He now found himself the target of indignant critics who not only questioned the accuracy of his mathematics, but who also accused him of "defending" wars, famines, and plagues as agents in depopulation and of denying to the poor even the solace of charity.

Stung by these criticisms, Malthus proceeded to strengthen his case. He gathered material bearing on "general checks to population." He read Greek and Roman history and added to his store of information regarding birth rates in Asiatic races. In 1799 he traveled on the continent of Europe, collecting facts and figures in relation to what was becoming his mental obsession—the problem of population.

In 1803 Malthus published a second edition of his *Essay,* embodying in it about four times as much matter as that contained in the original version. He spoke now of "moral restraint" as a major factor in bringing about a reduction of population, and by moral restraint he meant "a restraint from marriage from prudential motives, with a conduct strictly moral during the period of this restraint." The new edition was really an entirely new work, and Malthus acknowledged its authorship. Four more editions, substantially the same as the second edition, were to appear before he died in 1834. The present digest is based on the eighth edition.

At the age of thirty-eight Malthus married his cousin, Harriet Eckersall. This late marriage resulted in three children. In 1805, the year following his marriage, he became professor of history and political economy at Haileybury College, an institution established by the East India Company for the purpose of training young men who were to enter its service. With Grote, Ricardo, James Mill, and Tooke he helped to found the Political Economy Club in London in 1821.

Apart from the *Essay on the Principle of Population,* Malthus wrote voluminously on economic topics. Among his works are *Observations on the Effects of the Corn Laws* (1814), *An Inquiry into the Nature and Progress of Rent* (1815), *Principles of Political Economy* (1820), and *The Measure of Value Stated and Illustrated* (1823).

Charles Darwin made public acknowledgment of his intellectual debt to Malthus. "In October 1838," he writes in his autobiography, "that is, fifteen months after I had begun my systematic inquiry, I happened to read for amusement Malthus on *Population,* and being well prepared to appreciate the struggle for existence which everywhere goes on, from long-continued observation of the habits of animals and plants, it at once struck me that under these circumstances favourable variations would tend to be preserved and unfavourable ones to be destroyed." Alfred Russel Wallace, co-discoverer of the theory of evolution, also acknowledged his indebtedness to Malthus.

AN ESSAY ON THE PRINCIPLE OF POPULATION

Part One: Of the Checks to Population in the Less Civilised Parts of the World and in Past Times

I. Statement of the Subject. Ratios of the Increase of Population and Food

In an inquiry concerning the improvement of society, the mode of conducting the subject which naturally presents itself, is—

1. To investigate the causes that have hitherto impeded the progress of mankind towards happiness; and,

2. To examine the probability of the total or partial removal of these causes in future.

To enter fully into this question, and to enumerate all the causes that have hitherto influenced human improvement, would be much beyond the power of an individual. The principal object of the present essay is to examine the effects of one great cause intimately united with the very nature of man; which, though it has been constantly and powerfully operating since the commencement of society, has been little noticed by the writers who have treated this subject. The facts which establish the existence of this cause have, indeed, been repeatedly stated and acknowledged; but its natural and necessary effects have been almost totally overlooked; though probably among these effects may be reckoned a very considerable portion of that vice and misery, and of that unequal distribution of the bounties of nature, which it has been the unceasing object of the enlightened philanthropist in all ages to correct.

The cause to which I allude, is the constant tendency in all animated life to increase beyond the nourishment prepared for it.

It is observed by Dr. [Benjamin] Franklin, that there is no bound to the prolific nature of plants or animals but what is made by their crowding and interfering with each other's means of subsistence. Were the face of the earth, he says, vacant of other plants, it might be gradually sowed and overspread with one kind only, as, for instance, with fennel: and were it empty of other inhabitants, it might in a few ages be replenished from one nation only, as, for instance, with Englishmen.

This is incontrovertibly true. Throughout the animal and vegetable kingdoms Nature has scattered the seeds of life abroad with the most profuse and liberal hand; but has been comparatively sparing in the room and the nourishment necessary to rear them. The germs of existence contained in this earth, if they could freely develop themselves, would fill millions of worlds in the course of a few thousand years. Necessity, that imperious, all-pervading law of nature, restrains them within the prescribed bounds. The race of plants and the race of animals shrink under this great restrictive law; and man cannot by any efforts of reason escape from it.

In plants and irrational animals, the view of the subject is simple. They are all impelled by a powerful instinct to the increase of their species, and this instinct is interrupted by no doubts about providing for their offspring. Wherever, therefore, there is liberty, the power of increase is exerted, and the superabundant effects are repressed afterwards by want of room and nourishment.

The effects of this check on man are more complicated. Impelled to the increase of his species by an equally powerful instinct, reason interrupts his career, and asks him whether he may not bring beings into the world for whom he cannot provide the means of support. If he attend to this natural suggestion, the restriction too frequently produces vice. If he hear it not, the human race will be constantly endeavouring to increase beyond the means of subsistence. But as, by that law of our nature which makes food necessary to the life of man, population can never actually increase beyond the lowest nourishment capable of supporting it, a strong check on population, from the difficulty of acquiring food, must be constantly in operation. This difficulty must fall somewhere, and must necessarily be severely felt in some or other of the various forms of misery, or the fear of misery, by a large portion of mankind.

That population has this constant tendency to increase beyond the means of subsistence, and that it is kept to its necessary level by these causes, will sufficiently appear from a review of the different states of society in which man has existed. But, before we proceed to this review, the subject will perhaps be seen in a clearer light, if we endeavour to ascertain what would be the natural increase of population, if left to exert itself with perfect freedom; and what might be expected to be the rate of increase in the productions of the earth, under the most favourable circumstances of human industry.

It will be allowed that no country has hitherto been known, where the manners were so pure and simple, and the means of subsistence so abundant, that no check whatever has existed to early marriages from the difficulty of providing for a family, and that no waste of the human species has been occasioned by vicious customs, by towns, by unhealthy occupations, or too severe labour. Consequently in no state that we have yet known, has the power of population been left to exert itself with perfect freedom.

Whether the law of marriage be instituted or not, the dictate of nature and virtue seems to be an early attachment to one woman; and where there were no impediments of any kind in the way of a union to which such an attachment would lead, and no causes of depopulation afterwards, the increase of the human species would be evidently much greater than any increase which has been hitherto known.

In the northern states of America, where the means of subsistence have been more ample, the manners of the people more pure, and the checks to early marriages fewer, than in any of the modern states of Europe, the population has been found to double itself, for above a century and a half successively, in less than twenty-five years. Yet, even during these periods, in some of the towns, the deaths exceeded the births, a circumstance which clearly proves that in those parts of the country which supplied this deficiency, the increase must have been much more rapid than the general average.

In the back settlements, where the sole employment is agriculture, and vicious customs and unwholesome occupations are little known, the population has been found to double itself in fifteen years. Even this extraordinary rate of increase is probably short of the utmost power of population. Very severe labour is requisite to clear a fresh country; such situations are not in general considered as particularly healthy; and the inhabitants, probably, are occasionally subject to the incursions of the Indians, which may destroy some lives, or at any rate diminish the fruits of industry.

According to a table of Euler, calculated on a mortality of 1 in 36, if the births be to the deaths in the proportion of 3 to 1, the period of doubling will be only twelve years and four-fifths. And this proportion is not only a possible supposition, but has actually occurred for short periods in more countries than one.

Sir William Petty supposes a doubling possible in so short a time as ten years.

But, to be perfectly sure that we are far within the truth, we will take the slowest of these rates of increase, a rate in which all concurring testimonies agree, and which has been repeatedly ascertained to be from procreation only.

It may safely be pronounced, therefore, that population, when unchecked, goes on doubling itself every twenty-five years, or increases in a geometrical ratio.

The rate according to which the productions of the earth may be supposed to increase, will not be so easy to determine. Of this, however, we may be perfectly certain, that the ratio of their increase in a limited territory must be of a totally different nature from the ratio of the increase of population. A thousand millions are just as easily doubled every twenty-five years by the power of population as a thousand. But the food to support the increase from the greater number will by no means be obtained with the same facility. Man is necessarily confined in room. When acre has been added to acre till all the fertile land is occupied, the yearly increase of food must depend upon the melioration of the land already in possession. This is a fund, which, from the nature of all soils, instead of increasing, must be gradually diminishing. But population, could it be supplied with food, would go on with unexhausted vigour; and the increase of one period would furnish the power of a greater increase the next, and this without any limit.

From the accounts we have of China and Japan, it may be fairly doubted, whether the best directed efforts of human industry could double the produce of these countries even once in any number of years. There are many parts of the globe, indeed, hitherto uncultivated and almost unoccupied; but the right of exterminating, or driving into a corner where they must starve, even the inhabitants of these thinly peopled regions, will be questioned in a moral view. The process of improving their minds and directing their industry would necessarily be slow; and during this time, as population would regularly keep pace with the increasing produce, it would rarely happen that a great degree of knowledge and industry would have to operate at once upon rich unappropriated soil. Even where this might take place, as it does sometimes in new colonies, a geometrical ratio increases with such extraordinary rapidity, that the advantage could not last long. If the United States of America continue increasing, which they certainly will do, though not with the same rapidity as formerly, the Indians will be driven farther and farther back into the country, till the whole race is ultimately exterminated, and the territory is incapable of further extension.

These observations are, in a degree, applicable to all the parts of the earth where the soil is imperfectly cultivated. To exterminate the inhabitants of the greatest part of Asia and Africa, is a thought that could not be admitted for a moment. To civilise and direct the industry of the various tribes of Tartars and Negroes, would certainly be a work of considerable time, and of variable and uncertain success.

Europe is by no means so fully peopled as it might be. In Europe there is the fairest chance that human industry may receive its best direction. The science of agriculture has been much studied in England and Scotland; and there is still a great portion of uncultivated land in these countries. Let us consider at what rate the produce of this island (Great Britain) might be supposed to increase under circumstances the most favourable to improvement.

If it be allowed that by the best possible policy, and great encouragements to agriculture, the average produce of the island could be doubled in the first twenty-five years, it will be allowing, probably, a greater increase than could with reason be expected.

In the next twenty-five years, it is impossible to suppose that the produce could be quadrupled. It would be contrary to all our knowledge of the properties of land. The improvement of the barren parts would be a work of time and labour; and it must be evident to those who have the slightest acquaintance with agricultural subjects, that in proportion as cultivation extended, the additions that could yearly be made to the former average produce must be gradually and regularly diminishing. That we may be the better able to compare the increase of population and food, let us make a supposition, which, without pretending to accuracy, is clearly more favourable to the power of production in the earth than any experience we have had of its qualities will warrant.

Let us suppose that the yearly additions which might be made to the former average produce, instead of decreasing, which they certainly would do, were to remain the same; and that the produce of this island might be increased every twenty-five years, by a quantity equal to what it at present produces. The most enthusiastic speculator cannot suppose a greater increase than this. In a few centuries it would make every acre of land in the island like a garden.

If this supposition be applied to the whole earth, and if it be allowed that the subsistence for man which the earth affords might be increased every twenty-five years by a quantity equal to what it at present produces, this will be supposing a rate of increase much greater than we can imagine that any possible exertions of mankind could make it.

It may be fairly pronounced, therefore, that, considering the present average state of the earth, the means of subsistence, under circumstances the most favourable to human industry, could not possibly be made to increase faster than in an arithmetical ratio.

The necessary effects of these two different rates of increase, when brought together, will be very striking. Let us call the population of this island eleven millions; and suppose the present produce equal to the easy support of such a number. In the first twenty-five years the population would be twenty-two millions, and the food being also doubled, the means of subsistence would be equal to this increase. In the next twenty-five years, the population would be forty-four millions, and the means of subsistence only equal to the support of thirty-three millions. In the next period the population would be eighty-eight millions, and the means of subsistence just equal to the support of half that number. And, at the conclusion of the first century, the population would be a hundred and seventy-six millions, and the means of subsistence only equal to the support of fifty-five millions, leaving a population of a hundred and twenty-one millions totally unprovided for.

Taking the whole earth, instead of this island, emigration would of course be excluded; and, supposing the present population equal to a thousand millions, the human species would increase as the numbers, 1, 2, 4, 8, 16, 32, 64, 128, 256; and subsistence as 1, 2, 3, 4, 5, 6, 7, 8, 9. In two centuries the population would be to the means of subsistence as 256 to 9; in three centuries as 4096 to 13, and in two thousand years the difference would be almost incalculable.

In this supposition no limits whatever are placed to the produce of the earth. It may increase for ever, and be greater than any assignable quantity; yet still the power of population being in every period so much superior, the increase of the human species can only be kept down to the level of the means of subsistence by the constant operation of the strong law of necessity, acting as a check upon the greater power.

II. Of the General Checks to Population, and the Mode of Their Operation

The ultimate check to population appears then to be a want of food, arising necessarily from the different ratios according to which population and food increase. But this ultimate check is never the immediate check, except in cases of actual famine.

The immediate check may be stated to consist in all those customs, and all those diseases, which seem to be generated by a scarcity of the means of subsistence; and all those causes, independent of this scarcity, whether of a moral or physical nature, which tend prematurely to weaken and destroy the human frame.

These checks to population, which are constantly operating with more or less force in every society, and keep down the number to the level of the means of subsistence, may be classed under two general heads—the preventive and the positive checks.

The preventive check, as far as it is voluntary, is peculiar to man, and arises from that distinctive superiority in his reasoning faculties which enables him to calculate distant consequences. The checks to the indefinite increase of plants and irrational animals are all either positive or, if preventive, involuntary. But man cannot look around him, and see the distress which frequently presses upon those who have large families; he cannot contemplate his present possessions or earnings, which he now nearly consumes himself, and calculate the amount of each share, when with very little addition they must be divided, perhaps, among seven or eight, without feeling a doubt whether, if he follow the bent of his inclinations, he may be able to support the offspring which he will probably bring into the world. In a state of equality, if such can exist, this would be the simple question. In the present state of society other considerations occur. Will he not lower his rank in life, and be obliged to give up in great measure his former habits? Does any mode of employment present itself by which he may reasonably hope to maintain a family? Will he not at any rate subject himself to greater difficulties, and more severe labour, than in his single state? Will he not be unable to transmit to his children the same advantages of education and improvement that he had himself possessed? Does he even feel secure that, should he have a large family, his utmost exertions can save them from rags and squalid poverty, and their consequent degradation in the community? And may he not be reduced to the grating necessity of forfeiting his independence, and of being obliged to the sparing hand of charity for support?

These considerations are calculated to prevent, and certainly do prevent, a great number of persons in all civilised nations from pursuing the dictate of nature in an early attachment to one woman.

If this restraint do not produce vice, it is undoubtedly the least evil that can arise from the principle of population. Considered as a restraint on a strong natural inclination, it must be allowed to produce a certain degree of temporary unhappiness; but evidently slight, compared with the evils which result from any of the other checks to population; and merely of the same nature as many other sacrifices of temporary to permanent gratification, which it is the business of a moral agent continually to make.

When this restraint produces vice, the evils which follow are but too conspicuous. A promiscuous intercourse to such a degree as to prevent the birth of children, seems to lower, in the most marked manner, the dignity of human nature. It cannot be without its effect on men, and nothing can be more obvious than its tendency to degrade the female character, and to destroy all its most amiable and distinguishing characteristics. Add to which, that among those unfortunate females with which all great towns abound, more real distress and aggravated misery are, perhaps, to be found, than in any other department of human life.

When a general corruption of morals, with regard to the sex, pervades all the classes of society, its effects must necessarily be to poison the springs of domestic happiness, to weaken conjugal and parental affection, and to lessen the united exertions and ardour of parents in the care and education of their children;—effects which cannot take place without a decided diminution of the general happiness and virtue of society; particularly as the necessity of art in the accomplishment and conduct of intrigues, and in the concealment of their consequences, necessarily leads to many other vices.

The positive checks to population are extremely various, and include every cause, whether arising from vice or misery, which in any degree contribute to shorten the natural duration of human life. Under this head, therefore, may be enumerated all unwholesome occupations, severe labour and exposure to the seasons, extreme poverty, bad nursing of children, large towns, excesses of all kinds, the whole train of common diseases and epidemics, wars, plague, and famine.

On examining these obstacles to the increase of population which are classed under the heads of preventive and positive checks, it will appear that they are all resolvable into moral restraint, vice, and misery.

Of the preventive checks, the restraint from marriage which is not followed by irregular gratifications may properly be termed moral restraint.

Promiscuous intercourse, unnatural passions, violations of the marriage bed, and improper arts to conceal the consequences of irregular connections, are preventive checks that clearly come under the head of vice.

Of the positive checks, those which appear to arise unavoidably from the laws of nature, may be called exclusively misery; and those which we obviously bring upon ourselves, such as wars, excesses, and many others which it would be in our power to avoid, are of a mixed nature. They are brought upon us by vice, and their consequences are misery.

The sum of all these preventive and positive checks, taken together, forms the immediate check to population; and it is evident that, in every country where the whole of the procreative power cannot be called into action, the preventive and the positive checks must vary inversely as each other; that is, in countries either naturally unhealthy, or subject to a great mortality, from whatever cause it may arise, the preventive check will prevail very little. In those countries, on the contrary, which are naturally healthy, and where the preventive check is found to prevail with considerable force, the positive check will prevail very little, or the mortality be very small.

In every country some of these checks are, with more or less force, in constant operation; yet, notwithstanding their general prevalence, there are few states in which there is not a constant effort in the population to increase beyond the means of subsistence. This constant effort as constantly tends to subject the lower classes of society to distress, and to prevent any great permanent melioration of their condition.

These effects, in the present state of society, seem to be produced in the following manner. We will suppose the means of subsistence in any country just equal to the easy support of its inhabitants. The constant effort towards population, which is found to act even in the most vicious societies, increases the number of people before the means of subsistence are increased. The food, therefore, which before supported eleven millions, must now be divided among eleven millions and a half. The poor consequently must live much worse, and many of them be reduced to severe distress. The number of labourers also being above the proportion of work in the market, the price of labour must tend to fall, while the price of provisions would at the same time tend to rise. The labourer therefore must do more work to earn the same as he did before. During this season of distress, the discouragements to marriage and the difficulty of rearing a family are so great, that the progress of population is retarded. In the meantime, the cheapness of labour, the plenty of labourers, and the necessity of an increased industry among them, encourage cultivators to employ more labour upon their land, to turn up fresh soil, and to manure and improve more completely what is already in tillage, till ultimately the means of subsistence may become in the same proportion to the population as at the period from which we set out. The situation of the labourer being then again tolerably comfortable, the restraints to population are in some degree loosened; and, after a short period, the same retrograde and progressive movements with respect to happiness are repeated.

This sort of oscillation will not probably be obvious to common view; and it may be difficult even for the most attentive observer to calculate its periods. Yet that, in the generality of old states, some alternation of this kind does exist, though in a much less marked, and in a much more irregular manner, than I have described it, no reflecting man, who considers the subject deeply, can well doubt.

One principal reason why this oscillation has been less remarked, and less decidedly confirmed by experience than might naturally be expected, is, that the histories of mankind which we possess are, in general, histories only of the higher classes. We have not many accounts that can be depended upon, of the manners and customs of that part of mankind where these retrograde and progressive movements chiefly take place. A satisfactory history of this kind, of one people and of one period, would require the constant and minute attention of many observing minds in local and general remarks on the state of the lower classes of society, and the causes that influenced it; and, to draw accurate inferences upon this subject, a succession of such historians for some centuries would be necessary. This branch of statistical knowledge has, of late years, been attended to in some countries, and we may promise ourselves a clearer insight into the internal structure of human society from the progress of these inquiries. But the science may be said yet to be in its infancy, and many of the objects on which it would be desirable to have information, have been either omitted or not stated with sufficient accuracy. Among these, perhaps, may be reckoned the proportion of the number of adults to the number of marriages; the extent to which vicious customs have prevailed in consequence of the restraints upon matrimony; the comparative mortality among the children of the most distressed part of the community, and of those who live rather more at their ease; the variations in the real price of labour; the observable differences in the state of the lower classes of society, with respect to ease and happiness, at different times during a certain period; and very accurate registers of births, deaths, and marriages, which are of the utmost importance in this subject.

A faithful history, including such particulars, would tend greatly to elucidate the manner in which the constant check upon population acts; and would probably prove the existence of the retrograde and progressive movements that have been mentioned; though the times of their vibration must necessarily be rendered irregular from the operation of many interrupting causes; such as, the introduction or failure of certain manufactures; a greater or less prevalent spirit of agricultural enterprise; years of plenty, or years of scarcity; wars, sickly seasons, poor-laws, emigrations and other causes of a similar nature.

A circumstance which has, perhaps, more than any other, contributed to conceal this oscillation from common view, is the difference between the nominal and real price of labour. It very rarely happens that the nominal price of labour universally falls; but we well know that it frequently remains the same, while the nominal price of provisions has been gradually rising. This, indeed, will generally be the case, if the increase of manufactures and commerce be sufficient to employ the new labourers that are thrown into the market, and to prevent the increased supply from lowering the money price. But an increased number of labourers receiving the same money wages will necessarily, by their competition, increase the money price of corn. This is, in fact, a real fall in the price of labour; and, during this period, the condition of the lower classes of the community must be gradually growing worse. But the farmers and capitalists are growing rich from the real cheapness of labour. Their increasing capitals enable them to employ a greater number of men; and, as the population had probably suffered some check from the greater difficulty of supporting a family, the demand for labour, after a certain period, would be great in proportion to the supply, and its price would of course rise, if left to find its natural level; and thus the wages of labour, and consequently the condition of the lower classes of society, might have progressive and retrograde movements, though the price of labour might never nominally fall.

In savage life, where there is no regular price of labour, it is little to be doubted that similar oscillations take place. When population has increased nearly to the utmost limits of the food, all the preventive and the positive checks will naturally operate with increased force. Vicious habits with respect to the sex will be more general, the exposing of children more frequent, and both the probability and fatality of wars and epidemics will be considerably greater; and these causes will probably continue their operation till the population is sunk below the level of the food; and then the return to comparative plenty will again produce an increase, and, after a certain period, its further progress will again be checked by the same causes.

But without attempting to establish these progressive and retrograde movements in different countries, which would evidently require more minute histories than we possess, and which the progress of civilisation naturally tends to counteract, the following propositions are intended to be proved:—

1. Population is necessarily limited by the means of subsistence.

2. Population invariably increases where the means of subsistence increase, unless prevented by some very powerful and obvious checks.

3. These checks, and the checks which repress the superior power of population, and keep its effects on a level with the means of subsistence, are all resolvable into moral restraint, vice, and misery.

III. General Deductions from the Preceding View of Society

That the checks which have been mentioned are the immediate causes of the slow increase of population, and that these checks result principally from an insufficiency of subsistence, will be evident from the comparatively rapid increase which has invariably taken place, whenever, by some sudden enlargement in the means of subsistence, these checks have in any considerable degree been removed.

It has been universally remarked that all new colonies settled in healthy countries, where room and food were abundant, have constantly made a rapid progress in population. Many of the colonies from ancient Greece, in the course of one or two centuries, appear to have rivalled, and even surpassed, their mother cities. Syracuse and Agrigentum in Sicily, Tarentum and Locri in Italy, Ephesus and Miletus in Lesser Asia, were by all accounts at least equal to any of the cities of ancient Greece. All these colonies had established themselves in countries inhabited by savage and barbarous nations, which easily gave place to the new settlers, who had of course plenty of good land. It is calculated that the Israelites, though they increased very slowly while they were wandering in the land of Canaan, on settling in a fertile district of Egypt, doubled their numbers every fifteen years during the whole period of their stay. But not to dwell on remote instances, the European settlements in America bear ample testimony to the truth of a remark, that has never I believe been doubted. Plenty of rich land to be had for little or nothing is so powerful a cause of population, as generally to overcome all obstacles.

No settlements could easily have been worse managed than those of Spain, in Mexico, Peru, and Quito. The tyranny, superstition, and vices of the mother country were introduced in ample quantities among her children. Exorbitant taxes were exacted by the crown, the most arbitrary restrictions were imposed on their trade, and the governors were not behind hand in rapacity and extortion for themselves as well as their masters. Yet under all these difficulties the colonies made a quick progress in population. The city of Quito, which was but a hamlet of Indians, is represented by Ulloa as containing fifty or sixty thousand inhabitants above fifty years ago. Lima, which was founded since the conquest, is mentioned by the same author as equally or more populous before the fatal earthquake in 1746. Mexico is said to contain a hundred thousand inhabitants, which, notwithstanding the exaggerations of the Spanish writers, is supposed to be five times greater than what it contained in the time of Montezuma.

In the Portuguese colony of Brazil, governed with almost equal tyranny, there were supposed to be above thirty years ago six hundred thousand inhabitants of European extraction.

The Dutch and French colonies, though under the government of exclusive companies of merchants, still persisted in thriving under every disadvantage.

But the English North American colonies, now the powerful people of the United States of America, far outstripped all the others in the progress of their population. To the quantity of rich land which they possessed in common with the Spanish and Portuguese colonies, they added a greater degree of liberty and equality. Though not without some restrictions on their foreign commerce, they were allowed the liberty of managing their own internal affairs. The political institutions which prevailed were favourable to the alienation and division of property. Lands which were not cultivated by the proprietor within a limited time were declared grantable to any other person. In Pennsylvania there was no right of primogeniture, and in the provinces of New England the eldest son had only a double share. There were no tithes in any of the states, and scarcely any taxes. And on account of the extreme cheapness of good land, and a situation favourable to the exportation of grain, a capital could not be more advantageously employed than in agriculture, which, at the same time that it affords the greatest quantity of healthy work, supplies the most valuable produce to the society.

The consequence of these favourable circumstances united was a rapidity of increase almost without parallel in history. Throughout all the northern provinces the population was found to double itself in 25 years. The original number of persons which had settled in the four provinces of New England in 1643 was 21,200. Afterwards it was calculated that more left them than went to them. In the year 1760 they were increased to half a million. They had therefore all along doubled their number in 25 years. In New Jersey the period of doubling appeared to be 22 years, and in Rhode Island still less. In the back settlements, where the inhabitants applied themselves solely to agriculture, and luxury was not known, they were supposed to double their number in 15 years. Along the seacoast, which would naturally be first inhabited, the period of doubling was about 35 years, and in some of the maritime towns the population was absolutely at a stand. From the late census made in America it appears that, taking all the states together, they have still continued to double their numbers within 25 years; and as the whole population is now so great as not to be materially affected by the emigrations from Europe, and as it is known that in some of the towns and districts near the seacoast the progress of population has been comparatively slow, it is evident that in the interior of the country in general the period of doubling from procreation only must have been considerably less than 25 years.

The population of the United States of America, according to the fourth census in 1820, was 7,861,710. We have no reason to believe that Great Britain is less populous at present for the emigration of the small parent stock which produced these numbers. On the contrary, a certain degree of emigration is known to be favourable to the population of the mother country. It has been particularly remarked that the two Spanish provinces from which the greatest number of people emigrated to America became in consequence more populous.

Whatever was the original number of British emigrants which increased so fast in North America, let us ask, Why does not an equal number produce an equal increase in the same time in Great Britain? The obvious reason to be assigned is the want of food; and that this want is the most efficient cause of the three immediate checks to population, which have been observed to prevail in all societies, is evident from the rapidity with which even old states recover the desolations of war, pestilence, famine, and the convulsions of nature. They are then for a short time placed a little in the situation of new colonies, and the effect is always answerable to what might be expected. If the industry of the inhabitants be not destroyed, subsistence will soon increase beyond the wants of the reduced numbers; and the invariable consequence will be that population, which before perhaps was nearly stationary, will begin immediately to increase, and will continue its progress till the former population is recovered.

The fertile province of Flanders, which has been so often the seat of the most destructive wars, after a respite of a few years has always appeared as rich and populous as ever. The undiminished population of France, is an instance very strongly in point. The effects of the dreadful plague in London in 1666 were not perceptible 15 or 20 years afterwards. It may even be doubted whether Turkey and Egypt are upon an average much less populous for the plagues which periodically lay them waste. If the number of people which they contain be considerably less now than formerly, it is rather to be attributed to the tyranny and oppression of the governments under which they groan, and the consequent discouragements to agriculture, than to the losses which they sustain by the plague. The traces of the most destructive famines in China, Indostan, Egypt, and other countries, are by all accounts very soon obliterated; and the most tremendous convulsions of nature, such as volcanic eruptions and earthquakes, if they do not happen so frequently as to drive away the inhabitants or destroy their spirit of industry, have been found to produce but a trifling effect on the average population of any state.

It has appeared from the registers of different countries that the progress of their population is checked by the periodical though irregular returns of plagues and sickly seasons. Dr. Short, in his curious researches into bills of mortality, often uses the expression "terrible correctives of the redundance of mankind;" and in a table of all the plagues, pestilences, and famines of which he could collect accounts, shows the constancy and universality of their operation.

The epidemical years in his table, or the years in which the plague or some great and wasting epidemic prevailed (for smaller sickly seasons seem not to be included) are 431, of which 32 were before the Christian era. If we divide therefore the years of the present era by 399, it will appear that the periodical returns of such epidemics, to some countries that we are acquainted with, have been on an average only at the interval of about 4½ years.

Of the 254 great famines and dearths enumerated in the table, 15 were before the Christian era, beginning with that which occurred in Palestine in the time of Abraham. If, subtracting these 15, we divide the years of the present era by the remainder, it will appear that the average interval between the visits of this dreadful scourge has been only about 7½ years.

How far these "terrible correctives to the redundance of mankind" have been occasioned by the too rapid increase of population, is a point which it would be very difficult to determine with any degree of precision. The causes of most of our diseases appear to us to be so mysterious, and probably are really so various, that it would be rashness to lay too much stress on any single one; but it will not perhaps be too much to say that *among* these causes we ought certainly to rank crowded houses and insufficient or unwholesome food, which are the natural consequences of an increase of population faster than the accommodations of a country with respect to habitations and food will allow.

Almost all the histories of epidemics which we possess tend to confirm this supposition, by describing them in general as making their principal ravages among the lower classes of people. In Dr. Short's tables this circumstance is frequently mentioned; and it further appears that a very considerable proportion of the epidemic years either followed or were accompanied by seasons of dearth and bad food. In other places he also mentions great plagues as diminishing particularly the numbers of the lower or servile sort of people; and in speaking of different diseases he observes that those which are occasioned by bad and unwholesome food generally last the longest.

We know from constant experience that fevers are generated in our jails, our manufactories, our crowded workhouses, and in the narrow and close streets of our large towns—all which situations appear to be similar in their effects to squalid poverty; and we cannot doubt that causes of this kind aggravated in degree contributed to the production and prevalence of those great and wasting plagues formerly so common in Europe, but which now from the mitigation of these causes are everywhere considerably abated, and in many places appear to be completely extirpated.

Of the other great scourge of mankind, famine, it may be observed that it is not in the nature of things that the increase of population should absolutely produce one. This increase though rapid is necessarily gradual; and as the human frame cannot be supported even for a very short time without food, it is evident that no more human beings can grow up than there is provision to maintain. But though the principle of population cannot absolutely produce a famine, it prepares the way for one, and by frequently obliging the lower classes of people to subsist nearly on the smallest quantity of food that will support life, turns even a slight deficiency from the failure of the seasons into a severe dearth, and may be fairly said therefore to be one of the principal causes of famine.

It also appears that when the increasing produce of a country and the increasing demand for labour so far meliorate the condition of the labourer as greatly to encourage marriage, the custom of early marriages is generally continued till the population has gone beyond the increased produce, and sickly seasons appear to be the natural and necessary consequence. The continental registers exhibit many instances of rapid increase interrupted in this manner by mortal diseases; and the inference seems to be that those countries where subsistence is increasing sufficiently to encourage population, but not to answer all its demands, will be more subject to periodical epidemics than those where the increase of population is more nearly accommodated to the average produce.

The converse of this will of course be true. In those countries which are subject to periodical sicknesses, the increase of population, or the excess of births above the deaths, will be greater in the intervals of these periods than is usual in countries not so much subject to these diseases. If Turkey and Egypt have been nearly stationary in their average population for the last century in the intervals of their periodical plagues, the births must have exceeded the deaths in a much greater proportion than in such countries as France and England.

Europe was without doubt formerly more subject to plagues and wasting epidemics than at present, and this will account in a great measure for the greater proportion of births to deaths in former times mentioned by many authors, as it has always been a common practice to estimate these proportions from too short periods, and generally to reject the years of plague as accidental.

The average proportion of births to deaths in England during the last century may be considered as about 12 to 10, or 120 to 100. The proportion in France for ten years, ending in 1780, was about 115 to 100. Though these proportions undoubtedly varied at different periods during the century, yet we have reason to think that they did not vary in any very considerable degree; and it will appear therefore that the population of France and England had accommodated itself more nearly to the average produce of each country than many other states. The operation of the preventive check—wars—the silent though certain destruction of life in large towns and manufactories, and the close habitations and insufficient food of many of the poor, prevent population from outrunning the means of subsistence, and, if I may use an expression which certainly at first appears strange, supersede the necessity of great and ravaging epidemics to destroy what is redundant. If a wasting plague were to sweep off two millions in England, and six millions in France, it cannot be doubted that after the inhabitants had recovered from the dreadful shock, the proportion of births to deaths would rise much above the usual average in either country during the last century.

In New Jersey the proportion of births to deaths, on an average of 7 years ending with 1743, was 300 to 100. In France and England the average proportion cannot be reckoned at more than 120 to 100. Great and astonishing as this difference is, we ought not to be so wonder-struck at it as to attribute it to the miraculous interposition of Heaven. The causes of it are not remote, latent, and mysterious, but near us, round about us, and open to the investigation of every inquiring mind. It accords with the most liberal spirit of philosophy to believe that no stone can fall, or plant rise, without the immediate agency of divine power. But we know from experience that these operations of what we call Nature have been conducted almost invariably according to fixed laws. And since the world began, the causes of population and depopulation have been probably as constant as any of the laws of nature with which we are acquainted.

The passion between the sexes has appeared in every age to be so nearly the same that it may always be considered in algebraic language as a given quantity. The great law of necessity which prevents population from increasing in any country beyond the food which it can either produce or acquire is a law so open to our view, so obvious and evident to our understandings, that we cannot for a moment doubt it. The different modes which nature takes to repress a redundant population do not indeed appear to us so certain and regular; but though we cannot always predict the mode, we may with certainty predict the fact. If the proportion of the births to the deaths for a few years indicates an increase of numbers much beyond the proportional increased or acquired food of the country, we may be perfectly certain that unless an emigration take place, the deaths will shortly exceed the births, and that the increase which had been observed for a few years cannot be the real average increase of the population of the country. If there were no other depopulating causes, and if the preventive check did not operate very strongly, every country would without doubt be subject to periodical plagues and famines.

The only true criterion of a real and permanent increase in the population of any country is the increase of the means of subsistence. But even this criterion is subject to some slight variations, which however are completely open to our observation. In some countries population seems to have been forced; that is, the people have been habituated by degrees to live almost upon the smallest possible quantity of food. There must have been periods in such countries when population increased permanently without an increase in the means of subsistence. China, India, and the countries possessed by the Bedoween Arabs appear to answer to this description. The average produce of these countries seems to be but barely sufficient to support the lives of the inhabitants, and of course any deficiency from the badness of the seasons must be fatal. Nations in this state must necessarily be subject to famines.

In America, where the reward of labour is at present so liberal, the lower classes might retrench very considerably in a year of scarcity without materially distressing themselves. A famine therefore seems to be almost impossible. It may be expected that in the progress of the population of America the labourers will in time be much less liberally rewarded. The numbers will in this case permanently increase without a proportional increase in the means of subsistence.

In the different countries of Europe there must be some variations in the proportion of the number of inhabitants, and the quantity of food consumed arising from the different habits of living which prevail in each state. The labourers in the south of England are so accustomed to eat fine wheaten bread, that they will suffer themselves to be half starved before they will submit to live like the Scotch peasants.

They might perhaps in time, by the constant operation of the hard law of necessity, be reduced to live even like the lower classes of the Chinese, and the country would then with the same quantity of food support a greater population. But to effect this must always be a difficult, and every friend to humanity will hope an abortive, attempt.

I have mentioned some cases where population may permanently increase without a proportional increase in the means of subsistence. But it is evident that the variation in different states between the food and the numbers supported by it is restricted to a limit beyond which it cannot pass. In every country the population of which is not absolutely decreasing the food must be necessarily sufficient to support and continue the race of labourers.

Other circumstances being the same, it may be affirmed that countries are populous according to the quantity of human food which they produce or can acquire; and happy according to the liberality with which this food is divided, or the quantity which a day's labour will purchase. Corn countries are more populous than pasture countries, and rice countries more populous than corn countries. But their happiness does not depend either upon their being thinly or fully inhabited, upon their poverty or their riches, their youth or their age, but on the proportion which the population and the food bear to each other.

This proportion is generally the most favourable in new colonies, where the knowledge and industry of an old state operate on the fertile unappropriated land of a new one. In other cases the youth or the age of a state is not in this respect of great importance. It is probable that the food of Great Britain is divided in more liberal shares to her inhabitants at the present period than it was two thousand, three thousand, or four thousand years ago. And it has appeared that the poor and thinly inhabited tracts of the Scotch Highlands are more distressed by a redundant population than the most populous parts of Europe.

If a country were never to be overrun by a people more advanced in arts, but left to its own natural progress in civilisation, from the time that its produce might be considered as an unit to the time that it might be considered as a million, during the lapse of many thousand years, there might not be a single period when the mass of the people could be said to be free from distress, either directly or indirectly, for want of food. In every state in Europe since we have first had accounts of it, millions and millions of human existences have been repressed from this simple cause, though perhaps in some of these states an absolute famine may never have been known.

Must it not then be acknowledged by an attentive examiner of the histories of mankind that in every age and in every state in which man has existed or does now exist,

The increase to population is necessarily limited by the means of subsistence:

Population invariably increases when the means of subsistence increase, unless prevented by powerful and obvious checks:

These checks, and the checks which keep the population down to the level of the means of subsistence, are moral restraint, vice, and misery?

Part Two: Of Our Future Prospects Respecting the Removal or Mitigation of the Evils Arising from the Principle of Population

I. Of Moral Restraint, and Our Obligation to Practise This Virtue

As it appears that in the actual state of every society which has come within our review the natural progress of population has been constantly and powerfully checked, and as it seems evident that no improved form of government, no plans of emigration, no benevolent institutions, and no degree or direction of national industry can prevent the continued action of a great check to population in some form or other, it follows that we must submit to it as an inevitable law of nature; and the only inquiry that remains is how it may take place with the least possible prejudice to the virtue and happiness of human society.

All the immediate checks to population which have been observed to prevail in the same and different countries seem to be resolvable into moral restraint, vice, and misery; and if our choice be confined to these three, we cannot long hesitate in our decision respecting which it would be most eligible to encourage.

In the first edition of this essay I observed that as from the laws of nature it appeared that some check to population must exist, it was better that this check should arise from a foresight of the difficulties attending a family and the fear of dependent poverty than from the actual presence of want and sickness. This idea will admit of being pursued farther; and I am inclined to think that from the prevailing opinions respecting population, which undoubtedly originated in barbarous ages, and have been continued and circulated by that part of every community which may be supposed to be interested in their support, we have been prevented from attending to the clear dictates of reason and nature on this subject.

Natural and moral evil seem to be the instruments employed by the Deity in admonishing us to avoid any mode of conduct which is not suited to our being, and will consequently injure our happiness. If we are intemperate in eating and drinking, our health is disordered; if we indulge the transports of anger, we seldom fail to commit acts of which we afterwards repent; if we multiply too fast, we die miserably of poverty and contagious diseases. The laws of nature in all these cases are similar and uniform. They indicate to us that we have followed these impulses too far, so as to trench upon some other law, which equally demands attention. The uneasiness we feel from repletion, the injuries that we inflict on ourselves or others in anger, and the inconveniences we suffer on the approach of poverty, are all admonitions to us to regulate these impulses better; and if we heed not this admonition, we justly incur the penalty of our disobedience, and our sufferings operate as a warning to others.

From the inattention of mankind hitherto to the consequences of increasing too fast, it must be presumed that these consequences are not so immediately and powerfully connected with the conduct which leads to them as in the other instances; but the delayed knowledge of particular effects does not alter their nature, or our obligation to regulate our conduct accordingly, as soon as we are satisfied of what this conduct ought to be. In many other instances it has not been till after long and painful experience that the conduct most favourable to the happiness of man has been forced upon his attention. The kind of food and the mode of preparing it best suited to the purposes of nutrition and the gratification of the palate, the treatment and remedies of different disorders, the bad effects on the human frame of low and marshy situations, the invention of the most convenient and comfortable clothing, the construction of good houses, and all the advantages and extended enjoyments which distinguish civilised life, were not pointed out to the attention of man at once, but were the slow and late result of experience and of the admonitions received by repeated failures.

Diseases have been generally considered as the inevitable inflictions of Providence, but perhaps a great part of them may more justly be considered as indications that we have offended against some of the laws of nature. The plague at Constantinople and in other towns of the East is a constant admonition of this kind to the inhabitants. The human constitution cannot support such a state of filth and torpor; and as dirt, squalid poverty, and indolence are in the highest degree unfavourable to happiness and virtue, it seems a benevolent dispensation that such a state should by the laws of nature produce disease and death as a beacon to others to avoid splitting on the same rock.

The prevalence of the plague in London till the year 1666 operated in a proper manner on the conduct of our ancestors; and the removal of nuisances, the construction of drains, the widening of the streets, and the giving more room and air to the houses, had the effect of eradicating completely this dreadful disorder, and of adding greatly to the health and happiness of the inhabitants.

In the history of every epidemic it has almost invariably been observed that the lower classes of people, whose food was poor and insufficient, and who lived crowded together in small and dirty houses, were the principal victims. In what other manner can Nature point out to us that, if we increase too fast for the means of subsistence so as to render it necessary for a considerable part of the society to live in this miserable manner, we have offended against one of her laws? This law she has declared exactly in the same manner as she declares that intemperance in eating and drinking will be followed by ill health, and that, however grateful it may be to us at the moment to indulge this propensity to excess, such indulgence will ultimately produce unhappiness. It is as much a law of nature that repletion is bad for the human frame, as that eating and drinking, unattended with this consequence, are good for it.

An implicit obedience to the impulses of our natural passions would lead us into the wildest and most fatal extravagances, and yet we have the strongest reasons for believing that all these passions are so necessary to our being that they could not be generally weakened or diminished without injuring our happiness. The most powerful and universal of all our desires is the desire of food, and of those things—such as clothing, houses, &c.—which are immediately necessary to relieve us from the pains of hunger and cold. It is acknowledged by all that these desires put in motion the greatest part of that activity from which the multiplied improvements and advantages of civilised life are derived, and that the pursuit of these objects and the gratification of these desires form the principal happiness of the larger half of mankind, civilised or uncivilised, and are indispensably necessary to the more refined enjoyments of the other half. We are all conscious of the inestimable benefits that we derive from these desires when directed in a certain manner, but we are equally conscious of the evils resulting from them when not directed in this manner—so much so that society has taken upon itself to punish most severely what it considers as an irregular gratification of them. And yet the desires in both cases are equally natural, and, abstractedly considered, equally virtuous. The act of the hungry man who satisfies his appetite by taking a loaf from the shelf of another is in no respect to be distinguished from the act of him who does the same thing with a loaf of his own, but by its consequences. From the consideration of these consequences we feel the most perfect conviction that if people were not prevented from gratifying their natural desires with the loaves in the possession of others, the number of loaves would universally diminish. This experience is the foundation of the laws relating to property and of the distinctions of virtue and vice in the gratification of desires otherwise perfectly the same.

If the pleasure arising from the gratification of these propensities were universally diminished in vividness, violations of property would become less frequent; but this advantage would be greatly overbalanced by the narrowing of the sources of enjoyment. The diminution in the quantity of all those productions which contribute to human gratification would be much greater in proportion than the diminution of thefts, and the loss of general happiness on the one side would be beyond comparison greater than the gain of happiness on the other. When we contemplate the constant and severe toils of the greatest part of mankind, it is impossible not to be forcibly impressed with the reflection that the sources of human happiness would be most cruelly diminished if the prospect of a good meal, a warm house, and a comfortable fireside in the evening were not incitements sufficiently vivid to give interest and cheerfulness to the labours and privations of the day.

After the desire of food, the most powerful and general of our desires is the passion between the sexes, taken in an enlarged sense. Of the happiness spread over human life by this passion very few are unconscious. Virtuous love, exalted by friendship, seems to be that sort of mixture of sensual and intellectual enjoyment particularly suited to the nature of man, and most powerfully calculated to awaken the sympathies of the soul, and produce the most exquisite gratifications. Perhaps there is scarcely a man who has once experienced the genuine delight of virtuous love, however great his intellectual pleasures may have been, who does not look back to that period as the sunny spot in his whole life, where his imagination loves most to bask, which he recollects and contemplates with the fondest regret, and which he would wish to live over again.

It has been said by Mr. [William] Godwin, in order to show the evident inferiority of the pleasures of sense, "Strip the commerce of the sexes of all its attendant circumstances, and it would be generally despised." He might as well say to a man who admires trees, Strip them of their spreading branches and lovely foliage, and what beauty can you see in a bare pole? But it was the tree with the branches and foliage, and not without them, that excited admiration. It is "the symmetry of person, the vivacity, the voluptuous softness of temper, the affectionate kindness of feeling, the imagination, and the wit" of a woman, as Mr. Godwin says, which excites the passion of love and not the mere distinction of her being a female.

It is a very great mistake to suppose that the passion between the sexes only operates and influences human conduct when the immediate gratification of it is in contemplation. The formation and steady pursuit of some particular plan of life has been justly considered as one of the most permanent sources of happiness; but I am inclined to believe that there are not many of these plans formed which are not connected in a considerable degree with the prospect of the gratification of this passion, and with the support of children arising from it. The evening meal, the warm house, and the comfortable fireside would lose half their interest if we were to exclude the idea of some object of affection with whom they were to be shared.

We have also great reason to believe that the passion between the sexes has the most powerful tendency to soften and meliorate the human character, and keep it more alive to all the kindlier emotions of benevolence and pity. Observations on savage life have generally tended to prove that nations in which this passion appeared to be less vivid, were distinguished by a ferocious and malignant spirit, and particularly by tyranny and cruelty to the sex. If indeed this bond of conjugal affection were considerably weakened, it seems probable either that the man would make use of his superior physical strength, and turn his wife into a slave, as among the generality of savages, or at best that every little inequality of temper, which must necessarily occur between two persons, would produce a total alienation of affection; and this could hardly take place without a diminution of parental fondness and care, which would have the most fatal effect on the happiness of society.

It may be further remarked, and observations on the human character in different countries warrant us in the conclusion, that the passion is stronger, and its general effects in producing gentleness, kindness, and suavity of manners, much more powerful, where obstacles are thrown in the way of very early and universal gratification. In some of the southern countries, where every impulse may be almost immediately indulged, the passion sinks into mere animal desire, is soon weakened and almost extinguished by excess, and its influence on the character is extremely confined. But in European countries, where, though the women are not secluded, yet manners have imposed considerable restraints on this gratification, the passion not only rises in force, but in the universality and beneficial tendency of its effects; and has often the greatest influence in the formation and improvement of the character, where it is the least gratified.

Considering then the passion between the sexes in all its bearings and relations, and including the endearing engagement of parent and child resulting from it, few will be disposed to deny that it is one of the principal ingredients of human happiness. Yet experience teaches us that much evil flows from the irregular gratification of it; and though the evil be of little weight in the scale when compared with the good, yet its absolute quantity cannot be inconsiderable, on account of the strength and universality of the passion. It is evident however from the general conduct of all governments in their distribution of punishments, that the evil resulting from this cause is not so great and so immediately dangerous to society, as the irregular gratification of the desire of property; but placing this evil in the most formidable point of view, we should evidently purchase a diminution of it at a very high price by the extinction or diminution of the passion which causes it; a change which would probably convert human life either into a cold and cheerless blank or a scene of savage and merciless ferocity.

A careful attention to the remote as well as immediate effect of all the human passions and all the general laws of nature, leads us strongly to the conclusion that under the present constitution of things few or none of them will admit of being greatly diminished, without narrowing the sources of good more powerfully than the sources of evil. And the reason seems to be obvious. They are in fact the materials of all our pleasures as well as of all our pains; of all our happiness as well as of all our misery; of all our virtues as well as of all our vices. It must therefore be regulation and direction that are wanted, not diminution or extinction.

It is justly observed by Paley [in his *Natural Theology*] that "Human passions are either necessary to human welfare, or capable of being made, and in a great majority of instances are in fact made, conducive to its happiness. These passions are strong and general; and perhaps would not answer their purpose unless they were so. But strength and generality, when it is expedient that particular circumstances should be respected, become if left to themselves excess and misdirection. From which excess and misdirection the vices of mankind (the causes no doubt of much misery) appear to spring. This account, while it shows us the principle of vice, shows us at the same time the province of reason and self-government."

Our virtue therefore as reasonable beings evidently consists in educing from the general materials which the Creator has placed under our guidance the greatest sum of human happiness; and as natural impulses are abstractedly considered good, and only to be distinguished by their consequences, a strict attention to these consequences and the regulation of our conduct conformably to them must be considered as our principal duty.

The fecundity of the human species is in some respects a distinct consideration from the passion between the sexes, as it evidently depends more upon the power of women in bearing children than upon the strength and weakness of this passion. It is a law however exactly similar in its great features to all the other laws of nature. It is strong and general, and apparently would not admit of any very considerable diminution without being inadequate to its object; the evils arising from it are incidental to those necessary qualities of strength and generality; and these evils are capable of being very greatly mitigated and rendered comparatively light by human energy and virtue. We cannot but conceive that it is an object of the Creator that the earth should be replenished; and it appears to me clear that this could not be effected without a tendency in population to increase faster than food; and as, with the present law of increase, the peopling of the earth does not proceed very rapidly, we have undoubtedly some reason to believe that this law is not too powerful for its apparent object. The desire of the means of subsistence would be comparatively confined in its effects, and would fail of producing that general activity so necessary to the improvement of the human faculties, were it not for the strong and universal effort of population to increase with greater rapidity than its supplies. If these two tendencies were exactly balanced, I do not see what motive there would be sufficiently strong to overcome the acknowledged indolence of man, and make him proceed in the cultivation of the soil. The population of any large territory, however fertile, would be as likely to stop at five hundred or five thousand, as at five millions or fifty millions. Such a balance therefore would clearly defeat one great purpose of creation; and if the question be merely a question of degree, a question of a little more or a little less strength, we may fairly distrust our competence to judge of the precise quantity necessary to answer the object with the smallest sum of incidental evil. In the present state of things we appear to have under our guidance a great power, capable of peopling a desert region in a small number of years; and yet under other circumstances capable of being confined by human energy and virtue to any limits, however narrow, at the expense of a small comparative quantity of evil. The analogy of all the other laws of nature would be completely violated, if in this instance alone there were no provision for accidental failures, no resources against the vices of mankind, or the partial mischiefs resulting from other general laws. To effect the apparent object without any attendant evil, it is evident that a perpetual change in the law of increase would be necessary, varying with the varying circumstances of each country. But instead of this it is not only more consonant to the analogy of the other parts of nature, but we have reason to think that it is more conducive to the formation and improvement of the human mind, that the laws should be uniform and the evils incidental to it, under certain circumstances, left to be mitigated or removed by man himself. His duties in this case vary with his situation; he is thus kept more alive to the consequences of his actions; and his faculties have evidently greater play and opportunity of improvement, than if the evil were removed by a perpetual change of the law according to circumstances.

Even if from passions too easily subdued, or the facility of illicit intercourse, a state of celibacy were a matter of indifference, and not a state of some privation, the end of nature in the peopling of the earth would be apparently liable to be defeated. It is of the very utmost importance to the happiness of mankind that population should not increase too fast; but it does not appear that the object to be accomplished would admit of any considerable diminution in the desire of marriage. It is clearly the duty of each individual not to marry till he has a prospect of supporting his children; but it is at the same time to be wished that he should retain undiminished his desire of marriage, in order that he may exert himself to realise this prospect, and be stimulated to make provision for the support of greater numbers.

It is evidently therefore regulation and direction which are required with regard to the principle of population, not diminution or alteration. And if moral restraint be the only virtuous mode of avoiding the incidental evils arising from this principle, our obligation to practise it will evidently rest exactly upon the same foundation as our obligation to practise any of the other virtues.

Whatever indulgence we may be disposed to allow to occasional failures in the discharge of a duty of acknowledged difficulty, yet of the strict line of duty we cannot doubt. Our obligation not to marry till we have a fair prospect of being able to support our children will appear to deserve the attention of the moralist, if it can be proved that an attention to this obligation is of most powerful effect in the prevention of misery; and that if it were the general custom to follow the first impulse of nature and marry at the age of puberty, the universal prevalence of every known virtue in the greatest conceivable degree, would fail of rescuing society from the most wretched and desperate state of want, and all the diseases and famines which usually accompany it.

II. Of the Effects Which Would Result to Society from the Prevalence of Moral Restraint

One of the principal reasons which have prevented an assent to the doctrine of the constant tendency of population to increase beyond the means of subsistence, is a great unwillingness to believe that the Deity would by the laws of nature bring beings into existence, which by the laws of nature could not be supported in that existence. But if, in addition to that general activity and direction of our industry put in motion by these laws, we further consider that the incidental evils arising from them are constantly directing our attention to the proper check to population, moral restraint; and if it appear that by a strict obedience to the duties pointed out to us by the light of nature and reason, and confirmed and sanctioned by revelation, these evils may be avoided, the objection will, I trust, be removed, and all apparent imputation on the goodness of the Deity be done away.

The heathen moralists never represented happiness as attainable on earth but through the medium of virtue; and among their virtues prudence ranked in the first class, and by some was even considered as including every other. The Christian religion places our present as well as future happiness in the exercise of those virtues which tend to fit us for a state of superior enjoyment; and the subjection of the passions to the guidance of reason, which, if not the whole, is a principal branch of prudence, is in consequence most particularly inculcated.

If, for the sake of illustration, we might be permitted to draw a picture of society in which each individual endeavoured to attain happiness by the strict fulfillment of those duties which the most enlightened of the ancient philosophers deduced from the laws of nature, and which have been directly taught and received such powerful sanctions in the moral code of Christianity, it would present a very different scene from that which we now contemplate. Every act which was prompted by the desire of immediate gratification, but which threatened an ultimate overbalance of pain, would be considered as a breach of duty, and consequently no man whose earnings were only sufficient to maintain two children would put himself in a situation in which he might have to maintain four or five, however he might be prompted to it by the passion of love. This prudential restraint, if it were generally adopted, by narrowing the supply of labour in the market, would in the natural course of things soon raise its price. The period of delayed gratification would be passed in saving the earnings which were above the wants of a single man, and in acquiring habits of sobriety, industry, and economy, which would enable him in a few years to enter into the matrimonial contract without fear of its consequences. The operation of the preventive check in this way, by constantly keeping the population within the limits of the food though constantly following its increase, would give a real value to the rise of wages and the sums saved by labourers before marriage, very different from those forced advances in the price of labour or arbitrary parochial donations which, in proportion to their magnitude and extensiveness, must of necessity be followed by a proportional advance in the price of provisions. As the wages of labour would thus be sufficient to maintain with decency a large family, and as every married couple would set out with a sum for contingencies, all abject poverty would be removed from society, or would at least be confined to a very few who had fallen into misfortunes against which no prudence or foresight could provide.

The interval between the age of puberty and the period at which each individual might venture on marriage must, according to the supposition, be passed in strict chastity, because the law of chastity cannot be violated without producing evil. The effect of anything like a promiscuous intercourse, which prevents the birth of children, is evidently to weaken the best affections of the heart, and in a very marked manner to degrade the female character; and any other intercourse would, without improper arts, bring as many children into the society as marriage, with a much greater probability of their becoming a burden to it.

These considerations show that the virtue of chastity is not, as some have supposed, a forced produce of artificial society, but that it has the most real and solid foundation in nature and reason, being apparently the only virtuous means of avoiding the vice and misery which result so often from the principle of population.

In such a society as we have been supposing it might be necessary for some of both sexes to pass many of the early years of life in the single state, and if this were general there would certainly be room for a much greater number to marry afterwards, so that fewer, upon the whole, would be condemned to pass their lives in celibacy. If the custom of not marrying early prevailed generally, and if violations of chastity were equally dishonourable in both sexes, a more familiar and friendly intercourse between them might take place without danger. Two young people might converse together intimately without its being immediately supposed that they either intended marriage or intrigue, and a much better opportunity would thus be given to both sexes of finding out kindred dispositions, and of forming those strong and lasting attachments without which the married state is generally more productive of misery than of happiness. The earlier years of life would not be spent without love, though without the full gratification of it. The passion, instead of being extinguished as it now too frequently is by early sensuality, would only be repressed for a time that it might afterwards burn with a brighter, purer, and steadier flame, and the happiness of the married state, instead of only affording the means of immediate indulgence, would be looked forward to as the prize of industry and virtue, and the reward of a genuine and constant attachment.

The passion of love is a powerful stimulus in the formation of character and often prompts to the most noble and generous exertions, but this is only when the affections are centred in one object, and generally when full gratification is delayed by difficulties. The heart is perhaps never so much disposed to virtuous conduct, and certainly at no time is the virtue of chastity so little difficult to men as when under the influence of such a passion. Late marriages taking place in this way would be very different from those of the same name at present, where the union is too frequently prompted solely by interested views, and the parties meet not unfrequently with exhausted constitutions and generally with exhausted affections. The late marriages at present are indeed principally confined to the men, of whom there are few, however advanced in life, who if they determine to marry do not fix their choice on a young wife. A young woman without fortune, when she has passed her twenty-fifth year, begins to fear, and with reason, that she may lead a life of celibacy, and with a heart capable of forming a strong attachment feels as each year creeps on her hopes of finding an object on which to rest her affections gradually diminishing, and the uneasiness of her situation aggravated by the silly and unjust prejudices of the world. If the general age of marriage among women were later the period of youth and hope would be prolonged, and fewer would be ultimately disappointed.

That a change of this kind would be a most decided advantage to the more virtuous half of society we cannot for a moment doubt. However impatiently the privation might be borne by the men, it would be supported by the women readily and cheerfully, and if they could look forward with just confidence to marriage at twenty-seven or twenty-eight, I fully believe that if the matter were left to their free choice, they would clearly prefer waiting till this period to the being involved in all the cares of a large family at twenty-five. The most eligible age of marriage however could not be fixed, but must depend entirely on circumstances and situation. There is no period of human life at which nature most strongly prompts to an union of the sexes than from seventeen or eighteen to twenty. In every society above that state of depression, which almost excludes reason and foresight, these early tendencies must necessarily be restrained; and if in the actual state of things such a restraint on the impulses of nature be found unavoidable, at what time can we be consistently released from it but at that period, whatever it may be, when in the existing circumstances of the society a fair prospect presents itself of maintaining a family?

The difficulty of moral restraint will perhaps be objected to this doctrine. To him who does not acknowledge the authority of the Christian religion I have only to say that after the most careful investigation this virtue appears to be absolutely necessary in order to avoid certain evils which would otherwise result from the general laws of nature. According to his own principles it is his duty to pursue the greatest good consistent with these laws, and not to fail in this important end, and produce an overbalance of misery by a partial obedience to some of the dictates of nature while he neglects others. The path of virtue, though it be the only path which leads to permanent happiness, has always been represented by the heathen moralists as of difficult ascent.

To the Christian I would say that the Scriptures most clearly and precisely point it out to us as our duty to restrain our passions within the bounds of reason, and it is a palpable disobedience of this law to indulge our desires in such a manner as reason tells us will unavoidably end in misery. The Christian cannot consider the difficulty of moral restraint as any argument against its being his duty, since in almost every page of the sacred writings man is described as encompassed on all sides by temptations which it is extremely difficult to resist; and though no duties are enjoined which do not contribute to his happiness on earth as well as in a future state, yet an undeviating obedience is never represented as an easy task.

There is in general so strong a tendency to love in early youth that it is extremely difficult at this period to distinguish a genuine from a transient passion. If the earlier years of life were passed by both sexes in moral restraint, from the greater facility that this would give to the meeting of kindred dispositions, it might even admit of a doubt whether more happy marriages would not take place, and consequently more pleasure from the passion of love, than in a state such as that of America the circumstances of which allow of a very early union of the sexes. But if we compare the intercourse of the sexes in such a society as I have been supposing with that which now exists in Europe, taken under all its circumstances, it may safely be asserted that, independently of the load of misery which would be removed, the sum of pleasurable sensations from the passion of love would be increased in a very great degree.

If we could suppose such a system general, the accession of happiness to society in its internal economy would scarcely be greater than in its external relations. It might fairly be expected that war, that great pest of the human race, would under such circumstances soon cease to extend its ravages so widely and so frequently as it does at present.

One of its first causes and most powerful impulses was undoubtedly an insufficiency of room and food; and greatly as the circumstances of mankind have changed since it first began, the same cause still continues to operate and to produce, though in a smaller degree, the same effects. The ambition of princes would want instruments of destruction if the distresses of the lower classes of people did not drive them under their standards. A recruiting sergeant always prays for a bad harvest and a want of employment, or in other words a redundant population.

In the earlier ages of the world when war was the great business of mankind, and the drains of population from this cause were beyond comparison greater than in modern times, the legislators and statesmen of each country, adverting principally to the means of offence and defence, encouraged an increase of people in every possible way, fixed a stigma on barrenness and celibacy, and honoured marriage. The popular religions followed these prevailing opinions. In many countries the prolific power of nature was the object of solemn worship. In the religion of Mahomet, which was established by the sword, and the promulgation of which in consequence could not be unaccompanied by an extraordinary destruction of its followers, the procreation of children to glorify the Creator was laid down as one of the principal duties of man, and he who had the most numerous offspring was considered as having best answered the end of his creation. The prevalence of such moral sentiments had naturally a great effect in encouraging marriage, and the rapid procreation which followed was partly the effect and partly the cause of incessant war. The vacancies occasioned by former desolations made room for the rearing of fresh supplies, and the overflowing rapidity with which these supplies followed constantly furnished fresh incitements and fresh instruments for renewed hostilities. Under the influence of such moral sentiments, it is difficult to conceive how the fury of incessant war should ever abate.

It is a pleasing confirmation of the truth and divinity of the Christian religion, and of its being adapted to a more improved state of human society, that it places our duties respecting marriage and the procreation of children in a different light from that in which they were before beheld.

Without entering minutely into the subject, which would evidently lead too far, I think it will be admitted that if we apply the spirit of St. Paul's declarations respecting marriage to the present state of society and the known constitution of our nature, the natural inference seems to be that, when marriage does not interfere with higher duties, it is right; when it does, it is wrong. According to the general principles of moral science, says Paley [in his *Moral Philosophy*], "the method of coming at the will of God from the light of nature is to inquire into the tendency of the action to promote or diminish the general happiness." There are perhaps few actions that tend so directly to diminish the general happiness as to marry without the means of supporting children. He who commits this act therefore clearly offends against the will of God; and having become a burden on the society in which he lives, and plunged himself and family into a situation in which virtuous habits are preserved with more difficulty than in any other, he appears to have violated his duty to his neighbours and to himself, and thus to have listened to the voice of passion in opposition to his higher obligations.

In a society such as I have supposed, all the members of which endeavour to obtain happiness by obedience to the moral code derived from the light of nature, and enforced by strong sanctions in revealed religion, it is evident that no such marriages could take place; and the prevention of a redundant population in this way would remove one of the principal encouragements to offensive war, and at the same time tend powerfully to eradicate those two fatal political disorders, internal tyranny and internal tumult, which mutually produce each other.

Indisposed to a war of offence, in a war of defence such a society would be strong as a rock of adamant. Where every family possessed the necessaries of life in plenty, and a decent portion of its comforts and conveniences, there could not exist that hope of change, or at best that melancholy and disheartening indifference to it, which sometimes prompts the lower classes of people to say, "Let what will come, we cannot be worse off than we are now." Every heart and hand will be united to repel an invader when each individual felt the value of the solid advantages which he enjoyed, and a prospect of change presented only a prospect of being deprived of them.

As it appears therefore that it is in the power of each individual to avoid all the evil consequences to himself and society resulting from the principle of population by the practice of a virtue clearly dictated to him by the light of nature and expressly enjoined in revealed religion, and as we have reason to think that the exercise of this virtue to a certain degree would tend rather to increase than diminish individual happiness, we can have no reason to impeach the justice of the Deity because his general laws make this virtue necessary, and punish our offences against it by the evils attendant upon vice and the pains that accompany the various forms of premature death. A really virtuous society such as I have supposed would avoid these evils. It is the apparent object of the Creator to deter us from vice by the pains which accompany it, and to lead us to virtue by the happiness that it produces. This object appears to our conceptions to be worthy of a benevolent Creator. The laws of nature respecting population tend to promote this object. No imputation therefore on the benevolence of the Deity can be founded on these laws which is not equally applicable to any of the evils necessarily incidental to an imperfect state of existence.

III. Of the Only Effectual Mode of Improving the Condition of the Poor

He who publishes a moral code or system of duties, however firmly he may be convinced of the strong obligation on each individual strictly to conform to it, has never the folly to imagine that it will be universally or even generally practised. But this is no valid objection against the publication of the code. If it were, the same objection would always have applied, we should be totally without general rules, and to the vices of mankind arising from temptation would be added a much longer list than we have at present of vices from ignorance.

Judging merely from the light of nature, if we feel convinced of the misery arising from a redundant population on the one hand, and of the evils and unhappiness, particularly to the female sex, arising from promiscuous intercourse, on the other, I do not see how it is possible for any person who acknowledges the principle of utility as the great criterion of moral rules, to escape the conclusion that moral restraint, or the abstaining from marriage till we are in a condition to support a family, with a perfectly moral conduct during that period, is the strict line of duty; and when revelation is taken into the question, this duty undoubtedly receives very powerful confirmation. At the same time I believe that few of my readers can be less sanguine than I am in their expectations of any sudden and great change in the general conduct of men on this subject; and the chief reason why in the last chapter I allowed myself to suppose the universal prevalence of this virtue was that I might endeavour to remove any imputation on the goodness of the Deity, by showing that the evils arising from the principle of population were exactly of the same nature as the generality of other evils which excite fewer complaints, that they were increased by human ignorance and indolence, and diminished by human knowledge and virtue; and on the supposition that each individual strictly fulfilled his duty would be almost totally removed, and this without any general diminution of those sources of pleasure arising from the regulated indulgence of the passions, which have been justly considered as the principal ingredients of human happiness.

If it will answer any purpose of illustration, I see no harm in drawing the picture of a society, in which each individual is supposed strictly to fulfil his duties; nor does a writer appear to be justly liable to the imputation of being visionary, unless he make such universal or general obedience necessary to the practical utility of his system, and to that degree of moderate and partial improvement which is all that can rationally be expected from the most complete knowledge of our duties.

But in this respect there is an essential difference between that improved state of society which I have supposed in the last chapter and most of the other speculations on this subject. The improvement there supposed, if we ever should make approaches towards it, is to be effected in the way in which we have been in the habit of seeing all the greatest improvements effected by a direct application to the interest and happiness of each individual. It is not required of us to act from motives to which we are unaccustomed; to pursue a general good which we may not distinctly comprehend, or the effect of which may be weakened by distance and diffusion. The happiness of the whole is to be the result of the happiness of individuals, and to begin first with them. No co-operation is required. Every step tells. He who performs his duty faithfully will reap the full fruits of it, whatever may be the number of others who fail. This duty is intelligible to the humblest capacity. It is merely that he is not to bring beings into the world for whom he cannot find the means of support. When once this subject is cleared from the obscurity thrown over it by parochial laws and private benevolence, every man must feel the strongest conviction of such an obligation. If he cannot support his children, they must starve; and if he marry in the face of a fair probability that he shall not be able to support his children, he is guilty of all the evils which he thus brings upon himself, his wife, and his offspring. It is clearly his interest, and will tend greatly to promote his happiness, to defer marrying, till by industry and economy he is in a capacity to support the children that he may reasonably expect from his marriage; and as he cannot in the meantime gratify his passions without violating an express command of God, and running a great risk of injuring himself or some of his fellow creatures, considerations of his own interest and happiness will dictate to him the strong obligation to a moral conduct while he remains unmarried.

However powerful may be the impulses of passion, they are generally in some degree modified by reason. And it does not seem entirely visionary to suppose that, if the true and permanent cause of poverty were clearly explained and forcibly brought home to each man's bosom, it would have some and perhaps not an inconsiderable influence on his conduct; at least the experiment has never yet been fairly tried. Almost everything that has been hitherto done for the poor has tended, as if with solicitous care, to throw a veil of obscurity over this subject and to hide from them the true cause of their poverty. When the wages of labour are hardly sufficient to maintain two children, a man marries and has five or six; he of course finds himself miserably distressed. He accuses the insufficiency of the price of labour to maintain a family. He accuses his parish for their tardy and sparing fulfilment of their obligation to assist him. He accuses the avarice of the rich who suffer him to want what they can so well spare. He accuses the partial and unjust institutions of society which have awarded him an inadequate share of the produce of the earth. He accuses perhaps the dispensations of Providence which have assigned to him a place in society so beset with unavoidable distress and dependence. In searching for objects of accusation, he never adverts to the quarter from which his misfortunes originate. The last person that he would think of accusing is himself, on whom in fact the principal blame lies except so far as he has been deceived by the higher classes of society. He may perhaps wish that he had not married, because he now feels the inconveniences of it; but it never enters into his head that he can have done anything wrong. He has always been told that to raise up subjects for his king and country is a very meritorious act. He has done this and yet is suffering for it; and it cannot but strike him as most extremely unjust and cruel in his king and country to allow him thus to suffer in return for giving them what they are continually declaring that they particularly want.

Till these erroneous ideas have been corrected, and the language of nature and reason has been generally heard on the subject of population, instead of the language of error and prejudice, it cannot be said that any fair experiment has been made with the understandings of the common people; and we cannot justly accuse them of improvidence and want of industry, till they act as they do now, after it has been brought home to their comprehensions, that they are themselves the cause of their own poverty; that the means of redress are in their own hands, and in the hands of no other persons whatever; that the society in which they live, and the government which presides over it, are without any *direct* power in this respect; and that however ardently they may desire to relieve them, and whatever attempts they may make to do so, they are really and truly unable to execute what they benevolently wish, but unjustly promise; that when the wages of labour will not maintain a family it is an incontrovertible sign that their king and country do not want more subjects, or at least that they cannot support them; that, if they marry in this case, so far from fulfilling a duty to society, they are throwing a useless burden on it, at the same time that they are plunging themselves into distress, and that they are acting directly contrary to the will of God, and bringing down upon themselves various diseases, which might all, or the greater part, have been avoided if they had attended to the repeated admonitions which he gives by the general laws of nature to every being capable of reason.

Paley, in his *Moral Philosophy,* observes that "in countries in which subsistence is become scarce, it behoves the state to watch over the public morals with increased solicitude; for nothing but the instinct of nature, under the restraint of chastity, will induce men to undertake the labour, or consent to the sacrifice of personal liberty and indulgence, which the support of a family in such circumstances requires." That it is always the duty of a state to use every exertion likely to be effectual in discouraging vice and promoting virtue, and that no temporary circumstances ought to cause any relaxation in these exertions, is certainly true. The means therefore proposed are always good; but the particular end in view in this case appears to be absolutely criminal. We wish to force people into marriage, when from the acknowledged scarcity of subsistence they will have little chance of being able to support their children. We might as well force people into the water who are unable to swim. In both cases we rashly tempt Providence. Nor have we more reason to believe that a miracle will be worked to save us from the misery and mortality resulting from our conduct in the one case than in the other.

The object of those who really wish to better the condition of the lower classes of society must be to raise the relative proportion between the price of labour and the price of provisions, so as to enable the labourer to command a larger share of the necessaries and comforts of life. We have hitherto principally attempted to attain this end by encouraging the married poor, and consequently increasing the number of labourers, and overstocking the market with a commodity which we still say that we wish to be dear. It would seem to have required no great spirit of divination to foretell the certain failure of such a plan of proceeding. There is nothing, however, like experience. It has been tried in many different countries and for many hundred years, and the success has always been answerable to the nature of the scheme. It is really time now to try something else.

When it was found that oxygen or pure vital air would not cure consumption as was expected, but rather aggravated their symptoms, trial was made of an air of the most opposite kind. I wish we had acted with the same philosophical spirit in our attempts to cure the disease of poverty; and having found that the pouring in of fresh supplies of labour only tended to aggravate the symptoms, had tried what would be the effect of withholding a little these supplies.

In all old and fully peopled states it is from this method and this alone that we can rationally expect any essential and permanent melioration in the condition of the labouring classes of the people.

In an endeavour to raise the proportion of the quantity of provisions to the number of consumers in any country, our attention would naturally be first directed to the increasing of the absolute quantity of provisions; but finding that as fast as we did this the number of consumers more than kept pace with it, and that with all our exertions we were still as far as ever behind, we should be convinced that our efforts directed only in this way would never succeed. It would appear to be setting the tortoise to catch the hare. Finding therefore that from the laws of nature we could not proportion the food to the population, our next attempt should naturally be to proportion the population to the food. If we can persuade the hare to go to sleep, the tortoise may have some chance of overtaking her.

We are not however to relax our efforts in increasing the quantity of provisions, but to combine another effort with it, that of keeping the population, when once it has been overtaken, at such a distance behind as to effect the relative proportion which we desire, and thus unite the two grand *desiderata,* a great actual population and a state of society in which abject poverty and dependence are comparatively but little known, two objects which are far from being incompatible.

If we be really serious in what appears to be the object of such general research, the mode of essentially and permanently bettering the condition of the poor, we must explain to them the true nature of their situation, and show them that the withholding of the supplies of labour is the only possible way of really raising its price, and that they themselves being the possessors of this commodity have alone the power to do this.

I cannot but consider this mode of diminishing poverty as so perfectly clear in theory, and so invariably confirmed by the analogy of every other commodity which is brought to market, that nothing but its being shown to be calculated to produce greater evils than it proposes to remedy can justify us in not making the attempt to put it into execution.

IV. Objections to This Mode Considered

One objection which perhaps will be made to this plan is that from which alone it derives its value—a market rather understocked with labour. This must undoubtedly take place in a certain degree; but by no means in such a degree as to affect the wealth and prosperity of the country. But putting this subject of a market understocked with labour in the most unfavourable point of view, if the rich will not submit to a slight inconvenience necessarily attendant on the attainment of what they profess to desire, they cannot really be in earnest in their professions. Their benevolence to the poor must be either childish play or hypocrisy; it must be either to amuse themselves or to pacify the minds of the common people with a mere show of attention to their wants. To wish to better the condition of the poor by enabling them to command a greater quantity of the necessaries and comforts of life, and then to complain of higher wages, is the act of a silly boy who gives away his cake and then cries for it. A market overstocked with labour, and an ample remuneration to each labourer, are objects perfectly incompatible with each other. In the annals of the world they never existed together: and to couple them even in imagination betrays a gross ignorance of the simplest principles of political economy.

A second objection that may be made to this plan is the diminution of population that it would cause. It is to be considered however that this diminution is merely relative; and when once this relative diminution has been effected by keeping the population stationary while the supply of food has increased, it might then start afresh and continue increasing for ages with the increase of food, maintaining always nearly the same relative proportion to it. I can easily conceive that this country, with a proper direction of the national industry, might in the course of some centuries contain two or three times its present population, and yet every man in the kingdom be much better fed and clothed than he is at present. While the springs of industry continue in vigour, and a sufficient part of that industry is directed to agriculture, we need be under no apprehensions of a deficient population; and nothing perhaps would tend so strongly to excite a spirit of industry and economy among the poor as a thorough knowledge that their happiness must always depend principally upon themselves; and that, if they obey their passions in opposition to their reason, or be not industrious and frugal while they are single to save a sum for the common contingencies of the married state, they must expect to suffer the natural evils which Providence has prepared for those who disobey its repeated admonitions.

A third objection which may be started to this plan, and the only one which appears to me to have any kind of plausibility, is that, by endeavouring to urge the duty of moral restraint on the poor, we may increase the quantity of vice relating to the sex.

I should be extremely sorry to say anything which could either directly or remotely be construed unfavourably to the cause of virtue; but I certainly cannot think that the vices which relate to the sex are the only vices which are to be considered in a moral question; or that they are even the greatest and most degrading to the human character. They can rarely or never be committed without producing unhappiness somewhere or other, and therefore ought always to be strongly reprobated; but there are other vices the effects of which are still more pernicious; and there are other situations which lead more certainly to moral offences than the refraining from marriage. Powerful as may be the temptations to a breach of chastity, I am inclined to think that they are impotent in comparison of the temptations arising from continued distress. A large class of women and many men, I have no doubt, pass a considerable part of their lives consistently with the laws of chastity; but I believe there will be found very few who pass through the ordeal of squalid and hopeless poverty, or even of long-continued embarrassed circumstances, without a great moral degradation of character.

In the higher and middle classes of society it is a melancholy and distressing sight to observe not unfrequently a man of a noble and ingenuous disposition, once feelingly alive to a sense of honour and integrity, gradually sinking under the pressure of circumstances, making his excuses at first with a blush of conscious shame, afraid of seeing the faces of his friends from whom he may have borrowed money, reduced to the meanest tricks and subterfuges to delay or avoid the payment of his just debts, till ultimately grown familiar with falsehood and at enmity with the world he loses all the grace and dignity of man.

To the general prevalence of indigence, and the extraordinary encouragements which we afford in this country to a total want of foresight and prudence among the common people, is to be attributed a considerable part of those continual depredations on property, and other more atrocious crimes, which drive us to the painful resource of such a number of executions. According to Mr. [Patrick] Colquhoun, above twenty thousand miserable individuals of various classes rise up every morning without knowing how or by what means they are to be supported during the passing day, or where in many instances they are to lodge on the succeeding night. It is by these unhappy persons that the principal depredations on the public are committed; and supposing but few of them to be married, and driven to these acts from the necessity of supporting their children, yet still it is probably true that the too great frequency of marriage amongst the poorest classes of society is one of the principal causes of the temptations to these crimes. A considerable part of these unhappy wretches will probably be found to be the offspring of such marriages, educated in workhouses where every vice is propagated, or bred up at home in filth and rags, with an utter ignorance of every moral obligation. A still greater part perhaps consists of persons who, being unable for some time to get employment owing to the full supply of labour, have been urged to these extremities by their temporary wants; and having thus lost their characters, are rejected even when their labour may be wanted by the well-founded caution of civil society.

When indigence does not produce overt acts of vice, it palsies every virtue. Under the continued temptations to a breach of chastity, occasional failures may take place, and the moral sensibility in other respects not be very strikingly impaired; but the continued temptations which beset hopeless poverty, and the strong sense of injustice that generally accompanies it from an ignorance of its true cause, tend so powerfully to sour the disposition, to harden the heart, and deaden the moral sense, that generally speaking virtue takes her flight clear away from the tainted spot, and does not often return.

Even with respect to the vices which relate to the sex, marriage has been found to be by no means a complete remedy. Among the higher classes, our Doctors' Commons, and the lives that many married men are known to lead, sufficiently prove this; and the same kind of vice, though not so much heard of among the lower classes of people, is probably in all our great towns not much less frequent.

Add to this that abject poverty, particularly when joined with idleness, is a state the most unfavourable to chastity that can well be conceived. The passion is as strong, or nearly so, as in other situations; and every restraint on it from personal respect, or a sense of morality, is generally removed. There is a degree of squalid poverty in which, if a girl was brought up, I should say that her being really modest at twenty was an absolute miracle. Those persons must have extraordinary minds indeed, and such as are not usually formed under similar circumstances, who can continue to respect themselves when no other person whatever respects them. If the children thus brought up were even to marry at twenty, it is probable that they would have passed some years in vicious habits before that period.

If after all, however, these arguments should appear insufficient, if we reprobate the idea of endeavouring to encourage the virtue of moral restraint among the poor from a fear of producing vice; and if we think that to facilitate marriage by all possible means is a point of the first consequence to the morality and happiness of the people, let us act consistently, and before we proceed endeavour to make ourselves acquainted with the mode by which alone we can effect our object.

V. Of the Consequences of Pursuing the Opposite Mode

It is an evident truth that, whatever may be the rate of increase in the means of subsistence, the increase of population must be limited by it, at least after the food has once been divided into the smallest shares that will support life. All the children born beyond what would be required to keep up the population to this level must necessarily perish, unless room be made for them by the deaths of grown persons. It has appeared indeed clearly in the course of this work, that in all old states the marriages and births depend principally upon the deaths, and that there is no encouragement to early unions so powerful as a great mortality. To act consistently therefore we should facilitate, instead of foolishly and vainly endeavouring to impede, the operations of nature in producing this mortality; and if we dread the too frequent visitation of the horrid form of famine, we should sedulously encourage the other forms of destruction which we compel nature to use. Instead of recommending cleanliness to the poor, we should encourage contrary habits. In our towns we should make the streets narrower, crowd more people into the houses, and court the return of the plague. In the country we should build our villages near stagnant pools, and particularly encourage settlements in all marshy and unwholesome situations. But above all we should reprobate specific remedies for ravaging diseases; and those benevolent, but much mistaken men, who have thought they were doing a service to mankind by projecting schemes for the total extirpation of particular disorders. If by these and similar means the annual mortality were increased from 1 in 36 or 40, to one in 18 or 20, we might probably every one of us marry at the age of puberty, and yet few be absolutely starved.

If however we all marry at this age and yet still continue our exertions to impede the operations of nature, we may rest assured that all our efforts will be vain. Nature will not, nor cannot, be defeated in her purposes. The necessary mortality must come in some form or other; and the extirpation of one disease will only be the signal for the birth of another perhaps more fatal. We cannot lower the waters of misery by pressing them down in different places, which must necessarily make them rise somewhere else; the only way in which we can hope to effect our purpose, is by drawing them off. To this course nature is constantly directing our attention by the chastisements which await a contrary conduct. These chastisements are more or less severe, in proportion to the degree in which her admonitions produce their intended effect. In this country at present these admonitions are by no means entirely neglected. The preventive check to population prevails to a considerable degree, and her chastisements are in consequence moderate: but if we were all to marry at the age of puberty they would be severe indeed. Political evils would probably be added to physical. A people goaded by constant distress, and visited by frequent returns of famine, could not be kept down but by a cruel despotism. We should approach to the state of the people in Egypt or Abyssinia; and I would ask whether in that case it is probable that we should be more virtuous?

Physicians have long remarked the great changes which take place in diseases; and that while some appear to yield to the efforts of human care and skill, others seem to become in proportion more malignant and fatal. Dr. William Heberden published not long since some valuable observations on this subject deduced from the London bills of mortality. In his preface, speaking of these bills, he says, "The gradual changes they exhibit in particular diseases correspond to the alterations, which in time are known to take place in the channels through which the great stream of mortality is constantly flowing." In the body of his work afterwards, speaking of some particular diseases, he observes with that candour which always distinguishes true science: "It is not easy to give a satisfactory reason for all the changes which may be observed to take place in the history of diseases. Nor is it any disgrace to physicians if their causes are often so gradual in their operation, or so subtle as to elude investigation."

I hope I shall not be accused of presumption in venturing to suggest that under certain circumstances such changes must take place; and perhaps without any alteration in those proximate causes which are usually looked to on these occasions. If this should appear to be true, it will not seem extraordinary that the most skilful and scientific physicians, whose business it is principally to investigate proximate causes, should sometimes search for these causes in vain.

In the country which keeps its population at a certain standard, if the average number of marriages and births be given, it is evident that the average number of deaths will also be given; and, to use Dr. Heberden's metaphor, the channels through which the great stream of mortality is constantly flowing, will always convey off a given quantity. Now if we stop up any of these channels it is perfectly clear that the stream of mortality must run with greater force through some of the other channels; that is, if we eradicate some diseases others will become proportionally more fatal. In this case the only distinguishable cause is the damming up a necessary outlet of mortality. Nature, in the attainment of her great purposes, seems always to seize upon the weakest part. If this part be made strong by human skill, she seizes upon the next weakest part, and so on in succession; not like a capricious deity, with an intention to sport with our sufferings and constantly to defeat our labours; but like a kind though sometimes severe instructor, with the intention of teaching us to make all parts strong, and to chase vice and misery from the earth. In avoiding one fault we are too apt to run into some other; but we always find Nature faithful to her great object at every false step we commit, ready to admonish us of our errors by the infliction of some physical or moral evil. If the prevalence of the preventive check to population in a sufficient degree were to remove many of those diseases which now afflict us, yet be accompanied by a considerable increase of the vice of promiscuous intercourse, it is probable that the disorders and unhappiness, the physical and moral evils arising from this vice would increase in strength and degree; and admonishing us severely of our error would point to the only line of conduct approved by nature, reason, and religion, abstinence from marriage till we can support our children, and chastity till that period arrives.

In the case just stated, in which the population and the number of marriages are supposed to be fixed, the necessity of a change in the mortality of some diseases from the diminution or extinction of others is capable of mathematical demonstration. The only obscurity which can possibly involve this subject, arises from taking into consideration the effect that might be produced by a diminution of mortality in increasing the population or in decreasing the number of marriages. That the removal of any of the particular causes of mortality can have no further effect upon population than the means of subsistence will allow, and that it has no certain and necessary influence on these means of subsistence, are facts of which the reader must be already convinced. Of its operation in tending to prevent marriage by diminishing the demand for fresh supplies of children I have no doubt; and there is reason to think that it had this effect in no inconsiderable degree on the extinction of the plague, which had so long and so dreadfully ravaged this country.

If on contemplating the increase of vice which might contingently follow an attempt to inculcate the duty of moral restraint, and the increase of misery that must necessarily follow the attempts to encourage marriage and population, we come to the conclusion not to interfere in any respect, but to leave every man to his own free choice and responsible only to God for the evil which he does in either way; this is all I contend for; I would on no account do more; but I contend that at present we are very far from doing this.

Among the lower classes of society, where the point is of the greatest importance, the poor-laws afford a direct, constant, and systematical encouragement to marriage by removing from each individual that heavy responsibility which he would incur by the laws of nature for bringing beings into the world which he could not support. Our private benevolence has the same direction as the poor-laws, and almost invariably tends to encourage marriage and to equalise as much as possible the circumstances of married and single men.

Among the higher classes of people the superior distinctions which married women receive, and the marked inattentions to which single women of advanced age are exposed, enable many men who are agreeable neither in mind nor person and are besides in the wane of life to choose a partner among the young and fair, instead of being confined as nature seems to dictate to persons of nearly their own age and accomplishments. It is scarcely to be doubted that the fear of being an old maid, and of that silly and unjust ridicule which folly sometimes attaches to this name, drives many women into the marriage union with men whom they dislike, or at best to whom they are perfectly indifferent. Such marriages must to every delicate mind appear little better than legal prostitutions, and they often burden the earth with unnecessary children, without compensating for it by an accession of happiness and virtue to the parties themselves.

Throughout all the ranks of society the prevailing opinions respecting the duty and obligation of marriage cannot but have a very powerful influence. The man who thinks that in going out of the world without leaving representatives behind him he shall have failed in an important duty to society, will be disposed to force rather than to repress his inclinations on this subject; and when his reason represents to him the difficulties attending a family he will endeavour not to attend to these suggestions, will still determine to venture, and will hope that in the discharge of what he conceives to be his duty he shall not be deserted by Providence.

In a civilised country such as England, where a taste for the decencies and comforts of life prevails among a very large class of people, it is not possible that the encouragements to marriage from positive institutions and prevailing opinions should entirely obscure the light of nature and reason on this subject; but still they contribute to make it comparatively weak and indistinct. And till this obscurity is removed, and the poor are undeceived with respect to the principal cause of their poverty, and taught to know that their happiness or misery must depend chiefly upon themselves, it cannot be said that with regard to the great question of marriage we leave every man to his own free and fair choice.

VI. Effects of the Knowledge of the Principal Cause of Poverty on Civil Liberty

It may appear, perhaps, that a doctrine which attributes the greatest part of the sufferings of the lower classes of society exclusively to themselves is unfavourable to the cause of liberty, as affording a tempting opportunity to governments of oppressing their subjects at pleasure and laying the whole blame on the laws of nature and the imprudence of the poor. We are not, however, to trust to first appearances; and I am strongly disposed to believe that those who will be at the pains to consider this subject deeply will be convinced that nothing would so powerfully contribute to the advancement of rational freedom as a thorough knowledge generally circulated of the principal cause of poverty, and that the ignorance of this cause, and the natural consequences of this ignorance, form at present one of the chief obstacles to its progress.

The pressure of distress on the lower classes of people, together with the habit of attributing this distress to their rulers, appears to me to be the rock of defence, the castle, the guardian spirit of despotism. It affords to the tyrant the fatal and unanswerable plea of necessity. It is the reason why every free government tends constantly to destruction, and that its appointed guardians become daily less jealous of the encroachments of power. It is the reason why so many noble efforts in the cause of freedom have failed, and why almost every revolution after long and painful sacrifices has terminated in a military despotism. While any dissatisfied man of talents has power to persuade the lower classes of people that all their poverty and distress arise solely from the iniquity of the government, though, perhaps, the greatest part of what they suffer is unconnected with this cause, it is evident that the seeds of fresh discontents and fresh revolutions are continually sowing. When an established government has been destroyed, finding that their poverty is not removed, their resentment naturally falls upon the successors to power; and when these have been immolated without producing the desired effect, other sacrifices are called for, and so on without end. Are we to be surprised that under such circumstances the majority of well-disposed people, finding that a government with proper restrictions is unable to support itself against the revolutionary spirit, and weary and exhausted with perpetual change to which they can see no end, should give up the struggle in despair, and throw themselves into the arms of the first power which can afford them protection against the horrors of anarchy?

A mob, which is generally the growth of a redundant population goaded by resentment for real sufferings, but totally ignorant of the quarter from which they originate, is of all monsters the most fatal to freedom. It fosters a prevailing tyranny, and engenders one where it was not; and though in its dreadful fits of resentment it appears occasionally to devour its unsightly offspring, yet no sooner is the horrid deed committed than, however unwilling it may be to propagate such a breed, it immediately groans with a new birth.

Of the tendency of mobs to produce tyranny we may not, perhaps, be long without an example in this country. As a friend to freedom, and naturally an enemy to large standing armies, it is with extreme reluctance that I am compelled to acknowledge that, had it not been for the great organised force in the country, the distresses of the people during the late scarcities [of 1800 and 1801], encouraged by the extreme ignorance and folly of many among the higher classes, might have driven them to commit the most dreadful outrages, and ultimately to involve the country in all the horrors of famine. Should such periods often recur (a recurrence which we have too much reason to apprehend from the present state of the country), the prospect which opens to our view is melancholy in the extreme. The English constitution will be seen hastening with rapid strides to the *Euthanasia* foretold by [David] Hume, unless its progress be interrupted by some popular commotion; and this alternative presents a picture still more appalling to the imagination. If political discontents were blended with the cries of hunger, and a revolution were to take place by the instrumentality of a mob clamouring for want of food, the consequences would be unceasing change and unceasing carnage, the bloody career of which nothing but the establishment of some complete despotism could arrest.

We can scarcely believe that the appointed guardians of British liberty should quietly have acquiesced in those gradual encroachments of power which have taken place of late years, but from the apprehension of these still more dreadful evils. Great as has been the influence of corruption, I cannot yet think so meanly of the country gentlemen of England, as to believe that they would thus have given up a part of their birthright of liberty, if they had not been actuated by a real and genuine fear that it was then in greater danger from the people than from the crown. They appeared to surrender themselves to government, on condition of being protected from the mob; but they never would have made this melancholy and disheartening surrender, if such a mob had not existed either in reality or in imagination. That the fears on this subject were artfully exaggerated and increased beyond the limits of just apprehension is undeniable; but I think it is also undeniable that the frequent declamations which were heard against the unjust institutions of society, and the delusive arguments on equality which were circulated among the lower classes, gave us just reason to suppose that if the *vox populi* had been allowed to speak, it would have appeared to be the voice of error and absurdity instead of the *vox Dei*.

To say that our conduct is not to be regulated by circumstances is to betray an ignorance of the most solid and incontrovertible principles of morality. Though the admission of this principle may sometimes afford a cloak to changes of opinion that do not result from the purest motives, yet the admission of a contrary principle would be productive of infinitely worse consequences. The phrase of "existing circumstances" has, I believe, not unfrequently created a smile in the English House of Commons, but the smile should have been reserved for the application of the phrase, and not have been excited by the phrase itself. A very frequent repetition of it has indeed of itself rather a suspicious air; and its application should always be watched with the most jealous and anxious attention; but no man ought to be judged *in limine* for saying that existing circumstances had obliged him to alter his opinions and conduct. The country gentlemen were perhaps too easily convinced that existing circumstances called upon them to give up some of the most valuable privileges of Englishmen; but as far as they were really convinced of this obligation, they acted consistently with the clearest rule of morality.

The degree of power to be given to the civil government and the measure of our submission to it, must be determined by general expediency; and, in judging of this expediency, every circumstance is to be taken into consideration, particularly the state of public opinion and the degree of ignorance and delusion prevailing among the common people. The patriot who might be called upon by the love of his country to join with heart and hand in a rising of the people for some specific attainable object of reform, if he knew that they were enlightened respecting their own situation and would stop short when they had attained their demand, would be called upon by the same motive to submit to very great oppression rather than give the slightest countenance to a popular tumult, the members of which, at least the greater number of them, were persuaded that the destruction of the Parliament, the Lord Mayor, and the monopolisers, would make bread cheap, and that a revolution would enable them all to support their families. In this case it is more the ignorance and delusion of the lower classes of the people that occasion the oppression, than the actual disposition of the government to tyranny. That there is, however, in all power a constant tendency to encroach is an incontrovertible truth, and cannot be too strongly inculcated. The checks which are necessary to secure the liberty of the subject will always in some degree embarrass and delay the operations of the executive government. The members of this government feeling these inconveniences while they are exerting themselves, as they conceive, in the service of their country, and conscious perhaps of no ill intention towards the people, will naturally be disposed on every occasion to demand the suspension or abolition of these checks; but if once the convenience of ministers be put in competition with the liberties of the people and we get into a habit of relying on fair assurances and personal character, instead of examining with the most scrupulous and jealous care the merits of each particular case, there is an end of British freedom. If we once admit the principle that the government must know better with regard to the quantity of power which it wants than we can possibly do with our limited means of information, and that therefore it is our duty to surrender up our private judgments, we may just as well at the same time surrender up the whole of our constitution. Government is a quarter in which liberty is not nor cannot be very faithfully preserved. If we are wanting to ourselves, and inattentive to our great interest in this respect, it is the height of folly and unreasonableness to expect that government will attend to them for us. Should the British constitution ultimately lapse into a despotism as has been prophesied, I shall think that the country gentlemen of England will have much more to answer for than the ministers.

To do the country gentlemen justice, however, I should readily acknowledge that in the partial desertion of their posts as guardians of British freedom, which has already taken place, they have been actuated more by fear than corruption: And the principal reason of this fear was, I conceive, the ignorance and delusions of the common people, and the prospective horrors which were contemplated if in such a state of mind they should by any revolutionary movement obtain an ascendant.

The circulation of [Thomas] Paine's *Rights of Man* it is supposed has done great mischief among the lower and middling classes of people in this country. This is probably true; but not because man is without rights or that these rights ought not to be known; but because Mr. Paine has fallen into some fundamental errors respecting the principles of government, and in many important points has shown himself totally unacquainted with the structure of society, and the different moral effects to be expected from the physical difference between this country and America. Mobs of the same description as those collections of people known by this name in Europe could not exist in America. The number of people without property is there, from the physical state of the country, comparatively small: and therefore the civil power, which is to protect property, cannot require the same degree of strength. Mr. Paine very justly observes that whatever the apparent cause of any riots may be, the real one is always want of happiness; but when he goes on to say it shows that something is wrong in the system of government that injures the felicity by which society is to be preserved, he falls into the common error of attributing all want of happiness to government. It is evident that this want of happiness might have existed, and from ignorance might have been the principal cause of the riots, and yet be almost wholly unconnected with any of the proceedings of government. The redundant population of an old state furnishes materials of unhappiness unknown to such a state as that of America; and if an attempt were to be made to remedy this unhappiness by distributing the produce of the taxes to the poorer classes of society, according to the plan proposed by Mr. Paine, the evil would be aggravated a hundredfold, and in a very short time no sum that the society could possibly raise would be adequate to the proposed object.

Nothing would so effectually counteract the mischiefs occasioned by Mr. Paine's *Rights of Man* as a general knowledge of the real rights of man. What these rights are it is not my business at present to explain; but there is one right which man has generally been thought to possess, which I am confident he neither does nor can possess—a right to subsistence when his labour will not fairly purchase it. Our laws indeed say that he has this right, and bind the society to furnish employment and food to those who cannot get them in the regular market; but in so doing they attempt to reverse the laws of nature, and it is in consequence to be expected not only that they should fail in their object, but that the poor, who were intended to be benefited, should suffer most cruelly from the inhuman deceit thus practised upon them.

The Abbé Raynal has said that "*Avant toutes les loix sociales l'homme avoit le droit de subsister.*" He might with just as much propriety have said that before the institution of social laws every man had a right to live a hundred years. Undoubtedly he had then and has still a good right to live a hundred years, nay a thousand *if he can,* without interfering with the right of others to live; but the affair in both cases is principally an affair of power not of right. Social laws very greatly increase this power, by enabling a much greater number to subsist than could subsist without them, and so far very greatly enlarge *le droit de subsister;* but neither before nor after the institution of social laws could an unlimited number subsist; and before as well as since, he who ceased to have the power ceased to have the right.

If the great truths on these subjects were more generally circulated and the lower classes of people could be convinced that by the laws of nature, independently of any particular institutions except the great one of property, which is absolutely necessary in order to attain any considerable produce, no person has any claim of *right* on society for subsistence if his labour will not purchase it, the greatest part of the mischievous declamation on the unjust institutions of society would fall powerless to the ground. The poor are by no means inclined to be visionary. Their distresses are always real, though they are not attributed to the real causes. If these causes were properly explained to them, and they were taught to know what part of their present distress was attributable to government, and what part to causes totally unconnected with it, discontent and irritation among the lower classes of people would show themselves much less frequently than at present; and when they did show themselves would be much less to be dreaded. The efforts of turbulent and discontented men in the middle classes of society might safely be disregarded if the poor were so far enlightened respecting the real nature of their situation as to be aware that by aiding them in their schemes of renovation they would probably be promoting the ambitious views of others without in any respect benefiting themselves. The country gentlemen and men of property in England might securely return to a wholesome jealousy of the encroachments of power; and instead of daily sacrificing the liberties of the subject on the altar of public safety, might without any just apprehension from the people not only tread back their late steps, but firmly insist upon those gradual reforms which the lapse of time and the storms of the political world have rendered necessary to prevent the gradual destruction of the British constitution.

All improvements in governments must necessarily originate with persons of some education, and these will of course be found among the people of property. Whatever may be said of a few, it is impossible to suppose that the great mass of the people of property should be really interested in the abuses of government. They merely submit to them from the fear that an endeavour to remove them might be productive of greater evils. Could we but take away this fear, reform and improvement would proceed with as much facility as the removal of nuisances or the paving and lighting of the streets. In human life we are continually called upon to submit to a lesser evil in order to avoid a greater; and it is the part of a wise man to do this readily and cheerfully; but no wise man will submit to any evil if he can get rid of it without danger. Remove all apprehension from the tyranny or folly of the people, and the tyranny of government could not stand a moment. It would then appear in its proper deformity, without palliation, without pretext, without protector. Naturally feeble in itself, when it was once stripped naked and deprived of the support of public opinion and of the great plea of necessity, it would fall without a struggle. Its few interested defenders would hide their heads abashed, and would be ashamed any longer to support a cause for which no human ingenuity could invent a plausible argument.

The most successful supporters of tyranny are without doubt those general declaimers who attribute the distresses of the poor, and almost all the evils to which society is subject, to human institutions and the iniquity of governments. The falsity of these accusations and the dreadful consequences that would result from their being generally admitted and acted upon, make it absolutely necessary that they should at all events be resisted, not only on account of the immediate revolutionary horrors to be expected from a movement of the people acting under such impressions (a consideration which must at all times have very great weight), but also on account of the extreme probability that such a revolution would terminate in a much worse despotism than that which it had destroyed. On these grounds a genuine friend of freedom, a zealous advocate for the real rights of man, might be found among the defenders of a considerable degree of tyranny. A cause bad in itself might be supported by the good and the virtuous, merely because that which was opposed to it was much worse; and because it was absolutely necessary at the moment to make a choice between the two. Whatever therefore may be the intention of those indiscriminate accusations against governments, their real effect undoubtedly is to add a weight of talents and principles to the prevailing power which it never would have received otherwise.

It is a truth which I trust has been sufficiently proved in the course of this work, that under a government constructed upon the best and purest principles and executed by men of the highest talents and integrity, the most squalid poverty and wretchedness might universally prevail from an inattention to the prudential check to population. And as this cause of unhappiness has hitherto been so little understood that the efforts of society have always tended rather to aggravate than to lessen it, we have the strongest reasons for supposing that in all the governments with which we are acquainted a great part of the misery to be observed among the lower classes of the people arises from this cause.

The inference therefore which Mr. Paine and others have drawn against governments from the unhappiness of the people is palpably unfair; and before we give a sanction to such accusations it is a debt we owe to truth and justice to ascertain how much of this unhappiness arises from the principle of population, and how much is fairly to be attributed to government. When this distinction has been properly made, and all the vague, indefinite, and false accusations removed, government would remain, as it ought to be, clearly responsible for the rest; and the amount of this would still be such as to make the responsibility very considerable. Though government has but little power in the direct and immediate relief of poverty, yet its indirect influence on the prosperity of its subjects is striking and incontestable. And the reason is, that though it is comparatively impotent in its efforts to make the food of a country keep pace with an unrestricted increase of population, yet its influence is great in giving the best direction to those checks which in some form or other must necessarily take place. It has clearly appeared in the former part of this work that the most despotic and worst-governed countries, however low they might be in actual population, were uniformly the most populous in proportion to their means of subsistence, and the necessary effect of this state of things must of course be very low wages. In such countries the checks to population arise more from the sickness and mortality consequent on poverty than from the prudence and foresight which restrain the frequency and universality of early marriages. The checks are more of the positive and less of the preventive kind.

The first grand requisite to the growth of prudential habits is the perfect security of property, and the next perhaps is that respectability and importance which are given to the lower classes by equal laws and the possession of some influence in the framing of them. The more excellent therefore is the government, the more does it tend to generate that prudence and elevation of sentiment by which alone in the present state of our being poverty can be avoided.

It has been sometimes asserted that the only reason why it is advantageous that the people should have some share in the government is that a representation of the people tends best to secure the framing of good and equal laws, but that if the same object could be attained under a despotism the same advantage would accrue to the community. If, however, the representative system, by securing to the lower classes of society a more equal and liberal mode of treatment from their superiors, gives to each individual a greater personal respectability and a greater fear of personal degradation, it is evident that it will powerfully co-operate with the security of property in animating the exertions of industry and in generating habits of prudence, and thus more powerfully tend to increase the riches and prosperity of the lower classes of the community than if the same laws had existed under a despotism.

But though the tendency of a free constitution and a good government to diminish poverty be certain, yet their effect in this way must necessarily be indirect and slow, and very different from the direct and immediate relief which the lower classes of people are too frequently in the habit of looking forward to as the consequence of a revolution. This habit of expecting too much, and the irritation occasioned by disappointment, continually give a wrong direction to their efforts in favour of liberty, and constantly tend to defeat the accomplishment of those gradual reforms in government and that slow melioration of the condition of the lower classes of society which are really attainable. It is of the very highest importance therefore to know distinctly what government cannot do as well as what it can. If I were called upon to name the cause which in my conception had more than any other contributed to the very slow progress of freedom, so disheartening to every liberal mind, I should say that it was the confusion that had existed respecting the causes of the unhappiness and discontents which prevail in society, and the advantage which governments had been able to take and indeed had been compelled to take of this confusion to confirm and strengthen their power. I cannot help thinking therefore that a knowledge generally circulated that the principal cause of want and unhappiness is only indirectly connected with government and totally beyond its power directly to remove, and that it depends upon the conduct of the poor themselves, would, instead of giving any advantage to governments, give a great additional weight to the popular side of the question by removing the dangers with which from ignorance it is at present accompanied, and thus tend in a very powerful manner to promote the cause of rational freedom.

VII. Continuation of the Same Subject

The reasonings of the foregoing chapter have been strikingly confirmed by the events of the last two or three years [1815–17]. Perhaps there never was a period when more erroneous views were formed by the lower classes of society of the effects to be expected from reforms in the government when these erroneous views were more immediately founded on a total misapprehension of the principal cause of poverty, and when they more directly led to results unfavourable to liberty.

One of the main causes of complaint against the government has been that a considerable number of labourers, who are both able and willing to work, are wholly out of employment and unable consequently to command the necessaries of life. That this state of things is one of the most afflicting events that can occur in civilised life, that it is a natural and pardonable cause of discontent among the lower classes of society, and that every effort should be made by the higher classes to mitigate it, consistently with a proper care not to render it permanent, no man of humanity can doubt. But that such a state of things may occur in the best conducted and most economical government that ever existed is as certain as that governments have not the power of commanding with effect the resources of a country to be progressive when they are naturally stationary or declining.

It will be allowed that periods of prosperity may occur in any well-governed state, during which an extraordinary stimulus may be given to its wealth and population which cannot in its nature be permanent. If for instance new channels of trade are opened, new colonies are possessed, new inventions take place in machinery, and new and great improvements are made in agriculture, it is quite obvious that while the markets at home and abroad will readily take off at advantageous prices the increasing produce, there must be a rapid increase of capital and an unusual stimulus given to the population. On the other hand, if subsequently these channels of trade are either closed by accident or contracted by foreign competition; if colonies are lost, or the same produce is supplied from other quarters; if the markets, either from glut or competition, cease to extend with the extension of the new machinery; and if the improvements in agriculture from any cause whatever cease to be progressive, it is as obvious that just at the time when the stimulus to population has produced its greatest effect the means of employing and supporting this population may, in the natural course of things and without any fault whatever in the government, become deficient. This failure must unavoidably produce great distress among the labouring classes of society, but it is quite clear that no inference can be drawn from this distress that a radical change is required in the government, and the attempt to accomplish such a change might only aggravate the evil.

It has been supposed in this case that the government has in no respect by its conduct contributed to the pressure in question, a supposition which in practice perhaps will rarely be borne out by the fact. It is unquestionably in the power of a government to produce great distress by war and taxation, and it requires some skill to distinguish the distress which is the natural result of these causes from that which is occasioned in the way just described. In our own case unquestionably both descriptions of causes have combined, but the former in a greater degree than the latter. War and taxation, as far as they operate directly and simply, tend to destroy or retard the progress of capital, produce, and population; but during the late war these checks to prosperity have been much more than overbalanced by a combination of circumstances which has given an extraordinary stimulus to production: that for this overbalance of advantages the country cannot be considered as much indebted to the government is most certain. The government during the last twenty-five years has shown no very great love either of peace or liberty, and no particular economy in the use of the national resources. It has proceeded in a very straightforward manner to spend great sums in war and to raise them by very heavy taxes. It has no doubt done its part towards the dilapidation of the national resources. But still the broad fact must stare every impartial observer in the face that at the end of the war in 1814 the national resources were not dilapidated, and that not only were the wealth and population of the country considerably greater than they were at the commencement of the war, but that they had increased in the interval at a more rapid rate than was ever experienced before.

Perhaps this may justly be considered as one of the most extraordinary facts in history; and it certainly follows from it that the sufferings of the country since the peace have not been occasioned so much by the usual and most natural effects to be expected from war and taxation as by the sudden ceasing of an extraordinary stimulus to production, the distresses consequent upon which, though increased no doubt by the weight of taxation, do not essentially arise from it, and are not directly therefore and immediately to be relieved by its removal.

That the labouring classes of society should not be fully aware that the main causes of their distress are to a certain extent and for a certain time irremediable is natural enough, and that they should listen much more readily and willingly to those who confidently promise immediate relief rather than to those who can only tell them unpalatable truths is by no means surprising. But it must be allowed that full advantage has been taken by the popular orators and writers of a crisis which has given them so much power. Partly from ignorance and partly from design, everything that could tend to enlighten the labouring classes as to the real nature of their situation, and encourage them to bear an unavoidable pressure with patience, has been either sedulously kept out of their view or clamorously reprobated; and everything that could tend to deceive them, to aggravate and encourage their discontents, and to raise unreasonable and extravagant expectations as to the relief to be expected from reform, has been as sedulously brought forward. If under these circumstances the reforms proposed had been accomplished, it is impossible that the people should not have been most cruelly disappointed; and under a system of universal suffrage and annual parliaments, a general disappointment of the people would probably lead to every sort of experiment in government till the career of change was stopped by a military despotism. The warmest friends of genuine liberty might justly feel alarmed at such a prospect. To a cause conducted on such principles, and likely to be attended with such results, they could not of course consistently with their duty lend any assistance. And if with great difficulty, and against the sense of the great mass of petitioners, they were to effect a more moderate and more really useful reform, they could not but feel certain that the unavoidable disappointment of the people would be attributed to the half measures which had been pursued, and that they would be either forced to proceed to more radical changes or submit to a total loss of their influence and popularity by stopping short while the distresses of the people were unrelieved, their discontents unallayed, and the great *panacea* on which they had built their sanguine expectations untried.

These considerations have naturally paralysed the exertions of the best friends of liberty; and those salutary reforms which are acknowledged to be necessary in order to repair the breaches of time and improve the fabric of our constitution are thus rendered much more difficult and consequently much less probable.

But not only have the false expectations and extravagant demands suggested by the leaders of the people given an easy victory to government over every proposition for reform, whether violent or moderate, but they have furnished the most fatal instruments of offensive attack against the constitution itself. They are naturally calculated to excite some alarm and to check moderate reform; but alarm, when once excited, seldom knows where to stop, and the causes of it are particularly liable to be exaggerated. There is reason to believe that it has been under the influence of exaggerated statements, and of inferences drawn by exaggerated fears from these statements, that acts unfavourable to liberty have been passed without an adequate necessity. But the power of creating these exaggerated fears and of passing these acts has been unquestionably furnished by the extravagant expectations of the people. And it must be allowed that the present times furnish a very striking illustration of the doctrine that an ignorance of the principal cause of poverty is peculiarly unfavourable, and that a knowledge of it must be peculiarly favourable to the cause of civil liberty.

VIII. Plan of the Gradual Abolition of the Poor-Laws Proposed

If the principles in the preceding chapters should stand the test of examination, and we should ever feel the obligation of endeavouring to act upon them, the next inquiry would be in what way we ought practically to proceed. The first grand obstacle which presents itself in this country is the system of the poor-laws, which has been justly stated to be an evil, in comparison of which the national debt, with all its magnitude of terror, is of little moment. The rapidity with which the poor's rates have increased of late years presents us indeed with the prospect of such an extraordinary proportion of paupers in the society as would seem to be incredible in a nation flourishing in arts, agriculture, and commerce, and with a government which has generally been allowed to be the best that has hitherto stood the test of experience.

Greatly as we may be shocked at such a prospect, and ardently as we may wish to remove it, the evil is now so deeply seated, and the relief given by the poor-laws so widely extended, that no man of humanity could venture to propose their immediate abolition. To mitigate their effects, however, and stop their future increase, to which if left to continue upon their present plan we can see no probable termination, it has been proposed to fix the whole sum to be raised at its present rate, or any other that might be determined upon, and to make a law that on no account this sum should be exceeded. The objection to this plan is that a very large sum would be still to be raised and a great number of people to be supported, the consequence of which would be that the poor would not be easily able to distinguish the alteration that had been made. Each individual would think that he had as good a right to be supported when he was in want as any other person; and those who unfortunately chanced to be in distress when the fixed sum had been collected would think themselves particularly ill-used on being excluded from all assistance while so many others were enjoying this advantage. If the sum collected were divided among all that were in want, however their numbers might increase, though such a plan would not be so unfair with regard to those who became dependent after the sum had been fixed, it would undoubtedly be very hard upon those who had been in the habit of receiving a more liberal supply, and had done nothing to justify its being taken from them; and in both cases it would certainly be unjust in the society to undertake the support of the poor, and yet if their numbers increased to feed them so sparingly that they must necessarily die of hunger and disease.

I have reflected much on the subject of the poor-laws, and hope therefore that I shall be excused in venturing to suggest a mode of their gradual abolition, to which I confess that at present I can see no material objection. Of this indeed I feel nearly convinced, that should we ever become so fully sensible of the wide-spreading tyranny, dependence, indolence, and unhappiness which they create as seriously to make an effort to abolish them, we shall be compelled by a sense of justice to adopt the principle, if not the plan, which I shall mention. It seems impossible to get rid of so extensive a system of support, consistently with humanity, without applying ourselves directly to its vital principle, and endeavouring to counteract that deeply seated cause which occasions the rapid growth of all such establishments, and invariably renders them inadequate to their object.

As a previous step even to any considerable alteration in the present system, which would contract or stop the increase of the relief to be given, it appears to me that we are bound in justice and honour formally to disclaim the *right* of the poor to support.

To this end, I should propose a regulation to be made, declaring that no child born from any marriage taking place after the expiration of a year from the date of the law, and no illegitimate child born two years from the same date, should ever be entitled to parish assistance. And to give a more general knowledge of this law, and to enforce it more strongly on the minds of the lower classes of people, the clergyman of each parish should, after the publication of banns, read a short address, stating the strong obligation on every man to support his own children; the impropriety, and even immorality, of marrying without a prospect of being able to do this; the evils which had resulted to the poor themselves from the attempt which had been made to assist by public institutions in a duty which ought to be exclusively appropriated to parents, and the absolute necessity which had at length appeared of abandoning all such institutions on account of their producing effects totally opposite to those which were intended.

This would operate as a fair, distinct, and precise notice, which no man could well mistake, and without pressing hard on any particular individuals would at once throw off the rising generation from that miserable and helpless dependence upon the government and the rich, the moral as well as physical consequences of which are almost incalculable.

After the public notice which I have proposed had been given, and the system of poor-laws had ceased with regard to the rising generation, if any man choose to marry without a prospect of being able to support a family he should have the most perfect liberty so to do. Though to marry in this case is in my opinion clearly an immoral act, yet it is not one which society can justly take upon itself to prevent or punish; because the punishment provided for it by the laws of nature falls directly and most severely upon the individual who commits the act, and through him, only more remotely and feebly, on the society. When nature will govern and punish for us, it is a very miserable ambition to wish to snatch the rod from her hands, and draw upon ourselves the odium of executioner. To the punishment therefore of nature he should be left, the punishment of want. He has erred in the face of a most clear and precise warning, and can have no just reason to complain of any person but himself when he feels the consequences of his error. All parish assistance should be denied him, and he should be left to the uncertain support of private charity. He should be taught to know that the laws of nature, which are the laws of God, had doomed him and his family to suffer for disobeying their repeated admonitions; that he had no claim of *right* on society for the smallest portion of food beyond that which his labour would fairly purchase, and that if he and his family were saved from feeling the natural consequences of his imprudence, he would owe it to the pity of some kind benefactor, to whom therefore he ought to be bound by the strongest ties of gratitude.

If the plan which I have proposed were adopted, the poor's rates in a few years would begin very rapidly to decrease, and in no great length of time would be completely extinguished; and yet as far as it appears to me at present no individual would be either deceived or injured, and consequently no person could have a just right to complain.

The abolition of the poor-laws however is not of itself sufficient; and the obvious answer to those who lay too much stress on this system is, to desire them to look at the state of the poor in some other countries where such laws do not prevail, and to compare it with their condition in England. But this comparison it must be acknowledged is in many respects unfair; and would by no means decide the question of the utility or inutility of such a system. England possesses very great natural and political advantages, in which perhaps the countries that we should in this case compare with her, would be found to be palpably deficient. The nature of her soil and climate is such, that those almost universal failures in the crops of grain which are known in some countries never occur in England. Her insular situation and extended commerce are peculiarly favourable for importation. Her numerous manufactures employ nearly all the hands that are not engaged in agriculture, and afford the means of a regular distribution of the annual produce of the land and labour to the whole of her inhabitants. But above all, throughout a very large class of people, a decided taste for the conveniences and comforts of life, a strong desire of bettering their condition (that master spring of public prosperity), and in consequence a most laudable spirit of industry and foresight, are observed to prevail. These dispositions, so contrary to the hopeless indolence remarked in despotic countries, are generated by the constitution of the English government and the excellence of its laws, which secure to every individual the produce of his industry. When therefore on a comparison with other countries England appears to have the advantage in the state of her poor, the superiority is entirely to be attributed to these favourable circumstances and not to the poor-laws. A woman with one bad feature may greatly excel in beauty some other who may have this individual feature tolerably good, but it would be rather strange to assert in consequence that the superior beauty of the former was occasioned by this particular deformity. The poor-laws have constantly tended to counteract the natural and acquired advantages of this country. Fortunately these disadvantages have been so considerable that though weakened they could not be overcome, and to these advantages, together with the checks to marriage which the laws themselves create, it is owing that England has been able to bear up so long against this pernicious system. Probably there is not any other country in the world, except perhaps Holland before the revolution, which could have acted upon it so completely for the same period of time without utter ruin.

It has been proposed by some to establish poor-laws in Ireland, but from the depressed state of the common people there is little reason to doubt that, on the establishment of such laws, the whole of the landed property would very soon be absorbed or the system be given up in despair.

In Sweden, from the dearths which are not unfrequent owing to the general failure of crops in an unpropitious climate and the impossibility of great importations in a poor country, an attempt to establish a system of parochial relief such as that in England (if it were not speedily abandoned from the physical impossibility of executing it) would level the property of the kingdom from one end to the other, and convulse the social system in such a manner as absolutely to prevent it from recovering its former state on the return of plenty.

Even in France, with all her advantages of situation and climate, the tendency to population is so great and the want of foresight among the lower classes of the people so remarkable, that if poor-laws were established the landed property would soon sink under the burden, and the wretchedness of the people at the same time be increased. On these considerations the committee *de Mendicité,* at the beginning of the revolution, very properly and judiciously rejected the establishment of such a system which had been proposed.

The exception of Holland, if it were an exception, would arise from very particular circumstances—her extensive foreign trade and her numerous colonial emigrations, compared with the smallness of her territory, together with the extreme unhealthiness of a great part of the country, which occasions a much greater average mortality than is common in other states. These, I conceive, were the unobserved causes which principally contributed to render Holland so famous for the management of her poor, and able to employ and support all who applied for relief.

No part of Germany is sufficiently rich to support an extensive system of parochial relief, but I am inclined to think that from the absence of it the lower classes of the people, in some parts of Germany, are in a better situation than those of the same class in England. In Switzerland for the same reason their condition before the late troubles was perhaps universally superior; and in a journey through the duchies of Holstein and Sleswick belonging to Denmark, the houses of the lower classes of people appeared to me to be neater and better, and in general there were fewer indications of poverty and wretchedness among them, than among the same ranks in this country.

Even in Norway, notwithstanding the disadvantage of a severe and uncertain climate, from the little that I saw in a few weeks' residence in the country and the information that I could collect from others, I am inclined to think that the poor are on the average better off than in England. Their houses and clothing are often superior, and though they have no white bread they have much more meat, fish, and milk than our labourers, and I particularly remarked that the farmers' boys were much stouter and healthier-looking lads than those of the same description in England. This degree of happiness, superior to what could be expected from the soil and climate, arises almost exclusively from the degree in which the preventive check to population operates. The establishment of a system of poor-laws, which would destroy this check, would at once sink the lower classes of the people into a state of the most miserable poverty and wretchedness, would diminish their industry and consequently the produce of the land and labour of the country, would weaken the resources of ingenuity in times of scarcity, and ultimately involve the country in all the horrors of continual famines.

If, as in Ireland, Spain, and many countries of the more southern climates, the people are in so degraded a state as to propagate their species without regard to consequences, it matters little whether they have poor-laws or not. Misery in all its various forms must be the predominant check to their increase. Poor-laws indeed will always tend to aggravate the evil by diminishing the general resources of the country, and in such a state of things can exist only for a very short time; but with or without them no stretch of human ingenuity and exertion can rescue the people from the most extreme poverty and wretchedness.

IX. Of the Modes of Correcting the Prevailing Opinions on Population

It is not enough to abolish all the positive institutions which encourage population, but we must endeavour at the same time to correct the prevailing opinions which have the same or perhaps even a more powerful effect. This must necessarily be a work of time, and can only be done by circulating juster notions on these subjects in writings and conversation, and by endeavouring to impress as strongly as possible on the public mind that it is not the duty of man simply to propagate his species but to propagate virtue and happiness, and that if he has not a tolerably fair prospect of doing this he is by no means called upon to leave descendants.

Among the higher ranks of society we have not much reason to apprehend the too great frequency of marriage. Though the circulation of juster notions on this subject might even in this part of the community do much good and prevent many unhappy marriages, yet whether we make particular exertions for this purpose or not we may rest assured that the degree of proper pride and spirit of independence, almost invariably connected with education and a certain rank in life, will secure the operation of the prudential check to marriage to a considerable extent. All that the society can reasonably require of its members is that they should not have families without being able to support them. This may be fairly enjoined as a positive duty. Every restraint beyond this must be considered as a matter of choice and taste; but from what we already know of the habits which prevail among the higher ranks of life we have reason to think that little more is wanted to attain the object required than to award a greater degree of respect and of personal liberty to single women and to place them nearer upon a level with married women,—a change which, independently of any particular purpose in view, the plainest principles of equity seem to demand.

If among the higher classes of society the object of securing the operation of the prudential check to marriage to a sufficient degree appears to be attainable without much difficulty, the obvious mode of proceeding with the lower classes of society, where the point is of the principal importance, is to endeavour to infuse into them a portion of that knowledge and foresight which so much facilitates the attainment of this object in the educated part of the community.

The fairest chance of accomplishing this end would probably be by the establishment of a system of parochial education upon a plan similar to that proposed by Adam Smith [in the *Wealth of Nations*]. In addition to the usual subjects of instruction and those which he has mentioned, I should be disposed to lay considerable stress on the frequent explanation of the real state of the lower classes of society as affected by the principle of population, and their consequent dependence on themselves for the chief part of their happiness or misery. It would be by no means necessary or proper in these explanations to underrate in the smallest degree the desirableness of marriage. It should always be represented as what it really is, a state peculiarly suited to the nature of man, and calculated greatly to advance his happiness and remove the temptations to vice; but like property or any other desirable object its advantages should be shown to be unattainable except under certain conditions. And a strong conviction in a young man of the great desirableness of marriage, with a conviction at the same time that the power of supporting a family was the only condition which would enable him really to enjoy its blessings, would be the most effectual motive imaginable to industry and sobriety before marriage, and would powerfully urge him to save that superfluity of income which single labourers necessarily possess for the accomplishment of a rational and desirable object instead of dissipating it as is now usually done in idleness and vice.

If in the course of time a few of the simplest principles of political economy could be added to the instructions given in these schools the benefit to society would be almost incalculable. In some conversations with labouring men during the late scarcities, I confess that I was to the last degree disheartened at observing their inveterate prejudices on the subject of grain, and I felt very strongly the almost absolute incompatibility of a government really free with such a degree of ignorance. The delusions are of such a nature that if acted upon they must at all events be repressed by force, and it is extremely difficult to give such a power to the government as will be sufficient at all times for this purpose without the risk of its being employed improperly and endangering the liberty of the subject.

We have lavished immense sums on the poor, which we have every reason to think have constantly tended to aggravate their misery. But in their education and in the circulation of those important political truths that most nearly concern them, which are perhaps the only means in our power of really raising their condition, and of making them happier men and more peaceable subjects, we have been miserably deficient.

The principal argument which I have heard advanced against a system of national education in England is that the common people would be put in a capacity to read such works as those of Paine, and that the consequences would probably be fatal to government. But on this subject I agree most cordially with Adam Smith in thinking that an instructed and well-informed people would be much less likely to be led away by inflammatory writings, and much better able to detect the false declamation of interested and ambitious demagogues than an ignorant people. One or two readers in a parish are sufficient to circulate any quantity of sedition; and if these be gained to the democratic side, they will probably have the power of doing much more mischief by selecting the passages best suited to their hearers, and choosing the moments when their oratory is likely to have the most effect than if each individual in the parish had been in a capacity to read and judge of the whole work himself; and at the same time to read and judge of the opposing arguments which we may suppose would also reach him.

But in addition to this a double weight would undoubtedly be added to the observation of Adam Smith if these schools were made the means of instructing the people in the real nature of their situation; if they were taught what is really true, that without an increase of their own industry and prudence no change of government could essentially better their condition; that though they might get rid of some particular grievance, yet in the great point of supporting their families they would be but little or perhaps not at all benefited; that a revolution would not alter in their favour the proportion of the supply of labour to the demand, or the quantity of food to the number of the consumers; and that if the supply of labour were greater than the demand, and the demand for food greater than the supply, they might suffer the utmost severity of want under the freest, the most perfect, and best executed government that the human imagination could conceive.

A knowledge of these truths so obviously tends to promote peace and quietness, to weaken the effect of inflammatory writings, and to prevent all unreasonable and ill-directed opposition to the constituted authorities, that those who would still object to the instruction of the people may fairly be suspected of a wish to encourage their ignorance as a pretext for tyranny, and an opportunity of increasing the power and the influence of the executive government.

Besides explaining the real situation of the lower classes of society as depending principally upon themselves for their happiness or misery, the parochial schools would, by early instruction and the judicious distribution of rewards, have the fairest chance of training up the rising generation in habits of sobriety, industry, independence, and prudence, and in a proper discharge of their religious duties, which would raise them from their present degraded state, and approximate them in some degree to the middle classes of society, whose habits generally speaking are certainly superior.

In most countries, among the lower classes of people, there appears to be something like a standard of wretchedness, a point below which they will not continue to marry and propagate their species. This standard is different in different countries, and is formed by various concurring circumstances of soil, climate, government, degree of knowledge, civilisation, &c. The principal circumstances which contribute to raise it are liberty, security of property, the diffusion of knowledge, and a taste for the conveniences and the comforts of life. Those which contribute principally to lower it are despotism and ignorance.

In an attempt to better the condition of the labouring classes of society our object should be to raise this standard as high as possible by cultivating a spirit of independence, a decent pride, and a taste for cleanliness and comfort. The effect of a good government in increasing the prudential habits and personal respectability of the lower classes of society has already been insisted on; but certainly this effect will always be incomplete without a good system of education; and indeed it may be said that no government can approach to perfection that does not provide for the instruction of the people. The benefits derived from education are among those which may be enjoyed without restriction of numbers; and as it is in the power of governments to confer these benefits, it is undoubtedly their duty to do it.

X. Of the Direction of Our Charity

An important and interesting inquiry yet remains, relating to the mode of directing our private charity, so as not to interfere with the great object in view, of meliorating the condition of the labouring classes of people by preventing the population from pressing too hard against the limits of the means of subsistence.

The emotion which prompts us to relieve our fellow creatures in distress is like all our other natural passions general, and in some degree indiscriminate and blind. Our feelings of compassion may be worked up to a higher pitch by a well-wrought scene in a play or a fictitious tale in a novel than by almost any events in real life; and if among ten petitioners we were to listen only to the first impulses of our feelings without making further inquiries we should undoubtedly give our assistance to the best actor of the party. It is evident therefore that the impulse of benevolence, like the impulses of love, of anger, of ambition, the desire of eating and drinking, or any other of our natural propensities, must be regulated by experience and frequently brought to the test of utility, or it will defeat its intended purpose.

The apparent object of the passion between the sexes is the continuation of the species, and the formation of such an intimate union of views and interests between two persons as will best promote their happiness, and at the same time secure the proper degree of attention to the helplessness of infancy and the education of the rising generation; but if every man were to obey at all times the impulses of nature in the gratification of this passion without regard to consequences, the principal part of these important objects would not be attained, and even the continuation of the species might be defeated by a promiscuous intercourse.

The apparent end of the impulse of benevolence is to draw the whole human race together, but more particularly that part of it which is of our own nation and kindred, in the bonds of brotherly love, and by giving men an interest in the happiness and misery of their fellow creatures, to prompt them as they have power to mitigate the partial evils arising from general laws, and thus to increase the sum of human happiness; but if our benevolence be indiscriminate, and the degree of apparent distress be made the sole measure of our liberality, it is evident that it will be exercised almost exclusively upon common beggars, while modest, unobtrusive merit, struggling with unavoidable difficulties, yet still maintaining some slight appearances of decency and cleanliness, will be totally neglected. We shall raise the worthless above the worthy, we shall encourage indolence and check industry, and in the most marked manner subtract from the sum of human happiness.

Our experience has indeed informed us that the impulse of benevolence is not so strong as the passion between the sexes, and that generally speaking there is much less danger to be apprehended from the indulgence of the former than of the latter: but independently of this experience and of the moral codes founded upon it, we should be as much justified in a general indulgence of the former passion as in following indiscriminately every impulse of our benevolence. They are both natural passions excited by their appropriate objects, and to the gratification of which we are prompted by the pleasurable sensations which accompany them. As animals, or till we know their consequences, our only business is to follow these dictates of nature; but as reasonable beings we are under the strongest obligations to attend to their consequences; and if they be evil to ourselves or others, we may justly consider it as an indication that such a mode of indulging these passions is not suited to our state or conformable to the will of God. As moral agents therefore it is clearly our duty to restrain their indulgence in these particular directions; and by thus carefully examining the consequences of our natural passions, and frequently bringing them to the test of utility, gradually to acquire a habit of gratifying them only in that way which, being unattended with evil, will clearly add to the sum of human happiness and fulfil the apparent purpose of the Creator.

Though utility therefore can never be the immediate excitement to the gratification of any passion, it is the test by which alone we can know, independently of the revealed will of God, whether it ought or ought not to be indulged, and is therefore the surest criterion of moral rules which can be collected from the light of nature. All the moral codes which have inculcated the subjection of the passions to reason have been as I conceive really built upon this foundation, whether the promulgators of them were aware of it or not.

I remind the reader of these truths in order to apply them to the habitual direction of our charity; and if we keep the criterion of utility constantly in view, we may find ample room for the exercise of our benevolence without interfering with the great purpose which we have to accomplish.

One of the most valuable parts of charity is its effect upon the giver. It is more blessed to give than to receive. Supposing it to be allowed that the exercise of our benevolence in acts of charity is not upon the whole really beneficial to the poor, yet we could never sanction any endeavour to extinguish an impulse, the proper gratification of which has so evident a tendency to purify and exalt the human mind. But it is particularly satisfactory and pleasing to find that the mode of exercising our charity, which when brought to the test of utility will appear to be most beneficial to the poor, is precisely that which will have the best and most improving effect on the mind of the donor.

The quality of charity, like that of mercy,

> *Is not strained;*
> *It droppeth as the gentle rain from Heav'n*
> *Upon the earth beneath.*

The immense sums distributed to the poor in this country by the parochial laws are improperly called charity. They want its most distinguishing attribute; and as might be expected from an attempt to force that which loses its essence the moment it ceases to be voluntary, their effects upon those from whom they are collected are as prejudicial as on those to whom they are distributed. On the side of the receivers of this miscalled charity, instead of real relief, we find accumulated distress and more extended poverty; on the side of the givers, instead of pleasurable sensations, unceasing discontent and irritation.

In the great charitable institutions supported by voluntary contributions, some of which are certainly of a prejudicial tendency, the subscriptions I am inclined to fear are sometimes given grudgingly, and rather because they are expected by the world from certain stations and certain fortunes than because they are prompted by motives of genuine benevolence; and as the greater part of the subscribers do not interest themselves in the management of the funds or in the fate of the particular objects relieved, it is not to be expected that this kind of charity should have any strikingly beneficial influence on the minds of the majority who exercise it.

Even in the relief of common beggars we shall find that we are often as much influenced by the desire of getting rid of the importunities of a disgusting object as by the pleasure of relieving it. We wish that it had not fallen in our way rather than rejoice in the opportunity given us of assisting a fellow creature. We feel a painful emotion at the sight of so much apparent misery, but the pittance we give does not relieve it. We know that it is totally inadequate to produce any essential effect. We know besides that we shall be addressed in the same manner at the corner of the next street, and we know that we are liable to the grossest impositions. We hurry therefore sometimes by such objects, and shut our ears to their importunate demands. We give no more than we can help giving without doing actual violence to our feelings. Our charity is in some degree forced, and like forced charity it leaves no satisfactory impression on the mind, and cannot therefore have any very beneficial and improving effect on the heart and affections.

But it is far otherwise with that voluntary and active charity which makes itself acquainted with the objects which it relieves; which seems to feel and to be proud of the bond that unites the rich with the poor; which enters into their houses, informs itself not only of their wants but of their habits and dispositions, checks the hopes of clamorous and obtrusive poverty with no other recommendation but rags, and encourages with adequate relief the silent and retiring sufferer labouring under unmerited difficulties. This mode of exercising our charity presents a very different picture from that of any other; and its contrast with the common mode of parish relief cannot be better described than in the words of Mr. [Joseph] Townsend in the conclusion of his admirable *Dissertation on the Poor-laws:*—"Nothing in nature can be more disgusting than a parish pay table, attendant upon which, in the same objects of misery, are too often found combined snuff, gin, rags, vermin, insolence, and abusive language; nor in nature can anything be more beautiful than the mild complacency of benevolence hastening to the humble cottage to relieve the wants of industry and virtue, to feed the hungry, to clothe the naked, and to soothe the sorrows of the widow with her tender orphans; nothing can be more pleasing unless it be their sparkling eyes, their bursting tears, and their uplifted hands, the artless expressions of unfeigned gratitude for unexpected favours. Such scenes will frequently occur whenever men shall have power to dispose of their own property."

I conceive it to be almost impossible that any person could be much engaged in such scenes without daily making advances in virtue. No exercise of our affections can have a more evident tendency to purify and exalt the human mind. It is almost exclusively this species of charity that blesseth him that gives; and in a general view it is almost exclusively this species of charity which blesseth him that takes; at least it may be asserted that there are but few other modes of exercising our charity, in which large sums can be distributed, without a greater chance of producing evil than good.

The discretionary power of giving or withholding relief, which is to a certain extent vested in parish officers and justices, is of a very different nature and will have a very different effect from the discrimination which may be exercised by voluntary charity. Every man in this country under certain circumstances is entitled by law to parish assistance; and unless his disqualification is clearly proved, has a right to complain if it be withheld. The inquiries necessary to settle this point, and the extent of the relief to be granted, too often produce evasion and lying on the part of the petitioner, and afford an opening to partiality and oppression in the overseer. If the proposed relief be given, it is of course received with unthankfulness; and if it be denied the party generally thinks himself severely aggrieved and feels resentment and indignation at his treatment.

In the distribution of voluntary charity nothing of this kind can take place. The person who receives it is made the proper subject of the pleasurable sensation of gratitude; and those who do not receive it cannot possibly conceive themselves in the slightest degree injured. Every man has a right to do what he will with his own, and cannot in justice be called upon to render a reason why he gives in the one case and abstains from it in the other. This kind of despotic power, essential to voluntary charity, gives the greatest facility to the selection of worthy objects of relief without being accompanied by any ill consequences; and has further a most beneficial effect from the degree of uncertainty which must necessarily be attached to it. It is in the highest degree important to the general happiness of the poor that no man should look to charity as a fund on which he may confidently depend. He should be taught that his own exertions, his own industry and foresight, are his only just grounds of dependence; that if these fail assistance in his distresses can only be the subject of rational hope; and that even the foundation of this hope will depend in a considerable degree on his own good conduct, and the consciousness that he has not involved himself in these difficulties by his indolence or imprudence.

That in the distribution of our charity we are under a strong moral obligation to inculcate this lesson on the poor by a proper discrimination is a truth of which I cannot feel a doubt. If all could be completely relieved, and poverty banished from the country, even at the expense of three fourths of the fortunes of the rich, I would be the last person to say a single syllable against relieving all, and making the degree of distress alone the measure of our bounty. But as experience has proved, I believe without a single exception, that poverty and misery have always increased in proportion to the quantity of indiscriminate charity, are we not bound to infer, reasoning as we usually do from the laws of nature, that it is an intimation that such a mode of distribution is not the proper office of benevolence?

The laws of nature say with St. Paul, "If a man will not work, neither shall he eat." They also say that he is not rashly to trust to Providence. They appear indeed to be constant and uniform for the express purpose of telling him what he is to trust to, and that if he marry without a reasonable prospect of supporting a family he must expect to suffer want. These intimations appear from the constitution of human nature to be absolutely necessary and to have a strikingly beneficial tendency. If in the direction either of our public or our private charity we say that though a man will not work yet he shall eat; and though he marry without being able to support a family, yet his family shall be supported; it is evident that we do not merely endeavour to mitigate the partial evils arising from general laws, but *regularly* and *systematically* to counteract the obviously beneficial effects of these general laws themselves. And we cannot easily conceive that the Deity should implant any passion in the human breast for such a purpose.

In the great course of human events, the best-founded expectations will sometimes be disappointed; and industry, prudence, and virtue not only fail of their just reward but be involved in unmerited calamities. Those who are thus suffering in spite of the best-directed endeavours to avoid it, and from causes which they could not be expected to foresee, are the genuine objects of charity. In relieving these we exercise the appropriate office of benevolence, that of mitigating the partial evils arising from general laws; and in this direction of our charity therefore we need not apprehend any ill consequences. Such objects ought to be relieved, according to our means, liberally and adequately, even though the worthless were in much more severe distress.

When indeed this first claim on our benevolence was satisfied, we might then turn our attention to the idle and improvident; but the interests of human happiness most clearly require that the relief which we afford them should not be abundant. We may perhaps take upon ourselves with great caution to mitigate the punishments which they are suffering from the laws of nature, but on no account to remove them entirely. They are deservedly at the bottom in the scale of society; and if we raise them from this situation, we not only palpably defeat the end of benevolence, but commit a most glaring injustice to those who are above them. They should on no account be enabled to command so much of the necessaries of life as can be obtained by the wages of common labour.

It is evident that these reasonings do not apply to those cases of urgent distress arising from disastrous accidents, unconnected with habits of indolence and improvidence. If a man break a leg or an arm, we are not to stop to inquire into his moral character before we lend him our assistance; but in this case we are perfectly consistent, and the touchstone of utility completely justifies our conduct. By affording the most indiscriminate assistance in this way we are in little danger of encouraging people to break their arms and legs. According to the touchstone of utility, the high approbation which Christ gave to the conduct of the good Samaritan, who followed the immediate impulse of his benevolence in relieving a stranger in the urgent distress of an accident, does not in the smallest degree contradict the expression of St. Paul, "If a man will not work, neither shall he eat."

We are not, however, in any case to lose a present opportunity of doing good from the mere supposition that we may meet possibly with a worthier object. In all doubtful cases it may safely be laid down as our duty to follow the natural impulse of our benevolence; but when in fulfilling our obligations as reasonable beings to attend to the consequences of our actions, we have from our own experience and that of others drawn the conclusion that the exercise of our benevolence in one mode is prejudicial and in another is beneficial in its effects, we are certainly bound as moral agents to check our natural propensities in the one direction, and to encourage them and acquire the habits of exercising them in the other.

XI. Of Our Rational Expectations Respecting the Future Improvement of Society

In taking a general and concluding view of our rational expectations respecting the mitigation of the evils arising from the principle of population, it may be observed that though the increase of population in a geometrical ratio be incontrovertible, and the period of doubling when unchecked has been uniformly stated in this work rather below than above the truth; yet there are some natural consequences of the progress of society and civilisation, which necessarily repress its full effects. These are more particularly great towns and manufactures, in which we can scarcely hope, and certainly not expect to see any very material change. It is undoubtedly our duty and in every point of view highly desirable, to make towns and manufacturing employments as little injurious as possible to the duration of human life; but after all our efforts it is probable that they will always remain less healthy than country situations and country employments, and consequently operating as positive checks will diminish in some degree the necessity of the preventive check.

In every old state it is observed that a considerable number of grown-up people remain for a time unmarried. The duty of practising the common and acknowledged rules of morality during this period has never been controverted in theory, however it may have been opposed in practice. This branch of the duty of moral restraint has scarcely been touched by the reasonings of this work. It rests on the same foundation as before, neither stronger nor weaker. And knowing how incompletely this duty has hitherto been fulfilled, it would certainly be visionary to expect that in future it would be completely fulfilled.

The part which has been affected by the reasonings of this work is not therefore that which relates to our conduct during the period of celibacy, but to the duty of extending this period till we have a prospect of being able to maintain our children. And it is by no means visionary to indulge a hope of some favourable change in this respect; because it is found by experience that the prevalence of this kind of prudential restraint is extremely different in different countries, and in the same countries at different periods.

It cannot be doubted that throughout Europe in general, and most particularly in the northern states, a decided change has taken place in the operation of prudential restraint, since the prevalence of those warlike and enterprising habits which destroyed so many people. In later times the gradual diminution and almost total extinction of the plagues, which so frequently visited Europe in the seventeenth and beginning of the eighteenth centuries, produced a change of the same kind. And in this country it is not to be doubted that the proportion of marriages has become smaller since the improvement of our towns, the less frequent returns of epidemics, and the adoption of habits of greater cleanliness. During the late scarcities it appears that the number of marriages diminished; and the same motives which prevented many people from marrying during such a period, would operate precisely in the same way, if in future the additional number of children reared to manhood from the introduction of the cowpox, were to be such as to crowd all employments, lower the price of labour, and make it more difficult to support a family.

Universally, the practice of mankind on the subject of marriage has been much superior to their theories; and however frequent may have been the declamations on the duty of entering into this state, and the advantage of early unions to prevent vice, each individual has practically found it necessary to consider of the means of supporting a family before he ventured to take so important a step. That great *vis medicatrix reipublicæ,* the desire of bettering our condition, and the fear of making it worse, has been constantly in action, and has been constantly directing people into the right road in spite of all the declamations which tended to lead them aside. Owing to this powerful spring of health in every state, which is nothing more than an inference from the general course of the laws of nature irresistibly forced on each man's attention, the prudential check to marriage has increased in Europe; and it cannot be unreasonable to conclude that it will still make further advances. If this take place without any marked and decided increase of a vicious intercourse with the sex, the happiness of society will evidently be promoted by it; and with regard to the danger of such increase, it is consolatory to remark that those countries in Europe where marriages are the latest or least frequent, are by no means particularly distinguished by vices of this kind. It has appeared that Norway, Switzerland, England, and Scotland, are above all the rest in the prevalence of the preventive check; and though I do not mean to insist particularly on the virtuous habits of these countries, yet I think that no person would select them as the countries most marked for profligacy of manners. Indeed from the little that I know of the continent, I should have been inclined to select them as most distinguished for contrary habits, and as rather above than below their neighbours in the chastity of their women, and consequently in the virtuous habits of their men. Experience therefore seems to teach us that it is possible for moral and physical causes to counteract the effects that might at first be expected from an increase of the check to marriage; but allowing all the weight to these effects which is in any degree probable, it may be safely asserted that the diminution of the vices arising from indigence would fully counterbalance them; and that all the advantages of diminished mortality and superior comforts, which would certainly result from an increase of the preventive check, may be placed entirely on the side of the gains to the cause of happiness and virtue.

It is less the object of the present work to propose new plans of improving society than to inculcate the necessity of resting contented with that mode of improvement which already has in part been enacted upon as dictated by the course of nature, and of not obstructing the advances which would otherwise be made in this way.

It would be undoubtedly highly advantageous that all our positive institutions, and the whole tenor of our conduct to the poor, should be such as actively to co-operate with that lesson of prudence inculcated by the common course of human events; and if we take upon ourselves sometimes to mitigate the natural punishments of imprudence, that we could balance it by increasing the rewards of an opposite conduct. But much would be done if merely the institutions which directly tend to encourage marriage were gradually changed and we ceased to circulate opinions and inculcate doctrines which positively counteract the lessons of nature.

The limited good which it is sometimes in our power to effect is often lost by attempting too much, and by making the adoption of some particular plan essentially necessary even to a partial degree of success. In the practical application of the reasonings of this work I hope that I have avoided this error. I wish to press on the recollection of the reader that though I may have given some new views of old facts, and may have indulged in the contemplation of a considerable degree of *possible* improvement that I might not shut out that prime cheerer hope, yet in my expectations of probable improvement and in suggesting the means of accomplishing it I have been very cautious. The gradual abolition of the poor-laws has already often been proposed in consequence of the practical evils which have been found to flow from them, and the danger of their becoming a weight absolutely intolerable on the landed property of the kingdom. The establishment of a more extensive system of national education has neither the advantage of novelty with some nor its disadvantages with others to recommend it. The practical good effects of education have long been experienced in Scotland, and almost every person who has been placed in a situation to judge has given his testimony that education appears to have a considerable effect in the prevention of crimes, and the promotion of industry, morality, and regular conduct. Yet these are the only plans which have been offered, and though the adoption of them in the modes suggested would very powerfully contribute to forward the object of this work and better the condition of the poor, yet if nothing be done in this way I shall not absolutely despair of some partial good resulting from the general effects of the reasoning.

If the principles which I have endeavoured to establish be false I most sincerely hope to see them completely refuted; but if they be true, the subject is so important and interests the question of human happiness so nearly, that it is impossible they should not in time be more fully known and more generally circulated, whether any particular efforts be made for the purpose or not.

Among the higher and middle classes of society the effect of this knowledge will I hope be to direct without relaxing their efforts in bettering the condition of the poor; to show them what they can and what they cannot do; and that although much may be done by advice and instruction, by encouraging habits of prudence and cleanliness, by discriminate charity, and by any mode of bettering the present condition of the poor which is followed by an increase of the preventive check; yet that without this last effect all the former efforts would be futile; and that in any old and well-peopled state to assist the poor in such a manner as to enable them to marry as early as they please and rear up large families, is a physical impossibility. This knowledge, by tending to prevent the rich from destroying the good effects of their own exertions and wasting their efforts in a direction where success is unattainable, would confine their attention to the proper objects, and thus enable them to do more good.

Among the poor themselves its effects would be still more important. That the principal and most permanent cause of poverty has little or no *direct* relation to forms of government or the unequal division of property; and that as the rich do not in reality possess the *power* of finding employment and maintenance for the poor, the poor cannot in the nature of things possess the *right* to demand them, are important truths flowing from the principle of population which when properly explained would by no means be above the most ordinary comprehensions. And it is evident that every man in the lower classes of society who became acquainted with these truths would be disposed to bear the distresses in which he might be involved with more patience; would feel less discontent and irritation at the government and the higher classes of society on account of his poverty; would be on all occasions less disposed to insubordination and turbulence; and if he received assistance either from any public institution or from the hand of private charity, he would receive it with more thankfulness, and more justly appreciate its value.

If these truths were by degrees more generally known (which in the course of time does not seem to be improbable from the natural effects of the mutual interchange of opinions), the lower classes of people as a body would become more peaceable and orderly, would be less inclined to tumultuous proceedings in seasons of scarcity, and would at all times be less influenced by inflammatory and seditious publications from knowing how little the price of labour and the means of supporting a family depend upon a revolution. The mere knowledge of these truths, even if they did not operate sufficiently to produce any marked change in the prudential habits of the poor with regard to marriage, would still have a most beneficial effect on their conduct in a political light; and undoubtedly one of the most valuable of these effects would be the power that would result to the higher and middle classes of society of gradually improving their governments without the apprehension of those revolutionary excesses, the fear of which at present threatens to deprive Europe even of that degree of liberty which she had before experienced to be practicable, and the salutary effects of which she had long enjoyed.

From a review of the state of society in former periods compared with the present, I should certainly say that the evils resulting from the principle of population have rather diminished than increased, even under the disadvantage of an almost total ignorance of the real cause. And if we can indulge the hope that this ignorance will be gradually dissipated, it does not seem unreasonable to expect that they will be still further diminished. The increase of absolute population, which will of course take place, will evidently tend but little to weaken this expectation, as everything depends upon the relative proportion between population and food, and not on the absolute number of people. In the former part of this work it appeared that the countries which possessed the fewest people often suffered the most from the effects of the principle of population; and it can scarcely be doubted that, taking Europe throughout, fewer famines and fewer diseases arising from want have prevailed in the last century than in those which preceded it.

On the whole, therefore, though our future prospects respecting the mitigation of the evils arising from the principle of population may not be so bright as we could wish, yet they are far from being entirely disheartening, and by no means preclude that gradual and progressive improvement in human society, which before the late wild speculations on this subject was the object of rational expectation. To the laws of property and marriage, and to the apparently narrow principle of self-interest which prompts each individual to exert himself in bettering his condition, we are indebted for all the noblest exertions of human genius, for everything that distinguishes the civilised from the savage state. A strict inquiry into the principle of population obliges us to conclude that we shall never be able to throw down the ladder by which we have risen to this eminence; but it by no means proves that we may not rise higher by the same means. The structure of society in its great features will probably always remain unchanged. We have every reason to believe that it will always consist of a class of proprietors and a class of labourers; but the condition of each and the proportion which they bear to each other may be so altered as greatly to improve the harmony and beauty of the whole. It would indeed be a melancholy reflection that, while the views of physical science are daily enlarging so as scarcely to be bounded by the most distant horizon, the science of moral and political philosophy should be confined within such narrow limits, or at best be so feeble in its influence as to be unable to counteract the obstacles to human happiness arising from a single cause. But however formidable these obstacles may have appeared in some parts of this work, it is hoped that the general result of the inquiry is such as not to make us give up the improvement of human society in despair. The partial good which seems to be attainable is worthy of all our exertions, is sufficient to direct our efforts and animate our prospects. And although we cannot expect that the virtue and happiness of mankind will keep pace with the brilliant career of physical discovery; yet if we are not wanting to ourselves, we may confidently indulge the hope that to no unimportant extent they will be influenced by its progress and will partake in its success.

PRINCIPLES OF POLITICAL ECONOMY AND TAXATION

by

DAVID RICARDO

CONTENTS

Principles of Political Economy and Taxation

DAVID RICARDO

1772–1823

DAVID RICARDO, leading exponent of the classical school of English economists and one of the keenest minds that ever worked on economic problems, was born in London in 1772. His father was a prosperous Dutch Jew, a member of the Stock Exchange. The son was sent to school for a while in Holland, but he never went to college and he entered his father's business in London at the age of fourteen. In 1793 his marriage to a non-Jew, Priscilla Anne Wilkinson, led to alienation from his father. He continued to operate on the Stock Exchange and was so successful that in a few years he was a rich man, able to devote himself to scientific pursuits. At first his interests lay in the direction of geology, but a chance perusal of Adam Smith's *Wealth of Nations* turned his attention to economics.

Ricardo's earliest contribution to economic theory took the form of an unsigned paper published in 1809 in the London *Morning Chronicle.* It dealt with what was then a burning issue, the relation of gold to paper money, and was expanded into a pamphlet entitled *The High Price of Bullion a Proof of the Depreciation of Bank-notes.* This pamphlet indirectly led to the appointment of a Bullion Committee in the House of Commons, and brought its author into touch with Malthus, James Mill, J. R. MacCulloch, and other well-known economists.

Later, Ricardo took a prominent part in the Corn Law controversy. His *Essay on the Influence of a Low Price of Corn on the Profits of Stock,* published in 1815, leaned far in the direction of free trade and opposed Malthus's protectionist views.

In 1819 Ricardo, who had by this time become a landed proprietor, entered the House of Commons as a member for a small Irish borough and took part in debates on parliamentary issues. He opposed the Factory Acts; he urged the repeal of the laws against combinations of labor; and his arguments in favor of free trade influenced legislation that led to the repeal of the Corn Laws.

Ricardo has been called "the Newton of economics," an economist's economist. His magnum opus, *The Principles of Political Economy and Taxation,* was published in 1817. This work is informed by an individualist spirit. Unlike Adam Smith, who preceded him, and John Stuart Mill, who followed him, Ricardo confines himself, in the main, to strict economic analysis. He assumes that under a system of perfectly free commerce men will continue to be motivated by self-interest. The status quo, rather than the past or the future, holds his attention. The workingman he regards as merely an instrument of the capitalist.

In the preface to his *Principles* Ricardo states that the main problem of political economy is to determine the laws which regulate the distribution of the produce of the earth. This distribution, he says, affects three classes of the community—namely, the proprietor of the land, the owner of the stock or capital necessary for its cultivation, and the laborers by whose industry it is cultivated; but "in different stages of society the proportions of the whole produce of the earth which will be allotted to each of these classes, under the names of rent, profit, and wages, will be essentially different."

Following a preliminary chapter on value, or "embodied labor," Ricardo propounds the differential theory of rent. John Stuart Mill called this one of the cardinal doctrines of political economy. He added: "It is a theorem which may be called the *pons asinorum* of political economy, for there are, I am inclined to think, few persons who have refused their assent to it except from not having thoroughly understood it."

Implicit in the Ricardian theory of rent are the Malthusian concept that population tends to outstrip the means of subsistence, and the law of diminishing returns. Ricardo held that as a country grows and its population increases, society is forced to resort to poorer and poorer soils to obtain its food supply.

In a chapter on wages Ricardo formulates what Ferdinand Lassalle, German socialist leader, was later to call the iron law of wages. Ricardo says: "The natural price of labour is that price which is necessary to enable the labourers, one with another, to subsist and to perpetuate their race, without either increase or diminution."

As for profits, Ricardo, in a closely reasoned chapter, traces a downward trend. He calls them in one place "the leavings of wages." The capitalist will lose and the landlord will gain, he thinks, as time passes. He even goes so far as to speculate regarding the arrival of a period during which "the very low rate of profits will have arrested all accumulation, and almost the whole produce of the country, after paying the labourers, will be the property of the owners of land and the receivers of tithes and taxes."

It is strange, indeed, that the writings of this essentially conservative economist should have helped to buttress the contentions of Karl Marx and Henry George, two of the strongest radical thinkers of modern times. Karl Marx found in Ricardo's theory of value as "embodied labor" a foundation for his own doctrine of surplus value. Henry George's plea for a single tax on land values was based in part on Ricardo's differential theory of rent. It needs to be pointed out that Ricardo conceived of embodied labor not as the cause but as the measure of value. "So too, in the matter of economic rent," says Jacob H. Hollander, of Johns Hopkins University, "Ricardo insisted that with the progress of society capital tended to increase, and in consequence of limitation upon the productive capacity of the soil profits tended to fall and rents to rise; but he maintained that these phenomena, far from betokening any social injustice, were 'the most unequivocal truths of wealth and prosperity.' "

Apart from the impetus that Ricardo gave to the principle of free trade, his most influential contributions to economic theory and practice were probably in the fields of currency and taxation. The "economical and secure currency" which he advocated underlies modern monetary and banking systems, and his emphasis on the "ultimate incidence," rather than the immediate productivity, of taxation has furnished a generally accepted criterion for judging the value of fiscal proposals.

PRINCIPLES OF POLITICAL ECONOMY AND TAXATION

Preface

THE PRODUCE of the earth—all that is derived from its surface by the united application of labour, machinery, and capital, is divided among three classes of the community, namely, the proprietor of the land, the owner of the stock or capital necessary for its cultivation, and the labourers by whose industry it is cultivated.

But in different stages of society, the proportions of the whole produce of the earth which will be allotted to each of these classes, under the names of rent, profit, and wages, will be essentially different; depending mainly on the actual fertility of the soil, on the accumulation of capital and population, and on the skill, ingenuity, and instruments employed in agriculture.

To determine the laws which regulate this distribution is the principal problem in Political Economy: much as the science has been improved by the writings of Turgot, Stuart, Smith, Say, Sismondi, and others, they afford very little satisfactory information respecting the natural course of rent, profit, and wages.

In 1815, Mr. Malthus, in his *Inquiry into the Nature and Progress of Rent,* and [Sir Edward West] a Fellow of University College, Oxford, in his *Essay on the Application of Capital to Land,* presented to the world, nearly at the same moment, the true doctrine of rent; without a knowledge of which it is impossible to understand the effect of the progress of wealth on profits and wages, or to trace satisfactorily the influence of taxation on different classes of the community; particularly when the commodities taxed are the productions immediately derived from the surface of the earth. Adam Smith, and the other able writers to whom I have alluded, not having viewed correctly the principles of rent, have, it appears to me, overlooked many important truths, which can only be discovered after the subject of rent is thoroughly understood.

To supply this deficiency, abilities are required of a far superior cast to any possessed by the writer of the following pages; yet, after having given to this subject his best consideration—after the aid which he has derived from the works of the above-mentioned eminent writers—and after the valuable experience which a few late years, abounding in facts, have yielded to the present generation—it will not, he trusts, be deemed presumptuous in him to state his opinions on the laws of profits and wages, and on the operation of taxes. If the principles which he deems correct should be found to be so, it will be for others, more able than himself, to trace them to all their important consequences.

The writer, in combating received opinions, has found it necessary to advert more particularly to those passages in the writings of Adam Smith from which he sees reason to differ; but he hopes it will not, on that account, be suspected that he does not, in common with all those who acknowledge the importance of the science of Political Economy, participate in the admiration which the profound work of this celebrated author so justly excites.

The same remark may be applied to the excellent works of M. [Jean Baptiste] Say, who not only was the first, or among the first, of continental writers who justly appreciated and applied the principles of Smith, and who has done more than all other continental writers taken together to recommend the principles of that enlightened and beneficial system to the nations of Europe; but who has succeeded in placing the science in a more logical and more instructive order, and has enriched it by several discussions, original, accurate, and profound. The respect, however, which the author entertains for the writings of this gentleman has not prevented him from commenting, with that freedom which he thinks the interests of science require, on such passages of the *Economie Politique* as appeared at variance with his own ideas.

I. ON VALUE

1. The value of a commodity, or the quantity of any other commodity for which it will exchange, depends on the relative quantity of labour which is necessary for its production, and not on the greater or less compensation which is paid for that labour

It has been observed by Adam Smith that "the word Value has two different meanings, and sometimes expresses the utility of some particular object, and sometimes the power of purchasing other goods which the possession of that object conveys. The one may be called *value in use;* the other *value in exchange*. The things," he continues, "which have the greatest value in use, have frequently little or no value in exchange; and, on the contrary, those which have the greatest value in exchange, have little or no value in use." Water and air are abundantly useful; they are indeed indispensable to existence, yet, under ordinary circumstances, nothing can be obtained in exchange for them. Gold, on the contrary, though of little use compared with air or water, will exchange for a great quantity of other goods.

Utility then is not the measure of exchangeable value, although it is absolutely essential to it. If a commodity were in no way useful—in other words, if it could in no way contribute to our gratification—it would be destitute of exchangeable value, however scarce it might be, or whatever quantity of labour might be necessary to procure it.

Possessing utility, commodities derive their exchangeable value from two sources: from their scarcity, and from the quantity of labour required to obtain them.

There are some commodities, the value of which is determined by their scarcity alone. No labour can increase the quantity of such goods, and therefore their value cannot be lowered by an increased supply. Some rare statues and pictures, scarce books and coins, wines of a peculiar quality, which can be made only from grapes grown on a particular soil, of which there is a very limited quantity, are all of this description. Their value is wholly independent of the quantity of labour originally necessary to produce them, and varies with the varying wealth and inclinations of those who are desirous to possess them.

These commodities, however, form a very small part of the mass of commodities daily exchanged in the market. By far the greatest part of those goods which are the objects of desire are procured by labour; and they may be multiplied, not in one country alone, but in many, almost without any assignable limit, if we are disposed to bestow the labour necessary to obtain them.

In speaking, then, of commodities, of their exchangeable value, and of the laws which regulate their relative prices, we mean always such commodities only as can be increased in quantity by the exertion of human industry, and on the production of which competition operates without restraint.

In the early stages of society, the exchangeable value of these commodities, or the rule which determines how much of one shall be given in exchange for another, depends almost exclusively on the comparative quantity of labour expended on each.

"The real price of everything," says Adam Smith, "what everything really costs to the man who wants to acquire it, is the toil and trouble of acquiring it. What everything is really worth to the man who has acquired it, and who wants to dispose of it, or exchange it for something else, is the toil and trouble which it can save to himself, and which it can impose upon other people." "Labour was the first price—the original purchase-money that was paid for all things." Again, "in that early and rude state of society which precedes both the accumulation of stock and the appropriation of land, the proportion between the quantities of labour necessary for acquiring different objects seems to be the only circumstance which can afford any rule for exchanging them for one another. If, among a nation of hunters, for example, it usually cost twice the labour to kill a beaver which it does to kill a deer, one beaver should naturally exchange for, or be worth, two deer. It is natural that what is usually the produce of two days' or two hours' labour should be worth double of what is usually the produce of one day's or one hour's labour."

That this is really the foundation of the exchangeable value of all things, excepting those which cannot be increased by human industry, is a doctrine of the utmost importance in political economy; for from no source do so many errors, and so much difference of opinion in that science proceed, as from the vague ideas which are attached to the word value.

If the quantity of labour realised in commodities regulate their exchangeable value, every increase of the quantity of labour must augment the value of that commodity on which it is exercised, as every diminution must lower it.

Adam Smith, who so accurately defined the original source of exchangeable value, and who was bound in consistency to maintain that all things became more or less valuable in proportion as more or less labour was bestowed on their production, has himself erected another standard measure of value, and speaks of things being more or less valuable in proportion as they will exchange for more or less of this standard measure. Sometimes he speaks of corn, at other times of labour, as a standard measure; not the quantity of labour bestowed on the production of any object, but the quantity which it can command in the market: as if these were two equivalent expressions, and as if, because a man's labour had become doubly efficient, and he could therefore produce twice the quantity of a commodity, he would necessarily receive twice the former quantity in exchange for it.

If this indeed were true, if the reward of the labourer were always in proportion to what he produced, the quantity of labour bestowed on a commodity, and the quantity of labour which that commodity would purchase, would be equal, and either might accurately measure the variations of other things; but they are not equal; the first is under many circumstances an invariable standard, indicating correctly the variations of other things; the latter is subject to as many fluctuations as the commodities compared with it. Adam Smith, after most ably showing the insufficiency of a variable medium, such as gold and silver, for the purpose of determining the varying value of other things, has himself, by fixing on corn or labour, chosen a medium no less variable.

Gold and silver are no doubt subject to fluctuations from the discovery of new and more abundant mines; but such discoveries are rare, and their effects, though powerful, are limited to periods of comparatively short duration. They are subject also to fluctuation from improvements in the skill and machinery with which the mines may be worked; as in consequence of such improvements a greater quantity may be obtained with the same labour. They are further subject to fluctuation from the decreasing produce of the mines, after they have yielded a supply to the world for a succession of ages. But from which of these sources of fluctuation is corn exempted? Does not that also vary, on one hand, from improvements in agriculture, from improved machinery and implements used in husbandry, as well as from the discovery of new tracts of fertile land, which in other countries may be taken into cultivation, and which will affect the value of corn in every market where importation is free? Is it not on the other hand subject to be enhanced in value from prohibitions of importation, from increasing population and wealth, and the greater difficulty of obtaining the increased supplies, on account of the additional quantity of labour which the cultivation of inferior land requires? Is not the value of labour equally variable; being not only affected, as all other things are, by the proportion between the supply and demand, which uniformly varies with every change in the condition of the community, but also by the varying price of food and other necessaries, on which the wages of labour are expended?

In the same country double the quantity of labour may be required to produce a given quantity of food and necessaries at one time that may be necessary at another and a distant time; yet the labourer's reward may possibly be very little diminished. If the labourer's wages at the former period were a certain quantity of food and necessaries, he probably could not have subsisted if that quantity had been reduced. Food and necessaries in this case will have risen 100 per cent. if estimated by the *quantity* of labour necessary to their production, while they will scarcely have increased in value if measured by the quantity of labour for which they will *exchange.*

The same remark may be made respecting two or more countries. In America and Poland, on the land last taken into cultivation, a year's labour of any given number of men will produce much more corn than on land similarly circumstanced in England. Now, supposing all other necessaries to be equally cheap in those three countries, would it not be a great mistake to conclude that the quantity of corn awarded to the labourer would in each country be in proportion to the facility of production?

If the shoes and clothing of the labourer could, by improvements in machinery, be produced by one fourth of the labour now necessary to their production, they would probably fall 75 per cent.; but so far is it from being true that the labourer would thereby be enabled permanently to consume four coats, or four pair of shoes, instead of one, that it is probable his wages would in no long time be adjusted by the effects of competition, and the stimulus to population, to the new value of the necessaries on which they were expended. If these improvements extended to all the objects of the labourer's consumption, we should find him probably, at the end of a very few years, in possession of only a small, if any, addition to his enjoyments, although the exchangeable value of those commodities, compared with any other commodity, in the manufacture of which no such improvement were made, had sustained a very considerable reduction; and though they were the produce of a very considerably diminished quantity of labour.

It cannot then be correct to say with Adam Smith, "that as labour may sometimes *purchase* a greater and sometimes a smaller quantity of goods, it is their value which varies, not that of the labour which purchases them"; and therefore, "that labour, *alone never varying in its own value,* is alone the ultimate and real standard by which the value of all commodities can at all times and places be estimated and compared";—but it is correct to say, as Adam Smith had previously said, "that the proportion between the quantities of labour necessary for acquiring different objects seems to be the only circumstance which can afford any rule for exchanging them for one another"; or in other words that it is the comparative quantity of commodities which labour will produce that determines their present or past relative value, and not the comparative quantities of commodities which are given to the labourer in exchange for his labour.

Two commodities vary in relative value, and we wish to know in which the variation has really taken place. If we compare the present value of one with shoes, stockings, hats, iron, sugar, and all other commodities, we find that it will exchange for precisely the same quantity of all these things as before. If we compare the other with the same commodities, we find it has varied with respect to them all: we may then with great probability infer that the variation has been in this commodity, and not in the commodities with which we have compared it. If on examining still more particularly into all the circumstances connected with the production of these various commodities, we find that precisely the same quantity of labour and capital are necessary to the production of the shoes, stockings, hats, iron, sugar, etc.; but that the same quantity as before is not necessary to produce the single commodity whose relative value is altered, probability is changed into certainty, and we are sure that the variation is in the single commodity: we then discover also the cause of its variation.

If I found that an ounce of gold would exchange for a less quantity of all the commodities above enumerated and many others; and if, moreover, I found that by the discovery of a new and more fertile mine, or by the employment of machinery to great advantage, a given quantity of gold could be obtained with a less quantity of labour, I should be justified in saying that the cause of the alteration in the value of gold relatively to other commodities was the greater facility of its production, or the smaller quantity of labour necessary to obtain it. In like manner, if labour fell very considerably in value, relatively to all other things, and if I found that its fall was in consequence of an abundant supply, encouraged by the great facility with which corn, and the other necessaries of the labourer, were produced, it would, I apprehend, be correct for me to say that corn and necessaries had fallen in value in consequence of less quantity of labour being necessary to produce them, and that this facility of providing for the support of the labourer had been followed by a fall in the value of labour. No, say Adam Smith and Mr. Malthus, in the case of the gold you were correct in calling its variation a fall of its value, because corn and labour had not then varied; and as gold would command a less quantity of them, as well as of all other things, than before, it was correct to say that all things had remained stationary and that gold only had varied; but when corn and labour fall, things which we have selected to be our standard measure of value, notwithstanding all the variations to which we acknowledge they are subject, it would be highly improper to say so; the correct language will be to say that corn and labour have remained stationary, and all other things have risen in value.

Now it is against this language that I protest. I find that precisely, as in the case of the gold, the cause of the variation between corn and other things is the smaller quantity of labour necessary to produce it, and therefore, by all just reasoning, I am bound to call the variation of corn and labour a fall in their value, and not a rise in the value of the things with which they are compared. If I have to hire a labourer for a week, and instead of ten shillings I pay him eight, no variation having taken place in the value of money, the labourer can probably obtain more food and necessaries with his eight shillings than he before obtained for ten: but this is owing, not to a rise in the real value of his wages, as stated by Adam Smith, and more recently by Mr. Malthus, but to a fall in the value of the things on which his wages are expended, things perfectly distinct; and yet for calling this a fall in the real value of wages, I am told that I adopt new and unusual language, not reconcilable with the true principles of the science. To me it appears that the unusual and, indeed, inconsistent language is that used by my opponents.

Suppose a labourer to be paid a bushel of corn for a week's work when the price of corn is 80*s*. per quarter, and that he is paid a bushel and a quarter when the price falls to 40*s*. Suppose, too, that he consumes half a bushel of corn a week in his own family, and exchanges the remainder for other things, such as fuel, soap, candles, tea, sugar, salt, etc. etc.; if the three fourths of a bushel which will remain to him, in one case, cannot procure him as much of the above commodities as half a bushel did in the other, which it will not, will labour have risen or fallen in value? Risen, Adam Smith must say, because his standard is corn, and the labourer receives more corn for a week's labour. Fallen, must the same Adam Smith say, "because the value of a thing depends on the power of purchasing other goods which the possession of that object conveys," and labour has a less power of purchasing such other goods.

II. Labour of different qualities differently rewarded. This no cause of variation in the relative value of commodities

In speaking, however, of labour, as being the foundation of all value, and the relative quantity of labour as almost exclusively determining the relative value of commodities, I must not be supposed to be inattentive to the different qualities of labour, and the difficulty of comparing an hour's or a day's labour in one employment with the same duration of labour in another. The estimation in which different qualities of labour are held comes soon to be adjusted in the market with sufficient precision for all practical purposes, and depends much on the comparative skill of the labourer and intensity of the labour performed. The scale, when once formed, is liable to little variation. If a day's labour of a working jeweller be more valuable than a day's labour of a common labourer, it has long ago been adjusted and placed in its proper position in the scale of value.

In comparing, therefore, the value of the same commodity at different periods of time, the consideration of the comparative skill and intensity of labour required for that particular commodity needs scarcely to be attended to, as it operates equally at both periods. One description of labour at one time is compared with the same description of labour at another; if a tenth, a fifth, or a fourth has been added or taken away, an effect proportioned to the cause will be produced on the relative value of the commodity.

If a piece of cloth be now of the value of two pieces of linen, and if, in ten years hence, the ordinary value of a piece of cloth should be four pieces of linen, we may safely conclude that either more labour is required to make the cloth, or less to make the linen, or that both causes have operated.

As the inquiry to which I wish tc draw the reader's attention relates to the effect of the variations in the relative value of commodities, and not in their absolute value, it will be of little importance to examine into the comparative degree of estimation in which the different kinds of human labour are held. We may fairly conclude that whatever inequality there might originally have been in them, whatever the ingenuity, skill, or time necessary for the acquirement of one species of manual dexterity more than another, it continues nearly the same from one generation to another; or at least that the variation is very inconsiderable from year to year, and therefore can have little effect, for short periods, on the relative value of commodities.

III. Not only the labour applied immediately to commodities affect their value, but the labour also which is bestowed on the implements, tools, and buildings, with which such labour is assisted

Even in that early state to which Adam Smith refers, some capital, though possibly made and accumulated by the hunter himself, would be necessary to enable him to kill his game. Without some weapon, neither the beaver nor the deer could be destroyed, and therefore the value of these animals would be regulated, not solely by the time and labour necessary to their destruction, but also by the time and labour necessary for providing the hunter's capital, the weapon, by the aid of which their destruction was effected.

Suppose the weapon necessary to kill the beaver was constructed with much more labour than that necessary to kill the deer, on account of the greater difficulty of approaching near to the former animal, and the consequent necessity of its being more true to its mark; one beaver would naturally be of more value than two deer, and precisely for this reason, that more labour would, on the whole, be necessary to its destruction. Or suppose that the same quantity of labour was necessary to make both weapons, but that they were of very unequal durability; of the durable implement only a small portion of its value would be transferred to the commodity, a much greater portion of the value of the less durable implement would be realised in the commodity which it contributed to produce.

All the implements necessary to kill the beaver and deer might belong to one class of men, and the labour employed in their destruction might be furnished by another class; still, their comparative prices would be in proportion to the actual labour bestowed, both on the formation of the capital and on the destruction of the animals. Under different circumstances of plenty or scarcity of capital, as compared with labour, under different circumstances of plenty or scarcity of the food and necessaries essential to the support of men, those who furnished an equal value of capital for either one employment or for the other might have a half, a fourth, or an eighth of the produce obtained, the remainder being paid as wages to those who furnished the labour; yet this division could not affect the relative value of these commodities, since whether the profits of capital were greater or less, whether they were 50, 20, or 10 per cent., or whether the wages of labour were high or low, they would operate equally on both employments.

If we suppose the occupations of the society extended, that some provide canoes and tackle necessary for fishing, others the seed and rude machinery first used in agriculture, still the same principle would hold true, that the exchangeable value of the commodities produced would be in proportion to the labour bestowed on their production; not on their immediate production only, but on all those implements or machines required to give effect to the particular labour to which they were applied.

If we look to a state of society in which greater improvements have been made, and in which arts and commerce flourish, we shall still find that commodities vary in value conformably with this principle: in estimating the exchangeable value of stockings, for example, we shall find that their value, comparatively with other things, depends on the total quantity of labour necessary to manufacture them and bring them to market. First, there is the labour necessary to cultivate the land on which the raw cotton is grown; secondly, the labour of conveying the cotton to the country where the stockings are to be manufactured, which includes a portion of the labour bestowed in building the ship in which it is conveyed, and which is charged in the freight of the goods; thirdly, the labour of the spinner and weaver; fourthly, a portion of the labour of the engineer, smith, and carpenter, who erected the buildings and machinery, by the help of which they are made; fifthly, the labour of the retail dealer, and of many others, whom it is unnecessary further to particularise. The aggregate sum of these various kinds of labour determines the quantity of other things for which these stockings will exchange, while the same consideration of the various quantities of labour which have been bestowed on those other things will equally govern the portion of them which will be given for the stockings.

To convince ourselves that this is the real foundation of exchangeable value, let us suppose any improvement to be made in the means of abridging labour in any one of the various processes through which the raw cotton must pass before the manufactured stockings come to the market to be exchanged for other things, and observe the effects which will follow. If fewer men were required to cultivate the raw cotton, or if fewer sailors were employed in navigating, or shipwrights in constructing the ship, in which it was conveyed to us; if fewer hands were employed in raising the buildings and machinery, or if these, when raised, were rendered more efficient, the stockings would inevitably fall in value, and consequently command less of other things. They would fall, because a less quantity of labour was necessary to their production, and would therefore exchange for a smaller quantity of those things in which no such abridgment of labour had been made.

Economy in the use of labour never fails to reduce the relative value of a commodity, whether the saving be in the labour necessary to the manufacture of the commodity itself, or in that necessary to the formation of the capital by the aid of which it is produced. In either case the price of stockings would fall, whether there were fewer men employed as bleachers, spinners, and weavers, persons immediately necessary to their manufacture; or as sailors, carriers, engineers, and smiths, persons more indirectly concerned. In the one case, the whole saving of labour would fall on the stockings, because that portion of labour was wholly confined to the stockings; in the other, a portion only would fall on the stockings, the remainder being applied to all those other commodities, to the production of which the buildings, machinery, and carriage were subservient.

Suppose that, in the early stages of society, the bows and arrows of the hunter were of equal value, and of equal durability, with the canoe and implements of the fisherman, both being the produce of the same quantity of labour. Under such circumstances the value of the deer, the produce of the hunter's day's labour, would be exactly equal to the value of the fish, the produce of the fisherman's day's labour. The comparative value of the fish and the game would be entirely regulated by the quantity of labour realised in each, whatever might be the quantity of production or however high or low general wages or profits might be. If, for example, the canoes and implements of the fisherman were of the value of £100, and were calculated to last for ten years, and he employed ten men, whose annual labour cost £100, and who in one day obtained by their labour twenty salmon: If the weapons employed by the hunter were also of £100 value, and calculated to last ten years, and if he also employed ten men, whose annual labour cost £100, and who in one day procured him ten deer; then the natural price of a deer would be two salmon, whether the proportion of the whole produce bestowed on the men who obtained it were large or small. The proportion which might be paid for wages is of the utmost importance in the question of profits; for it must at once be seen that profits would be high or low exactly in proportion as wages were low or high; but it could not in the least affect the relative value of fish and game, as wages would be high or low at the same time in both occupations. If the hunter urged the plea of his paying a large proportion, or the value of a large proportion of his game for wages, as an inducement to the fisherman to give him more fish in exchange for his game, the latter would state that he was equally affected by the same cause; and therefore, under all variations of wages and profits, under all the effects of accumulation of capital, as long as they continued by a day's labour to obtain respectively the same quantity of fish and the same quantity of game, the natural rate of exchange would be one deer for two salmon.

If with the same quantity of labour a less quantity of fish or a greater quantity of game were obtained, the value of fish would rise in comparison with that of game. If, on the contrary, with the same quantity of labour a less quantity of game or a greater quantity of fish was obtained, game would rise in comparison with fish.

If there were any other commodity which was invariable in its value, we should be able to ascertain, by comparing the value of fish and game with this commodity, how much of the variation was to be attributed to a cause which affected the value of fish, and how much to a cause which affected the value of game.

Suppose money to be that commodity. If a salmon were worth £1 and a deer £2, one deer would be worth two salmon. But a deer might become of the value of three salmon, for more labour might be required to obtain the deer, or less to get the salmon, or both these causes might operate at the same time. If we had this invariable standard, we might easily ascertain in what degree either of these causes operated. If salmon continued to sell for £1 whilst deer rose to £3, we might conclude that more labour was required to obtain the deer. If deer continued at the same price of £2 and salmon sold for 13*s*. 4*d*., we might then be sure that less labour was required to obtain the salmon; and if deer rose to £2 10*s*. and salmon fell to 16*s*. 8 *d*., we should be convinced that both causes had operated in producing the alteration of the relative value of these commodities.

No alteration in the wages of labour could produce any alteration in the relative value of these commodities; for suppose them to rise, no greater quantity of labour would be required in any of these occupations but it would be paid for at a higher price, and the same reasons which should make the hunter and fisherman endeavour to raise the value of their game and fish would cause the owner of the mine to raise the value of his gold. This inducement acting with the same force on all these three occupations, and the relative situation of those engaged in them being the same before and after the rise of wages, the relative value of game, fish, and gold would continue unaltered. Wages might rise twenty per cent., and profits consequently fall in a greater or less proportion, without occasioning the least alteration in the relative value of these commodities.

Now suppose that, with the same labour and fixed capital, more fish could be produced, but no more gold or game, the relative value of fish would fall in comparison with gold or game. If, instead of twenty salmon, twenty-five were the produce of one day's labour, the price of a salmon would be sixteen shillings instead of a pound, and two salmon and a half, instead of two salmon, would be given in exchange for one deer, but the price of deer would continue at £2 as before. In the same manner, if fewer fish could be obtained with the same capital and labour, fish would rise in comparative value. Fish then would rise or fall in exchangeable value, only because more or less labour was required to obtain a given quantity; and it never could rise or fall beyond the proportion of the increased or diminished quantity of labour required.

If we had then an invariable standard, by which we could measure the variation in other commodities, we should find that the utmost limit to which they could permanently rise, if produced under the circumstances supposed, was proportioned to the additional quantity of labour required for their production; and that unless more labour were required for their production they could not rise in any degree whatever. A rise of wages would not raise them in money value, nor relatively to any other commodities, the production of which required no additional quantity of labour, which employed the same proportion of fixed and circulating capital, and fixed capital of the same durability. If more or less labour were required in the production of the other commodity, we have already stated that this will immediately occasion an alteration in its relative value, but such alteration is owing to the altered quantity of requisite labour, and not to the rise of wages.

IV. The principle that the quantity of labour bestowed on the production of commodities regulates their relative value considerably modified by the employment of machinery and other fixed and durable capital

In the former section we have supposed the implements and weapons necessary to kill the deer and salmon to be equally durable, and to be the result of the same quantity of labour, and we have seen that the variations in the relative value of deer and salmon depended solely on the varying quantities of labour necessary to obtain them, but in every state of society, the tools, implements, buildings, and machinery employed in different trades may be of various degrees of durability, and may require different portions of labour to produce them. The proportions, too, in which the capital that is to support labour, and the capital that is invested in tools, machinery, and buildings, may be variously combined. This difference in the degree of durability of fixed capital, and this variety in the proportions in which the two sorts of capital may be combined, introduce another cause, besides the greater or less quantity of labour necessary to produce commodities, for the variations in their relative value—this cause is the rise or fall in the value of labour.

The food and clothing consumed by the labourer, the buildings in which he works, the implements with which his labour is assisted, are all of a perishable nature. There is, however, a vast difference in the time for which these different capitals will endure: a steam engine will last longer than a ship, a ship than the clothing of the labourer, and the clothing of the labourer longer than the food which he consumes.

According as capital is rapidly perishable, and requires to be frequently reproduced, or is of slow consumption, it is classed under the heads of circulating or of fixed capital. A brewer whose buildings and machinery are valuable and durable is said to employ a large portion of fixed capital: on the contrary, a shoemaker, whose capital is chiefly employed in the payment of wages, which are expended on food and clothing, commodities more perishable than buildings and machinery, is said to employ a large proportion of his capital as circulating capital.

It is also to be observed that the circulating capital may circulate, or be returned to its employer, in very unequal times. The wheat bought by a farmer to sow is comparatively a fixed capital to the wheat purchased by a baker to make into loaves. One leaves it in the ground and can obtain no return for a year; the other can get it ground into flour, sell it as bread to his customers, and have his capital free to renew the same or commence any other employment in a week.

Two trades then may employ the same amount of capital; but it may be very differently divided with respect to the portion which is fixed and that which is circulating.

In one trade very little capital may be employed as circulating capital, that is to say, in the support of labour—it may be principally invested in machinery, implements, buildings, etc., capital of a comparatively fixed and durable character. In another trade the same amount of capital may be used, but it may be chiefly employed in the support of labour, and very little may be invested in implements, machines, and buildings. A rise in the wages of labour cannot fail to affect unequally commodities produced under such different circumstances.

Again, two manufacturers may employ the same amount of fixed and the same amount of circulating capital; but the durability of their fixed capitals may be very unequal. One may have steam engines of the value of £10,000, the other, ships of the same value.

If men employed no machinery in production but labour only, and were all the same length of time before they brought their commodities to market, the exchangeable value of their goods would be precisely in proportion to the quantity of labour employed.

If they employed fixed capital of the same value and of the same durability, then, too, the value of the commodities produced would be the same, and they would vary with the greater or less quantity of labour employed on their production.

But although commodities produced under similar circumstances would not vary with respect to each other from any cause but an addition or diminution of the quantity of labour necessary to produce one or other of them, yet, compared with others not produced with the same proportionate quantity of fixed capital, they would vary from the other cause also which I have before mentioned, namely, a rise in the value of labour, although neither more nor less labour were employed in the production of either of them. Barley and oats would continue to bear the same relation to each other under any variation of wages. Cotton goods and cloth would do the same, if they also were produced under circumstances precisely similar to each other, but yet with a rise or fall of wages barley might be more or less valuable compared with cotton goods and oats compared with cloth.

Suppose two men employ one hundred men each for a year in the construction of two machines, and another man employs the same number of men in cultivating corn, each of the machines at the end of the year will be of the same value as the corn, for they will each be produced by the same quantity of labour. Suppose one of the owners of one of the machines to employ it, with the assistance of one hundred men, the following year in making cloth, and the owner of the other machine to employ his also, with the assistance likewise of one hundred men, in making cotton goods, while the farmer continues to employ one hundred men as before in the cultivation of corn. During the second year they will all have employed the same quantity of labour, but the goods and machine together of the clothier, and also of the cotton manufacturer, will be the result of the labour of two hundred men employed for a year; or, rather, of the labour of one hundred men for two years; whereas the corn will be produced by the labour of one hundred men for one year, consequently if the corn be of the value of £500, the machine and cloth of the clothier together ought to be of the value of £1000, and the machine and cotton goods of the cotton manufacturer ought to be also of twice the value of the corn. But they will be of more than twice the value of the corn, for the profit on the clothier's and cotton manufacturer's capital for the first year has been added to their capitals, while that of the farmer has been expended and enjoyed. On account then of the different degrees of durability of their capitals, or, which is the same thing, on account of the time which must elapse before one set of commodities can be brought to market, they will be valuable, not exactly in proportion to the quantity of labour bestowed on them—they will not be as two to one, but something more, to compensate for the greater length of time which must elapse before the most valuable can be brought to market.

Suppose that for the labour of each workman £50 per annum were paid, or that £5000 capital were employed and profits were 10 per cent., the value of each of the machines as well as of the corn, at the end of the first year, would be £5500. The second year the manufacturers and farmers will again employ £5000 each in the support of labour, and will therefore again sell their goods for £5500; but the men using the machines, to be on a par with the farmer, must not only obtain £5500 for the equal capitals of £5000 employed on labour, but they must obtain a further sum of £550 for the profit on £5500, which they have invested in machinery, and consequently their goods must sell for £6050. Here, then, are capitalists employing precisely the same quantity of labour annually on the production of their commodities, and yet the goods they produce differ in value on account of the different quantities of fixed capital, or accumulated labour, employed by each respectively. The cloth and cotton goods are of the same value, because they are the produce of equal quantities of labour and equal quantities of fixed capital; but corn is not of the same value as these commodities, because it is produced, as far as regards fixed capital, under different circumstances.

But how will their relative value be affected by a rise in the value of labour? It is evident that the relative values of cloth and cotton goods will undergo no change, for what affects one must equally affect the other under the circumstances supposed; neither will the relative values of wheat and barley undergo any change, for they are produced under the same circumstances as far as fixed and circulating capital are concerned; but the relative value of corn to cloth, or to cotton goods, must be altered by a rise of labour.

There can be no rise in the value of labour without a fall of profits. If the corn is to be divided between the farmer and the labourer, the larger the proportion that is given to the latter the less will remain for the former. So, if cloth or cotton goods be divided between the workman and his employer, the larger the proportion given to the former the less remains for the latter. Suppose then, that owing to a rise of wages, profits fall from 10 to 9 per cent., instead of adding £550 to the common price of their goods (to £5500) for the profits on their fixed capital, the manufacturers would add only 9 per cent. on that sum, or £495, consequently the price would be £5995 instead of £6050. As the corn would continue to sell for £5500 the manufactured goods in which more fixed capital was employed would fall relatively to corn or to any other goods in which a less portion of fixed capital entered. The degree of alteration in the relative value of goods, on account of a rise or fall of labour, would depend on the proportion which the fixed capital bore to the whole capital employed. All commodities which are produced by very valuable machinery, or in very valuable buildings, or which require a great length of time before they can be brought to market, would fall in relative value, while all those which were chiefly produced by labour, or which would be speedily brought to market, would rise in relative value.

The reader, however, should remark that this cause of the variation of commodities is comparatively slight in its effects. With such a rise of wages as should occasion a fall of 1 per cent. in profits, goods produced under the circumstances I have supposed vary in relative value only 1 per cent.; they fall with so great a fall of profits from £6050 to £5995. The greatest effects which could be produced on the relative prices of these goods from a rise of wages could not exceed 6 or 7 per cent.; for profits could not, probably, under any circumstances, admit of a greater general and permanent depression than to that amount.

Not so with the other great cause of the variation in the value of commodities, namely, the increase or diminution in the quantity of labour necessary to produce them. If to produce the corn, eighty, instead of one hundred men, should be required, the value of the corn would fall 20 per cent., or from £5500 to £4400. If to produce the cloth, the labour of eighty instead of one hundred men would suffice, cloth would fall from £6050 to £4950. An alteration in the permanent rate of profits, to any great amount, is the effect of causes which do not operate but in the course of years, whereas alterations in the quantity of labour necessary to produce commodities are of daily occurrence. Every improvement in machinery, in tools, in buildings, in raising the raw material, saves labour, and enables us to produce the commodity to which the improvement is applied with more facility, and consequently its value alters. In estimating, then, the causes of the variations in the value of commodities, although it would be wrong wholly to omit the consideration of the effect produced by a rise or fall of labour, it would be equally incorrect to attach much importance to it; and consequently, in the subsequent part of this work, though I shall occasionally refer to this cause of variation, I shall consider all the great variations which take place in the relative value of commodities to be produced by the greater or less quantity of labour which may be required from time to time to produce them.

It is hardly necessary to say that commodities which have the same quantity of labour bestowed on their production will differ in exchangeable value if they cannot be brought to market in the same time.

Suppose I employ twenty men at an expense of £1000 for a year in the production of a commodity, and at the end of the year I employ twenty men again for another year, at a further expense of £1000 in finishing or perfecting the same commodity, and that I bring it to market at the end of two years, if profits be 10 per cent., my commodity must sell for £2310; for I have employed £1000 capital for one year, and £2100 capital for one year more. Another man employs precisely the same quantity of labour, but he employs it all in the first year; he employs forty men at an expense of £2000, and at the end of the first year he sells it with 10 per cent. profit, or for £2200. Here, then, are two commodities having precisely the same quantity of labour bestowed on them, one of which sells for £2310—the other for £2200.

This case appears to differ from the last, but is, in fact, the same. In both cases the superior price of one commodity is owing to the greater length of time which must elapse before it can be brought to market. In the former case the machinery and cloth were more than double the value of the corn, although only double the quantity of labour was bestowed on them. In the second case, one commodity is more valuable than the other, although no more labour was employed on its production. The difference in value arises in both cases from the profits being accumulated as capital, and is only a just compensation for the time that the profits were withheld.

It appears, then, that the division of capital into different proportions of fixed and circulating capital, employed in different trades, introduces a considerable modification to the rule, which is of universal application when labour is almost exclusively employed in production; namely, that commodities never vary in value unless a greater or less quantity of labour be bestowed on their production, it being shown in this section that, without any variation in the quantity of labour, the rise of its value merely will occasion a fall in the exchangeable value of those goods in the production of which fixed capital is employed; the larger the amount of fixed capital, the greater will be the fall.

V. The principle that value does not vary with the rise or fall of wages, modified also by the unequal durability of capital, and by the unequal rapidity with which it is returned to its employer

In the last section we have supposed that, of two equal capitals, in two different occupations, the proportions of fixed and circulating capitals were unequal; now let us suppose them to be in the same proportion, but of unequal durability. In proportion as fixed capital is less durable it approaches to the nature of circulating capital. It will be consumed and its value reproduced in a shorter time, in order to preserve the capital of the manufacturer. We have just seen that in proportion as fixed capital preponderates in a manufacture, when wages rise the value of commodities produced in that manufacture is relatively lower than that of commodities produced in manufactures where circulating capital preponderates. In proportion to the less durability of fixed capital, and its approach to the nature of circulating capital, the same effect will be produced by the same cause.

If fixed capital be not of a durable nature it will require a great quantity of labour annually to keep it in its original state of efficiency; but the labour so bestowed may be considered as really expended on the commodity manufactured, which must bear a value in proportion to such labour. If I had a machine worth £20,000 which with very little labour was efficient to the production of commodities, and if the wear and tear of such machine were of trifling amount, and the general rate of profit 10 per cent., I should not require much more than £2000 to be added to the price of the goods, on account of the employment of my machine; but if the wear and tear of the machine were great, if the quantity of labour requisite to keep it in an efficient state were that of fifty men annually, I should require an additional price for my goods equal to that which would be obtained by any other manufacturer who employed fifty men in the production of other goods, and who used no machinery at all.

But a rise in the wages of labour would not equally affect commodities produced with machinery quickly consumed, and commodities produced with machinery slowly consumed. In the production of the one, a great deal of labour would be continually transferred to the commodity produced—in the other very little would be so transferred. Every rise of wages, therefore, or, which is the same thing, every fall of profits, would lower the relative value of those commodities which were produced with a capital of a durable nature, and would proportionally elevate those which were produced with capital more perishable. A fall of wages would have precisely the contrary effect.

I have already said that fixed capital is of various degrees of durability—suppose now a machine which could in any particular trade be employed to do the work of one hundred men for a year, and that it would last only for one year. Suppose, too, the machine to cost £5000, and the wages annually paid to one hundred men to be £5000, it is evident that it would be a matter of indifference to the manufacturer whether he bought the machine or employed the men. But suppose labour to rise, and consequently the wages of one hundred men for a year to amount to £5500, it is obvious that the manufacturer would now no longer hesitate, it would be for his interest to buy the machine and get his work done for £5000. But will not the machine rise in price, will not that also be worth £5500 in consequence of the rise of labour? It would rise in price if there were no stock employed on its construction, and no profits to be paid to the maker of it. If, for example, the machine were the produce of the labour of one hundred men, working one year upon it with wages of £50 each, and its price were consequently £5000; should those wages rise to £55, its price would be £5500, but this cannot be the case; less than one hundred men are employed or it could not be sold for £5000, for out of the £5000 must be paid the profits of stock which employed the men. Suppose then that only eighty-five men were employed at an expense of £50 each, or £4250 per annum, and that the £750 which the sale of the machine would produce over and above the wages advanced to the men constituted the profits of the engineer's stock. When wages rose 10 per cent., he would be obliged to employ an additional capital of £425, and would therefore employ £4675 instead of £4250, on which capital he would only get a profit of £325 if he continued to sell his machine for £5000; but this is precisely the case of all manufacturers and capitalists; the rise of wages affects them all. If therefore the maker of the machine should raise the price of it in consequence of a rise of wages, an unusual quantity of capital would be employed in the construction of such machines, till their price afforded only the common rate of profits. We see then that machines would not rise in price in consequence of a rise of wages.

The manufacturer, however, who in a general rise of wages can have recourse to a machine which shall not increase the charge of production on his commodity, would enjoy peculiar advantages if he could continue to charge the same price for his goods; but he, as we have already seen, would be obliged to lower the price of his commodities, or capital would flow to his trade till his profits had sunk to the general level. Thus then is the public benefited by machinery: these mute agents are always the produce of much less labour than that which they displace, even when they are of the same money value. Through their influence an increase in the price of provisions which raises wages will affect fewer persons; it will reach, as in the above instance, eighty-five men instead of a hundred, and the saving which is the consequence shows itself in the reduced price of the commodity manufactured. Neither machines, nor the commodities made by them, rise in real value, but all commodities made by machines fall, and fall in proportion to their durability.

It will be seen then, that in the early stages of society, before much machinery or durable capital is used, the commodities produced by equal capitals will be nearly of equal value, and will rise or fall only relatively to each other on account of more or less labour being required for their production; but after the introduction of these expensive and durable instruments, the commodities produced by the employment of equal capitals will be of very unequal value, and although they will still be liable to rise or fall relatively to each other, as more or less labour becomes necessary to their production, they will be subject to another, though a minor variation, also from the rise or fall of wages and profits. Since goods which sell for £5000 may be the produce of a capital equal in amount to that from which are produced other goods which sell for £10,000, the profits on their manufacture will be the same; but those profits would be unequal if the prices of the goods did not vary with a rise or fall in the rate of profits.

It appears, too, that in proportion to the durability of capital employed in any kind of production the relative prices of those commodities on which such durable capital is employed will vary inversely as wages; they will fall as wages rise, and rise as wages fall; and, on the contrary, those which are produced chiefly by labour with less fixed capital, or with fixed capital of a less durable character than the medium in which price is estimated, will rise as wages rise, and fall as wages fall.

VI. On an invariable measure of value

When commodities varied in relative value it would be desirable to have the means of ascertaining which of them fell and which rose in real value, and this could be effected only by comparing them one after another with some invariable standard measure of value, which should itself be subject to none of the fluctuations to which other commodities are exposed. Of such a measure it is impossible to be possessed, because there is no commodity which is not itself exposed to the same variations as the things the value of which is to be ascertained; that is, there is none which is not subject to require more or less labour for its production. But if this cause of variation in the value of a medium could be removed—if it were possible that in the production of our money, for instance, the same quantity of labour should at all times be required, still it would not be a perfect standard or invariable measure of value, because, as I have already endeavoured to explain, it would be subject to relative variations from a rise or fall of wages, on account of the different proportions of fixed capital which might be necessary to produce it, and to produce those other commodities whose alteration of value we wished to ascertain. It might be subject to variations, too, from the same cause, on account of the different degrees of durability of the fixed capital employed on it, and the commodities to be compared with it—or the time necessary to bring the one to market might be longer or shorter than the time necessary to bring the other commodities to market, the variations of which were to be determined; all which circumstances disqualify any commodity that can be thought of from being a perfectly accurate measure of value.

If, for example, we were to fix on gold as a standard, it is evident that it is but a commodity obtained under the same contingencies as every other commodity, and requiring labour and fixed capital to produce it. Like every other commodity, improvements in the saving of labour might be applied to its production, and consequently it might fall in relative value to other things merely on account of the greater facility of producing it.

If we suppose this cause of variation to be removed, and the same quantity of labour to be always required to obtain the same quantity of gold, still gold would not be a perfect measure of value, by which we could accurately ascertain the variations in all other things, because it would not be produced with precisely the same combinations of fixed and circulating capital as all other things; nor with fixed capital of the same durability; nor would it require precisely the same length of time before it could be brought to market. It would be a perfect measure of value for all things produced under the same circumstances precisely as itself, but for no others. If, for example, it were produced under the same circumstances as we have supposed necessary to produce cloth and cotton goods, it would be a perfect measure of value for those things, but not so for corn, for coals, and other commodities produced with either a less or a greater proportion of fixed capital, because, as we have shown, every alteration in the permanent rate of profits would have some effect on the relative value of all these goods, independently of any alteration in the quantity of labour employed on their production. If gold were produced under the same circumstances as corn, even if they never changed, it would not, for the same reasons, be at all times a perfect measure of the value of cloth and cotton goods. Neither gold, then, nor any other commodity, can ever be a perfect measure of value for all things; but I have already remarked that the effect on the relative prices of things, from a variation in profits, is comparatively slight; that by far the most important effects are produced by the varying quantities of labour required for production; and therefore, if we suppose this important cause of variation removed from the production of gold, we shall probably possess as near an approximation to a standard measure of value as can be theoretically conceived. May not gold be considered as a commodity produced with such proportions of the two kinds of capital as approach nearest to the average quantity employed in the production of most commodities? May not these proportions be so nearly equally distant from the two extremes, the one where little fixed capital is used, the other where little labour is employed, as to form a just mean between them?

If, then, I may suppose myself to be possessed of a standard so nearly approaching to an invariable one, the advantage is that I shall be enabled to speak of the variations of other things without embarrassing myself on every occasion with the consideration of the possible alteration in the value of the medium in which price and value are estimated.

To facilitate, then, the object of this inquiry, although I fully allow that money made of gold is subject to most of the variations of other things, I shall suppose it to be invariable, and therefore all alterations in price to be occasioned by some alteration in the value of the commodity of which I may be speaking.

Before I quit this subject, it may be proper to observe that Adam Smith, and all the writers who have followed him, have, without one exception that I know of, maintained that a rise in the price of labour would be uniformly followed by a rise in the price of all commodities. I hope I have succeeded in showing that there are no grounds for such an opinion, and that only those commodities would rise which had less fixed capital employed upon them than the medium in which price was estimated, and that all those which had more would positively fall in price when wages rose. On the contrary, if wages fell, those commodities only would fall which had a less proportion of fixed capital employed on them than the medium in which price was estimated; all those which had more would positively rise in price.

It is necessary for me also to remark that I have not said because one commodity has so much labour bestowed upon it as will cost £1000, and another so much as will cost £2000, that therefore one would be of the value of £1000, and the other of the value of £2000; but I have said that their value will be to each other as two to one, and that in those proportions they will be exchanged. It is of no importance to the truth of this doctrine whether one of these commodities sells for £1100 and the other for £2200, or one for £1500 and the other for £3000; into that question I do not at present inquire; I affirm only that their relative values will be governed by the relative quantities of labour bestowed on their production.

VII. Different effects from the alteration in the value of money, the medium in which PRICE *is always expressed, or from the alteration in the value of the commodities which money purchases*

Although I shall, as I have already explained, have occasion to consider money as invariable in value, for the purpose of more distinctly pointing out the causes of relative variations in the value of other things, it may be useful to notice the different effects which will follow from the prices of goods being altered by the causes to which I have already adverted, namely, the different quantities of labour required to produce them, and their being altered by a variation in the value of money itself.

Money being a variable commodity, the rise of money wages will be frequently occasioned by a fall in the value of money. A rise of wages from this cause will, indeed, be invariably accompanied by a rise in the price of commodities; but in such cases it will be found that labour and all commodities have not varied in regard to each other, and that the variation has been confined to money.

Money, from its being a commodity obtained from a foreign country, from its being the general medium of exchange between all civilised countries, and from its being also distributed among those countries in proportions which are ever changing with every improvement in commerce and machinery, and with every increasing difficulty of obtaining food and necessaries for an increasing population, is subject to incessant variations. In stating the principles which regulate exchangeable value and price, we should carefully distinguish between those variations which belong to the commodity itself, and those which are occasioned by a variation in the medium in which value is estimated or price expressed.

A rise in wages, from an alteration in the value of money, produces a general effect on price, and for that reason it produces no real effect whatever on profits. On the contrary, a rise of wages, from the circumstance of the labourer being more liberally rewarded, or from a difficulty of procuring the necessaries on which wages are expended, does not, except in some instances, produce the effect of raising price, but has a great effect in lowering profits. In the one case, no greater proportion of the annual labour of the country is devoted to the support of the labourers; in the other case, a larger portion is so devoted.

It is according to the division of the whole produce of the land of any particular farm, between the three classes, of landlord, capitalist, and labourer, that we are to judge of the rise or fall of rent, profit, and wages, and not according to the value at which that produce may be estimated in a medium which is confessedly variable.

It is not by the absolute quantity of produce obtained by either class that we can correctly judge of the rate of profit, rent, and wages, but by the quantity of labour required to obtain that produce. By improvements in machinery and agriculture the whole produce may be doubled; but if wages, rent, and profit be also doubled, these three will bear the same proportions to one another as before, and neither could be said to have relatively varied. But if wages partook not of the whole of this increase; if they, instead of being doubled, were only increased one half; if rent, instead of being doubled, were only increased three fourths, and the remaining increase went to profit, it would, I apprehend, be correct for me to say that rent and wages had fallen while profits had risen; for if we had an invariable standard by which to measure the value of this produce we should find that a less value had fallen to the class of labourers and landlords, and a greater to the class of capitalists, than had been given before. We might find, for example, that though the absolute quantity of commodities had been doubled, they were the produce of precisely the former quantity of labour. Of every hundred hats, coats, and quarters of corn produced, if

The labourers had before	25
The landlords	25
And the capitalists	50
	100:

And if, after these commodities were double the quantity, of every 100

The labourers had only	22
The landlords	22
And the capitalists	56
	100:

In that case I should say that wages and rent had fallen and profits risen; though, in consequence of the abundance of commodities, the quantity paid to the labourer and landlord would have increased in the proportion of 25 to 44. Wages are to be estimated by their real value, viz., by the quantity of labour and capital employed in producing them, and not by their nominal value either in coats, hats, money, or corn. Under the circumstances I have just supposed, commodities would have fallen to half their former value, and if money had not varied, to half their former price also. If then in this medium, which had not varied in value, the wages of the labourer should be found to have fallen, it will not the less be a real fall because they might furnish him with a greater quantity of cheap commodities than his former wages.

The variation in the value of money, however great, makes no difference in the *rate* of profits; for suppose the goods of the manufacturer to rise from £1000 to £2000, or 100 per cent., if his capital, on which the variations of money have as much effect as on the value of produce, if his machinery, buildings, and stock in trade rise also a 100 per cent., his rate of profits will be the same, and he will have the same quantity, and no more, of the produce of the labour of the country at his command.

If, with a capital of a given value, he can, by economy in labour, double the quantity of produce, and it fall to half its former price, it will bear the same proportion to the capital that produced it which it did before, and consequently profits will still be at the same rate.

If, at the same time that he doubles the quantity of produce by the employment of the same capital, the value of money is by any accident lowered one half, the produce will sell for twice the money value that it did before; but the capital employed to produce it will also be of twice its former money value; and therefore in this case, too, the value of the produce will bear the same proportion to the value of the capital as it did before; and although the produce be doubled, rent, wages, and profits will only vary as the proportions vary, in which this double produce may be divided among the three classes that share it.

II. ON RENT

It remains, however, to be considered whether the appropriation of land, and the consequent creation of rent, will occasion any variation in the relative value of commodities independently of the quantity of labour necessary to production. In order to understand this part of the subject we must inquire into the nature of rent, and the laws by which its rise or fall is regulated.

Rent is that portion of the produce of the earth which is paid to the landlord for the use of the original and indestructible powers of the soil. It is often, however, confounded with the interest and profit of capital, and, in popular language, the term is applied to whatever is annually paid by a farmer to his landlord. If, of two adjoining farms of the same extent, and of the same natural fertility, one had all the conveniences of farming buildings, and, besides, were properly drained and manured, and advantageously divided by hedges, fences, and walls, while the other had none of these advantages, more remuneration would naturally be paid for the use of one than for the use of the other; yet in both cases this remuneration would be called rent. But it is evident that a portion only of the money annually to be paid for the improved farm would be given for the original and indestructible powers of the soil; the other portion would be paid for the use of the capital which had been employed in ameliorating the quality of the land, and in erecting such buildings as were necessary to secure and preserve the produce. Adam Smith sometimes speaks of rent in the strict sense to which I am desirous of confining it, but more often in the popular sense in which the term is usually employed. He tells us that the demand for timber, and its consequent high price, in the more southern countries of Europe caused a rent to be paid for forests in Norway which could before afford no rent. Is it not, however, evident that the person who paid what he thus calls rent, paid it in consideration of the valuable commodity which was then standing on the land, and that he actually repaid himself with a profit by the sale of the timber? If, indeed, after the timber was removed, any compensation were paid to the landlord for the use of the land, for the purpose of growing timber or any other produce, with a view to future demand, such compensation might justly be called rent, because it would be paid for the productive powers of the land; but in the case stated by Adam Smith, the compensation was paid for the liberty of removing and selling the timber, and not for the liberty of growing it. He speaks also of the rent of coal mines, and of stone quarries, to which the same observation applies—that the compensation given for the mine or quarry is paid for the value of the coal or stone which can be removed from them, and has no connection with the original and indestructible powers of the land. This is a distinction of great importance in an inquiry concerning rent and profits; for it is found that the laws which regulate the progress of rent are widely different from those which regulate the progress of profits, and seldom operate in the same direction. In all improved countries, that which is annually paid to the landlord, partaking of both characters, rent and profit, is sometimes kept stationary by the effects of opposing causes; at other times advances or recedes as one or the other of these causes preponderates. In the future pages of this work, then, whenever I speak of the rent of land, I wish to be understood as speaking of that compensation which is paid to the owner of land for the use of its original and indestructible powers.

On the first settling of a country in which there is an abundance of rich and fertile land, a very small proportion of which is required to be cultivated for the support of the actual population, or indeed can be cultivated with the capital which the population can command, there will be no rent; for no one would pay for the use of land when there was an abundant quantity not yet appropriated, and, therefore, at the disposal of whosoever might choose to cultivate it.

On the common principles of supply and demand, no rent could be paid for such land, for the reason stated why nothing is given for the use of air and water, or for any other of the gifts of nature which exist in boundless quantity. With a given quantity of materials, and with the assistance of the pressure of the atmosphere, and the elasticity of steam, engines may perform work, and abridge human labour to a very great extent; but no charge is made for the use of these natural aids, because they are inexhaustible and at every man's disposal. In the same manner, the brewer, the distiller, the dyer, make incessant use of the air and water for the production of their commodities; but as the supply is boundless, they bear no price. If all land had the same properties, if it were unlimited in quantity, and uniform in quality, no charge could be made for its use, unless where it possessed peculiar advantages of situation. It is only, then, because land is not unlimited in quantity and uniform in quality, and because, in the progress of population, land of an inferior quality, or less advantageously situated, is called into cultivation, that rent is ever paid for the use of it. When, in the progress of society, land of the second degree of fertility is taken into cultivation, rent immediately commences on that of the first quality, and the amount of that rent will depend on the difference in the quality of these two portions of land.

When land of the third quality is taken into cultivation, rent immediately commences on the second, and it is regulated as before by the difference in their productive powers. At the same time, the rent of the first quality will rise, for that must always be above the rent of the second by the difference between the produce which they yield with a given quantity of capital and labour. With every step in the progress of population, which shall oblige a country to have recourse to land of a worse quality, to enable it to raise its supply of food, rent, on all the more fertile land, will rise.

Thus suppose land—No. 1, 2, 3—to yield, with an equal employment of capital and labour, a net produce of 100, 90, and 80 quarters of corn. In a new country, where there is an abundance of fertile land compared with the population, and where therefore it is only necessary to cultivate No. 1, the whole net produce will belong to the cultivator, and will be the profits of the stock which he advances. As soon as population had so far increased as to make it necessary to cultivate No. 2, from which ninety quarters only can be obtained after supporting the labourers, rent would commence on No. 1; for either there must be two rates of profit on agricultural capital, or ten quarters, or the value of ten quarters must be withdrawn from the produce of No. 1 for some other purpose. Whether the proprietor of the land, or any other person, cultivated No. 1, these ten quarters would equally constitute rent; for the cultivator of No. 2 would get the same result with his capital whether he cultivated No. 1, paying ten quarters for rent, or continued to cultivate No. 2, paying no rent. In the same manner it might be shown that when No. 3 is brought into cultivation, the rent of No. 2 must be ten quarters, or the value of ten quarters, whilst the rent of No. 1 would rise to twenty quarters; for the cultivator of No. 3 would have the same profits whether he paid twenty quarters for the rent of No. 1, ten quarters for the rent of No. 2, or cultivated No. 3 free of all rent.

It often, and, indeed, commonly happens, that before No. 2, 3, 4, or 5, or the inferior lands are cultivated, capital can be employed more productively on those lands which are already in cultivation. It may perhaps be found that by doubling the original capital employed on No. 1, though the produce will not be doubled, will not be increased by 100 quarters, it may be increased by eighty-five quarters, and that this quantity exceeds what could be obtained by employing the same capital on land No. 3.

In such case, capital will be preferably employed on the old land, and will equally create a rent; for rent is always the difference between the produce obtained by the employment of two equal quantities of capital and labour. If, with a capital of £1000 a tenant obtain 100 quarters of wheat from his land, and by the employment of a second capital of £1000 he obtain a further return of eighty-five, his landlord would have the power, at the expiration of his lease, of obliging him to pay fifteen quarters or an equivalent value for additional rent; for there cannot be two rates of profit. If he is satisfied with a diminution of fifteen quarters in the return for his second £1000, it is because no employment more profitable can be found for it. The common rate of profit would be in that proportion, and if the original tenant refused, some other person would be found willing to give all which exceeded that rate of profit to the owner of the land from which he derived it.

In this case, as well as in the other, the capital last employed pays no rent. For the greater productive powers of the first £1000, fifteen quarters, is paid for rent, for the employment of the second £1000 no rent whatever is paid. If a third £1000 be employed on the same land, with a return of seventy-five quarters, rent will then be paid for the second £1000, and will be equal to the difference between the produce of these two, or ten quarters; and at the same time the rent for the first £1000 will rise from fifteen to twenty-five quarters; while the last £1000 will pay no rent whatever.

If, then, good land existed in a quantity much more abundant than the production of food for an increasing population required, or if capital could be indefinitely employed without a diminished return on the old land, there could be no rise of rent; for rent invariably proceeds from the employment of an additional quantity of labour with a proportionally less return.

The most fertile and most favourably situated land will be first cultivated, and the exchangeable value of its produce will be adjusted in the same manner as the exchangeable value of all other commodities, by the total quantity of labour necessary in various forms, from first to last, to produce it and bring it to market. When land of an inferior quality is taken into cultivation, the exchangeable value of raw produce will rise, because more labour is required to produce it.

The exchangeable value of all commodities, whether they be manufactured, or the produce of the mines, or the produce of land, is always regulated, not by the less quantity of labour that will suffice for their production under circumstances highly favourable, and exclusively enjoyed by those who have peculiar facilities of production; but by the greater quantity of labour necessarily bestowed on their production by those who have no such facilities; by those who continue to produce them under the most unfavourable circumstances; meaning—by the most unfavourable circumstances, the most unfavourable under which the quantity of produce required renders it necessary to carry on the production.

Thus, in a charitable institution, where the poor are set to work with the funds of benefactors, the general prices of the commodities, which are the produce of such work, will not be governed by the peculiar facilities afforded to these workmen, but by the common, usual, and natural difficulties which every other manufacturer will have to encounter. The manufacturer enjoying none of these facilities might indeed be driven altogether from the market if the supply afforded by these favoured workmen were equal to all the wants of the community; but if he continued the trade, it would be only on condition that he should derive from it the usual and general rate of profits on stock; and that could only happen when his commodity sold for a price proportioned to the quantity of labour bestowed on its production.

It is true, that on the best land, the same produce would still be obtained with the same labour as before, but its value would be enhanced in consequence of the diminished returns obtained by those who employed fresh labour and stock on the less fertile land. Notwithstanding, then, that the advantages of fertile over inferior lands are in no case lost, but only transferred from the cultivator, or consumer, to the landlord, yet, since more labour is required on the inferior lands, and since it is from such land only that we are enabled to furnish ourselves with the additional supply of raw produce, the comparative value of that produce will continue permanently above its former level, and make it exchange for more hats, cloth, shoes, etc., etc., in the production of which no such additional quantity of labour is required.

The reason, then, why raw produce rises in comparative value is because more labour is employed in the production of the last portion obtained, and not because a rent is paid to the landlord. The value of corn is regulated by the quantity of labour bestowed on its production on that quality of land, or with that portion of capital, which pays no rent. Corn is not high because a rent is paid, but a rent is paid because corn is high; and it has been justly observed that no reduction would take place in the price of corn although landlords should forego the whole of their rent. Such a measure would only enable some farmers to live like gentlemen, but would not diminish the quantity of labour necessary to raise raw produce on the least productive land in cultivation.

Nothing is more common than to hear of the advantages which the land possesses over every other source of useful produce, on account of the surplus which it yields in the form of rent. Yet when land is most abundant, when most productive, and most fertile, it yields no rent; and it is only when its powers decay, and less is yielded in return for labour, that a share of the original produce of the more fertile portions is set apart for rent. It is singular that this quality in the land, which should have been noticed as an imperfection compared with the natural agents by which manufacturers are assisted, should have been pointed out as constituting its peculiar pre-eminence. If air, water, the elasticity of steam, and the pressure of the atmosphere were of various qualities; if they could be appropriated, and each quality existed only in moderate abundance, they, as well as the land, would afford a rent, as the successive qualities were brought into use. With every worse quality employed, the value of the commodities in the manufacture of which they were used would rise, because equal quantities of labour would be less productive. Man would do more by the sweat of his brow and nature perform less; and the land would be no longer pre-eminent for its limited powers.

If the surplus produce which land affords in the form of rent be an advantage, it is desirable that, every year, the machinery newly constructed should be less efficient than the old, as that would undoubtedly give a greater exchangeable value to the goods manufactured, not only by that machinery but by all the other machinery in the kingdom; and a rent would be paid to all those who possessed the most productive machinery.

The rise of rent is always the effect of the increasing wealth of the country, and of the difficulty of providing food for its augmented population. It is a symptom, but it is never a cause of wealth; for wealth often increases most rapidly while rent is either stationary, or even falling. Rent increases most rapidly as the disposable land decreases in its productive powers. Wealth increases most rapidly in those countries where the disposable land is most fertile, where importation is least restricted, and where, through agricultural improvements, productions can be multiplied without any increase in the proportional quantity of labour, and where consequently the progress of rent is slow.

If the high price of corn were the effect, and not the cause of rent, price would be proportionally influenced as rents were high or low, and rent would be a component part of price. But that corn which is produced by the greatest quantity of labour is the regulator of the price of corn; and rent does not and cannot enter in the least degree as a component part of its price. Adam Smith, therefore, cannot be correct in supposing that the original rule which regulated the exchangeable value of commodities, namely, the comparative quantity of labour by which they were produced, can be at all altered by the appropriation of land and the payment of rent. Raw material enters into the composition of most commodities, but the value of that raw material, as well as corn, is regulated by the productiveness of the portion of capital last employed on the land and paying no rent; and therefore rent is not a component part of the price of commodities.

We have been hitherto considering the effects of the natural progress of wealth and population on rent in a country in which the land is of variously productive powers, and we have seen that with every portion of additional capital which it becomes necessary to employ on the land with a less productive return rent would rise. It follows from the same principles that any circumstances in the society which should make it unnecessary to employ the same amount of capital on the land, and which should therefore make the portion last employed more productive, would lower rent. Any great reduction in the capital of a country which should materially diminish the funds destined for the maintenance of labour would naturally have this effect. Population regulates itself by the funds which are to employ it, and therefore always increases or diminishes with the increase or diminution of capital. Every reduction of capital is therefore necessarily followed by a less effective demand for corn, by a fall of price, and by diminished cultivation. In the reverse order to that in which the accumulation of capital raises rent will the diminution of it lower rent. Land of a less unproductive quality will be in succession relinquished, the exchangeable value of produce will fall, and land of a superior quality will be the land last cultivated, and that which will then pay no rent.

The same effects may, however, be produced when the wealth and population of a country are increased, if that increase is accompanied by such marked improvements in agriculture as shall have the same effect of diminishing the necessity of cultivating the poorer lands, or of expending the same amount of capital on the cultivation of the more fertile portions.

If a million of quarters of corn be necessary for the support of a given population, and it be raised on land of the qualities of No. 1, 2, 3; and if an improvement be afterwards discovered by which it can be raised on No. 1 and 2, without employing No. 3, it is evident that the immediate effect must be a fall of rent; for No. 2, instead of No. 3, will then be cultivated without paying any rent; and the rent of No. 1, instead of being the difference between the produce of No. 3 and No. 1, will be the difference only between No. 2 and 1. With the same population, and no more, there can be no demand for any additional quantity of corn; the capital and labour employed on No. 3 will be devoted to the production of other commodities desirable to the community, and can have no effect in raising rent, unless the raw material from which they are made cannot be obtained without employing capital less advantageously on the land, in which case No. 3 must again be cultivated.

It is undoubtedly true that the fall in the relative price of raw produce, in consequence of the improvement in agriculture, or rather in consequence of less labour being bestowed on its production, would naturally lead to increased accumulation; for the profits of stock would be greatly augmented. This accumulation would lead to an increased demand for labour, to higher wages, to an increased population, to a further demand for raw produce, and to an increased cultivation. It is only, however, after the increase in the population that rent would be as high as before; that is to say, after No. 3 was taken into cultivation. A considerable period would have elapsed, attended with a positive diminution of rent.

But improvements in agriculture are of two kinds: those which increase the productive powers of the land and those which enable us, by improving our machinery, to obtain its produce with less labour. They both lead to a fall in the price of raw produce; they both affect rent, but they do not affect it equally. If they did not occasion a fall in the price of raw produce they would not be improvements; for it is the essential quality of an improvement to diminish the quantity of labour before required to produce a commodity; and this diminution cannot take place without a fall of its price or relative value.

The improvements which increased the productive powers of the land are such as the more skilful rotation of crops or the better choice of manure. These improvements absolutely enable us to obtain the same produce from a smaller quantity of land. If, by the introduction of a course of turnips, I can feed my sheep besides raising my corn, the land on which the sheep were before fed becomes unnecessary, and the same quantity of raw produce is raised by the employment of a less quantity of land. If I discover a manure which will enable me to make a piece of land produce 20 per cent. more corn, I may withdraw at least a portion of my capital from the most unproductive part of my farm. But, as I before observed, it is not necessary that land should be thrown out of cultivation in order to reduce rent: to produce this effect, it is sufficient that successive portions of capital are employed on the same land with different results, and that the portion which gives the least results should be withdrawn. If, by the introduction of the turnip husbandry, or by the use of a more invigorating manure, I can obtain the same produce with less capital, and without disturbing the difference between the productive powers of the successive portions of capital, I shall lower rent; for a different and more productive portion will be that which will form the standard from which every other will be reckoned. If, for example, the successive portions of capital yielded 100, 90, 80, 70; whilst I employed these four portions, my rent would be 60, or the difference between

70 and 100 = 30	whilst the produce would be 340	100
70 and 90 = 20		90
70 and 80 = 10		80
—		70
60		—
		340

and while I employed these portions, the rent would remain the same, although the produce of each should have an equal augmentation. If, instead of 100, 90, 80, 70, the produce should be increased to 125, 115, 105, 95, the rent would still be 60, or the difference between

95 and 125 = 30	whilst the produce would be increased to 440	125
95 and 115 = 20		115
95 and 105 = 10		105
—		95
60		—
		440

But with such an increase of produce, without an increase of demand, there could be no motive for employing so much capital on the land; one portion would be withdrawn, and consequently the last portion of capital would yield 105 instead of 95, and rent would fall to 30, or the difference between

105 and 125 = 20	whilst the produce will be still adequate to the wants of the population, for it would be 345 quarters, or	125
105 and 115 = 10		115
—		105
30		—
		345

the demand being only for 340 quarters.—But there are improvements which may lower the relative value of produce without lowering the corn rent, though they will lower the money rent of land. Such improvements do not increase the productive powers of the land, but they enable us to obtain its produce with less labour. They are rather directed to the formation of the capital applied to the land than to the cultivation of the land itself. Improvements in agricultural implements, such as the plough and the thrashing machine, economy in the use of horses employed in husbandry, and a better knowledge of the veterinary art, are of this nature. Less capital, which is the same thing as less labour, will be employed on the land; but to obtain the same produce, less land cannot be cultivated. Whether improvements of this kind, however, affect corn rent must depend on the question whether the difference between the produce obtained by the employment of different portions of capital be increased, stationary, or diminished. If four portions of capital, 50, 60, 70, 80, be employed on the land, giving each the same results, and any improvement in the formation of such capital should enable me to withdraw 5 from each, so that they should be 45, 55, 65, and 75, no alteration would take place in the corn rent; but if the improvements were such as to enable me to make the whole saving on that portion of capital which is least productively employed, corn rent would immediately fall, because the difference between the capital most productive and the capital least productive would be diminished; and it is this difference which constitutes rent.

Without multiplying instances, I hope enough has been said to show that whatever diminishes the inequality in the produce obtained from successive portions of capital employed on the same or on new land tends to lower rent; and that whatever increases that inequality necessarily produces an opposite effect, and tends to raise it.

In speaking of the rent of the landlord, we have rather considered it as the proportion of the produce, obtained with a given capital on any given farm, without any reference to its exchangeable value; but since the same cause, the difficulty of production, raises the exchangeable value of raw produce, and raises also the proportion of raw produce paid to the landlord for rent, it is obvious that the landlord is doubly benefited by difficulty of production. First, he obtains a greater share, and, secondly, the commodity in which he is paid is of greater value.

III. ON WAGES

Labour, like all other things which are purchased and sold, and which may be increased or diminished in quantity, has its natural and its market price. The natural price of labour is that price which is necessary to enable the labourers, one with another, to subsist and to perpetuate their race, without either increase or diminution.

The power of the labourer to support himself, and the family which may be necessary to keep up the number of labourers, does not depend on the quantity of money which he may receive for wages, but on the quantity of food, necessaries, and conveniences become essential to him from habit which that money will purchase. The natural price of labour, therefore, depends on the price of the food, necessaries, and conveniences required for the support of the labourer and his family. With a rise in the price of food and necessaries, the natural price of labour will rise; with the fall in their price, the natural price of labour will fall.

With the progress of society the natural price of labour has always a tendency to rise, because one of the principal commodities by which its natural price is regulated has a tendency to become dearer from the greater difficulty of producing it. As, however, the improvements in agriculture, the discovery of new markets, whence provisions may be imported, may for a time counteract the tendency to a rise in the price of necessaries, and may even occasion their natural price to fall, so will the same causes produce the correspondent effects on the natural price of labour.

The natural price of all commodities, excepting raw produce and labour, has a tendency to fall in the progress of wealth and population; for though, on one hand, they are enhanced in real value, from the rise in the natural price of the raw material of which they are made, this is more than counterbalanced by the improvements in machinery, by the better division and distribution of labour, and by the increasing skill, both in science and art, of the producers.

The market price of labour is the price which is really paid for it, from the natural operation of the proportion of the supply to the demand; labour is dear when it is scarce and cheap when it is plentiful. However much the market price of labour may deviate from its natural price, it has, like commodities, a tendency to conform to it.

It is when the market price of labour exceeds its natural price that the condition of the labourer is flourishing and happy, that he has it in his power to command a greater proportion of the necessaries and enjoyments of life, and therefore to rear a healthy and numerous family. When, however, by the encouragement which high wages give to the increase of population, the number of labourers is increased, wages again fall to their natural price, and indeed from a reaction sometimes fall below it.

When the market price of labour is below its natural price, the condition of the labourers is most wretched: then poverty deprives them of those comforts which custom renders absolute necessaries. It is only after their privations have reduced their number, or the demand for labour has increased, that the market price of labour will rise to its natural price, and that the labourer will have the moderate comforts which the natural rate of wages will afford.

Notwithstanding the tendency of wages to conform to their natural rate, their market rate may, in an improving society, for an indefinite period, be constantly above it; for no sooner may the impulse which an increased capital gives to a new demand for labour be obeyed, than another increase of capital may produce the same effect; and thus, if the increase of capital be gradual and constant, the demand for labour may give a continued stimulus to an increase of people.

Capital is that part of the wealth of a country which is employed in production, and consists of food, clothing, tools, raw materials, machinery, etc., necessary to give effect to labour.

Capital may increase in quantity at the same time that its value rises. An addition may be made to the food and clothing of a country at the same time that more labour may be required to produce the additional quantity than before; in that case not only the quantity but the value of capital will rise.

Or capital may increase without its value increasing, and even while its value is actually diminishing; not only may an addition be made to the food and clothing of a country, but the addition may be made by the aid of machinery, without any increase, and even with an absolute diminution in the proportional quantity of labour required to produce them. The quantity of capital may increase, while neither the whole together, nor any part of it singly, will have a greater value than before, but may actually have a less.

In the first case, the natural price of labour, which always depends on the price of food, clothing, and other necessaries, will rise; in the second, it will remain stationary or fall; but in both cases the market rate of wages will rise, for in proportion to the increase of capital will be the increase in the demand for labour; in proportion to the work to be done will be the demand for those who are to do it.

In both cases, too, the market price of labour will rise above its natural price; and in both cases it will have a tendency to conform to its natural price, but in the first case this agreement will be most speedily effected. The situation of the labourer will be improved, but not much improved; for the increased price of food and necessaries will absorb a large portion of his increased wages; consequently a small supply of labour, or a trifling increase in the population, will soon reduce the market price to the then increased natural price of labour.

In the second case, the condition of the labourer will be very greatly improved; he will receive increased money wages without having to pay any increased price, and perhaps even a diminished price for the commodities which he and his family consume; and it will not be till after a great addition has been made to the population that the market price of labour will again sink to its then low and reduced natural price.

Thus, then, with every improvement of society, with every increase in its capital, the market wages of labour will rise; but the permanence of their rise will depend on the question whether the natural price of labour has also risen; and this again will depend on the rise in the natural price of those necessaries on which the wages of labour are expended.

It is not to be understood that the natural price of labour, estimated even in food and necessaries, is absolutely fixed and constant. It varies at different times in the same country, and very materially differs in different countries. It essentially depends on the habits and customs of the people. An English labourer would consider his wages under their natural rate, and too scanty to support a family, if they enabled him to purchase no other food than potatoes, and to live in no better habitation than a mud cabin; yet these moderate demands of nature are often deemed sufficient in countries where "man's life is cheap" and his wants easily satisfied. Many of the conveniences now enjoyed in an English cottage would have been thought luxuries at an earlier period of our history.

From manufactured commodities always falling and raw produce always rising, with the progress of society, such a disproportion in their relative value is at length created, that in rich countries a labourer, by the sacrifice of a very small quantity only of his food, is able to provide liberally for all his other wants.

Independently of the variations in the value of money, which necessarily affect money wages, but which we have here supposed to have no operation, as we have considered money to be uniformly of the same value, it appears then that wages are subject to a rise or fall from two causes:—

First, the supply and demand of labourers.

Secondly, the price of the commodities on which the wages of labour are expended.

In different stages of society, the accumulation of capital, or of the means of employing labour, is more or less rapid, and must in all cases depend on the productive powers of labour. The productive powers of labour are generally greatest when there is an abundance of fertile land: at such periods accumulation is often so rapid that labourers cannot be supplied with the same rapidity as capital.

It has been calculated that under favourable circumstances population may be doubled in twenty-five years; but under the same favourable circumstances the whole capital of a country might possibly be doubled in a shorter period. In that case, wages during the whole period would have a tendency to rise, because the demand for labour would increase still faster than the supply.

In new settlements, where the arts and knowledge of countries far advanced in refinement are introduced, it is probable that capital has a tendency to increase faster than mankind; and if the deficiency of labourers were not supplied by more populous countries, this tendency would very much raise the price of labour. In proportion as these countries become populous, and land of a worse quality is taken into cultivation, the tendency to an increase of capital diminishes; for the surplus produce remaining, after satisfying the wants of the existing population, must necessarily be in proportion to the facility of production, viz. to the smaller number of persons employed in production. Although, then, it is probable that, under the most favourable circumstances, the power of production is still greater than that of population, it will not long continue so; for the land being limited in quantity, and differing in quality, with every increased portion of capital employed on it there will be a decreased rate of production, whilst the power of population continues always the same.

In those countries where there is abundance of fertile land, but where, from the ignorance, indolence, and barbarism of the inhabitants, they are exposed to all the evils of want and famine, and where it has been said that population presses against the means of subsistence, a very different remedy should be applied from that which is necessary in long settled countries, where, from the diminishing rate of the supply of raw produce, all the evils of a crowded population are experienced. In the one case, the evil proceeds from bad government, from the insecurity of property, and from a want of education in all ranks of the people. To be made happier they require only to be better governed and instructed, as the augmentation of capital, beyond the augmentation of people, would be the inevitable result. No increase in the population can be too great, as the powers of production are still greater. In the other case, the population increases faster than the funds required for its support. Every exertion of industry, unless accompanied by a diminished rate of increase in the population, will add to the evil, for production cannot keep pace with it.

With a population pressing against the means of subsistence, the only remedies are either a reduction of people or a more rapid accumulation of capital. In rich countries, where all the fertile land is already cultivated, the latter remedy is neither very practicable nor very desirable, because its effect would be, if pushed very far, to render all classes equally poor. But in poor countries, where there are abundant means of production in store, from fertile land not yet brought into cultivation, it is the only safe and efficacious means of removing the evil, particularly as its effect would be to elevate all classes of the people.

The friends of humanity cannot but wish that in all countries the labouring classes should have a taste for comforts and enjoyments, and that they should be stimulated by all legal means in their exertions to procure them. There cannot be a better security against a superabundant population. In those countries where the labouring classes have the fewest wants, and are contented with the cheapest food, the people are exposed to the greatest vicissitudes and miseries. They have no place of refuge from calamity; they cannot seek safety in a lower station; they are already so low that they can fall no lower. On any deficiency of the chief article of their subsistence there are few substitutes of which they can avail themselves and dearth to them is attended with almost all the evils of famine.

In the natural advance of society, the wages of labour will have a tendency to fall, as far as they are regulated by supply and demand; for the supply of labourers will continue to increase at the same rate, whilst the demand for them will increase at a slower rate. If, for instance, wages were regulated by a yearly increase of capital at the rate of 2 per cent., they would fall when it accumulated only at the rate of 1½ per cent. They would fall still lower when it increased only at the rate of 1 or ½ per cent., and would continue to do so until the capital became stationary, when wages also would become stationary, and be only sufficient to keep up the numbers of the actual population. I say that, under these circumstances, wages would fall if they were regulated only by the supply and demand of labourers; but we must not forget that wages are also regulated by the prices of the commodities on which they are expended.

As population increases, these necessaries will be constantly rising in price, because more labour will be necessary to produce them. If, then, the money wages of labour should fall, whilst every commodity on which the wages of labour were expended rose, the labourer would be doubly affected, and would be soon totally deprived of subsistence. Instead, therefore, of the money wages of labour falling, they would rise; but they would not rise sufficiently to enable the labourer to purchase as many comforts and necessaries as he did before the rise in the price of those commodities. If his annual wages were before £24, or six quarters of corn when the price was £4 per quarter, he would probably receive only the value of five quarters when corn rose to £5 per quarter. But five quarters would cost £25; he would, therefore, receive an addition in his money wages, though with that addition he would be unable to furnish himself with the same quantity of corn and other commodities which he had before consumed in his family.

Notwithstanding, then, that the labourer would be really worse paid, yet this increase in his wages would necessarily diminish the profits of the manufacturer; for his goods would sell at no higher price, and yet the expense of producing them would be increased. This, however, will be considered in our examination into the principles which regulate profits.

It appears, then, that the same cause which raises rent, namely, the increasing difficulty of providing an additional quantity of food with the same proportional quantity of labour, will also raise wages; and therefore, if money be of an unvarying value, both rent and wages will have a tendency to rise with the progress of wealth and population.

But there is this essential difference between the rise of rent and the rise of wages. The rise in the money value of rent is accompanied by an increased share of the produce; not only is the landlord's money rent greater, but his corn rent also; he will have more corn, and each defined measure of that corn will exchange for a greater quantity of all other goods which have not been raised in value. The fate of the labourer will be less happy; he will receive more money wages, it is true, but his corn wages will be reduced; and not only his command of corn, but his general condition will be deteriorated, by his finding it more difficult to maintain the market rate of wages above their natural rate. While the price of corn rises 10 per cent., wages will always rise less than 10 per cent., but rent will always rise more; the condition of the labourer will generally decline, and that of the landlord will always be improved.

When wheat was at £4 per quarter, suppose the labourer's wages to be £24 per annum, or the value of six quarters of wheat, and suppose half his wages to be expended on wheat, and the other half, or £12, on other things. He would receive

£24 14*s.*	when wheat was at	£4 4*s.* 8*d.*	or the value of	5.83 quarters.
£25 10*s.*		£4 10*s.*		5.66 quarters.
£26 8*s.*		£4 16*s.*		5.50 quarters.
£27 8*s.* 6*d.*		£5 2*s.* 10*d.*		5.33 quarters.

He would receive these wages to enable him to live just as well, and no better, than before; for when corn was at £4 per quarter, he would

expend for three quarters of corn, at £4 per quarter	£12
and on other things	£12
	£24

When wheat was £4 4*s.* 8*d.*, three quarters, which he and his family consumed, would cost him	£12 14*s.*
other things not altered in price	£12
	£24 14*s.*

When at £4 10*s.*, three quarters of wheat would cost	£13 10*s.*
and other things	£12
	£25 10*s.*

When at £4 16*s.*, three quarters of wheat	£14 8*s.*
other things	£12
	£26 8*s.*

When at £5 2*s.* 10*d.*, three quarters of wheat would cost . . .	£15 8*s.* 6*d.*
other things	£12
	£27 8*s.* 6*d.*

In proportion as corn became dear, he would receive less corn wages, but his money wages would always increase, whilst his enjoyments, on the above supposition, would be precisely the same. But as other commodities would be raised in price in proportion as raw produce entered into their composition, he would have more to pay for some of them. Although his tea, sugar, soap, candles, and house rent would probably be no dearer, he would pay more for his bacon, cheese, butter, linen, shoes, and cloth;

and therefore, even with the above increase of wages, his situation would be comparatively worse. But it may be said that I have been considering the effect of wages on price on the supposition that gold, or the metal from which money is made, is the produce of the country in which wages varied; and that the consequences which I have deduced agree little with the actual state of things, because gold is a metal of foreign production. The circumstance, however, of gold being a foreign production will not invalidate the truth of the argument, because it may be shown that whether it were found at home, or were imported from abroad, the effects ultimately, and, indeed, immediately, would be the same.

When wages rise it is generally because the increase of wealth and capital have occasioned a new demand for labour, which will infallibly be attended with an increased production of commodities. To circulate these additional commodities, even at the same prices as before, more money is required, more of this foreign commodity from which money is made, and which can only be obtained by importation. Whenever a commodity is required in greater abundance than before, its relative value rises comparatively with those commodities with which its purchase is made. If more hats were wanted, their price would rise, and more gold would be given for them. If more gold were required, gold would rise, and hats would fall in price, as a greater quantity of hats and of all other things would then be necessary to purchase the same quantity of gold. But in the case supposed, to say that commodities will rise because wages rise, is to affirm a positive contradiction; for we, first, say that gold will rise in relative value in consequence of demand, and, secondly, that it will fall in relative value because prices will rise, two effects which are totally incompatible with each other. To say that commodities are raised in price is the same thing as to say that money is lowered in relative value; for it is by commodities that the relative value of gold is estimated. If, then, all commodities rose in price, gold could not come from abroad to purchase those dear commodities, but it would go from home to be employed with advantage in purchasing the comparatively cheaper foreign commodities. It appears, then, that the rise of wages will not raise the prices of commodities, whether the metal from which money is made be produced at home or in a foreign country. All commodities cannot rise at the same time without an addition to the quantity of money. This addition could not be obtained at home, as we have already shown; nor could it be imported from abroad. To purchase any additional quantity of gold from abroad, commodities at home must be cheap, not dear. The importation of gold, and a rise in the price of all homemade commodities with which gold is purchased or paid for, are effects absolutely incompatible. The extensive use of paper money does not alter this question, for paper money conforms, or ought to conform, to the value of gold, and therefore its value is influenced by such causes only as influence the value of that metal.

These, then, are the laws by which wages are regulated, and by which the happiness of far the greatest part of every community is governed. Like all other contracts, wages should be left to the fair and free competition of the market, and should never be controlled by the interference of the legislature.

The clear and direct tendency of the poor-laws is in direct opposition to these obvious principles: it is not, as the legislature benevolently intended, to amend the condition of the poor, but to deteriorate the condition of both poor and rich; instead of making the poor rich, they are calculated to make the rich poor; and whilst the present laws are in force, it is quite in the natural order of things that the fund for the maintenance of the poor should progressively increase till it has absorbed all the net revenue of the country, or at least so much of it as the state shall leave to us, after satisfying its own never-failing demands for the public expenditure.

This pernicious tendency of these laws is no longer a mystery, since it has been fully developed by the able hand of Mr. Malthus; and every friend to the poor must ardently wish for their abolition. Unfortunately, however, they have been so long established, and the habits of the poor have been so formed upon their operation, that to eradicate them with safety from our political system requires the most cautious and skilful management. It is agreed by all who are most friendly to a repeal of these laws that, if it be desirable to prevent the most overwhelming distress to those for whose benefit they were erroneously enacted, their abolition should be effected by the most gradual steps.

It is a truth which admits not a doubt that the comforts and well-being of the poor cannot be permanently secured without some regard on their part, or some effort on the part of the legislature, to regulate the increase of their numbers, and to render less frequent among them early and improvident marriages. The operation of the system of poor-laws has been directly contrary to this. They have rendered restraint superfluous, and have invited imprudence, by offering it a portion of the wages of prudence and industry.

The nature of the evil points out the remedy. By gradually contracting the sphere of the poor-laws; by impressing on the poor the value of independence, by teaching them that they must look not to systematic or casual charity, but to their own exertions for support, that prudence and forethought are neither unnecessary nor unprofitable virtues, we shall by degrees approach a sounder and more healthful state.

No scheme for the amendment of the poor-laws merits the least attention which has not their abolition for its ultimate object; and he is the best friend of the poor, and to the cause of humanity, who can point out how this end can be attained with the most security, and at the same time with the least violence. It is not by raising in any manner different from the present the fund from which the poor are supported that the evil can be mitigated. It would not only be no improvement, but it would be an aggravation of the distress which we wish to see removed, if the fund were increased in amount or were levied according to some late proposals, as a general fund from the country at large. The present mode of its collection and application has served to mitigate its pernicious effects. Each parish raises a separate fund for the support of its own poor. Hence it becomes an object of more interest and more practicability to keep the rates low than if one general fund were raised for the relief of the poor of the whole kingdom. A parish is much more interested in an economical collection of the rate, and a sparing distribution of relief, when the whole saving will be for its own benefit, than if hundreds of other parishes were to partake of it.

It is to this cause that we must ascribe the fact of the poor-laws not having yet absorbed all the net revenue of the country; it is to the rigour with which they are applied that we are indebted for their not having become overwhelmingly oppressive. If by law every human being wanting support could be sure to obtain it, and obtain it in such a degree as to make life tolerably comfortable, theory would lead us to expect that all other taxes together would be light compared with the single one of poor rates. The principle of gravitation is not more certain than the tendency of such laws to change wealth and power into misery and weakness; to call away the exertions of labour from every object, except that of providing mere subsistence; to confound all intellectual distinction; to busy the mind continually in supplying the body's wants; until at last all classes should be infected with the plague of universal poverty. Happily these laws have been in operation during a period of progressive prosperity, when the funds for the maintenance of labour have regularly increased, and when an increase of population would be naturally called for. But if our progress should become more slow; if we should attain the stationary state, from which I trust we are yet far distant, then will the pernicious nature of these laws become more manifest and alarming; and then, too, will their removal be obstructed by many additional difficulties.

IV. ON PROFITS

The profits of stock, in different employments, having been shown to bear a proportion to each other, and to have a tendency to vary all in the same degree and in the same direction, it remains for us to consider what is the cause of the permanent variations in the rate of profit, and the consequent permanent alterations in the rate of interest.

We have seen that the price of corn is regulated by the quantity of labour necessary to produce it, with that portion of capital which pays no rent. We have seen, too, that all manufactured commodities rise and fall in price in proportion as more or less labour becomes necessary to their production. Neither the farmer who cultivates that quantity of land which regulates price, nor the manufacturer who manufactures goods, sacrifices any portion of the produce for rent. The whole value of their commodities is divided into two portions only: one constitutes the profits of stock, the other the wages of labour.

Supposing corn and manufactured goods always to sell at the same price, profits would be high or low in proportion as wages were low or high. But suppose corn to rise in price because more labour is necessary to produce it; that cause will not raise the price of manufactured goods in the production of which no additional quantity of labour is required. If, then, wages continued the same, the profits of manufacturers would remain the same; but if, as is absolutely certain, wages should rise with the rise of corn, then their profits would necessarily fall.

If a manufacturer always sold his goods for the same money, for £1000, for example, his profits would depend on the price of the labour necessary to manufacture those goods. His profits would be less when wages amounted to £800 than when he paid only £600. In proportion then as wages rose would profits fall. But if the price of raw produce would increase, it may be asked whether the farmer at least would not have the same rate of profits, although he should pay an additional sum for wages? Certainly not: for he will not only have to pay, in common with the manufacturer, an increase of wages to each labourer he employs, but he will be obliged either to pay rent, or to employ an additional number of labourers to obtain the same produce; and the rise in the price of raw produce will be proportioned only to that rent, or that additional number, and will not compensate him for the rise of wages.

If both the manufacturer and farmer employed ten men, on wages rising from £24 to £25 per annum per man, the whole sum paid by each would be £250 instead of £240. This is, however, the whole addition that would be paid by the manufacturer to obtain the same quantity of commodities; but the farmer on new land would probably be obliged to employ an additional man, and therefore to pay an additional sum of £25 for wages; and the farmer on the old land would be obliged to pay precisely the same additional sum of £25 for rent; without which additional labour corn would not have risen nor rent have been increased. One will therefore have to pay £275 for wages alone, the other for wages and rent together; each £25 more than the manufacturer: for this latter £25 the farmer is compensated by the addition to the price of raw produce, and therefore his profits still conform to the profits of the manufacturer. As this proposition is important, I will endeavour still further to elucidate it.

We have shown that in early stages of society, both the landlord's and the labourer's share of the *value* of the produce of the earth would be but small; and that it would increase in proportion to the progress of wealth and the difficulty of procuring food. We have shown, too, that although the value of the labourer's portion will be increased by the high value of food, his real share will be diminished; whilst that of the landlord will not only be raised in value, but will also be increased in quantity.

The remaining quantity of the produce of the land, after the landlord and labourer are paid, necessarily belongs to the farmer, and constitutes the profits of his stock. But it may be alleged, that though, as society advances, his proportion of the whole produce will be diminished yet as it will rise in value, he, as well as the landlord and labourer, may, notwithstanding, receive a greater value.

It may be said, for example, that when corn rose from £4 to £10, the 180 quarters obtained from the best land would sell for £1800 instead of £720; and, therefore, though the landlord and labourer be proved to have a greater value for rent and wages, still the value of the farmer's profit might also be augmented. This, however, is impossible, as I shall now endeavour to show.

In the first place, the price of corn would rise only in proportion to the increased difficulty of growing it on land of a worse quality.

It has been already remarked, that if the labour of ten men will, on land of a certain quality, obtain 180 quarters of wheat, and its value be £4 per quarter, or £720; and if the labour of ten additional men will, on the same or any other land, produce only 170 quarters in addition, wheat would rise from £4 to £4 4s *8d.;* for 170 : 180 : : £4 : £4 4s. 8*d*. In other words, as for the production of 170 quarters the labour of ten men is necessary in the one case, and only that of 9.44 in the other, the rise would be as 9.44 to 10, or as £4 to £4 4*s*. 8*d*. In the same manner it might be shown that, if the labour of ten additional men would only produce 160 quarters, the price would further rise to £4 10*s*.; if 150, to £4 16*s*., etc., etc.

But when 180 quarters were produced on the land paying no rent, and its price was £4 per quarter, it is sold for . .	£720
And when 170 quarters were produced on the land paying no rent, and the price rose to £4 4*s*. 8*d*., it still sold for . .	720
So 160 quarters at £4 10*s*. produce	720
And 150 quarters at £4 16*s*. produce the same sum of . . .	720

Now, it is evident that if, out of these equal values, the farmer is at one time obliged to pay wages regulated by the price of wheat at £4, and at other times at higher prices, the rate of his profits will diminish in proportion to the rise in the price of corn.

In this case, therefore, I think it is clearly demonstrated that a rise in the price of corn, which increases the money wages of the labourer, diminishes the money value of the farmer's profits.

But the case of the farmer of the old and better land will be in no way different; he also will have increased wages to pay, and will never retain more of the value of the produce, however high may be its price, than £720 to be divided between himself and his always equal number of labourers; in proportion therefore as they get more, he must retain less.

When the price of corn was at £4, the whole 180 quarters belonged to the cultivator, and he sold it for £720. When corn rose to £4 4*s.* 8*d.*, he was obliged to pay the value of ten quarters out of his 180 for rent, consequently the remaining 170 yielded him no more than £720: when it rose further to £4 10*s.*, he paid twenty quarters, or their value, for rent, and consequently only retained 160 quarters, which yielded the same sum of £720.

It will be seen, then, that whatever rise may take place in the price of corn, in consequence of the necessity of employing more labour and capital to obtain a given additional quantity of produce, such rise will always be equalled in value by the additional rent or additional labour employed; so that whether corn sells for £4, £4 10*s.*, or £5 2*s.* 10*d.*, the farmer will obtain for that which remains to him, after paying rent, the same real value. Thus we see that whether the produce belonging to the farmer be 180, 170, 160, or 150 quarters, he always obtains the same sum of £720 for it; the price increasing in an inverse proportion to the quantity.

Rent, then, it appears, always falls on the consumer, and never on the farmer; for if the produce of his farm should uniformly be 180 quarters, with the rise of price he would retain the value of a less quantity for himself, and give the value of a larger quantity to his landlord; but the deduction would be such as to leave him always the same sum of £720.

It will be seen too, that, in all cases, the same sum of £720 must be divided between wages and profits. If the value of the raw produce from the land exceed this value it belongs to rent, whatever may be its amount. If there be no excess, there will be no rent. Whether wages or profits rise or fall, it is this sum of £720 from which they must both be provided. On the one hand, profits can never rise so high as to absorb so much of this £720 that enough will not be left to furnish the labourers with absolute necessaries; on the other hand, wages can never rise so high as to leave no portion of this sum for profits.

Thus in every case, agricultural as well as manufacturing profits are lowered by a rise in the price of raw produce, if it be accompanied by a rise of wages. If the farmer gets no additional value for the corn which remains to him after paying rent, if the manufacturer gets no additional value for the goods which he manufactures, and if both are obliged to pay a greater value in wages, can any point be more clearly established than that profits must fall with a rise of wages?

The farmer, then, although he pays no part of his landlord's rent, that being always regulated by the price of produce, and invariably falling on the consumers, has however a very decided interest in keeping rent low, or rather in keeping the natural price of produce low. As a consumer of raw produce, and of those things into which raw produce enters as a component part, he will, in common with all other consumers, be interested in keeping the price low. But he is most materially concerned with the high price of corn as it affects wages. With every rise in the price of corn, he will have to pay, out of an equal and unvarying sum of £720, an additional sum for wages to the ten men whom he is supposed constantly to employ. We have seen, in treating on wages, that they invariably rise with the rise in the price of raw produce. On a basis assumed for the purpose of calculation, page 316, it will be seen that if when wheat is at £4 per quarter, wages should be £24 per annum,

	£	s.	d.		£	s.	d.
When wheat is at	4	4	8	wages would be	24	14	0
	4	10	0		25	10	0
	4	16	0		26	8	0
	5	2	10		27	8	6

Now, of the unvarying fund of £720 to be distributed between labourers and farmers,

	£	s.	d.		£	s.	d.		£	s.	d.
When the price of wheat is at	4	0	0	the labourers will receive	240	0	0	the farmer will receive	480	0	0
	4	4	8		247	0	0		473	0	0
	4	10	0		255	0	0		465	0	0
	4	16	0		264	0	0		456	0	0
	5	2	10		274	5	0		445	15	

And supposing that the original capital of the farmer was £3000, the profits of his stock being in the first instance £480, would be at the rate of 16 per cent. When his profits fell to £473, they would be at the rate of 15.7 per cent.

£465	15.5
£456	15.2
£445	14.8

But the *rate* of profits will fall still more, because the capital of the farmer, it must be recollected, consists in a great measure of raw produce, such as his corn and hayricks, his unthreshed wheat and barley, his horses and cows, which would all rise in price in consequence of the rise of produce. His absolute profits would fall from £480 to £445 15*s*.; but if, from the cause which I have just stated, his capital should rise from £3000 to £3200, the rate of his profits would, when corn was at £5 2*s*. 10*d*., be under 14 per cent.

If a manufacturer had also employed £3000 in his business, he would be obliged, in consequence of the rise of wages, to increase his capital, in order to be enabled to carry on the same business. If his commodities sold before for £720 they would continue to sell at the same price; but the wages of labour, which were before £240, would rise, when corn was at £5 2*s*. 10*d*., to £274 5*s*. In the first case he would have a balance of £480 as profit on £3000, in the second he would have a profit only of £445 15*s*., on an increased capital, and therefore his profits would conform to the altered rate of those of the farmer.

There are few commodities which are not more or less affected in their price by the rise of raw produce, because some raw material from the land enters into the composition of most commodities. Cotton goods, linen, and cloth will all rise in price with the rise of wheat; but they rise on account of the greater quantity of labour expended on the raw material from which they are made, and not because more was paid by the manufacturer to the labourers whom he employed on those commodities.

In all cases, commodities rise because more labour is expended on them, and not because the labour which is expended on them is at a higher value. Articles of jewellery, of iron, of plate, and of copper, would not rise, because none of the raw produce from the surface of the earth enters into their composition.

It may be said that I have taken it for granted that money wages would rise with a rise in the price of raw produce, but that this is by no means a necessary consequence, as the labourer may be contented with fewer enjoyments. It is true that the wages of labour may previously have been at a high level, and that they may bear some reduction. If so, the fall of profits will be checked; but it is impossible to conceive that the money price of wages should fall or remain stationary with a gradually increasing price of necessaries; and therefore it may be taken for granted that, under ordinary circumstances, no permanent rise takes place in the price of necessaries without occasioning, or having been preceded by, a rise in wages.

The effects produced on profits would have been the same, or nearly the same, if there had been any rise in the price of those other necessaries, besides food, on which the wages of labour are expended. The necessity which the labourer would be under of paying an increased price for such necessaries would oblige him to demand more wages; and whatever increases wages, necessarily reduces profits. But suppose the price of silks, velvets, furniture, and any other commodities, not required by the labourer, to rise in consequence of more labour being expended on them, would not that affect profits? Certainly not: for nothing can affect profits but a rise in wages; silks and velvets are not consumed by the labourer, and therefore cannot raise wages.

It is to be understood that I am speaking of profits generally. I have already remarked that the market price of a commodity may exceed its natural or necessary price, as it may be produced in less abundance than the new demand for it requires. This, however, is but a temporary effect. The high profits on capital employed in producing that commodity will naturally attract capital to that trade; and as soon as the requisite funds are supplied, and the quantity of the commodity is duly increased, its price will fall, and the profits of the trade will conform to the general level. A fall in the general rate of profits is by no means incompatible with a partial rise of profits in particular employments. It is through the inequality of profits that capital is moved from one employment to another. Whilst, then, general profits are falling, and gradually settling at a lower level in consequence of the rise of wages, and the increasing difficulty of supplying the increasing population with necessaries, the profits of the farmer may, for an interval of some little duration, be above the former level. An extraordinary stimulus may be also given for a certain time to a particular branch of foreign and colonial trade; but the admission of this fact by no means invalidates the theory that profits depend on high or low wages, wages on the price of necessaries, and the price of necessaries chiefly on the price of food, because all other requisites may be increased almost without limit.

It should be recollected that prices always vary in the market, and in the first instance, through the comparative state of demand and supply. Although cloth could be furnished at 40*s.* per yard, and give the usual profits of stock, it may rise to 60*s.* or 80*s.* from a general change of fashion, or from any other cause which should suddenly and unexpectedly increase the demand or diminish the supply of it. The makers of cloth will for a time have unusual profits, but capital will naturally flow to that manufacture, till the supply and demand are again at their fair level, when the price of cloth will again sink to 40*s.*, its natural or necessary price. In the same manner, with every increased demand for corn, it may rise so high as to afford more than the general profits to the farmer. If there be plenty of fertile land, the price of corn will again fall to its former standard, after the requisite quantity of capital has been employed in producing it, and profits will be as before; but if there be not plenty of fertile land, if, to produce this additional quantity, more than the usual quantity of capital and labour be required, corn will not fall to its former level. Its natural price will be raised, and the farmer, instead of obtaining permanently larger profits, will find himself obliged to be satisfied with the diminished rate which is the inevitable consequence of the rise of wages, produced by the rise of necessaries.

The natural tendency of profits then is to fall; for, in the progress of society and wealth, the additional quantity of food required is obtained by the sacrifice of more and more labour. This tendency, this gravitation as it were of profits, is happily checked at repeated intervals by the improvements in machinery connected with the production of necessaries, as well as by discoveries in the science of agriculture, which enable us to relinquish a portion of labour before required, and therefore to lower the price of the prime necessary of the labourer. The rise in the price of necessaries and in the wages of labour is, however, limited; for as soon as wages should be equal (as in the case formerly stated) to £720, the whole receipts of the farmer, there must be an end of accumulation; for no capital can then yield any profit whatever, and no additional labour can be demanded, and consequently population will have reached its highest point. Long, indeed, before this period, the very low rate of profits will have arrested all accumulation, and almost the whole produce of the country, after paying the labourers, will be the property of the owners of land and the receivers of tithes and taxes.

Thus, taking the former very imperfect basis as the grounds of my calculation, it would appear that when corn was at £20 per quarter, the whole net income of the country would belong to the landlords, for then the same quantity of labour that was originally necessary to produce 180 quarters would be necessary to produce 36; since £20 : £4 : : 180 : 36. The farmer, then, who produced 180 quarters (if any such there were, for the old and new capital employed on the land would be so blended that it could in no way be distinguished), would sell the

180 qrs. at £20 per qr. or	£3600
the value of 144 qrs. { to landlord for rent, being the difference between 36 and 180 qrs. }	2880
—	—
36 qrs.	720
the value of 36 qrs. to labourers, ten in number	720
leaving nothing whatever for profit.	—

I have supposed that at this price of £20 the labourers would continue to consume three quarters each per annum, or	£60
And that on the other commodities they would expend	12
	—
	72 for each labourer.

And therefore ten labourers would cost £720 per annum.

In all these calculations I have been desirous only to elucidate the principle, and it is scarcely necessary to observe that my whole basis is assumed at random, and merely for the purpose of exemplification. The results, though different in degree, would have been the same in principle, however accurately I might have set out in stating the difference in the number of labourers necessary to obtain the successive quantities of corn required by an increasing population, the quantity consumed by the labourer's family, etc., etc. My object has been to simplify the subject, and I have therefore made no allowance for the increasing price of the other necessaries, besides food, of the labourer; an increase which would be the consequence of the increased value of the raw materials from which they are made, and which would of course further increase wages and lower profits.

I have already said that long before this state of prices was become permanent there would be no motive for accumulation; for no one accumulates but with a view to make his accumulation productive, and it is only when so employed that it operates on profits. Without a motive there could be no accumulation, and consequently such a state of prices never could take place. The farmer and manufacturer can no more live without profit than the labourer without wages. Their motive for accumulation will diminish with every diminution of profit, and will cease altogether when their profits are so low as not to afford them an adequate compensation for their trouble, and the risk which they must necessarily encounter in employing their capital productively.

I must again observe that the rate of profits would fall much more rapidly than I have estimated in my calculation; for the value of the produce being what I have stated it under the circumstances supposed, the value of the farmer's stock would be greatly increased from its necessarily consisting of many of the commodities which had risen in value. Before corn could rise from £4 to £12, his capital would probably be doubled in exchangeable value, and be worth £6000 instead of £3000. If then his profit were £180, or 6 per cent. on his original capital, profits would not at that time be really at a higher *rate* than 3 per cent.; for £6000 at 3 per cent. gives £180; and on those terms only could a new farmer with £6000 money in his pocket enter into the farming business.

Many trades would derive some advantage, more or less, from the same source. The brewer, the distiller, the clothier, the linen manufacturer, would be partly compensated for the diminution of their profits by the rise in the value of their stock of raw and finished materials; but a manufacturer of hardware, of jewellery, and of many other commodities, as well as those whose capitals uniformly consisted of money, would be subject to the whole fall in the rate of profits, without any compensation whatever.

We should also expect that, however the rate of the profits of stock might diminish in consequence of the accumulation of capital on the land, and the rise of wages, yet that the aggregate amount of profits would increase. Thus, supposing that, with repeated accumulations of £100,000, the rate of profit should fall from 20 to 19, to 18, to 17 per cent., a constantly diminishing rate, we should expect that the whole amount of profits received by those successive owners of capital would be always progressive; that it would be greater when the capital was £200,000 than when £100,000; still greater when £300,000; and so on, increasing, though at a diminishing rate, with every increase of capital. This progression, however, is only true for a certain time; thus, 19 per cent. on £200,000 is more than 20 on £100,000; again, 18 per cent. on £300,000 is more than 19 per cent. on £200,000; but after capital has accumulated to a large amount, and profits have fallen, the further accumulation diminishes the aggregate of profits. Thus, suppose the accumulation should be £1,000,000, and the profits 7 per cent., the whole amount of profits will be £70,000; now if an addition of £100,000 capital be made to the million, and profits should fall to 6 per cent., £66,000 or a diminution of £4000 will be received by the owners of stock, although the whole amount of stock will be increased from £1,000,000 to £1,100,000.

There can, however, be no accumulation of capital so long as stock yields any profit at all, without its yielding not only an increase of produce, but an increase of value. By employing £100,000 additional capital, no part of the former capital will be rendered less productive. The produce of the land and labour of the country must increase, and its value will be raised, not only by the value of the addition which is made to the former quantity of productions, but by the new value which is given to the whole produce of the land, by the increased difficulty of producing the last portion of it. When the accumulation of capital, however, becomes very great, notwithstanding this increased value, it will be so distributed that a less value than before will be appropriated to profits, while that which is devoted to rent and wages will be increased. Thus with successive additions of £100,000 to capital, with a fall in the rate of profits, from 20 to 19, to 18, to 17 per cent., etc., the productions annually obtained will increase in quantity, and be of more than the whole additional value which the additional capital is calculated to produce. From £20,000 it will rise to more than £39,000, and then to more than £57,000, and when the capital employed is a million, as we before supposed, if £100,000 more be added to it, and the aggregate of profits is actually lower than before, more than £6000 will nevertheless be added to the revenue of the country, but it will be to the revenue of the landlords and labourers; they will obtain more than the additional produce, and will from their situation be enabled to encroach even on the former gains of the capitalist. Thus, suppose the price of corn to be £4 per quarter, and that therefore, as we before calculated, of every £720 remaining to the farmer after payment of his rent, £480 were retained by him, and £240 were paid to his labourers; when the price rose to £6 per quarter, he would be obliged to pay his labourers £300 and retain only £420 for profits: he would be obliged to pay them £300 to enable them to consume the same quantity of necessaries as before, and no more. Now if the capital employed were so large as to yield a hundred thousand times £720, or £72,000,000, the aggregate of profits would be £48,000,000 when wheat was at £4 per quarter; and if by employing a larger capital 105,000 times £720 were obtained when wheat was at £6, or £75,600,000, profits would actually fall from £48,000,000 to £44,100,000 or 105,000 times £420, and wages would rise from £24,000,000 to £31,500,000. Wages would rise because more labourers would be employed in proportion to capital; and each labourer would receive more money wages; but the condition of the labourer, as we have already shown, would be worse, inasmuch as he would be able to command a less quantity of the produce of the country. The only real gainers would be the landlords; they would receive higher rents, first, because produce would be of a higher value, and secondly, because they would have a greatly increased proportion of that produce.

Although a greater value is produced, a greater proportion of what remains of that value, after paying rent, is consumed by the producers, and it is this, and this alone, which regulates profits. Whilst the land yields abundantly, wages may temporarily rise, and the producers may consume more than their accustomed proportion; but the stimulus which will thus be given to population will speedily reduce the labourers to their usual consumption. But when poor lands are taken into cultivation, or when more capital and labour are expended on the old land, with a less return of produce, the effect must be permanent. A greater proportion of that part of the produce which remains to be divided, after paying rent, between the owners of stock and the labourers, will be apportioned to the latter. Each man may, and probably will, have a less absolute quantity; but as more labourers are employed in proportion to the whole produce retained by the farmer, the value of a greater proportion of the whole produce will be absorbed by wages, and consequently the value of a smaller proportion will be devoted to profits. This will necessarily be rendered permanent by the laws of nature, which have limited the productive powers of the land.

Thus we again arrive at the same conclusion which we have before attempted to establish:—that in all countries, and all times, profits depend on the quantity of labour requisite to provide necessaries for the labourers on that land or with that capital which yields no rent. The effects then of accumulation will be different in different countries, and will depend chiefly on the fertility of the land. However extensive a country may be where the land is of a poor quality, and where the importation of food is prohibited, the most moderate accumulations of capital will be attended with great reductions in the rate of profit and a rapid rise in rent; and on the contrary a small but fertile country, particularly if it freely permits the importation of food, may accumulate a large stock of capital without any great diminution in the rate of profits, or any great increase in the rent of land. In the chapter on Wages we have endeavoured to show that the money price of commodities would not be raised by a rise of wages, either on the supposition that gold, the standard of money, was the produce of this country, or that it was imported from abroad. But if it were otherwise, if the prices of commodities were permanently raised by high wages, the proposition would not be less true, which asserts that high wages invariably affect the employers of labour by depriving them of a portion of their real profits. Supposing the hatter, the hosier, and the shoemaker each paid £10 more wages in the manufacture of a particular quantity of their commodities, and that the price of hats, stockings, and shoes rose by a sum sufficient to repay the manufacturer the £10; their situation would be no better than if no such rise took place. If the hosier sold his stockings for £110 instead of £100, his profits would be precisely the same money amount as before; but as he would obtain in exchange for this equal sum, one tenth less of hats, shoes, and every other commodity, and as he could with his former amount of savings employ fewer labourers at the increased wages, and purchase fewer raw materials at the increased prices, he would be in no better situation than if his money profits had been really diminished in amount and everything had remained at its former price. Thus, then, I have endeavoured to show, first, that a rise of wages would not raise the price of commodities, but would invariably lower profits; and secondly, that if the prices of all commodities could be raised, still the effect on profits would be the same; and that, in fact, the value of the medium only in which prices and profits are estimated would be lowered.

V. ON FOREIGN TRADE

No extension of foreign trade will immediately increase the amount of value in a country, although it will very powerfully contribute to increase the mass of commodities, and therefore the sum of enjoyments. As the value of all foreign goods is measured by the quantity of the produce of our land and labour which is given in exchange for them, we should have no greater value if, by the discovery of new markets, we obtained double the quantity of foreign goods in exchange for a given quantity of ours. If by the purchase of English goods to the amount of £1000 a merchant can obtain a quantity of foreign goods, which he can sell in the English market for

£1200, he will obtain 20 per cent. profit by such an employment of his capital; but neither his gains, nor the value of the commodities imported, will be increased or diminished by the greater or smaller quantity of foreign goods obtained. Whether, for example, he imports twenty-five or fifty pipes of wine, his interest can be no way affected if at one time the twenty-five pipes, and at another the fifty pipes, equally sell for £1200. In either case his profit will be limited to £200, or 20 per cent. on his capital; and in either case the same value will be imported into England. If the fifty pipes sold for more than £1200, the profits of this individual merchant would exceed the general rate of profits, and capital would naturally flow into this advantageous trade, till the fall of the price of wine had brought everything to the former level.

It has indeed been contended that the great profits which are sometimes made by particular merchants in foreign trade will elevate the general rate of profits in the country, and that the abstraction of capital from other employments, to partake of the new and beneficial foreign commerce, will raise prices generally, and thereby increase profits. It has been said, by high authority, that less capital being necessarily devoted to the growth of corn, to the manufacture of cloth, hats, shoes, etc., while the demand continues the same, the price of these commodities will be so increased that the farmer, hatter, clothier, and shoemaker will have an increase of profits as well as the foreign merchant.

They who hold this argument agree with me that the profits of different employments have a tendency to conform to one another; to advance and recede together. Our variance consists in this: They contend that the equality of profits will be brought about by the general rise of profits; and I am of opinion that the profits of the favoured trade will speedily subside to the general level.

For, first, I deny that less capital will necessarily be devoted to the growth of corn, to the manufacture of cloth, hats, shoes, etc., unless the demand for these commodities be diminished; and if so, their price will not rise. In the purchase of foreign commodities, either the same, a larger, or a less portion of the produce of the land and labour of England will be employed. If the same portion be so employed, then will the same demand exist for cloth, shoes, corn, and hats as before, and the same portion of capital will be devoted to their production. If, in consequence of the price of foreign commodities being cheaper, a less portion of the annual produce of the land and labour of England is employed in the purchase of foreign commodities, more will remain for the purchase of other things. If there be a greater demand for hats, shoes, corn, etc., than before, which there may be, the consumers of foreign commodities having an additional portion of their revenue disposable, the capital is also disposable with which the greater value of foreign commodities was before purchased; so that with the increased demand for corn, shoes, etc., there exists also the means of procuring an increased supply, and therefore neither prices nor profits can permanently rise. If more of the produce of the land and labour of England be employed in the purchase of foreign commodities, less can be employed in the purchase of other things, and therefore fewer hats, shoes, etc., will be required. At the same time that capital is liberated from the production of shoes, hats, etc., more must be employed in manufacturing those commodities with which foreign commodities are purchased; and, consequently, in all cases the demand for foreign and home commodities together, as far as regards value, is limited by the revenue and capital of the country. If one increases the other must diminish. If the quantity of wine imported in exchange for the same quantity of English commodities be doubled, the people of England can either consume double the quantity of wine that they did before or the same quantity of wine and a greater quantity of English commodities. If my revenue had been £1000, with which I purchased annually one pipe of wine for £100, and a certain quantity of English commodities for £900; when wine fell to £50 per pipe, I might lay out the £50 saved, either in the purchase of an additional pipe of wine or in the purchase of more English commodities. If I bought more wine, and every wine drinker did the same, the foreign trade would not be in the least disturbed; the same quantity of English commodities would be exported in exchange for wine, and we should receive double the quantity, though not double the value of wine. But if I, and others, contented ourselves with the same quantity of wine as before, fewer English commodities would be exported, and the wine drinkers might either consume the commodities which were before exported, or any others for which they had an inclination. The capital required for their production would be supplied by the capital liberated from the foreign trade.

There are two ways in which capital may be accumulated; it may be saved either in consequence of increased revenue or of diminished consumption. If my profits are raised from £1000 to £1200, while my expenditure continues the same, I accumulate annually £200 more than I did before. If I save £200 out of my expenditure, while my profits continue the same, the same effect will be produced; £200 per annum will be added to my capital. The merchant who imported wine after profits had been raised from 20 per cent. to 40 per cent., instead of purchasing his English goods for £1000, must purchase them for £857 2*s.* 10*d.*, still selling the wine which he imports in return for those goods for £1200; or, if he continued to purchase his English goods for £1000, must raise the price of his wine to £1400; he would thus obtain 40 instead of 20 per cent. profit on his capital; but if, in consequence of the cheapness of all the commodities on which his revenue was expended, he and all other consumers could save the value of £200 out of every £1000 they before expended, they would more effectually add to the real wealth of the country; in one case, the savings would be made in consequence of an increase of revenue, in the other, in consequence of diminished expenditure.

If, by the introduction of machinery, the generality of the commodities on which revenue was expended fell 20 per cent. in value, I should be enabled to save as effectually as if my revenue had been raised 20 per cent.; but in one case the rate of profits is stationary, in the other it is raised 20 per cent.—If, by the introduction of cheap foreign goods, I can save 20 per cent. from my expenditure, the effect will be precisely the same as if machinery had lowered the expense of their production, but profits would not be raised.

It is not, therefore, in consequence of the extension of the market that the rate of profit is raised, although such extension may be equally efficacious in increasing the mass of commodities, and may thereby enable us to augment the funds destined for the maintenance of labour, and the materials on which labour may be employed. It is quite as important to the happiness of mankind that our enjoyments should be increased by the better distribution of labour, by each country producing those commodities for which by its situation, its climate, and its other natural or artificial advantages it is adapted, and by their exchanging them for the commodities of other countries, as that they should be augmented by a rise in the rate of profits.

It has been my endeavour to show throughout this work that the rate of profits can never be increased but by a fall in wages, and that there can be no permanent fall of wages but in consequence of a fall of the necessaries on which wages are expended. If, therefore, by the extension of foreign trade, or by improvements in machinery, the food and necessaries of the labourer can be brought to market, at a reduced price, profits will rise. If, instead of growing our own corn, or manufacturing the clothing and other necessaries of the labourer, we discover a new market from which we can supply ourselves with these commodities at a cheaper price, wages will fall and profits rise; but if the commodities obtained at a cheaper rate, by the extension of foreign commerce, or by the improvement of machinery, be exclusively the commodities consumed by the rich, no alteration will take place in the rate of profits. The rate of wages would not be affected, although wine, velvets, silks, and other expensive commodities should fall 50 per cent., and consequently profits would continue unaltered.

Foreign trade, then, though highly beneficial to a country, as it increases the amount and variety of the objects on which revenue may be expended, and affords, by the abundance and cheapness of commodities, incentives to saving, and to the accumulation of capital, has no tendency to raise the profits of stock unless the commodities imported be of that description on which the wages of labour are expended.

VI. ON TAXES

Taxes are a portion of the produce of the land and labour of a country placed at the disposal of the government, and are always ultimately paid either from the capital or from the revenue of the country.

We have already shown how the capital of a country is either fixed or circulating, according as it is of a more or of a less durable nature. It is difficult to define strictly where the distinction between circulating and fixed capital begins, for there are almost infinite degrees in the durability of capital. The food of a country is consumed and reproduced at least once in every year; the clothing of the labourer is probably not consumed and reproduced in less than two years; whilst his house and furniture are calculated to endure for a period of ten or twenty years.

When the annual productions of a country more than replace its annual consumption, it is said to increase its capital; when its annual consumption is not at least replaced by its annual production, it is said to diminish its capital. Capital may therefore be increased by an increased production or by a diminished unproductive consumption.

If the consumption of the government when increased by the levy of additional taxes be met either by an increased production or by a diminished consumption on the part of the people, the taxes will fall upon revenue, and the national capital will remain unimpaired; but if there be no increased production or diminished unproductive consumption on the part of the people, the taxes will necessarily fall on capital, that is to say, they will impair the fund allotted to productive consumption.

In proportion as the capital of a country is diminished, its productions will be necessarily diminished; and, therefore, if the same unproductive expenditure on the part of the people and of the government continue, with a constantly diminishing annual reproduction, the resources of the people and the state will fall away with increasing rapidity, and distress and ruin will follow.

Notwithstanding the immense expenditure of the English government during the last twenty years, there can be little doubt but that the increased production on the part of the people has more than compensated for it. The national capital has not merely been unimpaired, it has been greatly increased, and the annual revenue of the people, even after the payment of their taxes, is probably greater at the present time than at any former period of our history.

For the proof of this, we might refer to the increase of population—to the extension of agriculture—to the increase of shipping and manufactures—to the building of docks—to the opening of numerous canals, as well as to many other expensive undertakings; all denoting an increase both of capital and of annual production.

Still, however, it is certain that, but for taxation, this increase of capital would have been much greater. There are no taxes which have not a tendency to lessen the power to accumulate. All taxes must either fall on capital or revenue. If they encroach on capital, they must proportionably diminish that fund by whose extent the extent of the productive industry of the country must always be regulated; and if they fall on revenue, they must either lessen accumulation or force the contributors to save the amount of the tax, by making a corresponding diminution of their former unproductive consumption of the necessaries and luxuries of life. Some taxes will produce these effects in a much greater degree than others; but the great evil of taxation is to be found, not so much in any selection of its objects as in the general amount of its effects taken collectively.

Taxes are not necessarily taxes on capital because they are laid on capital, nor on income because they are laid on income. If from my income of £1000 per annum I am required to pay £100, it will really be a tax on my income should I be content with the expenditure of the remaining £900; but it will be a tax on capital if I continue to spend £1000.

The capital from which my income of £1000 is derived may be of the value of £10,000; a tax of one per cent. on such capital would be £100; but my capital would be unaffected if, after paying this tax, I in like manner contented myself with the expenditure of £900.

The desire which every man has to keep his station in life, and to maintain his wealth at the height which it has once attained, occasions most taxes, whether laid on capital or on income, to be paid from income; and, therefore, as taxation proceeds, or as government increases its expenditure, the annual enjoyments of the people must be diminished, unless they are enabled proportionally to increase their capitals and income. It should be the policy of governments to encourage a disposition to do this in the people, and never to lay such taxes as will inevitably fall on capital; since, by so doing, they impair the funds for the maintenance of labour, and thereby diminish the future production of the country.

In England this policy has been neglected in taxing the probates of wills, in the legacy duty, and in all taxes affecting the transference of property from the dead to the living. If a legacy of £1000 be subject to a tax of £100, the legatee considers his legacy as only £900 and feels no particular motive to save the £100 duty from his expenditure, and thus the capital of the country is diminished; but if he had really received £1000, and had been required to pay £100 as a tax on income, on wine, on horses, or on servants, he would probably have diminished, or rather not increased his expenditure by that sum, and the capital of the country would have been unimpaired.

For the general prosperity there cannot be too much facility given to the conveyance and exchange of all kinds of property, as it is by such means that capital of every species is likely to find its way into the hands of those who will best employ it in increasing the productions of the country. "Why," asks M. Say, "does an individual wish to sell his land? it is because he has another employment in view in which his funds will be more productive. Why does another wish to purchase this same land? It is to employ a capital which brings him in too little, which was unemployed, or the use of which he thinks susceptible of improvement. This exchange will increase the general income, since it increases the income of these parties. But if the charges are so exorbitant as to prevent the exchange, they are an obstacle to this increase of the general income." Those taxes, however, are easily collected; and this by many may be thought to afford some compensation for their injurious effects.

VII. VALUE AND RICHES, THEIR DISTINCTIVE PROPERTIES

"A MAN is rich or poor," says Adam Smith, "according to the degree in which he can afford to enjoy the necessaries, conveniences, and amusements of human life."

Value, then, essentially differs from riches, for value depends not on abundance, but on the difficulty or facility of production. The labour of a million of men in manufactures will always produce the same value, but will not always produce the same riches. By the invention of machinery, by improvements in skill, by a better division of labour, or by the discovery of new markets, where more advantageous exchanges may be made, a million of men may produce double or treble the amount of riches, of "necessaries, conveniences, and amusements," in one state of society that they could produce in another, but they will not on that account add anything to value; for everything rises or falls in value in proportion to the facility or difficulty of producing it, or, in other words, in proportion to the quantity of labour employed on its production. Suppose, with a given capital, the labour of a certain number of men produced 1000 pair of stockings, and that by inventions in machinery the same number of men can produce 2000 pair, or that they can continue to produce 1000 pair, and can produce besides 500 hats; then the value of the 2000 pair of stockings, or of the 1000 pair of stockings and 500 hats, will be neither more nor less than that of the 1000 pair of stockings before the introduction of machinery; for they will be the produce of the same quantity of labour. But the value of the general mass of commodities will nevertheless be diminished; for, although the value of the increased quantity produced in consequence of the improvement will be the same exactly as the value would have been of the less quantity that would have been produced, had no improvement taken place, an effect is also produced on the portion of goods still unconsumed, which were manufactured previously to the improvement; the value of those goods will be reduced, inasmuch as they must fall to the level, quantity for quantity, of the goods produced under all the advantages of the improvement: and the society will, notwithstanding the increased quantity of commodities, notwithstanding its augmented riches, and its augmented means of enjoyment, have a less amount of value. By constantly increasing the facility of production, we constantly diminish the value of some of the commodities before produced, though by the same means we not only add to the national riches, but also to the power of future production. Many of the errors in political economy have arisen from errors on this subject, from considering an increase of riches and an increase of value as meaning the same thing, and from unfounded notions as to what constituted a standard measure of value. One man considers money as a standard of value, and a nation grows richer or poorer, according to him, in proportion as its commodities of all kinds can exchange for more or less money. Others represent money as a very convenient medium for the purpose of barter, but not as a proper measure by which to estimate the value of other things; the real measure of value according to them is corn, and a country is rich or poor according as its commodities will exchange for more or less corn. There are others again who consider a country rich or poor according to the quantity of labour that it can purchase. But why should gold, or corn, or labour, be the standard measure of value, more than coals or iron?—more than cloth, soap, candles, and the other necessities of the labourer?—why, in short, should any commodity, or all commodities together, be the standard, when such a standard is itself subject to fluctuations in value? Corn, as well as gold, may from difficulty or facility of production vary 10, 20, or 30 per cent. relatively to other things; why should we always say that it is those other things which have varied, and not the corn? That commodity is alone invariable which at all times requires the same sacrifice of toil and labour to produce it. Of such a commodity we have no knowledge, but we may hypothetically argue and speak about it as if we had; and may improve our knowledge of the science by showing distinctly the absolute inapplicability of all the standards which have been hitherto adopted. But supposing either of these to be a correct standard of value, still it would not be a standard of riches, for riches do not depend on value. A man is rich or poor according to the abundance of necessaries and luxuries which he can command; and whether the exchangeable value of these for money, for corn, or for labour be high or low, they will equally contribute to the enjoyment of their possessor. It is through confounding the ideas of value and wealth, or riches, that it has been asserted that by diminishing the quantity of commodities, that is to say, of the necessaries, conveniences, and enjoyments of human life, riches may be increased. If value were the measure of riches, this could not be denied, because by scarcity the value of commodities is raised; but if Adam Smith be correct, if riches consist in necessaries and enjoyments, then they cannot be increased by a diminution of quantity.

It is true that the man in possession of a scarce commodity is richer if by means of it he can command more of the necessaries and enjoyments of human life; but as the general stock out of which each man's riches are drawn is diminished in quantity by all that any individual takes from it, other men's shares must necessarily be reduced in proportion as this favoured individual is able to appropriate a greater quantity to himself.

Let water become scarce, says Lord Lauderdale, and be exclusively possessed by an individual, and you will increase his riches, because water will then have value; and if wealth be the aggregate of individual riches, you will by the same means also increase wealth. You undoubtedly will increase the riches of this individual, but inasmuch as the farmer must sell a part of his corn, the shoemaker a part of his shoes, and all men give up a portion of their possessions for the sole purpose of supplying themselves with water, which they before had for nothing, they are poorer by the whole quantity of commodities which they are obliged to devote to this purpose, and the proprietor of water is benefited precisely by the amount of their loss. The same quantity of water, and the same quantity of commodities, are enjoyed by the whole society, but they are differently distributed. This is, however, supposing rather a monopoly of water than a scarcity of it. If it should be scarce, then the riches of the country and of individuals would be actually diminished, inasmuch as it would be deprived of a portion of one of its enjoyments. The farmer would not only have less corn to exchange for the other commodities which might be necessary or desirable to him, but he, and every other individual, would be abridged in the enjoyment of one of the most essential of their comforts. Not only would there be a different distribution of riches, but an actual loss of wealth.

It may be said, then, of two countries possessing precisely the same quantity of all the necessaries and comforts of life, that they are equally rich, but the value of their respective riches would depend on the comparative facility or difficulty with which they were produced. For if an improved piece of machinery should enable us to make two pair of stockings instead of one, without additional labour, double the quantity would be given in exchange for a yard of cloth. If a similar improvement be made in the manufacture of cloth, stockings and cloth will exchange in the same proportions as before, but they will both have fallen in value; for in exchanging them for hats, for gold, or other commodities in general, twice the former quantity must be given. Extend the improvement to the production of gold, and every other commodity, and they will all regain their former proportions. There will be double the quantity of commodities annually produced in the country, and therefore the wealth of the country will be doubled, but this wealth will not have increased in value.

Although Adam Smith has given the correct description of riches which I have more than once noticed, he afterwards explains them differently, and says, "that a man must be rich or poor according to the quantity of labour which he can afford to purchase." Now, this description differs essentially from the other and is certainly incorrect; for suppose the mines were to become more productive, so that gold and silver fell in value, from the greater facility of their production; or that velvets were to be manufactured with so much less labour than before that they fell to half their former value; the riches of all those who purchased those commodities would be increased; one man might increase the quantity of his plate, another might buy double the quantity of velvet; but with the possession of this additional plate and velvet, they could employ no more labour than before; because, as the exchangeable value of velvet and of plate would be lowered, they must part with proportionally more of these species of riches to purchase a day's labour. Riches, then, cannot be estimated by the quantity of labour which they can purchase.

From what has been said, it will be seen that the wealth of a country may be increased in two ways: it may be increased by employing a greater portion of revenue in the maintenance of productive labour, which will not only add to the quantity but to the value of the mass of commodities; or it may be increased, without employing any additional quantity of labour, by making the same quantity more productive, which will add to the abundance but not to the value of commodities.

In the first case, a country would not only become rich, but the value of its riches would increase. It would become rich by parsimony—by diminishing its expenditure on objects of luxury and enjoyment, and employing those savings in reproduction.

In the second case, there will not necessarily be either any diminished expenditure on luxuries and enjoyments or any increased quantity of productive labour employed, but, with the same labour, more would be produced; wealth would increase, but not value. Of these two modes of increasing wealth, the last must be preferred, since it produces the same effect without the privation and diminution of enjoyments which can never fail to accompany the first mode. Capital is that part of the wealth of a country which is employed with a view to future production, and may be increased in the same manner as wealth. An additional capital will be equally efficacious in the production of future wealth, whether it be obtained from improvements in skill and machinery or from using more revenue reproductively; for wealth always depends on the quantity of commodities produced, without any regard to the facility with which the instruments employed in production may have been procured. A certain quantity of clothes and provisions will maintain and employ the same number of men, and will therefore procure the same quantity of work to be done, whether they be produced by the labour of 100 or 200 men; but they will be of twice the value if 200 have been employed on their production.

VIII. ON CURRENCY AND BANKS

So MUCH has already been written on currency that of those who give their attention to such subjects none but the prejudiced are ignorant of its true principles. I shall, therefore, take only a brief survey of some of the general laws which regulate its quantity and value.

Gold and silver, like all other commodities, are valuable only in proportion to the quantity of labour necessary to produce them and bring them to market. Gold is about fifteen times dearer than silver, not because there is a greater demand for it, nor because the supply of silver is fifteen times greater than that of gold, but solely because fifteen times the quantity of labour is necessary to procure a given quantity of it.

The quantity of money that can be employed in a country must depend on its value: if gold alone were employed for the circulation of commodities, a quantity would be required one fifteenth only of what would be necessary if silver were made use of for the same purpose.

A circulation can never be so abundant as to overflow; for by diminishing its value in the same proportion you will increase its quantity, and by increasing its value, diminish its quantity.

While the state coins money and charges no seignorage, money will be of the same value as any other piece of the same metal of equal weight and fineness; but if the state charges a seignorage for coinage, the coined piece of money will generally exceed the value of the uncoined piece of metal by the whole seignorage charged, because it will require a greater quantity of labour, or, which is the same thing, the value of the produce of a greater quantity of labour, to procure it.

While the state alone coins, there can be no limit to this charge of seignorage; for by limiting the quantity of coin, it can be raised to any conceivable value.

It is on this principle that paper money circulates: the whole charge for paper money may be considered as seignorage. Though it has no intrinsic value, yet, by limiting its quantity, its value in exchange is as great as an equal denomination of coin, or of bullion in that coin. On the same principle, too, namely, by a limitation of its quantity, a debased coin would circulate at the value it should bear if it were of the legal weight and fineness, and not at the value of the quantity of metal which it actually contained. In the history of the British coinage we find, accordingly, that the currency was never depreciated in the same proportion that it was debased; the reason of which was, that it never was increased in quantity in proportion to its diminished intrinsic value.

There is no point more important in issuing paper money than to be fully impressed with the effects which follow from the principle of limitation of quantity. It will scarcely be believed fifty years hence that bank directors and ministers gravely contended in our times, both in Parliament and before committees of Parliament, that the issues of notes by the Bank of England, unchecked by any power in the holders of such notes to demand in exchange either specie or bullion, had not, nor could have, any effect on the prices of commodities, bullion, or foreign exchanges.

After the establishment of banks, the state has not the sole power of coining or issuing money. The currency may as effectually be increased by paper as by coin; so that if a state were to debase its money, and limit its quantity, it could not support its value, because the banks would have an equal power of adding to the whole quantity of circulation.

On these principles, it will be seen that it is not necessary that paper money should be payable in specie to secure its value; it is only necessary that its quantity should be regulated according to the value of the metal which is declared to be the standard. If the standard were gold of a given weight and fineness, paper might be increased with every fall in the value of gold, or, which is the same thing in its effects, with every rise in the price of goods.

"By issuing too great a quantity of paper," says Dr. Smith, "of which the excess was continually returning in order to be exchanged for gold and silver, the Bank of England was, for many years together, obliged to coin gold to the extent of between eight hundred thousand pounds and a million a year, or, at an average, about eight hundred and fifty thousand pounds. For this great coinage, the Bank, in consequence of the worn and degraded state into which the gold coin had fallen a few years ago, was frequently obliged to purchase bullion at the high price of four pounds an ounce, which it soon after issued in coin at £3 17*s*. 10½*d*. an ounce, losing in this manner between two and a half and three per cent. upon the coinage of so very large a sum. Though the Bank, therefore, paid no seignorage, though the government was properly at the expense of the coinage, this liberality of government did not prevent altogether the expense of the Bank."

On the principle above stated, it appears to me most clear that by not reissuing the paper thus brought in, the value of the whole currency, of the degraded as well as the new gold coin, would have been raised, when all demands on the Bank would have ceased.

Experience shows that neither a state nor a bank ever has had the unrestricted power of issuing paper money without abusing that power; in all states, therefore, the issue of paper money ought to be under some check and control; and none seems so proper for that purpose as that of subjecting the issuers of paper money to the obligation of paying their notes either in gold coin or bullion.

A currency is in its most perfect state when it consists wholly of paper money, but of paper money of an equal value with the gold which it professes to represent. The use of paper instead of gold substitutes the cheapest in place of the most expensive medium, and enables the country, without loss to any individual, to exchange all the gold which it before used for this purpose for raw materials, utensils, and food; by the use of which both its wealth and its enjoyments are increased.

A NEW VIEW OF SOCIETY

by

ROBERT OWEN

CONTENTS

A New View of Society

ROBERT OWEN

1771–1858

ROBERT OWEN, factory reformer, "utopian" socialist, and pioneer of industrial co-operation and of trade-unionism, was the outstanding figure in radical social movements in England and America during the early nineteenth century. His father was a saddler and ironmonger in Newtown in central Wales. Young Robert was only nine years old when he started work in a neighbor's shop, and a year later he was apprenticed to a linen draper in Stamford, Lincolnshire. At the age of eighteen, in Manchester, he set up his own business. Before he was thirty he bought from David Dale, of Glasgow, the famous New Lanark cotton mills and married Dale's daughter.

The guiding principle of Owen's life was his conviction that "man's character is made for, and not by, him," and at New Lanark he seized the opportunity to apply this principle. He found that Dale had taken into his mills more than four hundred pauper children. Some of the children were only six years old, and all of them worked from six o'clock in the morning until seven o'clock at night. In addition to the children some thirteen hundred adult employees and their families were crowded in barracklike structures adjoining the mills.

Owen changed all this. He improved the housing, ended the employment of young children, and established progressive schools. In his view a return of 5 per cent on invested capital was sufficient, and anything beyond that percentage should be applied to the welfare of employees. His business associates regarded him as eccentric, but he thought that the world, not he, was odd. In severing relations with William Allen, one of his partners, several years later he said: "All the world is queer save thee and me, and even thou art a little queer."

Owen appealed, over the heads of his associates, to social reformers of influence and to the rich and powerful. The Duke of Kent, father of Queen Victoria, was one of his sponsors. The Archbishop of Canterbury was another. Jeremy Bentham, utilitarian philosopher, and John Quincy Adams, American ambassador to England and later President of the United States, were his friends. The Grand Duke Nicholas, later czar of Russia, came to New Lanark to see with his own eyes what Owen had accomplished.

Moral support was one thing; the actual improvement of social conditions was another. When Owen tried to get his proposals embodied in parliamentary legislation he was unsuccessful. When he attacked religion as a barrier to social progress on the ground that it treated man as a free moral agent instead of as the creature of his environment, some of his friends fell away. He began to argue that only a social revolution could remedy the manifold evils and injustices of the rapidly expanding capitalist system. He wanted to make it a peaceful and voluntary revolution. In his *New View of Society* (published in 1813) he wrote that humanity must be educated in the principles of a new social order. His system was based on agriculture, and he proposed in his *Report to the County of Lanark* (published in 1821) that the spade be substituted for the plow in the cultivation of the soil. These two works are so closely related that we have combined them under the title of the principal work, *A New View of Society.* The section headed "An Essay on the Formation of Character" is taken directly from *A New View of Society,* and the section headed "A Plan for the Regeneration of Society" is taken from the *Report to the County of Lanark.*

The period was one of economic distress following the Napoleonic Wars. All kinds of remedies were being suggested. The example of America was invoked, and the possibilities of communistic colonization in the New World were debated.

In the spirit of the time, Robert Owen, in 1825, bought a tract of some twenty thousand acres on the Wabash River in the state of Indiana. This had been the site of a Rappite community under the name "New Harmony" and was to be the proving ground of Owen's theories. His watchword, then as always, was education, and he induced distinguished scholars to participate in the organization of the colony's schools. On his way to New Harmony, Owen was invited to give two addresses in the House of Representatives at Washington, which were attended by President Adams and other officials. He invited all and sundry to aid him in building the new commonwealth, and as a result a heterogeneous collection of some nine hundred radicals, enthusiasts, and adventurers gathered at New Harmony. The outcome must have been a bitter disappointment to Robert Owen. New Harmony was not harmonious. The colonists could not agree among themselves, and the parent community broke into several lesser communities. After two years the colony collapsed.

In England, after the failure of the New Harmony experiment, Owen found a great working-class audience ready to listen to him. Co-operative societies and stores inspired by his teachings were springing up. These helped to prepare the way for the world-wide consumers' co-operative movement which issued from the Rochdale Pioneers Co-operative Society founded in 1844. A great trade-union movement was in its infancy. The political movement known as Chartism was also under way.

Owen's contribution (in 1832) to this new social era was the organization in London of a National Equitable Labor Exchange, based on the principle that the natural standard of value is labor. "Labor notes," instead of ordinary currency, were used as a medium of exchange, and for a while were widely accepted. But excessive demands from a London landlord, the thievery of dishonest employees, and the difficulties involved in pricing goods in terms of labor-time brought the experiment to an end.

Two years later Owen led in the formation of a Grand National Consolidated Trades Union. More than half a million rallied to his leadership, but it was a mushroom growth. The violent language of some of Owen's followers and the bitter hostility of employers and of government defeated the movement.

In his old age Owen became a spiritualist and told of his conversations on social problems with the Duke of Kent and others of his friends who had passed to the Great Beyond.

Robert Owen may have been "a little mad," as G. D. H. Cole, one of his biographers, suggests; but few, if any, among the world's great humanitarians can show a more consistent record. From the years of his boyhood until the time of his death at the age of eighty-seven, he was indefatigable in his efforts to improve the lot of his fellow men. The repeated failure of his schemes seemed only to strengthen his purpose.

He was a pioneer not only of trade-unionism and of co-operative movements but also of the doctrine that social environment is a dominant factor in shaping character. "In fact," says Mr. Cole, "this doctrine, now regarded as distinctively Marxian, is in effect Owenite; and it is impossible to doubt that Marx, although he regarded Owen as a utopian socialist, owed far more to him in the formulation of the materialistic conception of history than has generally been admitted."

A NEW VIEW OF SOCIETY

AN ESSAY ON THE FORMATION OF CHARACTER

"Any general character, from the best to the worst, from the most ignorant to the most enlightened, may be given to any community, even to the world at large, by the application of proper means; which means are to a great extent at the command and under the control of those who have influence in the affairs of men."

According to the last returns under the Population Act, the poor and working classes of Great Britain and Ireland have been found to exceed fifteen millions of persons, or nearly three fourths of the population of the British Islands.

The characters of these persons are now permitted to be very generally formed without proper guidance or direction, and, in many cases, under circumstances which directly impel them to a course of extreme vice and misery; thus rendering them the worst and most dangerous subjects in the empire; while the far greater part of the remainder of the community are educated upon the most mistaken principles of human nature, such, indeed, as cannot fail to produce a general conduct throughout society, totally unworthy of the character of rational beings.

The first thus unhappily situated are the poor and the uneducated profligate among the working classes, who are now trained to commit crimes, for the commission of which they are afterwards punished.

The second is the remaining mass of the population, who are now instructed to believe, or at least to acknowledge, that certain principles are unerringly true, and to act as though they were grossly false; thus filling the world with folly and inconsistency, and making society, throughout all its ramifications, a scene of insincerity and counteraction.

In this state the world has continued to the present time; its evils have been and are continually increasing; they cry aloud for efficient corrective measures, which if we longer delay, general disorder must ensue.

"But," say those who have not deeply investigated the subject, "attempts to apply remedies have been often made, yet all of them have failed. The evil is now of a magnitude not to be controlled; the torrent is already too strong to be stemmed; and we can only wait with fear or calm resignation to see it carry destruction in its course, by confounding all distinctions of right and wrong."

Such is the language now held, and such are the general feelings on this most important subject.

These, however, if longer suffered to continue, must lead to the most lamentable consequences. Rather than pursue such a course, the character of legislators would be infinitely raised, if, forgetting the petty and humiliating contentions of sects and parties, they would thoroughly investigate the subject, and endeavour to arrest and overcome these mighty evils.

The chief object of these Essays is to assist and forward investigations of such vital importance to the well-being of this country, and of society in general.

The view of the subject which is about to be given has arisen from extensive experience for upwards of twenty years, during which period its truth and importance have been proved by multiplied experiments. That the writer may not be charged with precipitation or presumption, he has had the principle and its consequences examined, scrutinised, and fully canvassed, by some of the most learned, intelligent, and competent characters of the present day: who, on every principle of duty as well as of interest, if they had discovered error in either, would have exposed it;—but who, on the contrary, have fairly acknowledged their incontrovertible truth and practical importance.

Assured, therefore, that his principles are true, he proceeds with confidence, and courts the most ample and free discussion of the subject; courts it for the sake of humanity—for the sake of his fellow creatures—millions of whom experience sufferings which, were they to be unfolded, would compel those who govern the world to exclaim—"Can these things exist and we have no knowledge of them?" But they do exist—and even the heart-rending statements which were made known to the public during the discussions upon Negro slavery do not exhibit more afflicting scenes than those which, in various parts of the world, daily arise from the injustice of society towards itself; from the inattention of mankind to the circumstances which incessantly surround them; and from the want of a correct knowledge of human nature in those who govern and control the affairs of men.

If these circumstances did not exist to an extent almost incredible, it would be unnecessary now to contend for a principle regarding Man, which scarcely requires more than to be fairly stated to make it self-evident.

This principle is, that *"Any general character, from the best to the worst, from the most ignorant to the most enlightened, may be given to any community, even to the world at large, by the application of proper means; which means are to a great extent at the command and under the control of those who have influence in the affairs of men."*

The principle as now stated is a broad one, and, if it should be found to be true, cannot fail to give a new character to legislative proceedings, and such a character as will be most favourable to the well-being of society.

That this principle is true to the utmost limit of the terms is evident from the experience of all past ages, and from every existing fact.

Shall misery, then, most complicated and extensive, be experienced, from the prince to the peasant, throughout all the nations of the world, and shall its cause and the means of its prevention be known, and yet these means withheld? The undertaking is replete with difficulties which can only be overcome by those who have influence in society: who, by foreseeing its important practical benefits, may be induced to contend against those difficulties; and who, when its advantages are clearly seen and strongly felt, will not suffer individual considerations to be put in competition with their attainment. It is true their ease and comfort may be for a time sacrificed to those prejudices; but, if they persevere, the principles on which this knowledge is founded must ultimately universally prevail.

In preparing the way for the introduction of these principles, it cannot now be necessary to enter into the detail of facts to prove that children can be trained to acquire *"any language, sentiments, belief, or any bodily habits and manners, not contrary to human nature."*

For that this has been done, the history of every nation of which we have records, abundantly confirms; and that this is, and may be again done, the facts which exist around us and throughout all the countries in the world, prove to demonstration.

Possessing, then, the knowledge of a power so important, which, when understood, is capable of being wielded with the certainty of a law of nature, and which would gradually remove the evils which now chiefly afflict mankind, shall we permit it to remain dormant and useless, and suffer the plagues of society perpetually to exist and increase?

No: the time is now arrived when the public mind of this country, and the general state of the world, call imperatively for the introduction of this all-pervading principle, not only in theory, but into practice.

Nor can any human power now impede its rapid progress. Silence will not retard its course, and opposition will give increased celerity to its movements. The commencement of the work will, in fact, ensure its accomplishment; henceforth all the irritating angry passions, arising from ignorance of the true cause of bodily and mental character, will gradually subside, and be replaced by the most frank and conciliating confidence and good will.

Nor will it be possible hereafter for comparatively a few individuals unintentionally to occasion the rest of mankind to be surrounded by circumstances which inevitably form such characters as they afterwards deem it a duty and a right to punish even to death; and that, too, while they themselves have been the instruments of forming those characters. Such proceedings not only create innumerable evils to the directing few, but essentially retard them and the great mass of society from attaining the enjoyment of a high degree of positive happiness. Instead of punishing crimes after they have permitted the human character to be formed so as to commit them, they will adopt the only means which can be adopted to prevent the existence of those crimes; means by which they may be most easily prevented.

Happily for poor traduced and degraded human nature, the principle for which we now contend will speedily divest it of all the ridiculous and absurd mystery with which it has been hitherto enveloped by the ignorance of preceding times: and all the complicated and counteracting motives for good conduct, which have been multiplied almost to infinity, will be reduced to one single principle of action, which, by its evident operation and sufficiency, shall render this intricate system unnecessary, and ultimately supersede it in all parts of the earth. That principle is *the happiness of self, clearly understood and uniformly practised; which can only be attained by conduct that must promote the happiness of the community.*

For that Power which governs and pervades the universe has evidently so formed man that he must progressively pass from a state of ignorance to intelligence, the limits of which it is not for man himself to define; and in that progress to discover that his individual happiness can be increased and extended only in proportion as he actively endeavours to increase and extend the happiness of all around him. The principle admits neither of exclusion nor of limitation; and such appears evidently the state of the public mind that it will now seize and cherish this principle as the most precious boon which it has yet been allowed to attain. The errors of all opposing motives will appear in their true light, and the ignorance whence they arose will become so glaring that even the most unenlightened will speedily reject them.

For this state of matters, and for all the gradual changes contemplated, the extraordinary events of the present times have essentially contributed to prepare the way.

Even the late Ruler of France [Napoleon], although immediately influenced by the most mistaken principles of ambition, has contributed to this happy result, by shaking to its foundation that mass of superstition and bigotry, which on the continent of Europe had been accumulating for ages, until it had so overpowered and depressed the human intellect that to attempt improvement without its removal would have been most unavailing. And in the next place, by carrying the mistaken selfish principles in which mankind have been hitherto educated to the extreme in practice, he has rendered their error manifest, and left no doubt of the fallacy of the source whence they originated.

These transactions, in which millions have been immolated, or consigned to poverty and bereft of friends, will be preserved in the records of time, and impress future ages with a just estimation of the principles now about to be introduced into practice; and will thus prove perpetually useful to all succeeding generations.

For the direful effects of Napoleon's government have created the most deep-rooted disgust at notions which could produce a belief that such conduct was glorious, or calculated to increase the happiness of even the individual by whom it was pursued.

And the late discoveries and proceedings of the Rev. Dr. [Andrew] Bell and Mr. Joseph Lancaster, have also been preparing the way, in a manner the most opposite, but yet not less effectual, by directing the public attention to the beneficial effects, on the young and unresisting mind, of even the limited education which their systems embrace.

They have already effected enough to prove that all which is now in contemplation respecting the training of youth may be accomplished without fear of disappointment. And by so doing, as the consequences of their improvements cannot be confined within the British Isles, they will forever be ranked among the most important benefactors of the human race. But henceforward to contend for any new exclusive system will be in vain: the public mind is already too well informed, and has too far passed the possibility of retrogression, much longer to permit the continuance of any such evil.

For it is now obvious that such a system must be destructive of the happiness of the excluded, by their seeing others enjoy what they are not permitted to possess; and also that it tends, by creating opposition from the justly injured feelings of the excluded, in proportion to the extent of the exclusion, to diminish the happiness even of the privileged: the former therefore can have no rational motive for its continuance.

If, however, owing to the irrational principles by which the world has been hitherto governed, individuals, or sects, or parties, shall yet by their plans of exclusion attempt to retard the amelioration of society, and prevent the introduction into PRACTICE of that truly just spirit which knows no exclusion, such facts shall yet be brought forward as cannot fail to render all their efforts vain.

It will therefore be the essence of wisdom in the privileged class to co-operate sincerely and cordially with those who desire not to touch one iota of the supposed advantages which they now possess; and whose first and last wish is to increase the particular happiness of those classes, as well as the general happiness of society. A very little reflection on the part of the privileged will ensure this line of conduct; whence, without domestic revolution—without war or bloodshed—nay, without prematurely disturbing any thing which exists, the world will be prepared to receive principles which are alone calculated to build up a system of happiness, and to destroy those irritable feelings which have so long afflicted society,—solely because society has hitherto been ignorant of the true means by which the most useful and valuable character may be formed.

This ignorance being removed, experience will soon teach us how to form character, individually and generally, so as to give the greatest sum of happiness to the individual and to mankind.

These principles require only to be known in order to establish themselves; the outline of our future proceedings then becomes clear and defined, nor will they permit us henceforth to wander from the right path. They direct that the governing powers of all countries should establish rational plans for the education and general formation of the characters of their subjects. *These plans must be devised to train children from their earliest infancy in good habits of every description (which will of course prevent them from acquiring those of falsehood and deception). They must afterwards be rationally educated, and their labour be usefully directed. Such habits and education will impress them with an active and ardent desire to promote the happiness of every individual, and that without the* shadow of exception *for sect, or party, or country, or climate. They will also ensure, with the fewest possible exceptions, health, strength, and vigour of body; for the happiness of man can be erected only on the foundations of health of body and peace of mind.*

And that health of body and peace of mind may be preserved sound and entire, through youth and manhood, to old age, it becomes equally necessary that the irresistible propensities which form a part of his nature, and which now produce the endless and ever-multiplying evils with which humanity is afflicted, should be so directed as to increase and not to counteract his happiness.

The knowledge, however, thus introduced will make it evident to the understanding that by far the greater part of the misery with which man is encircled *may* be easily dissipated and removed; and that with mathematical precision he *may* be surrounded with those circumstances which must gradually increase his happiness.

Hereafter, when the public at large shall be satisfied that these principles *can* and *will* withstand the ordeal through which they must inevitably pass; when they shall prove themselves true to the clear comprehension and certain conviction of the unenlightened as well as the learned; and when, by the irresistible power of truth, detached from falsehood, they shall establish themselves in the mind, no more to be removed but by the entire annihilation of human intellect; then the consequent practice which they direct shall be explained, and rendered easy of adoption.

In the meantime, let no one anticipate evil, even in the slightest degree, from these principles; they are not innoxious only, but pregnant with consequences to be wished and desired beyond all others by *every* individual in society.

Some of the best intentioned among the various classes in society may still say, "All this is *very delightful and very beautiful in theory,* but *visionaries* alone expect to see it *realized.*" To this remark only one reply *can* or *ought* to be made: that *these principles have been carried most successfully into practice.*

(The beneficial effects of this practice have been experienced for many years among a population of between two and three thousand at New Lanark, in Scotland; at Munich, in Bavaria; and in the Pauper Colonies at Fredericks-oord.)

The present Essays, therefore, are not brought forward as mere matter of speculation, to amuse the idle visionary who *thinks* in his closet, and never *acts* in the world; but to create universal activity, pervade society with a knowledge of its true interests, and direct the public mind to the most important object to which it can be directed,—to a national proceeding for rationally forming the character of that immense mass of population which is now allowed to be so formed as to fill the world with crimes.

Shall questions of merely local and temporary interest, whose ultimate results are calculated only to withdraw pecuniary profits from one set of individuals and give them to others, engage day after day the attention of politicians and ministers; call forth petitions and delegates from the widely spread agricultural and commercial interests of the empire;—and shall the well-being of millions of the poor, half-naked, half-famished, untaught, and untrained, hourly increasing to a most alarming extent in these islands, not call forth *one* petition, *one* delegate, or *one* rational effective legislative measure?

No! For such has been our education that we hesitate not to devote years and expend millions in the *detection* and *punishment* of crimes, and in the attainment of objects whose ultimate results are, in comparison with this, insignificancy itself: and yet we have not moved one step in the true path to *prevent* crimes, and to diminish the innumerable evils with which mankind are now afflicted.

Are these false principles of conduct in those who govern the world to influence mankind permanently? And if not, *how* and *when* is the change to commence?

A PLAN FOR THE REGENERATION OF SOCIETY

1. Outlines of the Plan

It is admitted that under the present system no more hands can be employed advantageously in agriculture or manufactures; and that both interests are on the eve of bankruptcy.

It is also admitted that the prosperity of the country, or rather that which ought to create prosperity, the improvement in mechanical and chemical science, has enabled the population to produce more than the present system permits to be consumed.

In consequence, new arrangements become necessary, by which *consumption* may be made to keep pace with *production,* and the following are recommended:

First.—To cultivate the soil with the spade instead of the plough.

Second.—To make such changes as the spade cultivation requires, to render it easy and profitable to individuals, and beneficial to the country.

Third.—To adopt a standard of value by means of which the exchange of the products of labour may proceed without check or limit, until wealth shall become so abundant that any further increase to it will be considered useless, and will not be desired.

We proceed to give the reasons for recommending these arrangements in preference to all others.

And first, those for preferring the spade to the plough for the universal cultivation of the soil.

Practical cultivators of the soil know that the most favourable circumstance for promoting the growth of vegetation is a due supply of moisture, and that when this is provided for, a good general crop seldom, if ever, fails.

Water enters so largely into the food of all plants that if its gradual supply can be secured, the farmer and horticulturist feel assured of a fair return for their labour. Whatever mode of cultivation, therefore, can best effect the object of drawing off from the seed or plant an excess of water, and retaining this surplus as a reservoir from which a gradual supply of moisture may be obtained as required, must possess decided advantages.

It is also known to all practical agriculturists that to obtain the best crops, the soil ought to be well broken and separated; and that the nearer it is brought to a garden mould, the more perfect is the cultivation.

These facts no one will dispute, nor will any deny that the spade is calculated to prepare a better recipient than the plough for an excess of water in rainy seasons, and to return it to the seed or plant afterwards in a manner most favourable to vegetation.

The spade, whenever there is sufficient soil, opens it to a depth that allows the water to pass freely below the bed of the seed or plant, and to remain there until a long continuance of heat draws it forth again to replenish the crop in the ground when it most requires to be gradually supplied with moisture; and the greater the depth to which the soil is opened, the greater will be the advantage of this important operation. Hence the increased crops after deep ploughing, and after trenching, although the latter process may be also in some degree assisted by the new or rested soil which it brings into action; yet both these effects are obtained by the use of the spade.

The action of the plough upon the soil is the reverse of that of the spade in the following important particulars:

Instead of *loosening* the subsoil, it *hardens* it; the heavy smooth surface of the plough, and the frequent trampling of the horses' feet, tend to form a surface on the subsoil, well calculated to prevent the water from penetrating below it; and in many soils, after a few years' ploughing, it is there retained to drown the seed or plant in rainy seasons, and to be speedily evaporated when it would be the most desirable to retain it. Thus the crop is injured, and often destroyed, in dry weather, for the want of that moisture which, under a different system, might have been retained in the subsoil.

It is evident, therefore, that the plough conceals from the eye its own imperfections, and deceives its employers, being in truth a *mere surface implement,* and extremely defective in principle.

The spade, on the contrary, makes a good subsoil, as well as a superior surface, and the longer it is used on the same soil, the more easily will it be worked; and by occasional trenching, where there is sufficient depth of soil, new earth will be brought into action, and the benefits to be derived from a well-prepared subsoil will be increased.

Closet theorists and inexperienced persons suppose that to exchange the plough for the spade would be to turn back in the road of improvement,—to give up a superior for an inferior implement of cultivation. Little do they imagine that the introduction of the spade, with the scientific arrangements which it requires, will produce far greater improvements in agriculture than the steam engine has effected in manufactures. Still less do they imagine that the change from the plough to the spade will prove to be a far more extensive and beneficial innovation than that which the invention of the spinning machine has occasioned, by the introduction of which, instead of the single wheel in a corner of a farmhouse, we now see thousands of spindles revolving with the noise of a waterfall in buildings palace-like for their cost, magnitude, and appearance.

Yet this extraordinary change is at hand. It will immediately take place; for the interest and well-being of all classes require it. Society cannot longer proceed another step in advance without it; and until it is adopted, civilization must retrograde, and the working classes starve for want of employment.

The next consideration which demands our attention is,—what constitutes a proper system of spade husbandry?—or, in other words, *how these new cultivators can be placed on the soil and associated, that their exertions may have the most beneficial result for themselves and the community.*

The leading principle which should direct us in the outline of this arrangement, and from which there should be no deviation in any of its parts, is the public good, or the general interest of the whole population.

To this end, the following considerations must be combined.

First.—Where, in general, can the labourers be best placed for spade cultivation?

Second.—What is the quantity of land which it may be the most advantageous to cultivate *in cumulo* by the spade?

Third.—What number of workmen can be the most beneficially employed together with a view to all the objects of their labour?

Fourth.—What are the best arrangements under which these men and their families can be well and economically *lodged, fed, clothed, trained, educated, employed, and governed?*

Fifth.—What is the best mode of disposing of the surplus produce to be thus created by their labour?

Sixth.—What are the means best calculated to render the conduct and industry of these workmen beneficial to their neighbours, to their country, and to foreign nations?

These are some of the leading objects which naturally arise for our consideration in forming arrangements for the introduction of the spade as a substitute for the plough cultivation.

To substitute the spade for the plough may seem most trivial in the expression; and to inexperienced, and even to learned men,—to my respected friends the Edinburgh Reviewers, for instance, who cannot be supposed to have much useful practical knowledge,—will appear to indicate a change equally simple and unimportant in practice.

It generally happens, however, that when a great calamity overwhelms a country, relief is obtained from practical men, and not from mere theorists, however acute, learned, and eloquent. In the present case, simple as at first appears to be the alteration proposed, yet, when the mind of the practical agriculturist, of the commercial man, of the man of science, of the political economist, of the statesman, and of the philosopher, shall be directed to the subject as its importance demands, the change will be found to be one of the deepest interest to society, involving consequences of much higher concernment to the well-being of mankind than the change from hunting to the pastoral state, or from the pastoral state to the plough cultivation.

The change comes, too, at a crisis most momentous for the safety of the civilized world, to reunite the most jarring interests, which were on the extreme point of severing all the old connexions of society.

Having given the outline of the considerations which show the superiority in principle of the spade over the plough as a scientific and economical instrument of cultivation;—having also described briefly the objects to be attended to in forming economical arrangements for the change proposed:—it now remains that the principle should be generally explained by which an advantageous interchange and exchange may be made of the greatly increased products of labour which will be created by the spade cultivation aided by the improved arrangements now contemplated.

These incalculably increased products will render gold, the old artificial standard of value, far more unfit for the task which is to be performed than it was in 1797, when it ceased to be the British legal standard of value, or than it is now, when wealth has so much increased.

Your Reporter is of opinion that *the natural standard of human labour,* fixed to represent its natural worth, or power of creating new wealth, will alone be found adequate to the purposes required.

To a mind coming first to this subject, innumerable and apparently insurmountable difficulties will occur; but by the steady application of that fixed and persevering attention which is alone calculated successfully to contend against and overcome difficulties, every obstacle will vanish, and the practice will prove simple and easy.

That which can create new wealth is, of course, worth the wealth which it creates. Human labour, whenever common justice shall be done to human beings, can now be applied to produce, advantageously for all ranks in society, many times the amount of wealth that is necessary to support the individual in considerable comfort. Of this new wealth, so created, the labourer who produces it is justly entitled to his fair proportion; and the best interests of every community require that the producer should have a fair and fixed proportion of all the wealth which he creates. This can be assigned to him on no other principle than by forming arrangements by which the *natural* standard of value shall become the *practical* standard of value. To make labour the standard of value it is necessary to ascertain the amount of it in all articles to be bought and sold. This is, in fact, already accomplished, and is denoted by what in commerce is technically termed "the prime cost," or the net value of the whole labour contained in any article of value,—the material contained in or consumed by the manufacture of the article forming a part of the whole labour.

The great object of society is, to obtain wealth, and to enjoy it.

The genuine principle of barter was, to exchange the supposed prime cost of, or value of labour in, one article, against the prime cost of, or amount of labour contained in, any other article. This is the only equitable principle of exchange; but, as inventions increased and human desires multiplied, it was found to be inconvenient in practice. Barter was succeeded by commerce, the principle of which is, to produce or procure every article at the *lowest,* and to obtain for it, in exchange, the *highest* amount of labour. To effect this, an artificial standard of value was necessary; and metals were, by common consent among nations, permitted to perform the office.

This principle, in the progress of its operation, has been productive of important advantages, and of very great evils; but, like barter, it has been suited to a certain stage of society.

It has stimulated invention; it has given industry and talent to the human character; and has secured the future exertion of those energies which otherwise might have remained dormant and unknown.

But it has made man ignorantly, individually selfish; placed him in opposition to his fellows; engendered fraud and deceit; blindly urged him forward to create, but deprived him of the wisdom to enjoy. In striving to take advantage of others he has overreached himself. The strong hand of necessity will now force him into the path which conducts to that wisdom in which he has been so long deficient. He will discover the advantages to be derived from uniting in practice the best parts of the principles of barter and commerce, and dismissing those which experience has proved to be inconvenient and injurious.

This substantial improvement in the progress of society may be easily effected by exchanging all articles with each other at their prime cost, or with reference to the amount of labour in each, which can be equitably ascertained, and by permitting the exchange to be made through a convenient medium to represent this value, and which will thus represent a real and unchanging value, and be issued only as substantial wealth increases.

The profit of production will arise, in all cases, from the value of the labour contained in the article produced, and it will be for the interest of society that this profit should be most ample. Its exact amount will depend upon what, by strict examination, shall be proved to be the present real value of a day's labour; calculated with reference to the amount of wealth, in the necessaries and comforts of life, which an average labourer may, by temperate exertions, be now made to produce.

It would require an accurate and extended consideration of the existing state of society to determine the exact value of the unit or day's labour which society ought now to fix as a standard of value:—but a more slight and general view of the subject is sufficient to show, that this unit need not represent a less value than the wealth contained in the necessaries and comforts of life which may now be purchased with five shillings.

The landholder and capitalist would be benefited by this arrangement in the same degree with the labourer; because labour is the foundation of all values, and it is only from labour, liberally remunerated, that high profits can be paid for agricultural and manufactured products.

Depressed as the value of labour now is, there is no proposition in Euclid more true, than that society would be immediately benefited, in a great variety of ways, to an incalculable extent, by making labour the standard of value.

By this expedient all the markets in the world, which are now virtually closed against offering a profit to the producers of wealth, would be opened to an unlimited extent; and in each individual exchange all the parties interested would be sure to receive ample remuneration for their labour.

Before this change can be carried into effect, various preparatory measures will be necessary; the explanatory details of which will naturally succeed the development of those arrangements which your Reporter has to propose, to give all the advantages to the spade cultivation, of which that system of husbandry is susceptible.

2. *Details of the Plan*

This part of the Report naturally divides itself under the following heads, each of which shall be considered separately, and the whole, afterwards, in connexion, as forming an improved practical system for the working classes, highly beneficial, in whatever light it may be viewed, to every part of society.

First.—The number of persons who can be associated to give the greatest advantages to themselves and to the community.

Second.—The extent of the land to be cultivated by such association.

Third.—The arrangements for feeding, lodging, and clothing the population, and for training and educating the children.

Fourth.—Those for forming and superintending the establishments.

Fifth.—The disposal of the surplus produce, and the relation which will subsist between the several establishments.

Sixth.—Their connexion with the Government of the country and with general society.

The first object, then, of the political economist, in forming these arrangements, must be, to consider well *under what limitation of numbers, individuals should be associated to form the first nucleus or division of society.*

All his future proceedings will be materially influenced by the decision of this point, which is one of the most difficult problems in the science of political economy. It will affect essentially the future character of individuals, and influence the general proceedings of mankind.

It is, in fact, the cornerstone of the whole fabric of human society. The consequences, immediate and remote, which depend upon it, are so numerous and important, that to do justice to this part of the arrangement alone would require a work of many volumes.

To form anything resembling a rational opinion on this subject, the mind must steadily survey the various effects which have arisen from associations which accident has hitherto combined in the history of the human species; and it should have a distinct idea of the results which other associations are capable of producing.

Thus impressed with the magnitude and importance of the subject, after many years of deep and anxious reflection, and viewing it with reference to an improved spade cultivation, and to all the purposes of society, your Reporter ventures to recommend the formation of such arrangements as will unite about 300 men, women, and children, in their natural proportions, as the *minimum,* and about 2,000 as the *maximum,* for the future associations of the cultivators of the soil, who will be employed also in such additional occupations as may be advantageously annexed to it.

In coming to this conclusion your Reporter never lost sight of that only sure guide to the political economist, the principle, *that it is the interest of all men, whatever may be their present artificial station in society, that there should be the largest amount of intrinsically valuable produce created, at the least expense of labour, and in a way the most advantageous to the producers and society.*

Whatever fanciful notions may govern the mere closet theorist, who so often leads the public mind astray from its true course, the practical economist will never come to any one conclusion that is inconsistent with the foregoing fundamental principle of his science, well knowing that where there is inconsistency there *must be* error.

It is with reference to this principle that the minimum and maximum above stated (viz. 300 and 2,000) have been fixed upon, as will be more particularly developed under the subsequent heads.

Within this range more advantages can be given to the individuals and to society than by the association of any greater or lesser number.

But from 800 to 1,200 will be found the most desirable number to form into agricultural villages; and unless some very strong local causes interfere, the permanent arrangements should be adapted to the complete accommodation of that amount of population only.

Villages of this extent, in the neighbourhood of others of a similar description, at due distances, will be found capable of combining within themselves all the advantages that city and country residences now afford, without any of the numerous inconveniences and evils which necessarily attach to both those modes of society.

But a very erroneous opinion will be formed of the proposed arrangements and the social advantages which they will exhibit, if it should be imagined from what has been said that they will in any respect resemble any of the present agricultural villages of Europe, or the associated communities in America, except in so far as the latter may be founded *on the principle of united labour, expenditure, and property, and equal privileges.*

Recommending, then, from 300 to 2,000, according to the localities of the farm or village, as the number of persons who should compose the associations for the new system of spade husbandry, we now proceed to consider—

Second.—*The extent of land to be cultivated by such association.*

This will depend upon the quality of the soil and other local considerations.

Great Britain and Ireland, however, do not possess a population nearly sufficient to cultivate our *best* soils in the most advantageous manner. It would therefore be nationally impolitic to place these associations upon *inferior* lands, which, in consequence, may be dismissed from present consideration.

Society, ever misled by closet theorists, has committed almost every kind of error in practice, and in no instance perhaps a greater, than in separating the workman from his food, and making his existence depend upon the labour and uncertain supplies of others, as is the case under our present manufacturing system; and it is a vulgar error to suppose that a single individual more can be supported by means of such a system than without it; on the contrary, a whole population engaged in agriculture, with manufactures as an appendage, will, in a given district, support many more, and in a much higher degree of comfort, than the same district could do with its agricultural separate from its manufacturing population.

Improved arrangements for the working classes will, in almost all cases, place the workman in the midst of his food, which it will be as beneficial for him to create as to consume.

Sufficient land, therefore, will be allotted to these cultivators, to enable them to raise an abundant supply of food and the necessaries of life for themselves, and as much additional agricultural produce as the public demands may require from such a portion of the population.

Under a well-devised arrangement for the working classes they will all procure for themselves the necessaries and comforts of life in so short a time, and so easily and pleasantly, that the occupation will be experienced to be little more than a recreation, sufficient to keep them in the best health and spirits for rational enjoyment of life.

The surplus produce from the soil will be required only for the higher classes, those who live without manual labour, and those whose nice manual operations will not permit them at any time to be employed in agriculture and gardening.

Of the latter, very few, if any, will be necessary, as mechanism may be made to supersede such operations, which are almost always injurious to health.

Under this view of the subject, the quantity of land which it would be the most beneficial for these associations to cultivate, with reference to their own well-being and the interests of society, will probably be from half an acre to an acre and a half for each individual.

An association, therefore, of 1,200 persons, would require from 600 to 1,800 statute acres, according as it may be intended to be more or less agricultural.

Thus, when it should be thought expedient that the chief surplus products should consist in manufactured commodities, the lesser quantity of land would be sufficient; if a large surplus from the produce of the soil were deemed desirable, the greater quantity would be allotted; and when the localities of the situation should render it expedient for the association to create an equal surplus quantity of each, the medium quantity, or 1,200 acres, would be the most suitable.

It follows that land under the proposed system of husbandry would be divided into farms of from 150 to 3,000 acres, but generally perhaps from 800 to 1,500 acres. This division of the land will be found to be productive of incalculable benefits in practice; it will give all the advantages, without any of the disadvantages of small and large farms.

The next head for consideration is—

Third.—*The arrangement for feeding, lodging, and clothing the population, and for training and educating the children.*

It being always most convenient for the workman to reside near to his employment, the site for the dwellings of the cultivators will be chosen as near to the centre of the land, as water, proper levels, dry situation, &c., &c., may admit; and as courts, alleys, lanes, and streets create many unnecessary inconveniences, are injurious to health, and destructive to almost all the natural comforts of human life, they will be excluded, and a disposition of the buildings free from these objections and greatly more economical will be adopted.

As it will afterwards appear that the food for the whole population can be provided better and cheaper under one general arrangement of cooking, and that the children can be better trained and educated together under the eye of their parents than under any other circumstances, a large square, or rather parallelogram, will be found to combine the greatest advantages in its form for the domestic arrangements of the association.

This form, indeed, affords so many advantages for the comfort of human life, that if great ignorance respecting the means necessary to secure good conduct and happiness among the working classes had not prevailed in all ranks, it must long ago have become universal.

It admits of a most simple, easy, convenient, and economical arrangement for all the purposes required.

The four sides of this figure may be adapted to contain all the private apartments or sleeping and sitting rooms for the adult part of the population; general sleeping apartments for the children while under tuition; storerooms, or warehouses in which to deposit various products; an inn, or house for the accommodation of strangers; an infirmary; &c., &c.

In a line across the centre of the parallelogram, leaving free space for air and light and easy communication, might be erected the church, or places for worship; the schools; kitchen and apartments for eating; all in the most convenient situation for the whole population, and under the best possible public superintendence, without trouble, expense, or inconvenience to any party.

The advantages of this general domestic arrangement can only be known and appreciated by those who have had great experience in the beneficial results of extensive combinations in improving the condition of the working classes, and whose minds, advancing beyond the petty range of individual party interests, have been calmly directed to consider what may now be attained by a well-devised association of human powers for the benefit of all ranks. It is such individuals only who can detect the present total want of foresight in the conduct of society, and its gross misapplication of the most valuable and abundant means of securing prosperity. They can distinctly perceive that the blind are leading the blind from difficulties to dangers, which they feel to increase at every step.

The parallelogram being found to be the best form in which to dispose the dwelling and chief domestic arrangements for the proposed associations of cultivators, it will be useful now to explain the principles on which those arrangements have been formed.

The first in order, and the most necessary, are those respecting food.

It has been, and still is, a received opinion among theorists in political economy, that man can provide better for himself, and more advantageously for the public, when left to his own individual exertions, opposed to and in competition with his fellows, than when aided by any social arrangement which shall unite his interests individually and generally with society.

This principle of individual interest, opposed as it is perpetually to the public good, is considered, by the most celebrated political economists, to be the cornerstone to the social system, and without which society could not subsist.

Yet when they shall know themselves, and discover the wonderful effects which combination and union can produce, they will acknowledge that the present arrangement of society is the most antisocial, impolitic, and irrational that can be devised; that under its influence all the superior and valuable qualities of human nature are repressed from infancy, and that the most unnatural means are used to bring out the most injurious propensities; in short, that the utmost pains are taken to make that which by nature is the most delightful compound for producing excellence and happiness, absurd, imbecile, and wretched.

It is upon these principles that arrangements are now proposed for the new agricultural villages, by which the food of the inhabitants may be prepared in one establishment, where they will eat together as one family.

Various objections have been urged against this practice; but they have come from those only who, whatever may be their pretensions in other respects, are mere children in the knowledge of the principles and economy of social life.

By such arrangements the members of these new associations may be supplied with food at far less expense and with much more comfort than by any individual or family arrangements; and when the parties have been once trained and accustomed, as they easily may be, to the former mode, they will never afterwards feel any inclination to return to the latter.

If a saving in the quantity of food,—the obtaining of a superior quality of prepared provisions from the same materials,—and the operation of preparing them being effected in much less time, with far less fuel, and with greater ease, comfort, and health to all the parties employed,—be advantages, these will be obtained in a remarkable manner by the new arrangements proposed.

And if to partake of viands so prepared, served up with every regard to comfort, in clean, spacious, well-lighted, and pleasantly ventilated apartments, and in the society of well-dressed, well-trained, well-educated, and well-informed associates, possessing the most benevolent dispositions and desirable habits, can give zest and proper enjoyment to meals, then will the inhabitants of the proposed villages experience all this in an eminent degree.

We now proceed to describe the interior accommodations of the private lodging houses, which will occupy three sides of the parallelogram.

As it is of essential importance that there should be abundance of space within the line of the private dwellings, the parallelogram, in all cases, whether the association is intended to be near the maximum or the minimum in numbers, should be of large dimensions; and to accommodate a greater or less population, the private dwellings should be of one, two, three, or four stories, and the interior arrangements formed accordingly.

These will be very simple.

No kitchen will be necessary, as the public arrangements for cooking will supersede the necessity for any.

The apartments will be always well-ventilated, and, when necessary, heated or cooled on the improved principles lately introduced in the Derby Infirmary.

The expense and trouble, to say nothing of the superior health and comforts which these improvements will give, will be very greatly less than attach to the present practice.

To heat, cool, and ventilate their apartments, the parties will have no further trouble than to open or shut two slides, or valves, in each room, the atmosphere of which, by this simple contrivance, may always be kept temperate and pure.

One stove of proper dimensions, judiciously placed, will supply the apartments of several dwellings, with little trouble and at a very little expense, when the buildings are originally adapted for this arrangement.

Thus will all the inconveniences and expense of separate fires and fireplaces, and their appendages, be avoided, as well as the trouble and disagreeable effects of mending fires and removing ashes, &c., &c.

Good sleeping apartments looking over the gardens in the country, and sitting rooms of proper dimensions fronting the square, will afford as much lodging accommodation as, with the other public arrangements, can be useful to, or desired by, these associated cultivators.

Food and lodging being thus provided for, the next consideration regards dress.

This, too, is a subject, the utility and disadvantages of which seem to be little understood by the Public generally; and, in consequence, the most ridiculous and absurd notions and practices have prevailed respecting it.

Most persons take it for granted, without thinking on the subject, that to be warm and healthy it is necessary to cover the body with thick clothing and to exclude the air as much as possible; and first appearances favour this conclusion. Facts, however, prove, that under the same circumstances, those who from infancy have been the most lightly clad, and who, by their form of dress, have been the most exposed to the atmosphere, are much stronger, more active, in better general health, warmer in cold weather, and far less incommoded by heat, than those who from constant habit have been dressed in such description of clothing as excludes the air from their bodies. The more the air is excluded by clothing, although at first the wearer feels warmer by each additional covering he puts on, yet in a few weeks, or months at most, the less capable he becomes of bearing cold than before.

The Romans and the Highlanders of Scotland appear to be the only two nations who adopted a national dress on account of its utility, without, however, neglecting to render it highly becoming and ornamental. The form of the dress of these nations was calculated first to give strength and manly beauty to the figure, and afterwards to display it to advantage. The time, expense, thought, and labour now employed to create a variety of dress, the effects of which are to deteriorate the physical powers, and to render the human figure an object of pity and commiseration, are a certain proof of the low state of intellect among all classes in society. The whole of this gross misapplication of the human faculties serves no one useful or rational purpose. On the contrary, it essentially weakens all the physical and mental powers, and is, in all respects, highly pernicious to society.

All other circumstances remaining the same, sexual delicacy and virtue will be found much higher in nations among whom the person, *from infancy,* is the most exposed, than among those people who exclude from sight every part of the body except the eyes.

Although your Reporter is satisfied that the principle now stated is derived from the unchanging laws of nature, and is true to the utmost extent to which it can be carried; yet mankind must be trained in different habits, dispositions, and sentiments before they can be permitted to act rationally on this, or almost any other law of nature.

The intermediate stage of society which your Reporter now recommends, admits, however, of judicious practical approximations towards the observance of these laws.

In the present case he recommends that the male children of the new villagers should be clothed in a dress somewhat resembling the Roman and Highland garb, in order that the limbs may be free from ligatures, and the air may circulate over every part of the body, and that they may be trained to become strong, active, well-limbed, and healthy.

And the females should have a well-chosen dress to secure similar important advantages.

The inhabitants of these villages, under the arrangements which your Reporter has in view, may be better dressed, for all the acknowledged purposes of dress, at much less than the one hundredth part of the labour, inconvenience, and expense that are now required to clothe the same number of persons in the middle ranks of life; while the form and material of the new dress will be acknowledged to be superior to any of the old.

Your Reporter has now to enter upon the most interesting portion of this division of the subject, and, he may add, the most important part of the economy of human life, with reference to the science of the influence of circumstances over the well-being and happiness of mankind, and to the full power and control which men may now acquire over those circumstances, and by which they may direct them to produce among the human race, with ease and certainty, either universal good or evil.

No one can mistake the application of these terms to the training and education of the children.

Since men began to think and write, much has been thought and written on this subject; and yet all that has been thought and written has failed to make the subject understood, or to disclose the principles on which we should proceed. Even now, the minds of the most enlightened are scarcely prepared to begin to think rationally respecting it. The circumstances of the times, however, require that a substantial advance should now be made in this part of the economy of human life.

Before any rational plan can be devised for the proper training and education of children, it should be distinctly known what capabilities and qualities infants and children possess, or, in fact, what they really are by nature.

If this knowledge is to be attained, as all human knowledge has been acquired, through the evidence of our senses, then is it evident that infants receive from a source and power over which they have no control, all the natural qualities they possess, and that from birth they are continually subjected to impressions derived from the circumstances around them; which impressions, combined with their natural qualities (whatever fanciful speculative men may say to the contrary), do truly determine the character of the individual through every period of life.

The knowledge thus acquired will give to men the same kind of control over the combination of the natural powers and faculties of infants as they now possess over the formation of animals: and although, from the nature of the subject, it must be slow in its progress and limited in extent, yet the time is not perhaps far distant when it may be applied to an important rational purpose, that is, to improve the breed of men, more than men have yet improved the breed of domestic animals.

But whatever knowledge may be attained to enable man to improve the breed of his progeny at birth, facts exist in endless profusion to prove to every mind capable of reflection, that men may now possess a most extensive control over those circumstances which affect the infant after birth; and that, as far as such circumstances can influence the human character, the day has arrived when the existing generation may so far control them, that the rising generations may become in character, without any individual exceptions, whatever men can now desire them to be, that is not contrary to human nature.

It is upon these grounds that your Reporter, in educating the rising generation within his influence, has long adopted principles different from those which are usually acted upon.

He considers all children as beings whose dispositions, habits, and sentiments are to be formed *for* them; that these can be well formed only by excluding all notions of reward, punishment, and emulation; and that, if their characters are not such as they ought to be, the error proceeds from their instructors and the other circumstances which surround them. He knows that principles as certain as those upon which the science of mathematics is founded may be applied to the forming of any given general character, and that by the influence of other circumstances, not a few individuals only, but the whole population of the world, may in a few years be rendered a very far superior race of beings to any now upon the earth, or which has been made known to us by history.

The children in these new schools should be therefore trained systematically to acquire useful knowledge through the means of sensible signs, by which their powers of reflection and judgment may be habituated to draw accurate conclusions from the facts presented to them. This mode of instruction is founded in nature, and will supersede the present defective and tiresome system of book learning, which is ill calculated to give either pleasure or instruction to the minds of children. When arrangements founded on these principles shall be judiciously formed and applied to practice, children will, with ease and delight to themselves, acquire more real knowledge in a day than they have yet attained under the old system in many months. They will not only thus acquire valuable knowledge, but the best habits and dispositions will be at the same time imperceptibly created in every one; and they will be trained to fill every office and to perform every duty that the well-being of their associates and the establishments can require. It is only by education, rightly understood, that communities of men can ever be well governed, and by means of such education every object of human society will be attained with the least labour and the most satisfaction.

It is obvious that training and education must be viewed as intimately connected with the employments of the association. The latter, indeed, will form an essential part of education under these arrangements. Each association, generally speaking, should create for itself a full supply of the usual necessaries, conveniences, and comforts of life.

The dwelling houses and domestic arrangements being placed as near the centre of the land to be cultivated as circumstances will permit, it is concluded that the most convenient situation for the gardens will be adjoining the houses on the outside of the square; that these should be bounded by the principal roads; and that beyond them, at a sufficient distance to be covered by a plantation, should be placed the workshops and manufactory.

All will take their turn at *some one or more* of the occupations in this department, aided by every improvement that science can afford, alternately with employment in agriculture and gardening.

It has been a popular opinion to recommend a minute division of labour and a division of interests. It will presently appear, however, that this minute division of labour and division of interests are only other terms for poverty, ignorance, waste of every kind, universal opposition throughout society, crime, misery, and great bodily and mental imbecility.

To avoid these evils, which, while they continue, must keep mankind in a most degraded state, each child will receive a general education, early in life, that will fit him for the proper purposes of society, make him the most useful to it, and the most capable of enjoying it.

Before he is twelve years old he may with ease be trained to acquire a correct view of the outline of all the knowledge which men have yet attained.

By this means he will early learn what he is in relation to past ages, to the period in which he lives, to the circumstances in which he is placed, to the individuals around him, and to future events. *He will then only have any pretensions to the name of a rational being.*

His physical powers may be equally enlarged in a manner as beneficial to himself as to those around him. As his strength increases he will be initiated in the practice of all the leading operations of his community, by which his services, at all times and under all circumstances, will afford a great gain to society beyond the expense of his subsistence; while at the same time he will be in the continual possession of more substantial comforts and real enjoyments than have ever yet appertained to any class in society.

The new wealth which one individual, by comparatively light and always healthy employment, may create under the arrangements now proposed is indeed incalculable. They would give him giant powers compared with those which the working class or any other now possesses. There would at once be an end of all mere animal machines, who could only follow a plough, or turn a sod, or make some insignificant part of some insignificant manufacture or frivolous article which society could better spare than possess. Instead of the unhealthy pointer of a pin,—header of a nail,—piecer of a thread—or clodhopper, senselessly gazing at the soil or around him, without understanding or rational reflection, there would spring up a working class full of activity and useful knowledge, with habits, information, manners, and dispositions that would place the lowest in the scale many degrees above the best of any class which has yet been formed by the circumstances of past or present society.

Such are a few only of the advantages which a rational mode of training and education, combined with the other parts of this system, would give to all the individuals within the action of its influence.

The next object of attention is—

Fourth.—*The formation and superintendence of these establishments.*

These new farming and general working arrangements may be formed by one or any number of landed proprietors or large capitalists; by established companies having large funds to expend for benevolent and public objects; by parishes and counties, to relieve themselves from paupers and poor's rates; and by associations of the middle and working classes of farmers, mechanics, and tradesmen, to relieve themselves from the evils of the present system.

As land, capital, and labour may be applied *to far greater pecuniary advantage* under the proposed arrangements than under any other at present known to the public, all parties will readily unite in carrying them into execution as soon as they shall be so plainly developed in principle as to be generally understood, and as parties who possess sufficient knowledge of the practical details to direct them advantageously can be found or trained to superintend them.

The chief difficulty lies in the latter part of the business. The principles may be made plain to every capacity. They are simple principles of nature, in strict unison with all we see or know from facts to be true. But the practice of everything new, however trifling, requires time and experience to perfect it. It cannot be expected that arrangements which comprehend the whole business of life, and reduce to practice the entire science of political economy, can at once be combined and executed in the best manner. Many errors will be at first committed; and, as in every other attempt by human means to unite a great variety of parts to produce one grand general result, many partial failures may be anticipated.

In all probability in the first experiment many of the parts will be out of due proportion to the whole; and experience will suggest a thousand improvements. No union of minds previously to actual practice can correctly adjust such a multiplicity of movements as will be combined in this new machine, which is to perform so many important offices for society.

A machine it truly is, that will simplify and facilitate, in a very remarkable manner, all the operations of human life, and multiply rational and permanently desirable enjoyments to an extent that cannot be yet calmly contemplated by ordinary minds.

If the invention of various machines has multiplied the power of labour, in several instances, to the apparent advantage of particular individuals, while it has deteriorated the condition of many others, THIS is an invention which will at once multiply the physical and mental powers of the whole society to an incalculable extent, without injuring any one by its introduction or its most rapid diffusion.

Surely when the power of this extraordinary machine shall be estimated, and the amount of the work shall be ascertained which it will perform for society, some exertions may be made to acquire a knowledge of its practice.

The same class of minds that can be trained to direct any of the usual complicated business of life, may be with ease rendered competent to take a part in the management and superintendence of these new establishments.

The principal difficulty will be to set the first establishment in motion; and much care and circumspection will be requisite in bringing each part into action at the proper time, and with the guards and checks which a change from one set of habits to another renders necessary.

Yet, the principles being understood, a man of fair ordinary capacity would superintend such arrangements with more ease than most large commercial or manufacturing establishments are now conducted.

In these there is a continual opposition of various interests and feelings, and extensive principles of counteraction, among the parties themselves, and between the parties and the public.

On the contrary, in the new arrangements each part will give facility to all the others, and unity of interest and design will be seen and felt in every one of the operations. The mental, manual, and scientific movements will all harmonise, and produce with ease results which must appear inexplicable to those who remain ignorant of the principles which govern the proceedings.

In the first instance men must be sought who, in addition to a practical knowledge of gardening, agriculture, manufactures, the ordinary trades, &c., &c., can comprehend the principles in which these associations are formed, and, comprehending them, can feel an interest and a pleasure in putting them into execution. Such individuals may be found; for there is nothing new in the separate parts of the proposed practice—the arrangement alone can be considered new.

When one establishment shall have been formed, there will be no great difficulty in providing superintendents for many other establishments. All the children will be trained to be equal to the care of any of the departments, more particularly as there will be no counteraction between those who direct and those who perform the various operations.

They will have minds so well informed—their power of accurately tracing cause and effect will be so much increased, that they must clearly perceive that to be raised to one of the privileged orders would be to themselves a serious evil, and to their posterity would certainly occasion an incalculable loss of intellect and enjoyment, equally injurious to themselves and to society.

They will therefore have every motive not to interfere with the honours and privileges of the existing higher orders, but to remain well satisfied with their own station in life.

The only distinction which can be found of the least utility in these associations is that of age or experience. It is the only just and natural distinction; and any other would be inconsistent with the enlarged and superior acquirements of the individuals who would compose these associations. The deference to age or experience will be natural, and readily given; and many advantageous regulations may be formed in consequence, for apportioning the proper employments to the period of life best calculated for them, and diminishing the labour of the individual as age advances beyond the term when the period of governing is concluded.

Fifth.—*The disposal of the surplus produce, and the connexion which will subsist between the several establishments.*

Under the proposed system the facilities of production, the absence of all the counteracting circumstances which so abundantly exist in common society, with the saving of time and waste in all the domestic arrangements, will secure, other circumstances being equal, *a much larger amount of wealth at a greatly reduced expenditure.* The next question is, in what manner is this produce to be disposed of?

Society has been hitherto so constituted that all parties are afraid of being overreached by others, and, without great care to secure their individual interests, of being deprived of the means of existence. This feeling has created a universal selfishness of the most ignorant nature, for it almost *ensures* the evils which it means to prevent.

These new associations can scarcely be formed before it will be discovered that by the most simple and easy regulations all the natural wants of human nature may be abundantly supplied; and the principle of selfishness (in the sense in which that term is here used) will cease to exist for want of an adequate motive to produce it.

It will be quite evident to all that wealth of that kind which will alone be held in any estimation amongst them may be so easily created to exceed all their wants that every desire for individual accumulation will be extinguished. To them individual accumulation of wealth will appear as irrational as to bottle up or store water in situations where there is more of this invaluable fluid than all can consume.

The peculiar produce to be raised in each establishment, beyond the general supply of the necessaries and comforts of life, which, if possible, will be abundantly created in each, will be adapted to afford the greatest variety of intrinsically valuable objects to exchange with each other; and the particular surplus products which will serve to give energy and pleasure to the industry of the members of each association will be regulated by the nature of the soil and climate and other local capabilities of the situation of each establishment. In all these labour will be the standard of value, and as there will always be a progressive advance in the amount of labour, manual, mental, and scientific, if we suppose population to increase under these arrangements, there will be in the same proportion a perpetually extending market or demand for all the industry of society, whatever may be its extent. Under such arrangements what are technically called "bad times" can never occur.

These establishments will be provided with granaries and warehouses, which will always contain a supply sufficient to protect the population against the occurrence even of more unfavourable seasons than have ever yet been experienced since agriculture has been general in society. In these granaries and storehouses proper persons will be appointed to receive, examine, deposit, and deliver out again the wealth of these communities.

Arrangements will be formed to distribute this wealth among the members of the association which created it, and to exchange the surplus for the surplus of the other communities, by general regulations that will render these transactions most simple and easy, to whatever distance these communities may extend.

A paper representative of the value of labour, manufactured on the principle of the new notes of the Bank of England, will serve for every purpose of their domestic commerce or exchanges, and will be issued only for intrinsic value received and in store. It has been mentioned already that all motives to deception will be effectually removed from the minds of the inhabitants of these new villages, and, of course, forgeries, though not guarded against by this new improvement, would not have any existence among them; and as this representative would be of no use in old society, no injury could come from that quarter.

But these associations must contribute their fair quota to the exigencies of the state. This consideration leads your Reporter to the next general head, or—

Sixth.—*The connexion of the new establishments with the Government of the country and with old society.*

Under this head are to be noticed, the amount and collection of the revenue, and the public or legal duties of the associations in peace and war.

Your Reporter concludes that whatever taxes are paid from land, capital, and labour, under the existing arrangements of society, the same amount for the same proportion of each may be collected with far more ease under those now proposed. The Government would, of course, require its revenue to be paid in the legal circulating medium, to obtain which, the associations would have to dispose of as much of their surplus produce to common society for the legal coin or paper of the realm as would discharge the demands of Government.

In time of peace these associations would give no trouble to Government; their internal regulations being founded on principles of prevention, not only with reference to public crimes, but to the private evils and errors which so fatally abound in common society. Courts of law, prisons, and punishments would not be required. These are requisite only where human nature is greatly misunderstood; where society rests on the demoralizing system of individual competition, rewards, and punishments;—they are necessary only in a stage of existence previous to the discovery of the science of the certain and overwhelming influence of circumstances over the whole character and conduct of mankind. Whatever courts of law, prisons, and punishments have yet effected for society, the influence of other circumstances, which may now be easily introduced, will accomplish infinitely more; for they will effectually prevent the growth of those evils of which our present institutions do not take cognizance till they are already full-formed and in baneful activity. In time of peace, therefore, these associations will save much charge and trouble to Government.

In reference to war also, they will be equally beneficial. Bodily exercises, adapted to improve the dispositions and increase the health and strength of the individual, will form part of the training and education of the children. In these exercises they may be instructed to acquire facility in the execution of combined movements, a habit which is calculated to produce regularity and order in time of peace, as well as to aid defensive and offensive operations in war. The children, therefore, at an early age, will acquire, *through their amusements,* those habits which will render them capable of becoming, in a short time, at any future period of life, the best defenders of their country, if necessity should again arise to defend it; since they would, in all probability, be far more to be depended upon than those whose physical, intellectual, and moral training had been less carefully conducted. In furnishing their quotas for the militia or common army they would probably adopt the pecuniary alternative; by which means they would form a reserve that, in proportion to their numbers, would be a great security for the nation's safety. They would prefer this alternative, to avoid the demoralizing effects of recruiting.

But the knowledge of the science of the influence of circumstances over mankind will speedily enable all nations to discover, not only the evils of war, but the folly of it. Of all modes of conduct adopted by mankind to obtain advantages in the present stage of society, this is the most certain to defeat its object. It is, in truth, a system of direct demoralization and of destruction; while it is the highest interest of all individuals and of all countries to *remoralize and conserve*. Men surely cannot with truth be termed rational beings until they shall discover and put in practice the principles which shall enable them to conduct their affairs without war. The arrangements we are considering would speedily show how easily these principles and practices may be introduced into general society.

From what has been stated it is evident that these associations would not subject the Government to the same proportion of trouble and expense that an equal population would do in old society; on the contrary, they would relieve the Government of the whole burthen; and by the certain and decisive influence of these arrangements upon the character and conduct of the parties, would materially add to the political strength, power, and resources of the country into which they shall be introduced.

What, then, to sum up the whole in a few words, does your Reporter now propose to his fellow creatures?

After a life spent in the investigation of the causes of the evils with which society is afflicted, and of the means of removing them,—and being now in possession of facts demonstrating the practicability and the efficacy of the arrangements now exhibited, which have been the fruit of that investigation, aided by a long course of actual experiments,—he offers to exchange their poverty for wealth, their ignorance for knowledge, their anger for kindness, their divisions for union. He offers to effect this change without subjecting a single individual even to temporary inconvenience. No one shall suffer by it for an hour; all shall be essentially benefited within a short period from its introduction; and yet not any part of the existing system shall be prematurely disturbed.

His practical operations will commence with those who are now a burthen to the country for want of employment. He will enable these persons to support themselves and families, and pay the interest of the capital requisite to put their labour in activity. From the effects which will be thus produced on the character and circumstances of this oppressed class, the public will soon see and acknowledge that he has promised far less than will be realised; and when, by these arrangements, the vicious, the idle, and the pauper shall be made virtuous, industrious, and independent, those who shall be still the lowest in the scale of old society may place themselves under the new arrangements, when they have evidence before them that these offer greater advantages than the old.

Upon this principle the change from the old system to the new will be checked in its progress whenever the latter ceases to afford decided inducements to embrace it; for long-established habits and prejudices will continue to have a powerful influence over those who have been trained in them. The change, then, beyond the beneficial employment of those who now cannot obtain work, will proceed solely from proof, in practice, of the very great superiority of the new arrangements over the old. Unlike, therefore, all former great changes, this may be effected without a single evil or inconvenience. It calls for no sacrifice of principle or property to any individual in any rank or condition; through every step of its progress it effects unmixed good only.

Acting on principles merely *approximating* to those of the new system, and at the same time powerfully counteracted by innumerable errors of the old system, he has succeeded in giving to a population originally of the most wretched description, and placed under the most unfavourable circumstances, such habits, feelings, and dispositions as enable them to enjoy more happiness than is to be found among any other population of the same extent in any part of the world; a degree of happiness, indeed, which it is utterly impossible for the old system to create among any class of persons placed under the most favourable circumstances.

Seeing, therefore, on the one hand, the sufferings which are now experienced, and the increasing discontent which prevails, especially among the most numerous and most useful class of our population, and, on the other, the relief and the extensive benefits which are offered to society on the authority of facts open to inspection,—can the public any longer with decency decline investigation? Can those who profess a sincere desire to improve the condition of the poor and working classes longer refuse to examine a proposal which, on the most rational grounds, promises them ample relief, accompanied with unmixed good to every other part of society?

Your Reporter solicits no favour from any party; he belongs to none. He merely calls upon those who are the most competent to the task, honestly, as men valuing their own interests and the interests of society, to investigate, without favour or affection, a "Plan (derived from thirty years' study and practical experience) for relieving public distress and removing discontent, by giving permanent productive employment to the poor and working classes, under arrangements which will essentially improve their character and ameliorate their condition, diminish the expenses of production and consumption, and create markets coextensive with production."

PRINCIPLES OF POLITICAL ECONOMY

by

JOHN STUART MILL

CONTENTS

Principles of Political Economy

JOHN STUART MILL

1806–1873

JOHN STUART MILL, connecting link between the English economists of the classical school and the militant radicals Karl Marx and Henry George, was born in London in 1806. His father, James Mill, of whom he gives an elaborate account in his *Autobiography,* was himself an economist of some distinction and an intimate friend of Jeremy Bentham, English philosopher and jurist, and of David Ricardo. The son was subjected to a rigorous education planned and carried out by his father. He says that he began the study of Greek when he was three years old. He took up Latin a few years later and read widely in Greek and in Latin before he was ten years old. He studied algebra and geometry during the same period and turned to books on natural science for mental diversion. At the age of thirteen he was called upon by his father to assess the comparative merits of the economic doctrines of Adam Smith and Ricardo. At the age of fifteen he was reading with intellectual rapture an exposition of the "utilitarianism" of Bentham.

The elder Mill had written a *History of British India,* published in 1817, which led to his being appointed to a post in India House, London. The son received a similar appointment in 1822 and worked in India House for thirty-six years. This position left him time for reading and mental activities. He helped to organize discussion groups. Among the men with whom he came into personal contact during his youth were Ricardo, Bentham, Thomas Carlyle, Grote, John Austin, Macaulay, Frederick Denison Maurice, and John Sterling.

Mill was thirty-seven years old when he published his first important book, *A System of Logic.* In this he aligned himself with the psychological school of Locke, Hartley, and Hume, which rejected the principle of innate ideas and asserted the principle of association of ideas based on experience.

In 1844 appeared Mill's *Essays on Some Unsettled Questions of Political Economy.* This book deals with such topics as the laws of interchange between nations, the influence of consumption on production, and the terms "productive" and "unproductive." It reflects, in the main, the ideas of Ricardo.

Mill cherished the ambition to write a book on economics that would do for his generation something of what *The Wealth of Nations* had done for a previous generation. The result of his efforts was *Principles of Political Economy,* published in 1848.

With his *Principles* John Stuart Mill may be said to have brought to a close a line of development that started with Adam Smith and proceeded through Malthus and Ricardo. We shall find him unduly optimistic when he writes: "Wars, and the destruction they cause, are now usually confined, in almost every country, to those distant and outlying possessions at which it comes into contact with savages." But when he speaks of progress in the physical sciences and arts, "combined with the greater security of property, and greater freedom in disposing of it, which are obvious features in the civilization of modern nations," he talks in twentieth-century language. "The peculiar characteristic of civilized beings," he says, "is the capacity of co-operation; and this like other faculties tends to improve by practice, and becomes capable of assuming a constantly wider sphere of action."

Two of the most significant chapters in the work are entitled "On the Probable Futurity of the Labouring Classes" and "Of the Grounds and Limits of the Laisser-Faire or Non-Interference Principle." In the first of these chapters Mill expresses faith in the co-operative movement and describes the successful operations of French co-operative groups as well as of the Rochdale Pioneers. He declares in the same chapter that while he agrees with socialist writers in their conception of the form which industrial operations tend to assume in the advance of improvement, he utterly dissents from what he calls "the most conspicuous and vehement part of their teaching"—their declamations against competition. "If competition," he says, "has its evils, it prevents greater evils." In the second of the chapters cited above, Mill shows how *laissez faire* as a social principle is inevitably giving way before the extension of governmental functions.

During the latter part of his life Mill devoted much of his thought and writing to feminist issues. In this trend he was strongly influenced by Mrs. John Taylor (Harriet Hardy), who became his wife in 1851. A notable essay on the enfranchisement of women, published in 1853, was inspired by her, and *On Liberty,* published in 1859, is dedicated to her. *The Subjection of Women,* published ten years later, is another of Mill's books that shows her influence. Seven years after her death, in 1865, Mill was elected to Parliament.

Toward the end of his life Mill met Auguste Comte, French sociologist, and was strongly influenced by positivist doctrines. He was willing now to call himself a socialist. Writing in his *Autobiography* (posthumously published) regarding the thoughts that he and his wife shared in their maturity, he says: "Our ideal of ultimate improvement went far beyond Democracy, and would class us decidedly under the general designation of Socialists. The social problem of the future we considered to be, how to unite the greatest individual liberty of action with a common ownership of the raw material of the globe, and an equal participation of all in the benefits of combined labour."

PRINCIPLES OF POLITICAL ECONOMY

Preliminary Remarks

In every department of human affairs, Practice long precedes Science: systematic enquiry into the modes of action of the powers of nature, is the tardy product of a long course of efforts to use those powers for practical ends. The conception, accordingly, of Political Economy as a branch of science, is extremely modern; but the subject with which its enquiries are conversant has in all ages necessarily constituted one of the chief practical interests of mankind, and, in some, a most unduly engrossing one.

That subject is Wealth. Writers on Political Economy profess to teach, or to investigate, the nature of Wealth, and the laws of its production and distribution: including, directly or remotely, the operation of all the causes by which the condition of mankind, or of any society of human beings, in respect to this universal object of human desire, is made prosperous or the reverse. Not that any treatise on Political Economy can discuss or even enumerate all these causes; but it undertakes to set forth as much as is known of the laws and principles according to which they operate.

The world now contains several extensive regions, provided with the various ingredients of wealth in a degree of abundance of which former ages had not even the idea. Without compulsory labour, an enormous mass of food is annually extracted from the soil, and maintains, besides the actual producers, an equal, sometimes a greater number of labourers, occupied in producing conveniences and luxuries of innumerable kinds, or in transporting them from place to place; also a multitude of persons employed in directing and superintending these various labours; and over and above all these, a class more numerous than in the most luxurious ancient societies, of persons whose occupations are of a kind not directly productive, and of persons who have no occupation at all. The food thus raised, supports a far larger population than had ever existed (at least in the same regions) on an equal space of ground; and supports them with certainty, exempt from those periodically recurring famines so abundant in the early history of Europe, and in Oriental countries even now not unfrequent. Besides this great increase in the quantity of food, it has greatly improved in quality and variety; while conveniences and luxuries, other than food, are no longer limited to a small and opulent class, but descend, in great abundance, through many widening strata in society. The collective resources of one of these communities, when it chooses to put them forth for any unexpected purpose; its ability to maintain fleets and armies, to execute public works, either useful or ornamental, to perform national acts of beneficence like the ransom of the West India slaves; to found colonies, to have its people taught, to do anything in short which requires expense, and to do it with no sacrifice of the necessaries or even the substantial comforts of its inhabitants, are such as the world never saw before.

But in all these particulars, characteristic of the modern industrial communities, those communities differ widely from one another. Though abounding in wealth as compared with former ages, they do so in very different degrees. Even of the countries which are justly accounted the richest, some have made a more complete use of their productive resources, and have obtained, relatively to their territorial extent, a much larger produce, than others; nor do they differ only in amount of wealth, but also in the rapidity of its increase. The diversities in the distribution of wealth are still greater than in the production. There are great differences in the condition of the poorest class in different countries; and in the proportional numbers and opulence of the classes which are above the poorest. The very nature and designation of the classes who originally share among them the produce of the soil, vary not a little in different places. In some, the landowners are a class in themselves, almost entirely separate from the classes engaged in industry: in others, the proprietor of the land is almost universally its cultivator, owning the plough, and often himself holding it. Where the proprietor himself does not cultivate, there is sometimes, between him and the labourer, an intermediate agency, that of the farmer, who advances the subsistence of the labourers, supplies the instruments of production, and receives, after paying a rent to the landowner, all the produce: in other cases, the landlord, his paid agents, and the labourers, are the only sharers. Manufactures, again, are sometimes carried on by scattered individuals, who own or hire the tools or machinery they require, and employ little labour besides that of their own family; in other cases, by large numbers working together in one building, with expensive and complex machinery owned by rich manufacturers. The same difference exists in the operations of trade. The wholesale operations indeed are everywhere carried on by large capitals, where such exist; but the retail dealings, which collectively occupy a very great amount of capital, are sometimes conducted in small shops, chiefly by the personal exertions of the dealers themselves, with their families, and perhaps an apprentice or two; and sometimes in large establishments, of which the funds are supplied by a wealthy individual or association, and the agency is that of numerous salaried shopmen or shopwomen. Besides these differences in the economical phenomena presented by different parts of what is usually called the civilized world, all those earlier states which we previously passed in review, have continued in some part or other of the world, down to our own time. Hunting communities still exist in America, nomadic in Arabia and the steppes of Northern Asia; Oriental society is in essentials what it has always been; the great empire of Russia is even now, in many respects, the scarcely modified image of feudal Europe. Every one of the great types of human society, down to that of the Esquimaux or Patagonians, is still extant.

These remarkable differences in the state of different portions of the human race, with regard to the production and distribution of wealth, must, like all other phenomena, depend on causes. And it is not a sufficient explanation to ascribe them exclusively to the degrees of knowledge, possessed at different times and places, of the laws of nature and the physical arts of life. Many other causes co-operate; and that very progress and unequal distribution of physical knowledge, are partly the effects, as well as partly the causes, of the state of the production and distribution of wealth.

In so far as the economical condition of nations turns upon the state of physical knowledge, it is a subject for the physical sciences, and the arts founded on them. But in so far as the causes are moral or psychological, dependent on institutions and social relations, or on the principles of human nature, their investigation belongs not to physical, but to moral and social science, and is the object of what is called Political Economy.

Book One: Production

1. OF THE REQUISITES OF PRODUCTION

THE REQUISITES of production are two: labour, and appropriate natural objects.

Labour is either bodily or mental; or, to express the distinction more comprehensively, either muscular or nervous; and it is necessary to include in the idea, not solely the exertion itself, but all feelings of a disagreeable kind, all bodily inconvenience or mental annoyance, connected with the employment of one's thoughts, or muscles, or both, in a particular occupation. Of the other requisite—appropriate natural objects

—it is to be remarked, that some objects exist or grow up spontaneously, of a kind suited to the supply of human wants. There are caves and hollow trees capable of affording shelter; fruit, roots, wild honey, and other natural products, on which human life can be supported; but even here a considerable quantity of labour is generally required, not for the purpose of creating, but of finding and appropriating them. In all but these few and (except in the very commencement of human society) unimportant cases, the objects supplied by nature are only instrumental to human wants, after having undergone some degree of transformation by human exertion. Even the wild animals of the forest and of the sea, from which the hunting and fishing tribes derive their sustenance—though the labour of which they are the subject is chiefly that required for appropriating them—must yet, before they are used as food, be killed, divided into fragments, and subjected in almost all cases to some culinary process, which are operations requiring a certain degree of human labour. The amount of transformation which natural substances undergo before being brought into the shape in which they are directly applied to human use, varies from this or a still less degree of alteration in the nature and appearance of the object, to a change so total that no trace is perceptible of the original shape and structure. There is little resemblance between a piece of a mineral substance found in the earth, and a plough, an axe, or a saw. There is less resemblance between porcelain and the decomposing granite of which it is made, or between sand mixed with seaweed, and glass. The difference is greater still between the fleece of a sheep, or a handful of cotton seeds, and a web of muslin or broad cloth; and the sheep and seeds themselves are not spontaneous growths, but results of previous labour and care. In these several cases the ultimate product is so extremely dissimilar to the substance supplied by nature, that in the custom of language nature is represented as only furnishing materials.

Nature, however, does more than supply materials; she also supplies powers. The matter of the globe is not an inert recipient of forms and properties impressed by human hands; it has active energies by which it co-operates with, and may even be used as a substitute for, labour. In the early ages people converted their corn into flour by pounding it between two stones; they next hit on a contrivance which enabled them, by turning a handle, to make one of the stones revolve upon the other; and this process, a little improved, is still the common practice of the East. The muscular exertion, however, which it required, was very severe and exhausting, insomuch that it was often selected as a punishment for slaves who had offended their masters. When the time came at which the labour and sufferings of slaves were thought worth economizing, the greater part of this bodily exertion was rendered unnecessary, by contriving that the upper stone should be made to revolve upon the lower, not by human strength, but by the force of the wind or of falling water. In this case, natural agents, the wind or the gravitation of the water, are made to do a portion of the work previously done by labour.

Cases like this, in which a certain amount of labour has been dispensed with, its work being devolved upon some natural agent, are apt to suggest an erroneous notion of the comparative functions of labour and natural powers; as if the co-operation of those powers with human industry were limited to the cases in which they are made to perform what would otherwise be done by labour; as if, in the case of things made (as the phrase is) by hand, nature only furnished passive materials. This is an illusion. The powers of nature are as actively operative in the one case as in the other. A workman takes a stalk of the flax or hemp plant, splits it into separate fibres, twines together several of these fibres with his fingers, aided by a simple instrument called a spindle; having thus formed a thread, he lays many such threads side by side, and places other similar threads directly across them, so that each passes alternately over and under those which are at right angles to it; this part of the process being facilitated by an instrument called a shuttle. He has now produced a web of cloth, either linen or sackcloth, according to the material. He is said to have done this by hand, no natural force being supposed to have acted in concert with him. But by what force is each step of this operation rendered possible, and the web, when produced, held together? By the tenacity, or force of cohesion, of the fibres: which is one of the forces of nature, and which we can measure exactly against other mechanical forces, and ascertain how much of any of them it suffices to neutralize or counterbalance.

If we examine any other case of what is called the action of man upon nature, we shall find in like manner that the powers of nature, or in other words the properties of matter, do all the work, when once objects are put into the right position. This one operation, of putting things into fit places for being acted upon by their own internal forces, and by those residing in other natural objects, is all that man does, or can do, with matter. He only moves one thing to or from another. He moves a seed into the ground; and the natural forces of vegetation produce in succession a root, a stem, leaves, flowers, and fruit. He moves an axe through a tree, and it falls by the natural force of gravitation; he moves a saw through it, in a particular manner, and the physical properties by which a softer substance gives way before a harder, make it separate into planks, which he arranges in certain positions, with nails driven through them, or adhesive matter between them, and produces a table, or a house. He moves a spark to fuel, and it ignites, and by the force generated in combustion it cooks the food, melts or softens the iron, converts into beer or sugar the malt or cane juice, which he has previously moved to the spot. He has no other means of acting on matter than by moving it. Motion, and resistance to motion, are the only things which his muscles are constructed for. By muscular contraction he can create a pressure on an outward object, which, if sufficiently powerful, will set it in motion, or if it be already moving, will check or modify or altogether arrest its motion, and he can do no more. But this is enough to have given all the command which mankind have acquired over natural forces immeasurably more powerful than themselves; a command which, great as it is already, is without doubt destined to become indefinitely greater. He exerts this power either by availing himself of natural forces in existence, or by arranging objects in those mixtures and combinations by which natural forces are generated; as when by putting a lighted match to fuel, and water into a boiler over it, he generates the expansive force of steam, a power which has been made so largely available for the attainment of human purposes.

Labour, then, in the physical world, is always and solely employed in putting objects in motion; the properties of matter, the laws of nature, do the rest. The skill and ingenuity of human beings are chiefly exercised in discovering movements, practicable by their powers, and capable of bringing about the effects which they desire.

II. OF LABOUR AS AN AGENT OF PRODUCTION

The labour which terminates in the production of an article fitted for some human use, is either employed directly about the thing, or in previous operations destined to facilitate, perhaps essential to the possibility of, the subsequent ones. In making bread, for example, the labour employed about the thing itself is that of the baker; but the labour of the miller, though employed directly in the production not of bread but of flour, is equally part of the aggregate sum of labour by which the bread is produced; as is also the labour of the sower, and of the reaper. Some may think that all these persons ought to be considered as employing their labour directly about the thing; the corn, the flour, and the bread being one substance in three different states. Without disputing about this question of mere language, there is still the ploughman, who prepared the ground for the seed, and whose labour never came in contact with the substance in any of its states; and the ploughmaker, whose share in the result was still more remote. All these persons ultimately derive the remuneration of their labour from the bread, or its price: the ploughmaker as much as the rest; for since ploughs are of no use except for tilling the soil, no one would make or use ploughs for any other reason than because the increased returns, thereby obtained from the ground, afforded a source from which an adequate equivalent could be assigned for the labour of the ploughmaker. If the produce is to be used or consumed in the form of bread, it is from the bread that this equivalent must come. The bread must suffice to remunerate all these labours, and several others; such as the carpenters and bricklayers who erected the farm buildings; the hedgers and ditchers who made the fences necessary for the protection of the crop; the miners and smelters who extracted or prepared the iron of which the plough and other implements were made. These, however, and the ploughmaker, do not depend for their remuneration upon the bread made from the produce of a single harvest, but upon that made from the produce of all the harvests which are successively gathered until the plough, or the buildings and fences, are worn out. We must add yet another kind of labour; that of transporting the produce from the place of its production to the place of its destined use: the labour of carrying the corn to market, and from market to the miller's, the flour from the miller's to the baker's, and the bread from the baker's to the place of its final consumption. This labour is sometimes very considerable: flour is transported to England from beyond the Atlantic, corn from the heart of Russia; and in addition to the labourers immediately employed, the waggoners and sailors, there are also costly instruments, such as ships, in the construction of which much labour has been expended: that labour, however, not depending for its whole remuneration upon the bread, but for a part only; ships being usually, during the course of their existence, employed in the transport of many different kinds of commodities.

To estimate, therefore, the labour of which any given commodity is the result, is far from a simple operation. The items in the calculation are very numerous—as it may seem to some persons, infinitely so; for if, as a part of the labour employed in making bread, we count the labour of the blacksmith who made the plough, why not also (it may be asked) the labour of making the tools used by the blacksmith, and the tools used in making those tools, and so back to the origin of things? But after mounting one or two steps in this ascending scale, we come into a region of fractions too minute for calculation. Suppose, for instance, that the same plough will last, before being worn out, a dozen years. Only one twelfth of the labour of making the plough must be placed to the account of each year's harvest. A twelfth part of the labour of making a plough is an appreciable quantity. But the same set of tools, perhaps, suffice to the ploughmaker for forging a hundred ploughs, which serve during the twelve years of their existence to prepare the soil of as many different farms. A twelve hundredth part of the labour of making the tools, is as much, therefore, as has been expended in procuring one year's harvest of a single farm: and when this fraction comes to be further apportioned among the various sacks of corn and loaves of bread, it is seen at once that such quantities are not worth taking into the account for any practical purpose connected with the commodity. It is true that if the toolmaker had not laboured, the corn and bread never would have been produced; but they will not be sold a tenth part of a farthing dearer in consideration of his labour.

Another of the modes in which labour is indirectly or remotely instrumental to the production of a thing, requires particular notice: namely, when it is employed in producing subsistence, to maintain the labourers while they are engaged in the production. This previous employment of labour is an indispensable condition to every productive operation, on any other than the very smallest scale. Except the labour of the hunter and fisher, there is scarcely any kind of labour to which the returns are immediate. Productive operations require to be continued a certain time, before their fruits are obtained. Unless the labourer, before commencing his work, possesses a store of food, or can obtain access to the stores of some one else, in sufficient quantity to maintain him until the production is completed, he can undertake no labour but such as can be carried on at odd intervals, concurrently with the pursuit of his subsistence. He cannot obtain food itself in any abundance; for every mode of so obtaining it, requires that there be already food in store. Agriculture only brings forth food after the lapse of months; and though the labours of the agriculturist are not necessarily continuous during the whole period, they must occupy a considerable part of it. Not only is agriculture impossible without food produced in advance, but there must be a very great quantity in advance to enable any considerable community to support itself wholly by agriculture. A country like England or France is only able to carry on the agriculture of the present year, because that of past years has provided, in those countries or somewhere else, sufficient food to support their agricultural population until the next harvest. They are only enabled to produce so many other things besides food, because the food which was in store at the close of the last harvest suffices to maintain not only the agricultural labourers, but a large industrious population besides.

From these considerations it appears, that in an enumeration and classification of the kinds of industry which are intended for the indirect or remote furtherance of other productive labour, we need not include the labour of producing subsistence or other necessaries of life to be consumed by productive labourers; for the main end and purpose of his labour is the subsistence itself; and though the possession of a store of it enables other work to be done, this is but an incidental consequence. The remaining modes in which labour is indirectly instrumental to production, may be arranged under five heads.

First: Labour employed in producing materials, on which industry is to be afterwards employed. This is, in many cases, a labour of mere appropriation; *extractive* industry, as it has been aptly named by M. Dunoyer. The labour of the miner, for example, consists of operations for digging out of the earth substances convertible by industry into various articles fitted for human use.

The second kind of indirect labour is that employed in making tools or implements for the assistance of labour. I use these terms in their most comprehensive sense, embracing all permanent instruments or helps to production, from a flint and steel for striking a light, to a steam ship, or the most complex apparatus of manufacturing machinery.

Thirdly: Besides materials for industry to employ itself on, and implements to aid it, provision must be made to prevent its operations from being disturbed and its products injured, either by the destroying agencies of nature, or by the violence or rapacity of men. This gives rise to another mode in which labour not employed directly about the product itself, is instrumental to its production; namely, when employed for the *protection* of industry. Such is the object of all buildings for industrial purposes; all manufactories, warehouses, docks, granaries, barns, farm buildings devoted to cattle, or to the operations of agricultural labour.

Fourthly: There is a very great amount of labour employed, not in bringing the product into existence, but in rendering it, when in existence, accessible to those for whose use it is intended. Many important classes of labourers find their sole employment in some function of this kind. There is first the whole class of carriers, by land or water: muleteers, waggoners, bargemen, sailors, wharfmen, coal heavers, porters, railway establishments, and the like. Next, there are the constructors of all the implements of transport; ships, barges, carts, locomotives, &c., to which must be added roads, canals, and railways.

We have now completed the enumeration of the modes in which labour employed on external nature is subservient to production. But there is yet another mode of employing labour, which conduces equally, though still more remotely, to that end: this is, labour of which the subject is human beings. Every human being has been brought up from infancy at the expense of much labour to some person or persons, and if this labour, or part of it, had not been bestowed, the child would never have attained the age and strength which enable him to become a labourer in his turn. To the community at large, the labour and expense of rearing its infant population form a part of the outlay which is a condition of production, and which is to be replaced with increase from the future produce of their labour. By the individuals, this labour and expense are usually incurred from other motives than to obtain such ultimate return, and, for most purposes of political economy, need not be taken into account as expenses of production. But the technical or industrial education of the community; the labour employed in learning and in teaching the arts of production, in acquiring and communicating skill in those arts; this labour is really, and in general solely, undergone for the sake of the greater or more valuable produce thereby attained, and in order that a remuneration, equivalent or more than equivalent, may be reaped by the learner, besides an adequate remuneration for the labour of the teacher, when a teacher has been employed.

Another kind of labour, usually classed as mental, but conducing to the ultimate product as directly, though not so immediately, as manual labour itself, is the labour of the inventors of industrial processes. I say, usually classed as mental, because in reality it is not exclusively so. All human exertion is compounded of some mental and some bodily elements. The stupidest hodman, who repeats from day to day the mechanical act of climbing a ladder, performs a function partly intellectual; the most intelligent dog or elephant could not, probably, be taught to do it. The dullest human being, instructed beforehand, is capable of turning a mill; but a horse cannot drive it without somebody to drive and watch him. On the other hand, there is some bodily ingredient in the labour most purely mental, when it generates any external result. Newton could not have produced the *Principia* without the bodily exertion either of penmanship or of dictation; and he must have drawn many figures, and written out many calculations and demonstrations, while he was preparing it in his mind. Inventors, besides the labour of their brains, generally go through much labour with their hands, in the models which they construct and the experiments they have to make before their idea can realize itself successfully in act. Whether mental, however, or bodily, their labour is a part of that by which the production is brought about. The labour of Watt in contriving the steam engine was as essential a part of production as that of the mechanics who build or the engineers who work the instrument; and was undergone, no less than theirs, in the prospect of a remuneration from the produce. The labour of invention is often estimated and paid on the very same plan as that of execution. Many manufacturers of ornamental goods have inventors in their employment, who receive wages or salaries for designing patterns, exactly as others do for copying them. All this is strictly part of the labour of production; as the labour of the author of a book is equally a part of its production with that of the printer and binder.

In a national, or universal point of view, the labour of the savant, or speculative thinker, is as much a part of production in the very narrowest sense, as that of the inventor of a practical art; many such inventions having been the direct consequences of theoretic discoveries, and every extension of knowledge of the powers of nature being fruitful of applications to the purposes of outward life. The electromagnetic telegraph was the wonderful and most unexpected consequence of the experiments of Œrsted and the mathematical investigations of Ampère: and the modern art of navigation is an unforeseen emanation from the purely speculative and apparently merely curious inquiry, by the mathematicians of Alexandria, into the properties of three curves formed by the intersection of a plane surface and a cone. No limit can be set to the importance, even in a purely productive and material point of view, of mere thought. Inasmuch, however, as these material fruits, though the result, are seldom the direct purpose of the pursuits of savants, nor is their remuneration in general derived from the increased production which may be caused incidentally, and mostly after a long interval, by their discoveries; this ultimate influence does not, for most of the purposes of political economy, require to be taken into consideration; and speculative thinkers are generally classed as the producers only of the books, or other useable or saleable articles, which directly emanate from them. But when (as in political economy one should always be prepared to do) we shift our point of view, and consider not individual acts, and the motives by which they are determined, but national and universal results, intellectual speculation must be looked upon as a most influential part of the productive labour of society, and the portion of its resources employed in carrying on and in remunerating such labour, as a highly productive part of its expenditure.

III. OF CAPITAL

It has been seen in the preceding chapters that besides the primary and universal requisites of production, labour and natural agents, there is another requisite without which no productive operations beyond the rude and scanty beginnings of primitive industry, are possible: namely, a stock, previously accumulated, of the products of former labour. This accumulated stock of the produce of labour is termed Capital. The function of Capital in production, it is of the utmost importance thoroughly to understand, since a number of the erroneous notions with which our subject is invested, originate in an imperfect and confused apprehension of this point.

Capital, by persons wholly unused to reflect on the subject, is supposed to be synonymous with money. Money is no more synonymous with capital than it is with wealth. Money cannot in itself perform any part of the office of capital, since it can afford no assistance to production. To do this, it must be exchanged for other things; and anything, which is susceptible of being exchanged for other things, is capable of contributing to production in the same degree. What capital does for production, is to afford the shelter, protection, tools and materials which the work requires, and to feed and otherwise maintain the labourers during the process. These are the services which present labour requires from past, and from the produce of past, labour. Whatever things are destined for this use—destined to supply productive labour with these various prerequisites—are Capital.

To familiarize ourselves with the conception, let us consider what is done with the capital invested in any of the branches of business which compose the productive industry of a country. A manufacturer, for example, has one part of his capital in the form of buildings, fitted and destined for carrying on this branch of manufacture. Another part he has in the form of machinery. A third consists, if he be a spinner, of raw cotton, flax, or wool; if a weaver, of flaxen, woollen, silk, or cotton, thread; and the like, according to the nature of the manufacture. Food and clothing for his operatives, it is not the custom of the present age that he should directly provide; and few capitalists, except the producers of food or clothing, have any portion worth mentioning of their capital in that shape. Instead of this, each capitalist has money, which he pays to his workpeople, and so enables them to supply themselves: he has also finished goods in his warehouses, by the sale of which he obtains more money, to employ in the same manner, as well as to replenish his stock of materials, to keep his buildings and machinery in repair, and to replace them when worn out. His money and finished goods, however, are not wholly capital, for he does not wholly devote them to these purposes: he employs a part of the one, and of the proceeds of the other, in supplying his personal consumption and that of his family, or in hiring grooms or valets, or maintaining hunters and hounds, or in educating his children, or in paying taxes, or in charity. What then is his capital? Precisely that part of his possessions, whatever it be, which he designs to employ in carrying on fresh production. It is of no consequence that a part, or even the whole of it, is in a form in which it cannot directly supply the wants of labourers.

Suppose, for instance, that the capitalist is a hardware manufacturer, and that his stock in trade, over and above his machinery, consists at present wholly in iron goods. Iron goods cannot feed labourers. Nevertheless, by a mere change of the destination of the iron goods, he can cause labourers to be fed. Suppose that with a portion of the proceeds he intended to maintain a pack of hounds, or an establishment of servants; and that he changes his intention, and employs it in his business, paying it in wages to additional workpeople. These workpeople are enabled to buy and consume the food which would otherwise have been consumed by the hounds or by the servants; and thus without the employer's having seen or touched one particle of the food, his conduct has determined that so much more of the food existing in the country has been devoted to the use of productive labourers, and so much less consumed in a manner wholly unproductive. Now vary the hypothesis, and suppose that what is thus paid in wages would otherwise have been laid out not in feeding servants or hounds, but in buying plate and jewels; and in order to render the effect perceptible, let us suppose that the change takes place on a considerable scale, and that a large sum is diverted from buying plate and jewels to employing productive labourers, whom we shall suppose to have been previously, like the Irish peasantry, only half employed and half fed. The labourers, on receiving their increased wages, will not lay them out in plate and jewels, but in food. There is not, however, additional food in the country; nor any unproductive labourers or animals, as in the former case, whose food is set free for productive purposes. Food will therefore be imported if possible; if not possible, the labourers will remain for a season on their short allowance: but the consequence of this change in the demand for commodities, occasioned by the change in the expenditure of capitalists from unproductive to productive, is that next year more food will be produced, and less plate and jewellery. So that again, without having had anything to do with the food of the labourers directly, the conversion by individuals of a portion of their property, no matter of what sort, from an unproductive destination to a productive, has had the effect of causing more food to be appropriated to the consumption of productive labourers. The distinction, then, between Capital and Not-capital, does not lie in the kind of commodities, but in the mind of the capitalist—in his will to employ them for one purpose rather than another; and all property, however ill adapted in itself for the use of labourers, is a part of capital, so soon as it, or the value to be received from it, is set apart for productive reinvestment. The sum of all the values so destined by their respective possessors, composes the capital of the country. Whether all those values are in a shape directly applicable to productive uses, makes no difference. Once appropriated to that end, they do not fail to find a way of transforming themselves into things fitted to be applied to it.

As whatever of the produce of the country is devoted to production is capital, so, conversely, the whole of the capital of the country is devoted to production. This second proposition, however, must be taken with some limitations and explanations. A fund may be seeking for productive employment, and find none, adapted to the inclinations of its possessor: it then is capital still, but unemployed capital. Or the stock may consist of unsold goods, not susceptible of direct application to productive uses, and not, at the moment, marketable: these, until sold, are in the condition of unemployed capital. Again, artificial or accidental circumstances may render it necessary to possess a larger stock in advance, that is, a larger capital before entering on production, than is required by the nature of things. Suppose that the government lays a tax on the production in one of its earlier stages, as for instance by taxing the material. The manufacturer has to advance the tax, before commencing the manufacture, and is therefore under a necessity of having a larger accumulated fund than is required for, or is actually employed in, the production which he carries on. He must have a larger capital, to maintain the same quantity of productive labour; or (what is equivalent) with a given capital he maintains less labour. This mode of levying taxes, therefore, limits unnecessarily the industry of the country: a portion of the fund destined by its owners for production being diverted from its purpose, and kept in a constant state of advance to the government.

For another example: a farmer may enter on his farm at such a time of the year, that he may be required to pay one, two, or even three quarters' rent before obtaining any return from the produce. This, therefore, must be paid out of his capital. Now rent, when paid for the land itself, and not for improvements made in it by labour, is not a productive expenditure. It is not an outlay for the support of labour, or for the provision of implements or materials the produce of labour. It is the price paid for the use of an appropriated natural agent. This natural agent is indeed as indispensable (and even more so) as any implement: but the having to pay a price for it, is not. In the case of the implement (a thing produced by labour) a price of some sort is the necessary condition of its existence: but the land exists by nature. The payment for it, therefore, is not one of the expenses of production; and the necessity of making the payment out of capital, makes it requisite that there should be a greater capital, a greater antecedent accumulation of the produce of past labour, than is naturally necessary, or than is needed where land is occupied on a different system. This extra capital, though intended by its owners for production, is in reality employed unproductively, and annually replaced, not from any produce of its own, but from the produce of the labour supported by the remainder of the farmer's capital.

Finally, that large portion of the productive capital of a country which is employed in paying the wages and salaries of labourers, evidently is not, all of it, strictly and indispensably necessary for production. As much of it as exceeds the actual necessaries of life and health (an excess which in the case of skilled labourers is usually considerable) is not expended in supporting labour, but in remunerating it, and the labourers could wait for this part of their remuneration until the production is completed; it needs not necessarily pre-exist as capital: and if they unfortunately had to forego it altogether, the same amount of production might take place. In order that the whole remuneration of the labourers should be advanced to them in daily or weekly payments, there must exist in advance, and be appropriated to productive use, a greater stock, or capital, than would suffice to carry on the existing extent of production: greater, by whatever amount of remuneration the labourers receive, beyond what the self-interest of a prudent slave master would assign to his slaves. In truth, it is only after an abundant capital had already been accumulated, that the practice of paying in advance any remuneration of labour beyond a bare subsistence, could possibly have arisen: since whatever is so paid, is not really applied to production, but to the unproductive consumption of productive labourers, indicating a fund for production sufficiently ample to admit of habitually diverting a part of it to a mere convenience.

It will be observed that I have assumed, that the labourers are always subsisted from capital: and this is obviously the fact, though the capital needs not necessarily be furnished by a person called a capitalist. When the labourer maintains himself by funds of his own, as when a peasant-farmer or proprietor lives on the produce of his land, or an artisan works on his own account, they are still supported by capital, that is, by funds provided in advance. The peasant does not subsist this year on the produce of this year's harvest, but on that of the last. The artisan is not living on the proceeds of the work he has in hand, but on those of work previously executed and disposed of. Each is supported by a small capital of his own, which he periodically replaces from the produce of his labour. The large capitalist is, in like manner, maintained from funds provided in advance. If he personally conducts his operations, as much of his personal or household expenditure as does not exceed a fair remuneration of his labour at the market price, must be considered a part of his capital, expended, like any other capital, for production: and his personal consumption, so far as it consists of necessaries, is productive consumption.

Book Two: Distribution

I. OF PROPERTY

THE PRINCIPLES which have been set forth in the first part of this Treatise, are, in certain respects, strongly distinguished from those, on the consideration of which we are now about to enter. The laws and conditions of the production of wealth, partake of the character of physical truths. There is nothing optional or arbitrary in them. Whatever mankind produce, must be produced in the modes, and under the conditions, imposed by the constitution of external things, and by the inherent properties of their own bodily and mental structure. Whether they like it or not, their productions will be limited by the amount of their previous accumulation, and, that being given, it will be proportional to their energy, their skill, the perfection of their machinery, and their judicious use of the advantages of combined labour. Whether they like it or not, a double quantity of labour will not raise, on the same land, a double quantity of food, unless some improvement takes place in the processes of cultivation. Whether they like it or not, the unproductive expenditure of individuals will *pro tanto* tend to impoverish the community, and only their productive expenditure will enrich it. The opinions, or the wishes, which may exist on these different matters, do not control the things themselves. We cannot, indeed, foresee to what extent the modes of production may be altered, or the productiveness of labour increased, by future extensions of our knowledge of the laws of nature suggesting new processes of industry of which we have at present no conception. But howsoever we may succeed in making for ourselves more space within the limits set by the constitution of things, we know that there must be limits. We cannot alter the ultimate properties either of matter or mind, but can only employ those properties more or less successfully, to bring about the events in which we are interested.

It is not so with the Distribution of Wealth. That is a matter of human institution solely. The things once there, mankind, individually or collectively, can do with them as they like. They can place them at the disposal of whomsoever they please, and on whatever terms. Further, in the social state, in every state except total solitude, any disposal whatever of them can only take place by the consent of society, or rather of those who dispose of its active force. Even what a person has produced by his individual toil, unaided by any one, he cannot keep, unless by the permission of society. Not only can society take it from him, but individuals could and would take it from him, if society only remained passive; if it did not either interfere *en masse,* or employ and pay people for the purpose of preventing him from being disturbed in the possession. The distribution of wealth, therefore, depends on the laws and customs of society. The rules by which it is determined, are what the opinions and feelings of the ruling portion of the community make them, and are very different in different ages and countries; and might be still more different, if mankind so chose.

The opinions and feelings of mankind, doubtless, are not a matter of chance. They are consequences of the fundamental laws of human nature, combined with the existing state of knowledge and experience, and the existing condition of social institutions and intellectual and moral culture. But the laws of the generation of human opinions are not within our present subject. They are part of the general theory of human progress, a far larger and more difficult subject of inquiry than political economy. We have here to consider, not the causes, but the consequences, of the rules according to which wealth may be distributed. Those, at least, are as little arbitrary, and have as much the character of physical laws, as the laws of production. Human beings can control their own acts, but not the consequences of their acts either to themselves or to others. Society can subject the distribution of wealth to whatever rules it thinks best; but what practical results will flow from the operation of those rules, must be discovered, like any other physical or mental truths, by observation and reasoning.

We proceed, then, to the consideration of the different modes of distributing the produce of land and labour, which have been adopted in practice, or may be conceived in theory. Among these, our attention is first claimed by that primary and fundamental institution, on which, unless in some exceptional and very limited cases, the economical arrangements of society have always rested, though in its secondary features it has varied, and is liable to vary. I mean, of course, the institution of individual property.

Private property, as an institution, did not owe its origin to any of those considerations of utility, which plead for the maintenance of it when established. Enough is known of rude ages, both from history and from analogous states of society in our own time, to show, that tribunals (which always precede laws) were originally established, not to determine rights, but to repress violence and terminate quarrels. With this object chiefly in view, they naturally enough gave legal effect to first occupancy, by treating as the aggressor the person who first commenced violence, by turning, or attempting to turn, another out of possession. The preservation of the peace, which was the original object of civil government, was thus attained; while by confirming, to those who already possessed it, even what was not the fruit of personal exertion, a guarantee was incidentally given to them and others that they would be protected in what was so.

In considering the institution of property as a question in social philosophy, we must leave out of consideration its actual origin in any of the existing nations of Europe. We may suppose a community unhampered by any previous possession; a body of colonists, occupying for the first time an uninhabited country; bringing nothing with them but what belonged to them in common, and having a clear field for the adoption of the institutions and polity which they judged most expedient; required, therefore, to choose whether they would conduct the work of production on the principle of individual property, or on some system of common ownership and collective agency.

If private property were adopted, we must presume that it would be accompanied by none of the initial inequalities and injustice which obstruct the beneficial operation of the principle in old society. Every full-grown man or woman, we must suppose, would be secured in the unfettered use and disposal of his or her bodily and mental faculties; and the instruments of production, the land and tools, would be divided fairly among them, so that all might start, in respect to outward appliances, on equal terms. It is possible also to conceive that in this original apportionment, compensation might be made for the injuries of nature, and the balance redressed by assigning to the less robust members of the community advantages in the distribution, sufficient to put them on a par with the rest. But the division, once made, would not again be interfered with; individuals would be left to their own exertions and to the ordinary chances, for making an advantageous use of what was assigned to them. If individual property, on the contrary, were excluded, the plan which must be adopted would be to hold the land and all instruments of production as the joint property of the community, and to carry on the operations of industry on the common account. The direction of the labour of the community would devolve upon a magistrate or magistrates, whom we may suppose elected by the suffrages of the community, and whom we must assume to be voluntarily obeyed by them. The division of the produce would in like manner be a public act. The principle might either be that of complete equality, or of apportionment to the necessities or deserts of individuals, in whatever manner might be conformable to the ideas of justice or policy prevailing in the community.

Examples of such associations, on a small scale, are the monastic orders, the Moravians, the followers of Rapp, and others: and from the hopes which they hold out of relief from the miseries and iniquities of a state of much inequality of wealth, schemes for a larger application of the same idea have reappeared and become popular at all periods of active speculation on the first principles of society. In an age like the present, when a general reconsideration of all first principles is felt to be inevitable, and when more than at any former period of history the suffering portions of the community have a voice in the discussion, it was impossible but that ideas of this nature should spread far and wide. The late revolutions in Europe have thrown up a great amount of speculation of this character, and an unusual share of attention has consequently been drawn to the various forms which these ideas have assumed: nor is this attention likely to diminish, but on the contrary, to increase more and more.

The assailants of the principle of individual property may be divided into two classes: those whose scheme implies absolute equality in the distribution of the physical means of life and enjoyment, and those who admit inequality, but grounded on some principle, or supposed principle, of justice or general expediency, and not, like so many of the existing social inequalities, dependent on accident alone. At the head of the first class, as the earliest of those belonging to the present generation, must be placed Mr. [Robert] Owen and his followers. M. Louis Blanc and M. [Etienne] Cabet have more recently become conspicuous as apostles of similar doctrines (though the former advocates equality of distribution only as a transition to a still higher standard of justice, that all should work according to their capacity, and receive according to their wants). The characteristic name for this economical system is Communism, a word of continental origin, only of late introduced into this country. The word Socialism, which originated among the English Communists, and was assumed by them as a name to designate their own doctrine, is now, on the Continent, employed in a larger sense; not necessarily implying Communism, or the entire abolition of private property, but applied to any system which requires that the land and the instruments of production should be the property, not of individuals, but of communities or associations, or of the government. Among such systems, the two of highest intellectual pretension are those which, from the name of their real or reputed authors, have been called Saint-Simonism and Fourierism; the former, defunct as a system, but which during the few years of its public promulgation, sowed the seeds of nearly all the Socialist tendencies which have since spread so widely in France: the second, now flourishing in the number, talent, and zeal of its adherents.

Whatever may be the merits or defects of these various schemes, they cannot be truly said to be impracticable. No reasonable person can doubt that a village community, composed of a few thousand inhabitants cultivating in joint ownership the same extent of land which at present feeds the number of people, and producing by combined labour and the most improved processes the manufactured articles which they required, could raise an amount of productions sufficient to maintain them in comfort; and would find the means of obtaining, and if need be, exacting, the quantity of labour necessary for this purpose, from every member of the association who was capable of work.

The objection ordinarily made to a system of community of property and equal distribution of the produce, that each person would be incessantly occupied in evading his fair share of the work, points, undoubtedly, to a real difficulty. But those who urge this objection, forget to how great an extent the same difficulty exists under the system on which nine tenths of the business of society is now conducted. The objection supposes, that honest and efficient labour is only to be had from those who are themselves individually to reap the benefit of their own exertions. But how small a part of all the labour performed in England, from the lowest paid to the highest, is done by persons working for their own benefit. From the Irish reaper or hodman to the chief justice or the minister of state, nearly all the work of society is remunerated by day wages or fixed salaries. A factory operative has less personal interest in his work than a member of a Communist association, since he is not, like him, working for a partnership of which he is himself a member. It will no doubt be said, that though the labourers themselves have not, in most cases, a personal interest in their work, they are watched and superintended, and their labour directed, and the mental part of the labour performed, by persons who have. Even this, however, is far from being universally the fact. In all public, and many of the largest and most successful private undertakings, not only the labours of detail but the control and superintendence are entrusted to salaried officers. And though the "master's eye," when the master is vigilant and intelligent, is of proverbial value, it must be remembered that in a Socialist farm or manufactory, each labourer would be under the eye not of one master, but of the whole community. In the extreme case of obstinate perseverance in not performing the due share of work, the community would have the same resources which society now has for compelling conformity to the necessary conditions of the association. Dismissal, the only remedy at present, is no remedy when any other labourer who may be engaged does no better than his predecessor: the power of dismissal only enables an employer to obtain from his workmen the customary amount of labour, but that customary labour may be of any degree of inefficiency. Even the labourer who loses his employment by idleness or negligence, has nothing worse to suffer, in the most unfavourable case, than the discipline of a workhouse, and if the desire to avoid this be a sufficient motive in the one system, it would be sufficient in the other. I am not undervaluing the strength of the incitement given to labour when the whole or a large share of the benefit of extra exertion belongs to the labourer. But under the present system of industry this incitement, in the great majority of cases, does not exist. If Communistic labour might be less vigorous than that of a peasant proprietor, or a workman labouring on his own account, it would probably be more energetic than that of a labourer for hire, who has no personal interest in the matter at all. The neglect by the uneducated classes of labourers for hire, of the duties which they engage to perform, is in the present state of society most flagrant. Now it is an admitted condition of the Communist scheme that all shall be educated: and this being supposed, the duties of the members of the association would doubtless be as diligently performed as those of the generality of salaried officers in the middle or higher classes; who are not supposed to be necessarily unfaithful to their trust, because so long as they are not dismissed, their pay is the same in however lax a manner their duty is fulfilled. Undoubtedly, as a general rule, remuneration by fixed salaries does not in any class of functionaries produce the maximum of zeal: and this is as much as can be reasonably alleged against Communistic labour.

That even this inferiority would necessarily exist, is by no means so certain as is assumed by those who are little used to carry their minds beyond the state of things with which they are familiar. Mankind are capable of a far greater amount of public spirit than the present age is accustomed to suppose possible. History bears witness to the success with which large bodies of human beings may be trained to feel the public interest their own. And no soil could be more favourable to the growth of such a feeling, than a Communist association, since all the ambition, and the bodily and mental activity, which are now exerted in the pursuit of separate and self-regarding interests, would require another sphere of employment, and would naturally find it in the pursuit of the general benefit of the community. The same cause, so often assigned in explanation of the devotion of the Catholic priest or monk to the interest of his order —that he has no interest apart from it—would, under Communism, attach the citizen to the community. And independently of the public motive, every member of the association would be amenable to the most universal, and one of the strongest, of personal motives, that of public opinion. The force of this motive in deterring from any act or omission positively reproved by the community, no one is likely to deny; but the power also of emulation, in exciting to the most strenuous exertions for the sake of the approbation and admiration of others, is borne witness to by experience in every situation in which human beings publicly compete with one another, even if it be in things frivolous, or from which the public derive no benefit. A contest, who can do most for the common good, is not the kind of competition which Socialists repudiate. To what extent, therefore, the energy of labour would be diminished by Communism, or whether in the long run it would be diminished at all, must be considered for the present an undecided question.

Another of the objections to Communism is similar to that, so often urged against poor-laws: that if every member of the community were assured of subsistence for himself and any number of children, on the sole condition of willingness to work, prudential restraint on the multiplication of mankind would be at an end, and population would start forward at a rate which would reduce the community through successive stages of increasing discomfort to actual starvation. There would certainly be much ground for this apprehension if Communism provided no motives of restraint, equivalent to those which it would take away. But Communism is precisely the state of things in which opinion might be expected to declare itself with greatest intensity against this kind of selfish intemperance. An augmentation of numbers which diminished the comfort or increased the toil of the mass, would then cause (which now it does not) immediate and unmistakable inconvenience to every individual in the association; inconvenience which could not then be imputed to the avarice of employers, or the unjust privileges of the rich. In such altered circumstances opinion could not fail to reprobate, and if reprobation did not suffice, to repress by penalties of some description, this or any other culpable self-indulgence at the expense of the community. The Communistic scheme, instead of being peculiarly open to the objection drawn from danger of overpopulation, has the recommendation of tending in an especial degree to the prevention of that evil.

A more real difficulty is that of fairly apportioning the labour of the community among its members. There are many kinds of work, and by what standard are they to be measured one against another? Who is to judge how much cotton spinning, or distributing goods from the stores, or bricklaying, or chimney sweeping, is equivalent to so much ploughing? The difficulty of making the adjustment between different qualities of labour is so strongly felt by Communist writers, that they have usually thought it necessary to provide that all should work by turns at every description of useful labour: an arrangement which by putting an end to the division of employments, would sacrifice so much of the advantage of co-operative production as greatly to diminish the productiveness of labour. Besides, even in the same kind of work, nominal equality of labour would be so great a real inequality, that the feeling of justice would revolt against its being enforced. All persons are not equally fit for all labour; and the same quantity of labour is an unequal burthen on the weak and the strong, the hardy and the delicate, the quick and the slow, the dull and the intelligent.

But these difficulties, though real, are not necessarily insuperable. The apportionment of work to the strength and capacities of individuals, the mitigation of a general rule to provide for cases in which it would operate harshly, are not problems to which human intelligence, guided by a sense of justice, would be inadequate. And the worst and most unjust arrangement which could be made of these points, under a system aiming at equality, would be so far short of the inequality and injustice with which labour (not to speak of remuneration) is now apportioned, as to be scarcely worth counting in the comparison. We must remember too that Communism, as a system of society, exists only in idea; that its difficulties, at present, are much better understood than its resources; and that the intellect of mankind is only beginning to contrive the means of organizing it in detail, so as to overcome the one and derive the greatest advantage from the other.

If, therefore, the choice were to be made between Communism with all its chances, and the present state of society with all its sufferings and injustices; if the institution of private property necessarily carried with it as a consequence, that the produce of labour should be apportioned as we now see it, almost in an inverse ratio to the labour—the largest portions to those who have never worked at all, the next largest to those whose work is almost nominal, and so in a descending scale, the remuneration dwindles as the work grows harder and more disagreeable, until the most fatiguing and exhausting bodily labour cannot count with certainty on being able to earn even the necessaries of life; if this, or Communism, were the alternative, all the difficulties, great or small, of Communism, would be but as dust in the balance.

II. OF WAGES

UNDER the head of Wages are to be considered, first, the causes which determine or influence the wages of labour generally, and secondly, the differences that exist between the wages of different employments. It is convenient to keep these two classes of considerations separate; and in discussing the law of wages, to proceed in the first instance as if there were no other kind of labour than common unskilled labour, of the average degree of hardness and disagreeableness.

Wages, like other things, may be regulated either by competition or by custom. In this country there are few kinds of labour of which the remuneration would not be lower than it is, if the employer took the full advantage of competition. Competition, however, must be regarded, in the present state of society, as the principal regulator of wages, and custom or individual character only as a modifying circumstance, and that in a comparatively slight degree.

Wages, then, depend mainly upon the demand and supply of labour; or, as it is often expressed, on the proportion between population and capital. By population is here meant the number only of the labouring class, or rather of those who work for hire; and by capital, only circulating capital, and not even the whole of that, but the part which is expended in the direct purchase of labour. To this, however, must be added all funds which, without forming a part of capital, are paid in exchange for labour, such as the wages of soldiers, domestic servants, and all other unproductive labourers. There is unfortunately no mode of expressing by one familiar term, the aggregate of what may be called the wages fund of a country: and as the wages of productive labour form nearly the whole of that fund, it is usual to overlook the smaller and less important part, and to say that wages depend on population and capital. It will be convenient to employ this expression, remembering, however, to consider it as elliptical, and not as a literal statement of the entire truth.

With these limitations of the terms, wages not only depend upon the relative amount of capital and population, but cannot, under the rule of competition, be affected by anything else. Wages (meaning, of course, the general rate) cannot rise, but by an increase of the aggregate funds employed in hiring labourers, or a diminution in the number of the competitors for hire; nor fall, except either by a diminution of the funds devoted to paying labour, or by an increase in the number of labourers to be paid.

There are, however, some facts in apparent contradiction to this doctrine, which it is incumbent on us to consider and explain.

For instance, it is a common saying that wages are high when trade is good. The demand for labour in any particular employment is more pressing, and higher wages are paid, when there is a brisk demand for the commodity produced; and the contrary when there is what is called a stagnation: then workpeople are dismissed, and those who are retained must submit to a reduction of wages: though in these cases there is neither more nor less capital than before. This is true; and is one of those complications in the concrete phenomena, which obscure and disguise the operation of general causes; but it is not really inconsistent with the principles laid down. Capital which the owner does not employ in purchasing labour, but keeps idle in his hands, is the same thing to the labourers, for the time being, as if it did not exist. All capital is, from the variations of trade, occasionally in this state. A manufacturer, finding a slack demand for his commodity, forbears to employ labourers in increasing a stock which he finds it difficult to dispose of; or if he goes on until all his capital is locked up in unsold goods, then at least he must of necessity pause until he can get paid for some of them. But no one expects either of these states to be permanent; if he did, he would at the first opportunity remove his capital to some other occupation, in which it would still continue to employ labour. The capital remains unemployed for a time, during which the labour market is overstocked, and wages fall. Afterwards the demand revives, and perhaps becomes unusually brisk, enabling the manufacturer to sell his commodity even faster than he can produce it: his whole capital is then brought into complete efficiency, and if he is able, he borrows capital in addition, which would otherwise have gone into some other employment. At such times wages, in his particular occupation, rise. If we suppose, what in strictness is not absolutely impossible, that one of these fits of briskness or of stagnation should affect all occupations at the same time, wages altogether might undergo a rise or a fall. These, however, are but temporary fluctuations: the capital now lying idle will next year be in active employment, that which is this year unable to keep up with the demand will in its turn be locked up in crowded warehouses; and wages in these several departments will ebb and flow accordingly: but nothing can permanently alter general wages, except an increase or a diminution of capital itself (always meaning by the term, the funds of all sorts, destined for the payment of labour) compared with the quantity of labour offering itself to be hired.

Again, it is another common notion that high prices make high wages; because the producers and dealers, being better off, can afford to pay more to their labourers. I have already said that a brisk demand, which causes temporary high prices, causes also temporary high wages. But high prices, in themselves, can only raise wages if the dealers, receiving more, are induced to save more, and make an addition to their capital, or at least to their purchases of labour. This is indeed likely enough to be the case; and if the high prices came direct from heaven, or even from abroad, the labouring class might be benefited, not by the high prices themselves, but by the increase of capital occasioned by them. The same effect, however, is often attributed to a high price which is the result of restrictive laws, or which is in some way or other to be paid by the remaining members of the community; they having no greater means than before to pay it with. High prices of this sort, if they benefit one class of labourers, can only do so at the expense of others; since if the dealers by receiving high prices are enabled to make greater savings, or otherwise increase their purchases of labour, all other people by paying those high prices have their means of saving, or of purchasing labour, reduced in an equal degree; and it is a matter of accident whether the one alteration or the other will have the greatest effect on the labour market. Wages will probably be temporarily higher in the employment in which prices have risen, and somewhat lower in other employments: in which case, while the first half of the phenomenon excites notice, the other is generally overlooked, or if observed, is not ascribed to the cause which really produced it. Nor will the partial rise of wages last long: for though the dealers in that one employment gain more, it does not follow that there is room to employ a greater amount of savings in their own business: their increasing capital will probably flow over into other employments, and there counterbalance the diminution previously made in the demand for labour by the diminished savings of other classes.

Another opinion often maintained is, that wages (meaning of course money wages) vary with the price of food; rising when it rises, and falling when it falls. This opinion is, I conceive, only partially true; and in so far as true, in no way affects the dependence of wages on the proportion between capital and labour: since the price of food, when it affects wages at all, affects them through that law. Dear or cheap food caused by variety of seasons does not affect wages (unless they are artificially adjusted to it by law or charity): or rather, it has some tendency to affect them in the contrary way to that supposed; since in times of scarcity people generally compete more violently for employment, and lower the labour market against themselves. But dearness or cheapness of food, when of a permanent character, and capable of being calculated on beforehand, may affect wages. In the first place, if the labourers have, as is often the case, no more than enough to keep them in working condition and enable them barely to support the ordinary number of children, it follows that if food grows permanently dearer without a rise of wages, a greater number of the children will prematurely die; and thus wages will ultimately be higher, but only because the number of people will be smaller, than if food had remained cheap. But, secondly, even though wages were high enough to admit of food's becoming more costly without depriving the labourers and their families of necessaries; though they could bear, physically speaking, to be worse off, perhaps they would not consent to be so. They might have habits of comfort which were to them as necessaries, and sooner than forego which, they would put an additional restraint on their power of multiplication; so that wages would rise, not by increase of deaths but by diminution of births. In these cases, then, wages do adapt themselves to the price of food, though after an interval of almost a generation. Mr. Ricardo considers these two cases to comprehend all cases. He assumes, that there is everywhere a minimum rate of wages: either the lowest with which it is physically possible to keep up the population, or the lowest with which the people will choose to do so. To this minimum he assumes that the general rate of wages always tends; that they can never be lower, beyond the length of time required for a diminished rate of increase to make itself felt, and can never long continue higher. This assumption contains sufficient truth to render it admissible for the purposes of abstract science; and the conclusion which Mr. Ricardo draws from it, namely, that wages in the long run rise and fall with the permanent price of food, is, like almost all his conclusions, true hypothetically, that is, granting the suppositions from which he sets out. But in the application to practice, it is necessary to consider that the minimum of which he speaks, especially when it is not a physical, but what may be termed a moral minimum, is itself liable to vary. If wages were previously so high that they could bear reduction, to which the obstacle was a high standard of comfort habitual among the labourers, a rise of the price of food, or any other disadvantageous change in their circumstances, may operate in two ways: it may correct itself by a rise of wages, brought about through a gradual effect on the prudential check to population; or it may permanently lower the standard of living of the class, in case their previous habits in respect of population prove stronger than their previous habits in respect of comfort. In that case the injury done to them will be permanent, and their deteriorated condition will become a new minimum, tending to perpetuate itself as the more ample minimum did before. It is to be feared that of the two modes in which the cause may operate, the last is the most frequent, or at all events sufficiently so, to render all propositions ascribing a self-repairing quality to the calamities which befall the labouring classes, practically of no validity. There is considerable evidence that the circumstances of the agricultural labourers in England have more than once in our history sustained great permanent deterioration, from causes which operated by diminishing the demand for labour, and which, if population had exercised its power of self-adjustment in obedience to the previous standard of comfort, could only have had a temporary effect: but unhappily the poverty in which the class was plunged during a long series of years brought that previous standard into disuse; and the next generation, growing up without having possessed those pristine comforts, multiplied in turn without any attempt to retrieve them.

The converse case occurs when, by improvements in agriculture, the repeal of corn laws, or other such causes, the necessaries of the labourers are cheapened, and they are enabled with the same wages, to command greater comforts than before. Wages will not fall immediately; it is even possible that they may rise; but they will fall at last, so as to leave the labourers no better off than before, unless during this interval of prosperity the standard of comfort regarded as indispensable by the class, is permanently raised. Unfortunately this salutary effect is by no means to be counted upon: it is a much more difficult thing to raise, than to lower, the scale of living which the labourers will consider as more indispensable than marrying and having a family. If they content themselves with enjoying the greater comfort while it lasts, but do not learn to require it, they will people down to their old scale of living. If from poverty their children had previously been insufficiently fed or improperly nursed, a greater number will now be reared, and the competition of these, when they grow up, will depress wages, probably in full proportion to the greater cheapness of food. If the effect is not produced in this mode, it will be produced by earlier and more numerous marriages, or by an increased number of births to a marriage. According to all experience, a great increase invariably takes place in the number of marriages, in seasons of cheap food and full employment. I cannot, therefore, agree in the importance so often attached to the repeal of the corn laws, considered merely as a labourer's question, or to any of the schemes, of which some one or other is at all times in vogue, for making the labourers a very little better off. Things which only affect them a very little, make no permanent impression upon their habits and requirements, and they soon slide back into their former state. To produce permanent advantage, the temporary cause operating upon them must be sufficient to make a great change in their condition—a change such as will be felt for many years, notwithstanding any stimulus which it may give during one generation to the increase of people. When, indeed, the improvement is of this signal character, and a generation grows up which has always been used to an improved scale of comfort, the habits of this new generation in respect to population become formed upon a higher minimum, and the improvement in their condition becomes permanent.

Wages depend, then, on the proportion between the number of the labouring population, and the capital or other funds devoted to the purchase of labour; we will say, for shortness, the capital. If wages are higher at one time or place than at another, if the subsistence and comfort of the class of hired labourers are more ample, it is for no other reason than because capital bears a greater proportion to population. It is not the absolute amount of accumulation or of production, that is of importance to the labouring class; it is not the amount even of the funds destined for distribution among the labourers: it is the proportion between those funds and the numbers among whom they are shared. The condition of the class can be bettered in no other way than by altering that proportion to their advantage: and every scheme for their benefit, which does not proceed on this as its foundation, is, for all permanent purposes, a delusion.

In countries like North America and the Australian colonies, where the knowledge and arts of civilized life, and a high effective desire of accumulation, co-exist with a boundless extent of unoccupied land, the growth of capital easily keeps pace with the utmost possible increase of population, and is chiefly retarded by the impracticability of obtaining labourers enough. All, therefore, who can possibly be born, can find employment without overstocking the market: every labouring family enjoys in abundance the necessaries, many of the comforts, and some of the luxuries of life; and, unless in case of individual misconduct, or actual inability to work, poverty does not, and dependence needs not, exist. A similar advantage, though in a less degree, is occasionally enjoyed by some special class of labourers in old countries, from an extraordinary rapid growth, not of capital generally, but of the capital employed in a particular occupation. So gigantic has been the progress of the cotton manufacture since the inventions of Watt and Arkwright, that the capital engaged in it has probably quadrupled in the time which population requires for doubling. While, therefore, it has attracted from other employments nearly all the hands which geographical circumstances and the habits or inclinations of the people rendered available; and while the demand it created for infant labour has enlisted the immediate pecuniary interest of the operatives in favour of promoting, instead of restraining, the increase of population; nevertheless wages in the great seats of the manufacture are still so high, that the collective earnings of a family amount, on an average of years, to a very satisfactory sum; and there is, as yet, no sign of decrease, while the effect has also been felt in raising the general standard of agricultural wages in the counties adjoining.

But those circumstances of a country, or of an occupation, in which population can with impunity increase at its utmost rate, are rare, and transitory. Very few are the countries presenting the needful union of conditions. Either the industrial arts are backward and stationary, and capital therefore increases slowly; or the effective desire of accumulation being low, the increase soon reaches its limit; or, even though both these elements are at their highest known degree, the increase of capital is checked, because there is not fresh land to be resorted to, of as good quality as that already occupied. Though capital should for a time double itself simultaneously with population, if all this capital and population are to find employment on the same land, they cannot without an unexampled succession of agricultural inventions continue doubling the produce; therefore, if wages do not fall, profits must; and when profits fall, increase of capital is slackened. Besides, even if wages did not fall, the price of food (as will be shown more fully hereafter) would in these circumstances necessarily rise; which is equivalent to a fall of wages.

Except, therefore, in the very peculiar cases which I have just noticed, of which the only one of any practical importance is that of a new colony, or a country in circumstances equivalent to it; it is impossible that population should increase at its utmost rate without lowering wages. Nor will the fall be stopped at any point, short of that which either by its physical or its moral operation, checks the increase of population. In no old country, therefore, does population increase at anything like its utmost rate; in most, at a very moderate rate: in some countries, not at all. These facts are only to be accounted for in two ways. Either the whole number of births which nature admits of, and which happen in some circumstances, do not take place; or if they do, a large proportion of those who are born, die. The retardation of increase results either from mortality or prudence; from Mr. Malthus's positive, or from his preventive check: and one or the other of these must and does exist, and very powerfully too, in all old societies. Wherever population is not kept down by the prudence either of individuals or of the state, it is kept down by starvation or disease.

Mr. Malthus has taken great pains to ascertain, for almost every country in the world, which of these checks it is that operates; and the evidence which he collected on the subject, in his *Essay on Population,* may even now be read with advantage. Throughout Asia, and formerly in most European countries in which the labouring classes were not in personal bondage, there is, or was, no restrainer of population but death. The mortality was not always the result of poverty: much of it proceeded from unskilful and careless management of children, from uncleanly and otherwise unhealthy habits of life among the adult population, and from the almost periodical occurrence of destructive epidemics. Throughout Europe these causes of shortened life have much diminished, but they have not ceased to exist. Until a period not very remote, hardly any of our large towns kept up its population, independently of the stream always flowing into them from the rural districts: this was still true of Liverpool until very recently; and even in London, the mortality is larger, and the average duration of life shorter, than in rural districts where there is much greater poverty. In Ireland, epidemic fevers, and deaths from the exhaustion of the constitution by insufficient nutriment, have always accompanied even the most moderate deficiency of the potato crop. Nevertheless, it cannot now be said that in any part of Europe, population is principally kept down by disease, still less by starvation, either in a direct or in an indirect form. The agency by which it is limited is chiefly preventive, not (in the language of Mr. Malthus) positive. But the preventive remedy seldom, I believe, consists in the unaided operation of prudential motives on a class wholly or mainly composed of labourers for hire, and looking forward to no other lot. In England, for example, I much doubt if the generality of agricultural labourers practise any prudential restraint whatever. They generally marry as early, and have as many children to a marriage, as they would or could do if they were settlers in the United States. During the generation which preceded the enactment of the present Poor Law, they received the most direct encouragement to this sort of improvidence: being not only assured of support, on easy terms, whenever out of employment, but even when in employment, very commonly receiving from the parish a weekly allowance proportioned to their number of children; and the married with large families being always, from a shortsighted economy, employed in preference to the unmarried; which last premium on population still exists. Under such prompting, the rural labourers acquired habits of recklessness, which are so congenial to the uncultivated mind, that in whatever manner produced, they in general long survive their immediate causes. There are so many new elements at work in society, even in those deeper strata which are inaccessible to the mere movements on the surface, that it is hazardous to affirm anything positive on the mental state or practical impulses of classes and bodies of men, when the same assertion may be true today, and may require great modification in a few years' time. It does, however, seem, that if the rate of increase of population depended solely on the agricultural labourers, it would, as far as dependent on births, and unless repressed by deaths, be as rapid in the southern counties of England as in America. The restraining principle lies in the very great proportion of the population composed of the middle classes and the skilled artizans, who in this country almost equal in number the common labourers, and on whom prudential motives do, in a considerable degree, operate.

So long as mankind remained in a semibarbarous state, with the indolence and the few wants of the savage, it probably was not desirable that population should be restrained; the pressure of physical want may have been a necessary stimulus, in that stage of the human mind, to the exertion of labour and ingenuity required for accomplishing that greatest of all past changes in human modes of existence, by which industrial life attained predominance over the hunting, the pastoral, and the military or predatory state. Want, in that age of the world, had its uses, as even slavery had; and there may be corners of the earth where those uses are not yet superseded, though they might easily be so were a helping hand held out by more civilized communities. But in Europe the time, if it ever existed, is long past, when a life of privation had the smallest tendency to make men either better workmen or more civilized beings. It is, on the contrary, evident, that if the agricultural labourers were better off, they would both work more efficiently and be better citizens. I ask, then, is it true, or not, that if their numbers were fewer they would obtain higher wages? This is the question, and no other: and it is idle to divert attention from it, by attacking any incidental position of Malthus or some other writer, and pretending that to refute that, is to disprove the principle of population. Some, for instance, have achieved an easy victory over a passing remark of Mr. Malthus, hazarded chiefly by way of illustration, that the increase of food may perhaps be assumed to take place in an arithmetical ratio, while population increases in a geometrical: when every candid reader knows that Mr. Malthus laid no stress on this unlucky attempt to give numerical precision to things which do not admit of it, and every person capable of reasoning must see that it is wholly superfluous to his argument. Others have attached immense importance to a correction which more recent political economists have made in the mere language of the earlier followers of Mr. Malthus. Several writers had said that it is the tendency of population to *increase faster* than the means of subsistence. The assertion was true in the sense in which they meant it, namely that population would in most circumstances increase faster than the means of subsistence, if it were not checked either by mortality or by prudence. But inasmuch as these checks act with unequal force at different times and places, it was possible to interpret the language of these writers as if they had meant that population is usually gaining ground upon subsistence, and the poverty of the people becoming greater. Under this interpretation of their meaning, it was urged that the reverse is the truth: that as civilization advances, the prudential check tends to become stronger, and population to slacken its rate of increase, relatively to subsistence; and that it is an error to maintain that population, in any improving community, tends to increase faster than, or even so fast as, subsistence. The word tendency is here used in a totally different sense from that of the writers who affirmed the proposition: but waiving the verbal question, is it not allowed on both sides, that in old countries, population presses too closely upon the means of subsistence? And though its pressure diminishes, the more the ideas and habits of the poorest class of labourers can be improved, to which it is to be hoped that there is always some tendency in a progressive country, yet since that tendency has hitherto been, and still is, extremely faint, and (to descend to particulars) has not yet extended to giving to the Wiltshire labourers higher wages than eight shillings a week, the only thing which it is necessary to consider is, whether that is a sufficient and suitable provision for a labourer? For if not, population does, as an existing fact, bear too great a proportion to the wages fund; and whether it pressed still harder or not quite so hard at some former period, is practically of no moment, except that, if the ratio is an improving one, there is the better hope that by proper aids and encouragements it may be made to improve more and faster.

III. OF PROFITS

Having treated of the labourer's share of the produce, we next proceed to the share of the capitalist; the profits of capital or stock; the gains of the person who advances the expenses of production—who, from funds in his possession, pays the wages of the labourers, or supports them during the work; who supplies the requisite buildings, materials, and tools or machinery; and to whom, by the usual terms of the contract, the produce belongs, to be disposed of at his pleasure. After indemnifying him for his outlay, there commonly remains a surplus, which is his profit; the net income from his capital: the amount which he can afford to expend in necessaries or pleasures, or from which by further saving he can add to his wealth.

A large portion of the expenditure of every capitalist consists in the direct payment of wages. What does not consist of this, is composed of materials and implements, including buildings. But materials and implements are produced by labour; and as our supposed capitalist is not meant to represent a single employment, but to be a type of the productive industry of the whole country, we may suppose that he makes his own tools, and raises his own materials. He does this by means of previous advances, which, again, consist wholly of wages. If we suppose him to buy the materials and tools instead of producing them, the case is not altered: he then repays to a previous producer the wages which that previous producer has paid. It is true, he repays it to him with a profit; and if he had produced the things himself, he himself must have had that profit, on this part of his outlay, as well as on every other part. The fact, however, remains, that in the whole process of production, beginning with the materials and tools, and ending with the finished product, all the advances have consisted of nothing but wages; except that certain of the capitalists concerned have, for the sake of general convenience, had their share of profit paid to them before the operation was completed. Whatever, of the ultimate product, is not profit, is repayment of wages.

It thus appears that the two elements on which, and which alone, the gains of the capitalists depend, are, first, the magnitude of the produce, in other words, the productive power of labour; and secondly, the proportion of that produce obtained by the labourers themselves; the ratio, which the remuneration of the labourers bears to the amount they produce. These two things form the data for determining the gross amount divided as profit among all the capitalists of the country; but the *rate* of profit, the percentage on the capital, depends only on the second of the two elements, the labourer's proportional share, and not on the amount to be shared. If the produce of labour were doubled, and the labourers obtained the same proportional share as before, that is, if their remuneration was also doubled, the capitalists, it is true, would gain twice as much; but as they would also have had to advance twice as much, the rate of their profit would be only the same as before.

We thus arrive at the conclusion of Ricardo and others, that the rate of profits depends upon wages; rising as wages fall, and falling as wages rise. In adopting, however, this doctrine, I must insist upon making a most necessary alteration in its wording. Instead of saying that profits depend on wages, let us say (what Ricardo really meant) that they depend on the *cost of labour*.

Wages, and the cost of labour; what labour brings in to the labourer, and what it costs to the capitalist; are ideas quite distinct, and which it is of the utmost importance to keep so. For this purpose it is essential not to designate them, as is almost always done, by the same name. Wages, in public discussions, both oral and printed, being looked upon from the same point of view of the payers, much oftener than from that of the receivers, nothing is more common than to say that wages are high or low, meaning only that the cost of labour is high or low. The reverse of this would be oftener the truth: the cost of labour is frequently at its highest where wages are lowest. This may arise from two causes. In the first place, the labour, though cheap, may be inefficient. In no European country are wages so low as they are (or at least were) in Ireland; the remuneration of an agricultural labourer in the west of Ireland not being more than half the wages of even the lowest-paid Englishman, the Dorsetshire labourer. But if, from inferior skill and industry, two days' labour of an Irishman accomplished no more work than an English labourer performed in one, the Irishman's labour cost as much as the Englishman's, though it brought in so much less to himself. The capitalist's profit is determined by the former of these two things, not by the latter. That a difference to this extent really existed in the efficiency of the labour, is proved not only by abundant testimony, but by the fact, that notwithstanding the lowness of wages, profits of capital have never been higher in Ireland than in England.

The other cause which renders wages, and the cost of labour, no real criteria of one another, is the varying costliness of the articles which the labourer consumes. If these are cheap, wages, in the sense which is of importance to the labourer, may be high, and yet the cost of labour may be low; if dear, the labourer may be wretchedly off, though his labour may cost much to the capitalist. This last is the condition of a country overpeopled in relation to its land; in which, food being dear, the poorness of the labourer's real reward does not prevent labour from costing much to the purchaser, and low wages and low profits co-exist. The opposite case is exemplified in the United States of America. The labourer there enjoys a greater abundance of comforts than in any other country of the world, except some of the newest colonies; but, owing to the cheap price at which these comforts can be obtained (combined with the great efficiency of the labour), the cost of labour to the capitalist is considerably lower than in Europe. It must be so, since the rate of profit is higher; as indicated by the rate of interest, which is six per cent at New York when it is three, or three and a quarter per cent in London.

The cost of labour, then, is, in the language of mathematics, a function of three variables: the efficiency of labour; the wages of labour (meaning thereby the real reward of the labourer); and the greater or less cost at which the articles composing that real reward can be produced or purchased. It is plain that the cost of labour to the capitalist must be influenced by each of these three circumstances, and by no others. These, therefore, are also the circumstances which determine the rate of profit; and it cannot be in any way affected except through one or other of them. If labour generally became more efficient, without being more highly rewarded; if, without its becoming less efficient, its remuneration fell, no increase taking place in the cost of the articles composing that remuneration; or if those articles became less costly, without the labourer's obtaining more of them; in any one of these three cases, profits would rise. If, on the contrary, labour became less efficient (as it might do from diminished bodily vigour in the people, destruction of fixed capital, or deteriorated education); or if the labourer obtained a higher remuneration, without any increased cheapness in the things composing it; or if, without his obtaining more, that which he did obtain became more costly; profits, in all these cases, would suffer a diminution. And there is no other combination of circumstances, in which the general rate of profit of a country, in all employments indifferently, can either fall or rise.

IV. OF RENT

THE REQUISITES of production being labour, capital, and natural agents; the only person, besides the labourer and the capitalist, whose consent is necessary to production, and who can claim a share of the produce as the price of that consent, is the person who, by the arrangements of society, possesses exclusive power over some natural agent. The land is the principal of the natural agents which are capable of being appropriated, and the consideration paid for its use is called rent. Landed proprietors are the only class, of any numbers or importance, who have a claim to a share in the distribution of the produce, through their ownership of something which neither they nor any one else have produced. If there be any other cases of a similar nature, they will be easily understood, when the nature and laws of rent are comprehended.

It is at once evident, that rent is the effect of a monopoly; though the monopoly is a natural one, which may be regulated, which may even be held as a trust for the community generally, but which cannot be prevented from existing. The reason why landowners are able to require rent for their land, is that it is a commodity which many want, and which no one can obtain but from them. If all the land of the country belonged to one person, he could fix the rent at his pleasure. The whole people would be dependent on his will for the necessaries of life, and he might make what conditions he chose. This is the actual state of things in those Oriental kingdoms in which the land is considered the property of the state. Rent is then confounded with taxation, and the despot may exact the utmost which the unfortunate cultivators have to give. Indeed, the exclusive possessor of the land of a country could not well be other than despot of it. The effect would be much the same if the land belonged to so few people that they could, and did, act together as one man, and fix the rent by agreement among themselves. This case, however, is nowhere known to exist; and the only remaining supposition is that of free competition; the landowners being supposed to be, as in fact they are, too numerous to combine.

A thing which is limited in quantity, even though its possessors do not act in concert, is still a monopolized article. But even when monopolized, a thing which is the gift of nature, and requires no labour or outlay as the condition of its existence, will, if there be competition among the holders of it, command a price, only if it exists in less quantity than the demand. If the whole land of a country were required for cultivation, all of it might yield a rent. But in no country of any extent do the wants of the population require that all the land, which is capable of cultivation, should be cultivated. The food and other agricultural produce which the people need, and which they are willing and able to pay for at a price which remunerates the grower, may always be obtained without cultivating all the land; sometimes without cultivating more than a small part of it; the more fertile lands, or those in the more convenient situations, being of course preferred. There is always, therefore, some land which cannot, in existing circumstances, pay any rent; and no land ever pays rent, unless, in point of fertility or situation, it belongs to those superior kinds which exist in less quantity than the demand—which cannot be made to yield all the produce required for the community, unless on terms still less advantageous than the resort to less favoured soils.

There is land, such as the deserts of Arabia, which will yield nothing to any amount of labour; and there is land, like some of our hard sandy heaths, which would produce something, but, in the present state of the soil, not enough to defray the expenses of production. Such lands, unless by some application of chemistry to agriculture still remaining to be invented, cannot be cultivated for profit, unless some one actually creates a soil, by spreading new ingredients over the surface, or mixing them with the existing materials. If ingredients fitted for this purpose exist in the subsoil, or close at hand, the improvement even of the most unpromising spots may answer as a speculation: but if those ingredients are costly, and must be brought from a distance, it will seldom answer to do this for the sake of profit, though the "magic of property" will sometimes effect it. Land which cannot possibly yield a profit, is sometimes cultivated at a loss, the cultivators having their wants partially supplied from other sources; as in the case of paupers, and some monasteries or charitable institutions, among which may be reckoned the Poor Colonies of Belgium. The worst land which can be cultivated as a means of subsistence, is that which will just replace the seed, and the food of the labourers employed on it, together with what Dr. Chalmers calls their secondaries; that is, the labourers required for supplying them with tools, and with the remaining necessaries of life. Whether any given land is capable of doing more than this, is not a question of political economy, but of physical fact. The supposition leaves nothing for profits, nor anything for the labourers except necessaries: the land, therefore, can only be cultivated by the labourers themselves, or else at a pecuniary loss: and *à fortiori,* cannot in any contingency afford a rent. The worst land which can be cultivated as an investment for capital, is that which, after replacing the seed, not only feeds the agricultural labourers and their secondaries, but affords them the current rate of wages, which may extend to much more than mere necessaries; and leaves for those who have advanced the wages of these two classes of labourers, a surplus equal to the profit they could have expected from any other employment of their capital. Whether any given land can do more than this, is not merely a physical question, but depends partly on the market value of agricultural produce. What the land can do for the labourers and for the capitalist, beyond feeding all whom it directly or indirectly employs, of course depends upon what the remainder of the produce can be sold for. The higher the market value of produce, the lower are the soils to which cultivation can descend, consistently with affording to the capital employed, the ordinary rate of profit.

As, however, differences of fertility slide into one another by insensible gradations; and differences of accessibility, that is, of distance from markets do the same; and since there is land so barren that it could not pay for its cultivation at any price; it is evident that, whatever the price may be, there must in any extensive region be some land which at that price will just pay the wages of the cultivators, and yield to the capital employed the ordinary profit, and no more. Until, therefore, the price rises higher, or until some improvement raises that particular land to a higher place in the scale of fertility, it cannot pay any rent. It is evident, however, that the community needs the produce of this quality of land; since if the lands more fertile or better situated than it, could have sufficed to supply the wants of society, the price would not have risen so high as to render its cultivation profitable. This land, therefore, will be cultivated; and we may lay it down as a principle, that so long as any of the land of a country which is fit for cultivation, and not withheld from it by legal or other factitious obstacles, is not cultivated, the worst land in actual cultivation (in point of fertility and situation together) pays no rent.

If, then, of the land in cultivation, the part which yields least return to the labour and capital employed on it gives only the ordinary profit of capital, without leaving anything for rent; a standard is afforded for estimating the amount of rent which will be yielded by all other land. Any land yields just as much more than the ordinary profits of stock, as it yields more than what is returned by the worst land in cultivation. The surplus is what the farmer can afford to pay as rent to the landlord; and since, if he did not so pay it, he would receive more than the ordinary rate of profit, the competition of other capitalists, that competition which equalizes the profits of different capitals, will enable the landlord to appropriate it. The rent, therefore, which any land will yield, is the excess of its produce, beyond what would be returned to the same capital if employed on the worst land in cultivation. This is not, and never was pretended to be, the limit of metayer rents, or of cottier rents; but it is the limit of farmers' rents. No land rented to a capitalist farmer will permanently yield more than this; and when it yields less, it is because the landlord foregoes a part of what, if he chose, he could obtain.

This is the theory of rent, first propounded at the end of the last century by Dr. [James] Anderson, and which, neglected at the time, was almost simultaneously rediscovered, twenty years later, by Sir Edward West, Mr. Malthus, and Mr. Ricardo. It is one of the cardinal doctrines of political economy; and until it was understood, no consistent explanation could be given of many of the more complicated industrial phenomena. The evidence of its truth will be manifested with a great increase of clearness, when we come to trace the laws of the phenomena of Value and Price. Until that is done, it is not possible to free the doctrine from every difficulty which may present itself, nor perhaps to convey, to those previously unacquainted with the subject, more than a general apprehension of the reasoning by which the theorem is arrived at. Some, however, of the objections commonly made to it, admit of a complete answer even in the present stage of our inquiries.

It has been denied that there can be any land in cultivation which pays no rent; because landlords (it is contended) would not allow their land to be occupied without payment. Those who lay any stress on this as an objection, must think that land of the quality which can but just pay for its cultivation, lies together in large masses, detached from any land of better quality. If an estate consisted wholly of this land, or of this and still worse, it is likely enough that the owner would not give the use of it for nothing; he would probably (if a rich man) prefer keeping it for other purposes, as for exercise, or ornament, or perhaps as a game preserve. No farmer could afford to offer him anything for it, for purposes of culture; though something would probably be obtained for the use of its natural pasture, or other spontaneous produce. Even such land, however, would not necessarily remain uncultivated. It might be farmed by the proprietor; no unfrequent case even in England. Portions of it might be granted as temporary allotments to labouring families, either from philanthropic motives, or to save the poor rate; or occupation might be allowed to squatters, free of rent, in the hope that their labour might give it value at some future period. Both these cases are of quite ordinary occurrence. So that even if an estate were wholly composed of the worst land capable of profitable cultivation, it would not necessarily lie uncultivated because it could pay no rent. Inferior land, however, does not usually occupy, without interruption, many square miles of ground; it is dispersed here and there, with patches of better land intermixed, and the same person who rents the better land, obtains along with it the inferior soils which alternate with it. He pays a rent, nominally for the whole farm, but calculated on the produce of those parts alone (however small a portion of the whole) which are capable of returning more than the common rate of profit. It is thus scientifically true, that the remaining parts pay no rent.

Let us, however, suppose that there were a validity in this objection, which can by no means be conceded to it; that when the demand of the community had forced up food to such a price as would remunerate the expense of producing it from a certain quality of soil, it happened nevertheless that all the soil of that quality was withheld from cultivation, by the obstinacy of the owners in demanding rent for it, not nominal, nor trifling, but sufficiently onerous to be a material item in the calculations of a farmer. What would then happen? Merely that the increase of produce, which the wants of society required, would for the time be obtained wholly (as it always is partially), not by an extension of cultivation, but by an increased application of labour and capital to land already cultivated.

Now we have already seen that this increased application of capital, other things being unaltered, is always attended with a smaller proportional return. We are not to suppose some new agricultural invention made precisely at this juncture; nor a sudden extension of agricultural skill and knowledge, bringing into more general practice, just then, inventions already partially in use. We are to suppose no change, except a demand for more corn, and a consequent rise of its price. The rise of price enables measures to be taken for increasing the produce, which could not have been taken with profit at the previous price. The farmer uses more expensive manures, or manures land which he formerly left to nature; or procures lime or marl from a distance, as a dressing for the soil; or pulverizes or weeds it more thoroughly; or drains, irrigates, or subsoils portions of it, which at former prices would not have paid the cost of the operation; and so forth. These things, or some of them, are done, when, more food being wanted, cultivation has no means of expanding itself upon new lands. And when the impulse is given to extract an increased amount of produce from the soil, the farmer or improver will only consider whether the outlay he makes for the purpose will be returned to him with the ordinary profit, and not whether any surplus will remain for rent. Even, therefore, if it were the fact, that there is never any *land* taken into cultivation, for which rent, and that too of an amount worth taking into consideration, was not paid; it would be true, nevertheless, that there is always some *agricultural capital* which pays no rent, because it returns nothing beyond the ordinary rate of profit: this capital being the portion of capital last applied—that to which the last addition to the produce was due; or (to express the essentials of the case in one phrase), that which is applied in the least favourable circumstances. But the same amount of demand, and the same price, which enable this least productive portion of capital barely to replace itself with the ordinary profit, enable every other portion to yield a surplus proportioned to the advantage it possesses. And this surplus it is, which competition enables the landlord to appropriate. The rent of all land is measured by the excess of the return to the whole capital employed on it above what is necessary to replace the capital with the ordinary rate of profit, or in other words, above what the same capital would yield if it were all employed in as disadvantageous circumstances as the least productive portion of it: whether that least productive portion of capital is rendered so by being employed on the worst soil, or by being expended in extorting more produce from land which already yielded as much as it could be made to part with on easier terms.

It is not pretended that the facts of any concrete case conform with absolute precision to this or any other scientific principle. We must never forget that the truths of political economy are truths only in the rough.

Book Three: Exchange

I. OF VALUE

THE SUBJECT on which we are now about to enter fills so important and conspicuous a position in political economy, that in the apprehension of some thinkers its boundaries confound themselves with those of the science itself. One eminent writer has proposed as a name for Political Economy, "Catallactics," or the science of exchanges: by others it has been called the Science of Values. If these denominations had appeared to me logically correct, I must have placed the discussion of the elementary laws of value at the commencement of our enquiry, instead of postponing it to the Third Part; and the possibility of so long deferring it is alone a sufficient proof that this view of the nature of Political Economy is too confined. It is true that in the preceding Books we have not escaped the necessity of anticipating some small portion of the theory of Value, especially as to value of labour and of land. It is nevertheless evident, that of the two great departments of Political Economy, the production of wealth and its distribution, the consideration of Value has to do with the latter alone; and with that, only so far as competition, and not usage or custom, is the distributing agency. The conditions and laws of production would be the same as they are, if the arrangements of society did not depend on Exchange, or did not admit of it. Even in the present system of industrial life, in which employments are minutely subdivided, and all concerned in production depend for their remuneration on the price of a particular commodity, exchange is not the fundamental law of the distribution of the produce, no more than roads and carriages are the essential laws of motion, but merely a part of the machinery for effecting it. To confound these ideas, seems to me, not only a logical, but a practical blunder. It is a case of the error too common in political economy, of not distinguishing between necessities arising from the nature of things, and those created by social arrangements: an error, which appears to me to be at all times producing two opposite mischiefs; on the one hand, causing political economists to class the merely temporary truths of their subject among its permanent and universal laws; and on the other, leading many persons to mistake the permanent laws of production (such as those on which the necessity is grounded of restraining population) for temporary accidents arising from the existing constitution of society—which those who would frame a new system of social arrangements, are at liberty to disregard.

In a state of society, however, in which the industrial system is entirely founded on purchase and sale, each individual, for the most part, living not on things in the production of which he himself bears a part, but on things obtained by a double exchange, a sale followed by a purchase—the question of Value is fundamental. Almost every speculation respecting the economical interests of a society thus constituted, implies some theory of Value: the smallest error on that subject infects with corresponding error all our other conclusions; and anything vague or misty in our conception of it, creates confusion and uncertainty in everything else.

We must begin by settling our phraseology. Adam Smith, in a passage often quoted, has touched upon the most obvious ambiguity of the word value; which, in one of its senses, signifies usefulness, in another, power of purchasing; in his own language, value in use and value in exchange. But (as Mr. [Thomas] De Quincey has remarked) in illustrating this double meaning, Adam Smith has himself fallen into another ambiguity. Things (he says) which have the greatest value in use have often little or no value in exchange; which is true, since that which can be obtained without labour or sacrifice will command no price, however useful or needful it may be. But he proceeds to add, that things which have the greatest value in exchange, as a diamond for example, may have little or no value in use. This is employing the word use, not in the sense in which political economy is concerned with it, but in that other sense in which use is opposed to pleasure. Political economy has nothing to do with the comparative estimation of different uses in the judgment of a philosopher or of a moralist. The use of a thing, in political economy, means its capacity to satisfy a desire, or serve a purpose. Diamonds have this capacity in a high degree, and unless they had it, would not bear any price. Value in use, or as Mr. De Quincey calls it, *teleologic* value, is the extreme limit of value in exchange. The exchange value of a thing may fall short, to any amount, of its value in use; but that it can ever exceed the value in use, implies a contradiction; it supposes that persons will give, to possess a thing, more than the utmost value which they themselves put upon it, as a means of gratifying their inclinations.

The word Value, when used without adjunct, always means, in

political economy, value in exchange; or as it has been called by Adam Smith and his successors, exchangeable value, a phrase which no amount of authority that can be quoted for it can make other than bad English. Mr. De Quincey substitutes the term Exchange Value, which is unexceptionable.

Exchange value requires to be distinguished from Price. The words Value and Price were used as synonymous by the early political economists, and are not always discriminated even by Ricardo. But the most accurate modern writers, to avoid the wasteful expenditure of two good scientific terms on a single idea, have employed Price to express the value of a thing in relation to money; the quantity of money for which it will exchange. By the price of a thing, therefore, we shall henceforth understand its value in money; by the value, or exchange value of a thing, its general power of purchasing; the command which its possession gives over purchasable commodities in general.

But here a fresh demand for explanation presents itself. What is meant by command over commodities in general? The same thing exchanges for a greater quantity of some commodities, and for a very small quantity of others. A suit of clothes exchanges for a great quantity of bread, and for a very small quantity of precious stones. The value of a thing in exchange for some commodities may be rising, for others falling. A coat may exchange for less bread this year than last, if the harvest has been bad, but for more glass or iron, if a tax has been taken off those commodities, or an improvement made in their manufacture. Has the value of the coat, under these circumstances, fallen or risen? It is impossible to say: all that can be said is, that it has fallen in relation to one thing, and risen in respect to another. But there is another case, in which no one would have any hesitation in saying what sort of change had taken place in the value of the coat: namely, if the cause in which the disturbance of exchange values originated, was something directly affecting the coat itself, and not the bread, or the glass. Suppose, for example, that an invention had been made in machinery, by which broadcloth could be woven at half the former cost. The effect of this would be to lower the value of a coat, and if lowered by this cause, it would be lowered not in relation to bread only or to glass only, but to all purchasable things, except such as happened to be affected at the very time by a similar depressing cause. We should therefore say, that there had been a fall in the exchange value or general purchasing power of a coat. The idea of general exchange value originates in the fact, that there really are causes which tend to alter the value of a thing in exchange for things generally, that is, for all things which are not themselves acted upon by causes of similar tendency.

In considering exchange value scientifically, it is expedient to abstract from it all causes except those which originate in the very commodity under consideration. Those which originate in the commodities with which we compare it, affect its value in relation to those commodities; but those which originate in itself, affect its value in relation to all commodities. In order the more completely to confine our attention to these last, it is convenient to assume that all commodities but the one in question remain invariable in their relative values. When we are considering the causes which raise or lower the value of corn, we suppose that woollens, silks, cutlery, sugar, timber, &c., while varying in their power of purchasing corn, remain constant in the proportions in which they exchange for one another. On this assumption, any one of them may be taken as a representative of all the rest: since in whatever manner corn varies in value with respect to any one commodity, it varies in the same manner and degree with respect to every other; and the upward or downward movement of its value estimated in some one thing, is all that needs be considered. Its money value, therefore, or price, will represent as well as anything else its general exchange value, or purchasing power; and from an obvious convenience, will often be employed by us in that representative character; with the proviso that money itself do not vary in its general purchasing power, but that the prices of all things, other than that which we happen to be considering, remain unaltered.

The distinction between Value and Price, as we have now defined them, is so obvious, as scarcely to seem in need of any illustration. But in political economy the greatest errors arise from overlooking the most obvious truths. Simple as this distinction is, it has consequences with which a reader unacquainted with the subject would do well to begin early by making himself thoroughly familiar. The following is one of the principal. There is such a thing as a general rise of prices. All commodities may rise in their money price. But there cannot be a general rise of values. It is a contradiction in terms. A can only rise in value by exchanging for a greater quantity of B and C; in which case these must exchange for a smaller quantity of A. All things cannot rise relatively to one another. If one half of the commodities in the market rise in exchange value, the very terms imply a fall of the other half; and reciprocally, the fall implies a rise. Things which are exchanged for one another can no more all fall, or all rise, than a dozen runners can each outrun all the rest, or a hundred trees all overtop one another. Simple as this truth is, we shall presently see that it is lost sight of in some of the most accredited doctrines both of theorists and of what are called practical men. And as a first specimen, we may instance the great importance attached in the imagination of most people to a rise or fall of general prices. Because when the price of any one commodity rises, the circumstance usually indicates a rise of its value, people have an indistinct feeling when all prices rise, as if all things simultaneously had risen in value, and all the possessors had become enriched. That the money prices of all things should rise or fall, provided they all rise or fall equally, is in itself, and apart from existing contracts, of no consequence. It affects nobody's wages, profits, or rent. Every one gets more money in the one case and less in the other; but of all that is to be bought with money they get neither more nor less than before. It makes no other difference than that of using more or fewer counters to reckon by. The only thing which in this case is really altered in value is money; and the only persons who either gain or lose are the holders of money, or those who have to receive or to pay fixed sums of it. There is a difference to annuitants and to creditors the one way, and to those who are burthened with annuities, or with debts, the contrary way. There is a disturbance, in short, of fixed money contracts; and this is an evil, whether it takes place in the debtor's favour or in the creditor's. But as to future transactions there is no difference to anyone. Let it therefore be remembered (and occasions will often arise for calling it to mind) that a general rise or a general fall of values is a contradiction; and that a general rise or a general fall of prices is merely tantamount to an alteration in the value of money, and is a matter of complete indifference, save in so far as it affects existing contracts for receiving and paying fixed pecuniary amounts.

II. OF DEMAND AND SUPPLY IN THEIR RELATION TO VALUE

That a thing may have any value in exchange, two conditions are necessary. It must be of some use; that is (as already explained) it must conduce to some purpose, satisfy some desire. No one will pay a price, or part with anything which serves some of his purposes, to obtain a thing which serves none of them. But, secondly, the thing must not only have some utility, there must also be some difficulty in its attainment. "Any article whatever," says Mr. De Quincey [in his *Logic of Political Economy*], "to obtain that artificial sort of value which is meant by exchange value, must begin by offering itself as a means to some desirable purpose; and secondly, even though possessing incontestably this preliminary advantage, it will never ascend to an exchange value in cases where it can be obtained gratuitously and without effort; of which last terms both are necessary as limitations. For often it will happen that some desirable object may be obtained gratuitously; stoop, and you gather it at your feet; but still, because the continued iteration of this stooping exacts a laborious effort, very soon it is found, that to gather for yourself virtually is not gratuitous. In the vast forests of the Canadas, at intervals, wild strawberries may be gratuitously gathered by shiploads: yet such is the exhaustion of a stooping posture, and of a labour so monotonous, that everybody is soon glad to resign the service into mercenary hands."

As was pointed out in the last chapter, the utility of a thing in the estimation of the purchaser, is the extreme limit of its exchange value: higher the value cannot ascend; peculiar circumstances are required to raise it so high. This topic is happily illustrated by Mr. De Quincey. "Walk into almost any possible shop, buy the first article you see; what will determine its price? In the ninety-nine cases out of a hundred, simply the element D—difficulty of attainment. The other element, U, or intrinsic utility, will be perfectly inoperative. Let the thing (measured by its uses) be, for your purposes, worth ten guineas, so that you would rather give ten guineas than lose it; yet, if the difficulty of producing it be only worth one guinea, one guinea is the price which it will bear. But still not the less, though U is inoperative, can U be supposed absent? By no possibility; for, if it *had* been absent, assuredly you would not have bought the article even at the lowest price. U acts upon *you,* though it does not act upon the price. On the other hand, in the hundredth case, we will suppose the circumstances reversed: you are on Lake Superior in a steamboat, making your way to an unsettled region 800 miles ahead of civilization, and consciously with no chance at all of purchasing any luxury whatsoever, little luxury or big luxury, for the space of ten years to come. One fellow passenger, whom you will part with before sunset, has a powerful musical snuffbox; knowing by experience the power of such a toy over your own feelings, the magic with which at times it lulls your agitations of mind, you are vehemently desirous to purchase it. In the hour of leaving London you had forgot to do so; here is a final chance. But the owner, aware of your situation not less than yourself, is determined to operate by a strain pushed to the very uttermost upon U, upon the intrinsic worth of the article in your individual estimate for your individual purposes. He will not hear of D as any controlling power or mitigating agency in the case; and finally, although at six guineas apiece in London or Paris you might have loaded a waggon with such boxes, you pay sixty rather than lose it when the last knell of the clock has sounded, which summons you to buy now or to forfeit forever. Here, as before, only one element is operative: before it was D, now it is U. But after all, D was not absent, though inoperative. The inertness of D allowed U to put forth its total effect. The practical compression of D being withdrawn, U springs up like water in a pump when released from the pressure of air. Yet still that D was present to your thoughts, though the price was otherwise regulated, is evident; both because U and D must co-exist in order to found any case of exchange value whatever, and because undeniably you take into very particular consideration this D, the extreme difficulty of attainment (which here is the greatest possible, viz.

an impossibility) before you consent to have the price racked up to U. The special D has vanished; but it is replaced in your thoughts by an unlimited D. Undoubtedly you have submitted to U in extremity as the regulating force of the price; but it was under a sense of D's latent presence. Yet D is so far from exerting any positive force, that the retirement of D from all agency whatever on the price—this it is which creates as it were a perfect vacuum, and through that vacuum U rushes up to its highest and ultimate gradation."

This case, in which the value is wholly regulated by the necessities or desires of the purchaser, is the case of strict and absolute monopoly; in which, the article desired being only obtainable from one person, he can exact any equivalent, short of the point at which no purchaser could be found. But it is not a necessary consequence, even of complete monopoly, that the value should be forced up to this ultimate limit: as will be seen when we have considered the law of value in so far as depending on the other element, difficulty of attainment.

The difficulty of attainment which determines value, is not always the same kind of difficulty. It sometimes consists in an absolute limitation of the supply. There are things of which it is physically impossible to increase the quantity beyond certain narrow limits. Such are those wines which can be grown only in peculiar circumstances of soil, climate, and exposure. Such also are ancient sculptures; pictures by the old masters; rare books or coins, or other articles of antiquarian curiosity. Among such may also be reckoned houses and building ground, in a town of definite extent (such as Venice, or any fortified town where fortifications are necessary to security); the most desirable sites in any town whatever; houses and parks peculiarly favoured by natural beauty, in places where that advantage is uncommon. Potentially, all land whatever is a commodity of this class; and might be practically so, in countries fully occupied and cultivated.

But there is another category, (embracing the majority of all things that are bought and sold,) in which the obstacle to attainment consists only in the labour and expense requisite to produce the commodity. Without a certain labour and expense it cannot be had: but when anyone is willing to incur these, there needs be no limit to the multiplication of the product. If there were labourers enough and machinery enough, cottons, woollens, or linens might be produced by thousands of yards for every single yard now manufactured. There would be a point, no doubt, where further increase would be stopped by the incapacity of the earth to afford more of the material. But there is no need, for any purpose of political economy, to contemplate a time when this ideal limit could become a practical one.

There is a third case, intermediate between the two preceding, and rather more complex, which I shall at present merely indicate, but the importance of which in political economy is extremely great. There are commodities which can be multiplied to an indefinite extent by labour and expenditure, but not by a fixed amount of labour and expenditure. Only a limited quantity can be produced at a given cost; if more is wanted, it must be produced at a greater cost. To this class, as has been often repeated, agricultural produce belongs; and generally all the rude produce of the earth; and this peculiarity is a source of very important consequences; one of which is the necessity of a limit to population; and another, the payment of rent.

III. OF COST OF PRODUCTION IN ITS RELATION TO VALUE

When the production of a commodity is the effect of labour and expenditure, whether the commodity is susceptible of unlimited multiplication or not, there is a minimum value which is the essential condition of its being permanently produced. The value at any particular time is the result of supply and demand; and is always that which is necessary to create a market for the existing supply. But unless that value is sufficient to repay the Cost of Production, and to afford, besides, the ordinary expectation of profit, the commodity will not continue to be produced. Capitalists will not go on permanently producing at a loss. They will not even go on producing at a profit less than they can live upon. Persons whose capital is already embarked, and cannot be easily extricated, will persevere for a considerable time without profit, and have been known to persevere even at a loss, in hopes of better times. But they will not do so indefinitely, or when there is nothing to indicate that times are likely to improve. No new capital will be invested in an employment, unless there be an expectation not only of some profit, but of a profit as great (regard being had to the degree of eligibility of the employment in other respects) as can be hoped for in any other occupation at that time and place. When such profit is evidently not to be had, if people do not actually withdraw their capital, they at least abstain from replacing it when consumed. The cost of production, together with the ordinary profit, may therefore be called the *necessary* price, or value, of all things made by labour and capital. Nobody willingly produces in the prospect of loss. Whoever does so, does it under a miscalculation, which he corrects as fast as he is able.

When a commodity is not only made by labour and capital, but can be made by them in indefinite quantity, this Necessary Value, the minimum with which the producers will be content, is also, if competition is free and active, the maximum which they can expect. If the value of a commodity is such that it repays the cost of production not only with the customary but with a higher rate of profit, capital rushes to share in this extra gain, and by increasing the supply of the article, reduces its value. This is not a mere supposition or surmise, but a fact familiar to those conversant with commercial operations. Whenever a new line of business presents itself, offering a hope of unusual profits, and whenever any established trade or manufacture is believed to be yielding a greater profit than customary, there is sure to be in a short time so large a production or importation of the commodity, as not only destroys the extra profit, but generally goes beyond the mark, and sinks the value as much too low as it had before been raised too high; until the oversupply is corrected by a total or partial suspension of further production.

As a general rule, then, things tend to exchange for one another at such values as will enable each producer to be repaid the cost of production with the ordinary profit; in other words, such as will give to all producers the same rate of profit on their outlay. But in order that the profit may be equal where the outlay, that is, the cost of production, is equal, things must on the average exchange for one another in the ratio of their cost of production; things of which the cost of production is the same, must be of the same value. For only thus will an equal outlay yield an equal return. If a farmer with a capital equal to 1000 quarters of corn, can produce 1200 quarters, yielding him a profit of 20 per cent.; whatever else can be produced in the same time by a capital of 1000 quarters, must be worth, that is, must exchange for, 1200 quarters, otherwise the producer would gain either more or less than 20 per cent.

Adam Smith and Ricardo have called that value of a thing which is proportional to its cost of production, its Natural Value (or its Natural Price). They meant by this, the point about which the value oscillates, and to which it always tends to return; the centre value, towards which, as Adam Smith expresses it, the market value of a thing is constantly gravitating; and any deviation from which is but a temporary irregularity, which, the moment it exists, sets forces in motion tending to correct it. On an average of years sufficient to enable the oscillations on one side of the central line to be compensated by those on the other, the market value agrees with the natural value; but it very seldom coincides exactly with it at any particular time. The sea everywhere tends to a level; but it never is at an exact level; its surface is always ruffled by waves, and often agitated by storms. It is enough that no point, at least in the open sea, is permanently higher than another. Each place is alternately elevated and depressed; but the ocean preserves its level.

Book Four: Influence of the Progress of Society on Production and Distribution

1. OF THE STATIONARY STATE

THE PRECEDING CHAPTERS comprise the general theory of the economical progress of society, in the sense in which those terms are commonly understood; the progress of capital, of population, and of the productive arts. But in contemplating any progressive movement, not in its nature unlimited, the mind is not satisfied with merely tracing the laws of the movement; it cannot but ask the further question, to what goal? Towards what ultimate point is society tending by its industrial progress? When the progress ceases, in what condition are we to expect that it will leave mankind?

It must always have been seen, more or less distinctly, by political economists, that the increase of wealth is not boundless: that at the end of what they term the progressive state lies the stationary state, that all progress in wealth is but a postponement of this, and that each step in advance is an approach to it. We have now been led to recognize that this ultimate goal is at all times near enough to be fully in view; that we are always on the verge of it, and that if we have not reached it long ago, it is because the goal itself flies before us. The richest and most prosperous countries would very soon attain the stationary state, if no further improvements were made in the productive arts, and if there were a suspension of the overflow of capital from those countries into the uncultivated or ill-cultivated regions of the earth.

This impossibility of ultimately avoiding the stationary state—this irresistible necessity that the stream of human industry should finally spread itself out into an apparently stagnant sea—must have been, to the political economists of the last two generations, an unpleasing and discouraging prospect; for the tone and tendency of their speculations goes completely to identify all that is economically desirable with the progressive state, and with that alone. With Mr. [James Ramsay] McCulloch, for example, prosperity does not mean a large production and a good distribution of wealth, but a rapid increase of it; his test of prosperity is high profits; and as the tendency of that very increase of wealth, which he calls prosperity, is towards low profits, economical progress, according to him, must tend to the extinction of prosperity. Adam Smith always assumes that the condition of the mass of the people, though it may not be positively distressed, must be pinched and stinted in a stationary condition of wealth, and can only be satisfactory in a progressive state. The doctrine that, to however distant a time incessant struggling may put off our doom, the progress of society must "end in shallows and in miseries," far from being, as many people still believe, a wicked invention of Mr. Malthus, was either expressly or tacitly affirmed by his most distinguished predecessors, and can only be successfully combated on his principles. Before attention had been directed to the principle of population as the active force in determining the remuneration of labour, the increase of mankind was virtually treated as a constant quantity: it was, at all events, assumed that in the natural and normal state of human affairs population must constantly increase, from which it followed that a constant increase of the means of support was essential to the physical comfort of the mass of mankind. The publication of Mr. Malthus's *Essay* is the era from which better views of this subject must be dated; and notwithstanding the acknowledged errors of his first edition, few writers have done more than himself, in the subsequent editions, to promote these juster and more hopeful anticipations.

Even in a progressive state of capital, in old countries, a conscientious or prudential restraint on population is indispensable, to prevent the increase of numbers from outstripping the increase of capital, and the condition of the classes who are at the bottom of society from being deteriorated. Where there is not, in the people, or in some very large proportion of them, a resolute resistance to this deterioration—a determination to preserve an established standard of comfort—the condition of the poorest class sinks, even in a progressive state, to the lowest point which they will consent to endure. The same determination would be equally effectual to keep up their condition in the stationary state, and would be quite as likely to exist. Indeed, even now, the countries in which the greatest prudence is manifested in the regulating of population, are often those in which capital increases least rapidly. Where there is an indefinite prospect of employment for increased numbers, there is apt to appear less necessity for prudential restraint. If it were evident that a new hand could not obtain employment but by displacing, or succeeding to, one already employed, the combined influences of prudence and public opinion might in some measure be relied on for restricting the coming generation within the numbers necessary for replacing the present.

I cannot, therefore, regard the stationary state of capital and wealth with the unaffected aversion so generally manifested towards it by political economists of the old school. I am inclined to believe that it would be, on the whole, a very considerable improvement on our present condition. I confess I am not charmed with the ideal of life held out by those who think that the normal state of human beings is that of struggling to get on; that the trampling, crushing, elbowing, and treading on each other's heels, which form the existing type of social life, are the most desirable lot of human kind, or anything but the disagreeable symptoms of one of the phases of industrial progress. The northern and middle states of America are a specimen of this stage of civilization in very favourable circumstances; having, apparently, got rid of all social injustices and inequalities that affect persons of Caucasian race and of the male sex, while the proportion of population to capital and land is such as to ensure abundance to every able-bodied member of the community who does not forfeit it by misconduct. They have the six points of Chartism, and they have no poverty: and all that these advantages seem to have yet done for them (notwithstanding some incipient signs of a better tendency) is that the life of the whole of one sex is devoted to dollar-hunting, and of the other to breeding dollar-hunters. This is not a kind of social perfection which philanthropists to come will feel any very eager desire to assist in realizing. Most fitting, indeed, is it, that while riches are power, and to grow as rich as possible the universal object of ambition, the path to its attainment should be open to all, without favour or partiality. But the best state for human nature is that in which, while no one is poor, no one desires to be richer, nor has any reason to fear being thrust back, by the efforts of others to push themselves forward.

That the energies of mankind should be kept in employment by the struggle for riches, as they were formerly by the struggle of war, until the better minds succeed in educating the others into better things, is undoubtedly more desirable than that they should rust and stagnate. While minds are coarse they require coarse stimuli, and let them have them. In the meantime, those who do not accept the present very early stage of human improvement as its ultimate type, may be excused for being comparatively indifferent to the kind of economical progress which excites the congratulations of ordinary politicians; the mere increase of production and accumulation. For the safety of national independence it is essential that a country should not fall much behind its neighbours in these things. But in themselves they are of little importance, so long as either the increase of population or anything else prevents the mass of the people from reaping any part of the benefit of them. I know not why it should be matter of congratulation that persons who are already richer than anyone needs to be, should have doubled their means of consuming things which give little or no pleasure except as representative of wealth; or that numbers of individuals should pass over, every year, from the middle classes into a richer class, or from the class of the occupied rich to that of the unoccupied. It is only in the backward countries of the world that increased production is still an important object: in those most advanced, what is economically needed is a better distribution, of which one indispensable means is a stricter restraint on population.

Levelling institutions, either of a just or of an unjust kind, cannot alone accomplish it; they may lower the heights of society, but they cannot, of themselves, permanently raise the depths.

On the other hand, we may suppose this better distribution of property attained, by the joint effect of the prudence and frugality of individuals, and of a system of legislation favouring equality of fortunes, so far as is consistent with the just claim of the individual to the fruits, whether great or small, of his or her own industry. We may suppose, for instance, a limitation of the sum which any one person may acquire by gift or inheritance, to the amount sufficient to constitute a moderate independence. Under this twofold influence, society would exhibit these leading features: a well-paid and affluent body of labourers; no enormous fortunes, except what were earned and accumulated during a single lifetime; but a much larger body of persons than at present, not only exempt from the coarser toils, but with sufficient leisure, both physical and mental, from mechanical details, to cultivate freely the graces of life, and afford examples of them to the classes less favourably circumstanced for their growth. This condition of society, so greatly preferable to the present, is not only perfectly compatible with the stationary state, but, it would seem, more naturally allied with that state than with any other.

There is room in the world, no doubt, and even in old countries, for a great increase of population, supposing the arts of life to go on improving, and capital to increase. But even if innocuous, I confess I see very little reason for desiring it. The density of population necessary to enable mankind to obtain, in the greatest degree, all the advantages both of co-operation and of social intercourse, has, in all the most populous countries, been attained. A population may be too crowded, though all be amply supplied with food and raiment. It is not good for a man to be kept perforce at all times in the presence of his species. A world from which solitude is extirpated, is a very poor ideal. Solitude, in the sense of being often alone, is essential to any depth of meditation or of character; and solitude in the presence of natural beauty and grandeur, is the cradle of thoughts and aspirations which are not only good for the individual, but which society could ill do without. Nor is there much satisfaction in contemplating the world with nothing left to the spontaneous activity of nature; with every rood of land brought into cultivation, which is capable of growing food for human beings; every flowery waste or natural pasture ploughed up, all quadrupeds or birds which are not domesticated for man's use exterminated as his rivals for food, every hedgerow or superfluous tree rooted out, and scarcely a place left where a wild shrub or flower could grow without being eradicated as a weed in the name of improved agriculture. If the earth must lose that great portion of its pleasantness which it owes to things that the unlimited increase of wealth and population would extirpate from it, for the mere purpose of enabling it to support a larger, but not a better or a happier population, I sincerely hope, for the sake of posterity, that they will be content to be stationary, long before necessity compels them to it.

It is scarcely necessary to remark that a stationary condition of capital and population implies no stationary state of human improvement. There would be as much scope as ever for all kinds of mental culture, and moral and social progress; as much room for improving the Art of Living, and much more likelihood of its being improved, when minds ceased to be engrossed by the art of getting on. Even the industrial arts might be as earnestly and as successfully cultivated, with this sole difference, that instead of serving no purpose but the increase of wealth, industrial improvements would produce their legitimate effect, that of abridging labour. Hitherto it is questionable if all the mechanical inventions yet made have lightened the day's toil of any human being. They have enabled a greater population to live the same life of drudgery and imprisonment, and an increased number of manufacturers and others to make fortunes. They have increased the comforts of the middle classes. But they have not yet begun to effect those great changes in human destiny, which it is in their nature and in their futurity to accomplish. Only when, in addition to just institutions, the increase of mankind shall be under the deliberate guidance of judicious foresight, can the conquests made from the powers of nature by the intellect and energy of scientific discoverers, become the common property of the species, and the means of improving and elevating the universal lot.

II. ON THE PROBABLE FUTURITY OF THE LABOURING CLASSES

The observations in the preceding chapter had for their principal object to deprecate a false ideal of human society. Their applicability to the practical purposes of present times, consists in moderating the inordinate importance attached to the mere increase of production, and fixing attention upon improved distribution, and a large remuneration of labour, as the two desiderata. Whether the aggregate produce increases absolutely or not, is a thing in which, after a certain amount has been obtained, neither the legislator nor the philanthropist need feel any strong interest: but, that it should increase relatively to the number of those who share in it, is of the utmost possible importance; and this, (whether the wealth of mankind be stationary, or increasing at the most rapid rate ever known in an old country,) must depend on the opinions and habits of the most numerous class, the class of manual labourers.

When I speak, either in this place or elsewhere, of "the labouring classes," or of labourers as a "class," I use those phrases in compliance with custom, and as descriptive of an existing, but by no means a necessary or permanent, state of social relations. I do not recognize as either just or salutary, a state of society in which there is any "class" which is not labouring; any human beings, exempt from bearing their share of the necessary labours of human life, except those unable to labour, or who have fairly earned rest by previous toil. So long, however, as the great social evil exists of a non-labouring class, labourers also constitute a class, and may be spoken of, though only provisionally, in that character.

Considered in its moral and social aspect, the state of the labouring people has latterly been a subject of much more speculation and discussion than formerly; and the opinion, that it is not now what it ought to be, has become very general. The suggestions which have been promulgated, and the controversies which have been excited, on detached points rather than on the foundations of the subject, have put in evidence the existence of two conflicting theories, respecting the social position desirable for manual labourers. The one may be called the theory of dependence and protection, the other that of self-dependence.

According to the former theory, the lot of the poor, in all things which affect them collectively, should be regulated *for* them, not *by* them. They should not be required or encouraged to think for themselves, or give to their own reflection or forecast an influential voice in the determination of their destiny. It is supposed to be the duty of the higher classes to think for them, and to take the responsibility of their lot, as the commander and officers of an army take that of the soldiers composing it. This function, it is contended, the higher classes should prepare themselves to perform conscientiously, and their whole demeanour should impress the poor with a reliance on it, in order that, while yielding passive and active obedience to the rules prescribed for them, they may resign themselves in all other respects to a trustful *insouciance,* and repose under the shadow of their protectors. The relation between rich and poor, according to this theory, (a theory also applied to the relation between men and women) should be only partly authoritative; it should be amiable, moral, and sentimental: affectionate tutelage on the one side, respectful and grateful deference on the other. The rich should be *in loco parentis* to the poor, guiding and restraining them like children. Of spontaneous action on their part there should be no need. They should be called on for nothing but to do their day's work, and to be moral and religious. Their morality and religion should be provided for them by their superiors, who should see them properly taught it, and should do all that is necessary to ensure their being, in return for labour and attachment, properly fed, clothed, housed, spiritually edified, and innocently amused.

I am quite sensible of all that is seductive in the picture of society which this theory presents. Though the facts of it have no prototype in the past, the feelings have. In them lies all that there is of reality in the conception. As the idea is essentially repulsive of a society only held together by the relations and feelings arising out of pecuniary interests, so there is something naturally attractive in a form of society abounding in strong personal attachments and disinterested self-devotion. Of such feelings it must be admitted that the relation of protector and protected has hitherto been the richest source. The strongest attachments of human beings in general, are towards the things or the persons that stand between them and some dreaded evil. Hence, in an age of lawless violence and insecurity, and general hardness and roughness of manners, in which life is beset with dangers and sufferings at every step, to those who have neither a commanding position of their own, nor a claim on the protection of someone who has—a generous giving of protection, and a grateful receiving of it, are the strongest ties which connect human beings; the feelings arising from that relation are their warmest feelings; all the enthusiasm and tenderness of the most sensitive natures gather round it; loyalty on the one part and chivalry on the other are principles exalted into passions. I do not desire to depreciate these qualities. The error lies in not perceiving, that these virtues and sentiments, like the clanship and the hospitality of the wandering Arab, belong emphatically to a rude and imperfect state of the social union, and that the feelings between protector and protected, whether between kings and subjects, rich and poor, or men and women, can no longer have this beautiful and endearing character, where there are no longer any serious dangers from which to protect.

Of the workingmen, at least in the more advanced countries of Europe, it may be pronounced certain, that the patriarchal or paternal system of government is one to which they will not again be subject. That question was decided, when they were taught to read, and allowed access to newspapers and political tracts; when dissenting preachers were suffered to go among them, and appeal to their faculties and feelings in opposition to the creeds professed and countenanced by their superiors; when they were brought together in numbers, to work socially under the same roof; when railways enabled them to shift from place to place, and change their patrons and employers as easily as their coats; when they were encouraged to seek a share in the government, by means of the electoral franchise. The working classes have taken their interests into their own hands, and are perpetually showing that they think the interests of their employers not identical with their own, but opposite to them. Some among the higher classes flatter themselves that these tendencies may be counteracted by moral and religious education; but they have let the time go by for giving an education which can serve their purpose.

The principles of the Reformation have reached as low down in society as reading and writing, and the poor will not much longer accept morals and religion of other people's prescribing.

It is on a far other basis that the well-being and well-doing of the labouring people must henceforth rest. The poor have come out of leading strings, and cannot any longer be governed or treated like children. To their own qualities must now be commended the care of their destiny. Modern nations will have to learn the lesson, that the well-being of a people must exist by means of the justice and self-government, the *δικαιοσύνη* and *σωφροσύνη*, of the individual citizens. The theory of dependence attempts to dispense with the necessity of these qualities in the dependent classes. But now, when even in position they are becoming less and less dependent, and their minds less and less acquiescent in the degree of dependence which remains, the virtues of independence are those which they stand in need of. Whatever advice, exhortation, or guidance is held out to the labouring classes, must henceforth be tendered to them as equals, and accepted with their eyes open. The prospect of the future depends on the degree in which they can be made rational beings.

The political consequences of the increasing power and importance of the operative classes, and of the growing ascendancy of numbers, which even in England and under the present institutions, is rapidly giving to the will of the majority at least a negative voice in the acts of government, are too wide a subject to be discussed in this place. But, confining ourselves to economical considerations, and notwithstanding the effect which improved intelligence in the working classes, together with just laws, may have in altering the distribution of the produce to their advantage, I cannot think that they will be permanently contented with the condition of labouring for wages as their ultimate state. They may be willing to pass through the class of servants in their way to that of employers; but not to remain in it all their lives. To begin as hired labourers, then after a few years to work on their own account, and finally employ others, is the normal condition of labourers in a new country, rapidly increasing in wealth and population, like America or Australia. But in an old and fully peopled country, those who begin life as labourers for hire, as a general rule, continue such to the end, unless they sink into the still lower grade of recipients of public charity. In the present stage of human progress, when ideas of equality are daily spreading more widely among the poorer classes, and can no longer be checked by anything short of the entire suppression of printed discussion and even of freedom of speech, it is not to be expected that the division of the human race into two hereditary classes, employers and employed, can be permanently maintained. The relation is nearly as unsatisfactory to the payer of wages as to the receiver. If the rich regard the poor as, by a kind of natural law, their servants and dependants, the rich in their turn are regarded as a mere prey and pasture for the poor; the subject of demands and expectations wholly indefinite, increasing in extent with every concession made to them. The total absence of regard for justice or fairness in the relations between the two, is as marked on the side of the employed as on that of the employers. We look in vain among the working classes in general for the just pride which will choose to give good work for good wages: for the most part, their sole endeavour is to receive as much, and return as little in the shape of service, as possible. It will sooner or later become insupportable to the employing classes to live in close and hourly contact with persons whose interests and feelings are in hostility to them. Capitalists are almost as much interested as labourers, in placing the operations of industry on such a footing, that those who labour for them may feel the same interest in the work, which is felt by those who labour on their own account.

The aim of improvement should be not solely to place human beings in a condition in which they will be able to do without one another, but to enable them to work with or for one another in relations not involving dependence. Hitherto there has been no alternative for those who lived by their labour, but that of labouring either each for himself alone, or for a master. But the civilizing and improving influences of association, and the efficiency and economy of production on a large scale, may be obtained without dividing the producers into two parties with hostile interests and feelings, the many who do the work being mere servants under the command of the one who supplies the funds, and having no interest of their own in the enterprise except to earn their wages with as little labour as possible. The speculations and discussions of the last fifty years, and the events of the last ten, are abundantly conclusive on this point. If the improvement which even triumphant military despotism has only retarded, not stopped, shall continue its course, there can be little doubt that the status of hired labourers will gradually tend to confine itself to the description of workpeople whose low moral qualities render them unfit for anything more independent: and that the relation of masters and workpeople will be gradually superseded by partnership, in one of two forms: temporarily and in some cases, association of the labourers with the capitalist; in other cases, and perhaps finally in all, association of labourers among themselves.

The first of these forms of association has long been practised, not indeed as a rule, but as an exception. In several departments of industry there are already cases in which every one who contributes to the work, either by labour or by pecuniary resources, has a partner's interest in it, proportional to the value of his contribution. It is already a common practice to remunerate those in whom peculiar trust is reposed, by means of a percentage on the profits: and cases exist in which the principle is, with excellent success, carried down to the class of mere manual labourers.

In the American ships trading to China, it has long been the custom for every sailor to have an interest in the profits of the voyage; and to this has been ascribed the general good conduct of those seamen, and the extreme rarity of any collision between them and the government or people of the country. An instance in England, not so well known as it deserves to be, is that of the Cornish miners. "In Cornwall the mines are worked strictly on the system of joint adventure; gangs of miners contracting with the agent, who represents the owner of the mine, to execute a certain portion of a vein, and fit the ore for market, at the price of so much in the pound of the sum for which the ore is sold. These contracts are put up at certain regular periods, generally every two months, and taken by a voluntary partnership of men accustomed to the mine. This system has its disadvantages, in consequence of the uncertainty and irregularity of the earnings, and consequent necessity of living for long periods on credit; but it has advantages which more than counterbalance these drawbacks. It produces a degree of intelligence, independence, and moral elevation, which raise the condition and character of the Cornish miner far above that of the generality of the labouring class." (Samuel Laing on "The Causes and Remedies of National Distress" in *Report of the Children's Employment Commission.*)

Mr. Babbage, who also gives an account of this system, observes that the payment to the crews of whaling ships is governed by a similar principle; and that "the profits arising from fishing with nets on the south coast of England are thus divided: one half the produce belongs to the owner of the boat and net: the other half is divided in equal portions between the persons using it, who are also bound to assist in repairing the net when required." Mr. Babbage has the great merit of having pointed out [in his book, the *Economy of Machinery and Manufactures*], the practicability, and the advantage, of extending the principle to manufacturing industry generally.

Some attention has been excited by an experiment of this nature, commenced about sixteen years ago by a Paris tradesman, a house painter, M. Leclaire; and described by him in a pamphlet published in the year 1842. M. Leclaire, according to his statement, employs on an average two hundred workmen, whom he pays in the usual manner, by fixed wages or salaries. He assigns to himself, besides interest for his capital, a fixed allowance for his labour and responsibility as manager. At the end of the year, the surplus profits are divided among the body, himself included, in the proportion of their salaries.

Even in the first year during which M. Leclaire's experiment was in complete operation, the success was remarkable. Not one of his journeymen who worked as many as three hundred days, earned in that year less than 1500 francs, and some considerably more. His highest rate of daily wages being four francs, or 1200 francs for 300 days, the remaining 300 francs, or 12*l.*, must have been the smallest amount which any journeyman, who worked that number of days, obtained as his proportion of the surplus profit. M. Leclaire describes in strong terms the improvement which was already manifest in the habits and demeanour of his workmen, not merely when at work, and in their relations with their employer, but at other times and in other relations, showing increased respect both for others and for themselves.

The form of association, however, which if mankind continue to improve, must be expected in the end to predominate, is not that which can exist between a capitalist as chief, and workpeople without a voice in the management, but the association of the labourers themselves on terms of equality, collectively owning the capital with which they carry on their operations, and working under managers elected and removable by themselves. So long as this idea remained in a state of theory, in the writings of Owen or of Louis Blanc, it may have appeared, to the common modes of judgment, incapable of being realized, and not likely to be tried unless by seizing on the existing capital, and confiscating it for the benefit of the labourers; which is even now imagined by many persons, and pretended by more, both in England and on the Continent, to be the meaning and purpose of Socialism. But there is a capacity of exertion and self-denial in the masses of mankind, which is never known but on the rare occasions on which it is appealed to in the name of some great idea or elevated sentiment. Such an appeal was made by the French Revolution of 1848. For the first time it then seemed to the intelligent and generous of the working classes of a great nation, that they had obtained a government who sincerely desired the freedom and dignity of the many, and who did not look upon it as their natural and legitimate state to be instruments of production, worked for the benefit of the possessors of capital. Under this encouragement, the ideas sown by Socialist writers, of an emancipation of labour to be effected by means of association, throve and fructified; and many working people came to the resolution, not only that they would work for one another, instead of working for a master tradesman or manufacturer, but that they would also free themselves, at whatever cost of labour or privation, from the necessity of paying, out of the produce of their industry, a heavy tribute for the use of capital; that they would extinguish this tax, not by robbing the capitalists of what they or their predecessors had acquired by labour and preserved by economy, but by honestly acquiring capital for themselves. If only a few operatives had attempted this arduous task, or if, while many attempted it, a few only had succeeded, their success might have been deemed to furnish no argument for their system as a permanent mode of industrial organization. But, excluding all the instances of failure, there exist, or existed a short time ago, upwards of a hundred successful, and many eminently prosperous, associations of operatives in Paris alone, besides a considerable number in the departments.

It is the declared principle of most of these associations, that they do not exist for the mere private benefit of the individual members, but for the promotion of the co-operative cause. With every extension, therefore, of their business, they take in additional members, not to receive wages from them as hired labourers, but to enter at once into the full benefits of the association, without being required to bring anything in, except their labour: the only condition imposed is that of receiving during a few years a smaller share in the annual division of profits, as some equivalent for the sacrifices of the founders. When members quit the association, which they are always at liberty to do, they carry none of the capital with them: it remains an indivisible property, of which the members for the time being have the use, but not the arbitrary disposal: by the stipulations of most of the contracts, even if the association breaks up, the capital cannot be divided, but must be devoted entire to some work of beneficence or of public utility. A fixed, and generally a considerable, proportion of the annual profits, is not shared among the members, but added to the capital of the association, or devoted to the repayment of advances previously made to it: another portion is set aside to provide for the sick and disabled, and another to form a fund for extending the practice of association, or aiding other associations in their need. The managers are paid, like other members, for the time which is occupied in management, usually at the rate of the highest paid labour: but the rule is adhered to, that the exercise of power shall never be an occasion of profit.

The vitality of these associations must indeed be great, to have enabled about twenty of them to survive not only the anti-socialist reaction, which for the time discredited all attempts to enable workpeople to be their own employers—not only the *tracasseries* of the police, and the hostile policy of the government since the usurpation—but in addition to these obstacles, all the difficulties arising from the trying condition of financial and commercial affairs from 1854 to 1858. Of the prosperity attained by some of them even while passing through this difficult period, I have given examples which must be conclusive to all minds as to the brilliant future reserved for the principle of co-operation.

It is not in France alone that these associations have commenced a career of prosperity. To say nothing at present of Piedmont or of Germany, England can produce cases of success rivalling even those which

I have cited from France. Under the impulse commenced by Mr. Owen, and more recently propagated by the writings and personal efforts of a band of friends, chiefly clergymen and barristers, to whose noble exertions too much praise can scarcely be given, the good seed was widely sown; the necessary alterations in the English law of partnership were obtained from Parliament; many industrial associations, and a still greater number of co-operative stores for retail purchases, were founded. Among these are already many instances of remarkable prosperity, the most signal of which are the Leeds Flour Mill, and the Rochdale Society of Equitable Pioneers. Of this last association, the most successful of all, the history has been written in a very interesting manner by Mr. [George Jacob] Holyoake; and the notoriety which by this and other means has been given to facts so encouraging, is causing a rapid extension of associations with similar objects in Lancashire and Yorkshire.

It is hardly possible to take any but a hopeful view of the prospects of mankind, when in the two leading countries of the world, the obscure depths of society contain simple working men whose integrity, good sense, self-command, and honourable confidence in one another, have enabled them to carry these noble experiments to the triumphant issue which the facts recorded in the preceding pages attest. Their admirable history shows how vast an increase might be made even in the aggregate productiveness of labour, if the labourers as a mass were placed in a relation to their work which would make it (what now it is not) their principle and their interest to do the utmost, instead of the least possible, in exchange for their remuneration. In the co-operative movement, the permanency of which may now be considered as ensured, we see exemplified the process for bringing about a change in society, which would combine the freedom and independence of the individual, with the moral, intellectual, and economical advantages of aggregate production; and which, without violence or spoliation, or even any sudden disturbance of existing habits and expectations, would realize, at least in the industrial department, the best aspirations of the democratic spirit, by putting an end to the division of society into the industrious and the idle, and effacing all social distinctions but those fairly earned by personal services and exertions. Associations like those which we have described, by the very process of their success, are a course of education in those moral and active qualities by which alone success can be either deserved or attained. As associations multiplied, they would tend more and more to absorb all workpeople, except those who have too little understanding, or too little virtue, to be capable of learning to act on any other system than that of narrow selfishness. As this change proceeded, owners of capital would gradually find it to their advantage, instead of maintaining the struggle of the old system with workpeople of only the worst description, to lend their capital to the associations; to do this at a diminishing rate of interest, and at last, perhaps, even to exchange their capital for terminable annuities. In this or some such mode, the existing accumulations of capital might honestly, and by a kind of spontaneous process, become in the end the joint property of all who participate in their productive employment: a transformation which, thus effected, (and assuming of course that both sexes participate equally in the rights and in the government of the association) would be the nearest approach to social justice, and the most beneficial ordering of industrial affairs for the universal good, which it is possible at present to foresee.

I agree, then, with the Socialist writers in their conception of the form which industrial operations tend to assume in the advance of improvement; and I entirely share their opinion that the time is ripe for commencing this transformation, and that it should by all just and effectual means be aided and encouraged. But while I agree and sympathize with Socialists in this practical portion of their aims, I utterly dissent from the most conspicuous and vehement part of their teaching, their declamations against competition. With moral conceptions in many respects far ahead of the existing arrangements of society, they have in general very confused and erroneous notions of its actual working; and one of their greatest errors, as I conceive, is to charge upon competition all the economical evils which at present exist. They forget that wherever competition is not, monopoly is; and that monopoly, in all its forms, is the taxation of the industrious for the support of indolence, if not of plunder. They forget, too, that with the exception of competition among labourers, all other competition is for the benefit of the labourers, by cheapening the articles they consume; that competition even in the labour market is a source not of low but of high wages, wherever the competition *for* labour exceeds the competition *of* labour, as in America, in the colonies, and in the skilled trades; and never could be a cause of low wages, save by the overstocking of the labour market through the too great numbers of the labourers' families; while, if the supply of labourers is excessive, not even Socialism can prevent their remuneration from being low. Besides, if association were universal, there would be no competition between labourer and labourer; and that between association and association would be for the benefit of the consumers, that is, of the associations; of the industrious classes generally.

I do not pretend that there are no inconveniences in competition, or that the moral objections urged against it by Socialist writers, as a source of jealousy and hostility among those engaged in the same occupation, are altogether groundless. But if competition has its evils, it prevents greater evils. It is the common error of Socialists to overlook the natural indolence of mankind; their tendency to be passive, to be the slaves of habit, to persist indefinitely in a course once chosen. Let them once attain any state of existence which they consider tolerable, and the danger to be apprehended is that they will thenceforth stagnate; will not exert themselves to improve, and by letting their faculties rust, will lose even the energy required to preserve them from deterioration. Competition may not be the best conceivable stimulus, but it is at present a necessary one, and no one can foresee the time when it will not be indispensable to progress. Even confining ourselves to the industrial department, in which, more than in any other, the majority may be supposed to be competent judges of improvements; it would be difficult to induce the general assembly of an association to submit to the trouble and inconvenience of altering their habits by adopting some new and promising invention, unless their knowledge of the existence of rival associations made them apprehend that what they would not consent to do, others would, and that they would be left behind in the race.

Instead of looking upon competition as the baneful and anti-social principle which it is held to be by the generality of Socialists, I conceive that, even in the present state of society and industry, every restriction of it is an evil, and every extension of it, even if for the time injuriously affecting some class of labourers, is always an ultimate good. To be protected against competition is to be protected in idleness, in mental dulness; to be saved the necessity of being as active and as intelligent as other people; and if it is also to be protected against being underbid for employment by a less highly paid class of labourers, this is only where old custom or local and partial monopoly has placed some particular class of artisans in a privileged position as compared with the rest; and the time has come when the interest of universal improvement is no longer promoted by prolonging the privileges of a few. If the slopsellers and other of their class have lowered the wages of tailors, and some other artisans, by making them an affair of competition instead of custom, so much the better in the end. What is now required is not to bolster up old customs, whereby limited classes of labouring people obtain partial gains which interest them in keeping up the present organization of society, but to introduce new general practices beneficial to all; and there is reason to rejoice at whatever makes the privileged classes of skilled artisans feel, that they have the same interests, and depend for their remuneration on the same general causes, and must resort for the improvement of their condition to the same remedies, as the less fortunately circumstanced and comparatively helpless multitude.

Book Five: Of the Influence of Government

I. OF THE FUNCTIONS OF GOVERNMENT IN GENERAL

One of the most disputed questions both in political science and in practical statesmanship at this particular period, relates to the proper limits of the functions and agency of governments. At other times it has been a subject of controversy how governments should be constituted, and according to what principles and rules they should exercise their authority; but it is now almost equally a question, to what departments of human affairs that authority should extend. And when the tide sets so strongly towards changes in government and legislation, as a means of improving the condition of mankind, this discussion is more likely to increase than to diminish in interest. On the one hand, impatient reformers, thinking it easier and shorter to get possession of the government than of the intellects and dispositions of the public, are under a constant temptation to stretch the province of government beyond due bounds: while, on the other, mankind have been so much accustomed by their rulers to interference for purposes other than the public good, or under an erroneous conception of what that good requires, and so many rash proposals are made by sincere lovers of improvement, for attempting, by compulsory regulation, the attainment of objects which can only be effectually or only usefully compassed by opinion and discussion, that there has grown up a spirit of resistance *in limine* to the interference of government, merely as such, and a disposition to restrict its sphere of action within the narrowest bounds. From differences in the historical development of different nations, not necessary to be here dwelt upon, the former excess, that of exaggerating the province of government, prevails most, both in theory and in practice, among the Continental nations, while in England the contrary spirit has hitherto been predominant.

In attempting to enumerate the necessary functions of government, we find them to be considerably more multifarious than most people are at first aware of, and not capable of being circumscribed by those very definite lines of demarcation, which, in the inconsiderateness of popular discussion, it is often attempted to draw round them. We sometimes, for example, hear it said that governments ought to confine themselves to affording protection against force and fraud: that, these two things apart, people should be free agents, able to take care of themselves, and that so long as a person practises no violence or deception, to the injury of others in person or property, legislatures and governments are in no way called on to concern themselves about him. But why should people be protected by their government, that is, by their own collective strength, against violence and fraud, and not against other evils, except that the expediency is more obvious? If nothing, but what people cannot possibly do for themselves, can be fit to be done for them by government, people might be required to protect themselves by their skill and courage even against force, or to beg or buy protection against it, as they actually do where the government is not capable of protecting them: and against fraud everyone has the protection of his own wits. But without further anticipating the discussion of principles, it is sufficient on the present occasion to consider facts.

Under which of these heads, the repression of force or of fraud, are we to place the operation, for example, of the laws of inheritance? Some such laws must exist in all societies. It may be said, perhaps, that in this matter government has merely to give effect to the disposition which an individual makes of his own property by will. This, however, is at least extremely disputable; there is probably no country by whose laws the power of testamentary disposition is perfectly absolute. And suppose the very common case of there being no will: does not the law, that is, the government, decide on principles of general expediency, who shall take the succession? and in case the successor is in any manner incompetent, does it not appoint persons, frequently officers of its own, to collect the property and apply it to his benefit? There are many other cases in which the government undertakes the administration of property, because the public interest, or perhaps only that of the particular persons concerned, is thought to require it. This is often done in cases of litigated property; and in cases of judicially declared insolvency. It has never been contended that in doing these things, a government exceeds its province.

Nor is the function of the law in defining property itself, so simple a thing as may be supposed. It may be imagined, perhaps, that the law has only to declare and protect the right of everyone to what he has himself produced, or acquired by the voluntary consent, fairly obtained, of those who produced it. But is there nothing recognised as property except what has been produced? Is there not the earth itself, its forests and waters, and all other natural riches, above and below the surface? These are the inheritance of the human race, and there must be regulations for the common enjoyment of it. What rights, and under what conditions, a person shall be allowed to exercise over any portion of this common inheritance, cannot be left undecided. No function of government is less optional than the regulation of these things, or more completely involved in the idea of civilized society.

Again, the legitimacy is conceded of repressing violence or treachery; but under which of these heads are we to place the obligation imposed on people to perform their contracts? Non-performance does not necessarily imply fraud; the person who entered into the contract may have sincerely intended to fulfil it: and the term fraud, which can scarcely admit of being extended even to the case of voluntary breach of contract when no deception was practised, is certainly not applicable when the omission to perform is a case of negligence. Is it no part of the duty of governments to enforce contracts? Here the doctrine of non-interference would no doubt be stretched a little, and it would be said, that enforcing contracts is not regulating the affairs of individuals at the pleasure of government, but giving effect to their own expressed desire. Let us acquiesce in this enlargement of the restrictive theory, and take it for what it is worth. But governments do not limit their concern with contracts to a simple enforcement. They take upon themselves to determine what contracts are fit to be enforced. It is not enough that one person, not being either cheated or compelled, makes a promise to another. There are promises by which it is not for the public good that persons should have the power of binding themselves. To say nothing of engagements to do something contrary to law, there are engagements which the law refuses to enforce, for reasons connected with the interest of the promiser, or with the general policy of the state. A contract by which a person sells himself to another as a slave, would be declared void by the tribunals of this and of most other European countries. There are few nations whose laws enforce a contract for what is looked upon as prostitution, or any matrimonial engagement of which the conditions vary in any respect from those which the law has thought fit to prescribe. But when once it is admitted that there are any engagements which for reasons of expediency the law ought not to enforce, the same question is necessarily opened with respect to all engagements. Whether, for example, the law should enforce a contract to labour, when the wages are too low, or the hours of work too severe: whether it should enforce a contract by which a person binds himself to remain, for more than a very limited period, in the service of a given individual: whether a contract of marriage, entered into for life, should continue to be enforced against the deliberate will of the persons, or of either of the persons, who entered into it. Every question which can possibly arise as to the policy of contracts, and of the relations which they establish among human beings, is a question for the legislator; and one which he cannot escape from considering, and in some way or other deciding.

Again, the prevention and suppression of force and fraud afford appropriate employment for soldiers, policemen, and criminal judges; but there are also civil tribunals. The punishment of wrong is one business of an administration of justice, but the decision of disputes is another. Innumerable disputes arise between persons, without *mala fides* on either side, through misconception of their legal rights, or from not being agreed about the facts, on the proof of which those rights are legally dependent. Is it not for the general interest that the State should appoint persons to clear up these uncertainties and terminate these disputes? It cannot be said to be a case of absolute necessity. People might appoint an arbitrator, and engage to submit to his decision; and they do so where there are no courts of justice, or where the courts are not trusted, or where their delays and expenses, or the irrationality of their rules of evidence, deter people from resorting to them. Still, it is universally thought right that the State should establish civil tribunals; and if their defects often drive people to have recourse to substitutes, even then the power held in reserve of carrying the case before a legally constituted court, gives to the substitutes their principal efficacy.

Not only does the State undertake to decide disputes, it takes precautions beforehand that disputes may not arise. The laws of most countries lay down rules for determining many things, not because it is of much consequence in what way they are determined, but in order that they may be determined somehow, and there may be no question on the subject. The law prescribes forms of words for many kinds of contract, in order that no dispute or misunderstanding may arise about their meaning: it makes provision that if a dispute does arise, evidence shall be procurable for deciding it, by requiring that the document be attested by witnesses and executed with certain formalities. The law preserves authentic evidence of facts to which legal consequences are attached, by keeping a registry of such facts; as of births, deaths, and marriages, of wills and contracts, and of judicial proceedings. In doing these things, it has never been alleged that government oversteps the proper limits of its functions.

Again, however wide a scope we may allow to the doctrine that individuals are the proper guardians of their own interests, and that government owes nothing to them but to save them from being interfered with by other people, the doctrine can never be applicable to any persons but those who are capable of acting in their own behalf. The individual may be an infant or a lunatic, or fallen into imbecility. The law surely must look after the interest of such persons. It does not necessarily do this through officers of its own. It often devolves the trust upon some relative or connexion. But in doing so is its duty ended? Can it make over the interests of one person to the control of another, and be excused from supervision, or from holding the person thus trusted, responsible for the discharge of the trust?

There is a multitude of cases in which governments, with general approbation, assume powers and execute functions for which no reason can be assigned except the simple one, that they conduce to general convenience. We may take as an example, the function (which is a monopoly too) of coining money. This is assumed for no more recondite purpose than that of saving to individuals the trouble, delay, and expense of weighing and assaying. No one, however, even of those most jealous of state interference, has objected to this as an improper exercise of the powers of government. Prescribing a set of standard weights and measures is another instance. Paving, lighting, and cleansing the streets and thoroughfares, is another; whether done by the general government, or, as is more usual, and generally more advisable, by a municipal authority. Making or improving harbours, building lighthouses, making surveys in order to have accurate maps and charts, raising dykes to keep the sea out, and embankments to keep rivers in, are cases in point.

Examples might be indefinitely multiplied without intruding on any disputed ground. But enough has been said to show that the admitted functions of government embrace a much wider field than can easily be included within the ring fence of any restrictive definition, and that it is hardly possible to find any ground of justification common to them all, except the comprehensive one of general expediency; nor to limit the interference of government by any universal rule, save the simple and vague one that it should never be admitted but when the case of expediency is strong.

CAPITAL

by

KARL MARX

CONTENTS

Capital

KARL MARX

1818–1883

KARL MARX, the greatest thinker socialism has produced, was born in Trèves, near the Rhine River, in 1818. His father was a lawyer of Jewish origin but not of Jewish religious faith, and the son studied at the universities of Bonn and Berlin with a view, at first, to following his father's profession. In Berlin, however, he fell strongly under the influence of Hegel's philosophy, and he thought for a while of becoming a teacher of philosophy. From this thought he was swerved by the growing appeal of social and political problems and by his growing powers as a writer. In 1842 his articles in the Cologne *Rheinische Zeitung* led to the suppression of this newspaper by the Prussian Government. He married Jenny von Westphalen, daughter of a Trèves official and a woman of aristocratic background, and went with her to Paris. The French capital at that time was seething with radical social ideas and movements. Here he met Frederick Engels, son of a wealthy textile manufacturer operating in Manchester, England. Engels was destined to become his lifelong friend and collaborator. Here he also met the anarchists Pierre Joseph Proudhon and Michael Bakunin. A little later he was to write a book, *The Poverty of Philosophy,* attacking Proudhon's anarchist book, *The System of Economic Contradictions,* with its subtitle, *The Philosophy of Poverty,* and drawing a strong line of demarcation between anarchism and socialism. His immediate work was connected with the editing and publishing of a short-lived German-French yearbook.

In 1845 Marx was expelled from France at the request of the Prussian Government and went to Brussels. While living in this city he was approached by a representative of an organization known as the League of the Just. This league, a radical group composed of intellectuals and wageworkers from many countries, was holding a convention in London. It had been a conspiratorial group prior to the social upheavals of 1848, but now desired to come out into the open and publish its beliefs. It asked that Marx and Engels draw up a declaration of principles, and the result was the famous *Communist Manifesto*.

This is one of the great revolutionary documents of the world, addressed to wageworkers. It states at its outset: "The history of all hitherto existing society is the history of class struggles." It ends with the slogan: "The proletarians have nothing to lose but their chains. They have a world to win. Workingmen of all countries, unite!"

The fundamental idea of the manifesto is that of the so-called economic interpretation of history. Of this manifesto Engels wrote forty years later: "Being our joint production, I consider myself bound to state that the fundamental proposition which forms its nucleus belongs to Marx." He continued:

> That proposition is: That in every historical epoch the prevailing mode of economic production and exchange, and the social organization necessarily following from it, form the basis upon which is built up, and from which alone can be explained, the political and intellectual history of that epoch; that consequently the whole history of mankind (since the dissolution of primitive tribal society, holding land in common ownership) has been a history of class struggles, contests between exploiting and exploited, ruling and oppressed classes; that the history of these class struggles forms a development in which a stage has now been reached where the exploited and oppressed class—the proletariat—cannot attain its emancipation from the sway of the exploiting and ruling class—the bourgeoisie—without, at the same time, and once for all, emancipating society at large from all exploitation, oppression, class-distinction, and class struggles.
>
> This proposition which, in my opinion, is destined to do for history what Darwin's theory has done for biology, both of us had been gradually approaching for some years before 1845.

In 1849 Marx went to London and became absorbed in immense labors of economic and historical investigation. It was his custom to make daily visits to the British Museum reading room. The first fruit of his mental activity was a book entitled *Class Struggles in France,* dealing with the February revolution of 1848 and leading to a more complete study of the same period, *The Eighteenth Brumaire of Louis Napoleon.* By this time Marx was the father of young children, and he and his wife were enduring the rigors of extreme poverty. For a while his only regular income came from weekly letters on European affairs printed in Horace Greeley's New York *Tribune*. These letters were collected in book form more than thirty years later under the title *Revolution and Counter-Revolution in Germany*.

The League of the Just changed its name to Communist League and proved to be the forerunner of the International Workingmen's Association, organized in London in 1864, the year of a great international exhibition in Crystal Palace. Marx wrote the inaugural address and the statutes of the new association, as well as a number of economic and historical studies reflecting its attitude. One of these, *The Civil War in France,* published in 1871, deals with the Paris Commune.

During the stormy years which marked the growth and expansion of the International Workingmen's Association and which culminated in a bitter struggle for supremacy between Marx and Bakunin, Marx was at work on his magnum opus, *Capital*. A previous book, his *Contribution to the Critique of Political Economy,* published in 1859, had prepared the way for the larger work.

The first volume of *Capital,* here presented in condensed form, is subtitled *A Critique of Political Economy* and deals with "the process of capitalist production." It was first published in a German edition in 1867 and did not appear in an English translation until 1886—three years after Marx's death. The first volume is, as Engels says, in a great measure a whole in itself, and has ranked since its publication as an independent work. The second and third volumes of *Capital,* published posthumously and edited by Engels, deal respectively with "the process of capitalist circulation" and with "the process of capitalist production as a whole"; that is, of production and circulation in their interrelations. Material at first intended for a fourth volume has been issued in a separate work edited by Karl Kautsky under the title *Theories of Surplus Value.*

In its unabridged form the first volume of *Capital* is in parts an extremely difficult work. Some of the interest it evokes in a reader determined to fathom its meaning may be traced to its highly technical form. Marx often resorts to symbols and algebraic formulas. He is almost willfully obscure in certain passages, and at times he lays himself open to the charge of being prolix and repetitious. Even the Englishman William Morris, himself a leading socialist as well as a great poet and a great artist, confessed that he had suffered "agonies of confusion of the brain" in trying to understand the pure economics of *Capital*.

Marx opens *Capital* with definitions of the use-value and exchange value of commodities. He goes on to enunciate the labor theory of value and to tell what he means by "labour-power" and "surplus-value." The last-named value, he charges, is filched from the working class by the capitalist class.

Hundreds of books and articles have been written to demonstrate the "fallacies" of *Capital*. But it has its own authentic vitality. It furnished fundamental principles for great working-class movements in practically every nation of the world. Its doctrines were written into the literature of the three Internationals, which were formed to help bring socialism to the world. The epoch-making Russian Revolution, from its inception to the present day, has been inspired by Marx's teachings. The Marx-Engels Institute in Moscow is one of the shrines of Soviet Russia.

CAPITAL

PART ONE: COMMODITIES AND MONEY

I. *COMMODITIES*

1. *The Two Factors of a Commodity: Use-Value and Value (the Substance of Value and the Magnitude of Value)*

THE WEALTH of those societies in which the capitalist mode of production prevails presents itself as "an immense accumulation of commodities," its unit being a single commodity. Our investigation must therefore begin with the analysis of a commodity.

A commodity is, in the first place, an object outside us, a thing that by its properties satisfies human wants of some sort or another. The nature of such wants, whether, for instance, they spring from the stomach or from fancy, makes no difference. Neither are we here concerned to know how the object satisfies these wants, whether directly as means of subsistence, or indirectly as means of production.

Every useful thing, such as iron, paper, etc., may be looked at from the two points of view of quality and quantity. It is an assemblage of many properties, and may therefore be of use in various ways. To discover the various use of things is the work of history. So also is the establishment of socially recognised standards of measure for the quantities of these useful objects. The diversity of these measures has its origin partly in the diverse nature of the objects to be measured, partly in convention.

The utility of a thing makes it a use-value. But this utility is not a thing of air. Being limited by the physical properties of the commodity, it has no existence apart from that commodity. A commodity, such as iron, corn, or a diamond, is therefore, so far as it is a material thing, a use-value, something useful. This property of a commodity is independent of the amount of labour required to appropriate its useful qualities. When treating of use-value, we always assume to be dealing with definite quantities, such as dozens of watches, yards of linen, or tons of iron. The use-values of commodities furnish the material for a special study, that of the commercial knowledge of commodities. Use-values become a reality only by use or consumption: they also constitute the substance of all wealth, whatever may be the social form of that wealth. In the form of society we are about to consider, they are, in addition, the material depositories of exchange value.

Exchange value, at first sight, presents itself as a quantitative relation, as the proportion in which values in use of one sort are exchanged for those of another sort, a relation constantly changing with time and place. Hence exchange value appears to be something accidental and purely relative; and consequently an intrinsic value, i.e., an exchange value that is inseparably connected with, inherent in, commodities seems a contradiction in terms. Let us consider the matter a little more closely.

A given commodity, e.g., a quarter of wheat, is exchanged for x blacking, y silk, or z gold, etc.—in short, for other commodities in the most different proportions. Instead of one exchange value, the wheat has, therefore, a great many. But since x blacking, y silk, or z gold, etc., each represent the exchange value of one quarter of wheat, x blacking, y silk, z gold, etc., must as exchange values be replaceable by each other or equal to each other. Therefore, first: the valid exchange values of a given commodity express something equal; secondly, exchange value, generally, is only the mode of expression, the phenomenal form, of something contained in it, yet distinguishable from it.

Let us take two commodities, e.g., corn and iron. The proportions in which they are exchangeable, whatever those proportions may be, can always be represented by an equation in which a given quantity of corn is equated to some quantity of iron: e.g., 1 quarter corn=x cwt. iron. What does this equation tell us? It tells us that in two different things —in 1 quarter of corn and x cwt. of iron, there exists in equal quantities something common to both. The two things must therefore be equal to a third, which in itself is neither the one nor the other. Each of them, so far as it is exchange value, must therefore be reducible to this third.

A simple geometrical illustration will make this clear. In order to calculate and compare the areas of rectilinear figures, we decompose them into triangles. But the area of the triangle itself is expressed by something totally different from its visible figure, namely, by half the product of the base into the altitude. In the same way the exchange values of commodities must be capable of being expressed in terms of something common to them all, of which thing they represent a greater or less quantity.

This common "something" cannot be either a geometrical, a chemical, or any other natural property of commodities. Such properties claim our attention only in so far as they affect the utility of those commodities, make them use-values. But the exchange of commodities is evidently an act characterised by a total abstraction from use-value. Then one use-value is just as good as another, provided only it be present in sufficient quantity. Or, as old Barbon says, "one sort of wares are as good as another, if the values be equal. There is no difference or distinction in things of equal value. . . . An hundred pounds' worth of lead or iron is of as great value as one hundred pounds' worth of silver or gold." As use-values, commodities are, above all, of different qualities, but as exchange values they are merely different quantities, and consequently do not contain an atom of use-value.

If then we leave out of consideration the use-value of commodities, they have only one common property left, that of being products of labour. But even the product of labour itself has undergone a change in our hands. If we make abstraction from its use-value, we make abstraction at the same time from the material elements and shapes that make the product a use-value; we see in it no longer a table, a house, yarn, or any other useful thing. Its existence as a material thing is put out of sight. Neither can it any longer be regarded as the product of the labour of the joiner, the mason, the spinner, or of any other definite kind of productive labour. Along with the useful qualities of the products themselves, we put out of sight both the useful character of the various kinds of labour embodied in them and the concrete forms of that labour; there is nothing left but what is common to them all; all are reduced to one and the same sort of labour, human labour in the abstract.

Let us now consider the residue of each of these products; it consists of the same unsubstantial reality in each, a mere congelation of homogeneous human labour, of labour-power expended without regard to the mode of its expenditure. All that these things now tell us is that human labour-power has been expended in their production, that human labour is embodied in them. When looked at as crystals of this social substance, common to them all, they are—Values.

We have seen that when commodities are exchanged, their exchange value manifests itself as something totally independent of their use-value. But if we abstract from their use-value, there remains their Value as defined above. Therefore, the common substance that manifests itself in the exchange value of commodities, whenever they are exchanged, is their value. The progress of our investigation will show that exchange value is the only form in which the value of commodities can manifest itself or be expressed. For the present, however, we have to consider the nature of value independently of this, its form.

A use-value, or useful article, therefore, has value only because human labour in the abstract has been embodied or materialised in it. How, then, is the magnitude of this value to be measured? Plainly, by the quantity of the value-creating substance, the labour, contained in the article. The quantity of labour, however, is measured by its duration, and labour time in its turn finds its standard in weeks, days, and hours.

Some people might think that if the value of a commodity is determined by the quantity of labour spent on it, the more idle and unskilful the labourer, the more valuable would his commodity be, because more time would be required in its production. The labour, however, that forms the substance of value is homogeneous human labour, expenditure of one uniform labour-power. The total labour-power of society, which is embodied in the sum total of the values of all commodities produced by that society, counts here as one homogeneous mass of human labour-power, composed though it be of innumerable individual units. Each of these units is the same as any other, so far as it has the character of the average labour-power of society, and takes effect as such; that is, so far as it requires for producing a commodity no more time than is needed on an average, no more than is socially necessary. The labour time socially necessary is that required to produce an article under the normal conditions of production, and with the average degree of skill and intensity prevalent at the time. The introduction of power looms into England probably reduced by one half the labour required to weave a given quantity of yarn into cloth. The hand-loom weavers, as a matter of fact, continued to require the same time as before; but for all that, the product of one hour of their labour represented after the change only half an hour's social labour, and consequently fell to one-half its former value.

We see then that that which determines the magnitude of the value of any article is the amount of labour socially necessary, or the labour time socially necessary for its production.

The value of a commodity would therefore remain constant, if the labour time required for its production also remained constant. But the latter changes with every variation in the productiveness of labour. This productiveness is determined by various circumstances, amongst others, by the average amount of skill of the workmen, the state of science, and the degree of its practical application, the social organisation of production, the extent and capabilities of the means of production, and by physical conditions. For example, the same amount of labour in favourable seasons is embodied in 8 bushels of corn, and in unfavourable, only in 4. The same labour extracts from rich mines more metal than from poor mines. Diamonds are of very rare occurrence on the earth's surface, and hence their discovery costs, on an average, a great deal of labour time. Consequently much labour is represented in a small compass. Jacob doubts whether gold has ever been paid for at its full value. This applies still more to diamonds. According to Eschwege, the total produce of the Brazilian diamond mines for the eighty years, ending in 1823, had not realized the price of one and a half year's average produce of the sugar and coffee plantations of the same country, although the diamonds cost much more labour, and therefore represented more value. With richer mines, the same quantity of labour would embody itself in more diamonds and their value would fall. If we could succeed at a small expenditure of labour in converting carbon into diamonds, their value might fall below that of bricks. In general, the greater the productiveness of labour, the less is the labour time required for the production of an article, the less is the amount of labour crystallised in that article, and the less is its value; and vice versa, the less the productiveness of labour, the greater is the labour time required for the production of an article, and the greater is its value. The value of a commodity, therefore, varies directly as the quantity, and inversely as the productiveness, of the labour incorporated in it.

A thing can be a use-value without having value. This is the case whenever its utility to man is not due to labour. Such are air, virgin soil, natural meadows, etc. A thing can be useful, and the product of human labour, without being a commodity. Whoever directly satisfies his wants with the produce of his own labour, creates, indeed, use-values, but not commodities. In order to produce the latter, he must not only produce use-values, but use-values for others, social use-values. Lastly, nothing can have value, without being an object of utility. If the thing is useless, so is the labour contained in it; the labour does not count as labour, and therefore creates no value.

2. *The Twofold Character of the Labour Embodied in Commodities*

At first sight a commodity presented itself to us as a complex of two things—use-value and exchange value. Later on, we saw also that labour, too, possesses the same twofold nature; for, so far as it finds expression in value, it does not possess the same characteristics that belong to it as a creator of use-values. I was the first to point out and to examine critically this twofold nature of the labour contained in commodities. As this point is the pivot on which a clear comprehension of political economy turns, we must go more into detail.

Let us take two commodities such as a coat and 10 yards of linen, and let the former be double the value of the latter, so that, if 10 yards of linen=W, the coat=2W.

The coat is a use-value that satisfies a particular want. Its existence is the result of a special sort of productive activity, the nature of which is determined by its aim, mode of operation, subject, means, and result.

The labour whose utility is thus represented by the value in use of its product, or which manifests itself by making its product a use-value, we call useful labour. In this connection we consider only its useful effect.

As the coat and the linen are two qualitatively different use-values, so also are the two forms of labour that produce them, tailoring and weaving. Were these two objects not qualitatively different, not produced respectively by labour of different quality, they could not stand to each other in the relation of commodities.

The use-values, coat, linen, etc., i.e., the bodies of commodities, are combinations of two elements—matter and labour. If we take away the useful labour expended upon them, a material substratum is always left, which is furnished by Nature without the help of man. The latter can work only as Nature does, that is by changing the form of matter. Nay more, in this work of changing the form he is constantly helped by natural forces. We see, then, that labour is not the only source of material wealth, of use-values produced by labour. As William Petty puts it, labour is its father and the earth its mother.

Let us now pass from the commodity considered as a use-value to the value of commodities.

By our assumption, the coat is worth twice as much as the linen. But this is a mere quantitative difference, which for the present does not concern us. We bear in mind, however, that if the value of the coat is double that of 10 yards of linen, 20 yards of linen must have the same value as one coat. So far as they are values, the coat and the linen are things of a like substance, objective expressions of essentially identical labour. But tailoring and weaving are, qualitatively, different kinds of labour. There are, however, states of society in which one and the same man does tailoring and weaving alternately, in which case these two forms of labour are mere modifications of the labour of the same individual, and not special and fixed functions of different persons; just as the coat which our tailor makes one day, and the trousers which he makes another day, imply only a variation in the labour of one and the same individual. Moreover, we see at a glance that, in our capitalist society, a given portion of human labour is, in accordance with the varying demand, at one time supplied in the form of tailoring, at another in the form of weaving. This change may possibly not take place without friction, but take place it must.

Productive activity, if we leave out of sight its special form, viz., the useful character of the labour, is nothing but the expenditure of human labour-power. Tailoring and weaving, though qualitatively different productive activities, are each a productive expenditure of human brains, nerves, and muscles, and in this sense are human labour. They are but two different modes of expending human labour-power. Of course this labour-power, which remains the same under all its modifications, must have attained a certain pitch of development before it can be expended in a multiplicity of modes. But the value of a commodity represents human labour in the abstract, the expenditure of human labour in general. And just as in society a general or a banker plays a great part, but mere man, on the other hand, a very shabby part, so here with mere human labour. It is the expenditure of simple labour-power, i.e., of the labour-power which, on an average, apart from any special development, exists in the organism of every ordinary individual. Simple average labour, it is true, varies in character in different countries and at different times, but in a particular society it is given. Skilled labour counts only as simple labour intensified, or rather, as multipled simple labour, a given quantity of skilled being considered equal to a greater quantity of simple labour. Experience shows that this reduction is constantly being made. A commodity may be the product of the most skilled labour, but its value, by equating it to the product of simple unskilled labour, represents a definite quantity of the latter labour alone. The different proportions in which different sorts of labour are reduced to unskilled labour as their standard are established by a social process that goes on behind the backs of the producers and, consequently, appear to be fixed by custom. For simplicity's sake we shall henceforth account every kind of labour to be unskilled, simple labour; by this we do no more than save ourselves the trouble of making the reduction.

3. The Form of Value or Exchange Value

Commodities come into the world in the shape of use-values, articles, or goods, such as iron, linen, corn, etc. This is their plain, homely, bodily form. They are, however, commodities, only because they are something twofold, both objects of utility and, at the same time, depositories of value. They manifest themselves therefore as commodities, or have the form of commodities, only in so far as they have two forms, a physical or natural form, and a value form.

The reality of the value of commodities differs in this respect from Dame Quickly, that we don't know "where to have it." The value of commodities is the very opposite of the coarse materiality of their substance, not an atom of matter enters into its composition. Turn and examine a single commodity, by itself, as we will. Yet in so far as it remains an object of value, it seems impossible to grasp it. If, however, we bear in mind that the value of commodities has a purely social reality, and that they acquire this reality only in so far as they are expressions or embodiments of one identical social substance, viz., human labour, it follows as a matter of course that value can only manifest itself in the social relation of commodity to commodity. In fact we started from exchange value, or the exchange relation of commodities, in order to get at the value that lies hidden behind it. We must now return to this form under which value first appeared to us.

Everyone knows, if he knows nothing else, that commodities have a value form common to them all, and presenting a marked contrast with the varied bodily forms of their use-values. I mean their money form.

4. *The Fetishism of Commodities and the Secret Thereof*

A commodity appears, at first sight, a very trivial thing, and easily understood. Its analysis shows that it is, in reality, a very queer thing, abounding in metaphysical subtleties and theological niceties. So far as it is a value in use, there is nothing mysterious about it, whether we consider it from the point of view that by its properties it is capable of satisfying human wants, or from the point that those properties are the product of human labour. It is as clear as noonday that man, by his industry, changes the forms of the materials furnished by Nature in such a way as to make them useful to him. The form of wood, for instance, is altered, by making a table out of it. Yet for all that the table continues to be that common, everyday thing, wood. But so soon as it steps forth as a commodity, it is changed into something transcendent. It not only stands with its feet on the ground, but, in relation to all other commodities, it stands on its head, and evolves out of its wooden brain grotesque ideas, far more wonderful than "table-turning" ever was.

The mystical character of commodities does not originate, therefore, in their use-value. Just as little does it proceed from the nature of the determining factors of value.

Whence, then, arises the enigmatical character of the product of labour, so soon as it assumes the form of commodities? Clearly from this form itself. The equality of all sorts of human labour is expressed objectively by their products all being equally values; the measure of the expenditure of labour-power, by the duration of that expenditure, takes the form of the quantity of value of the products of labour; and finally, the mutual relations of the producers, within which the social character of their labour affirms itself, take the form of a social relation between the products.

A commodity is therefore a mysterious thing, simply because in it the social character of men's labour appears to them as an objective character stamped upon the product of that labour; because the relation of the producers to the sum total of their own labour is presented to them as a social relation, existing not between themselves, but between the products of their labour. This is the reason why the products of labour become commodities, social things whose qualities are at the same time perceptible and imperceptible by the senses. In the same way the light from an object is perceived by us not as the subjective excitation of our optic nerve, but as the objective form of something outside the eye itself. But, in the act of seeing, there is at all events an actual passage of light from one thing to another, from the external object to the eye. There is a physical relation between physical things. But it is different with commodities. There the existence of the things *qua* commodities, and the value relation between the products of labour which stamps them as commodities, have absolutely no connection with their physical properties and with the material relations arising therefrom. There it is a definite social relation between men that assumes, in their eyes, the fantastic form of a relation between things. In order, therefore, to find an analogy, we must have recourse to the mist-enveloped regions of the religious world. In that world the productions of the human brain appear as independent beings endowed with life, and entering into relation both with one another and the human race. So it is in the world of commodities with the products of men's hands. This I call the Fetishism which attaches itself to the products of labour, so soon as they are produced as commodities, and which is therefore inseparable from the production of commodities.

This Fetishism of commodities has its origin, as the foregoing analysis has already shown, in the peculiar social character of the labour that produces them.

As a general rule, articles of utility become commodities only because they are products of the labour of private individuals or groups of individuals who carry on their work independently of each other. The sum total of the labour of all these private individuals forms the aggregate labour of society. Since the producers do not come into social contact with each other until they exchange their products, the specific social character of each producer's labour does not show itself except in the act of exchange. In other words, the labour of the individual asserts itself as a part of the labour of society only by means of the relations which the act of exchange establishes directly between the products and indirectly, through them, between the producers. To the latter, therefore, the relations connecting the labour of one individual with that of the rest appear, not as direct social relations between individuals at work, but as what they really are, material relations between persons and social relations between things. It is only by being exchanged that the products of labour acquire, as values, one uniform social status, distinct from their varied forms of existence as objects of utility. This division of a product into a useful thing and a value becomes practically important only when exchange has acquired such an extension that useful articles are produced for the purpose of being exchanged, and their character as values has therefore to be taken into account, beforehand, during production. From this moment the labour of the individual producer acquires socially a twofold character. On the one hand, it must, as a definite useful kind of labour, satisfy a definite social want, and thus hold its place as part and parcel of the collective labour of all, as a branch of a social division of labour that has sprung up spontaneously. On the other hand, it can satisfy the manifold wants of the individual producer himself only in so far as the mutual exchangeability of all kinds of useful private labour is an established social fact, and therefore the private useful labour of each producer ranks on an equality with that of all others. The equalization of the most different kinds of labour can be the result only of an abstraction from their inequalities, or of reducing them to their common denominator, viz., expenditure of human labour-power or human labour in the abstract. The twofold social character of the labour of the individual appears to him, when reflected in his brain, only under those forms which are impressed upon that labour in everyday practice by the exchange of products. In this way the character that his own labour possesses of being socially useful takes the form of the condition that the product must be not only useful, but useful for others; and the social character that his particular labour has of being the equal of all other particular kinds of labour takes the form that all the physically different articles that are the products of labour, have one common quality, viz., that of having value.

Hence, when we bring the products of our labour into relation with each other as values, it is not because we see in these articles the material receptacles of homogeneous human labour. Quite the contrary; whenever, by an exchange, we equate as values our different products, by that very act we also equate, as human labour, the different kinds of labour expended upon them. We are not aware of this, nevertheless we do it. Value, therefore, does not stalk about with a label describing what it is. It is value, rather, that converts every product into a social hieroglyphic. Later on, we try to decipher the hieroglyphic, to get behind the secret of our own social products; for to stamp an object of utility as a value is just as much a social product as language. The recent scientific discovery that the products of labour, so far as they are values, are but material expressions of the human labour spent in their production, marks, indeed, an epoch in the history of the development of the human race, but, by no means, dissipates the mist through which the social character of labour appears to us to be an objective character of the products themselves. The fact that in the particular form of production with which we are dealing, viz., the production of commodities, the specific social character of private labour carried on independently consists in the equality of every kind of that labour, by virtue of its being human labour, which character, therefore, assumes in the product the form of value—this fact appears to the producers, notwithstanding the discovery above referred to, to be just as real and final as the fact that, after the discovery by science of the component gases of air, the atmosphere itself remained unaltered.

Man's reflections on the forms of social life, and consequently also his scientific analysis of those forms, take a course directly opposite to that of their actual historical development. He begins, *post festum,* with the results of the process of development ready to hand before him. The characters that stamp products as commodities, and whose establishment is a necessary preliminary to the circulation of commodities, have already acquired the stability of natural, self-understood forms of social life, before man seeks to decipher, not their historical character, for in his eyes they are immutable, but their meaning. Consequently it was the analysis of the prices of commodities that alone led to the determination of the magnitude of value, and it was the common expression of all commodities in money that alone led to the establishment of their characters as values. It is, however, just this ultimate money form of the world of commodities that actually conceals, instead of disclosing, the social character of private labour, and the social relations between the individual producers. When I state that coats or boots stand in a relation to linen, because it is the universal incarnation of abstract human labour, the absurdity of the statement is self-evident. Nevertheless, when the producers of coats and boots compare those articles with linen or, what is the same thing, with gold or silver, as the universal equivalent, they express the relation between their own private labour and the collective labour of society in the same absurd form.

The categories of bourgeois economy consist of such like forms. They are forms of thought expressing with social validity the conditions and relations of a definite, historically determined mode of production, viz., the production of commodities. The whole mystery of commodities, all the magic and necromancy that surround the products of labour as long as they take the form of commodities, vanishes, therefore, so soon as we come to other forms of production.

Since Robinson Crusoe's experiences are a favorite theme with political economists, let us take a look at him on his island. Moderate though he be, yet some few wants he has to satisfy, and must therefore do a little useful work of various sorts, such as making tools and furniture, taming goats, fishing and hunting. Of his prayers and the like we take no account, since they are a source of pleasure to him, and he looks upon them as so much recreation. In spite of the variety of his work, he knows that his labour, whatever its form, is but the activity of one and the same Robinson, and consequently that it consists of nothing but different modes of human labour. Necessity itself compels him to apportion his time accurately between his different kinds of work. Whether one kind occupies a greater space in his general activity than another depends on the difficulties, greater or less as the case may be, to be overcome in attaining the useful effect aimed at. This our friend Robinson soon learns by experience, and having rescued a watch, ledger, and pen and ink from the wreck, commences, like a true-born Briton, to keep a set of books. His stock-book contains a list of the objects of utility that belong to him, of the operations necessary for their production; and lastly, of the labour time that definite quantities of those objects have, on an average, cost him. All the relations between Robinson and the objects that form this wealth of his own creation are here so simple and clear. And yet those relations contain all that is essential to the determination of value.

Let us now transport ourselves from Robinson's island bathed in light to the European Middle Ages shrouded in darkness. Here, instead of the independent man, we find everyone dependent, serfs and lords, vassals and suzerains, laymen and clergy. Personal dependence here characterises the social relations of production just as much as it does the other spheres of life organized on the basis of that production. But for the very reason that personal dependence forms the groundwork of society, there is no necessity for labour and its products to assume a fantastic form different from their reality. They take the shape, in the transactions of society, of services in kind and payments in kind. Here the particular and natural form of labour, and not, as in a society based on production of commodities, its general abstract form, is the immediate social form of labour. Compulsory labour is just as properly measured by time as commodity-producing labour; but every serf knows that what he expends in the service of his lord is a definite quantity of his own personal labour-power. The tithe to be rendered to the priest is more matter of fact than his blessing. No matter, then, what we may think of the parts played by the different classes of people themselves in this society, the social relations between individuals in the performance of their labour appear at all events as their own mutual personal relations, and are not disguised under the shape of social relations between the products of labour.

For an example of labour in common or directly associated labour, we have no occasion to go back to that spontaneously developed form which we find on the threshold of the history of all civilized races. We have one close at hand in the patriarchal industries of a peasant family that produces corn, cattle, yarn, linen, and clothing for home use. These different articles are, as regards the family, so many products of its labour, but as between themselves they are not commodities. The different kinds of labour, such as tillage, cattle tending, spinning, weaving and making clothes, which result in the various products, are in themselves, and such as they are, direct social functions, because functions of the family, which, just as much as a society based on the production of commodities, possesses a spontaneously developed system of division of labour. The distribution of the work within the family and the regulation of the labour time of the several members depend as well upon differences of age and sex as upon natural conditions varying with the seasons. The labour-power of each individual, by its very nature, operates in this case merely as a definite portion of the whole labour-power of the family, and therefore the measure of the expenditure of individual labour-power by its duration appears here by its very nature as a social character of their labour.

Let us now picture to ourselves, by way of change, a community of free individuals, carrying on their work with the means of production in common, in which the labour-power of all the different individuals is consciously applied as the combined labour-power of the community. All the characteristics of Robinson's labour are here repeated, but with this difference, that they are social, instead of individual. Everything produced by him was exclusively the result of his own personal labour, and therefore simply an object of use for himself. The total product of our community is a social product. One portion serves as fresh means of production and remains social. But another portion is consumed by the members as means of subsistence. A distribution of this portion amongst them is consequently necessary. The mode of this distribution will vary with the productive organization of the community, and the degree of historical development attained by the producers. We will assume, but merely for the sake of a parallel with the production of commodities, that the share of each individual producer in the means of subsistence is determined by his labour time. Labour time would, in that case, play a double part. Its apportionment in accordance with a definite social plan maintains the proper proportion between the different kinds of work to be done and the various wants of the community. On the other hand, it also serves as a measure of the portion of the common labour borne by each individual and of his share in the part of the total product destined for individual consumption. The social relations of the individual producers, with regard both to their labour and to its products, are in this case perfectly simple and intelligible, and that with regard not only to production but also to distribution.

The religious world is but the reflex of the real world. And for a society based upon the production of commodities, in which the producers in general enter into social relations with one another by treating their products as commodities and values, whereby they reduce their individual private labour to the standard of homogeneous human labour—for such a society, Christianity with its *cultus* of abstract man, more especially in its bourgeois developments, Protestantism, Deism, etc., is the most fitting form of religion. In the ancient Asiatic and other ancient modes of production, we find that the conversion of products into commodities, and therefore the conversion of men into producers of commodities, holds a subordinate place, which, however, increases in importance as the primitive communities approach nearer and nearer to their dissolution. Trading nations, properly so called, exist in the ancient world only in its interstices, like the gods of Epicurus in the Intermundia, or like Jews in the pores of Polish society. Those ancient social organisms of production are, as compared with bourgeois society, extremely simple and transparent. But they are founded either on the immature development of man individually, who has not yet severed the umbilical cord that unites him with his fellow men in a primitive tribal community, or upon direct relations of subjection. They can arise and exist only when the development of the productive power of labour has not risen beyond a low stage, and when, therefore, the social relations within the sphere of material life, between man and man, and between man and Nature, are correspondingly narrow. This narrowness is reflected in the ancient worship of Nature and in the other elements of the popular religions. The religious reflex of the real world can, in any case, only then finally vanish, when the practical relations of everyday life offer to man none but perfectly intelligible and reasonable relations with regard to his fellow men and to Nature.

The life-process of society, which is based on the process of material production, does not strip off its mystical veil until it is treated as production by freely associated men, and is consciously regulated by them in accordance with a settled plan. This, however, demands for society a certain material groundwork, or set of conditions of existence, which in their turn are the spontaneous product of a long and painful process of development.

Political economy has indeed analysed, however incompletely, value and its magnitude, and has discovered what lies beneath these forms. But it has never once asked the question why labour is represented by the value of its product and labour time by the magnitude of that value. These formulæ, which bear stamped upon them in unmistakable letters that they belong to a state of society in which the process of production has the mastery over man, instead of being controlled by him, such formulæ appear to the bourgeois intellect to be as much a self-evident necessity imposed by Nature as productive labour itself. Hence forms of social production that preceded the bourgeois form are treated by the bourgeoisie in much the same way as the Fathers of the Church treated pre-Christian religions.

To what extent some economists are misled by the Fetishism inherent in commodities, or by the objective appearance of the social characteristics of labour, is shown, amongst other ways, by the dull and tedious quarrel over the part played by Nature in the formation of exchange value. Since exchange value is a definite social manner of expressing the amount of labour bestowed upon an object, Nature has no more to do with it than it has in fixing the course of exchange.

The mode of production in which the product takes the form of a commodity, or is produced directly for exchange, is the most general and most embryonic form of bourgeois production. It therefore makes its appearance at an early date in history, though not in the same predominating and characteristic manner as nowadays. Hence its Fetish character is comparatively easy to be seen through. But when we come to more concrete forms, even this appearance of simplicity vanishes. Whence arose the illusions of the monetary system? To it gold and silver, when serving as money, did not represent a social relation between producers, but were natural objects with strange social properties. And modern economy, which looks down with such disdain on the monetary system, does not its superstition come out as clear as noonday, whenever it treats of capital? How long is it since economy discarded the physiocratic illusion that rents grow out of the soil and not out of society?

But not to anticipate, we will content ourselves with yet another example relating to the commodity form. Could commodities themselves speak, they would say: Our use-value may be a thing that interests men. It is no part of us as objects. What, however, does belong to us as objects is our value. Our natural intercourse as commodities proves it. In the eyes of each other we are nothing but exchange values. Now listen how those commodities speak through the mouth of the economist. "Value" (i.e., exchange value) "is a property of things, riches" (i.e., use-value) "of man. Value, in this sense, necessarily implies exchanges, riches do not." "Riches" (use-value) "are the attribute of men, value is the attribute of commodities. A man or a community is rich, a pearl or a diamond is valuable." "A pearl or a diamond is valuable" as a pearl or diamond. So far no chemist has ever discovered exchange value either in a pearl or a diamond. The economical discoverers of this chemical element, who by the bye lay special claim to critical acumen, find however that the use-value of objects belongs to them independently of their material properties, while their value, on the other hand, forms a part of them as objects. What confirms them in this view is the peculiar circumstances that the use-value of objects is realised without exchange, by means of a direct relation between the objects and man, while, on the other hand, their value is realised only by exchange, that is, by means of a social process. Who fails here to call to mind our good friend, Dogberry, who informs neighbour Seacoal, that, "To be a well-favoured man is the gift of fortune; but reading and writing comes by nature."

II. EXCHANGE

It is plain that commodities cannot go to market and make exchanges of their own account. We must, therefore, have recourse to their guardians, who are also their owners. Commodities are things, and therefore without power of resistance against man. If they are wanting in docility he can use force; in other words, he can take possession of them. In order that these objects may enter into relation with each other as commodities, their guardians must place themselves in relation to one another, as persons whose will resides in those objects, and must behave in such a way that each does not appropriate the commodity of the other, and part with his own, except by means of an act done by mutual consent. They must, therefore, mutually recognise in each other the right of private proprietors. This juridical relation, which thus expresses itself in a contract, whether such contract be part of a developed legal system or not, is a relation between two wills, and is but the reflex of the real economical relation between the two. It is this economical relation that determines the subject matter comprised in each such juridical act. The persons exist for one another merely as representatives of, and, therefore, as owners of, commodities. In the course of our investigation we shall find, in general, that the characters who appear on the economic stage are but the personifications of the economical relations that exist between them.

What chiefly distinguishes a commodity from its owner is the fact that it looks upon every other commodity as but the form of appearance of its own value. A born leveller and a cynic, it is always ready to exchange not only soul, but body, with any and every other commodity, be the same more repulsive than Maritornes herself. The owner makes up for this lack in the commodity of a sense of the concrete by his own five and more senses. His commodity possesses for himself no immediate use-value. Otherwise, he would not bring it to the market. It has use-value for others; but for himself its only direct use-value is that of being a depository of exchange value, and consequently, a means of exchange. Therefore, he makes up his mind to part with it for commodities whose value in use is of service to him. All commodities are non-use-values for their owners, and use-values for their non-owners. Consequently, they must all change hands. But this change of hands is what constitutes their exchange, and the latter puts them in relation with each other as values and realises them as values. Hence commodities must be realised as values before they can be realised as use-values.

On the other hand, they must show that they are use-values before they can be realised as values. For the labour spent upon them counts effectively, only in so far as it is spent in a form that is useful for others. Whether that labour is useful for others and its product consequently capable of satisfying the wants of others can be proved only by the act of exchange.

Every owner of a commodity wishes to part with it in exchange only for those commodities whose use-value satisfies some want of his. Looked at in this way, exchange is for him simply a private transaction. On the other hand, he desires to realise the value of his commodity, to convert it into any other suitable commodity of equal value, irrespective of whether his own commodity has or has not any use-value for the owner of the other. From this point of view, exchange is for him a social transaction of a general character. But one and the same set of transactions cannot be simultaneously for all owners of commodities both exclusively private and exclusively social and general.

Let us look at the matter a little closer. To the owner of a commodity, every other commodity is, in regard to his own, a particular equivalent, and consequently his own commodity is the universal equivalent for all the others. But since this applies to every owner, there is, in fact, no commodity acting as universal equivalent, and the relative value of commodities possesses no general form under which they can be equated as values and have the magnitude of their values compared. So far, therefore, they do not confront each other as commodities, but only as products or use-values. In their difficulties our commodity owners think like Faust: "*Im Anfang war die That.*" They therefore acted and transacted before they thought. Instinctively they conform to the laws imposed by the nature of commodities. They cannot bring their commodities into relation as values, and therefore as commodities, except by comparing them with some one other commodity as the universal equivalent. That we saw from the analysis of a commodity. But a particular commodity cannot become the universal equivalent except by a social act. The social action therefore of all other commodities sets apart the particular commodity in which they all represent their values. Thereby the bodily form of this commodity becomes the form of the socially recognised universal equivalent. To be the universal equivalent becomes, by this social process, the specific function of the commodity thus excluded by the rest. Thus it becomes—money.

III. MONEY, OR THE CIRCULATION OF COMMODITIES

1. The Measure of Values

THROUGHOUT this work, I assume, for the sake of simplicity, gold as the money commodity.

The first chief function of money is to supply commodities with the material for the expression of their values, or to represent their values as magnitudes of the same denomination, qualitatively equal and quantitatively comparable. It thus serves as a *universal measure of value.* And only by virtue of this function does gold, the equivalent commodity *par excellence,* become money.

It is not money that renders commodities commensurable. Just the contrary. It is because all commodities, as values, are realised human labour, and therefore commensurable, that their values can be measured by one and the same special commodity, and the latter be converted into the common measure of their values, i.e., into money. Money as a measure of value is the phenomenal form that must of necessity be assumed by that measure of value which is immanent in commodities, labour time.

As *measure of value* and as *standard of price* money has two entirely distinct functions to perform. It is the measure of value inasmuch as it is the socially recognised incarnation of human labour; it is the standard of price inasmuch as it is a fixed weight of metal. As the measure of value it serves to convert the values of all the manifold commodities into prices, into imaginary quantities of gold; as the standard of price it measures those quantities of gold. The measure of values measures commodities considered as values; the standard of price measures, on the contrary, quantities of gold by a unit quantity of gold, not the value of one quantity of gold by the weight of another. In order to make gold a standard of price, a certain weight must be fixed upon as the unit. In this case, as in all cases of measuring quantities of the same denomination, the establishment of an unvarying unit of measure is all-important. Hence, the less the unit is subject to variation, so much the better does the standard of price fulfill its office.

Price is the money name of the labour realised in a commodity. Hence the expression of the equivalence of a commodity with the sum of money constituting its price is a tautology, just as in general the expression of the relative value of a commodity is a statement of the equivalence of two commodities. But although price, being the exponent of the magnitude of a commodity's value, is the exponent of its exchange ratio with money, it does not follow that the exponent of this exchange ratio is necessarily the exponent of the magnitude of the commodity's value. Suppose two equal quantities of socially necessary labour to be respectively represented by 1 quarter of wheat and £2 (nearly ½ oz. of gold), £2 is the expression in money of the magnitude of the value of the quarter of wheat, or is its price. If now circumstances allow of this price being raised to £3, or compel it to be reduced to £1, then although £1 and £3 may be too small or too great properly to express the magnitude of the wheat's value, nevertheless they are its prices, for they are, in the first place, the form under which its value appears, i.e., money; and in the second place, the exponents of its exchange ratio with money. If the conditions of production, in other words, if the productive power of labour remain constant, the same amount of social labour time must, both before and after the change in price, be expended in the reproduction of a quarter of wheat. This circumstance depends neither on the will of the wheat producer nor on that of the owners of other commodities.

Magnitude of value expresses a relation of social production, it expresses the connection that necessarily exists between a certain article and the portion of the total labour time of society required to produce it. As soon as magnitude of value is converted into price, the above necessary relation takes the shape of a more or less accidental exchange ratio between a single commodity and another, the money commodity. But this exchange ratio may express either the real magnitude of that commodity's value or the quantity of gold deviating from that value, for which, according to circumstances, it may be parted with. The possibility, therefore, of quantitative incongruity between price and magnitude of value, or the deviation of the former from the latter, is inherent in the price form itself. This is no defect, but, on the contrary, admirably adapts the price form to a mode of production whose inherent laws impose themselves only as the mean of apparently lawless irregularities that compensate one another.

The price form, however, is not only compatible with the possibility of a quantitative incongruity between magnitude of value and price, i.e., between the former and its expression in money, but it may also conceal a qualitative inconsistency, so much so, that, although money is nothing but the value form of commodities, price ceases altogether to express value. Objects that in themselves are no commodities, such as conscience, honour, etc., are capable of being offered for sale by their holders, and of thus acquiring, through their price, the form of commodities. Hence an object may have a price without having value. The price in that case is imaginary, like certain quantities in mathematics. On the other hand, the imaginary price-form may sometimes conceal either a direct or indirect real value-relation; for instance, the price of uncultivated land, which is without value, because no human labour has been incorporated in it.

Price, like relative value in general, expresses the value of a commodity (e.g., a ton of iron), by stating that a given quantity of the equivalent (e.g., an ounce of gold), is directly exchangeable for iron. But it by no means states the converse, that iron is directly exchangeable for gold. In order, therefore, that a commodity may in practice act effectively as exchange value, it must quit its bodily shape, must transform itself from mere imaginary into real gold, although to the commodity such transubstantiation may be more difficult than to the Hegelian "concept," the transition from "necessity" to "freedom," or to a lobster the casting of his shell, or to St. Jerome the putting off of the old Adam. Though a commodity may, side by side with its actual form (iron, for instance), take in our imagination the form of gold, yet it cannot at one and the same time actually be both iron and gold. To fix its price, it suffices to equate it to gold in imagination. But to enable it to render to its owner the service of a universal equivalent, it must be actually replaced by gold. If the owner of the iron were to go to the owner of some other commodity offered for exchange, and were to refer him to the price of the iron as proof that it was already money, he would get the same answer as St. Peter gave in heaven to Dante, when the latter recited the creed—

Assai bene è trascorsa
D'esta moneta già la lega e'l peso,
Ma dimmi se tu l'hai nella tua borsa.

A price therefore implies both that a commodity is exchangeable for money, and also that it must be so exchanged. On the other hand, gold serves as an ideal measure of value, only because it has already, in the process of exchange, established itself as the money commodity. Under the ideal measure of values there lurks the hard cash.

2. *The Medium of Circulation*

A. THE METAMORPHOSIS OF COMMODITIES

We saw in a former chapter that the exchange of commodities implies contradictory and mutually exclusive conditions. The differentiation of commodities into commodities and money does not sweep away these inconsistencies, but develops a *modus vivendi,* a form in which they can exist side by side. This is generally the way in which real contradictions are reconciled. For instance, it is a contradiction to depict one body as constantly falling towards another, and as, at the same time, constantly flying away from it. The ellipse is a form of motion which, while allowing this contradiction to go on, at the same time reconciles it.

In so far as exchange is a process by which commodities are transferred from hands in which they are non-use-values, to hands in which they become use-values, it is a social circulation of matter. The product of one form of useful labour replaces that of another. When once a commodity has found a resting place, where it can serve as a use-value, it falls out of the sphere of exchange into that of consumption. But the former sphere alone interests us at present. We have, therefore, now to consider exchange from a formal point of view; to investigate the change of form, or metamorphosis, of commodities which effectuates the social circulation of matter.

The comprehension of this change of form is, as a rule, very imperfect. The cause of this imperfection is, apart from indistinct notions of value itself, that every change of form in a commodity results from the exchange of two commodities, an ordinary one and the money commodity. If we keep in view the material fact alone that a commodity has been exchanged for gold we overlook the very thing that we ought to observe—namely, what has happened to the form of the commodity. We overlook the facts that gold, when a mere commodity, is not money, and that when other commodities express their prices in gold, this gold is but the money form of those commodities themselves.

Commodities, first of all, enter into the process of exchange just as they are. The process then differentiates them into commodities and money, and thus produces an external opposition corresponding to the internal opposition inherent in them, as being at once use-values and values. Commodities as use-values now stand opposed to money as exchange value. On the other hand, both opposing sides are commodities, unities of use-value and value. But this unity of differences manifests itself at two opposite poles, and at each pole in an opposite way. Being poles, they are as necessarily opposite as they are connected. On the one side of the equation we have an ordinary commodity, which is in reality a use-value. Its value is expressed only ideally in its price, by which it is equated to its opponent, the gold, as to the real embodiment of its value. On the other hand, the gold in its metallic reality ranks as the embodiment of value, as money. Gold, as gold, is exchange value itself. As to its use-value, that has only an ideal existence, represented by the series of expressions of relative value in which it stands face to face with all other commodities, the sum of whose uses makes up the sum of the various uses of gold. These antagonistic forms of commodities are the real forms in which the process of their exchange moves and takes place.

Let us now accompany the owner of some commodity—say, our old friend the weaver of linen—to the scene of action, the market. His 20 yards of linen has a definite price, £2. He exchanges it for the £2, and then, like a man of the good old stamp that he is, he parts with the £2 for a family Bible of the same price. The linen, which in his eyes is a mere commodity, a depository of value, he alienates in exchange for gold, which is the linen's value form, and this form he again parts with for another commodity, the Bible, which is destined to enter his house as an object of utility and of edification to its inmates. The exchange becomes an accomplished fact by two metamorphoses of opposite yet supplementary character—the conversion of the commodity into money, and the reconversion of the money into a commodity. The two phases of this metamorphosis are both of them distinct transactions of the weaver—selling, or the exchange of the commodity for money; buying, or the exchange of the money for a commodity; and the unity of the two acts, selling in order to buy.

The result of the whole transaction, as regards the weaver, is this, that instead of being in possession of the linen, he now has the Bible; instead of his original commodity, he now possesses another of the same value but of different utility. In like manner he procures his other means of subsistence and means of production. From his point of view, the whole process effectuates nothing more than the exchange of the product of his labour for the product of someone else's, nothing more than an exchange of products.

The exchange of commodities is therefore accompanied by the following changes in their form:

Commodity—Money—Commodity
C——M——C

The result of the whole process is, so far as concerns the objects themselves, C—C, the exchange of one commodity for another, the circulation of materialised social labour. When this result is attained, the process is at an end.

C—M. First Metamorphosis, or Sale.

The leap taken by value from the body of the commodity, into the body of the gold, is, as I have elsewhere called it, the *salto mortale* of the commodity. If it falls short, then, although the commodity itself is not harmed, its owner decidedly is. The social division of labour causes his labour to be as one-sided as his wants are many-sided. This is precisely the reason why the product of his labour serves him solely as exchange value. But it cannot acquire the properties of a socially recognised universal equivalent, except by being converted into money. That money, however, is in someone else's pocket. In order to entice the money out of that pocket, our friend's commodity must, above all things, be a use-value to the owner of the money. For this, it is necessary that the labour expended upon it be of a kind that is socially useful, of a kind that constitutes a branch of the social division of labour. But division of labour is a system of production which has grown up spontaneously and continues to grow behind the backs of the producers. The commodity to be exchanged may possibly be the product of some new kind of labour that pretends to satisfy newly arisen requirements, or even to give rise itself to new requirements. A particular operation, though yesterday, perhaps, forming one out of the many operations conducted by one producer in creating a given commodity, may today separate itself from this connection, may establish itself as an independent branch of labour and send its incomplete product to market as an independent commodity. The circumstances may or may not be ripe for such a separation. Today the product satisfies a social want. Tomorrow the article may, either altogether or partially, be superseded by some other appropriate product. Moreover, although our weaver's labour may be a recognised branch of the social division of labour, yet that fact is by no means sufficient to guarantee the utility of his 20 yards of linen. If the community's want of linen, and such a want has a limit like every other want, should already be saturated by the products of rival weavers, our friend's product is superfluous, redundant, and consequently useless. Although people do not look a gift horse in the mouth, our friend does not frequent the market for the purpose of making presents. But suppose his product turn out a real use-value, and thereby attracts money? The question arises, how much will it attract? No doubt the answer is already anticipated in the price of the article, in the exponent of the magnitude of its value. We leave out of consideration here any accidental miscalculation of value by our friend, a mistake that is soon rectified in the market. We suppose him to have spent on his product only that amount of labour time that is on an average socially necessary. The price, then, is merely the money name of the quantity of social labour realised in his commodity. But without the leave, and behind the back, of our weaver, the old fashioned mode of weaving undergoes a change. The labour time that yesterday was without doubt socially necessary to the production of a yard of linen, ceases to be so today, a fact which the owner of the money is only too eager to prove from the prices quoted by our friend's competitors. Unluckily for him, weavers are not few and far between. Lastly, suppose that every piece of linen in the market contains no more labour time than is socially necessary. In spite of this, all these pieces taken as a whole may have had superfluous labour time spent upon them. If the market cannot stomach the whole quantity at the normal price of 2 shillings a yard, this proves that too great a portion of the total labour of the community has been expended in the form of weaving. The effect is the same as if each individual weaver had expended more labour time upon his particular product than is socially necessary. Here we may say, with the German proverb: caught together, hung together. All the linen in the market counts but as one article of commerce, of which each piece is only an aliquot part. And as a matter of fact, the value also of each single yard is but the materialised form of the same definite and socially fixed quantity of homogeneous human labour.

We see, then, commodities are in love with money, but "the course of true love never did run smooth." The quantitative division of labour is brought about in exactly the same spontaneous and accidental manner as its qualitative division. The owners of commodities therefore find out that the same division of labour that turns them into independent private producers also frees the social process of production and the relations of the individual producers to each other within that process from all dependence on the will of those producers, and that the seeming mutual independence of the individuals is supplemented by a system of general and mutual dependence through or by means of the products.

The division of labour converts the product of labour into a commodity, and thereby makes necessary its further conversion into money. At the same time it also makes the accomplishment of this transubstantiation quite accidental. Here, however, we are only concerned with the phenomenon in its integrity, and we therefore assume its progress to be normal. Moreover, if the conversion take place at all, that is, if the commodity be not absolutely unsaleable, its metamorphosis does take place although the price realised may be abnormally above or below the value.

The seller has his commodity replaced by gold, the buyer has his gold replaced by a commodity. The fact which here stares us in the face is that a commodity and gold, 20 yards of linen and £2, have changed hands and places, in other words, that they have been exchanged. But for what is the commodity exchanged? For the shape assumed by its own value, for the universal equivalent. And for what is the gold exchanged? For a particular form of its own use-value. Why does gold take the form of money face to face with the linen? Because the linen's price of £2, its denomination in money, has already equated the linen to gold in its character of money. A commodity strips off its original commodity form on being alienated, i.e., on the instant its use-value actually attracts the gold that before existed only ideally in its price. The realisation of a commodity's price, or of its ideal value form, is therefore at the same time the realisation of the ideal use-value of money; the conversion of a commodity into money, is the simultaneous conversion of money into a commodity. The apparently single process is in reality a double one. From the pole of the commodity owner it is a sale, from the opposite pole of the money owner, it is a purchase. In other words, a sale is a purchase, C—M is also M—C.

Up to this point we have considered men in only one economical capacity, that of owners of commodities, a capacity in which they appropriate the produce of the labour of others, by alienating that of their own labour. Hence, for one commodity owner to meet with another who has money, it is necessary, either that the product of the labour of the latter person, the buyer, should be in itself money, should be gold, the material of which money consists, or that his product should already have changed its skin and have stripped off its original form of a useful object. In order that it may play the part of money, gold must of course enter the market at some point or other. This point is to be found at the source of production of the metal, at which place gold is bartered, as the immediate product of labour, for some other product of equal value. From that moment it always represents the realised price of some commodity. Apart from its exchange for other commodities at the source of its production, gold, in whose-so-ever hands it may be, is the transformed shape of some commodity alienated by its owner; it is the product of a sale or of the first metamorphosis C—M. Gold, as we saw, became ideal money, or a measure of values, in consequence of all commodities measuring their values by it, and thus contrasting it ideally with their natural shape as useful objects, and making it the shape of their value. It became real money, by the general alienation of commodities, by actually changing places with their natural forms as useful objects, and thus becoming in reality the embodiment of their values. When they assume this money-shape, commodities strip off every trace of their natural use-value, and of the particular kind of labour to which they owe their creation, in order to transform themselves into the uniform, socially recognised incarnation of homogeneous human labour. We cannot tell from the mere look of a piece of money for what particular commodity it has been exchanged. Under their money form all commodities look alike. Hence, money may be dirt, although dirt is not money. We will assume that the two gold pieces, in consideration of which our weaver has parted with his linen, are the metamorphosed shape of a quarter of wheat. The sale of the linen, C—M, is at the same time its purchase, M—C. But the sale is the first act of a process that ends with a transaction of an opposite nature, namely, the purchase of a Bible; the purchase of the linen, on the other hand, ends a movement that began with a transaction of an opposite nature, namely, with the sale of the wheat. C—M (linen—money), which is the first phase of C—M—C (linen—money—Bible), is also M—C (money—linen), the last phase of another movement C—M—C (wheat—money—linen). The first metamorphosis of one commodity, its transformation from a commodity into money, is therefore also invariably the second metamorphosis of some other commodity, the retransformation of the latter from money into a commodity.

M—C, or Purchase. The Second and Concluding Metamorphosis of a Commodity.

Because money is the metamorphosed shape of all other commodities, the result of their general alienation, for this reason it is alienable itself without restriction or condition. It reads all prices backwards, and thus, so to say, depicts itself in the bodies of all other commodities, which offer to it the material for the realisation of its own use-value. At the same time the prices, wooing glances cast at money by commodities, define the limits of its convertibility, by pointing to its quantity. Since every commodity, on becoming money, disappears as a commodity, it is impossible to tell from the money itself, how it got into the hands of its possessor, or what article has been changed into it. *Non olet,* from whatever source it may come. Representing on the one hand a sold commodity, it represents on the other hand a commodity to be bought.

M—C, a purchase, is, at the same time, C—M, a sale; the concluding metamorphosis of one commodity is the first metamorphosis of another. With regard to our weaver, the life of his commodity ends with the Bible, into which he has reconverted his £2. But suppose the seller of the Bible turns the £2 set free by the weaver into brandy. M—C, the concluding phase of C—M—C (linen—money—Bible), is also C—M, the first phase of C—M—C (Bible—money—brandy). The producer of a particular commodity has that one article alone to offer; this he sells very often in large quantities, but his many and various wants compel him to split up the price realised, the sum of money set free, into numerous purchases. Hence a sale leads to many purchases of various articles. The concluding metamorphosis of a commodity thus constitutes an aggregation of first metamorphoses of various other commodities.

If we now consider the completed metamorphosis of a commodity as a whole, it appears in the first place that it is made up of two opposite and complementary movements, C—M and M—C. These two antithetical transmutations of a commodity are brought about by two antithetical social acts on the part of the owner, and these acts in their turn stamp the character of the economical parts played by him. As the person who makes a sale, he is a seller; as the person who makes a purchase, he is a buyer. But just as, upon every such transmutation of a commodity, its two forms, commodity form and money form, exist simultaneously but at opposite poles, so every seller has a buyer opposed to him, and every buyer a seller. While one particular commodity is going through its two transmutations in succession, from a commodity into money and from money into another commodity, the owner of the commodity changes in succession his part from that of seller to that of buyer. These characters of seller and buyer are therefore not permanent, but attach themselves in turns to the various persons engaged in the circulation of commodities.

The complete metamorphosis of a commodity, in its simplest form, implies four extremes, and three dramatis personæ. First, a commodity comes face to face with money; the latter is the form taken by the value of the former, and exists in all its hard reality in the pocket of the buyer. A commodity owner is thus brought into contact with a possessor of money. So soon, now, as the commodity has been changed into money, the money becomes its transient equivalent form, the use-value of which equivalent form is to be found in the bodies of other commodities. Money, the final term of the first transmutation, is at the same time the starting point for the second. The person who is a seller in the first transaction thus becomes a buyer in the second, in which a third commodity owner appears on the scene as a seller.

The two phases, each inverse to the other, that make up the metamorphosis of a commodity constitute together a circular movement, a circuit: commodity form, stripping off of this form, and return to the commodity form. No doubt, the commodity appears here under two different aspects. At the starting point it is not a use-value to its owner; at the finishing point it is. So, too, the money appears in the first phase as a solid crystal of value, a crystal into which the commodity eagerly solidifies, and in the second, dissolves into the mere transient equivalent form destined to be replaced by a use-value.

The two metamorphoses constituting the circuit are at the same time two inverse partial metamorphoses of two other commodities. One and the same commodity, the linen, opens the series of its own metamorphoses, and completes the metamorphosis of another (the wheat). In the first phase or sale, the linen plays these two parts in its own person. But, then, changed into gold, it completes its own second and final metamorphosis, and helps at the same time to accomplish the first metamorphosis of a third commodity. Hence the circuit made by one commodity in the course of its metamorphoses is inextricably mixed up with the circuits of other commodities. The total of all the different circuits constitutes *the circulation of commodities.*

B. THE CURRENCY OF MONEY

The change of form, C—M—C, by which the circulation of the material products of labour is brought about, requires that a given value in the shape of a commodity shall begin the process, and shall, also in the shape of a commodity, end it. The movement of the commodity is therefore a circuit. On the other hand, the form of this movement precludes a circuit from being made by the money. The result is not the return of the money, but its continued removal further and further away from its starting point. So long as the seller sticks fast to his money, which is the transformed shape of his commodity, that commodity is still in the first phase of its metamorphosis, and has completed only half its course. But so soon as he completes the process, so soon as he supplements his sale by a purchase, the money again leaves the hands of its possessor. It is true that if the weaver, after buying the Bible, sells more linen, money comes back into his hands. But this return is not owing to the circulation of the first 20 yards of linen; that circulation resulted in the money getting into the hands of the seller of the Bible. The return of money into the hands of the weaver is brought about only by the renewal or repetition of the process of circulation with a fresh commodity, which renewed process ends with the same result as its predecessor did. Hence the movement directly imparted to money by the circulation of commodities takes the form of a constant motion away from its starting point, of course from the hands of one commodity owner into those of another. This course constitutes its currency (*cours de la monnaie*).

The currency of money is the constant and monotonous repetition of the same process. The commodity is always in the hands of the seller; the money, as a means of purchase, always in the hands of the buyer. And money serves as a means of purchase by realising the price of the commodity. This realisation transfers the commodity from the seller to the buyer, and removes the money from the hands of the buyer into those of the seller, where it again goes through the same process with another commodity. That this one-sided character of the money's motion arises out of the two-sided character of the commodity's motion is a circumstance that is veiled over.

C. COIN AND SYMBOLS OF VALUE

That money takes the shape of coin springs from its function as the circulating medium. The weight of gold represented in imagination by the prices or money-names of commodities must confront those commodities, within the circulation, in the shape of coins or pieces of gold of a given denomination. Coining, like the establishment of a standard of prices, is the business of the State. The different national uniforms worn at home by gold and silver as coins, and doffed again in the market of the world, indicate the separation between the internal or national spheres of the circulation of commodities, and their universal sphere.

The only difference, therefore, between coin and bullion, is one of shape, and gold can at any time pass from one form to the other. But no sooner does coin leave the mint, than it immediately finds itself on the highroad to the melting pot. During their currency coins wear away, some more, others less. Name and substance, nominal weight and real weight, begin their process of separation. Coins of the same denomination become different in value, because they are different in weight. The weight of gold fixed upon as the standard of prices deviates from the weight that serves as the circulating medium, and the latter thereby ceases any longer to be a real equivalent of the commodities whose prices it realises. The history of coinage during the Middle Ages and down into the 18th century records the ever renewed confusion arising from this cause. The natural tendency of circulation to convert coins into a mere semblance of what they profess to be, into a symbol of the weight of metal they are officially supposed to contain, is recognised by modern legislation, which fixes the loss of weight sufficient to demonetise a gold coin, or to make it no longer legal tender.

The fact that the currency of coins itself effects a separation between their nominal and their real weight, creating a distinction between them as mere pieces of metal on the one hand, and as coins with a definite function on the other—this fact implies the latent possibility of replacing metallic coins by tokens of some other material, by symbols serving the same purposes as coins. The practical difficulties in the way of coining extremely minute quantities of gold or silver, and the circumstance that at first the less precious metal is used as a measure of value instead of the more precious, copper instead of silver, silver instead of gold, and that the less precious circulates as money until dethroned by the more precious—all these facts explain the parts historically played by silver and copper tokens as substitutes for gold coins. Silver and copper tokens take the place of gold in those regions of the circulation where coins pass from hand to hand most rapidly, and are subject to the maximum amount of wear and tear. This occurs where sales and purchases on a very small scale are continually happening. In order to prevent these satellites from establishing themselves permanently in the place of gold, positive enactments determine the extent to which they must be compulsorily received as payment instead of gold. The particular tracks pursued by the different species of coin in currency run naturally into each other. The tokens keep company with gold, to pay fractional parts of the smallest gold coin; gold is, on the one hand, constantly pouring into retail circulation, and on the other hand is as constantly being thrown out again by being changed into tokens.

3. *Money*

A. HOARDING

The continual movement in circuits of the two antithetical metamorphoses of commodities, or the never ceasing alternation of sale and purchase, is reflected in the restless currency of money, or in the function that money performs of a *perpetuum mobile* of circulation. But so soon as the series of metamorphoses is interrupted, so soon as sales are not supplemented by subsequent purchases, money ceases to be mobilized; it is transformed, as Boisguillebert says, from *meuble* into *immeuble,* from movable into immovable, from coin into money.

With the very earliest development of the circulation of commodities, there is also developed the necessity, and the passionate desire, to hold fast the product of the first metamorphosis. This product is the transformed shape of the commodity, or its gold chrysalis. Commodities are thus sold not for the purpose of buying others, but in order to replace their commodity form by their money form. From being the mere means of effecting the circulation of commodities, this change of form becomes the end and aim. The changed form of the commodity is thus prevented from functioning as its unconditionally alienable form, or as its merely transient money form. The money becomes petrified into a hoard, and the seller becomes a hoarder of money.

In the early stages of the circulation of commodities, it is the surplus use-values alone that are converted into money. Gold and silver thus become of themselves social expressions for superfluity of wealth. This naïve form of hoarding becomes perpetuated in those communities in which the traditional mode of production is carried on for the supply of a fixed and limited circle of home wants. It is thus with the people of Asia, and particularly of the East Indies. Vanderlint, who fancies that the prices of commodities in a country are determined by the quantity of gold and silver to be found in it, asks himself why Indian commodities are so cheap. Answer: Because the Hindus bury their money. From 1602 to 1734, he remarks, they buried 150 millions of pounds sterling of silver, which originally came from America to Europe. In the 10 years from 1856 to 1866, England exported to India and China £120,000,000 in silver, which had been received in exchange for Australian gold. Most of the silver exported to China makes its way to India.

As the production of commodities further develops, every producer of commodities is compelled to make sure of the *nexus rerum,* or the social pledge. His wants are constantly making themselves felt, and necessitate the continual purchase of other people's commodities, while the production and sale of his own goods require time and depend upon circumstances. In order then to be able to buy without selling, he must have sold previously without buying. This operation, conducted on a general scale, appears to imply a contradiction. But the precious metals at the sources of their production are directly exchanged for other commodities. And here we have sales (by the owners of commodities) without purchases (by the owners of gold or silver). And subsequent sales, by other producers, unfollowed by purchases, merely bring about the distribution of the newly produced precious metals among all the owners of commodities. In this way, all along the line of exchange, hoards of gold and silver of varied extent are accumulated. With the possibility of holding and storing up exchange value in the shape of a particular commodity arises also the greed for gold. Along with the extension of circulation increases the power of money, that absolutely social form of wealth ever ready for use. "Gold is a wonderful thing! Whoever possesses it is lord of all he wants. By means of gold one can even get souls into Paradise." (Columbus in his letter from Jamaica, 1503.) Since gold does not disclose what has been transformed into it, everything, commodity or not, is convertible into gold. Everything becomes saleable and buyable. The circulation becomes the great social retort into which everything is thrown, to come out again as a gold-crystal. Not even are the bones of saints, and still less are more delicate *res sacrosanctæ extra commercium hominum,* able to withstand this alchemy. Just as every qualitative difference between commodities is extinguished in money, so money, on its side, like the radical leveller that it is, does away with all distinctions. But money itself is a commodity, an external object, capable of becoming the private property of any individual. Thus social power becomes the private power of private persons. The ancients therefore denounced money as subversive of the economical and moral order of things. Modern society, which soon after its birth pulled Plutus by the hair of his head from the bowels of the earth, greets gold as its Holy Grail, as the glittering incarnation of the very principle of its own life.

B. MEANS OF PAYMENT

In the simple form of the circulation of commodities hitherto considered, we found a given value always presented to us in a double shape, as a commodity at one pole, as money at the opposite pole. The owners of commodities came therefore into contact as the respective representatives of what were already equivalents. But with the development of circulation conditions arise under which the alienation of commodities becomes separated, by an interval of time, from the realisation of their prices. It will be sufficient to indicate the most simple of these conditions. One sort of article requires a longer, another a shorter, time for its production. Again, the production of different commodities depends on different seasons of the year. One sort of commodity may be born on its own market place, another has to make a long journey to market. Commodity owner No. 1 may therefore be ready to sell before No. 2 is ready to buy. When the same transactions are continually repeated between the same persons, the conditions of sale are regulated in accordance with the conditions of production. On the other hand, the use of a given commodity, of a house, for instance, is sold (in common parlance, let) for a definite period. Here, it is only at the end of the term that the buyer has actually received the use-value of the commodity. He therefore buys it before he pays for it. The vendor sells an existing commodity, the purchaser buys as the mere representative of money, or rather of future money. The vendor becomes a creditor, the purchaser becomes a debtor. Since the metamorphosis of commodities, or the development of their value-form, appears here under a new aspect, money also acquires a fresh function; it becomes the means of payment.

C. UNIVERSAL MONEY

When money leaves the home sphere of circulation, it strips off the local garbs which it there assumes, of a standard of prices, of coin, of tokens, and of a symbol of value, and returns to its original form of bullion. In the trade between the markets of the world, the value of commodities is expressed so as to be universally recognised. Hence their independent value form also, in these cases, confronts them under the shape of universal money. It is only in the markets of the world that money acquires to the full extent the character of the commodity whose bodily form is also the immediate social incarnation of human labour in the abstract. Its real mode of existence in this sphere adequately corresponds to its ideal concept.

PART TWO: THE TRANSFORMATION OF MONEY INTO CAPITAL

IV. THE GENERAL FORMULA FOR CAPITAL

THE CIRCULATION of commodities is the starting point of capital. The production of commodities, their circulation, and that more developed form of their circulation called commerce, these form the historical groundwork from which it rises. The modern history of capital dates from the creation in the 16th century of a world-embracing commerce and a world-embracing market.

If we abstract from the material substance of the circulation of commodities, that is, from the exchange of the various use-values, and consider only the economic forms produced by this process of circulation, we find its final result to be money: this final product of the circulation of commodities is the first form in which capital appears.

As a matter of history, capital, as opposed to landed property, invariably takes the form at first of money; it appears as moneyed wealth, as the capital of the merchant and of the usurer. But we have no need to refer to the origin of capital in order to discover that the first form of appearance of capital is money. We can see it daily under our very eyes. All new capital, to commence with, comes on the stage, that is, on the market, whether of commodities, labour, or money, even in our days, in the shape of money that by a definite process has to be transformed into capital.

The first distinction we notice between money that is money only and money that is capital is nothing more than a difference in their form of circulation.

The simplest form of the circulation of commodities is C—M—C, the transformation of commodities into money, and the change of the money back again into commodities; or selling in order to buy. But alongside of this form we find another specifically different form: M—C—M, the transformation of money into commodities, and the change of commodities back again into money; or buying in order to sell. Money that circulates in the latter manner is thereby transformed into, becomes capital, and is already potentially capital.

The circuit C—M—C starts with one commodity, and finishes with another, which falls out of circulation and into consumption. Consumption, the satisfaction of wants, in one word, use-value, is its end and aim. The circuit M—C—M, on the contrary, commences with money and ends with money. Its leading motive, and the goal that attracts it, is therefore mere exchange value.

In the simple circulation of commodities, the two extremes of the circuit have the same economic form. They are both commodities, and commodities of equal value. But they are also use-values differing in their qualities, as, for example, corn and clothes. The exchange of products, of the different materials in which the labour of society is embodied, forms here the basis of the movement. It is otherwise in the circulation M—C—M, which at first sight appears purposeless, because tautological. Both extremes have the same economic form. They are both money, and therefore are not qualitatively different use-values; for money is but the converted form of commodities, in which their particular use-values vanish. To exchange £100 for cotton, and then this same cotton again for £100, is merely a roundabout way of exchanging money for money, the same for the same, and appears to be an operation just as purposeless as it is absurd. One sum of money is distinguishable from another only by its amount. The character and tendency of the process M—C—M is therefore not due to any qualitative difference between its extremes, both being money, but solely to their quantitative difference. More money is withdrawn from circulation at the finish than was thrown into it at the start. The cotton that was bought for £100 is perhaps resold for £100+£10 or £110. The exact form of this process is therefore M—C—M′, where M′=M+Δ M=the original sum advanced, plus an increment. This increment or excess over the original value I call "surplus-value." The value originally advanced, therefore, not only remains intact while in circulation, but adds to itself a surplus-value or expands itself. It is this movement that converts it into capital.

Value therefore now becomes value in process, money in process, and, as such, capital. It comes out of circulation, enters into it again, preserves and multiplies itself within its circuit, comes back out of it with expanded bulk, and begins the same round ever afresh. M—M′, money which begets money, such is the description of Capital from the mouths of its first interpreters, the Mercantilists.

Buying in order to sell, or, more accurately, buying in order to sell dearer, M—C—M′, appears certainly to be a form peculiar to one kind of capital alone, namely, merchants' capital. But industrial capital too is money that is changed into commodities, and by the sale of these commodities is reconverted into more money. The events that take place outside the sphere of circulation, in the interval between the buying and selling, do not affect the form of this movement. Lastly, in the case of interest-bearing capital, the circulation M—C—M′ appears abridged. We have its result without the intermediate stage, in the form M—M′, *en style lapidaire* so to say, money that is worth more money, value that is greater than itself.

M—C—M′ is therefore in reality the general formula of capital as it appears prima facie within the sphere of circulation.

V. THE BUYING AND SELLING OF LABOUR-POWER

The change of value that occurs in the case of money intended to be converted into capital cannot take place in the money itself, since in its function of means of purchase and of payment it does no more than realise the price of the commodity it buys or pays for; and, as hard cash, it is value petrified, never varying. Just as little can it originate in the second act of circulation, the resale of the commodity, which does no more than transform the article from its bodily form back again into its money form. The change must, therefore, take place in the commodity bought by the first act, M—C, but not in its value, for equivalents are exchanged, and the commodity is paid for at its full value. We are, therefore, forced to the conclusion that the change originates in the use-value, as such, of the commodity, i.e., in its consumption. In order to be able to extract value from the consumption of a commodity, our friend, Moneybags, must be so lucky as to find, within the sphere of circulation, in the market, a commodity, whose use-value possesses the peculiar property of being a source of value, whose actual consumption, therefore, is itself an embodiment of labour and, consequently, a creation of value. The possessor of money does find on the market such a special commodity in capacity for labour or labour-power.

By labour-power or capacity for labour is to be understood the aggregate of those mental and physical capabilities existing in a human being which he exercises whenever he produces a use-value of any description.

But in order that our owner of money may be able to find labour-power offered for sale as a commodity, various conditions must first be fulfilled. The exchange of commodities of itself implies no other relations of dependence than those which result from its own nature. On this assumption labour-power can appear upon the market as a commodity only if, and so far as, its possessor, the individual whose labour-power it is, offers it for sale, or sells it, as a commodity. In order that he may be able to do this, he must have it at his disposal, must be the untrammelled owner of his capacity for labour, i.e., of his person. He and the owner of money meet in the market, and deal with each other as on the basis of equal rights, with this difference alone, that one is buyer, the other seller; both, therefore, equal in the eyes of the law. The continuance of this relation demands that the owner of the labour-power should sell it only for a definite period, for if he were to sell it rump and stump, once for all, he would be selling himself, converting himself from a free man into a slave, from an owner of a commodity into a commodity. He must constantly look upon his labour-power as his own property, his own commodity, and this he can only do by placing it at the disposal of the buyer temporarily, for a definite period of time. By this means alone can he avoid renouncing his rights of ownership over it.

The second essential condition to the owner of money finding labour-power in the market as a commodity is this—that the labourer instead of being in the position to sell commodities in which his labour is incorporated, must be obliged to offer for sale as a commodity that very labour-power which exists only in his living self.

In order that a man may be able to sell commodities other than labour-power, he must of course have the means of production, such as raw material, implements, etc. No boots can be made without leather. He requires also the means of subsistence. Nobody—not even "a musician of the future"—can live upon future products or upon use-values in an unfinished state; and ever since the first moment of his appearance on the world's stage, man always has been and must still be a consumer, both before and while he is producing. In a society where all products assume the form of commodities, these commodities must be sold after they have been produced; it is only after their sale that they can serve in satisfying the requirements of their producer. The time necessary for their sale is superadded to that necessary for their production.

For the conversion of his money into capital, therefore, the owner of money must meet in the market with the free labourer, free in the double sense, that as a free man he can dispose of his labour-power as his own commodity, and that on the other hand he has no other commodity for sale, is short of everything necessary for the realisation of his labour-power.

The question why this free labourer confronts him in the market has no interest for the owner of money, who regards the labour market as a branch of the general market for commodities. And for the present it interests us just as little. We cling to the fact theoretically, as he does practically. One thing, however, is clear—nature does not produce on the one side owners of money or commodities, and on the other men possessing nothing but their own labour-power. This relation has no natural basis, neither is its social basis one that is common to all historical periods. It is clearly the result of a past historical development, the product of many economical revolutions, of the extinction of a whole series of older forms of social production.

We must now examine more closely this peculiar commodity, labour-power. Like all others it has a value. How is that value determined?

The value of labour-power is determined, as in the case of every other commodity, by the labour time necessary for the production, and consequently also the reproduction, of this special article. So far as it has value, it represents no more than a definite quantity of the average labour of society incorporated in it. Labour-power exists only as a capacity, or power of the living individual. Its production consequently presupposes his existence. Given the individual, the production of labour-power consists in his reproduction of himself or his maintenance. For his maintenance he requires a given quantity of the means of subsistence. Therefore the labour time requisite for the production of labour-power reduces itself to that necessary for the production of those means of subsistence; in other words, the value of labour-power is the value of the means of subsistence necessary for the maintenance of the labourer. Labour-power, however, becomes a reality only by its exercise; it sets itself in action only by working. But thereby a definite quantity of human muscle, nerve, brain, etc., is wasted, and these require to be restored. This increased expenditure demands a larger income. If the owner of labour-power works today, tomorrow he must again be able to repeat the same process in the same conditions as regards health and strength. His means of subsistence must therefore be sufficient to maintain him in his normal state as a labouring individual. His natural wants, such as food, clothing, fuel, and housing, vary according to the climatic and other physical conditions of his country. On the other hand, the number and extent of his so-called necessary wants, as also the modes of satisfying them, are themselves the product of historical development, and depend therefore to a great extent on the degree of civilization of a country, more particularly on the conditions under which, and consequently on the habits and degree of comfort in which, the class of free labourers has been formed. In contradistinction therefore to the case of other commodities, there enters into the determination of the value of labour-power a historical and moral element. Nevertheless, in a given country, at a given period, the average quantity of the means of subsistence necessary for the labourer is practically known.

The owner of labour-power is mortal. If then his appearance in the market is to be continuous, and the continuous conversion of money into capital assumes this, the seller of labour-power must perpetuate himself, "in the way that every living individual perpetuates himself, by procreation" (Petty). The labour-power withdrawn from the market by wear and tear and death must be continually replaced by, at the very least, an equal amount of fresh labour-power. Hence the sum of the means of subsistence necessary for the production of labour-power must include the means necessary for the labourer's substitutes, i.e., his children, in order that this race of peculiar commodity owners may perpetuate its appearance in the market.

In order to modify the human organism, so that it may acquire skill and handiness in a given branch of industry, and become labour-power of a special kind, a special education or training is requisite, and this, on its part, costs an equivalent in commodities of a greater or less amount. This amount varies according to the more or less complicated character of the labour-power. The expenses of this education (excessively small in the case of ordinary labour-power) enter *pro tanto* into the total value spent in its production.

The value of labour-power resolves itself into the value of a definite quantity of the means of subsistence. It therefore varies with the value of these means or with the quantity of labour requisite for their production.

Some of the means of subsistence, such as food and fuel, are consumed daily, and a fresh supply must be provided daily. Others, such as clothes and furniture, last for longer periods and require to be replaced only at longer intervals. One article must be bought or paid for daily, another weekly, another quarterly, and so on. But in whatever way the sum total of these outlays may be spread over the year, they must be covered by the average income, taking one day with another. If the total of the commodities required daily for the production of labour-power=A, and those required weekly=B, and those required quarterly=C, and so on, the daily average of these commodities$=\frac{365A+52B+4C+\text{etc.}}{365}$. Suppose that in this mass of commodities requisite for the average day there are embodied 6 hours of social labour, then there is incorporated daily in labour-power half a day's average social labour, in other words, half a day's labour is requisite for the daily production of labour-power. This quantity of labour forms the value of a day's labour-power or the value of the labour-power daily reproduced. If half a day's average social labour is incorporated in three shillings, then three shillings is the price corresponding to the value of a day's labour-power. If its owner therefore offers it for sale at three shillings a day, its selling price is equal to its value, and according to our supposition, our friend Moneybags, who is intent upon converting his three shillings into capital, pays this value.

The minimum limit of the value of labour-power is determined by the value of the commodities, without the daily supply of which the labourer cannot renew his vital energy, consequently by the value of those means of subsistence that are physically indispensable. If the price of labour-power fall to this minimum, it falls below its value, since under such circumstances it can be maintained and developed only in a crippled state. But the value of every commodity is determined by the labour time requisite to turn it out so as to be of normal quality.

We now know how the value paid by the purchaser to the possessor of this peculiar commodity, labour-power, is determined. The use-value which the former gets in exchange manifests itself only in the actual usufruct, in the consumption of the labour-power. The money owner buys everything necessary for this purpose, such as raw material, in the market, and pays for it at its full value. The consumption of labour-power is at one and the same time the production of commodities and of surplus-value. The consumption of labour-power is completed, as in the case of every other commodity, outside the limits of the market or of the sphere of circulation. Accompanied by Mr. Moneybags and by the possessor of labour-power, we therefore take leave for a time of this noisy sphere, where everything takes place on the surface and in view of all men, and follow them both into the hidden abode of production, on whose threshold there stares us in the face: "No admittance except on business."

Here we shall see not only how capital produces, but how capital is produced. We shall at last force the secret of profit making.

This sphere that we are deserting, within whose boundaries the sale and purchase of labour-power goes on, is in fact a very Eden of the innate rights of man. There alone rule Freedom, Equality, Property, and Bentham. Freedom, because both buyer and seller of a commodity, say of labour-power, are constrained only by their own free will. They contract as free agents, and the agreement they come to is but the form in which they give legal expression to their common will. Equality, because each enters into relation with the other, as with a simple owner of commodities, and they exchange equivalent for equivalent. Property, because each disposes only of what is his own. And Bentham, because each looks only to himself. The only force that brings them together and puts them in relation with each other is the selfishness, the gain, and the private interests of each. Each looks to himself only, and no one troubles himself about the rest, and just because they do so, do they all, in accordance with the pre-established harmony of things, or under the auspices of an all-shrewd providence, work together to their mutual advantage, for the common weal and in the interest of all.

On leaving this sphere of simple circulation or of exchange of commodities, which furnishes the "Free-trader Vulgaris" with his views and ideas, and with the standard by which he judges a society based on capital and wages, we think we can perceive a change in the physiognomy of our dramatis personæ. He who before was the money owner now strides in front as capitalist; the possessor of labour-power follows as his labourer. The one with an air of importance, smirking, intent on business; the other, timid and holding back, like one who is bringing his own hide to market and has nothing to expect but—a hiding.

PART THREE: THE PRODUCTION OF ABSOLUTE SURPLUS-VALUE

VI. THE LABOUR PROCESS AND THE PROCESS OF PRODUCING SURPLUS-VALUE

1. The Labour Process or the Production of Use-Values

THE ELEMENTARY FACTORS of the labour process are (1) the personal activity of man, i.e., work itself, (2) the subject of that work, and (3) its instruments.

The soil (and this, economically speaking, includes water) in the virgin state in which it supplies man with necessaries or the means of subsistence ready to hand exists independently of him, and is the universal subject of human labour. All those things which labour merely separates from immediate connection with their environment are subjects of labour spontaneously provided by Nature. Such are fish which we catch and take from their element, water, timber which we fell in the virgin forest, and ores which we extract from their veins. If, on the other hand, the subject of labour has, so to say, been filtered through previous labour, we call it raw material; such is ore already extracted and ready for washing. All raw material is the subject of labour, but not every subject of labour is raw material; it can only become so after it has undergone some alteration by means of labour.

An instrument of labour is a thing, or a complex of things, which the labourer interposes between himself and the subject of his labour, and which serves as the conductor of his activity. He makes use of the mechanical, physical, and chemical properties of some substances in order to make other substances subservient to his aims. Leaving out of consideration such ready-made means of subsistence as fruits, in gathering which a man's own limbs serve as the instruments of his labour, the first thing of which the labourer possesses himself is not the subject of labour but its instrument. Thus Nature becomes one of the organs of his activity, one that he annexes to his own bodily organs, adding stature to himself in spite of the Bible. As the earth is his original larder, so too it is his original tool house. It supplies him, for instance, with stones for throwing, grinding, pressing, cutting, etc. The earth itself is an instrument of labour, but when used as such in agriculture implies a whole series of other instruments and a comparatively high development of labour. No sooner does labour undergo the least development, than it requires specially prepared instruments. Thus in the oldest caves we find stone implements and weapons. In the earliest period of human history domesticated animals, i.e., animals which have been bred for the purpose, and have undergone modification by means of labour, play the chief part as instruments of labour along with specially prepared stones, wood, bones, and shells. The use and fabrication of instruments of labour, although existing in the germ among certain species of animals, are specifically characteristic of the human labour process, and Franklin therefore defines man as a tool-making animal. Relics of bygone instruments of labour possess the same importance for the investigation of extinct economical forms of society as do fossil bones for the determination of extinct species of animals. It is not the articles made, but how they are made, and by what instruments, that enables us to distinguish different economical epochs. Instruments of labour not only supply a standard of the degree of development to which human labour has attained, but they are also indicators of the social conditions under which that labour is carried on. Among the instruments of labour, those of a mechanical nature, which, taken as a whole, we may call the bone and muscles of production, offer much more decided characteristics of a given epoch of production than those which, like pipes, tubs, baskets, jars, etc., serve only to hold the materials for labour, which latter class we may, in a general way, call the vascular system of production. The latter first begins to play an important part in the chemical industries.

In a wider sense we may include among the instruments of labour, in addition to those things that are used for directly transferring labour to its subject, and which therefore, in one way or another, serve as conductors of activity, all such objects as are necessary for carrying on the labour process. These do not enter directly into the process, but without them it is either impossible for it to take place at all, or possible only to a partial extent. Once more we find the earth to be a universal instrument of this sort, for it furnishes a *locus standi* to the labourer and a field of employment for his activity. Among instruments that are the result of previous labour and also belong to this class, we find workshops, canals, roads, and so forth.

2. *The Production of Surplus-Value*

The product appropriated by the capitalist is a use-value, as yarn, for example, or boots. But, although boots are, in one sense, the basis of all social progress, and our capitalist is a decided "progressist," yet he does not manufacture boots for their own sake. Use-value is, by no means, the thing *"qu'on aime pour lui-même"* in the production of commodities. Use-values are only produced by capitalists, because, and in so far as, they are the material substratum, the depositaries of exchange-value. Our capitalist has two objects in view: in the first place, he wants to produce a use-value that has a value in exchange, that is to say, an article destined to be sold, a commodity; and secondly, he desires to produce a commodity whose value shall be greater than the sum of the values of the commodities used in its production, that is, of the means of production and the labour-power that he purchased with his good money in the open market. His aim is to produce not only a use-value, but a commodity also; not only use-value, but value; not only value, but at the same time surplus-value.

It must be borne in mind that we are now dealing with the production of commodities, and that, up to this point, we have only considered one aspect of the process. Just as commodities are, at the same time, use-values and values, so the process of producing them must be a labour process, and at the same time, a process of creating value.

Let us now examine production as a creation of value.

We know that the value of each commodity is determined by the quantity of labour expended on and materialised in it, by the working time necessary, under given social conditions, for its production. This rule also holds good in the case of the product that accrued to our capitalist, as the result of the labour process carried on for him. Assuming this product to be 10 lbs. of yarn, our first step is to calculate the quantity of labour realised in it.

For spinning the yarn, raw material is required; suppose in this case 10 lbs. of cotton. We have no need at present to investigate the value of this cotton, for our capitalist has, we will assume, bought it at its full value, say of 10 shillings. In this price the labour required for the production of the cotton is already expressed in terms of the average labour of society. We will further assume that the wear and tear of the spindle, which, for our present purpose, may represent all other instruments of labour employed, amounts to the value of 2 shillings. If, then, twenty-four hours' labour, or two working days, are required to produce the quantity of gold represented by 12 shillings, we have here, to begin with, 2 days' labour already incorporated in the yarn.

We must not let ourselves be misled by the circumstance that the cotton has taken a new shape while the substance of the spindle has to a certain extent been used up. By the general law of value, if the value of 40 lbs. of yarn=the value of 40 lbs. of cotton+the value of a whole spindle, i.e., if the same working time is required to produce the commodities on either side of this equation, then 10 lbs. of yarn are an equivalent for 10 lbs. of cotton, together with one fourth of a spindle. In the case we are considering the same working time is materialised in the 10 lbs. of yarn on the one hand, and in the 10 lbs. of cotton and the fraction of a spindle on the other. Therefore, whether value appears in cotton, in a spindle, or in yarn makes no difference in the amount of that value. The spindle and cotton, instead of resting quietly side by side, join together in the process, their forms are altered, and they are turned into yarn; but their value is no more affected by this fact than it would be if they had been simply exchanged for their equivalent in yarn.

The labour required for the production of the cotton, the raw material of the yarn, is part of the labour necessary to produce the yarn, and is therefore contained in the yarn. The same applies to the labour embodied in the spindle, without whose wear and tear the cotton could not be spun.

Hence, in determining the value of the yarn, or the labour-time required for its production, all the special processes carried on at various times and in different places, which were necessary, first to produce the cotton and the wasted portion of the spindle, and then with the cotton and spindle to spin the yarn, may together be looked on as different and successive phases of one and the same process. The whole of the labour in the yarn is past labour; and it is a matter of no importance that the operations necessary for the production of its constituent elements were carried on at times which, referred to the present, are more remote than the final operation of spinning. If a definite quantity of labour, say thirty days, is requisite to build a house, the total amount of labour incorporated in it is not altered by the fact that the work of the last day is done twenty-nine days later than that of the first. Therefore the labour contained in the raw material and the instruments of labour can be treated just as if it were labour expended in an earlier stage of the spinning process, before the labour of actual spinning commenced.

The values of the means of production, i.e., the cotton and the spindle, which values are expressed in the price of twelve shillings, are therefore constituent parts of the value of the yarn or, in other words, of the value of the product.

Two conditions must nevertheless be fulfilled. First, the cotton and spindle must concur in the production of a use-value; they must in the present case become yarn. Value is independent of the particular use-value by which it is borne, but it must be embodied in a use-value of some kind. Secondly, the time occupied in the labour of production must not exceed the time really necessary under the given social conditions of the case. Therefore, if no more than 1 lb. of cotton be requisite to spin 1 lb. of yarn, care must be taken that no more than this weight of cotton is consumed in the production of 1 lb. of yarn; and similarly with regard to the spindle. Though the capitalist have a hobby, and use a gold instead of a steel spindle, yet the only labour that counts for anything in the value of the yarn is that which would be required to produce a steel spindle, because no more is necessary under the given social conditions.

We now know what portion of the value of the yarn is owing to the cotton and the spindle. It amounts to twelve shillings or the value of two days' work. The next point for our consideration is what portion of the value of the yarn is added to the cotton by the labour of the spinner.

We have now to consider this labour under a very different aspect from that which it had during the labour process; there we viewed it solely as that particular kind of human activity which changes cotton into yarn; there the more the labour was suited to the work, the better the yarn, other circumstances remaining the same. The labour of the spinner was then viewed as specifically different from other kinds of productive labour, different on the one hand in its special aim, viz., spinning, different, on the other hand, in the special character of its operations, in the special nature of its means of production, and in the special use-value of its product. For the operation of spinning, cotton and spindles are a necessity, but for making rifled cannon they would be of no use whatever. Here, on the contrary, where we consider the labour of the spinner only so far as it is value-creating, i.e., a source of value, his labour differs in no respect from the labour of the man who bores cannon, or (what here more nearly concerns us) from the labour of the cotton planter and spindle maker incorporated in the means of production. It is solely by reason of this identity that cotton planting, spindle making, and spinning are capable of forming the component parts, differing only quantitatively from each other, of one whole, namely, the value of the yarn. Here we have nothing more to do with the quality, the nature, and the specific character of the labour, but merely with its quantity. And this simply requires to be calculated. We proceed upon the assumption that spinning is simple, unskilled labour, the average labour of a given state of society. Hereafter we shall see that the contrary assumption would make no difference.

While the labourer is at work, his labour constantly undergoes a transformation: from being motion it becomes an object without motion; from being the labourer working it becomes the thing produced. At the end of one hour's spinning, that act is represented by a definite quantity of yarn; in other words, a definite quantity of labour, namely that of one hour, has become embodied in the cotton. We say labour, i.e., the expenditure of his vital force by the spinner, and not spinning labour, because the special work of spinning counts here, only so far as it is the expenditure of labour-power in general, and not in so far as it is the specific work of the spinner.

In the process we are now considering it is of extreme importance that no more time be consumed in the work of transforming the cotton into yarn than is necessary under the given social conditions. If under normal, i.e., average social conditions of production, *a* pounds of cotton ought to be made into *b* pounds of yarn by one hour's labour, then a day's labour does not count as 12 hours' labour unless 12 *a* pounds of cotton have been made into 12 *b* pounds of yarn; for in the creation of value the time that is socially necessary alone counts.

Not only the labour, but also the raw material and the product now appear in quite a new light, very different from that in which we viewed them in the labour process pure and simple. The raw material serves now merely as an absorbent of a definite quantity of labour. By this absorption it is in fact changed into yarn, because it is spun, because labour-power in the form of spinning is added to it; but the product, the yarn, is now nothing more than a measure of the labour absorbed by the cotton. If in one hour 1⅔ lbs. of cotton can be spun into 1⅔ lbs. of yarn, then 10 lbs. of yarn indicate the absorption of 6 hours' labour. Definite quantities of product, these quantities being determined by experience, now represent nothing but definite quantities of labour, definite masses of crystallized labour time. They are nothing more than the materialisation of so many hours or so many days of social labour.

We are here no more concerned about the facts that the labour is the specific work of spinning, that its subject is cotton and its product yarn, than we are about the fact that the subject itself is already a product and therefore raw material. If the spinner, instead of spinning, were working in a coal mine, the subject of his labour, the coal, would be supplied by Nature; nevertheless, a definite quantity of extracted coal, a hundred weight, for example, would represent a definite quantity of absorbed labour.

We assumed, on the occasion of its sale, that the value of a day's labour-power is 3 shillings, and that 6 hours' labour are incorporated in that sum; and consequently that this amount of labour is requisite to produce the necessaries of life daily required on an average by the labourer. If now our spinner by working for one hour can convert 1⅔ lbs. of cotton into 1⅔ lbs. of yarn, it follows that in 6 hours he will convert 10 lbs. of cotton into 10 lbs. of yarn. Hence, during the spinning process, the cotton absorbs 6 hours' labour. The same quantity of labour is also embodied in a piece of gold of the value of 3 shillings. Consequently by the mere labour of spinning a value of 3 shillings is added to the cotton.

Let us now consider the total value of the product, the 10 lbs. of yarn. Two and a half days' labour have been embodied in it, of which two days were contained in the cotton and in the substance of the spindle worn away, and half a day was absorbed during the process of spinning. This 2½ days' labour is also represented by a piece of gold of the value of 15 shillings. Hence, 15 shillings is an adequate price for the 10 lbs. of yarn, or the price of one pound is eighteenpence.

Our capitalist stares in astonishment. The value of the product is exactly equal to the value of the capital advanced. The value so advanced has not expanded, no surplus-value has been created, and consequently money has not been converted into capital. The price of the yarn is 15 shillings, and 15 shillings were spent in the open market upon the constituent elements of the product, or, what amounts to the same thing, upon the factors of the labour process; 10 shillings were paid for the cotton, 2 shillings for the substance of the spindle worn away, and 3 shillings for the labour-power. The swollen value of the yarn is of no avail, for it is merely the sum of the values formerly existing in the cotton, the spindle, and the labour-power; out of such a simple addition of existing values, no surplus-value can possibly arise. These separate values are now all concentrated in one thing; but so they were also in the sum of 15 shillings, before it was split up into three parts, by the purchase of the commodities.

There is in reality nothing very strange in this result. The value of one pound of yarn being eighteenpence, if our capitalist buys 10 lbs. of yarn in the market, he must pay 15 shillings for them. It is clear that, whether a man buys his house ready built, or gets it built for him, in neither case will the mode of acquisition increase the amount of money laid out on the house.

Our capitalist, who is at home in his vulgar economy, exclaims: "Oh! but I advanced my money for the express purpose of making more money." The way to Hell is paved with good intentions, and he might just as easily have intended to make money without producing at all. He threatens all sorts of things. He won't be caught napping again. In future he will buy the commodities in the market, instead of manufacturing them himself. But if all his brother capitalists were to do the same, where would he find his commodities in the market? And his money he cannot eat. He tries persuasion. "Consider my abstinence; I might have played ducks and drakes with the 15 shillings; but instead of that I consumed it productively, and made yarn with it." Very well, and by way of reward he is now in possession of good yarn instead of a bad conscience; and as for playing the part of a miser, it would never do for him to relapse into such bad ways as that; we have seen before to what results such asceticism leads. Besides, where nothing is, the king has lost his rights: whatever may be the merit of his abstinence, there is nothing wherewith specially to remunerate it, because the value of the product is merely the sum of the values of the commodities that were thrown into the process of production. Let him therefore console himself with the reflection that virtue is its own reward. But no, he becomes importunate. He says: "The yarn is of no use to me: I produced it for sale." In that case let him sell it, or, still better, let him for the future produce only things for satisfying his personal wants, a remedy that his physician McCulloch has already prescribed as infallible against an epidemic of overproduction. He now gets obstinate. "Can the labourer," he asks, "merely with his arms and legs, produce commodities out of nothing? Did I not supply him with the materials, by means of which, and in which alone, his labour could be embodied? And as the greater part of society consists of such ne'er-do-wells, have I not rendered society incalculable service by my instruments of production, my cotton and my spindle, and not only society, but the labourer also, whom in addition I have provided with the necessaries of life? And am I to be allowed nothing in return for all this service?" Well, but has not the labourer rendered him the equivalent service of changing his cotton and spindle into yarn? Moreover, there is here no question of service. A service is nothing more than the useful effect of a use-value, be it of a commodity, or be it of labour. But here we are dealing with exchange-value. The capitalist paid to the labourer a value of 3 shillings, and the labourer gave him back an exact equivalent in the value of 3 shillings, added by him to the cotton: he gave him value for value. Our friend, up to this time so purse-proud, suddenly assumes the modest demeanour of his own workman, and exclaims: "Have I myself not worked? Have I not performed the labour of superintendence and of overlooking the spinner? And does not this labour, too, create value?" His overlooker and his manager try to hide their smiles. Meanwhile, after a hearty laugh, he reassumes his usual mien. Though he chanted to us the whole creed of the economists, in reality, he says, he would not give a brass farthing for it. He leaves this and all such like subterfuges and juggling tricks to the professors of political economy, who are paid for it. He himself is a practical man; and though he does not always consider what he says outside his business, yet in his business he knows what he is about.

Let us examine the matter more closely. The value of a day's labour-power amounts to 3 shillings, because on our assumption half a day's labour is embodied in that quantity of labour-power, i.e., because the means of subsistence that are daily required for the production of labour-power cost half a day's labour. But the past labour that is embodied in the labour-power and the living labour that it can call into action; the daily cost of maintaining it and its daily expenditure in work, are two totally different things. The former determines the exchange-value of the labour-power, the latter is its use-value. The fact that half a day's labour is necessary to keep the labourer alive during 24 hours does not in any way prevent him from working a whole day. Therefore, the value of labour-power and the value which that labour-power creates in the labour process are two entirely different magnitudes; and this difference of the two values was what the capitalist had in view, when he was purchasing the labour-power. The useful qualities that labour-power possesses, and by virtue of which it makes yarn or boots, were to him nothing more than a *conditio sine qua non;* for in order to create value, labour must be expended in a useful manner. What really influenced him was the specific use-value which this commodity possesses of being *a source not only of value, but of more value than it has itself.* This is the special service that the capitalist expects from labour-power, and in this transaction he acts in accordance with the "eternal laws" of the exchange of commodities. The seller of labour-power, like the seller of any other commodity, realises its exchange-value and parts with its use-value. He cannot take the one without giving the other. The use-value of labour-power, or in other words, labour, belongs just as little to its seller as the use-value of oil after it has been sold belongs to the dealer who has sold it. The owner of the money has paid the value of a day's labour-power; his, therefore, is the use of it for a day; a day's labour belongs to him. The circumstance that on the one hand the daily sustenance of labour-power costs only half a day's labour, while on the other hand the very same labour-power can work during a whole day, that consequently the value which its use during one day creates is double what he pays for that use, this circumstance is, without doubt, a piece of good luck for the buyer, but by no means an injury to the seller.

Our capitalist foresaw this state of things, and that was the cause of his laughter. The labourer therefore finds, in the workshop, the means of production necessary for working, not only during six, but during twelve hours. Just as during the six hours' process our 10 lbs. of cotton absorbed six hours' labour, and became 10 lbs. of yarn, so now 20 lbs. of cotton will absorb 12 hours' labour and be changed into 20 lbs. of yarn. Let us now examine the product of this prolonged process. There is now materialised in this 20 lbs. of yarn the labour of five days, of which four days are due to the cotton and the lost steel of the spindle, the remaining day having been absorbed by the cotton during the spinning process. Expressed in gold, the labour of five days is 30 shillings. This is therefore the price of the 20 lbs. of yarn, giving, as before, eighteenpence as the price of a pound. But the sum of the values of the commodities that entered into the process amounts to 27 shillings. The value of the yarn is 30 shillings. Therefore the value of the product is 1/9 greater than the value advanced for its production; 27 shillings have been transformed into 30 shillings; a surplus-value of 3 shillings has been created. The trick has at last succeeded; money has been converted into capital.

Every condition of the problem is satisfied, while the laws that regulate the exchange of commodities have been in no way violated. Equivalent has been exchanged for equivalent. For the capitalist as buyer paid for each commodity, for the cotton, the spindle, and the labour-power, its full value. He then did what is done by every purchaser of commodities; he consumed their use-value. The consumption of the labour-power, which was also the process of producing commodities, resulted in 20 lbs. of yarn, having a value of 30 shillings. The capitalist, formerly a buyer, now returns to market as a seller, of commodities. He sells his yarn at eighteenpence a pound, which is its exact value. Yet for all that he withdraws 3 shillings more from circulation than he originally threw into it. This metamorphosis, this conversion of money into capital, takes place both within the sphere of circulation and also outside it; within the circulation, because conditioned by the purchase of the labour-power in the market; outside the circulation, because what is done within it is only a steppingstone to the production of surplus-value, a process which is entirely confined to the sphere of production. Thus *"tout est pour le mieux dans le meilleur des mondes possibles."*

By turning his money into commodities that serve as the material elements of a new product, and as factors in the labour process, by incorporating living labour with their dead substance, the capitalist at the same time converts value, i.e., past, materialised, and dead labour into capital, into value big with value, a live monster that is fruitful and multiplies.

If we now compare the two processes of producing value and of creating surplus-value, we see that the latter is nothing but the continuation of the former beyond a definite point. If on the one hand the process be not carried beyond the point, where the value paid by the capitalist for the labour-power is replaced by an exact equivalent, it is simply a process of producing value; if, on the other hand, it be continued beyond that point, it becomes a process of creating surplus-value.

If we proceed further, and compare the process of producing value with the labour process, pure and simple, we find that the latter consists of the useful labour, the work, that produces use-values. Here we contemplate the labour as producing a particular article; we view it under its qualitative aspect alone, with regard to its end and aim. But viewed as a value-creating process, the same labour process presents itself under its quantitative aspect alone. Here it is a question merely of the time occupied by the labourer in doing the work; of the period during which the labour-power is usefully expended. Here the commodities that take part in the process do not count any longer as necessary adjuncts of labour-power in the production of a definite, useful object. They count merely as depositaries of so much absorbed or materialised labour; that labour, whether previously embodied in the means of production, or incorporated in them for the first time during the process by the action of labour-power, counts in either case only according to its duration; it amounts to so many hours or days as the case may be.

Moreover, only so much of the time spent in the production of any article is counted, as, under the given social conditions, is necessary. The consequences of this are various. In the first place, it becomes necessary that the labour should be carried on under normal conditions. If a self-acting mule is the implement in general use for spinning, it would be absurd to supply the spinner with a distaff and spinning wheel. The cotton too must not be such rubbish as to cause extra waste in being worked, but must be of suitable quality. Otherwise the spinner would be found to spend more time in producing a pound of yarn than is socially necessary, in which case the excess of time would create neither value nor money. But whether the material factors of the process are of normal quality or not depends not upon the labourer, but entirely upon the capitalist. Then again, the labour-power itself must be of average efficacy. In the trade in which it is being employed, it must possess the average skill, handiness, and quickness prevalent in that trade, and our capitalist took good care to buy labour-power of such normal goodness. This power must be applied with the average amount of exertion and with the usual degree of intensity; and the capitalist is as careful to see that this is done, as that his workmen are not idle for a single moment. He has bought the use of the labour-power for a definite period, and he insists upon his rights. He has no intention of being robbed. Lastly, and for this purpose our friend has a penal code of his own, all wasteful consumption of raw material or instruments of labour is strictly forbidden, because what is so wasted represents labour superfluously expended, labour that does not count in the product or enter into its value.

We now see that the difference between labour, considered on the one hand as producing utilities, and on the other hand as creating value, a difference which we discovered by our analysis of a commodity, resolves itself into a distinction between two aspects of the process of production.

The process of production, considered on the one hand as the unity of the labour process and the process of creating value, is production of commodities; considered on the other hand as the unity of the labour process and the process of producing surplus-value, it is the capitalist process of production, or capitalist production of commodities.

We stated, on a previous page, that in the creation of surplus-value it does not in the least matter, whether the labour appropriated by the capitalist be simple unskilled labour of average quality or more complicated skilled labour. All labour of a higher or more complicated character than average labour is expenditure of labour-power of a more costly kind, labour-power whose production has cost more time and labour, and which therefore has a higher value, than unskilled or simple labour-power. This power being of higher value, its consumption is labour of a higher class, labour that creates in equal times proportionally higher values than unskilled labour does. Whatever difference in skill there may be between the labour of a spinner and that of a jeweller, the portion of his labour by which the jeweller merely replaces the value of his own labour-power, does not in any way differ in quality from the additional portion by which he creates surplus-value. In the making of jewellery, just as in spinning, the surplus-value results only from a quantitative excess of labour, from a lengthening out of one and the same labour process, in the one case, of the process of making jewels, in the other of the process of making yarn.

But on the other hand, in every process of creating value, the reduction of skilled labour to average social labour, e.g., one day of skilled to six days of unskilled labour, is unavoidable. We therefore save ourselves a superfluous operation, and simplify our analysis, by the assumption that the labour of the workman employed by the capitalist is unskilled average labour.

VII. CONSTANT CAPITAL AND VARIABLE CAPITAL

By our explanation of the different parts played by the various factors of the labour process in the formation of the product's value, we have, in fact, disclosed the characters of the different functions allotted to the different elements of capital in the process of expanding its own value. The surplus of the total value of the product, over the sum of the values of its constituent factors, is the surplus of the expanded capital over the capital originally advanced. The means of production on the one hand, labour-power on the other, are merely the different modes of existence which the value of the original capital assumed when from being money it was transformed into the various factors of the labour process. That part of capital then, which is represented by the means of production, by the raw material, auxiliary material, and the instruments of labour does not, in the process of production, undergo any quantitative alteration of value. I therefore call it the constant part of capital, or, more shortly, *constant capital*.

On the other hand, that part of capital represented by labour-power does, in the process of production, undergo an alteration of value. It both reproduces the equivalent of its own value and also produces an excess, a surplus-value, which may itself vary, may be more or less according to circumstances. This part of capital is continually being transformed from a constant into a variable magnitude. I therefore call it the variable part of capital, or, shortly, *variable capital*. The same elements of capital which, from the point of view of the labour process, present themselves respectively as the objective and subjective factors, as means of production and labour-power, present themselves, from the point of view of the process of creating surplus-value, as constant and variable capital.

VIII. THE RATE OF SURPLUS-VALUE

1. The Degree of Exploitation of Labour-Power

The method of calculating the rate of surplus-value is, shortly, as follows. We take the total value of the product and put the constant capital which merely reappears in it equal to zero. What remains is the only value that has, in the process of producing the commodity, been actually created. If the amount of surplus-value be given, we have only to deduct it from this remainder, to find the variable capital. And vice versa, if the latter be given and we require to find the surplus-value. If both be given, we have only to perform the concluding operation, viz., to calculate $\frac{s}{v}$, the ratio of the surplus-value to the variable capital.

Though the method is so simple, yet it may not be amiss, by means of a few examples, to exercise the reader in the application of the novel principles underlying it.

First we will take the case of a spinning mill containing 10,000 mule spindles, spinning No. 32 yarn from American cotton and producing 1 lb. of yarn weekly per spindle. We assume the waste to be 6 per cent: under these circumstances 10,600 lbs. of cotton are consumed weekly, of which 600 lbs. go to waste. The price of the cotton in April, 1871, was 7¾d. per lb.; the raw material therefore costs in round numbers £342. The 10,000 spindles, including preparation machinery and motive power, cost, we will assume, £1 per spindle, amounting to a total of £10,000. The wear and tear we put at 10 per cent, or £1000 yearly=£20 weekly. The rent of the building we suppose to be £300 a year or £6 a week. Coal consumed (for 100 horsepower indicated, at 4 lbs. of coal per horsepower per hour during 60 hours, and inclusive of that consumed in heating the mill) 11 tons a week at 8s. 6d. a ton, amounts to about £4½ a week: gas, £1 a week, oil, etc., £4½ a week. Total cost of the above auxiliary materials, £10 weekly. Therefore the constant portion of the value of the week's product is £378. Wages amount to £52 a week. The price of the yarn is 12¼d. per lb., which gives for the value of 10,000 lbs. the sum of £510. The surplus-value is therefore in this case £510—£430=£80. We put the constant part of the value of the product=0, as it plays no part in the creation of value. There remains £132 as the weekly value created, which=£52 var.+£80 surpl. The rate of surplus-value is therefore 80/52=153 11/13 per cent. In a working day of 10 hours with average labour the result is: necessary labour=3 31/33 hours and surplus-labour =6 2/33.

One more example. Jacob gives the following calculation for the year 1815. Owing to the previous adjustment of several items it is very imperfect; nevertheless for our purpose it is sufficient. In it he assumes the price of wheat to be 8s. a quarter, and the average yield per acre to be 22 bushels.

VALUE PRODUCED PER ACRE

	£	s.	d.		£	s.	d.
Seed	£1	9	0	Tithes, Rates, and Taxes	£1	1	0
Manure	2	10	0	Rent	1	8	0
Wages	3	10	0	Farmer's Profit and Interest	1	2	0
Total	£7	9	0	Total	£3	11	0

Assuming that the price of the product is the same as its value, we here find the surplus-value distributed under the various heads of profit, interest, rent, etc. We have nothing to do with these in detail; we simply add them together, and the sum is a surplus-value of £3 11s. 0 d. The sum of £3 19s. 0 d., paid for seed and manure, is constant capital, and we put it equal to zero. There is left the sum of £3 10s. 0 d., which is the variable capital advanced: and we see that a new value of £3 10s. 0 d. + £3 11s. 0 d. has been produced in its place. Therefore $\frac{s}{v} = \frac{\text{£3 11s. 0d.}}{\text{£3 10s. 0d.}}$, giving a rate of surplus-value of more than 100 per cent. The labourer employs more than one half of his working day in producing the surplus-value, which different persons, under different pretexts, share amongst themselves.

2. *Senior's "Last Hour"*

One fine morning, in the year 1836, Nassau W. Senior, who may be called the *bel esprit* of English economists, well known, alike for his economical "science" and for his beautiful style, was summoned from Oxford to Manchester, to learn in the latter place the political economy that he taught in the former. The manufacturers elected him as their champion, not only against the newly passed Factory Act, but against the still more menacing Ten-hours' agitation. With their usual practical acuteness, they had found out that the learned professor "wanted a good deal of finishing"; it was this discovery that caused them to write for him. On his side the professor has embodied the lecture he received from the Manchester manufacturers in a pamphlet, entitled *Letters on the Factory Act, as it affects the cotton manufacture* (London, 1837). Here we find the following edifying passage: "Under the present law, no mill in which persons under 18 years of age are employed . . . can be worked more than 11½ hours a day, that is, 12 hours for 5 days in the week, and 9 on Saturday.

"Now the following analysis (!) will show that in a mill so worked, the whole net profit is derived *from the last hour*. I will suppose a manufacturer to invest £100,000:—£80,000 in his mill and machinery, and £20,000 in raw material and wages. The annual return of that mill, supposing the capital to be turned once a year and gross profits to be 15 per cent., ought to be goods worth £115,000. . . . Of this £115,000 each of the 23 half-hours of work produces 5-115ths or one twenty-third. Of these 23-23rds (constituting the whole £115,000) twenty, that is to say £100,000 out of the £115,000, simply replace the capital;—one twenty-third (or £5000 out of the £115,000) makes up for the deterioration of the mill and machinery. The remaining 2-23rds that is, the last two of the 23 half-hours of every day, produce the net profit of 10 per cent. If, therefore (prices remaining the same), the factory could be kept at work 13 hours instead of 11½, with an addition of about £2600 to the circulating capital, the net profit would be more than doubled. On the other hand, if the hours of working were reduced by one hour per day (prices remaining the same), the *net* profit would be destroyed—if they were reduced by one hour and a half, even the *gross* profit would be destroyed."

And the professor calls this an "analysis"! If, giving credence to the outcries of the manufacturers, he believed that the workmen spend the best part of the day in the production, i.e., the reproduction or replacement of the value of the buildings, machinery, cotton, coal, etc., then his analysis was superfluous. His answer would simply have been: Gentlemen! if you work your mills for 10 hours instead of 11½, then, other things being equal, the daily consumption of cotton, machinery, etc., will decrease in proportion. You gain just as much as you lose. Your work-people will in future spend one hour and a half less time in producing or replacing the capital that has been advanced. If, on the other hand, he did not believe them without further inquiry, but, as being an expert in such matters, deemed an analysis necessary, then he ought, in a question that is concerned exclusively with the relations of net profit to the length of the working day, before all things to have asked the manufacturers to be careful not to lump together machinery, workshops, raw material, and labour, but to be good enough to place the constant capital, invested in buildings, machinery, raw material, etc., on one side of the account, and the capital advanced in wages on the other side. If the professor then found that, in accordance with the calculation of the manufacturers, the workman reproduced or replaced his wages in 2 half-hours, in that case, he should have continued his analysis thus:

According to your figures, the workman in the last hour but one produces his wages, and in the last hour your surplus-value or net profit. Now, since in equal periods he produces equal values, the produce of the last hour but one must have the same value as that of the last hour. Further, it is only while he labours that he produces any value at all, and the amount of his labour is measured by his labour time. This, you say, amounts to 11½ hours a day. He employs one portion of these 11½ hours in producing or replacing his wages, and the remaining portion in producing your net profit. Beyond this he does absolutely nothing. But since, on your assumption, his wages and the surplus-value he yields are of equal value, it is clear that he produces his wages in 5¾ hours, and your net profit in the other 5¾ hours. Again, since the value of the yarn produced in 2 hours is equal to the sum of the values of his wages and of your net profit, the measure of the value of this yarn must be

11½ working hours, of which 5¾ hours measure the value of the yarn produced in the last hour but one, and 5¾, the value of the yarn produced in the last hour. We now come to a ticklish point; therefore, attention! The last working hour but one is, like the first, an ordinary working hour, neither more nor less. How then can the spinner produce in one hour, in the shape of yarn, a value that embodies 5¾ hours' labour? The truth is that he performs no such miracle. The use-value produced by him in one hour is a definite quantity of yarn. The value of this yarn is measured by 5¾ working hours, of which 4¾ were, without any assistance from him, previously embodied in the means of production, in the cotton, the machinery, and so on; the remaining one hour is added by him. Therefore, since his wages are produced in 5¾ hours, and the yarn produced in one hour also contains 5¾ hours' work, there is no witchcraft in the result, that the value created by his 5¾ hours' spinning is equal to the value of the product spun in one hour. You are altogether on the wrong track if you think that he loses a single moment of his working day in reproducing or replacing the values of the cotton, the machinery, and so on. On the contrary, it is because his labour converts the cotton and spindles into yarn, because he spins, that the values of the cotton and spindles go over to the yarn of their own accord. This result is owing to the quality of his labour, not to its quantity. It is true, he will in one hour transfer to the yarn more value, in the shape of cotton, than he will in half an hour; but that is only because in one hour he spins up more cotton than in half an hour. You see, then, your assertion that the workman produces, in the last hour but one, the value of his wages, and in the last hour your net profit, amounts to no more than this, that in the yarn produced by him in 2 working hours, whether they are the 2 first or the 2 last hours of the working day, in that yarn there are incorporated 11½ working hours, or just a whole day's work, i.e., 2 hours of his own work and 9½ hours of other people's. And my assertion that, in the first 5¾ hours, he produces his wages, and in the last 5¾ hours your net profit, amounts only to this, that you pay him for the former, but not for the latter. In speaking of payment of labour, instead of payment of labour-power, I only talk your own slang. Now, gentlemen, if you compare the working time you pay for with that which you do not pay for, you will find that they are to one another as half a day is to half a day; this gives a rate of 100 per cent, and a very pretty percentage it is. Further, there is not the least doubt that if you make your "hands" toil for 13 hours instead of 11½, and, as may be expected from you, treat the work done in that extra one hour and a half as pure surplus labour, then the latter will be increased from 5¾ hours' labour to 7¼ hours' labour, and the rate of surplus-value from 100 per cent to 126 2/23 per cent. So that you are altogether too sanguine, in expecting that by such an addition of 1½ hours to the working day the rate will rise from 100 per cent to 200 per cent and more, in other words that it will be "more than doubled." On the other hand—man's heart is a wonderful thing, especially when carried in the purse—you take too pessimistic a view when you fear that with a reduction of the hours of labour from 11½ to 10, the whole of your net profit will go to the dogs. Not at all. All other conditions remaining the same, the surplus-labour will fall from 5¾ hours to 4¾ hours, a period that still gives a very profitable rate of surplus-value, namely 82 14/32 per cent. But this dreadful "last hour," about which you have invented more stories than have the millenarians about the day of judgment, is "all bosh." If it goes, it will cost neither you, your net profit, nor the boys and girls whom you employ, their "purity of mind." Whenever *your* "last hour" strikes in earnest, think on the Oxford professor. And now, gentlemen, "farewell, and may we meet again in yonder better world, but not before."

3. *Surplus-Produce*

The portion of the product that represents the surplus-value we call "surplus-produce." Just as the rate of surplus-value is determined by its relation, not to the sum total of the capital, but to its variable part; in like manner, the relative quantity of surplus-produce is determined by the ratio that this produce bears, not to the remaining part of the total product, but to that part of it in which is incorporated the necessary labour. Since the production of surplus-value is the chief end and aim of capitalist production, it is clear that the greatness of a man's or a nation's wealth should be measured not by the absolute quantity produced, but by the relative magnitude of the surplus-produce.

IX. THE WORKING DAY

1. *The Limits of the Working Day*

THE CAPITALIST has bought the labour-power at its day rate. To him its use-value belongs during one working day. He has thus acquired the right to make the labourer work for him during one day. But what is a working day?

At all events, less than a natural day. By how much? The capitalist has his own views of this *ultima Thule,* the necessary limit of the working day. As capitalist, he is only capital personified. His soul is the soul of capital. But capital has one single life impulse, the tendency to create value and surplus-value, to make its constant factor, the means of production, absorb the greatest possible amount of surplus-labour.

Capital is dead labour, that vampire-like only lives by sucking living labour, and lives the more, the more labour it sucks. The time during which the labourer works is the time during which the capitalist consumes the labour power he has purchased of him.

If the labourer consumes his disposable time for himself, he robs the capitalist.

The capitalist then takes his stand on the law of the exchange of commodities. He, like all other buyers, seeks to get the greatest possible benefit out of the use-value of his commodity. Suddenly the voice of the labourer, which had been stifled in the storm and stress of the process of production, rises:

The commodity that I have sold to you differs from the crowd of other commodities in that its use creates value and a value greater than its own. That is why you bought it. That which on your side appears a spontaneous expansion of capital is on mine extra expenditure of labour-power. You and I know on the market only one law, that of the exchange of commodities. And the consumption of the commodity belongs not to the seller, who parts with it, but to the buyer, who acquires it. To you, therefore, belongs the use of my daily labour-power. But by means of the price that you pay for it each day, I must be able to reproduce it daily and to sell it again. Apart from natural exhaustion through age, etc., I must be able on the morrow to work with the same normal amount of force, health, and freshness as today. You preach to me constantly the gospel of "saving" and "abstinence." Good! I will, like a sensible saving owner, husband my sole wealth, labour-power, and abstain from all foolish waste of it. I will each day spend, set in motion, put into action only as much of it as is compatible with its normal duration, and healthy development. By an unlimited extension of the working day you may in one day use up a quantity of labour-power greater than I can restore in three. What you gain in labour I lose in substance. The use of my labour-power and the spoliation of it are quite different things. If the average time that (doing a reasonable amount of work) an average labourer can live is 30 years, the value of my labour-power, which you pay me from day to day, is $\frac{1}{365 \times 30}$ or $\frac{1}{10950}$ of its total value. But if you consume it in ten years, you pay me daily $\frac{1}{10950}$ instead of $\frac{1}{3650}$ of its total value, i.e., only ⅓ of its daily value, and you rob me, therefore, every day of ⅔ of the value of my commodity. You pay me for one day's labour-power, whilst you use that of 3 days. That is against our contract and the law of exchanges. I demand, therefore, a working day of normal length, and I demand it without any appeal to your heart, for in money matters sentiment is out of place. You may be a model citizen, perhaps a member of the Society for the Prevention of Cruelty to Animals, and in the odour of sanctity to boot; but the thing that you represent face to face with me has no heart in its breast. That which seems to throb there is my own heart-beating. I demand the normal working day because I, like every other seller, demand the value of my commodity.

We see then that, apart from extremely elastic bounds, the nature of the exchange of commodities itself imposes no limit to the working day, no limit to surplus-labour. The capitalist maintains his rights as a purchaser when he tries to make the working day as long as possible, and to make, whenever possible, two working days out of one. On the other hand, the peculiar nature of the commodity sold implies a limit to its consumption by the purchaser, and the labourer maintains his right as seller when he wishes to reduce the working day to one of definite normal duration. There is here, therefore, an antinomy, right against right, both equally bearing the seal of the law of exchanges. Between equal rights force decides. Hence is it that in the history of capitalist production, the determination of what is a working day, presents itself as the result of a struggle, a struggle between collective capital, i.e., the class of capitalists, and collective labour, i.e., the working class.

2. *The Greed for Surplus-Labour. Manufacturer and Boyar*

Capital has not invented surplus-labour. Wherever a part of society possesses the monopoly of the means of production, the labourer, free or not free, must add to the working time necessary for his own maintenance an extra working time in order to produce the means of subsistence for the owners of the means of production, whether this proprietor be the Athenian καλὸς κἀγαθός, Etruscan theocrat, *civis Romanus,* Norman baron, American slave owner, Wallachian Boyar, modern landlord, or capitalist. It is, however, clear that in any given economic formation of society, where not the exchange value but the use-value of the product predominates, surplus-labour will be limited by a given set of wants which may be greater or less, and that here no boundless thirst for surplus-labour arises from the nature of the production itself. Hence in antiquity overwork becomes horrible only when the object is to obtain exchange value in its specific independent money form: in the production of gold and silver. Compulsory working to death is here the recognized form of overwork. Only read Diodorus Siculus. Still these are exceptions in antiquity. But as soon as people, whose production still moves within the lower forms of slave labour, *corvée* labour, etc., are drawn into the whirlpool of an international market dominated by the capitalistic mode of production, the sale of their products for export becoming their principal interest, the civilized horrors of overwork are grafted on the barbaric horrors of slavery, serfdom, etc. Hence the Negro labour in the Southern States of the American Union preserved something of a patriarchal character, so long as production was chiefly directed to immediate local consumption. But in proportion as the export of cotton became of vital interest to these states, the overworking of the Negro and sometimes the using up of his life in 7 years' labour became a factor in a calculated and calculating system. It was no longer a question of obtaining from him a certain quantity of useful products. It was now a question of production of surplus-labour itself. So was it also with the *corvée,* e.g., in the Danubian Principalities (now Rumania).

The comparison of the greed for surplus-labour in the Danubian Principalities with the same greed in English factories has special interest, because surplus-labour in the *corvée* has an independent and palpable form.

Suppose the working day consists of 6 hours of necessary labour and 6 hours of surplus-labour. Then the free labourer gives the capitalist every week 6 × 6, or 36 hours, of surplus-labour. It is the same as if he worked 3 days in the week for himself, and 3 days in the week gratis for the capitalist. But this is not evident on the surface. Surplus-labour and necessary labour glide one into the other. I can, therefore, express the same relationship by saying, e.g., that the labourer in every minute works 30 seconds for himself and 30 for the capitalist, etc. It is otherwise with the *corvée.* The necessary labour which the Wallachian peasant does for his own maintenance is distinctly marked off from his surplus-labour on behalf of the Boyar. The one he does on his own field, the other on the seignorial estate. Both parts of the labour time exist, therefore, independently, side by side one with the other. In the *corvée* the surplus-labour is accurately marked off from the necessary labour. This, however, can make no difference with regard to the quantitative relation of surplus-labour to necessary labour. Three days' surplus-labour in the week remain three days that yield no equivalent to the labourer himself, whether it be called *corvée* or wage-labour. But in the capitalist the greed for surplus-labour appears in the straining after an unlimited extension of the working day, in the Boyar more simply in a direct hunting after days of *corvée.*

In the Danubian Principalities the *corvée* was mixed up with rents in kind and other appurtenances of bondage, but it formed the most important tribute paid to the ruling class. Where this was the case, the *corvée* rarely arose from serfdom; serfdom much more frequently on the other hand took origin from the *corvée.* This is what took place in the Rumanian Provinces. Their original mode of production was based on community of the soil, but not in the Slavonic or Indian form. Part of the land was cultivated in severalty as freehold by the members of the community, another part—*ager publicus*—was cultivated by them in common. The products of this common labour served partly as a reserve fund against bad harvests and other accidents, partly as a public store for providing the costs of war, religion, and other common expenses. In course of time military and clerical dignitaries usurped, along with the common land, the labour spent upon it. The labour of the free peasants on their common land was transformed into *corvée* for the thieves of the common land. This *corvée* soon developed into a servile relationship existing in point of fact, not in point of law, until Russia, the liberator of the world, made it legal under pretence of abolishing serfdom. The code of the *corvée,* which the Russian General Kisseleff proclaimed in 1831, was of course dictated by the Boyars themselves. Thus Russia conquered with one blow the magnates of the Danubian Provinces, and the applause of liberal cretins throughout Europe.

According to the Réglement Organique, as this code of the *corvée* is called, every Wallachian peasant owes to the so-called landlord, besides a mass of detailed payments in kind: (1) 12 days of general labour; (2) one day of field labour; (3) one day of wood carrying. In all, 14 days in the year. With deep insight into political economy, however, the working day is not taken in its ordinary sense, but as the working day necessary to the production of an average daily product; and that average daily product is determined in so crafty a way that no Cyclops would be done with it in 24 hours. In dry words, the Réglement itself declares with true Russian irony that by 12 working days one must understand the product of the manual labour of 36 days, by 1 day of field labour 3 days, and by 1 day of wood carrying in like manner three times as much. In all, 42 *corvée* days. To this had to be added the so-called *jobagie,* service due to the lord for extraordinary occasions. In proportion to the size of its population, every village has to furnish annually a definite contingent to the jobagie. This additional *corvée* is estimated at 14 days for each Wallachian peasant. Thus the prescribed *corvée* amounts to 56 working days yearly. But the agricultural year in Wallachia numbers in consequence of the severe climate only 210 days, of which 40 for Sundays and holidays, 30 on an average for bad weather, together 70 days, do not count. One hundred and forty working days remain. The ratio of the *corvée* to the necessary labour 56/84 or 66⅔ per cent gives a much smaller rate of surplus-value than that which regulates the labour of the English agricultural or factory labourer. This is, however, only the legally prescribed *corvée.* And in a spirit yet more "liberal" than the English Factory Acts, the Réglement Organique has known how to facilitate its own evasion. After it has made 56 days out of 12, the nominal day's work of each of the 56 *corvée* days is again so arranged that a portion of it must fall on the ensuing day. In one day, e.g., must be weeded an extent of land, which, for this work, especially in maize plantations, needs twice as much time. The legal day's work for some kinds of agricultural labour is interpretable in such a way that the day begins in May and ends in October. In Moldavia conditions are still harder. "The *corvée* days of the Réglement Organique," cried a Boyar, drunk with victory, "amount to 365 days in the year."

If the Réglement Organique of the Danubian Provinces was a positive expression of the greed for surplus-labour which every paragraph legalised, the English Factory Acts are the negative expression of the same greed. These acts curb the passion of capital for a limitless draining of labour-power, by forcibly limiting the working day by state regulations, made by a state that is ruled by capitalist and landlord. Apart from the working-class movement that daily grew more threatening, the limiting of factory labour was dictated by the same necessity which spread guano over the English fields. The same blind eagerness for plunder that in the one case exhausted the soil had, in the other, torn up by the roots the living force of the nation. Periodical epidemics speak on this point as clearly as the diminishing military standard in Germany and France.

3. *Branches of English Industry without Legal Limits to Exploitation*

We have hitherto considered the tendency to the extension of the working day, the werewolf's hunger for surplus-labour in a department where the monstrous exactions, not surpassed, says an English bourgeois economist, by the cruelties of the Spaniards to the American redskins, caused capital at last to be bound by the chains of legal regulations. Now, let us cast a glance at certain branches of production in which the exploitation of labour is either free from fetters to this day, or was so yesterday.

Mr. Broughton Charlton, county magistrate, declared as chairman of a meeting held at the Assembly Rooms, Nottingham, on the 14th of January, 1860, "that there was an amount of privation and suffering among that portion of the population connected with the lace trade, unknown in other parts of the kingdom, indeed, in the civilized world . . . Children of nine or ten years are dragged from their squalid beds at two, three, or four o'clock in the morning and compelled to work for a bare subsistence until ten, eleven, or twelve at night, their limbs wearing away, their frames dwindling, their faces whitening, and their humanity absolutely sinking into a stone-like torpor, utterly horrible to contemplate . . ."

The manufacture of lucifer matches dates from 1833, from the discovery of the method of applying phosphorus to the match itself. Since 1845 this manufacture has rapidly developed in England, and has extended especially amongst the thickly populated parts of London as well as in Manchester, Birmingham, Liverpool, Bristol, Norwich, Newcastle, and Glasgow. With it has spread the form of lockjaw, which a Vienna physician in 1845 discovered to be a disease peculiar to lucifer-matchmakers. Half the workers are children under thirteen, and young persons under eighteen. The manufacture is on account of its unhealthiness and unpleasantness in such bad odour that only the most miserable part of the labouring class, half-starved widows and so forth, deliver up their children to it, "the ragged, half-starved, untaught children."

Of the witnesses that Commissioner White examined (1863), 270 were under 18, 50 under 10, 10 only 8, and 5 only 6 years old. [They revealed] a range of the working day from 12 to 14 or 15 hours, night labour, irregular meal times, meals for the most part taken in the very workrooms that are pestilent with phosphorus. Dante would have found the worst horrors of his Inferno surpassed in this manufacture.

No branch of industry in England (we do not take into account the making of bread by machinery recently introduced) has preserved up to the present day a method of production so archaic, so—as we see from the poets of the Roman Empire—pre-Christian, as baking. But capital, as was said earlier, is at first indifferent as to the technical character of the labour process; it begins by taking it just as it finds it.

The incredible adulteration of bread, especially in London, was first revealed by the House of Commons Committee "on the adulteration of articles of food" (1855–56) and Dr. Hassall's work, *Adulterations Detected*. The consequence of these revelations was the act of August 6, 1860, "for preventing the adulteration of articles of food and drink," an inoperative law, as it naturally shows the tenderest consideration for every free trader who determines by the buying or selling of adulterated commodities "to turn an honest penny." The Committee itself formulated more or less naïvely its conviction that free trade meant essentially trade with adulterated, or as the English ingeniously put it, "sophisticated" goods. In fact this kind of sophistry knows better than Protagoras how to make white black, and black white, and better than the Eleatics how to demonstrate *ad oculos* that everything is only appearance.

At all events the committee had directed the attention of the public to its "daily bread," and therefore to the baking trade. At the same time in public meetings and in petitions to Parliament rose the cry of the London journeymen bakers against their overwork, etc. The cry was so urgent that Mr. H. S. Tremenheere, also a member of the Commission of 1863, was appointed Royal Commissioner of Inquiry. His report, together with the evidence given, roused not the heart of the public but its stomach. Englishmen, always well up in the Bible, knew well enough that man, unless by elective grace a capitalist, or landlord, or sinecurist, is commanded to eat his bread in the sweat of his brow, but they did not know that he had to eat daily in his bread a certain quantity of human perspiration mixed with the discharge of abscesses, cobwebs, dead black beetles, and putrid German yeast, without counting alum, sand, and other agreeable mineral ingredients. Without any regard to his holiness, Free-trade, the free baking trade was therefore placed under the supervision of the State inspectors (at the close of the Parliamentary session of 1863), and by the same Act of Parliament work from 9 in the evening to 5 in the morning was forbidden for journeymen bakers under 18. The last clause speaks volumes as to the overwork in this old-fashioned, homely line of business.

"The work of a London journeyman baker begins, as a rule, at about eleven at night. At that hour he 'makes the dough'—a laborious process, which lasts from half an hour to three quarters of an hour, according to the size of the batch or the labour bestowed upon it. He then lies down upon the kneading board, which is also the covering of the trough in which the dough is 'made'; and with a sack under him, and another rolled up as a pillow, he sleeps for about a couple of hours. He is then engaged in a rapid and continuous labour for about five hours—throwing out the dough, 'scaling it off,' moulding it, putting it into the oven, preparing and baking rolls and fancy bread, taking the batch bread out of the oven, and up into the shop, etc., etc. The temperature of a bake-house ranges from about 75 to upwards of 90 degrees, and in the smaller bakehouses approximates usually to the higher rather than to the lower degree of heat. When the business of making the bread, rolls, etc., is over, that of its distribution begins, and a considerable proportion of the journeymen in the trade, after working hard in the manner described during the night, are upon their legs for many hours during the day, carrying baskets, or wheeling handcarts, and sometimes again in the bakehouse, leaving off work at various hours between 1 and 6 P.M. according to the season of the year, or the amount and nature of their master's business; while others are again engaged in the bakehouse in 'bringing out' more batches until late in the afternoon. . . . During what is called 'the London season,' the operatives belonging to the 'full-priced' bakers at the West End of the town, generally begin work at 11 P.M., and are engaged in making the bread, with one or two short (sometimes very short) intervals of rest, up to 8 o'clock the next morning. They are then engaged all day long, up to 4, 5, 6, and as late as 7 o'clock in the evening carrying out bread, or sometimes in the afternoon in the bakehouse again, assisting in the biscuit-baking. They may have, after they have done their work, sometimes five or six, sometimes only four or five hours' sleep before they begin again. On Fridays they always begin sooner, some about ten o'clock, and continue in some cases, at work, either in making or delivering the bread up to 8 P.M. on Saturday night, but more generally up to 4 or 5 o'clock, Sunday morning. On Sundays the men must attend twice or three times during the day for an hour or two to make preparations for the next day's bread. . . . The men employed by the underselling masters (who sell their bread under the 'full price,' and who, as already pointed out, comprise three-fourths of the London bakers) have not only to work on the average longer hours, but their work is almost entirely confined to the bakehouse. The underselling masters generally sell their bread . . . in the shop. If they send it out, which is not common, except as supplying chandlers' shops, they usually employ other hands for that purpose. It is not their practice to deliver bread from house to house. Towards the end of the week . . . the men begin on Thursday night at 10 o'clock, and continue on with only slight intermission until late on Saturday evening." (*First Report . . . Relating to the Grievances Complained of by the Journeymen Bakers,* London, 1862.)

Even the bourgeois intellect understands the position of the "underselling" masters. "The unpaid labour of the men was made the source whereby the competition was carried on." (George Read, *The History of Baking,* London, 1848.) And the "full-priced" baker denounces his underselling competitors to the Commission of Inquiry as thieves of foreign labour and adulterators. "They only exist now by first defrauding the public, and next getting 18 hours' work out of their men for 12 hours' wages." (*Report* cited.)

In Scotland, the agricultural labourer, the ploughman, protests against his 13–14 hours' work in the most inclement climate, with 4 hours' additional work on Sunday (in this land of Sabbatarians!), whilst, at the same time, three railway men are standing before a London coroner's jury—a guard, an engine driver, a signalman. A tremendous railway accident has hurried hundreds of passengers into another world. The negligence of the employees is the cause of the misfortune. They declare with one voice before the jury that ten or twelve years before, their labour only lasted eight hours a day. During the last five or six years it had been screwed up to 14, 18, and 20 hours, and under a specially severe pressure of holidaymakers, at times of excursion trains, it often lasted for 40 or 50 hours without a break. They were ordinary men, not Cyclops. At a certain point their labour-power failed. Torpor seized them. Their brain ceased to think, their eyes to see. The thoroughly "respectable" British jurymen answered by a verdict that sent them to the next assizes on a charge of manslaughter, and, in a gentle "rider" to their verdict, expressed the pious hope that the capitalistic magnates of the railways would, in future, be more extravagant in the purchase of a sufficient quantity of labour-power and more "abstemious," more "self-denying," more "thrifty," in the draining of paid labour-power.

In the last week of June, 1863, all the London daily papers published a paragraph with the "sensational" heading "Death from Simple Overwork." It dealt with the death of the milliner, Mary Anne Walkley, 20 years of age, employed in a highly respectable dressmaking establishment, exploited by a lady with the pleasant name of Elise. The old, often told story was once more recounted. This girl worked, on an average, 16½ hours, during the season often 30 hours, without a break, whilst her failing labour-power was revived by occasional supplies of sherry, port, or coffee. It was just now the height of the season. It was necessary to conjure up in the twinkling of an eye the gorgeous dresses for the noble ladies bidden to the ball in honour of the newly imported Princess of Wales. Mary Anne Walkley had worked without intermission for 26½ hours, with 60 other girls, 30 in one room, that only afforded ⅓ of the cubic feet of air required for them. At night they slept in pairs in one of the stifling holes into which the bedroom was divided by partitions of board. And this was one of the best millinery establishments in London. Mary Anne Walkley fell ill on the Friday, died on Sunday, without, to the astonishment of Madame Elise, having previously completed the work in hand. The doctor, Mr. Keys, called too late to the deathbed, duly bore witness before the coroner's jury that "Mary Anne Walkley had died from long hours of work in an overcrowded workroom, and a too small and badly ventilated bedroom." In order to give the doctor a lesson in good manners, the coroner's jury thereupon brought in a verdict that "the deceased had died of apoplexy, but there was reason to fear that her death had been accelerated by overwork in an overcrowded workroom, etc." "Our white slaves," cried the *Morning Star,* the organ of the free traders, Cobden and Bright, "our white slaves, who are toiled into the grave, for the most part silently pine and die."

4. *Day and Night Work. The Relay System*

Constant capital, the means of production, considered from the standpoint of the creation of surplus-value, only exist to absorb labour, and with every drop of labour a proportional quantity of surplus-labour. While they fail to do this, their mere existence causes a relative loss to the capitalist, for they represent during the time they lie fallow a useless advance of capital. And this loss becomes positive and absolute as soon as the intermission of their employment necessitates additional outlay at the recommencement of work. The prolongation of the working day beyond the limits of the natural day, into the night, only acts as a palliative. It quenches only in a slight degree the vampire thirst for the living blood of labour. To appropriate labour during all the 24 hours of the day is, therefore, the inherent tendency of capitalist production. But as it is physically impossible to exploit the same individual labour-power constantly during the night as well as the day, to overcome this physical hindrance, an alternation becomes necessary between the workpeople whose powers are exhausted by day and those who are used up by night. This alternation may be effected in various ways; e.g., it may be so arranged that part of the workers are one week employed on day work, the next week on night work. It is well known that this relay system, this alternation of two sets of workers, held full sway in the full-blooded youth time of the English cotton manufacture, and that at the present time it still flourishes, among others, in the cotton spinning of the Moscow district. This 24 hours' process of production exists today as a system in many of the branches of industry of Great Britain that are still "free," in the blast furnaces, forges, plate-rolling mills, and other metallurgical establishments in England, Wales, and Scotland. The working time here includes, besides the 24 hours of the 6 working days, a great part also of the 24 hours of Sunday. The workers consist of men and women, adults and children of both sexes. The ages of the children and young persons run through all intermediate grades, from 8 (in some cases from 6) to 18.

In some branches of industry, the girls and women work through the night together with the males.

Placing on one side the generally injurious influence of night labour, the duration of the process of production, unbroken during the 24 hours, offers very welcome opportunities of exceeding the limits of the normal working day, e.g., in the branches of industry already mentioned, which are of an exceedingly fatiguing nature; the official working day means for each worker usually 12 hours by night or day. But the overwork beyond this amount is in many cases, to use the words of the English official report, "truly fearful."

5. *The Struggle for a Normal Working Day. Compulsory Laws for the Extension of the Working Day from the Middle of the 14th to the End of the 17th Century*

"What is a working day? What is the length of time during which capital may consume the labour-power whose daily value it buys? How far may the working day be extended beyond the working time necessary for the reproduction of labour-power itself?" It has been seen that to these questions capital replies: the working day contains the full 24 hours, with the deduction of the few hours of repose without which labour-power absolutely refuses its services again. Hence it is self-evident that the labourer is nothing else, his whole life through, than labour-power, that therefore all his disposable time is by nature and law labour time, to be devoted to the self-expansion of capital. Time for education, for intellectual development, for the fulfilling of social functions and for social intercourse, for the free play of his bodily and mental activity, even the rest time of Sunday (and that in a country of Sabbatarians!)—moonshine! But in its blind unrestrainable passion, its werewolf hunger for surplus-labour, capital oversteps not only the moral but even the merely physical maximum bounds of the working day. It usurps the time for growth, development, and healthy maintenance of the body. It steals the time required for the consumption of fresh air and sunlight. It higgles over a mealtime, incorporating it where possible with the process of production itself, so that food is given to the labourer as to a mere means of production, as coal is supplied to the boiler, grease and oil to the machinery. It reduces the sound sleep needed for the restoration, reparation, refreshment of the bodily powers to just so many hours of torpor as the revival of an organism, absolutely exhausted, renders essential.

The slave owner buys his labourer as he buys his horse. If he loses his slave, he loses capital that can only be restored by new outlay in the slave mart. But "the rice-grounds of Georgia, or the swamps of the Mississippi may be fatally injurious to the human constitution; but the waste of human life which the cultivation of these districts necessitates, is not so great that it cannot be repaired from the teeming preserves of Virginia and Kentucky. Considerations of economy, moreover, which, under a natural system, afford some security for humane treatment by identifying the master's interest with the slave's preservation, when once trading in slaves is practised, become reasons for racking to the uttermost the toil of the slave; for, when his place can at once be supplied from foreign preserves, the duration of his life becomes a matter of less moment than its productiveness while it lasts. It is accordingly a maxim of slave management, in slave-importing countries, that the most effective economy is that which takes out of the human chattel in the shortest space of time the utmost amount of exertion it is capable of putting forth. It is in tropical culture, where annual profits often equal the whole capital of plantations, that Negro life is most recklessly sacrificed. It is the agriculture of the West Indies, which has been for centuries prolific of fabulous wealth, that has engulfed millions of the African race. It is in Cuba, at this day, whose revenues are reckoned by millions, and whose planters are princes, that we see in the servile class the coarsest fare, the most exhausting and unremitting toil, and even the absolute destruction of a portion of its numbers every year." (J. E. Cairnes, *The Slave Power,* London, 1862.)

Mutato nomine de te fabula narratur. For slave trade read labour market, for Kentucky and Virginia, Ireland and the agricultural districts of England, Scotland, and Wales, for Africa, Germany. We heard how overwork thinned the ranks of the bakers in London. Nevertheless, the London labour market is always overstocked with German and other candidates for death in the bakeries. Pottery is one of the shortest-lived industries. Is there any want therefore of potters? Josiah Wedgwood, the inventor of modern pottery, himself originally a common workman, said in 1785 before the House of Commons that the whole trade employed from 15,000 to 20,000 people. In the year 1861 the population alone of the town centers of this industry in Great Britain numbered 101,302. "The cotton trade has existed for ninety years. . . . It has existed for three generations of the English race, and I believe I may safely say that during that period it has destroyed nine generations of factory operatives." (Ferrand's Speech in the House of Commons, April 27, 1863.)

The establishment of a normal working day is the result of centuries of struggle between capitalist and labourer. The history of this struggle shows two opposed tendencies. Compare, e.g., the English factory legislation of our time with the English Labour Statutes from the 14th century to well into the middle of the 18th. Whilst the modern Factory Acts compulsorily shortened the working day, the earlier statutes tried to lengthen it by compulsion. Of course the pretensions of capital in embryo—when, beginning to grow, it secures the right of absorbing a *quantum sufficit* of surplus-labour, not merely by the force of economic relations, but by the help of the State—appear very modest when put face to face with the concessions that, growling and struggling, it has to make in its adult condition. It takes centuries ere the "free" labourer, thanks to the development of capitalistic production, agrees, i.e., is compelled by social conditions, to sell the whole of his active life, his very capacity for work, for the price of the necessaries of life, his birthright for a mess of pottage. Hence it is natural that the lengthening of the working day, which capital, from the middle of the 14th to the end of the 17th century, tries to impose by state measures on adult labourers, approximately coincides with the shortening of the working day which, in the second half of the 19th century, has here and there been effected by the State to prevent the coining of children's blood into capital. That which today, e.g., in the state of Massachusetts, until recently the freest state of the North American Republic, has been proclaimed as the statutory limit of the labour of children under 12 was in England, even in the middle of the 17th century, the normal working day of able-bodied artisans, robust labourers, athletic blacksmiths.

The first "Statute of Labourers" (23 Edward III, 1349) found its immediate pretext (not its cause, for legislation of this kind lasts centuries after the pretext for it has disappeared) in the great plague that decimated the people, so that, as a Tory writer says, "The difficulty of getting men to work on reasonable terms (i.e., at a price that left their employers a reasonable quantity of surplus-labour) grew to such a height as to be quite intolerable." Reasonable wages were, therefore, fixed by law as well as the limits of the working day. The latter point, the only one that here interests us, is repeated in the Statute of 1496 (Henry VIII). The working day for all artificers and field labourers from March to September ought, according to this statute (which, however, could not be enforced), to last from 5 in the morning to between 7 and 8 in the evening. But the mealtimes consist of 1 hour for breakfast, 1½ hours for dinner, and ½ an hour for "noon-meate," i.e., exactly twice as much as under the factory acts now in force. In winter, work was to last from 5 in the morning until dark, with the same intervals. A statute of Elizabeth of 1562 leaves the length of the working day for all labourers "hired for daily or weekly wage" untouched, but aims at limiting the intervals to 2½ hours in the summer, or to 2 in the winter. Dinner is only to last 1 hour, and the "afternoon-sleep of half an hour" is only allowed between the middle of May and the middle of August. For every hour of absence 1d. is to be subtracted from the wage. In practice, however, the conditions were much more favorable to the labourers than in the statute book. William Petty, the father of political economy and to some extent the founder of Statistics, says in a work that he published in the last third of the 17th century: "Labouring-men (then meaning field labourers) work 10 hours per diem, and make 20 meals per week, viz., 3 a day for working days, and 2 on Sundays; whereby it is plain, that if they could fast on Fryday nights, and dine in one hour and a half, whereas they take two, from eleven to one; thereby this working 1/20 more, and spending 1/20 less, the above-mentioned [tax] might be raised." Was not Dr. Andrew Ure right in crying down the 12 hours' bill of 1833 as a retrogression to the times of the Dark Ages? It is true, these regulations contained in the statute mentioned by Petty apply also to apprentices. But the condition of child labour, even at the end of the 17th century, is seen from the following complaint: "'Tis not their practice (in Germany) as with us in this kingdom, to bind an apprentice for seven years; three or four is their common standard: and the reason is, because they are educated from their cradle to something of employment, which renders them the more apt and docile, and consequently the more capable of attaining to a ripeness and quicker proficiency in business. Whereas our youth, here in England, being bred to nothing before they come to be apprentices, make a very slow progress and require much longer time wherein to reach the perfection of accomplished artists."

Still, during the greater part of the 18th century, up to the epoch of Modern Industry and machinism, capital in England had not succeeded in seizing for itself, by the payment of the weekly value of labour-power, the whole week of the labourer, with the exception, however, of the agricultural labourers. The fact that they could live for a whole week on the wage of four days did not appear to the labourers a sufficient reason that they should work the other two days for the capitalist. One party of English economists, in the interest of capital, denounces this obstinacy in the most violent manner; another party defends the labourers. Let us listen, e.g., to the contest between Postlethwayt, whose *Dictionary of Trade* then had the same reputation as the kindred works of McCulloch and McGregor today, and the author of the *Essay on Trade and Commerce.*

Postlethwayt says among other things: "We cannot put an end to those few observations, without noticing that trite remark in the mouth of too many; that if the industrious poor can obtain enough to maintain themselves in five days, they will not work the whole six. Whence they infer the necessity of even the necessaries of life being made dear by taxes, or any other means, to compel the working artisan and manufacturer to labour the whole six days in the week, without ceasing. I must beg leave to differ in sentiment from those great politicians, who contend for the perpetual slavery of the working people of this kingdom; they forget the vulgar adage, all work and no play. Have not the English boasted of the ingenuity and dexterity of her working artists and manufacturers which have heretofore given credit and reputation to British wares in general? What has this been owing to? To nothing more probably than the relaxation of the working people in their own way. Were they obliged to toil the year round, the whole six days in the week, in a repetition of the same work, might it not blunt their ingenuity, and render them stupid instead of alert and dexterous; and might not our workmen lose their reputation instead of maintaining it by such eternal slavery? . . . And what sort of workmanship could we expect from such hard-driven animals? . . . Many of them will execute as much work in four days as a Frenchman will in five or six. But if Englishmen are to be eternal drudges, 'tis to be feared they will degenerate below the Frenchmen. As our people are famed for bravery in war, do we not say that it is owing to good English roast beef and pudding in their bellies, as well as their constitutional spirit of liberty? And why may not the superior ingenuity and dexterity of our artists and manufacturers be owing to that freedom and liberty to direct themselves in their own way, and I hope we shall never have them deprived of such privileges and that good living from whence their ingenuity no less than their courage may proceed." Thereupon the author of the *Essay on Trade and Commerce* replies: "If the making of every seventh day an holiday is supposed to be of divine institution, as it implies the appropriating the other six days to labour" (he means capital as we shall soon see) "surely it will not be thought cruel to enforce it. . . . That mankind in general are naturally inclined to ease and indolence, we fatally experience to be true, from the conduct of our manufacturing populace, who do not labour, upon an average, above four days in a week, unless provisions happen to be very dear. . . . Put all the necessaries of the poor under one denomination; for instance, call them all wheat, or suppose that . . . the bushel of wheat shall cost five shillings and that he (a manufacturer) earns a shilling by his labour, he then would be obliged to work five days only in a week. If the bushel of wheat should cost but four shillings, he would be obliged to work but four days; but as wages in this kingdom are much higher in proportion to the price of necessaries . . . the manufacturer, who labours four days, has a surplus of money to live idle with the rest of the week. . . . I hope I have said enough to make it appear that the moderate labour of six days in a week is no slavery. Our labouring people do this, and to all appearance are the happiest of all our labouring poor, but the Dutch do this in manufactures, and appear to be a very happy people. The French do so, when holidays do not intervene. But our populace have adopted a notion, that as Englishmen they enjoy a birthright privilege of being more free and independent than in any country in Europe. Now this idea, as far as it may affect the bravery of our troops, may be of some use; but the less the manufacturing poor have of it, certainly the better for themselves and for the State. The labouring people should never think themselves independent of their superiors. . . . It is extremely dangerous to encourage mobs in a commercial state like ours, where, perhaps, seven parts out of eight of the whole are people with little or no property. The cure will not be perfect, till our manufacturing poor are contented to labour six days for the same sum which they now earn in four days." To this end, and for "extirpating idleness, debauchery and excess," promoting a spirit of industry, "lowering the price of labour in our manufactories, and easing the lands of the heavy burden of poor's rates," our "faithful Eckart" of capital proposes this approved device: to shut up such labourers as become dependent on public support, in a word, paupers, in "an *ideal workhouse.*" Such ideal workhouse must be made a "House of Terror," and not an asylum for the poor, "where they are to be plentifully fed, warmly and decently clothed, and where they do but little work." In this "House of Terror," this "ideal workhouse, the poor shall work 14 hours in a day, allowing proper time for meals, in such manner that there shall remain 12 hours of neat-labour."

Twelve working hours daily in the Ideal Workhouse, in the "House of Terror" of 1770! Sixty-three years later, in 1833, when the English Parliament reduced the working day for children of 13 to 18, in 4 branches of industry, to 12 full hours, the judgment day of English Industry had dawned! In 1852, when Louis Bonaparte sought to secure his position with the bourgeoisie by tampering with the legal working day, the French people cried out with one voice, "The law that limits the working day to 12 hours is the one good that has remained to us of the legislation of the Republic!" At Zurich the work of children over 10 is limited to 12 hours; in Aargau, in 1862, the work of children between 13 and 16 was reduced from 12½ to 12 hours; in Austria, in 1860, for children between 14 and 16, the same reduction was made. "What a progress" since 1770! Macaulay would shout with exultation!

The "House of Terror" for paupers, of which the capitalistic soul of 1770 only dreamed, was realised a few years later in the shape of a gigantic "Workhouse" for the industrial worker himself. It is called the Factory. And the ideal this time fades before the reality.

6. *The Struggle for the Normal Working Day. Reaction of the English Acts on Other Countries*

The reader will bear in mind that the production of surplus-value, or the extraction of surplus-labour, is the specific end and aim, the sum and substance, of capitalist production quite apart from any changes in the mode of production, which may arise from the subordination of labour to capital. He will remember that as far as we have at present gone, only the independent labourer, and therefore only the labourer legally qualified to act for himself, enters as a vendor of a commodity into a contract with the capitalist. If, therefore, in our historical sketch, modern industry, on the one hand, the labour of those who are physically and legally minors, on the other, play important parts, the former was to us only a special department, and the latter only a specially striking example of labour exploitation. Without, however, anticipating the subsequent development of our inquiry, from the mere connection of the historic facts before us, it follows:

First. The passion of capital for an unlimited and reckless extension of the working day is first gratified in the industries earliest revolutionised by water power, steam, and machinery, in those first creations of the modern mode of production, cotton, wool, flax, and silk spinning, and weaving. The changes in the material mode of production and the corresponding changes in the social relations of the producers gave rise first to an extravagance beyond all bounds and then, in opposition to this, called forth a control on the part of Society which legally limits, regulates, and makes uniform the working day and its pauses. This control appears, therefore, during the first half of the nineteenth century simply as exceptional legislation. As soon as this primitive dominion of the new mode of production was conquered, it was found that, in the meantime, not only had many other branches of production been made to adopt the same factory system, but that manufacturers with more or less obsolete methods, such as potteries, glassmaking, etc., that old-fashioned handicrafts, like baking, and, finally, even that the so-called domestic industries such as nailmaking, had long since fallen as completely under capitalist exploitation as the factories themselves. Legislation was, therefore, compelled to gradually get rid of its exceptional character, or where, as in England, it proceeds after the manner of the Roman Casuists, to declare any house in which work was done to be a factory.

Second. The history of the regulation of the working day in certain branches of production, and the struggle still going on in others in regard to this regulation, prove conclusively that the isolated labourer, the labourer as "free" vendor of his labour-power, when capitalist production has once attained a certain stage, succumbs without any power of resistance. The creation of a normal working day is, therefore, the product of a protracted civil war, more or less dissembled, between the capitalist class and the working class. As the contest takes place in the arena of modern industry, it first breaks out in the home of that industry—England. The English factory workers were the champions, not only of the English, but of the modern working class generally, as their theorists were the first to throw down the gauntlet to the theory of capital. Hence, the philosopher of the Factory, Ure, denounces as an ineffable disgrace to the English working class that they inscribed "the slavery of the Factory Acts" on the banner which they bore against capital, manfully striving for "perfect freedom of labour."

France limps slowly behind England. The February revolution [of 1848] was necessary to bring into the world the 12 hours' law, which is much more deficient than its English original. For all that, the French revolutionary method has its special advantages. It once for all commands the same limit to the working day in all shops and factories without distinction, whilst English legislation reluctantly yields to the pressure of circumstances, now on this point, now on that, and is getting lost in a hopelessly bewildering tangle of contradictory enactments. On the other hand, the French law proclaims as a principle that which in England was only won in the name of children, minors, and women, and has been only recently for the first time claimed as a general right.

In the United States of North America, every independent movement of the workers was paralysed so long as slavery disfigured a part of the Republic. Labour cannot emancipate itself in the white skin where in the black it is branded. But out of the death of slavery a new life at once arose. The first fruit of the Civil War was the 8 hours' agitation, that ran with the seven-leagued boots of the locomotive from the Atlantic to the Pacific, from New England to California. The General Congress of Labour at Baltimore (August 16, 1866) declared: "The first and great necessity of the present, to free the labour of this country from capitalistic slavery, is the passing of a law by which eight hours shall be the normal working day in all States of the American Union. We are resolved to put forth all our strength until this glorious result is attained." At the same time, the Congress of the International Working Men's Association at Geneva, on the proposition of the London General Council, resolved that "the limitation of the working day is a preliminary condition without which all further attempts at improvement and emancipation must prove abortive . . . the Congress proposes eight hours as the legal limit of the working day."

Thus the movement of the working class on both sides of the Atlantic, that had grown instinctively out of the conditions of production themselves, endorsed the words of the English Factory Inspector, R. J. Saunders: "Further steps towards a reformation of society can never be carried out with any hope of success, unless the hours of labour be limited, and the prescribed limit strictly enforced."

It must be acknowledged that our labourer comes out of the process of production other than he entered. In the market he stood as owner of the commodity "labour-power" face to face with other owners of commodities, dealer against dealer. The contract by which he sold to the capitalist his labour-power proved, so to say, in black and white that he disposed of himself freely. The bargain concluded, it is discovered that he was no "free agent," that the time for which he is free to sell his labour-power is the time for which he is forced to sell it, that in fact the vampire will not loose its hold on him "so long as there is a muscle, a nerve, a drop of blood to be exploited." For "protection" against "the serpent of their agonies," the labourers must put their heads together and, as a class, compel the passing of a law, an all-powerful social barrier that shall prevent the very workers from selling, by voluntary contract with capital, themselves and their families into slavery and death. In place of the pompous catalogue of the "inalienable rights of man" comes the modest Magna Charta of a legally limited working day, which shall make clear "when the time which the worker sells is ended, and when his own begins." *Quantum mutatus ab illo!*

PART FOUR: PRODUCTION OF RELATIVE SURPLUS-VALUE

X. THE CONCEPT OF RELATIVE SURPLUS-VALUE

THE SURPLUS-VALUE produced by prolongation of the working day, I call *absolute surplus-value*. On the other hand, the surplus-value arising from the curtailment of the necessary labour time, and from the corresponding alteration in the respective lengths of the two components of the working day, I call *relative surplus-value*.

XI. CO-OPERATION

WHEN numerous labourers work together side by side, whether in one and the same process or in different but connected processes, they are said to co-operate, or to work in co-operation.

Just as the offensive power of a squadron of cavalry, or the defensive power of a regiment of infantry, is essentially different from the sum of the offensive or defensive powers of the individual cavalry or infantry soldiers taken separately, so the sum total of the mechanical forces exerted by isolated workmen differs from the social force that is developed, when many hands take part simultaneously in one and the same undivided operation, such as raising a heavy weight, turning a winch, or removing an obstacle. In such cases the effect of the combined labour could either not be produced at all by isolated individual labour or it could only be produced by a great expenditure of time or on a very dwarfed scale. Not only have we here an increase in the productive power of the individual, by means of co-operation, but the creation of a new power, namely, the collective power of masses.

The colossal effects of simple co-operation are to be seen in the gigantic structures of the ancient Asiatics, Egyptians, Etruscans, etc. "It has happened in times past that these Oriental States, after supplying the expenses of their civil and military establishments, have found themselves in possession of a surplus which they could apply to works of magnificence or utility, and in the construction of these their command over the hands and arms of almost the entire non-agricultural population has produced stupendous monuments which still indicate their power. The teeming valley of the Nile . . . produced food for a swarming non-agricultural population, and this food, belonging to the monarch and the priesthood, afforded the means of erecting the mighty monuments which filled the land. . . . In moving the colossal statues and vast masses of which the transport creates wonder, human labour almost alone was prodigally used. . . . The number of the labourers and the concentration of their efforts sufficed. We see mighty coral reefs rising from the depths of the ocean into islands and firm land, yet each individual depositor is puny, weak, and contemptible. The non-agricultural labourers of an Asiatic monarchy have little but their individual bodily exertions to bring to the task, but their number is their strength, and the power of directing these masses gave rise to the palaces and temples, the pyramids, and the armies of gigantic statues of which the remains astonish and perplex us. It is that confinement of the revenues which feed them, to one or a few hands, which makes such undertakings possible." (Rev. Richard Jones, *Textbook of Lectures on the Political Economy of Nations,* Hertford, 1852.) This power of Asiatic and Egyptian kings, Etruscan theocrats, etc., has in modern society been transferred to the capitalist, whether he be an isolated or, as in joint stock companies, a collective capitalist.

Co-operation, such as we find it at the dawn of human development, among races who live by the chase, or say in the agriculture of Indian communities, is based, on the one hand, on ownership in common of the means of production and, on the other hand, on the fact that in those cases each individual has no more torn himself off from the navel string of his tribe or community than each bee has freed itself from connection with the hive. Such co-operation is distinguished from capitalistic co-operation by both of the above characteristics. The sporadic application of co-operation on a large scale in ancient times, in the Middle Ages, and in modern colonies reposes on relations of dominion and servitude, principally on slavery. The capitalistic form, on the contrary, presupposes from first to last the free wage labourer, who sells his labour-power to capital.

XII. DIVISION OF LABOUR AND MANUFACTURE

1. Twofold Origin of Manufacture

THAT CO-OPERATION which is based on division of labour, assumes its typical form in manufacture and is the prevalent characteristic form of the capitalist process of production throughout the manufacturing period properly so called. That period, roughly speaking, extends from the middle of the 16th to the last third of the 18th century.

Manufacture takes its rise in two ways:

(1) By the assemblage, in one workshop under the control of a single capitalist, of labourers belonging to various independent handi-

crafts, but through whose hands a given article must pass on its way to completion. A carriage, for example, was formerly the product of the labour of a great number of independent artificers, such as wheelwrights, harness makers, tailors, locksmiths, upholsterers, turners, fringe makers, glaziers, painters, polishers, gilders, etc. In the manufacture of carriages, however, all these different artificers are assembled in one building, where they work into one another's hands. It is true that a carriage cannot be gilt before it has been made. But if a number of carriages are being made simultaneously, some may be in the hands of the gilders while others are going through an earlier process. So far, we are still in the domain of simple co-operation, which finds its materials ready to hand in the shape of men and things. But very soon an important change takes place. The tailor, the locksmith, and the other artificers, being now exclusively occupied in carriage-making, each gradually loses, through want of practice, the ability to carry on, to its full extent, his old handicraft. But, on the other hand, his activity, now confined in one groove, assumes the form best adapted to the narrowed sphere of action. At first carriage manufacture is a combination of various independent handicrafts. By degrees it becomes the splitting up of carriage-making into its various detail processes, each of which crystallizes into the exclusive function of a particular workman, the manufacture, as a whole, being carried on by the men in conjunction. In the same way cloth manufacture, as also a whole series of other manufactures, arose by combining different handicrafts together under the control of a single capitalist.

(2) Manufacture also arises in a way exactly the reverse of this—namely, by one capitalist employing simultaneously in one workshop a number of artificers, who all do the same, or the same kind of work, such as making paper, type, or needles. This is co-operation in its most elementary form. Each of these artificers (with the help, perhaps, of one or two apprentices) makes the entire commodity, and he consequently performs in succession all the operations necessary for its production. He still works in his old handicraft-like way. But very soon external circumstances cause a different use to be made of the concentration of the workmen on one spot and of the simultaneousness of their work. An increased quantity of the article has perhaps to be delivered within a given time. The work is therefore redistributed. Instead of each man being allowed to perform all the various operations in succession, these operations are changed into disconnected, isolated ones, carried on side by side; each is assigned to a different artificer, and the whole of them together are performed simultaneously by the co-operating workmen. This accidental repartition gets repeated, develops advantages of its own, and gradually ossifies into a systematic division of labour. The commodity, from being the individual product of an independent

artificer, becomes the social product of a union of artificers, each of whom performs one, and only one, of the constituent partial operations. The same operations which, in the case of a papermaker belonging to a German Guild, merged one into the other as the successive acts of one artificer became in the Dutch paper manufacture so many partial operations carried on side by side by numerous co-operating labourers. The needlemaker of the Nuremberg Guild was the cornerstone on which the English needle manufacture was raised. But while in Nuremberg that single artificer performed a series of perhaps 20 operations one after another, in England it was not long before there were 20 needlemakers side by side, each performing one alone of those 20 operations; and in consequence of further experience, each of those 20 operations was again split up, isolated, and made the exclusive function of a separate workman.

The mode in which manufacture arises, its growth out of handicrafts, is therefore twofold. On the one hand, it arises from the union of various independent handicrafts, which become stripped of their independence and specialised to such an extent as to be reduced to mere supplementary partial processes in the production of one particular commodity. On the other hand, it arises from the co-operation of artificers of one handicraft; it splits up that particular handicraft into its various detail operations, isolating and making these operations independent of one another up to the point where each becomes the exclusive function of a particular labourer.

The productiveness of labour depends not only on the proficiency of the workman, but on the perfection of his tools. Tools of the same kind, such as knives, drills, gimlets, hammers, etc., may be employed in different processes; and the same tool may serve various purposes in a single process. But so soon as the different operations of a labour-process are disconnected the one from the other, and each fractional operation acquires in the hands of the detail labourer a suitable and peculiar form, alterations become necessary in the implements that previously served more than one purpose. The direction taken by this change is determined by the difficulties experienced in consequence of the unchanged form of the implement. Manufacture is characterised by the differentiation of the instruments of labour—a differentiation whereby implements of a given sort acquire fixed shapes, adapted to each particular application, and by the specialisation of those instruments, giving to each special instrument its full play only in the hands of a specific detail labourer. In Birmingham alone 500 varieties of hammers are produced, and not only is each adapted to one particular process, but several varieties often serve exclusively for the different operations in one and the same process. The manufacturing period simplifies, improves, and multiplies the implements of labour, by adapting them to the exclusively special functions of each detail labourer. It thus creates at the same time one of the material conditions for the existence of machinery, which consists of a combination of simple instruments.

The detail labourer and his implements are the simplest elements of manufacture. Let us now turn to its aspect as a whole.

2. *The Two Fundamental Forms of Manufacture: Heterogeneous Manufacture, Serial Manufacture*

The organisation of manufacture has two fundamental forms, which, in spite of occasional blending, are essentially different in kind, and, moreover, play very distinct parts in the subsequent transformation of manufacture into modern industry carried on by machinery. This double character arises from the nature of the article produced. This article either results from the mere mechanical fitting together of partial products made independently, or owes its completed shape to a series of connected processes and manipulations.

A locomotive, for instance, consists of more than 5000 independent parts. It cannot, however, serve as an example of the first kind of genuine manufacture, for it is a structure produced by modern mechanical industry. But a watch can; and William Petty used it to illustrate the division of labour in manufacture.

The second kind of manufacture, its perfected form, produces articles that go through connected phases of development, through a series of processes step by step, like the wire in the manufacture of needles, which passes through the hands of 72 and sometimes even 92 different detail workmen.

3. *Division of Labour in Manufacture, and Division of Labour in Society*

We first considered the origin of Manufacture, then its simple elements, then the detail labourer and his implements, and, finally, the totality of the mechanism. We shall now lightly touch upon the relation between the division of labour in manufacture and the social division of labour, which forms the foundation of all production of commodities.

If we keep labour alone in view, we may designate the separation of social production into its main division or *genera*—viz., agriculture, industries, etc.—as division of labour in general, and the splitting up of these families into species and sub-species, as division of labour in particular, and the division of labour within the workshop as division of labour in singular or in detail.

The foundation of every division of labour that is well developed, and brought about by the exchange of commodities, is the separation between town and country. It may be said that the whole economical history of society is summed up in the movement of this antithesis.

Just as a certain number of simultaneously employed labourers are the material prerequisites for division of labour in manufacture, so are the number and density of the population, which here correspond to the agglomeration in one workshop, a necessary condition for the division of labour in society. Nevertheless, this density is more or less relative. A relatively thinly populated country, with well-developed means of communication, has a denser population than a more numerously populated country, with badly developed means of communication; and in this sense the Northern States of the American Union, for instance, are more thickly populated than India.

But, in spite of the numberous analogies and links connecting them, division of labour in the interior of a society and that in the interior of a workshop differ not only in degree, but also in kind. The analogy appears most indisputable where there is an invisible bond uniting the various branches of trade. For instance, the cattle breeder produces hides, the tanner makes the hides into leather, and the shoemaker the leather into boots. Here the thing produced by each of them is but a step towards the final form, which is the product of all their labours combined. There are, besides, all the various industries that supply the cattle breeder, the tanner, and the shoemaker with the means of production. Now it is quite possible to imagine, with Adam Smith, that the difference between the above social division of labour and the division in manufacture is merely subjective, exists merely for the observer, who, in a manufacture, can see with one glance all the numerous operations being performed on one spot, while in the instance given above, the spreading out of the work over great areas and the great number of people employed in each branch of labour obscure the connection. But what is it that forms the bond between the independent labours of the cattle breeder, the tanner, and the shoemaker? It is the fact that their respective products are commodities. What, on the other hand, characterises division of labour in manufactures? The fact that the detail labourer produces no commodities. It is only the common product of all the detail labourers that becomes a commodity. Division of labour in a society is brought about by the purchase and sale of the products of different branches of industry, while the connection between the detail operations in a workshop is due to the sale of the labour-power of several workmen to one capitalist, who applies it as combined labour-power. The division of labour in the workshop implies concentration of the means of production in the hands of one capitalist; the division of labour in society implies their dispersion among many independent producers of commodities. While within the workshop, the iron law of proportionality subjects definite numbers of workmen to definite functions, in the society outside the workshop chance and caprice have full play in distributing the producers and their means of production among the various branches of industry.

4. *The Capitalistic Character of Manufacture*

In manufacture, as well as in simple co-operation, the collective working organism is a form of existence of capital. The mechanism that is made up of numerous individual detail labourers belongs to the capitalist. Hence, the productive power resulting from a combination of labourers appears to be the productive power of capital. Manufacture proper not only subjects the previously independent workman to the discipline and command of capital, but, in addition, creates a hierarchic gradation of the workmen themselves. While simple co-operation leaves the mode of working by the individual for the most part unchanged, manufacture thoroughly revolutionises it and seizes labour-power by its very roots. It converts the labourer into a crippled monstrosity by forcing his detail dexterity at the expense of a world of productive capabilities and instincts; just as in the States of La Plata they butcher a whole beast for the sake of his hide or his tallow. Not only is the detail work distributed to the different individuals, but the individual himself is made the automatic motor of a fractional operation, and the absurd fable of Menenius Agrippa, which makes man a mere fragment of his own body, becomes realised.

"The understandings of the greater part of men," says Adam Smith, "are necessarily formed by their ordinary employments. The man whose whole life is spent in performing a few simple operations . . . has no occasion to exert his understanding. . . . He generally becomes as stupid and ignorant as it is possible for a human creature to become." After describing the stupidity of the detail labourer he goes on: "The uniformity of his stationary life naturally corrupts the courage of his mind. . . . It corrupts even the activity of his body and renders him incapable of exerting his strength with vigour and perseverance in any other employments than that to which he has been bred. His dexterity at his own particular trade seems in this manner to be acquired at the expense of his intellectual, social, and martial virtues. But in every improved and civilised society, this is the state into which the labouring poor, that is, the great body of the people, must necessarily fall." For preventing the complete deterioration of the great mass of the people by division of labour, A. Smith commends education of the people by the State, but prudently, and in homeopathic doses. G. Garnier, his French translator and commentator, who, under the first French Empire, quite naturally developed into a senator, quite as naturally opposes him on this point. Education of the masses, he urges, violates the first law of the division of labour, and with it "our whole social system would be proscribed." "Like all other divisions of labour," he says, "that between hand labour and head labour is more pronounced and decided in proportion as society (he rightly uses this word, for capital, landed property, and their State) becomes richer. This division of labour, like every other, is an effect of past, and a cause of future progress . . . ought the government then to work in opposition to this division of labour, and to hinder its natural course? Ought it to expend a part of the public money in the attempt to confound and blend together two classes of labour, which are striving after division and separation?"

Some crippling of body and mind is inseparable even from division of labour in society as a whole. Since, however, manufacture carries this social separation of branches of labour much further, and also, by its peculiar division, attacks the individual at the very roots of his life, it is the first to afford the materials for, and to give a start to, industrial pathology.

"To subdivide a man is to execute him, if he deserves the sentence, to assassinate him if he does not. . . . The subdivision of labour is the assassination of a people" [Garnier].

Political economy, which as an independent science first sprang into being during the period of manufacture, views the social division of labour only from the standpoint of manufacture, and sees in it only the means of producing more commodities with a given quantity of labour, and, consequently, of cheapening commodities and hurrying on the accumulation of capital. In most striking contrast with this accentuation of quantity and exchange-value is the attitude of the writers of classical antiquity, who hold exclusively by quality and use-value. In consequence of the separation of the social branches of production, commodities are better made, the various bents and talents of men select a suitable field, and without some restraint no important results can be obtained anywhere. Hence both product and producer are improved by division of labour. If the growth of the quantity produced is occasionally mentioned, this is only done with reference to the greater abundance of use-values. There is not a word alluding to exchange-value or to the cheapening of commodities. This aspect, from the standpoint of use-value alone, is taken by Plato, who treats division of labour as the foundation on which the division of society into classes is based, as by Xenophon, who with characteristic bourgeois instinct approaches more nearly to division of labour within the workshop. Plato's *Republic*, in so far as division of labour is treated in it, as the formative principle of the State, is merely the Athenian idealisation of the Egyptian system of castes, Egypt having served as the model of an industrial country to many of his contemporaries also, amongst others to Isocrates, and it continued to have this importance to the Greeks of the Roman Empire.

XIII. MACHINERY AND MODERN INDUSTRY

1. The Development of Machinery

JOHN STUART MILL says in his *Principles of Political Economy:* "It is questionable if all the mechanical inventions yet made have lightened the day's toil of any human being." That is, however, by no means the aim of the capitalistic application of machinery. Like every other increase in the productiveness of labour, machinery is intended to cheapen commodities, and, by shortening that portion of the working day in which the labourer works for himself, to lengthen the other portion that he gives, without an equivalent, to the capitalist. In short, it is a means for producing surplus-value.

In manufacture the revolution in the mode of production begins with the labour-power; in modern industry it begins with the instruments of labour. Our first inquiry then is, How are the instruments of labour converted from tools into machines, or, What is the difference between a machine and the implements of a handicraft?

All fully developed machinery consists of three essentially different parts—the motor mechanism, the transmitting mechanism, and finally the tool or working machine. The motor mechanism is that which puts the whole in motion. It either generates its own motive power, like the steam engine, the caloric engine, the electromagnetic machine, etc., or it receives its impulse from some already existing natural force, like the water wheel from a head of water, the windmill from wind, etc. The transmitting mechanism, composed of flywheels, shafting, toothed wheels, pullies, straps, ropes, bands, pinions, and gearing of the most varied kinds, regulates the motion, changes its form where necessary, as, for instance, from linear to circular, and divides and distributes it among the working machines. These two first parts of the whole mechanism are there solely for putting the working machines in motion, by means of which motion the subject of labour is seized upon and modified as desired. The tool, or working machine, is that part of the machinery with which the industrial revolution of the 18th century started. And to this day it constantly serves as such a starting point, whenever a handicraft, or a manufacture, is turned into an industry carried on by machinery.

On a closer examination of the working machine proper, we find in it, as a general rule, though often, no doubt, under very altered forms, the apparatus and tools used by the handicraftsman, or manufacturing workman; with this difference, that instead of being human implements, they are the implements of a mechanism, or mechanical implements. Either the entire machine is only a more or less altered mechanical edition of the old handicraft tool, as, for instance, the power loom; or the working parts fitted in the frame of the machine are old acquaintances, as spindles are in a mule, needles in a stocking loom, saws in a sawing machine, and knives in a chopping machine. The distinction between these tools and the body proper of the machine exists from their very birth; for they continue for the most part to be produced by handicraft, or by manufacture, and are afterwards fitted into the body of the machine, which is the product of machinery. The machine proper is therefore a mechanism that, after being set in motion, performs with its tools the same operations that were formerly done by the workman with similar tools. Whether the motive power is derived from man, or from some other machine, makes no difference in this respect. From the moment that the tool proper is taken from man and fitted into a mechanism, a machine takes the place of a mere implement. The difference strikes one at once, even in those cases where man himself continues to be the prime mover. The number of implements that he himself can use simultaneously is limited by the number of his own natural instruments of production, by the number of his bodily organs. In Germany, they tried at first to make one spinner work two spinning wheels, that is, to work simultaneously with both hands and both feet. This was too difficult. Later a treadle spinning wheel with two spindles was invented, but adepts in spinning, who could spin two threads at once, were almost as scarce as two-headed men. The jenny, on the other hand, even at its very birth, spun with 12–18 spindles, and the stocking loom knits with many thousand needles at once. The number of tools that a machine can bring into play simultaneously is from the very first emancipated from the organic limits that hedge in the tools of a handicraftsman.

In many manual implements the distinction between man as mere motive power and man as the workman or operator properly so-called is brought into striking contrast. For instance, the foot is merely the prime mover of the spinning wheel, while the hand, working with the spindle and drawing and twisting, performs the real operation of spinning. It is this last part of the handicraftsman's implement that is first seized upon by the industrial revolution, leaving to the workman, in addition to his new labour of watching the machine with his eyes and correcting its mistakes with his hands, the merely mechanical part of being the moving power. On the other hand, implements, in regard to which man has always acted as a simple motive power, as, for instance, by turning the crank of a mill, by pumping, by moving up and down the arm of a bellows, by pounding with a mortar, etc., such implements soon call for the application of animals, water, and wind as motive powers. Here and there, long before the period of manufacture, and also to some extent during that period, these implements pass over into machines, but without creating any revolution in the mode of production. It becomes evident, in the period of Modern Industry, that these implements, even under their form of manual tools, are already machines. For instance, the pumps with which the Dutch, in 1836–37, emptied the Lake of Harlem, were constructed on the principle of ordinary pumps; the only difference being that their pistons were driven by cyclopean steam engines, instead of by men. The common and very imperfect bellows of the blacksmith is, in England, occasionally converted into a blowing engine by connecting its arm with a steam engine. The steam engine itself, such as it was at its invention during the manufacturing period at the close of the 17th century, and such as it continued to be down to 1780, did not give rise to any industrial revolution. It was, on the contrary, the invention of machines that made a revolution in the form of steam engines necessary.

If we now fix our attention on that portion of the machinery employed in the construction of machines, which constitutes the operating tool, we find the manual implements reappearing, but on a cyclopean scale. The operating part of the boring machine is an immense drill driven by a steam engine; without this machine, on the other hand, the cylinders of large steam engines and of hydraulic presses could not be made. The mechanical lathe is only a cyclopean reproduction of the ordinary foot lathe; the planing machine, an iron carpenter, that works on iron with the same tools that the human carpenter employs on wood; the instrument that, on the London wharves, cuts the veneers, is a gigantic razor; the tool of the shearing machine, which shears iron as easily as a tailor's scissors cut cloth, is a monster pair of scissors; and the steam hammer works with an ordinary hammer head, but of such a weight that not Thor himself could wield it. These steam hammers are an invention of Nasmyth, and there is one that weighs over 6 tons and strikes with a verticle fall of 7 feet, on an anvil weighing 36 tons. It is mere child's play for it to crush a block of granite into powder, yet it is no less capable of driving, with a succession of light taps, a nail into a piece of soft wood.

2. *The Value Transferred by Machinery to the Product*

The productive forces resulting from co-operation and division of labour cost capital nothing. They are natural forces of social labour. So also physical forces, like steam, water, etc., when appropriated to productive processes, cost nothing. But just as a man requires lungs to breathe with, so he requires something that is the work of man's hand in order to consume physical forces productively. A water wheel is necessary to exploit the force of water, and a steam engine to exploit the elasticity of steam. Once discovered, the law of the deviation of the magnetic needle in the field of an electric current, or the law of magnetisation of iron, around which an electric current circulates, cost never a penny. But the exploitation of these laws for the purposes of telegraphy, etc., necessitates a costly and expensive apparatus. The tool, as we have seen, is not exterminated by the machine. From being a dwarf implement of the human organism, it expands and multiplies into the implement of mechanism created by man. Capital now sets the labourer to work, not with a manual tool, but with a machine which itself handles the tools. Although, therefore, it is clear at the first glance that, by incorporating both stupendous physical forces, and the natural sciences, with the process of production, Modern Industry raises the productiveness of labour to an extraordinary degree, it is by no means equally clear that this increased productive force is not, on the other hand, purchased by an increased expenditure of labour. Machinery, like every other component of constant capital, creates no new value, but yields up its own value to the product that it serves to beget. In so far as the machine has value, and, in consequence, parts with value to the product, it forms an element in the value of that product. Instead of being cheapened, the product is made dearer in proportion to the value of the machine.

It is evident that whenever it costs as much labour to produce a machine as is saved by the employment of that machine, there is nothing but a transposition of labour; consequently the total labour required to produce a commodity is not lessened or the productiveness of labour is not increased. It is clear, however, that the difference between the labour a machine costs and the labour it saves, in other words that the degree of its productiveness, does not depend on the difference between its own value and the value of the implement it replaces. As long as the labour spent on a machine, and consequently the portion of its value added to the product, remains smaller than the value added by the workman to the product with his tool, there is always a difference of labour saved in favour of the machine. The productiveness of a machine is therefore measured by the human labour-power it replaces. Before Eli Whitney invented the cotton gin in 1793, the separation of the seed from a pound of cotton cost an average day's labour. By means of his invention one Negress was enabled to clean 100 lbs. daily; and since then the efficacy of the gin has been considerably increased. A pound of cotton wool, previously costing 50 cents to produce, included after that invention more unpaid labour, and was consequently sold with greater profit at 10 cents. In India they employ for separating the wool from the seed an instrument, half machine, half tool, called a churka; with this one man and a woman can clean 28 lbs. daily. With the churka, invented some years ago by Dr. Forbes, one man and a boy produce 250 pounds daily. If oxen, steam, or water be used for driving it, only a few boys and girls as feeders are required. Sixteen of these machines driven by oxen do as much work in a day as formerly 750 people did on an average.

3. *The Approximate Effects of Machinery on the Workman*

The starting point of Modern Industry is, as we have shown, the revolution in the instruments of labour, and this revolution attains its most highly developed form in the organised system of machinery in a factory. Before we inquire how human material is incorporated with this objective organism, let us consider some general effects of this revolution on the labourer himself.

A. APPROPRIATION OF SUPPLEMENTARY LABOUR-POWER BY CAPITAL. THE EMPLOYMENT OF WOMEN AND CHILDREN

In so far as machinery dispenses with muscular power, it becomes a means of employing labourers of slight muscular strength, and those whose bodily development is incomplete, but whose limbs are all the more supple. The labour of women and children was, therefore, the first thing sought for by capitalists who used machinery. That mighty substitute for labour and labourers was forthwith changed into a means for increasing the number of wage labourers by enrolling, under the direct sway of capital, every member of the workman's family, without distinction of age or sex. Compulsory work for the capitalist usurped the place not only of the children's play, but also of free labour at home within moderate limits for the support of the family.

Machinery also revolutionises out and out the contract between the labourer and the capitalist, which formally fixes their mutual relations. Taking the exchange of commodities as our basis, our first assumption was that capitalist and labourer met as free persons, as independent owners of commodities; the one possessing money and means of production, the other labour-power. But now the capitalist buys children and young persons under age. Previously, the workman sold his own labour-power, which he disposed of nominally as a free agent. Now he sells wife and child. He has become a slave dealer. The demand for children's labour often resembles in form the inquiries for Negro slaves, such as were formerly to be read among the advertisements in American journals.

The moral degradation caused by the capitalistic exploitation of women and children has been so exhaustively depicted by F. Engels, in his *Lage der Arbeitenden Klasse Englands* [Condition of the Working Class in England], and other writers, that I need only mention the subject in this place. But the intellectual desolation, artificially produced by converting immature human beings into mere machines for the fabrication of surplus-value, a state of mind clearly distinguishable from that natural ignorance which keeps the mind fallow without destroying its capacity for development, its natural fertility, this desolation finally compelled even the English Parliament to make elementary education a compulsory condition to the "productive" employment of children under 14 years, in every industry subject to the Factory Acts.

B. PROLONGATION OF THE WORKING DAY

If machinery be the most powerful means for increasing the productiveness of labour—i.e., for shortening the working time required in the production of a commodity, it becomes in the hands of capital the most powerful means, in those industries first invaded by it, for lengthening the working day beyond all bounds set by human nature. It creates, on the one hand, new conditions by which capital is enabled to give free scope to this its constant tendency and, on the other hand, new motives with which to whet capital's appetite for the labour of others.

In the first place, in form of machinery, the implements of labour become automatic, things moving and working independent of the workman. They are thenceforth an industrial *perpetuum mobile,* that would go on producing forever, did it not meet with certain natural obstructions in the weak bodies and the strong wills of its human attendants. The automaton, as capital and because it is capital, is endowed, in the person of the capitalist, with intelligence and will; it is therefore animated by the longing to reduce to a minimum the resistance offered by that repellant yet elastic natural barrier, man. This resistance is moreover lessened by the apparent lightness of machine work, and by the more pliant and docile character of the women and children employed on it.

If, then, the capitalistic employment of machinery, on the one hand, supplies new and powerful motives to an excessive lengthening of the working day, and radically changes as well the methods of labour, as also the character of the social working organism, in such a manner as to break down all opposition to this tendency, on the other hand it produces, partly by opening out to the capitalist new strata of the working class, previously inaccessible to him, partly by setting free the labourers it supplants, a surplus working population, which is compelled to submit to the dictation of capital. Hence that remarkable phenomenon in the history of Modern Industry, that machinery sweeps away every moral and natural restriction on the length of the working day. Hence, too, the economical paradox, that the most powerful instrument for shortening labour time becomes the most unfailing means for placing every moment of the labourer's time and that of his family at the disposal of the capitalist for the purpose of expanding the value of his capital. "If," dreamed Aristotle, the greatest thinker of antiquity, "if every tool, when summoned, or even of its own accord, could do the work that befits it, just as the creations of Dædalus moved of themselves, or the tripods of Hephæstos went of their own accord to their sacred work, if the weavers' shuttles were to weave of themselves, then there would be no need either of apprentices for the master workers, or of slaves for the lords." And Antipatros, a Greek poet of the time of Cicero, hailed the invention of the water wheel for grinding corn, an invention that is the elementary form of all machinery, as the giver of freedom to female slaves, and the bringer back of the golden age. Oh! those heathens! They understood, as the learned Bastiat and before him the still wiser McCulloch have discovered, nothing of political economy and Christianity. They did not, for example, comprehend that machinery is the surest means of lengthening the working day. They perhaps excused the slavery of one on the ground that it was a means to the full development of another. But to preach slavery of the masses, in order that a few crude and half-educated parvenus might become "eminent spinners," "extensive sausage-makers," and "influential shoe black dealers," to do this, they lacked the bump of Christianity.

C. INTENSIFICATION OF LABOUR

The immoderate lengthening of the working day, produced by machinery in the hands of capital, leads to a reaction on the part of society, the very sources of whose life are menaced, and thence to a normal working day whose length is fixed by law. Thenceforth a phenomenon that we have already met with, namely, the intensification of labour, develops into great importance. Our analysis of absolute surplus-value had reference primarily to the extension or duration of the labour, its intensity being assumed as given. We now proceed to consider the substitution of a more intensified labour for labour of more extensive duration, and the degree of the former.

The shortening of the hours of labour creates, to begin with, the subjective conditions for the condensation of labour, by enabling the workman to exert more strength in a given time. So soon as that shortening becomes compulsory, machinery becomes in the hands of capital the objective means, systematically employed for squeezing out more labour in a given time. This is effected in two ways: by increasing the speed of the machinery and by giving the workman more machinery to tend. Improved construction of the machinery is necessary, partly because without it greater pressure cannot be put on the workman, and partly because the shortened hours of labour force the capitalist to exercise the strictest watch over the cost of production. The improvements in the steam engine have increased the piston speed, and at the same time have made it possible, by means of a greater economy of power, to drive with the same or even a smaller consumption of coal more machinery with the same engine. The improvements in the transmitting mechanism have lessened friction and, what so strikingly distinguishes modern from the older machinery, have reduced the diameter and weight of the shafting to a constantly decreasing minimum. Finally, the improvements in the operative machines have, while reducing their size, increased their speed and efficiency, as in the modern power loom; or, while increasing the size of their framework, have also increased the extent and number of their working parts, as in spinning mules, or have added to the speed of these working parts by imperceptible alterations of detail.

Dr. [Andrew] Ure, the Pindar of the automatic factory, describes it, on the one hand, as "combined co-operation of many orders of work-people, adult and young, in tending with assiduous skill, a system of productive machines, continuously impelled by a central power" (the prime mover); on the other hand, as "a vast automaton, composed of various mechanical and intellectual organs, acting in uninterrupted concert for the production of a common object, all of them being subordinate to a self-regulated moving force." These two descriptions are far from being identical. In one, the collective labourer, or social body of labour, appears as the dominant subject and the mechanical automaton as the object; in the other, the automaton itself is the subject, and the workmen are merely conscious organs, co-ordinate with the unconscious organs of the automaton and, together with them, subordinated to the central moving power. The first description is applicable to every possible employment of machinery on a large scale; the second is characteristic of its use by capital and therefore of the modern factory system. Ure prefers, therefore, to describe the central machine, from which the motion comes, not only as an automaton, but as an autocrat. "In these spacious halls the benignant power of steam summons around him his myriads of willing menials."

Along with the tool, the skill of the workman in handling it passes over to the machine. The capabilities of the tool are emancipated from the restraints that are inseparable from human labour-power. In handicrafts and manufacture the workman makes use of a tool; in the factory the machine makes use of him. There the movements of the instrument of labour proceed from him; here it is the movements of the machine that he must follow. In manufacture the workmen are parts of a living mechanism. In the factory we have a lifeless mechanism independent of the workman, who becomes its mere living appendage. "The miserable routine of endless drudgery and toil, in which the same mechanical process is gone through over and over again, is like the labour of Sisyphus. The burden of labour, like the rock, keeps ever falling back on the worn-out labourer" (Frederick Engels). At the same time that factory work exhausts the nervous system to the uttermost, it does away with the many-sided play of the muscles, and confiscates every atom of freedom, both in bodily and intellectual activity. The lightening of the labour, even, becomes a sort of torture, since the machine does not free the labourer from work, but deprives the work of all interest. Every kind of capitalist production, in so far as it is not only a labour process but also a process of creating surplus-value, has this in common, that it is not the workman that employs the instruments of labour, but the instruments of labour that employ the workman. But it is only in the factory system that this inversion for the first time acquires technical and palpable reality. By means of its conversion into an automaton, the instrument of labour confronts the labourer, during the labour process, in the shape of capital, of dead labour, that dominates, and pumps dry, living labour-power.

We shall here merely allude to the material conditions under which factory labour is carried on. Every organ of sense is injured in an equal degree by artificial elevation of the temperature, by the dust-laden atmosphere, by the deafening noise, not to mention danger to life and limb among the thickly crowded machinery, which, with the regularity of the seasons, issues its list of the killed and wounded in the industrial battle. Economy of the social means of production, matured and forced as in a hothouse by the factory system, is turned, in the hands of capital, into systematic robbery of what is necessary for the life of the workman while he is at work, robbery of space, light, air, and of protection to his person against the dangerous and unwholesome accompaniments of the productive process, not to mention the robbery of appliances for the comfort of the workman. Is Fourier wrong when he calls factories "tempered bagnios"?

4. *The Strife between Workman and Machine*

The contest between the capitalist and the wage labourer dates back to the very origin of capital. It raged on throughout the whole manufacturing period. But only since the introduction of machinery has the workman fought against the instrument of labour itself, the material embodiment of capital. He revolts against this particular form of the means of production, as being the material basis of the capitalist mode of production.

In the 17th century nearly all Europe experienced revolts of the workpeople against the ribbon loom, a machine for weaving ribbons and trimmings, called in Germany *Bandmühle, Schnurmühle,* and *Mühlenstuhl.* These machines were invented in Germany. Abbé Lancellotti, in a work that appeared in Venice in 1636 but which was written in 1579, says: "Anthony Müller of Danzig saw about 50 years ago in that town a very ingenious machine, which weaves 4 to 6 pieces at once. But the Mayor, being apprehensive that this invention might throw a large number of workmen on the streets, caused the inventor to be secretly strangled or drowned." In Leyden, this machine was not used till 1629; there the riots of the ribbon weavers at length compelled the Town Council to prohibit it. In Hamburg it was burnt in public by order of the Senate. The Emperor Charles VI, on February 9, 1719, renewed the edict of 1685, and not till 1765 was its use openly allowed in the Electorate of Saxony. This machine, which shook Europe to its foundations, was in fact the precursor of the mule and the power loom and of the Industrial Revolution of the 18th century. It enabled a totally inexperienced boy to set the whole loom with all its shuttles in motion by simply moving a rod backwards and forwards, and in its improved form produced from 40 to 50 pieces at once.

5. *The Theory of Compensation as Regards the Workpeople Displaced by Machinery*

James Mill, McCulloch, Torrens, Senior, John Stuart Mill, and a whole series besides of bourgeois political economists insist that all machinery that displaces workmen simultaneously and necessarily sets free an amount of capital adequate to employ the same identical workmen.

Suppose a capitalist to employ 100 workmen, at £30 a year each, in a carpet factory. The variable capital annually laid out amounts, therefore, to £3000. Suppose, also, that he discharges 50 of his workmen, and employs the remaining 50 with machinery that costs him £1500. To simplify matters, we take no account of buildings, coal, etc. Further suppose that the raw material annually consumed costs £3000, both before and after the change. Is any capital set free by this metamorphosis? Before the change the total sum of £6000 consisted half of constant and half of variable capital. After the change it consists of £4500 constant

(£3000 raw material and £1500 machinery) and £1500 variable capital. The variable capital, instead of being one half, is only one quarter of the total capital. Instead of being set free, a part of the capital is here locked up in such a way as to cease to be exchanged against labour-power: variable has been changed into constant capital. Other things remaining unchanged, the capital of £6000, can, in future, employ no more than 50 men. With each improvement in the machinery, it will employ fewer. If the newly introduced machinery had cost less than did the labour-power and implements displaced by it, if, for instance, instead of costing £1500, it had cost only £1000, a variable capital of £1000 would have been converted into constant capital and locked up; and a capital of £500 would have been set free. The latter sum, supposing wages unchanged, would form a fund sufficient to employ about 16 out of the 50 men discharged; nay, less than 16, for, in order to be employed as capital, a part of this £500 must now become constant capital, thus leaving only the remainder to be laid out in labour-power.

But suppose, besides, that the making of the new machinery affords employment to a greater number of mechanics, can that be called compensation to the carpetmakers, thrown on the streets? At the best, its construction employs fewer men than its employment displaces. The sum of £1500, that formerly represented the wages of the discharged carpet-makers, now represents in the shape of machinery: (1) the value of the means of production used in the construction of that machinery, (2) the wages of the mechanics employed in its construction, and (3) the surplus-value falling to the share of their "master." Further, the machinery need not be renewed till it is worn out. Hence, in order to keep the increased number of mechanics in constant employment, one carpet manufacturer after another must displace workmen by machines.

As a matter of fact, the apologists do not mean this sort of setting free. They have in their minds the means of subsistence of the liberated workpeople. It cannot be denied, in the above instance, that the machinery not only liberates 50 men, thus placing them at others' disposal, but, at the same time, it withdraws from their consumption and sets free means of subsistence to the value of £1500. The simple fact, by no means a new one, that machinery cuts off the workmen from their means of subsistence is, therefore, in economical parlance tantamount to this, that machinery liberates means of subsistence for the workman, or converts those means into capital for his employment. The mode of expression, you see, is everything. *Nominibus mollire licet mala.*

The real facts, which are travestied by the optimism of economists, are as follows: The labourers, when driven out of the workshop by the machinery, are thrown upon the labour market, and there add to the number of workmen at the disposal of the capitalists. They can no doubt seek for employment in some other branch. If they find it, and thus renew the bond between them and the means of subsistence, this takes place only by the intermediary of a new and additional capital that is seeking investment; not at all by the intermediary of the capital that formerly employed them and was afterwards converted into machinery. And even should they find employment, what a poor lookout is theirs! Crippled as they are by division of labour, these poor devils are worth so little outside their old trade that they cannot find admission into any industries, except a few of inferior kind, that are oversupplied with underpaid workmen. Further, every branch of industry attracts each year a new stream of men, who furnish a contingent from which to fill up vacancies and to draw a supply for expansion. So soon as machinery sets free a part of the workmen employed in a given branch of industry, the reserve men are also diverted into new channels of employment, and become absorbed in other branches; meanwhile the original victims, during the period of transition, for the most part starve and perish.

6. *Revolution Effected in Manufacture, Handicrafts, and Domestic Industry by Modern Industry*

A. OVERTHROW OF CO-OPERATION BASED ON HANDICRAFT AND ON THE DIVISION OF LABOUR

We have seen how machinery does away with co-operation based on handicrafts and with manufacture based on the division of handicraft labour. An example of the first sort is the mowing machine; it replaces co-operation between mowers. A striking example of the second kind is the needle-making machine. According to Adam Smith, 10 men in his day made in co-operation over 48,000 needles a day. On the other hand, a single needle machine makes 145,000 in a working day of 11 hours. One woman or one girl superintends 4 such machines, and so produces near upon 600,000 needles in a day and upwards of 3,000,000 in a week. A single machine, when it takes the place of co-operation or of manufacture, may itself serve as the basis of an industry of a handicraft character. Still, such a return to handicrafts is but a transition to the factory system, which, as a rule, makes its appearance so soon as the human muscles are replaced, for the purpose of driving the machines, by a mechanical motive power, such as steam or water. Here and there, but in any case only for a time, an industry may be carried on, on a small scale, by means of mechanical power. This is effected by hiring steam power, as is done in some of the Birmingham trades, or by the use of small caloric engines, as in some branches of weaving. In the Coventry silk-weaving industry the experiment of "cottage factories" was tried. In the centre of a square surrounded by rows of cottages an engine house was built and the engine connected by shafts with the looms in the cottages. In all cases the power was hired at so much per loom. The rent was payable weekly, whether the looms worked or not. Each cottage held from 2 to 6 looms; some belonged to the weaver, some were bought on credit, some were hired. The struggle between these cottage factories and the factory proper lasted over 12 years. It ended with the complete ruin of the 300 cottage factories. Wherever the nature of the process did not involve production on a large scale, the new industries that have sprung up in the last few decades, such as envelope making, steel-pen making, etc., have, as a general rule, first passed through the handicraft stage and then the manufacturing stage, as short phases of transition to the factory stage. The transition is very difficult in those cases where the production of the article by manufacture consists not of a series of graduated processes, but of a great number of disconnected ones. This circumstance formed a great hindrance to the establishment of steel-pen factories. Nevertheless, about 15 years ago, a machine was invented that automatically performed 6 separate operations at once.

B. PASSAGE OF MODERN MANUFACTURE AND DOMESTIC INDUSTRY INTO MODERN MECHANICAL INDUSTRY

The cheapening of labour-power, by sheer abuse of the labour of women and children, by sheer robbery of every normal condition requisite for working and living, and by the sheer brutality of overwork and night-work, meets at last with natural obstacles that cannot be overstepped. So also, when based on these methods, do the cheapening of commodities and capitalist exploitation in general. So soon as this point is at last reached—and it takes many years—the hour has struck for the introduction of machinery, and for the thenceforth rapid conversion of the scattered domestic industries and also of manufactures into factory industries.

An example, on the most colossal scale, of this movement is afforded by the production of wearing apparel. The production of wearing apparel is carried on partly in manufactories in whose workrooms there is but a reproduction of that division of labour, the *membra disjecta* of which were found ready to hand; partly by small master handicraftsmen; these, however, do not, as formerly, work for individual consumers, but for manufactories and warehouses, and to such an extent that often whole towns and stretches of country carry on certain branches, such as shoemaking, as a specialty; finally, on a very great scale by the so-called domestic workers, who form an external department of the manufactories, warehouses, and even of the workshops of the smaller masters.

The raw material, etc., is supplied by mechanical industry; the mass of cheap human material (*taillable à merci et miséricorde*) is composed of the individuals "liberated" by mechanical industry and improved agriculture. The manufactures of this class owed their origin chiefly to the capitalist's need of having at hand an army ready equipped to meet any increase of demand. These manufactures, nevertheless, allowed the scattered handicrafts and domestic industries to continue to exist as a broad foundation. The great production of surplus-value in these branches of labour and the progressive cheapening of their articles were and are chiefly due to the minimum wages paid, no more than requisite for a miserable vegetation, and to the extension of working time up to the maximum endurable by the human organism. It was in fact by the cheapness of the human sweat and the human blood, which were converted into commodities, that the markets were constantly being extended and continue daily to be extended; more especially was this the case with England's colonial markets, where, besides, English tastes and habits prevail. At last the critical point was reached. The basis of the old method, sheer brutality in the exploitation of the workpeople, accompanied more or less by a systematic division of labour, no longer sufficed for the extending markets and for the still more rapidly extending competition of the capitalists. The hour struck for the advent of machinery. The decisively revolutionary machine, the machine which attacks in an equal degree the whole of the numberless branches of this sphere of production, dressmaking, tailoring, shoemaking, sewing, hat making, and many others, is the sewing machine.

Its immediate effect on the workpeople is like that of all machinery, which, since the rise of modern industry, has seized upon new branches of trade. Children of too tender an age are sent adrift. The wage of the machine hands rises compared with that of the house workers, many of whom belong to the poorest of the poor. That of the better situated handicraftsmen, with whom the machine competes, sinks. The new machine hands are exclusively girls and young women. With the help of mechanical force, they destroy the monopoly that male labour had of the heavier work, and they drive off from the lighter work numbers of old women and very young children. The overpowering competition crushes the weakest of the manual labourers. The fearful increase in death from starvation during the last 10 years in London runs parallel with the extension of machine sewing.

C. THE FACTORY ACTS

Factory legislation, that first conscious and methodical reaction of society against the spontaneously developed form of the process of production, is, as we have seen, just as much the necessary product of modern industry as cotton yarn, self-actors, and the electric telegraph.

What could possibly show better the character of the capitalist mode of production than the necessity that exists for forcing upon it, by Acts of Parliament, the simplest appliances for maintaining cleanliness and health? In the potteries the Factory Act of 1864 "has whitewashed and cleansed upwards of 200 workshops, after a period of abstinence from any such cleaning, in many cases of 20 years, and in some, entirely" (this is the "abstinence" of the capitalist!) "in which were employed 27,800 artisans, hitherto breathing through protracted days and often nights of labour a mephitic atmosphere, and which rendered an otherwise comparatively innocuous occupation pregnant with disease and death." (*Report* of Inspectors of Factories, October 31, 1865.)

One step already spontaneously taken is the establishment of technical and agricultural schools, and of *"écoles d'enseignement professionnel,"* in which the children of the workingmen receive some little instruction in technology and in the practical handling of the various implements of labour. Though the Factory Act, that first and meagre concession wrung from capital, is limited to combining elementary education with work in the factory, there can be no doubt that when the working class comes into power, as inevitably it must, technical instruction, both theoretical and practical, will take its proper place in the working-class schools. There is also no doubt that such revolutionary ferments, the final result of which is the abolition of the old division of labour, are diametrically opposed to the capitalistic form of production and to the economic status of the labourer corresponding to that form. But the historical development of the antagonisms, immanent in a given form of production, is the only way in which that form of production can be dissolved and a new form established. *"Ne sutor ultra crepidam"*—this *ne plus ultra* of handicraft wisdom became sheer nonsense, from the moment the watchmaker Watt invented the steam engine, the barber Arkwright, the throstle, and the working jeweller Fulton, the steamship.

So long as factory legislation is confined to regulating the labour in factories, manufactories, etc., it is regarded as a mere interference with the exploiting rights of capital. But when it comes to regulating the so-called "home labour," it is immediately viewed as a direct attack on the *patria potestas,* on parental authority. The tenderhearted English Parliament long affected to shrink from taking this step. The force of facts, however, compelled it at last to acknowledge that modern industry, in overturning the economical foundation on which was based the traditional family and the family labour corresponding to it, had also unloosened all traditional family ties. The rights of the children had to be proclaimed. The final report of the Child Employment Commission of

1866 states: "It is unhappily, to a painful degree, apparent throughout the whole of the evidence, that against no persons do the children of both sexes so much require protection as against their parents." The system of unlimited exploitation of children's labour in general and the so-called home labour in particular is "maintained only because the parents are able, without check or control, to exercise this arbitrary and mischievous power over their young and tender offspring. . . . Parents must not possess the absolute power of making their children mere 'machines to earn so much weekly wage.' . . . The children and young persons, therefore, in all such cases may justifiably claim from the legislature, as a natural right, that an exemption should be secured to them, from what destroys prematurely their physical strength and lowers them in the scale of intellectual and moral beings." It was not, however, the misuse of parental authority that created the capitalistic exploitation, whether direct or indirect, of children's labour; but, on the contrary, it was the capitalistic mode of exploitation which, by sweeping away the economical basis of parental authority, made its exercise degenerate into a mischievous misuse of power. However terrible and disgusting the dissolution, under the capitalist system, of the old family ties may appear, nevertheless, modern industry, by assigning as it does an important part in the process of production, outside the domestic sphere, to women, to young persons, and to children of both sexes, creates a new economical foundation for a higher form of the family and of the relations between the sexes. It is, of course, just as absurd to hold the Teutonic-Christian form of the family to be absolute and final as it would be to apply that character to the ancient Roman, the ancient Greek, or the Eastern forms which, moreover, taken together form a series in historic development. Moreover, it is obvious that the fact of the collective working group being composed of individuals of both sexes and all ages must necessarily, under suitable conditions, become a source of humane development; although in its spontaneously developed, brutal, capitalistic form, where the labourer exists for the process of production, and not the process of production for the labourer, that fact is a pestiferous source of corruption and slavery.

PART FIVE: THE PRODUCTION OF ABSOLUTE AND OF RELATIVE SURPLUS-VALUE

XIV. ABSOLUTE AND RELATIVE SURPLUS-VALUE

FROM one standpoint, any distinction between absolute and relative surplus-value appears illusory. Relative surplus-value is absolute, since it compels the absolute prolongation of the working day beyond the labour time necessary to the existence of the labourer himself. Absolute surplus-value is relative, since it makes necessary such a development of the productiveness of labour as will allow of the necessary labour time being confined to a portion of the working day. But if we keep in mind the behaviour of surplus-value, this appearance of identity vanishes. Once the capitalist mode of production has been established and has become general, the difference between absolute and relative surplus-value makes itself felt, whenever there is a question of raising the rate of surplus-value. Assuming that labour-power is paid for at its value, we are confronted by this alternative: Given the productiveness of labour and its normal intensity, the rate of surplus-value can be raised only by the actual prolongation of the working day; on the other hand, given the length of the working day, that rise can be effected only by a change in the relative magnitudes of the components of the working day, viz., necessary labour and surplus labour; a change which, if the wages are not to fall below the value of labour-power, presupposes a change either in the productiveness or in the intensity of the labour.

If the labourer wants all his time to produce the necessary means of subsistence for himself and his race, he has no time left in which to work gratis for others. Without a certain degree of productiveness in his labour, he has no such superfluous time at his disposal; without such superfluous time no surplus labour, and therefore no capitalists, no slave-owners, no feudal lords, in one word, no class of large proprietors.

Thus we may say that surplus-value rests on a natural basis; but this is permissible only in the very general sense that there is no natural obstacle absolutely preventing one man from disburdening himself of the labour requisite for his own existence and burdening another with it, any more, for instance, than unconquerable natural obstacles prevent one man from eating the flesh of another. No mystical ideas must in any way be connected, as sometimes happens, with this historically developed productiveness of labour. It is only after men have raised themselves above the rank of animals, when therefore their labour has been to some extent socialised, that a state of things arises in which the surplus labour of the one becomes a condition of existence for the other. At the dawn of civilisation the productiveness acquired by labour is small, but so too are the wants which develop with and by the means of satisfying them. Further, at that early period, the portion of society that lives on the labour of others is infinitely small compared with the mass of direct producers. Along with the progress in the productiveness of labour, that small portion of society increases both absolutely and relatively. Besides, capital with its accompanying relations springs up from an economic soil that is the product of a long process of development. The productiveness of labour that serves as its foundation and starting point is a gift, not of nature, but of a history embracing thousands of centuries.

Apart from the degree of development, greater or less, in the form of social production, the productiveness of labour is fettered by physical conditions. These are all referable to the constitution of man himself (race, etc.), and to surrounding nature. The external physical conditions fall into two great economical classes: (1) Natural wealth in means of subsistence, i.e., a fruitful soil, waters teeming with fish, etc., and (2) natural wealth in the instruments of labour, such as waterfalls, navigable rivers, wood, metal, coal, etc. At the dawn of civilisation, it is the first class that turns the scale; at a higher stage of development, it is the second. Compare, for example, England with India or, in ancient times, Athens and Corinth with the shores of the Black Sea.

The fewer the number of natural wants imperatively calling for satisfaction, and the greater the natural fertility of the soil and the favourableness of the climate, so much less is the labour time necessary for the maintenance and reproduction of the producer. So much greater therefore can be the excess of his labour for others over his labour for himself. Diodorus long ago remarked this in relation to the ancient Egyptians. "It is altogether incredible how little trouble and expense the bringing up of their children causes them. They cook for them the first simple food at hand; they also give them the lower part of the papyrus stem to eat, so far as it can be roasted in the fire, and the roots and stalks of marsh plants, some raw, some boiled and roasted. Most of the children go without shoes and unclothed, for the air is so mild. Hence a child, until he is grown up, costs his parents not more, on the whole, than 20 drachmas. It is this, chiefly, which explains why the population of Egypt is so numerous, and, therefore, why so many great works can be undertaken." Nevertheless the grand structures of ancient Egypt are less due to the extent of its population than to the large proportion of it that was freely disposable. Just as the individual labourer can do more surplus labour in proportion as his necessary labour time is less, so with regard to the working population. The smaller the part of it which is required for the production of the necessary means of subsistence, so much the greater is the part that can be set to do other work.

Capitalist production once assumed then, all other circumstances remaining the same, and given the length of the working day, the quantity of surplus labour will vary with the physical conditions of labour, especially with the fertility of the soil. But it by no means follows from this that the most fruitful soil is the most fitted for the growth of the capitalist mode of production. This mode is based on the dominion of man over nature. Where nature is too lavish, she "keeps him in hand, like a child in leading strings." She does not impose upon him any necessity to develop himself. It is not the tropics with their luxuriant vegetation, but the temperate zone, that is the mother country of capital. It is not the mere fertility of the soil, but the differentiation of the soil, the variety of its natural products, the changes of the seasons, which form the physical basis for the social division of labour, and which, by changes in the natural surroundings, spur man on to the multiplication of his wants, his capabilities, his means and modes of labour. It is the necessity of bringing a natural force under the control of society, of economizing, of appropriating or subduing it on a large scale by the work of man's hand, that first plays the decisive part in the history of industry. Examples are the irrigation works in Egypt, Lombardy, Holland, or India and Persia, where irrigation by means of artificial canals not only supplies the soil with the water indispensable to it, but also carries down to it, in the shape of sediment from the hills, mineral fertilizers. The secret of the flourishing state of industry in Spain and Sicily under the dominion of the Arabs lay in their irrigation works.

Favourable natural conditions alone gave us only the possibility, never the reality, of surplus labour, nor, consequently, of surplus-value and a surplus product. The result of difference in the natural conditions of labour is this: that the same quantity of labour satisfies, in different countries, a different mass of requirements; consequently, that under circumstances in other respects analogous the necessary labour time is different. These conditions affect surplus labour only as natural limits, i.e., by fixing the points at which labour for others can begin. In proportion as industry advances, these natural limits recede. In the midst of our West European society, where the labourer purchases the right to work for his own livelihood only by paying for it in surplus labour, the idea easily takes root that it is an inherent quality of human labour to furnish a surplus product. But consider, for example, an inhabitant of the eastern islands of the Asiatic Archipelago, where sago grows wild in the forests. "When the inhabitants have convinced themselves, by boring a hole in the tree, that the pith is ripe, the trunk is cut down and divided into several pieces, the pith is extracted, mixed with water and filtered: it is then quite fit for use as sago. One tree commonly yields 300 lbs., and occasionally 500 to 600 lbs. There, then, people go into the forests, and cut bread for themselves, just as with us they cut firewood." (F. Schouw, *Die Erde, die Pflanze und der Mensch,* Leipzig, 1854.) Suppose now such an eastern bread cutter requires 12 working hours a week for the satisfaction of all his wants. Nature's direct gift to him is plenty of leisure time. Before he can apply this leisure time productively for himself, a whole series of historical events is required; before he spends it in surplus labour for strangers, compulsion is necessary. If capitalist production were introduced, the honest fellow would perhaps have to work six days a week, in order to appropriate to himself the product of one working day. The bounty of Nature does not explain why he would then have to work 6 days a week, or why he must furnish 5 days of surplus labor. It explains only why his necessary labour time would be limited to one day a week. But in no case would his surplus product arise from some occult quality inherent in human labour.

Thus, not only does the historically developed social productiveness of labour, but also its natural productiveness, appear to be productiveness of the capital with which that labour is incorporated.

Ricardo never concerns himself about the origin of surplus-value. He treats it as a thing inherent in the capitalist mode of production, which mode, in his eyes, is the natural form of social production. Whenever he discusses the productiveness of labour, he seeks in it not the cause of surplus-value, but the cause that determines the magnitude of that value. On the other hand, his school has openly proclaimed the productiveness of labour to be the originating cause of profit (read: surplus-value). This at all events is a progress as against the mercantilists who, on their side, derived the excess of the price over the cost of production of the product, from the act of exchange, from the product being sold above its value. Nevertheless, Ricardo's school simply shirked the problem, they did not solve it. In fact these bourgeois economists instinctively saw, and rightly so, that it is very dangerous to stir too deeply the burning question of the origin of surplus-value. But what are we to think of John Stuart Mill, who, half a century after Ricardo, solemnly claims superiority over the mercantilists by clumsily repeating the wretched evasions of Ricardo's earliest vulgarisers?

PART SIX: WAGES

XV. THE TRANSFORMATION OF THE VALUE (AND RESPECTIVELY THE PRICE) OF LABOUR-POWER INTO WAGES

On the surface of bourgeois society the wage of the labourer appears as the price of labour, a certain quantity of money that is paid for a certain quantity of labour. Thus people speak of the value of labour and call its expression in money its necessary or natural price. On the other hand, they speak of the market prices of labour, i.e., prices oscillating above or below its natural price.

But what is the value of a commodity? The objective form of the social labour expended in its production. And how do we measure the quantity of this value? By the quantity of the labour contained in it. How then is the value, e.g., of a 12 hours' working day to be determined?

By the 12 working hours contained in a working day of 12 hours, which is an absurd tautology.

In order to be sold as a commodity in the market, labour must at all events exist before it is sold. But could the labourer give it an independent objective existence, he would sell a commodity and not labour.

Apart from these contradictions, a direct exchange of money, i.e., of realised labour, with living labour would either do away with the law of value, which only begins to develop itself freely on the basis of capitalist production, or do away with capitalist production itself, which rests directly on wage labour. The working day of 12 hours embodies itself, e.g., in a money value of 6 shillings. Either equivalents are exchanged, and then the labourer receives 6 shillings for 12 hours' labour; the price of his labour would be equal to the price of his product. In this case he produces no surplus-value for the buyer of his labour, the 6 shillings are not transformed into capital, the basis of capitalist production vanishes. But it is on this very basis that he sells his labour and that his labour is wage labour. Or else he receives for 12 hours' labour less than 6 shillings, i.e., less than 12 hours' labour. Twelve hours' labour is exchanged against 10, 6, etc., hours' labour. This equalisation of unequal quantities not merely does away with the determination of value. Such a self-destructive contradiction cannot be in any way even enunciated or formulated as a law.

It is of no avail to deduce the exchange of more labour against less from their difference of form, the one being realised, the other living. This is the more absurd as the value of a commodity is determined not by the quantity of labour actually realised in it, but by the quantity of living labour necessary for its production. A commodity represents, say 6 working hours. If an invention is made by which it can be produced in 3 hours, the value, even of the commodity already produced, falls by half. It represents now 3 hours of social labour instead of the 6 formerly necessary. It is the quantity of labour required for its production, not the realised form of that labour, by which the amount of the value of a commodity is determined.

That which comes directly face to face with the possessor of money on the market is in fact not labour, but the labourer. What the latter sells is his labour-power. As soon as his labour actually begins, it has already ceased to belong to him; it can therefore no longer be sold by him. Labour is the substance, and the immanent measure of value, but *has itself no value*.

In the expression "value of labour," the idea of value is not only completely obliterated, but actually reversed. It is an expression as imaginary as the value of the earth. These imaginary expressions arise, however, from the relations of production themselves. They are categories for the phenomenal forms of essential relations. That in their appearance things often represent themselves in inverted form is pretty well known in every science except political economy.

Classical political economy borrowed from everyday life the category "price of labour" without further criticism, and then simply asked the question, How is this price determined? It soon recognized that the change in the relations of demand and supply explained in regard to the price of labour, as of all other commodities, nothing except its changes, i.e., the oscillations of the market price above or below a certain mean. If demand and supply balance, the oscillation of prices ceases, all other conditions remaining the same. But then demand and supply also cease to explain anything. The price of labour, at the moment when demand and supply are in equilibrium, is its natural price, determined independently of the relation of demand and supply. And how this price is determined, is just the question. Or a larger period of oscillations in the market price is taken, e.g., a year, and they are found to cancel one the other, leaving a mean average quantity, a relatively constant magnitude. This had naturally to be determined otherwise than by its own compensating variations. This price which always finally predominates over the accidental market prices of labour and regulates them, this "necessary price" (physiocrats) or "natural price" of labour (Adam Smith) can, as with all other commodities, be nothing else than its value expressed in money. In this way political economy expected to penetrate athwart the accidental prices of labour, to the value of labour. As with other commodities, this value was determined by the cost of production. But what is the cost of production—of the labourer, i.e., the cost of producing or reproducing the labourer himself? This question unconsciously substituted itself in political economy for the original one; for the search after the cost of production of labour as such turned in a circle and never left the spot. What economists therefore call value of labour is in fact the value of labour-power as it exists in the personality of the labourer, which is as different from its function, labour, as a machine is from the work it performs. Occupied with the difference between the market price of labour and its so-called value, with the relation of this value to the rate of profit, and to the values of the commodities produced by means of labour, etc., they never discovered that the course of the analysis had led not only from the market prices of labour to its presumed value, but had led to the resolution of this value of labour itself into the value of labour-power. Classical economy never arrived at a consciousness of the results of its own analysis; it accepted uncritically the categories "value of labour," "natural price of labour," etc., as final and as adequate expressions for the value relation under consideration, and was thus led, as will be seen later, into inextricable confusion and contradiction, while it offered to the vulgar economists a secure basis of operations for their shallowness, which on principle worships appearances only.

Let us next see how value (and price) of labour-power, present themselves in this transformed condition as wages.

We know that the daily value of labour-power is calculated upon a certain length of the labourer's life, to which, again, corresponds a certain length of working day. Assume the habitual working day as 12 hours, the daily value of labour-power as 3 shillings, the expression in money of a value that embodies 6 hours of labour. If the labourer receives 3 shillings, then he receives the value of his labour-power functioning through 12 hours. If, now, this value of a day's labour-power is expressed as the value of a day's labour itself, we have the formula: Twelve hours' labour has a value of 3 shillings. The value of labour-power thus determines the value of labour, or, expressed in money, its necessary price. If, on the other hand, the price of labour-power differs from its value, in like manner the price of labour differs from its so-called value.

As the value of labour is only an irrational expression for the value of labour-power, it follows, of course, that the value of labour must always be less than the value it produces, for the capitalist always makes labour-power work longer than is necessary for the reproduction of its own value. In the above example, the value of the labour-power that functions through 12 hours is 3 shillings, a value for the reproduction of which 6 hours are required. The value which the labour-power produces is, on the other hand, 6 shillings, because it, in fact, functions during 12 hours, and the value it produces depends not on its own value, but on the length of time it is in action. Thus we have a result absurd at first sight—that labour which creates a value of 6 shillings possesses a value of 3 shillings.

We see, further: The value of 3 shillings, by which a part only of the working day—i.e., 6 hours' labour—is paid for, appears as the value or price of the whole working day of 12 hours, which thus includes 6 hours unpaid for. The wage form thus extinguishes every trace of the division of the working day into necessary labour and surplus labour into paid and unpaid labour. All labour appears as paid labour. In the *corvée* the labour of the worker for himself and his compulsory labour for his lord differ in space and time in the clearest possible way. In slave labour even that part of the working day in which the slave is only replacing the value of his own means of existence, in which, therefore, in fact, he works for himself alone, appears as labour for his master. All the slave's labour appears as unpaid labour. In wage labour, on the contrary, even surplus labour, or unpaid labour, appears as paid. There the property relation conceals the labour of the slave for himself; here the money relation conceals the unrequited labour of the wage labourer.

Hence, we may understand the decisive importance of the transformation of value and price of labour-power into the form of wages, or into the value and price of labour itself. This phenomenal form, which makes the actual relation invisible, and, indeed, shows the direct opposite of that relation, forms the basis of all the juridical notions of both labourer and capitalist, of all the mystifications of the capitalistic mode of production, of all its illusions as to liberty, of all the apologetic shifts of the vulgar economists.

If history took a long time to get at the bottom of the mystery of wages, nothing, on the other hand, is more easy to understand than the necessity, the *raison d'être,* of this phenomenon.

The exchange between capital and labour at first presents itself to the mind in the same guise as the buying and selling of all other commodities. The buyer gives a certain sum of money, the seller an article of a nature different from money. The jurist's consciousness recognises in this, at most, a material difference, expressed in the juridically equivalent formulæ: *"Do ut des, do ut facias, facio ut des, facio ut facias."*

Further. Exchange-value and use-value, being intrinsically incommensurable magnitudes, the expressions "value of labour," "price of labour," do not seem more irrational than the expressions "value of cotton," "price of cotton." Moreover, the labourer is paid after he has given his labour. In its function of means of payment, money realises subsequently the value or price of the article supplied—i.e., in this particular case, the value or price of the labour supplied. Finally, the use-value supplied by the labourer to the capitalist is not, in fact, his labour-power, but its function, some definite useful labour, the work of tailoring, shoemaking, spinning, etc. That this same labour is, on the other hand, the universal value-creating element, and thus possesses a property by which it differs from all other commodities, is beyond the cognisance of the ordinary mind.

Let us put ourselves in the place of the labourer who receives for 12 hours' labour say the value produced by 6 hours' labour, say 3 shillings. For him, in fact, his 12 hours' labour is the means of buying the 3 shillings. The value of his labour-power may vary, with the value of his usual means of subsistence, from 3 to 4 shillings, or from 3 to 2 shillings; or, if the value of his labour-power remains constant, its price may, in consequence of changing relations of demand and supply, rise to 4 shillings or fall to 2 shillings. He always gives 12 hours of labour. Every change in the amount of the equivalent that he receives appears to him, therefore, necessarily as a change in the value or price of his 12 hours' work. This circumstance misled Adam Smith, who treated the working day as a constant quantity, to the assertion that the value of labour is constant, although the value of the means of subsistence may vary, and the same working day, therefore, may represent itself in more or less money for the labourer.

Let us consider, on the other hand, the capitalist. He wishes to receive as much labour as possible for as little money as possible. Practically, therefore, the only thing that interests him is the difference between the price of labour-power and the value which its function creates. But, then, he tries to buy all commodities as cheaply as possible, and always accounts for his profit by simple cheating, by buying under and selling over the value. Hence, he never comes to see that, if such a thing as the value of labour really existed, and he really paid this value, no capital would exist, his money would not be turned into capital.

Moreover, the actual movement of wages presents phenomena which seem to prove that not the value of labour-power is paid, but the value of its function, of labour itself. We may reduce these phenomena to two great classes: (1) Change of wages with the changing length of the working day. One might as well conclude that not the value of a machine is paid, but that of its working, because it costs more to hire a machine for a week than for a day. (2) The individual difference in the wages of different labourers who do the same kind of work. We find this individual difference, but are not deceived by it, in the system of slavery, where, frankly and openly, without any circumlocution, labour-power itself is sold. Only, in the slave system, the advantage of a labour-power above the average, and the disadvantage of a labour-power below the average, affects the slaveowner; in the wage-labour system it affects the labourer himself, because his labour-power is, in the one case, sold by himself, in the other, by a third person.

For the rest, in respect to the phenomenal form, "value and price of labour," or "wages," as contrasted with the essential relation manifested therein, viz., the value and price of labour-power, the same difference holds that holds in respect to all phenomena and their hidden substratum. The former appear directly and spontaneously as current modes of thought; the latter must first be discovered by science. Classical political economy nearly touches the true relation of things, without, however, consciously formulating it. This it cannot so long as it sticks in its bourgeois skin.

XVI. TIME WAGES

Wages themselves, again, take many forms, a fact not recognisable in the ordinary economical treatises which, exclusively interested in the material side of the question, neglect every difference of form. We limit ourselves therefore to a few points characteristic of time wages.

The sum of money which the labourer receives for his daily or weekly labour forms the amount of his nominal wages, or of his wages estimated in value. But it is clear that according to the length of the working day, that is, according to the amount of actual labour daily supplied, the same daily or weekly wage may represent very different prices of labour, i.e., very different sums of money for the same quantity of labour. We must, therefore, in considering time wages, again distinguish between the sum total of the daily or weekly wages, etc., and the price of labour. How then to find this price, i.e., the money value of a given quantity of labour? The average price of labour is found, when the average daily value of the labour-power is divided by the average number of hours in the working day. If, e.g., the daily value of labour-power is 3 shillings, the value of the product of 6 working hours, and if the working day is 12 hours, the price of 1 working hour is $\frac{3}{12}$ shillings=3 pence. The price of the working hour thus found serves as the unit measure for the price of labour.

It follows therefore that the daily and weekly wages, etc., may remain the same, although the price of labour falls constantly. If, e.g., the habitual working day is 10 hours and the daily value of the labour-power 3 shillings, the price of the working hour is $3\frac{3}{5}$ pence. It falls to 3 pence as soon as the working day rises to 12 hours, to $2\frac{2}{5}$ pence as soon as it rises to 15 hours. Daily or weekly wages remain, despite all this, unchanged. On the contrary, the daily or weekly wages may rise, although the price of labour remains constant or even falls. If, e.g., the working day is 10 hours, and the daily value of labour-power 3 shillings, the price of one working hour is $3\frac{3}{5}$ pence. If the labourer in consequence of increase of trade works 12 hours, the price of labour remaining the same, his daily wage now rises to 3 shillings $7\frac{1}{5}$ pence without any variation in the price of labour. The same result might follow if, instead of the extensive amount of labour, its intensive amount increased. The rise of the nominal daily or weekly wages may therefore be accompanied by a price of labour that remains stationary or falls. The same holds as to the income of the labourer's family, as soon as the quantity of labour expended by the head of the family is increased by the labour of the members of his family. There are, therefore, methods of lowering the price of labour independent of the reduction of the nominal daily or weekly wages.

As a general law it follows that, given the amount of daily, weekly labour, etc., the daily or weekly wages depend on the price of labour, which itself varies either with the value of labour-power, or with the difference between its price and its value. Given, on the other hand, the price of labour, the daily or weekly wages depend on the quantity of the daily or weekly labour.

It is a fact generally known that, the longer the working days in any branch of industry, the lower are the wages. A. Redgrave, factory inspector, illustrates this by a comparative review of the 20 years from 1839 to 1859, according to which wages rose in the factories under the 10 hours' law, whilst they fell in the factories in which the work lasted 14 to 15 hours daily.

From the law, "the price of labour being given, the daily or weekly wage depends on the quantity of labour expended," it follows, first of all, that, the lower the price of labour, the greater must be the quantity of labour, or the longer must be the working day for the labourer to secure even a miserable average wage. The lowness of the price of labour acts here as a stimulus to the extension of the labour time.

On the other hand, the extension of the working time produces, in its turn, a fall in the price of labour, and with this a fall in the day's or week's wages.

XVII. PIECE WAGES

Wages by the piece are nothing else than a converted form of wages by time, just as wages by time are a converted form of the value or price of labour-power.

In piece wages it seems at first sight as if the use-value bought from the labourer was, not the function of his labour-power, living labour, but labour already realised in the product, and as if the price of this labour was determined not as with time wages by the fraction, $\frac{\text{daily value of labor power}}{\text{working day of given number of hours}}$ but by the capacity for work of the producer.

The confidence that trusts in this appearance ought to receive a first severe shock from the fact that both forms of wages exist side by side, simultaneously, in the same branches of industry; e.g., "the compositors of London, as a general rule, work by the piece, time-work being the exception, while those in the country work by the day, the exception being work by the piece. The shipwrights of the port of London work by the job or piece, while those of all other parts work by the day." (T. J. Dunning, *Trades Unions and Strikes,* London, 1860.)

In the same saddlery shops of London, often for the same work, piece wages are paid to the French, time wages to the English. In the regular factories in which throughout piece wages predominate, particular kinds of work are unsuitable to this form of wage, and are therefore paid by time. But it is moreover self-evident that the difference of form in the payment of wages alters in no way their essential nature, although the one form may be more favorable to the development of capitalist production than the other.

Let the ordinary working day contain 12 hours of which 6 are paid, 6 unpaid. Let its value product be 6 shillings, that of one hour's labour therefore 6 pence. Let us suppose that, as the result of experience, a labourer who works with the average amount of intensity and skill, who, therefore, gives in fact only the time socially necessary to the production of an article, supplies in 12 hours 24 pieces, either distinct products or measurable parts of a continuous whole. Then the value of these 24 pieces, after subtraction of the portion of constant capital contained in them, is 6 shillings, and the value of a single piece 3 pence. The labourer receives 1½ pence per piece, and thus earns in 12 hours 3 shillings. Just as, with time wages, it does not matter whether we assume that the labourer works 6 hours for himself and 6 hours for the capitalist, or half of every hour for himself and the other half for the capitalist, so here it does not matter whether we say that each individual piece is half paid and half unpaid for, or that the price of 12 pieces is the equivalent only of the value of the labour-power, whilst in the other 12 pieces surplus-value is incorporated.

The form of piece wages is just as irrational as that of time wages. Whilst in our example two pieces of a commodity, after subtraction of the value of the means of production consumed in them, are worth 6 pence as being the product of one hour, the labourer receives for them a price of 3 pence. Piece wages do not, in fact, distinctly express any relation of value. It is not, therefore, a question of measuring the value of the piece by the working time incorporated in it, but on the contrary of measuring the working time the labourer has expended, by the number of pieces he has produced. In time wages the labour is measured by its immediate duration, in piece wages by the quantity of products in which the labour has embodied itself during a given time. The price of labour time itself is finally determined by the equation: value of a day's labour= daily value of labour-power. Piece wage is, therefore, only a modified form of time wage.

PART SEVEN: THE ACCUMULATION OF CAPITAL

XVIII. CONVERSION OF SURPLUS-VALUE INTO CAPITAL

1. Capitalist Production on a Progressively Increasing Scale. Transition of the Laws of Property That Characterise Production of Commodities into Laws of Capitalist Appropriation

HITHERTO we have investigated how surplus-value emanates from capital; we have now to see how capital arises from surplus-value. Employing surplus-value as capital, reconverting it into capital, is called accumulation of capital.

First let us consider this transaction from the standpoint of the individual capitalist. Suppose a spinner to have advanced a capital of £10,000, of which four fifths (£8000) are laid out in cotton, machinery, etc., and one fifth (£2000) in wages. Let him produce 240,000 lbs. of yarn annually, having a value of £12,000. The rate of surplus-value being 100 per cent., the surplus-value lies in the surplus or net product of 40,000 lbs. of yarn, one sixth of the gross product, with a value of £2000 which will be realised by a sale. £2000 is £2000. We can neither see nor smell in this sum of money a trace of surplus-value. When we know that a given value is surplus-value, we know how its owner came by it; but that does not alter the nature either of value or of money.

In order to convert this additional sum of £2000 into capital, the master spinner will, all circumstances remaining as before, advance four fifths of it (£1600) in the purchase of cotton, etc., and one fifth (£400) in the purchase of additional spinners, who will find in the market the necessaries of life whose value the master has advanced to them. Then the new capital of £2000 functions in the spinning mill, and brings in, in its turn, a surplus-value of £400.

The capital value was originally advanced in the money form. The surplus-value on the contrary is, originally, the value of a definite portion of the gross product. If this gross product be sold, converted into money, the capital value regains its original form. From this moment the capital value and the surplus-value are both of them sums of money, and their reconversion into capital takes place in precisely the same way. The one, as well as the other, is laid out by the capitalist in the purchase of commodities that place him in a position to begin afresh the fabrication of his goods, and this time, on an extended scale. But in order to be able to buy those commodities, he must find them ready in the market.

His own yarns circulate only because he brings his annual product to market, as all other capitalists likewise do with their commodities. But these commodities, before coming to market, were part of the general annual product, part of the total mass of objects of every kind, into which the sum of the individual capitals, i.e., the total capital of society, had been converted in the course of the year, and of which each capitalist had in hand only an aliquot part. The transactions in the market effectuate only the interchange of the individual components of this annual product, transfer them from one hand to another, but can neither augment the total annual production, nor alter the nature of the objects produced. Hence the use that can be made of the total annual product depends entirely upon its own composition, but in no way upon circulation.

The annual production must in the first place furnish all those objects (use-values) from which the material components of capital, used up in the course of the year, have to be replaced. Deducting these there remains the net or surplus product, in which the surplus-value lies. And of what does this surplus product consist? Only of things destined to satisfy the wants and desires of the capitalist class, things which, consequently, enter into the consumption fund of the capitalists? Were that the case, the cup of surplus-value would be drained to the very dregs, and nothing but simple reproduction would ever take place.

To accumulate it is necessary to convert a portion of the surplus product into capital. But we cannot, except by a miracle, convert into capital anything but such articles as can be employed in the labour process (i.e., means of production), and such further articles as are suitable for the sustenance of the labourer (i.e., means of subsistence). Consequently, a part of the annual surplus-labour must have been applied to the production of additional means of production and subsistence, over and above the quantity of these things required to replace the capital advanced. In one word, surplus-value is convertible into capital solely because the surplus product, whose value it is, already comprises the material elements of new capital.

Now in order to allow of these elements actually functioning as capital, the capitalist class requires additional labour. If the exploitation of the labourers already employed do not increase, either extensively or intensively, then additional labour-power must be found. For this the mechanism of capitalist production provides beforehand, by converting the working class into a class dependent on wages, a class whose ordinary wages suffice, not only for its maintenance, but for its increase. It is only necessary for capital to incorporate this additional labour-power, annually supplied by the working class in the shape of labourers of all ages, with the surplus means of production comprised in the annual produce, and the conversion of surplus-value into capital is complete. From a concrete point of view, accumulation resolves itself into the reproduction of capital on a progressively increasing scale. The circle in which simple reproduction moves, alters its form, and, to use Sismondi's expression, changes into a spiral.

Let us now return to our illustration. It is the old story: Abraham begat Isaac, Isaac begat Jacob, and so on. The original capital of £10,000 brings in a surplus-value of £2000, which is capitalised. The new capital of £2000 brings in a surplus-value of £400, and this, too, is capitalised, converted into a second additional capital, which, in its turn, produces a further surplus-value of £80. And so the ball rolls on.

We here leave out of consideration the portion of the surplus-value consumed by the capitalist. Just as little does it concern us, for the moment, whether the additional capital is joined on to the original capital, or is separated from it to function independently; whether the same capitalist, who accumulated it, employs it, or whether he hands it over to another. This only we must not forget, that by the side of the newly formed capital the original capital continues to reproduce itself and to produce surplus-value, and that this is also true of all accumulated capital and the additional capital engendered by it.

The original capital was formed by the advance of £10,000. How did the owner become possessed of it? "By his own labour and that of his forefathers," answer unanimously the spokesmen of political economy. And, in fact, their supposition appears the only one consonant with the laws of the production of commodities.

But it is quite otherwise with regard to the additional capital of £2000. How that originated we know perfectly well. There is not one single atom of its value that does not owe its existence to unpaid labour. The means of production, with which the additional labour-power is incorporated, as well as the necessaries with which the labourers are sustained, are nothing but component parts of the surplus product, of the tribute annually exacted from the working class by the capitalist class. Though the latter with a portion of that tribute purchases the additional labour-power even at its full price, so that equivalent is exchanged for equivalent, yet the transaction is for all that only the old dodge of every conqueror who buys commodities from the conquered with the money he has robbed them of.

If the additional capital employs the person who produced it, this producer must not only continue to augment the value of the original capital, but must buy back the fruits of his previous labour with more labour than they cost. When viewed as a transaction between the capitalist class and the working class, it makes no difference that additional labourers are employed by means of the unpaid labour of the previously employed labourers. The capitalist may even convert the additional capital into a machine that throws the producers of that capital out of work, and that replaces them by a few children. In every case the working class creates by the surplus labour of one year the capital destined to employ additional labour in the following year. And this is what is called: creating capital out of capital.

The accumulation of the first additional capital of £2000 presupposes a value of £10,000 belonging to the capitalist by virtue of his "primitive labour," and advanced by him. The second additional capital of £400 presupposes, on the contrary, only the previous accumulation of the £2000, of which the £400 is the surplus-value capitalised. The ownership of past unpaid labour is thenceforth the sole condition for the appropriation of living unpaid labour on a constantly increasing scale. The more the capitalist has accumulated, the more is he able to accumulate.

In so far as the surplus-value, of which the additional capital, No. 1, consists, is the result of the purchase of labour-power with part of the original capital, a purchase that conformed to the laws of the exchange of commodities, and that, from a legal standpoint, presupposes nothing beyond the free disposal, on the part of the labourer, of his own capacities, and on the part of the owner of money or commodities, of the values that belong to him; in so far as the additional capital, No. 2, etc., is the mere result of No. 1, and, therefore, a consequence of the above condition; in so far as each single transaction invariably conforms to the laws of the exchange of commodities, the capitalist buying labour-power, the labourer selling it, and we will assume at its real value; in so far as all this is true, it is evident that the laws of appropriation or of private property, laws that are based on the production and circulation of commodities, become by their own inner and inexorable dialectic changed into their very opposite. The exchange of equivalents, the original operation with which we started, has now become turned round in such a way that there is only an apparent exchange. This is owing to the fact, first, that the capital which is exchanged for labour-power is itself but a portion of the product of others' labour appropriated without an equivalent; and, secondly, that this capital must not only be replaced by its producer, but replaced together with an added surplus. The relation of exchange subsisting between capitalist and labourer becomes a mere semblance appertaining to the process of circulation, a mere form, foreign to the real nature of the transaction, and only mystifies it. The ever repeated purchase and sale of labour-power is now the mere form; what really takes place is this—the capitalist again and again appropriates, without equivalent, a portion of the previously materialised labour of others, and exchanges it for a greater quantity of living labour. At first the rights of property seemed to us to be based on a man's own labour. At least, some such assumption was necessary since only commodity owners with equal rights confronted each other, and the sole means by which a man could become possessed of the commodities of others, was by alienating his own commodities; and these could be replaced by labour alone. Now, however, property turns out to be the right, on the part of the capitalist, to appropriate the unpaid labour of others or its product and to be the impossibility, on the part of the labourer, of appropriating his own product. The separation of property from labour has become the necessary consequence of a law that apparently originated in their identity.

No matter how severely the capitalist mode of appropriation may seem to slap the face of the fundamental laws of the production of commodities, it does not arise from a violation, but from an application of these laws. A brief retrospect upon the succession of phases, whose climax the capitalist accumulation is, may serve once more to make this clear.

We have seen, in the first place, that the original transformation of a certain quantity of values into capital proceeded strictly according to the laws of exchange. One of the contracting parties sells his labour-power, the other buys it. The first receives the exchange-value of his commodity, while its use-value, labour, passes into the possession of the other. This second party then converts means of production belonging to him into a new product belonging to him by right through the instrumentality of labour also belonging to him.

The value of this product comprizes, in the first place, the value of the consumed means of production. Useful labour cannot consume these means of production without transferring their value to the new product. But in order to be saleable labour-power must be able to furnish useful labour in that line of industry in which it is to be employed.

The value of the new product comprizes, furthermore, the equivalent of the value of labour-power and a surplus-value. It does so for the reason that the labour-power sold for a certain length of time, such as a day, a week, etc., has less value than is produced by its employment during that time. The labourer, however, has received the exchange-value of his labour-power and given up its use-value in return, as happens in every sale and purchase.

The fact that this particular commodity labour-power has the peculiar use-value of supplying labour and creating value cannot affect the general law of the production of commodities. Hence, if the sum of values advanced in wages is not merely reproduced in the product, but also increased by a surplus-value, this is not due to an advantage gained over the seller, who received the value of his commodity, but simply to the consumption of this commodity by the buyer.

The law of exchange requires equality only for the exchange-values of the commodities passed from hand to hand. But it requires at the outset a disparity of their use-values, and has nothing to do with their consumption, which does not begin until after the trade has been made.

The original transformation of money into capital proceeds therefore, in strict compliance with the economic laws of the production of commodities and with the property right derived therefrom. Nevertheless it has the following results:

(1) That the product belongs to the capitalist, not to the labourer;

(2) That the value of this product comprizes a surplus-value over and above the value of the advanced capital. This surplus-value has cost the labourer labour, but the capitalist nothing, yet it becomes the lawful property of the capitalist;

(3) That the labourer has reproduced his labour-power and can sell it once more, if he finds a buyer for it.

Simple reproduction is but a periodical repetition of this first operation. Money is thereby transformed again and again into capital. The general law is not violated thereby, but rather finds an opportunity to manifest itself permanently. "Several successive exchanges have merely made of the last a representative of the first." (Simonde de Sismondi, *Nouveaux Principes de l'Économie Politique,* Paris, 1819.)

Nevertheless we have seen that this simple reproduction suffices to impregnate this first operation, so far as it was considered an isolated transaction, with a totally different character. "Of those, who divide the national revenue among themselves, some (the labourers) acquire each year a new title to it by new labour, while others (the capitalists) have previously acquired a permanent title to it by primitive work." (Sismondi.) The domain of labour is evidently not the only one in which primogeniture accomplishes wonders.

It does not alter matters any, if simple reproduction is replaced by reproduction on an enlarged scale, by accumulation. In the first instance the capitalist consumes the entire surplus-value, in the second he demonstrates his civic virtue by consuming only a part of it and converting the remainder into money.

The surplus-value is his property, it has never belonged to anybody else. If he advances it to production, he makes advances from his own funds just as he did on the day when he first came in the market. That this fund in the present case comes from the unpaid labour of his labourers, does not alter the matter in the least. If labourer B is employed with surplus-values produced by labourer A, then, in the first place, A supplied this surplus-value without having the just price of his commodity reduced by one farthing, and, in the second place, this transaction is none of B's concern. What B demands and has a right to demand is that the capitalist should pay him the value of his labour-power. "Both sides are gainers; the labourer, by having the fruit of his labour advanced to him" (that is, the fruit of the unpaid labour of others) "before he has performed any labour" (that is, before his own labour has borne any fruit); "the master, because the labour of this labourer was worth more than his wages" (that is, produced a value greater than that of his wages). (Sismondi.)

True, the matter assumes an entirely different aspect when we look upon capitalist production in the uninterrupted flow of its reproduction, and when we consider the capitalist class as a whole and its antagonist, the working class, instead of the individual capitalist and the individual labourer. But in so doing we should be applying a standard which is totally foreign to the production of commodities.

In the production of commodities only sellers and buyers, independent of one another, meet. Their mutual relations cease with the termination of their mutual contract. If the transaction is repeated, it is done by a new contract, which has nothing to do with the former one, and only an accident brings the same seller once more together with the same buyer.

Hence, if the production of commodities, or a transaction belonging to it, is to be judged by its own economic laws, we must consider each act of exchange by itself, outside of all connection with the act of exchange preceding it and following it. And since purchases and sales are transacted between individuals, it will not do to seek therein relations between entire classes of society.

No matter how long may be the series of periodical reproductions and former accumulations through which the capital now invested may have passed, it always retains its primal virginity. So long as the laws of exchange are observed in every act of exchange, individually considered, the mode of appropriation may be completely revolutionised without in the least affecting the property right bestowed by the production of commodities. The same right remains in force, whether it be at a time when the product belonged to the producer, and when this producer, exchanging equivalent for equivalent, could enrich himself only by his own labour, or whether it be under capitalism, where the social wealth becomes in an ever-increasing degree the property of those who are in a position to appropriate to themselves again and again the unpaid labour of others.

This result becomes inevitable, as soon as labour-power is sold as a commodity by the "free" labourer himself. It is from that time on that the production of commodities becomes universal and a typical form of production. Henceforth every product is intended at the outset for sale, and all produced wealth passes through the circulation. The production of commodities does not impose itself upon the whole society, until wage labour becomes its basis. And only then does it unfold all its powers. To say that the intervention of wage labour adulterates the production of commodities means to say that the production of commodities must not develop, if it wishes to remain unadulterated. To the same extent that it continues to develop by its own inherent laws into a capitalist production, the property laws of the production of commodities are converted into the laws of capitalistic appropriation.

We have seen that even in the case of simple reproduction, all capital, whatever its original source, becomes converted into accumulated capital, capitalised surplus-value. But in the flood of production all the capital originally advanced becomes a vanishing quantity (*magnitudo evanescens,* in the mathematical sense), compared with the directly accumulated capital, i.e., with the surplus-value or surplus product that is reconverted into capital, whether it function in the hands of its accumulator, or in those of others. Hence, political economy describes capital in general as "accumulated wealth" (converted surplus-value or revenue), "that is employed over again in the production of surplus-value," and the capitalist as "the owner of surplus-value." It is merely another way of expressing the same thing to say that all existing capital is accumulated or capitalised interest, for interest is a mere fragment of surplus-value.

2. *Erroneous Conception by Political Economy of Reproduction on a Progressively Increasing Scale*

Before we further investigate accumulation or the reconversion of surplus-value into capital, we must brush on one side an ambiguity introduced by the classical economists.

Just as little as the commodities that the capitalist buys with a part of the surplus-value for his own consumption, serve the purpose of production and of creation of value, so little is the labour that he buys for the satisfaction of his natural and social requirements, productive labour. Instead of converting surplus-value into capital, he, on the contrary, by the purchase of those commodities and that labour, consumes or expends it as revenue. In the face of the habitual mode of life of the old feudal nobility, which, as Hegel rightly says, "consists in consuming what is in hand," and more especially displays itself in the luxury of personal retainers, it was extremely important for bourgeois economy to promulgate the doctrine that accumulation of capital is the first duty of every citizen, and to preach without ceasing, that a man cannot accumulate, if he eats up all his revenue, instead of spending a good part of it in the acquisition of additional productive labourers, who bring in more than they cost. On the other hand, the economists had to contend against the popular prejudice, that confuses capitalist production with hoarding, and fancies that accumulated wealth is either wealth that is rescued from being destroyed in its existing form, i.e., from being consumed, or wealth that is withdrawn from circulation. Exclusion of money from circulation would also exclude absolutely its self-expansion as capital, while accumulation of a hoard in the shape of commodities would be sheer tomfoolery. The accumulation of commodities in great masses is the result either of overproduction or of a stoppage of circulation. It is true that the popular mind is impressed by the sight, on the one hand, of the mass of goods that are stored up for gradual consumption by the rich, and, on the other hand, by the formation of reserve stocks; the latter, a phenomenon that is common to all modes of production, and on which we shall dwell for a moment, when we come to analyse circulation. Classical economy is therefore quite right, when it maintains that the consumption of surplus products by productive, instead of by unproductive labourers, is a characteristic feature of the process of accumulation. But at this point the mistakes also begin. Adam Smith has made it the fashion, to represent accumulation as nothing more than consumption of surplus-products by productive labourers, which amounts to saying, that the capitalising of surplus-value consists in merely turning surplus-value into labour-power. Let us see what Ricardo, e.g., says: "It must be understood that all the productions of a country are consumed; but it makes the greatest difference imaginable whether they are consumed by those who reproduce, or by those who do not reproduce another value. When we say that revenue is saved, and added to capital, what we mean is, that the portion of revenue, so said to be added to capital, is consumed by productive instead of unproductive labourers. There can be no greater error than in supposing that capital is increased by non-consumption." There can be no greater error than that which Ricardo and all subsequent economists repeat after A. Smith, viz., that "the part of revenue, of which it is said, it has been added to capital, is consumed by productive labourers." According to this, all surplus-value that is changed into capital becomes variable capital. So far from this being the case, the surplus-value, like the original capital, divides itself into constant capital and variable capital, into means of production and labour-power. Labour-power is the form under which variable capital exists during the process of production. In this process the labour-power is itself consumed by the capitalist while the means of production are consumed by the labour-power in the exercise of its function, labour. At the same time, the money paid for the purchase of the labour-power, is converted into necessaries, that are consumed, not by "productive labour," but by the "productive labourer." Adam Smith, by a fundamentally perverted analysis, arrives at the absurd conclusion, that even though each individual capital is divided into a constant and a variable part, the capital of society resolves itself only into variable capital, i.e., is laid out exclusively in payment of wages. For instance, suppose a cloth manufacturer converts £2000 into capital. One portion he lays out in buying weavers, the other in woollen yarn, machinery, etc. But the people, from whom he buys the yarn and the machinery, pay for labour with a part of the purchase money, and so on until the whole £2000 are spent in the payment of wages, i.e., until the entire product represented by the £2000 has been consumed by productive labourers. It is evident that the whole gist of this argument lies in the words "and so on," which send us from pillar to post. In truth, Adam Smith breaks his investigation off just where its difficulties begin.

The annual process of reproduction is easily understood, so long as we keep in view merely the sum total of the year's production. But every single component of this product must be brought into the market as a commodity, and there the difficulty begins. The movements of the individual capitals, and of the personal revenues, cross and intermingle and are lost in the general change of places, in the circulation of the wealth of society; this dazes the sight, and propounds very complicated problems for solution. It is one of the great merits of the Physiocrats, that in their

Tableau économique they were the first to attempt to depict the annual production in the shape in which it is presented to us after passing through the process of circulation.

For the rest, it is a matter of course, that political economy, acting in the interests of the capitalist class, has not failed to exploit the doctrine of Adam Smith, viz., that the whole of that part of the surplus product which is converted into capital, is consumed by the working class.

3. Separation of Surplus-Value into Capital and Revenue. The Abstinence Theory

In the last preceding chapter we treated surplus-value (or the surplus product) solely as a fund for supplying the individual consumption of the capitalist. In this chapter we have, so far, treated it solely as a fund for accumulation. It is, however, neither the one nor the other, but is both together. One portion is consumed by the capitalist as revenue, the other is employed as capital, is accumulated.

Given the mass of surplus-value, then, the larger the one of these parts, the smaller is the other. *Cæteris paribus,* the ratio of these parts determines the magnitude of the accumulation. But it is by the owner of the surplus-value, by the capitalist alone, that the division is made. It is his deliberate act. That part of the tribute exacted by him which he accumulates, is said to be saved by him, because he does not eat it, i.e., because he performs the function of a capitalist, and enriches himself.

Except as personified capital, the capitalist has no historical value, and no right to that historical existence which, to use an expression of the witty Lichnowsky, "hasn't got no date." And so far only is the necessity for his own transitory existence implied in the transitory necessity for the capitalist mode of production. But, so far as he is personified capital, it is not values in use and the enjoyment of them but exchange-value and its augmentation, that spur him into action. Fanatically bent on making value expand itself, he ruthlessly forces the human race to produce for production's sake; he thus forces the development of the productive powers of society, and creates those material conditions which alone can form the real basis of a higher form of society, a society in which the full and free development of every individual forms the ruling principle. Only as personified capital is the capitalist respectable. As such, he shares with the miser the passion for wealth as wealth. But that which in the miser is a mere idiosyncrasy is in the capitalist the effect of the social mechanism, of which he is but one of the wheels. Moreover, the development of capitalist production makes it constantly necessary to keep increasing the amount of the capital laid out in a given industrial undertaking, and competition makes the immanent laws of capitalist production to be felt by each individual capitalist as external coercive laws. It compels him to keep constantly extending his capital in order to preserve it, but extend it he cannot, except by means of progressive accumulation.

So far, therefore, as his actions are a mere function of capital—endowed as capital is, in his person, with consciousness and a will—his own private consumption is a robbery perpetrated on accumulation, just as in bookkeeping by double entry the private expenditure of the capitalist is placed on the debtor side of his account against his capital. To accumulate is to conquer the world of social wealth, to increase the mass of human beings exploited by him, and thus to extend both the direct and the indirect sway of the capitalist.

But original sin is at work everywhere. As capitalist production, accumulation, and wealth become developed, the capitalist ceases to be the mere incarnation of capital. He has a fellow feeling for his own Adam, and his education gradually enables him to smile at the rage for asceticism as a mere prejudice of the old-fashioned miser. While the capitalist of the classical type brands individual consumption as a sin against his function, and as "abstinence" from accumulating, the modernised capitalist is capable of looking upon accumulation as "abstinence" from pleasure.

Two souls, alas, do dwell within his breast;
The one is ever parting from the other.

At the historical dawn of capitalist production—and every capitalist upstart has personally to go through this historical stage—avarice and desire to get rich are the ruling passions. But the progress of capitalist production not only creates a world of delights; it lays open, in speculation and the credit system, a thousand sources of sudden enrichment. When a certain stage of development has been reached, a conventional degree of prodigality, which is also an exhibition of wealth and consequently a source of credit, becomes a business necessity to the "unfortunate" capitalist. Luxury enters into capital's expenses of representation. Moreover, the capitalist gets rich, not like the miser, in proportion to his personal labour and restricted consumption, but at the same rate as he squeezes out the labour-power of others and enforces on the labourer abstinence from all life's enjoyments. Although, therefore, the prodigality of the capitalist never possesses the bona fide character of the openhanded feudal lord's prodigality, but, on the contrary, has always lurking behind it the most sordid avarice and the most anxious calculation, yet his expenditure grows with his accumulation, without the one necessarily restricting the other. But along with this growth, there is at the same time developed in his breast a Faustian conflict between the passion for accumulation and the desire for enjoyment.

Accumulate, accumulate! That is Moses and the prophets! "Industry furnishes the material which saving accumulates." Therefore, save, save, i.e., reconvert the greatest possible portion of surplus-value or surplus product into capital! Accumulation for accumulation's sake, production for production's sake: by this formula classical economy expressed the historical mission of the bourgeoisie, and did not for a single instant deceive itself over the birth throes of wealth. But what avails lamentation in the face of historical necessity? If to classical economy the proletarian is but a machine for the production of surplus-value, on the other hand, the capitalist is in its eyes only a machine for the conversion of this surplus-value into additional capital. Political economy takes the historical function of the capitalist in bitter earnest. In order to charm out of his bosom the awful conflict between the desire for enjoyment and the chase after riches, Malthus, about the year 1820, advocated a division of labour, which assigns to the capitalist actually engaged in production the business of accumulating, and to the other sharers in surplus-value, to the landlords, the placemen, the beneficed clergy, etc., the business of spending. It is of the highest importance, he says, "to keep separate the passion for expenditure and the passion for accumulation." The capitalists having long been good livers and men of the world, uttered loud cries. What, exclaimed one of their spokesmen, a disciple of Ricardo, Mr. Malthus preaches high rents, heavy taxes, etc., so that the pressure of the spur may constantly be kept on the industrious by unproductive consumers! By all means, production, production on a constantly increasing scale, runs the shibboleth; but "production will, by such a process, be far more curbed in than spurred on. Nor is it quite fair thus to maintain in idleness a number of persons, only to pinch others, who are likely, from their characters, if you can force them to work, to work with success." (*An Inquiry into those principles respecting the nature of Demand as lately advocated by Mr. Malthus*, London, 1821.) Unfair as he finds it to spur on the industrial capitalist, by depriving his bread of its butter, yet he thinks it necessary to reduce the labourer's wages to a minimum "to keep him industrious." Nor does he for a moment conceal the fact, that the appropriation of unpaid labour is the secret of surplus-value. "Increased demand on the part of the labourers means nothing more than their willingness to take less of their own product for themselves, and leave a greater part of it to their employer; and if it be said, that this begets glut, by lessening consumption" (on the part of the labourers), "I can only reply that glut is synonymous with large profits."

The learned disputation, how the booty pumped out of the labourer may be divided, with most advantage to accumulation, between the industrial capitalist and the rich idler, was hushed in face of the revolution of July [1830]. Shortly afterwards the town proletariat at Lyons sounded the tocsin of revolution, and the country proletariat in England began to set fire to farmyards and cornstacks. On this side of the Channel, Owenism began to spread; on the other side, Saint-Simonism and Fourierism. The hour of vulgar economy had struck. Exactly a year before Nassau W. Senior discovered at Manchester, that the profit (including interest) of capital is the product of the last hour of the twelve, he had announced to the world another discovery. "I substitute," he proudly says, "for the word capital, considered as an instrument of production, the word abstinence." An unparalleled sample this, of the discoveries of vulgar economy! It substitutes for an economic category, a sycophantic phrase—*voilà tout*. "When the savage," says Senior, "makes bows, he exercises an industry, but he does not practice abstinence." This explains how and why, in the earlier states of society, the implements of labour were fabricated without abstinence on the part of the capitalist. "The more society progresses, the more abstinence is demanded," namely, from those who ply the industry of appropriating the fruits of others' industry. All the conditions for carrying on the labour process are suddenly converted into so many acts of abstinence on the part of the capitalist. If the corn is not all eaten, but part of it also sown—abstinence of the capitalist. If the wine gets time to mature—abstinence of the capitalist. The capitalist robs his own self, whenever he "lends (!) the instruments of production to the labourer" [G. de Molinari], that is, whenever by incorporating labour-power with them, he uses them to extract surplus-value out of that labour-power, instead of eating them up, steam engines, cotton, railways, manure, horses, and all; or as the vulgar economist childishly puts it, instead of dissipating "their value" in luxuries and other articles of consumption. How the capitalists as a class are to perform that feat is a secret that vulgar economy has hitherto obstinately refused to divulge. Enough that the world still jogs on, solely through the self-chastisement of this modern penitent of Vishnu, the capitalist. Not only accumulation, but the simple "conservation of a capital requires a constant effort to resist the temptation of consuming it" [Courcelles-Seneuil]. The simple dictates of humanity therefore plainly enjoin the release of the capitalist from this martyrdom and temptation, in the same way that the Georgian slaveowner was lately delivered, by the abolition of slavery, from the painful dilemma, whether to squander the surplus product lashed out of his niggers entirely in champagne, or whether to reconvert a part of it into more niggers and more land.

In economic forms of society of the most different kinds, there occurs, not only simple reproduction, but, in varying degrees, reproduction on a progressively increasing scale. By degrees more is produced and more consumed, and consequently more products have to be converted into means of production. This process, however, does not present itself as accumulation of capital, nor as the function of a capitalist, so long as the labourer's means of production, and with them, his product and means of subsistence, do not confront him in the shape of capital. Richard Jones, who died a few years ago, and was the successor of Malthus in the chair of political economy at Haileybury College, discusses this point well in the light of two important facts. Since the great mass of the Hindu population are peasants cultivating their land themselves, their products, their instruments of labour and means of subsistence never take "the shape of a fund saved from revenue, which fund has, therefore, gone through a previous process of accumulation." On the other hand, the non-agricultural labourers in those provinces where the English rule has least disturbed the old system, are directly employed by the magnates, to whom a portion of the agricultural surplus product is rendered in the shape of tribute or rent. One portion of this product is consumed by the magnates in kind, another is converted, for their use, by the labourers, into articles of luxury and such like things; while the rest forms the wages of the labourers, who own their implements of labour. Here production and reproduction on a progressively increasing scale go on their way without any intervention from that queer saint, that knight of the woeful countenance, the capitalist "abstainer."

4. The So-Called Labour Fund

It has been shown in the course of this inquiry that capital is not a fixed magnitude, but is a part of social wealth, elastic and constantly fluctuating with the division of fresh surplus-value into revenue and additional capital. It has been seen further that, even with a given magnitude of functioning capital, the labour-power, the science, and the land (by which are to be understood, economically, all conditions of labour furnished by Nature independently of man) embodied in it, from elastic powers of capital, allow it, within certain limits, a field of action independent of its own magnitude. In this inquiry we have neglected all effects of the process of circulation, effects which may produce very different degrees of efficiency in the same mass of capital. And as we presupposed the limits set by capitalist production, that is to say, presupposed the process of social production in a form developed by purely spontaneous growth, we neglected any more rational combination, directly and systematically practicable with the means of production and the mass of labour-power at present disposable. Classical economy always loved to conceive social capital as a fixed magnitude of a fixed degree of efficiency. But this prejudice was first established as a dogma by the arch-Philistine, Jeremy Bentham, that insipid, pedantic, leather-tongued oracle of the ordinary bourgeois intelligence of the 19th century. Bentham is among philosophers what Martin Tupper is among poets. Both could only have been manufactured in England. In the light of his dogma the commonest phenomena of the process of production, as, e.g., its sudden expansions and contractions, nay, even accumulation itself, become perfectly inconceivable. The dogma was used by Bentham himself, as well as by Malthus, James Mill, McCulloch, etc., for an apologetic purpose, and especially in order to represent one part of capital, namely, variable capital, or that part convertible into labour-power, as a fixed magnitude. The material of variable capital, i.e., the mass of the means of subsistence it represents for the labourer, or the so-called labour fund, was fabled as a separate part of social wealth, fixed by natural laws and unchangeable. To set in motion the part of social wealth which is to function as constant capital, or, to express it in a material form, as means of production, a definite mass of living labour is required. This mass is given technologically. But neither is the number of labourers required to render fluid this mass of labour-power given (it changes with the degree of exploitation of the individual labour-power), nor is the price of this labour-power given, but only its minimum limit, which is moreover very variable. The facts that lie at the bottom of this dogma are these: on the one hand, the labourer has no right to interfere in the division of social wealth into means of enjoyment for the non-labourer and means of production. On the other hand, only in favourable and exceptional cases has he the power to enlarge the so-called labour fund at the expense of the "revenue" of the wealthy.

What silly tautology results from the attempt to represent the capitalistic limits of the labour fund as its natural and social limits may be seen, e.g., in Professor [Henry] Fawcett. "The circulating capital of a country," he says, "is its wage fund. Hence, if we desire to calculate the average money wages received by each labourer, we have simply to divide the amount of this capital by the number of the labouring population." That is to say we first add together the individual wages actually paid, and then we affirm that the sum thus obtained forms the total value of the "labour fund" determined and vouchsafed to us by God and Nature. Lastly, we divide the sum thus obtained by the number of labourers to find out again how much may come to each on the average. An uncommonly knowing dodge this. It did not prevent Mr. Fawcett saying in the same breath: "The aggregate wealth which is annually saved in England, is divided into two portions; one portion is employed as capital to maintain our industry, and the other portion is exported to foreign countries. . . . Only a portion, and perhaps, not a large portion of the wealth which is annually saved in this country, is invested in our own industry."

The greater part of the yearly accruing surplus product, embezzled, because abstracted without return of an equivalent, from the English labourer, is thus used as capital, not in England, but in foreign countries. But with the additional capital thus exported, a part of the "labour fund" invented by God and Bentham is also exported.

XIX. THE GENERAL LAW OF CAPITALIST ACCUMULATION

1. The Increased Demand for Labour-Power That Accompanies Accumulation, the Composition of Capital Remaining the Same

Growth of capital involves growth of its variable constituent or of the part invested in labour-power. A part of the surplus-value turned into additional capital must always be retransformed into variable capital, or additional labour fund. If we suppose that, all other circumstances remaining the same, the composition of capital also remains constant (i.e., that a definite mass of means of production constantly needs the same mass of labour-power to set in motion), then the demand for labour and the subsistence fund of the labourers clearly increase in the same proportion as the capital, and the more rapidly, the more rapidly the capital increases. Since the capital produces yearly a surplus-value, of which one part is yearly added to the original capital; since this increment itself grows yearly along with the augmentation of the capital already functioning; since lastly, under special stimulus to enrichment, such as the opening of new markets or of new spheres for the outlay of capital in consequence of newly developed social wants, etc., the scale of accumulation may be suddenly extended, merely by a change in the division of the surplus-value or surplus product into capital and revenue, the requirements of accumulating capital may exceed the increase of labour-power or of the number of labourers; the demand for labourers may exceed the supply, and, therefore, wages may rise. This must, indeed, ultimately be the case if the conditions supposed above continue. For since in each year more labourers are employed than in its predecessor, sooner or later a point must be reached at which the requirements of accumulation begin to surpass the customary supply of labour, and, therefore, a rise of wages takes place. A lamentation on this score was heard in England during the whole of the 15th, and the first half of the 18th centuries. The more or less favourable circumstances in which the wage-working class supports and multiplies itself, in no way alter the fundamental character of capitalist production. As simple reproduction constantly reproduces the capital relation itself, i.e., the relation of capitalists on the one hand, and wage-workers on the other, so reproduction on a progressive scale, i.e., accumulation, reproduces the capital relation on a progressive scale, more capitalists or larger capitalists at this pole, more wageworkers at that. The reproduction of a mass of labour-power, which must incessantly re-incorporate itself with capital for that capital's self-expansion; which cannot get free from capital, and whose enslavement to capital is only concealed by the variety of individual capitalists to whom it sells itself, this reproduction of labour-power forms, in fact, an essential of the reproduction of capital itself. Accumulation of capital is, therefore, increase of the proletariat.

Classical economy grasped this fact so thoroughly that Adam Smith, Ricardo, etc., as mentioned earlier, inaccurately identified accumulation with the consumption by the productive labourers of all the capitalised part of the surplus product, or with its transformation into additional wage-labourers. As early as 1696 John Bellers says: "For if one had a hundred thousand acres of land and as many pounds of money, and as many cattle, without a labourer, what would the rich man be, but a labourer? And as the labourers make men rich, so the more labourers, there will be the more rich men . . . the labour of the poor being the mines of the rich." So also Bernard de Mandeville at the beginning of the 18th century: "It would be easier, where property is well secured, to live without money than without poor; for who would do the work? . . . As they (the poor) ought to be kept from starving, so they should receive nothing worth saving. If here and there one of the lowest class by uncommon industry, and pinching his belly, lifts himself above the condition he was brought up in, nobody ought to hinder him; nay, it is undeniably the wisest course for every person in the society, and for every private family to be frugal; but it is the interest of all rich nations, that the greatest part of the poor should almost never be idle, and yet continually spend what they get." What Mandeville, an honest, clear-headed man, had not yet seen, is that the mechanism of the process of accumulation itself increases, along with the capital, the mass of "labouring poor," i.e., the wage labourers, who turn their labour-power into an increasing power of self-expansion of the growing capital, and even by doing so must eternize their dependent relation on their own product, as personified in the capitalists. In reference to this relation of dependence, Sir F. M. Eden, in his *The State of the Poor, an History of the Labouring Classes in England,* says: "The natural produce of our soil is certainly not fully adequate to our subsistence; we can neither be clothed, lodged nor fed but in consequence of some previous labour. A portion at least of the society must be indefatigably employed. . . . There are others who, though they 'neither toil nor spin,' can yet command the produce of industry, but who owe their exemption from labour solely to civilisation and order. . . . They are peculiarly the creatures of civil institutions, which have recognised that individuals may acquire property by various other means besides the exertion of labour. . . . Persons of independent fortune . . . owe their superior advantages by no means to any superior abilities of their own, but almost entirely . . . to the industry of others. It is not the possession of land, or of money, but the command of labour which distinguishes the opulent from the labouring part of the community. . . . This [scheme approved by Eden] would give the people of property sufficient (but by no means too much) influence and authority over those who . . . work for them; and it would place such labourers, not in an abject or servile condition, but in such a state of easy and liberal dependence as all who know human nature, and its history, will allow to be necessary for their own comfort." Sir F. M. Eden, it may be remarked in passing, is the only disciple of Adam Smith during the 18th century that produced any work of importance.

2. *Relative Diminution of the Variable Part of Capital Simultaneously with the Progress of Accumulation and of the Concentration That Accompanies It*

According to the economists themselves, it is neither the actual extent of social wealth nor the magnitude of the capital already functioning, that leads to a rise of wages, but only the constant growth of accumulation and the degree of rapidity of that growth. So far we have only considered one special phase of this process, that in which the increase of capital occurs along with a constant technical composition of capital. But the process goes beyond this phase.

Once given the general basis of the capitalistic system, then, in the course of accumulation, a point is reached at which the development of the productivity of social labour becomes the most powerful lever of accumulation. "The same cause," says Adam Smith, "which raises the wages of labour, the increase of stock, tends to increase its productive powers, and to make a smaller quantity of labour produce a greater quantity of work."

Apart from natural conditions, such as fertility of the soil, etc., and from the skill of independent and isolated producers (shown rather qualitatively in the goodness than quantitatively in the mass of their products), the degree of productivity of labour, in a given society, is expressed in the relative extent of the means of production that one labourer, during a given time, with the same tension of labour-power, turns into products. The mass of the means of production which he thus transforms, increases with the productiveness of his labour. But those means of production play a double part. The increase of some is a consequence, that of the others a condition of the increasing productivity of labour. For example, with the division of labour in manufacture, and with the use of machinery, more raw material is worked up in the same time, and, therefore, a greater mass of raw material and auxiliary substances enter into the labour process. That is the consequence of the increasing productivity of labour. On the other hand, the mass of machinery, beasts of burden, mineral manures, drain pipes, etc., is a condition of the increasing productivity of labour. So also is it with the means of production concentrated in buildings, furnaces, means of transport, etc. But whether condition or consequence, the growing extent of the means of production, as compared with the labour-power incorporated with them, is an expression of the growing productiveness of labour.

3. Progressive Production of a Relative Surplus Population or Industrial Reserve Army

Considering the social capital in its totality, the movement of its accumulation now causes periodical changes, affecting it more or less as a whole, now distributes its various phases simultaneously over the different spheres of production. In some spheres a change in the composition of capital occurs without increase of its absolute magnitude, as a consequence of simple centralisation; in others the absolute growth of capital is connected with absolute diminution of its variable constituent or of the labour-power absorbed by it; in others again, capital continues growing for a time on its given technical basis and attracts additional labour-power in proportion to its increase, while at other times it undergoes organic change and lessens its variable constituent; in all spheres the increase of the variable part of capital, and therefore of the number of labourers employed by it, is always connected with violent fluctuations and transitory production of surplus population, whether this takes the more striking form of the repulsion of labourers already employed or the less evident but not less real form of the more difficult absorption of the additional labouring population through the usual channels. With the magnitude of social capital already functioning, and the degree of its increase, with the extension of the scale of production, and the mass of the labourers set in motion, with the development of the productiveness of their labour, with the greater breadth and fulness of all sources of wealth, there is also an extension of the scale on which greater attraction of labourers by capital is accompanied by their greater repulsion; the rapidity of the change in the organic composition of capital and in its technical form increases, and an increasing number of spheres of production becomes involved in this change, now simultaneously, now alternately. The labouring population therefore produces, along with the accumulation of capital produced by it, the means by which itself is made relatively superfluous, is turned into a relative surplus population; and it does this to an always increasing extent. This is a law of population peculiar to the capitalist mode of production; and in fact every special historic mode of production has its own special laws of population, historically valid within its limits alone. An abstract law of population exists for plants and animals only, and only in so far as man has not interfered with them.

But if a surplus labouring population is a necessary product of accumulation or of the development of wealth on a capitalist basis, this surplus population becomes, conversely, the lever of capitalistic accumulation, nay, a condition of existence of the capitalist mode of production. It forms a disposable industrial reserve army that belongs to capital quite as absolutely as if the latter had bred it at its own cost. Independently of the limits of the actual increase of population, it creates, for the changing needs of the self-expansion of capital, a mass of human material always ready for exploitation. With accumulation, and the development of the productiveness of labour that accompanies it, the power of sudden expansion of capital grows also; it grows, not merely because the elasticity of the capital already functioning increases, not merely because the absolute wealth of society expands, of which capital only forms an elastic part, not merely because credit, under every special stimulus, at once places an unusual part of this wealth at the disposal of production in the form of additional capital; it grows, also, because the technical conditions of the process of production themselves—machinery, means of transport, etc.—now admit of the rapidest transformation of masses of surplus product into additional means of production. The mass of social wealth, overflowing with the advance of accumulation and transformable into additional capital, thrusts itself frantically into old branches of production, whose market suddenly expands, or into newly formed branches, such as railways, etc., the need for which grows out of the development of the old ones. In all such cases there must be the possibility of throwing great masses of men suddenly on the decisive points without injury to the scale of production in other spheres. Overpopulation supplies these masses. The course characteristic of modern industry, viz., a decennial cycle (interrupted by smaller oscillations) of periods of average activity, production at high pressure, crisis and stagnation, depends on the constant formation, the greater or less absorption, and the re-formation of the industrial reserve army of surplus population. In their turn, the varying phases of the industrial cycle recruit the surplus population and become one of the most energetic agents of its reproduction. This peculiar course of modern industry, which occurs in no earlier period of human history, was also impossible in the childhood of capitalist production. The composition of capital changed but very slowly. With its accumulation, therefore, there kept pace, on the whole, a corresponding growth in the demand for labour. Slow as was the advance of accumulation compared with that of more modern times, it found a check in the natural limits of the exploitable labouring population, limits which could only be got rid of by forcible means to be mentioned later. The expansion by fits and starts of the scale of production is the preliminary to its equally sudden contraction; the latter again evokes the former, but the former is impossible without disposable human material, without an increase in the number of labourers independently of the absolute growth of the population. This increase is effected by the simple process that constantly "sets free" a part of the labourers; by methods which lessen the number of labourers employed in proportion to the increased production. The whole form of the movement of modern industry depends, therefore, upon the constant transformation of a part of the labouring population into unemployed or half-employed hands. The superficiality of Political Economy shows itself in the fact that it looks upon the expansion and contraction of credit, which is a mere symptom of the periodic changes of the industrial cycle, as their cause. As the heavenly bodies, once thrown into a certain definite motion, always repeat this, so is it with social production as soon as it is once thrown into this movement of alternate expansion and contraction. Effects, in their turn, become causes, and the varying accidents of the whole process, which always reproduces its own conditions, take on the form of periodicity. When this periodicity is once consolidated, even Political Economy then sees that the production of a relative surplus population—i.e., surplus with regard to the average needs of the self-expansion of capital—is a necessary condition of modern industry.

4. *Illustrations of the General Law of Capitalist Accumulation*

A. ENGLAND FROM 1846 TO 1866

No period of modern society is so favourable for the study of capitalist accumulation as the period of the last twenty years. It is as if this period had found Fortunatus' purse. But of all countries England again furnishes the classical example, because it holds the foremost place in the world market, because capitalist production is here alone completely developed, and lastly, because the introduction of the Free Trade millennium since 1846 has cut off the last retreat of vulgar economy.

Although the absolute increase of the English population in the last half century was very great, the relative increase or rate of growth fell constantly, as the following table borrowed from the census shows.

Annual increase per cent. of the population of England and Wales in decimal numbers:

1811–1821	1.533 per cent.
1821–1831	1.446 "
1831–1841	1.326 "
1841–1851	1.216 "
1851–1861	1.141 "

Let us now, on the other hand, consider the increase of wealth. Here the movement of profit, rent of land, etc., that come under the income tax, furnishes the surest basis. The increase of profits liable to income tax (farmers and some other categories not included) in Great Britain from 1853 to 1864 amounted to 50.47 per cent or 4.58 per cent as the annual average, that of the population during the same period to about 1.2 per cent. The augmentation of the rent of land subject to taxation (including houses, railways, mines, fisheries, etc.) amounted for 1853 to 1864 to 38 per cent or 3⁵⁄₁₁ per cent annually. Under this head the following categories show the greatest increase:

Houses, 38.60%	3.50%
Quarries, 84.76%	7.70%
Mines, 68.85%	6.26%
Ironworks, 39.92%	3.63%
Fisheries, 57.37%	5.21%
Gasworks, 126.02%	11.45%
Railways, 83.29%	7.57%

If we compare the years from 1853 to 1864 in three sets of four consecutive years each, the rate of augmentation of the income increases constantly. It is, e.g., for that arising from profits between 1853 to 1857, 1.73 per cent yearly; 1857–61, 2.74 per cent, and for 1861–64, 9.30 per cent yearly. The sum of the incomes of the United Kingdom that come under the income tax was, in 1856, £307,068,898; in 1859, £328,127,416; in 1862, £351,745,241; in 1863, £359,142,897; in 1864, £362,462,279; in 1865, £385,530,020.

The accumulation of capital was attended at the same time by its concentration and centralisation. Although no official statistics of agriculture existed for England (they did for Ireland), they were voluntarily given in 10 counties. These statistics gave the result that from 1851 to 1861 the number of farms of less than 100 acres had fallen from 31,583 to 26,597, so that 5016 had been thrown together into larger farms. From 1815 to 1825 no personal estate of more than £1,000,000 came under the succession duty; from 1825 to 1855, however, 8 did; and 4 from 1856 to June 1859, i.e., in 4½ years. The centralisation will, however, be best seen from a short analysis of the Income Tax Schedule D (profits, exclusive of farms, etc.) in the years 1864 and 1865. I note beforehand that incomes from this source pay income tax on everything over £60. These incomes liable to taxation in England, Wales, and Scotland amounted in 1864 to £95,844,222, in 1865 to £105,435,579. The number of persons taxed were, in 1864, 308,416 out of a population of 23,891,009; in 1865, 332,431 out of a population of 24,127,003. The following table shows the distribution of these incomes in the two years:

Year ending April 5, 1864			Year ending April 5, 1865		
Income from profits		Persons	Income from profits		Persons
Total Income	£95,844,222	308,416	Total Income	£105,435,738	332,431
of these	57,028,289	23,334	of these	64,554,297	24,265
"	36,415,225	3619	"	42,535,576	4021
"	22,809,781	832	"	27,555,313	973
"	8,744,762	91	"	11,077,238	107

In 1855 there were produced in the United Kingdom 61,453,079 tons of coal, of value £16,113,167; in 1864, 92,787,873 tons, of value £23,197,-968; in 1855, 3,218,154 tons of pig iron, of value £8,045,385; 1864, 4,767,951 tons, of value £11,919,877. In 1854 the length of the railroads worked in the United Kingdom was 8054 miles, with a paid-up capital of £286,068,794; in 1864 the length was 12,789 miles, with capital paid up of £425,719,613. In 1854 the total sum of the exports and imports of the United Kingdom was £268,210,145; in 1865, £489,923,285. The following table shows the movement of the exports:

1846	£58,842,377
1849	63,596,052
1856	115,826,948
1860	135,842,817
1865	165,862,402
1866	188,917,563

After these few examples one understands the cry of triumph of the Registrar-General of the British people: "Rapidly as the population has increased, it has not kept pace with the progress of industry and wealth."

Let us turn now to the direct agents of this industry, or the producers of this wealth, to the working class. "It is one of the most melancholy features in the social state of this country," says [William Ewart] Gladstone, "that while there was a decrease in the consuming powers of the people, and while there was an increase in the privations and distress of the labouring class and operatives, there was at the same time a constant accumulation of wealth in the upper classes, and a constant increase of capital." Thus spake this unctuous minister in the House of Commons on February 13, 1843. On April 16, 1863, twenty years later, in the speech in which he introduced his Budget: "From 1842 to 1852 the taxable income of the country increased by 6 per cent. . . . In the eight years from 1853 to 1861 it had increased from the basis taken in 1853 by 20 per cent! The fact is so astonishing as to be almost incredible . . . this intoxicating augmentation of wealth and power . . . entirely confined to classes of property . . . must be of indirect benefit to the labouring population, because it cheapens the commodities of general consumption. While the rich have been growing richer, the poor have been growing less poor. At any rate, whether the extremes of poverty are less, I do not presume to say." How lame an anticlimax! If the working class has remained "poor," only "less poor" in proportion as it produces for the wealthy class "an intoxicating augmentation of wealth and power," then it has remained relatively just as poor. If the extremes of poverty have not lessened, they have increased, because the extremes of wealth have. As to the cheapening of the means of subsistence, the official statistics, e.g., the accounts of the London Orphan Asylum, show an increase in price of 20 per cent for the average of the three years 1860–62, compared with 1851–53. In the following three years, 1863–65, there was a progressive rise in the price of meat, butter, milk, sugar, salt, coals, and a number of other necessary means of subsistence. Gladstone's next Budget speech of April 7, 1864, is a Pindaric dithyrambus on the advance of surplus-value-making and the happiness of the people tempered by "poverty." He speaks of masses "on the border" of pauperism, of branches of trade in which "wages have not increased," and finally sums up the happiness of the working class in the words: "Human life is but, in nine cases out of ten, a struggle for existence." Professor Fawcett, not bound like Gladstone by official considerations, declares roundly: "I do not, of course, deny that money wages have been augmented by this increase of capital (in the last ten years), but this apparent advantage is to a great extent lost, because many of the necessaries of life are becoming dearer" (he believes because of the fall in value of the precious metals) . . . "the rich grow rapidly richer, whilst there is no perceptible advance in the comfort enjoyed by the industrial classes. . . . They (the labourers) become almost the slaves of the tradesman, to whom they owe money."

B. THE BRITISH AGRICULTURAL PROLETARIAT

Nowhere does the antagonistic character of capitalistic production and accumulation assert itself more brutally than in the progress of English agriculture (including cattle breeding) and the retrogression of the English agricultural labourer. Before I turn to his present situation, a rapid retrospect: Modern agriculture dates in England from the middle of the 18th century, although the revolution in landed property, from which the changed mode of production starts as a basis, has a much earlier date.

If we take the statements of Arthur Young, a careful observer, though a superficial thinker, as to the agricultural labourer of 1771, the latter plays a very pitiable part compared with his predecessor of the end of the 14th century, "when the labourer . . . could live in plenty, and accumulate wealth," not to speak of the 15th century, "the golden age of the English labourer in town and country," [according to James E. Thorold Rogers]. We need not, however, go back so far. In a very instructive work of the year 1777 we read: "The great farmer is nearly mounted to a level with him (the gentleman); while the poor labourer is depressed almost to the earth. His unfortunate situation will fully appear, by taking a comparative view of it, only forty years ago, and at present. . . . Landlord and tenant . . . have both gone hand in hand in keeping the labourer down." (*Reasons for the Late Increase of the Poor Rate,* London, 1777.) It is then proved in detail that the real agricultural wages between 1737 and 1777 fell nearly one fourth, or 25 per cent. "Modern policy," says Dr. Richard Price also, "is, indeed, more favourable to the higher classes of people; and the consequences may in time prove that the whole kingdom will consist of only gentry and beggars, or of grandees and slaves."

Nevertheless, the position of the English agricultural labourer from 1770 to 1780, with regard to his food and dwelling, as well as to his self-respect, amusements, etc., is an ideal never attained again since that time. His average wage is expressed in pints of what was from 1770 to 1771, 90 pints, in Eden's time (1797) only 65, in 1808 but 60.

The state of the agricultural labourer at the end of the Anti-Jacobin war, during which landed proprietors, farmers, manufacturers, merchants, bankers, stockbrokers, army contractors, etc., enriched themselves so extraordinarily, has been already indicated above. The nominal wages rose in consequence partly of the bank-note depreciation, partly of a rise in the price of the primary means of subsistence independent of this depreciation. But the actual wage variation can be evidenced in a very simple way, without entering into details that are here unnecessary. The

Poor Law and its administration were in 1795 and 1814 the same. It will be remembered how this law was carried out in the country districts: in the form of alms the parish made up the nominal wage to the nominal sum required for the simple vegetation of the labourer. The ratio between the wages paid by the farmer and the wage deficit made good by the parish shows us two things. First, the falling of wages below their minimum; second, the degree in which the agricultural labourer was a compound of wage labourer and pauper, or the degree in which he had been turned into a serf of his parish. Let us take one county that represents the average condition of things in all counties. In Northamptonshire, in 1795, the average weekly wage was 7s. 6d.; the total yearly expenditure of a family of 6 persons, £36 12s. 5d.; their total income, £29 18s.; deficit made good by the parish, £6 14s. 5d. In 1814, in the same county, the weekly wage was 12s. 2d.; the total yearly expenditure of a family of 5 persons, £54 18s. 4d.; their total income, £36 2s.; deficit made good by the parish, £18 16s. 4d. In 1795 the deficit was less than one fourth the wage, in 1814, more than half. It is self-evident that, under these circumstances, the meagre comforts that Eden still found in the cottage of the agricultural labourer, had vanished by 1814. Of all the animals kept by the farmer, the labourer, the *instrumentum vocale,* was, thenceforth, the most oppressed, the worst nourished, the most brutally treated.

The same state of things went on quietly until "the Swing riots, in 1830, revealed to us (i.e., the ruling classes) by the light of blazing corn stacks, that misery and black mutinous discontent smouldered quite as fiercely under the surface of agricultural as of manufacturing England." (S. Laing, *National Distress,* London, 1844.) At this time Sadler, in the House of Commons, christened the agricultural labourers "white slaves," and a bishop echoed the epithet in the Upper House. The most notable political economist of that period—E. G. Wakefield—says: "The peasant of the South of England . . . is not a freeman, nor is he a slave; he is a pauper." (*England and America,* London, 1833.)

The continual emigration to the towns, the continual formation of surplus population in the country through the concentration of farms, conversion of arable land into pasture, machinery, etc., and the continual eviction of the agricultural population by the destruction of their cottages, go hand in hand. The more empty the district is of men, the greater is its "relative surplus population," the greater is their pressure on the means of employment, the greater is the absolute excess of the agricultural population over the means for housing it, the greater, therefore, in the villages is the local surplus population and the most pestilential packing together of human beings. The packing together of knots of men in scattered little villages and small country towns corresponds to the forcible draining of men from the surface of the land. The continuous superseding of the agricultural labourers, in spite of their diminishing number and the increasing mass of their products, gives birth to their pauperism. Their pauperism is ultimately a motive to their eviction and the chief source of their miserable housing which breaks down their last power of resistance and makes them mere slaves of the landed proprietors and the farmers. Thus the minimum of wages becomes a law of Nature to them. On the other hand, the land, in spite of its constant "relative surplus population," is at the same time underpopulated. This is seen not only locally at the points where the efflux of men to towns, mines, railroad making, etc., is most marked. It is to be seen everywhere, in harvesttime as well as in spring and summer, at those frequently recurring times when English agriculture, so careful and intensive, wants extra hands. There are always too many agricultural labourers for the ordinary, and always too few for the exceptional or temporary needs of the cultivation of the soil. Hence we find in the official documents contradictory complaints from the same places of deficiency and excess of labour simultaneously. The temporary or local want of labour brings about no rise in wages, but a forcing of the women and children into the fields and exploitation at an age constantly lowered. As soon as the exploitation of the women and children takes place on a larger scale, it becomes in turn a new means of making a surplus population of the male agricultural labourer and of keeping down his wage. In the east of England thrives a beautiful fruit of this vicious circle—the so-called gang system, to which I must briefly refer here.

The gang system obtains almost exclusively in the counties of Lincoln, Huntingdon, Cambridge, Norfolk, Suffolk, and Nottingham, here and there in the neighbouring counties of Northampton, Bedford, and Rutland. Lincolnshire will serve us as an example. A large part of this county is new land, marsh formerly, or even, as in others of the eastern counties just named, won lately from the sea. The steam engine has worked wonders in the way of drainage. What were once fens and sandbanks bear now a luxuriant sea of corn and the highest of rents. The same thing holds of the alluvial lands won by human endeavour, as in the island of Axholme and other parishes on the banks of the Trent. In proportion as the new farms arose, not only were no new cottages built; old ones were demolished, and the supply of labour had to come from open villages, miles away, by long roads that wound along the sides of the hills. There alone had the population formerly found shelter from the incessant floods of the wintertime. The labourers that dwell on the farms of 400–1000 acres (they are called "confined labourers") are solely employed on such kinds of agricultural work as is permanent, difficult, and carried on by aid of horses. For every 100 acres there is, on an average, scarcely one cottage. A fen farmer, e.g., gave evidence before the Commission of Inquiry: "I farm 320 acres, all arable land. I have not one cottage on my farm. I have only one labourer on my farm now. I have four horsemen lodging about. We get light work done by gangs." The soil requires much light field labour, such as weeding, hoeing, certain processes of manuring, removing of stones, etc. This is done by the gangs, or organised bands that dwell in the open villages.

The gang consists of 10 to 40 or 50 persons, women, young persons of both sexes (13–18 years of age, although the boys are for the most part eliminated at the age of 13), and children of both sexes (6–13 years of age). At the head is the gangmaster, always an ordinary agricultural labourer, generally what is called a bad lot, a scapegrace, unsteady, drunken, but with a dash of enterprise and *savoir-faire*. He is the recruiting sergeant for the gang, which works under him, not under the farmer. He generally arranges with the latter for piecework, and his income, which on the average is not very much above that of an ordinary agricultural labourer, depends almost entirely upon the dexterity with which he manages to extract within the shortest time the greatest possible amount of labour from his gang. The farmers have discovered that women work steadily only under the direction of men, but that women and children, once set going, impetuously spend their life force—as Fourier knew—while the adult male labourer is shrewd enough to economise his as much as he can. The gangmaster goes from one farm to another, and thus employs his gang from 6 to 8 months in the year. Employment by him is, therefore, much more lucrative and more certain for the labouring families than employment by the individual farmer, who only employs children occasionally. This circumstance so completely rivets his influence in the open villages that children are generally only to be hired through his instrumentality. The lending out of these individually, independently of the gang, is his second trade.

The "drawbacks" of the system are the overwork of the children and young persons, the enormous marches that they make daily to and from the farms, 5, 6, and sometimes 7 miles distant, finally, the demoralisation of the gang. Although the gangmaster, who in some districts is called "the driver," is armed with a long stick, he uses it but seldom, and complaints of brutal treatment are exceptional. He is a democratic emperor, or a kind of Pied Piper of Hamelin. He must therefore be popular with his subjects, and he binds them to himself by the charms of the gypsy life under his direction. Coarse freedom, a noisy jollity, and obscenest impudence give attractions to the gang. Generally the gangmaster pays up in a public house; then he returns home at the head of the procession reeling drunk, propped up right and left by a stalwart virago, while children and young persons bring up the rear, boisterous and singing chaffing and bawdy songs. On the return journey what Fourier calls "phanerogamie" is the order of the day. The getting with child of girls of 13 and 14 by their male companions of the same age is common. The open villages which supply the contingent of the gang become Sodoms and Gomorrahs, and have twice as high a rate of illegitimate births as the rest of the kingdom.

PART EIGHT: THE SO-CALLED PRIMITIVE ACCUMULATION

XX. THE SECRET OF PRIMITIVE ACCUMULATION

We have seen how money is changed into capital; how through capital surplus-value is made, and from surplus-value more capital. But the accumulation of capital presupposes surplus-value; surplus-value presupposes capitalistic production; capitalistic production presupposes the pre-existence of considerable masses of capital and of labour-power in the hands of producers of commodities. The whole movement, therefore, seems to turn in a vicious circle, out of which we can only get by supposing a primitive accumulation (previous accumulation of Adam Smith) preceding capitalistic accumulation; an accumulation not the result of the capitalist mode of production, but its starting point.

This primitive accumulation plays in Political Economy about the same part as original sin in theology. Adam bit the apple, and thereupon sin fell on the human race. Its origin is supposed to be explained when it is told as an anecdote of the past. In times long gone by there were two sorts of people: one, the diligent, intelligent, and, above all, frugal elite; the other, lazy rascals, spending their substance and more in riotous living. The legend of theological original sin tells us certainly how man came to be condemned to eat his bread in the sweat of his brow; but the history of economic original sin reveals to us that there are people to whom this is by no means essential. Never mind! Thus it came to pass that the former sort accumulated wealth, and the latter sort had at last nothing to sell except their own skins. And from this original sin dates the poverty of the great majority that, despite all its labour, has up to now nothing to sell but itself, and the wealth of the few that increases constantly although they have long ceased to work. Such insipid childishness is every day preached to us in the defence of property. M. Thiers, e.g., had the assurance to repeat it with all the solemnity of a statesman to the French people, once so *spirituel*. But as soon as the question of property crops up, it becomes a sacred duty to proclaim the intellectual food of the infant as the one thing fit for all ages and for all stages of development. In actual history it is notorious that conquest, enslavement, robbery, murder, briefly force, play the great part. In the tender annals of Political Economy, the idyllic reigns from time immemorial. Right and "labour" were from all time the sole means of enrichment, the present year, of course, always excepted. As a matter of fact, the methods of primitive accumulation are anything but idyllic.

The economic structure of capitalistic society has grown out of the economic structure of feudal society. The dissolution of the latter set free the elements of the former.

The immediate producer, the labourer, could only dispose of his own person after he had ceased to be attached to the soil and ceased to be the slave, serf, or bondman of another. To become a free seller of labour-power, who carries his commodity wherever he finds a market, he must further have escaped from the regime of the guilds, their rules for apprentices and journeymen, and the impediments of their labour regulations. Hence the historical movement which changes the producers into wageworkers appears, on the one hand, as their emancipation from serfdom and from the fetters of the guilds, and this side alone exists for our bourgeois historians. But, on the other hand, these new freedmen became sellers of themselves only after they had been robbed of all their own means of production and of all the guarantees of existence afforded by the old feudal arrangements. And the history of this, their expropriation, is written in the annals of mankind in letters of blood and fire.

The industrial capitalists, these new potentates, had on their part not only to displace thc guild masters of handicrafts, but also the feudal lords, the possessors of the sources of wealth. In this respect their conquest of social power appears as the fruit of a victorious struggle both against feudal lordship and its revolting prerogatives, and against the guilds and the fetters they laid on the free development of production and the free exploitation of man by man. The *chevaliers d'industrie,* however, only succeed in supplanting the chevaliers of the sword by making use of events of which they themselves were wholly innocent. They have risen by means as vile as those by which the Roman freedman once on a time made himself the master of his *patronus.*

The starting point of the development that gave rise to the wage labourer as well as to the capitalist was the servitude of the labourer. The advance consisted in a change of form of this servitude, in the transformation of feudal exploitation into capitalist exploitation. To understand its march we need not go back very far. Although we come across the first beginnings of capitalist production as early as the 14th or 15th century, sporadically, in certain towns of the Mediterranean, the capitalistic era dates from the 16th century. Wherever it appears, the abolition of serfdom has been long effected, and the highest development of the Middle Ages, the existence of sovereign towns, has been long on the wane.

In the history of primitive accumulation all revolutions are epoch-making that act as levers for the capitalist class in course of formation; but, above all, those moments when great masses of men are suddenly and forcibly torn from their means of subsistence and hurled as free and "unattached" proletarians on the labour market. The expropriation of the agricultural producer, of the peasant, from the soil is the basis of the whole process.

XXI. EXPROPRIATION OF THE AGRICULTURAL POPULATION FROM THE LAND

In England serfdom had practically disappeared in the last part of the 14th century. The immense majority of the population consisted then, and to a still larger extent in the 15th century, of free peasant proprietors, whatever was the feudal title under which their right of property was hidden. In the larger seignorial domains the old bailiff, himself a serf, was displaced by the free farmer. The wage labourers of agriculture consisted partly of peasants, who utilised their leisure time by working on the large estates, partly of an independent special class of wage labourers, relatively and absolutely few in numbers. The latter also were practically at the same time peasant farmers, since, besides their wages, they had allotted to them arable land to the extent of 4 or more acres, together with their cottages. Besides they, with the rest of the peasants, enjoyed the usufruct of the common land, which gave pasture to their cattle, furnished them with timber, firewood, turf, etc. In all countries of Europe feudal production is characterised by division of the soil amongst the greatest possible number of subfeudatories. The might of the feudal lord, like that of the sovereign, depended not on the length of his rent roll, but on the number of his subjects, and the latter depended on the number of peasant proprietors. Although, therefore, the English land, after the Norman Conquest, was distributed in gigantic baronies, one of which often included some 900 of the old Anglo-Saxon lordships, it was bestrewn with small peasant properties, only here and there interspersed with great seignorial domains. Such conditions, together with the prosperity of the towns so characteristic of the 15th century, allowed of that wealth of the people which Chancellor Fortescue so eloquently paints in his *Laudes legum Angliæ;* but it excluded the possibility of capitalistic wealth.

The prelude of the revolution that laid the foundation of the capitalist mode of production was played in the last third of the 15th and the first decade of the 16th century. A mass of free proletarians was hurled on the labour market by the breaking up of the bands of feudal retainers, who, as Sir James Steuart well says, "everywhere uselessly filled house and castle." Although the royal power, itself a product of bourgeois development, in its strife after absolute sovereignty forcibly hastened on the dissolution of these bands of retainers, it was by no means the sole cause of it. In insolent conflict with king and parliament, the great feudal lords created an incomparably larger proletariat by the forcible driving of the peasantry from the land, to which the latter had the same feudal right as the lord himself, and by the usurpation of the common lands. The rapid rise of the Flemish wool manufactures, and the corresponding rise in the price of wool in England, gave the direct impulse to these evictions. The old nobility had been devoured by the great feudal wars. The new nobility was the child of its time, for which money was the power of all powers. Transformation of arable land into sheepwalks was, therefore, its cry. Harrison, in his "Description of England," prefixed to Holinshed's *Chronicle,* describes how the expropriation of small peasants is ruining the country. "What care our great encroachers?" The dwellings of the peasants and the cottages of the labourers were razed to the ground or doomed to decay. "If," says Harrison, "the old records of euerie manour be sought . . . it will soon appear that in some manour seventeene, eighteene, or twentie houses are shrunk . . . that England was neuer less furnished with people than at the present. . . . Of cities and townes either utterly decaied or more than a quarter or half diminished, though some one be a little increased here or there; of townes pulled downe for sheepe-walks, and no more but the lordships now standing in them . . . I could saie somewhat." The complaints of these old chroniclers are always exaggerated, but they reflect faithfully the impression made on contemporaries by the revolution in the conditions of production. A comparison of the writings of Chancellor Fortescue and Thomas More reveals the gulf between the 15th and 16th century. As Thornton rightly has it, the English working class was precipitated without any transition from its golden into its iron age.

XXII. BLOODY LEGISLATION AGAINST THE EXPROPRIATED, FROM THE END OF THE 15TH CENTURY. FORCING DOWN OF WAGES BY ACTS OF PARLIAMENT

The proletariat created by the breaking up of the bands of feudal retainers and by the forcible expropriation of the people from the soil, this "free" proletariat, could not possibly be absorbed by the nascent manufactures as fast as it was thrown upon the world. On the other hand, these men, suddenly dragged from their wonted mode of life, could not as suddenly adapt themselves to the discipline of their new condition. They were turned *en masse* into beggars, robbers, vagabonds, partly from inclination, in most cases from stress of circumstances. Hence at the end of the 15th and during the whole of the 16th century, throughout Western Europe a bloody legislation against vagabondage. The fathers of the present working class were chastised for their enforced transformation into vagabonds and paupers. Legislation treated them as "voluntary" criminals, and assumed that it depended on their own goodwill to go on working under the old conditions that no longer existed.

In England this legislation began under Henry VII.

Henry VIII, 1530: Beggars old and unable to work receive a beggar's licence. On the other hand, whipping and imprisonment for sturdy vagabonds. They are to be tied to the cart tail and whipped until the blood streams from their bodies, then to swear an oath to go back to their birthplace or to where they have lived the last three years and to "put themselves to labour." What grim irony! In 27 Henry VIII the former statute is repeated, but strengthened with new clauses. For the second arrest for vagabondage the whipping is to be repeated and half the ear sliced off; but for the third relapse the offender is to be executed as a hardened criminal and enemy of the common weal.

Edward VI: A statute of the first year of his reign, 1547, ordains that if anyone refuses to work, he shall be condemned as a slave to the person who has denounced him as an idler. The master shall feed his slave on bread and water, weak broth, and such refuse meat as he thinks fit. He has the right to force him to do any work, no matter how disgusting, with whip and chains. If the slave is absent a fortnight, he is condemned to slavery for life and is to be branded on forehead or back with the letter S; if he runs away thrice, he is to be executed as a felon. The master can sell him, bequeath him, let him out on hire as a slave, just as any other personal chattel, or cattle. If the slaves attempt anything against the masters, they are also to be executed. Justices of the peace, on information, are to hunt the rascals down. If it happens that a vagabond has been idling about for three days, he is to be taken to his birthplace, branded with a red-hot iron with the letter V on the breast and be set to work, in chains, in the streets or at some other labour. If the vagabond gives a false birthplace, he is then to become the slave for life of this place, of its inhabitants, or its corporation, and to be branded with an S. All persons have the right to take away the children of the vagabonds and to keep them as apprentices, the young men until the 24th year, the girls until the 20th. If they run away, they are to become up to this age the slaves of their masters, who can put them in irons, whip them, etc., if they like. Every master may put an iron ring round the neck, arms, or legs of his slave, by which to know him more easily and to be more certain of him. The last part of the statute provides that certain poor people may be employed by a place or by persons, who are willing to give them food and drink and to find them work. This kind of parish slaves was kept up in England until far into the 19th century under the name of "roundsmen."

Elizabeth, 1572: Unlicensed beggars above 14 years of age are to be severely flogged and branded on the left ear unless some one will take them into service for two years; in case of a repetition of the offence, if they are over 18, they are to be executed, unless some one will take them into service for two years; but for the third offence they are to be executed without mercy as felons. Similar statutes: 18 Elizabeth, c. 13, and another of 1597.

James I: Any one wandering about and begging is declared a rogue and a vagabond. Justices of the peace in petty sessions are authorised to have them publicly whipped and for the first offence to imprison them for 6 months, for the second for 2 years. Whilst in prison they are to be whipped as much and as often as the justices of the peace think fit . . . Incorrigible and dangerous rogues are to be branded with an R on the left shoulder and set to hard labour, and if they are caught begging again, to be executed without mercy. These statutes, legally binding until the beginning of the 18th century, were only repealed by 12 Ann, c. 23.

[There were] similar laws in France, where by the middle of the 17th century a kingdom of vagabonds (truands) was established in Paris. Even at the beginning of Louis XVI's reign (Ordinance of July 13, 1777) every man in good health from 16 to 60 years of age, if without means of subsistence and not practising a trade, is to be sent to the galleys. Of the same nature are the statute of Charles V for the Netherlands (October, 1537), the first edict of the States and Towns of Holland (March 10, 1614), the "Plakaat" of the United Provinces (June 26, 1649), etc.

Thus were the agricultural people, first forcibly expropriated from the soil, driven from their homes, turned into vagabonds, and then whipped, branded, tortured by laws grotesquely terrible, into the discipline necessary for the wage system.

XXIII. GENESIS OF THE CAPITALIST FARMER

Now that we have considered the forcible creation of a class of outlawed proletarians, the bloody discipline that turned them into wage labourers, the disgraceful action of the state which employed the police to accelerate the accumulation of capital by increasing the degree of exploitation of labour, the question remains: Whence came the capitalists originally? For the expropriation of the agricultural population creates, directly, none but great landed proprietors. As far, however, as concerns the genesis of the farmer, we can, so to say, put our hand on it, because it is a slow process evolving through many centuries. The serfs, as well as the free small proprietors, held land under very different tenures, and were therefore emancipated under very different economic conditions. In England the first form of the farmer is the bailiff, himself a serf. His position is similar to that of the old Roman *villicus,* only in a more limited sphere of action. During the second half of the 14th century he is replaced by a farmer, whom the landlord provides with seed, cattle, and implements. His condition is not very different from that of the peasant. Only he exploits more wage labour. Soon he becomes a *métayer,* a half farmer. He advances one part of the agricultural stock, the landlord the other. The two divide the total product in proportions determined by contract. This form quickly disappears in England, to give place to the farmer proper, who makes his own capital breed by employing wage labourers, and pays a part of the surplus product, in money or in kind, to the landlord as rent. So long, during the 15th century, as the independent peasant and the farm labourer working for himself as well as for wages enriched themselves by their own labour, the circumstances of the farmer and his field of production were equally mediocre. The agricultural revolution which commenced in the last third of the 15th century, and continued during almost the whole of the 16th (excepting, however, its last decade) enriched him just as speedily as it impoverished the mass of the agricultural people.

The usurpation of the common lands allowed him to augment greatly his stock of cattle, almost without cost, whilst they yielded him a richer supply of manure for the tillage of the soil. To this was added in the 16th century a very important element. At that time the contracts for farms ran for a long time, often for 99 years. The progressive fall in the value of the precious metals, and therefore of money, brought the farmers golden fruit. Apart from all the other circumstances discussed above, it lowered wages. A portion of the latter was now added to the profits of the farm. The continuous rise in the price of corn, wool, meat, in a word of all agricultural produce, swelled the money capital of the farmer without any action on his part, whilst the rent he paid (being calculated on the old value of money) diminished in reality. Thus they grew rich at the expense both of their labourers and their landlords. No wonder, therefore, that England, at the end of the 16th century had a class of capitalist farmers, rich considering the circumstances of the time.

XXIV. GENESIS OF THE INDUSTRIAL CAPITALIST

The genesis of the industrial capitalist did not proceed in such a gradual way as that of the farmer. Doubtless many small guild masters, and yet more independent small artisans, or even wage labourers, transformed themselves into small capitalists, and (by gradually extending exploitation of wage labour and corresponding accumulation) into full-blown capitalists. In the infancy of capitalist production, things often happened as in the infancy of mediæval towns, where the question which of the escaped serfs should be master and which servant was in great part decided by the earlier or later date of their flight. The snail's pace of this method corresponded in no wise with the commercial requirements of the new world market that the great discoveries of the end of the 15th century created. But the middle age had handed down two distinct forms of capital, which mature in the most different economic social formations and which, before the era of the capitalist mode of production, are considered as capital *quand même*—usurer's capital and merchant's capital.

"At present, all the wealth of society goes first into the possession of the capitalist . . . he pays the landowner his rent, the labourer his wages, the tax and tithe gatherer their claims, and keeps a large, indeed the largest, and a continually augmenting share, of the annual produce of labour for himself. The capitalist may now be said to be the first owner of all the wealth of the community, though no law has conferred on him the right to this property . . . this change has been effected by the taking of interest on capital . . . and it is not a little curious that all the lawgivers of Europe endeavoured to prevent this by statutes, viz., statutes against usury. . . . The power of the capitalist over all the wealth of the country is a complete change in the right of property, and by what law, or series of laws, was it effected?" (Thomas Hodgskin, *The Natural and Artificial Rights of Property Contrasted,* London, 1832.) The author should have remembered that revolutions are not made by laws.

The money capital formed by means of usury and commerce was prevented from turning into industrial capital, in the country by the feudal constitution, in the towns by the guild organization. These fetters vanished with the dissolution of feudal society, with the expropriation and partial eviction of the country population. The new manufacturers were established at seaports or in inland points beyond the control of the old municipalities and their guilds. Hence in England an embittered struggle of the corporate towns against these new industrial nurseries.

The discovery of gold and silver in America, the extirpation, enslavement, and entombment in mines of the aboriginal population, the beginning of the conquest and looting of the East Indies, the turning of Africa into a warren for the commercial hunting of black-skins, signalised the rosy dawn of the era of capitalist production. These idyllic proceedings are the chief momenta of primitive accumulation. On their heels treads the commercial war of the European nations, with the globe for a theatre. It begins with the revolt of the Netherlands from Spain, assumes giant dimensions in England's Anti-Jacobin war, and is still going on in the opium wars against China, etc.

The different momenta of primitive accumulation distribute themselves now, more or less in chronological order, particularly over Spain, Portugal, Holland, France, and England. In England at the end of the 17th century, they arrive at a systematical combination, embracing the colonies, the national debt, the modern mode of taxation, and the protectionist system. These methods depend in part on brute force, e.g., the colonial system. But they all employ the power of the State, the concentrated and organised force of society, to hasten, hothouse fashion, the process of transformation of the feudal mode of production into the capitalist mode, and to shorten the transition. Force is the midwife of every old society pregnant with a new one. It is itself an economic power.

Of the Christian colonial system, W. Howitt, a man who makes a specialty of Christianity, says: "The barbarities and desperate outrages of the so-called Christian race, throughout every region of the world, and upon every people they have been able to subdue, are not to be paralleled by those of any other race, however fierce, however untaught, and however reckless of mercy and of shame, in any age of the earth." The history of the colonial administration of Holland—and Holland was the head capitalistic nation of the 17th century—"is one of the most extraordinary relations of treachery, bribery, massacre, and meanness," [according to Thomas Stamford Raffles, formerly lieutenant governor of Java]. Nothing is more characteristic than their system of stealing men, to get slaves for Java. The men stealers were trained for this purpose. The thief, the interpreter, and the seller were the chief agents in this trade, native princes the chief sellers. The young people stolen were thrown into the secret dungeons of Celebes until they were ready for sending to the slave ships. An official report says: "This one town of Macassar, e.g., is full of secret prisons, one more horrible than the other, crammed with unfortunates, victims of greed and tyranny fettered in chains, forcibly torn from their families." To secure Malacca the Dutch corrupted the Portuguese governor. He let them into the town in 1641. They hurried at once to his house and assassinated him, to "abstain" from the payment of £21,875, the price of his treason. Wherever they set foot, devastation and depopulation followed. Banjuwangi, a province of Java, in 1750 numbered over 80,000 inhabitants, in 1811 only 18,000. Sweet commerce!

The English East India Company, as is well known, obtained, besides the political rule in India, the exclusive monopoly of the tea trade, as well as of the Chinese trade in general, and of the transport of goods to and from Europe. But the coasting trade of India and between the islands, as well as the internal trade of India, were the monopoly of the higher employees of the company. The monopolies of salt, opium, betel, and other commodities, were inexhaustible mines of wealth. The employees themselves fixed the price and plundered at will the unhappy Hindus. The Governor-General took part in this private traffic. His favourites received contracts under conditions whereby they, cleverer than the alchemists, made gold out of nothing. Great fortunes sprang up like mushrooms in a day; primitive accumulation went on without the advance of a shilling. The trial of Warren Hastings swarms with such cases. Here is an instance. A contract for opium was given to a certain Sullivan at the moment of his departure on an official mission to a part of India far removed from the opium district. Sullivan sold his contract to one Binn for £40,000; Binn sold it the same day for £60,000, and the ultimate purchaser who carried out the contract declared that after all he realised an enormous gain. According to one of the lists laid before Parliament, the Company and its employees from 1757 to 1766 got £6,000,000 from the Indians as gifts. Between 1769 and 1770 the English manufactured a famine by buying up all the rice and refusing to sell it again, except at fabulous prices.

The treatment of the aborigines was, naturally, most frightful in plantation colonies destined for export trade only, such as the West Indies, and in rich and well-populated countries, such as Mexico and India, that were given over to plunder. But even in the colonies properly so-called, the Christian character of primitive accumulation did not belie itself. Those sober virtuosi of Protestantism, the Puritans of New England, in 1703 by decrees of their assembly set a premium of £40 on every Indian scalp and every captured redskin: in 1720 a premium of £100 on every scalp; in 1744, after Massachusetts-Bay had proclaimed a certain tribe as rebels, the following prices: for a male scalp of 12 years and upwards £100 (new currency), for a male prisoner £105, for women and children prisoners £50, for scalps of women and children £50. Some decades later, the colonial system took its revenge on the descendants of the pious Pilgrim Fathers, who had grown seditious in the meantime. At English instigation and for English pay they were tomahawked by redskins. The British Parliament proclaimed bloodhounds and scalping as "means that God and Nature had given into its hand."

The colonial system ripened, like a hothouse, trade and navigation. The "societies Monopolia" of Luther were powerful levers for concentration of capital. The colonies secured a market for the budding manufactures and, through the monopoly of the market, an increased accumulation. The treasures captured outside Europe by undisguised looting, enslavement, and murder floated back to the mother country and were there turned into capital. Holland, which first fully developed the colonial system, in 1648 stood already in the acme of its commercial greatness. It was "in almost exclusive possession of the East Indian trade and the commerce between the southeast and northwest of Europe. Its fisheries, marine, manufactures, surpassed those of any other country. The total capital of the Republic was probably more important than that of all the rest of Europe put together." Gülich forgets to add that by 1648 the people of Holland were more overworked, poorer, and more brutally oppressed than those of all the rest of Europe put together.

Today industrial supremacy implies commercial supremacy. In the period of manufacture properly so-called, it is, on the other hand, the commercial supremacy that gives industrial predominance. Hence the preponderant role that the colonial system plays at that time. It was "the strange God" who perched himself on the altar cheek by jowl with the old Gods of Europe, and one fine day with a shove and a kick chucked them all of a heap. It proclaimed surplus-value-making as the sole end and aim of humanity.

The system of public credit, i.e., of national debts, whose origin we discover in Genoa and Venice as early as the Middle Ages, took possession of Europe generally during the manufacturing period. The colonial system with its maritime trade and commercial wars served as a forcing house for it. Thus it first took root in Holland. National debts, i.e., the alienation of the state—whether despotic, constitutional, or republican—marked with its stamp the capitalistic era. The only part of the so-called national wealth that actually enters into the collective possessions of modern peoples is—their national debt. Hence, as a necessary consequence, the modern doctrine that a nation becomes the richer the more deeply it is in debt. Public credit becomes the credo of capital. And with the rise of national debt-making, want of faith in the national debt takes the place of the blasphemy against the Holy Ghost, which may not be forgiven.

The public debt becomes one of the most powerful levers of primitive accumulation. As with the stroke of an enchanter's wand it endows barren money with the power of breeding and thus turns it into capital, without the necessity of its exposing itself to the troubles and risks inseparable from its employment in industry or even in usury. The state creditors actually give nothing away, for the sum lent is transformed into public bonds, easily negotiable, which go on functioning in their hands just as so much hard cash would. But further, apart from the class of lazy annuitants thus created, and from the improvised wealth of the financiers, middlemen between the government and the nation—as also apart from the tax farmers, merchants, private manufacturers, to whom a good part of every national loan renders the service of a capital fallen from heaven—the national debt has given rise to joint-stock companies, to dealings in negotiable effects of all kinds, and to agiotage, in a word to stock-exchange gambling and the modern bankocracy.

At their birth the great banks, decorated with national titles, were only associations of private speculators, who placed themselves by the side of governments and, thanks to the privileges they received, were in a position to advance money to the state. Hence the accumulation of the national debt has no more infallible measure than the successive rise in the stock of these banks, whose full development dates from the founding of the Bank of England in 1694. The Bank of England began with lending its money to the Government at 8 per cent.; at the same time it was empowered by Parliament to coin money out of the same capital, by lending it again to the public in the form of bank notes. It was allowed to use these notes for discounting bills, making advances on commodities, and for buying the precious metals. It was not long ere this credit money, made by the bank itself, became the coin in which the Bank of England made its loans to the state and paid, on account of the state, the interest on the public debt. It was not enough that the bank gave with one hand and took back more with the other; it remained, even whilst receiving, the eternal creditor of the nation down to the last shilling advanced. Gradually it became inevitably the receptacle of the metallic hoard of the country and the centre of gravity of all commercial credit. What effect was produced on their contemporaries by the sudden uprising of this brood of bankocrats, financiers, rentiers, brokers, stockjobbers, etc., is proved by the writings of that time, e.g., by Bolingbroke's.

With the national debt arose an international credit system, which often conceals one of the sources of primitive accumulation in this or that people. Thus the villainies of the Venetian thieving system formed one of the secret bases of the capital wealth of Holland to whom Venice in her decadence lent large sums of money. So also was it with Holland and England. By the beginning of the 18th century the Dutch manufactures were far outstripped. Holland had ceased to be the nation preponderant in commerce and industry. One of its main lines of business, therefore, from 1701 to 1776 is the lending out of enormous amounts of capital, especially to its great rival England. The same thing is going on today between England and the United States. A great deal of capital, which appears today in the United States without any certificate of birth, was yesterday, in England, the capitalized blood of children.

As the national debt finds its support in the public revenue, which must cover the yearly payments for interest, etc., the modern system of taxation was the necessary complement of the system of national loans.

The loans enable the government to meet extraordinary expenses, without the taxpayers feeling it immediately, but they necessitate, as a consequence, increased taxes. On the other hand, the raising of taxation caused by the accumulation of debts contracted one after another compels the government always to have recourse to new loans for new extraordinary expenses. Modern fiscality, whose pivot is formed by taxes on the most necessary means of subsistence (thereby increasing their price) thus contains within itself the germ of automatic progression. Overtaxation is not an incident, but rather a principle. In Holland, therefore, where this system was first inaugurated, the great patriot, De Witt, has in his *Maxims* extolled it as the best system for making the wage labourer submissive, frugal, industrious, and overburdened with labour. The destructive influence that it exercises on the condition of the wage labourer concerns us less, however, here than the forcible expropriation, resulting from it, of peasants, artisans, and, in a word, all elements of the lower middle class. On this there are not two opinions, even among the bourgeois economists. Its expropriating efficacy is still further heightened by the system of protection, which forms one of its integral parts.

The great part that the public debt, and the fiscal system corresponding with it, has played in the capitalisation of wealth and the expropriation of the masses, has led many writers, like Cobbett, Doubleday, and others, to seek in this, incorrectly, the fundamental cause of the misery of the modern peoples.

The system of protection was an artificial means of manufacturing manufacturers, of expropriating independent labourers, of capitalising the national means of production and subsistence, of forcibly abbreviating the transition from the mediæval to the modern mode of production. The European states tore one another to pieces about the patent of this invention, and, once entered into the service of the surplus-value makers, did not merely lay under contribution in the pursuit of this purpose their own people, indirectly through protective duties, directly through export premiums. They also forcibly rooted out, in their dependent countries, all industry, as, e.g., England did with the Irish woollen manufacture. On the continent of Europe, after Colbert's example, the process was much simplified. The primitive industrial capital, here, came in part directly out of the state treasury. "Why," cries Mirabeau, "why go so far to seek the cause of the manufacturing glory of Saxony before the war? 180,000,000 of debts contracted by the sovereigns!"

Colonial system, public debts, heavy taxes, protection, commercial wars, etc., these children of the true manufacturing period, increase gigantically during the infancy of Modern Industry. The birth of the latter is heralded by a great slaughter of the innocents. Like the royal navy, the factories were recruited by means of the press gang. Blasé as Sir F. M.

Eden is as to the horrors of the expropriation of the agricultural population from the soil, from the last third of the 15th century to his own time; with all the self-satisfaction with which he rejoices in this process, "essential" for establishing capitalistic agriculture and "the due proportion between arable and pasture land"—he does not show, however, the same economic insight in respect to the necessity of child-stealing and child-slavery for the transformation of manufacturing exploitation into factory exploitation, and the establishment of the "true relation" between capital and labour-power. He says: "It may, perhaps, be worthy the attention of the public to consider, whether any manufacture, which, in order to be carried on successfully, requires that cottages and workhouses should be ransacked for poor children; that they should be employed by turns during the greater part of the night and robbed of that rest which, though indispensable to all, is most required by the young; and that numbers of both sexes, of different ages and dispositions, should be collected together in such a manner that the contagion of example cannot but lead to profligacy and debauchery; will add to the sum of individual or national felicity."

"In the counties of Derbyshire, Nottinghamshire, and more particularly in Lancashire," says [John] Fielden, "the newly invented machinery was used in large factories built on the sides of streams capable of turning the water wheel. Thousands of hands were suddenly required in these places, remote from towns; and Lancashire, in particular, being, till then, comparatively thinly populated and barren, a population was all that she now wanted. The small and nimble fingers of little children being by very far the most in request, the custom instantly sprang up of procuring *apprentices* from the different parish workhouses of London, Birmingham, and elsewhere. Many, many thousands of these little, hapless creatures were sent down into the north, being from the age of 7 to the age of 13 or 14 years old. The custom was for the master to clothe his apprentices and to feed and lodge them in an 'apprentice house' near the factory; overseers were appointed to see to the works, whose interest it was to work the children to the utmost, because their pay was in proportion to the quantity of work that they could exact. Cruelty was, of course, the consequence. . . . In many of the manufacturing districts, but particularly, I am afraid, in the guilty county to which I belong [Lancashire], cruelties the most heartrending were practised upon the unoffending and friendless creatures who were thus consigned to the charge of master manufacturers; they were harassed to the brink of death by excess of labour . . . were flogged, fettered and tortured in the most exquisite refinement of cruelty; . . . they were in many cases starved to the bone while flogged to their work and . . . even in some instances . . . were driven to commit suicide. . . . The beautiful and romantic valleys of Derbyshire, Nottinghamshire and Lancashire, secluded from the public eye, became the dismal solitudes of torture, and of many a murder. The profits of manufactures were enormous; but this only whetted the appetite that it should have satisfied, and therefore the manufacturers had recourse to an expedient that seemed to secure to them those profits without any possibility of limit; they began the practice of what is termed 'night-working,' that is, having tired one set of hands, by working them throughout the day, they had another set ready to go on working throughout the night; the day-set getting into the beds that the night-set had just quitted, and in their turn again, the night-set getting into the beds that the day-set quitted in the morning. It is a common tradition in Lancashire, that the beds *never get cold.*"

With the development of capitalist production during the manufacturing period, the public opinion of Europe had lost the last remnant of shame and conscience. The nations bragged cynically of every infamy that served them as a means to capitalistic accumulation. Read, e.g., the naïve *Annals of Commerce* of the worthy A. Anderson. Here it is trumpeted forth as a triumph of English statecraft that at the Peace of Utrecht England extorted from the Spaniards by the Asiento Treaty the privilege of being allowed to ply the Negro trade, until then only carried on between Africa and the English West Indies, between Africa and Spanish America as well. England thereby acquired the right of supplying Spanish America until 1743 with 4800 Negroes yearly. This threw, at the same time, an official cloak over British smuggling. Liverpool waxed fat on the slave trade. This was its method of primitive accumulation. And, even to the present day, Liverpool "respectability" is the Pindar of the slave trade which "has coincided with that spirit of bold adventure which has characterised the trade of Liverpool and rapidly carried it to its present state of prosperity; has occasioned vast employment for shipping and sailors, and greatly augmented the demand for the manufactures of the country." Liverpool employed in the slave trade, in 1730, 15 ships; in 1751, 53; in 1760, 74; in 1770, 96; and in 1792, 132.

Whilst the cotton industry introduced child slavery in England, it gave in the United States a stimulus to the transformation of the earlier, more or less patriarchal slavery, into a system of commercial exploitation. In fact, the veiled slavery of the wage earners in Europe needed, for its pedestal, slavery pure and simple in the New World.

Tantæ molis erat, to establish the "eternal laws of Nature" of the capitalist mode of production, to complete the process of separation between labourers and conditions of labour, to transform, at one pole, the social means of production and subsistence into capital, at the opposite pole, the mass of the population into wage labourers, into "free labouring poor," that artificial product of modern society. If money, according to Augier, "comes into the world with a congenital blood-stain on one cheek," capital comes dripping from head to foot, from every pore, with blood and dirt.

XXV. HISTORICAL TENDENCY OF CAPITALIST ACCUMULATION

What does the primitive accumulation of capital, i.e., its historical genesis, resolve itself into? In so far as it is not immediate transformation of slaves and serfs into wage labourers, and therefore a mere change of form, it only means the expropriation of the immediate producers, i.e., the dissolution of private property based on the labour of its owner. Private property, as the antithesis to social, collective property, exists only where the means of labour and the external conditions of labour belong to private individuals. But according as these private individuals are labourers or not labourers, private property has a different character. The numberless shades, that it at first sight presents, correspond to the intermediate stages lying between these two extremes. The private property of the labourer in his means of production is the foundation of petty industry, whether agricultural, manufacturing, or both; petty industry, again, is an essential condition for the development of social production and of the free individuality of the labourer himself. Of course this petty mode of production exists also under slavery, serfdom, and other states of dependence. But it flourishes, it lets loose its whole energy, it attains its adequate classical form, only where the labourer is the private owner of his own means of labour set in action by himself: the peasant of the land which he cultivates, the artisan of the tool which he handles as a virtuoso. This mode of production presupposes parcelling of the soil and scattering of the other means of production. As it excludes the concentration of these means of production, so also it excludes co-operation, division of labour within each separate process of production, the control over and the productive application of the forces of Nature by society, and the free development of the social productive powers. It is compatible only with a system of production and a society moving within narrow and more or less primitive bounds. To perpetuate it would be, as Pecqueur rightly says, "to decree universal mediocrity." At a certain stage of development it brings forth the material agencies for its own dissolution. From that moment new forces and new passions spring up in the bosom of society; but the old social organization fetters them and keeps them down. It must be annihilated; it is annihilated. Its annihilation, the transformation of the individualised and scattered means of production into socially concentrated ones, of the pigmy property of the many into the huge property of the few, the expropriation of the great mass of the people from the soil, from the means of subsistence, and from the means of labour, this fearful and painful expropriation of the mass of the people forms the prelude to the history of capital. It comprises a series of forcible methods, of which we have passed in review only those that have been epoch-making as methods of the primitive accumulation of capital. The expropriation of the immediate producers was accomplished with merciless Vandalism, and under the stimulus of passions the most infamous, the most sordid, the pettiest, the most meanly odious. Self-earned private property, that is based, so to say, on the fusing together of the isolated, independent labouring individual with the conditions of his labour, is supplanted by capitalistic private property, which rests on exploitation of the nominally free labour of others, ie., on wages labour.

As soon as this process of transformation has sufficiently decomposed the old society from top to bottom, as soon as the labourers are turned into proletarians, their means of labour into capital, as soon as the capitalist mode of production stands on its own feet, then the further socialisation of labour and further transformation of the land and other means of production into socially exploited and, therefore, common means of production, as well as the further expropriation of private proprietors, takes a new form. That which is now to be expropriated is no longer the labourer working for himself, but the capitalist exploiting many labourers. This expropriation is accomplished by the action of the immanent laws of capitalistic production itself, by the centralisation of capital. One capitalist always kills many. Hand in hand with this centralisation, or this expropriation of many capitalists by few, develop, on an ever extending scale, the co-operative form of the labour process, the conscious technical application of science, the methodical cultivation of the soil, the transformation of the instruments of labour into instruments of labour only usable in common, the economising of all means of production by their use as the means of production of combined, socialised labour, the entanglement of all peoples in the net of the world market, and this, the international character of the capitalistic régime. Along with the constantly diminishing number of the magnates of capital, who usurp and monopolise all advantages of this process of transformation, grows the mass of misery, oppression, slavery, degradation, exploitation; but with this too grows the revolt of the working class, a class always increasing in numbers, and disciplined, united, organised by the very mechanism of the process of capitalist production itself. The monopoly of capital becomes a fetter upon the mode of production, which has sprung up and flourished along with, and under it. Centralisation of the means of production and socialisation of labour at last reach a point where they become incompatible with their capitalist integument. This integument is burst asunder. The knell of capitalist private property sounds. The expropriators are expropriated.

The capitalist mode of appropriation, the result of the capitalist mode of production, produces capitalist private property. This is the first negation of individual private property, as founded on the labour of the proprietor. But capitalist production begets, with the inexorability of a law of Nature, its own negation. It is the negation of negation. This does not re-establish private property for the producer, but gives him individual property based on the acquisitions of the capitalist era: i.e., on co-operation and the possession in common of the land and of the means of production.

The transformation of scattered private property, arising from individual labour, into capitalist private property is, naturally, a process, incomparably more protracted, violent, and difficult, than the transformation of capitalistic private property, already practically resting on socialised production, into socialised property. In the former case, we had the expropriation of the mass of the people by a few usurpers; in the latter, we have the expropriation of a few usurpers by the mass of the people.

PROGRESS AND POVERTY

by

HENRY GEORGE

CONTENTS

Progress and Poverty

HENRY GEORGE

1839–1897

HENRY GEORGE, advocate of the single tax and founder of the single-tax movement, was born in Philadelphia in 1839. He was the second child in a family that included ten children. Both his father and mother were strongly religious, and his father at one time published and sold religious books.

As a boy Henry George haunted the Philadelphia water front. His ambition was to go to sea, and his opportunity came when he was sixteen years old. His first voyage was to Australia and India. Two years later he sailed through the Strait of Magellan to San Francisco. It was the period of the "gold rush," and Henry George was caught in the stampede. He went to the Fraser River in British Columbia and worked for a while in a miners' supply store in Victoria, but he was not successful in his quest for gold.

The adventurous side of Henry George's character was balanced by his mental interests. In Philadelphia he had learned typesetting, and in San Francisco he started to work as a compositor. When he married Annie Fox in 1861 he was a poor man, sometimes without work and sometimes in debt. His status improved when he joined the staff of the San Francisco *Times* and rose to the position of managing editor.

In California land speculation was rife, and some men were making fortunes while others starved. The vivid contrasts of wealth and indigence were constantly thrust before the eyes of Henry George. Here was progress and here was poverty. Why were the two, he kept asking himself, so closely intertwined? It was during this period that in conversation with a teamster in Oakland he experienced a sudden mental illumination. "I saw," he says, "that with the growth of population land grows in value, and the men who work it must pay more for the privilege." In 1871 he elaborated this idea in a pamphlet entitled *Our Land and Land Policy.*

Henry George had seen a copy of Adam Smith's *Wealth of Nations* in a men's temperance hotel in San Francisco, but he had been so absorbed in trying to earn a living that he had never had time to study political economy. He now turned to Smith, Malthus, Ricardo, John Stuart Mill, and other leading economists, and began writing a book on the social problem. The result of his efforts was *Progress and Poverty,* published in 1879. This book was at first ignored and disparaged, but later led to world-wide discussion. In its pages Henry George emerges as a great literary stylist as well as a sincere thinker. No other economic work has had such a wide circulation. In faraway Russia Count Leo Tolstoy, who knew and admired it, declared: "People don't argue with George's teaching, they simply don't know it." John Dewey has gone so far as to say: "It would require less than the fingers of the two hands to enumerate those who, from Plato down, rank with Henry George among the world's social philosophers."

Progress and Poverty starts with an attack on the so-called wages-fund doctrine, advanced by the classical economists. According to this doctrine, wages depend on the ratio existing between the number of laborers in society at any given time and the amount of capital devoted to the employment of labor. George points out that labor precedes capital, and he tries to show that, despite appearances to the contrary, labor employs capital. He goes on to expose what he calls the fallacy of the Malthusian theory that population tends to outstrip the means of subsistence. He calls this theory "utterly inconsistent with all the facts." Then he says: "The reason why, in spite of the increase of productive power, wages constantly tend to a minimum which will give but a bare living, is that, with increase in productive power, rent tends to even greater increase, thus producing a constant tendency to the forcing down of wages." Apart from the economic phase of the argument, Henry George asserts that the Creator intended land to be used by all, and that private ownership of land is immoral. He proposes to make land common property by imposing a single tax on land values.

The single-tax doctrine was not original with Henry George. An *impôt unique* had been advocated by Quesnay and the French physiocrats, and at least four British writers

—Spence, Ogilvie, Paine, and Dove—had made similar proposals. But no predecessor had ever exerted the energy that George used in pushing the single tax.

Following the publication of *Progress and Poverty,* Henry George moved to New York and started his crusade. This crusade took the forms of organization, education, and agitation, and bore fruit in laws tending to increase taxes on land and to reduce taxes on everything else. Henry George thought nothing of crossing the ocean to preach his gospel, and he lectured not only in England and Scotland but even in Australia and New Zealand. At one time he courted arrest in Ireland by taking an active part in agitation directed against absentee and resident landlordism.

On two occasions Henry George entered the political arena. The first of these was in 1887, when he was nominated for mayor of New York by a United Labor party and polled more votes, in a three-cornered contest, than Theodore Roosevelt, the Republican candidate. Ten years later he was again nominated for mayor of New York, but died in the midst of the campaign.

Free trade was in Henry George's mind a corollary of the single tax, and he published in 1886 a book entitled *Protection or Free Trade* defending the free-trade doctrine. Some of his other books are: *The Irish Land Question* (1881), *Social Problems* (1883), and *The Science of Political Economy* (1897).

PROGRESS AND POVERTY

Introductory

THE PROBLEM

THE PRESENT CENTURY has been marked by a prodigious increase in wealth-producing power. The utilization of steam and electricity, the introduction of improved processes and labor-saving machinery, the greater subdivision and grander scale of production, the wonderful facilitation of exchanges, have multiplied enormously the effectiveness of labor.

At the beginning of this marvelous era it was natural to expect, and it was expected, that labor-saving inventions would lighten the toil and improve the condition of the laborer; that the enormous increase in the power of producing wealth would make real poverty a thing of the past. Could a man of the last century—a Franklin or a Priestley—have seen, in a vision of the future, the steamship taking the place of the sailing vessel, the railroad train of the wagon, the reaping machine of the scythe, the threshing machine of the flail; could he have heard the throb of the engines that in obedience to human will, and for the satisfaction of human desire, exert a power greater than that of all the men and all the beasts of burden of the earth combined; could he have seen the forest tree transformed into finished lumber—into doors, sashes, blinds, boxes, or barrels, with hardly the touch of a human hand; the great workshops where boots and shoes are turned out by the case with less labor than the old-fashioned cobbler could have put on a sole; the factories where, under the eye of a girl, cotton becomes cloth faster than hundreds of stalwart weavers could have turned it out with their hand-looms; could he have seen steam hammers shaping mammoth shafts and mighty anchors, and delicate machinery making tiny watches; the diamond drill cutting through the heart of the rocks, and coal oil sparing the whale; could he have realized the enormous saving of labor resulting from improved facilities of exchange and communication—sheep killed in Australia eaten fresh in England, and the order given by the London banker in the afternoon executed in San Francisco in the morning of the same day; could he have conceived of the hundred thousand improvements which these only suggest, what would he have inferred as to the social condition of mankind?

It would not have seemed like an inference; further than the vision went it would have seemed as though he saw; and his heart would have leaped and his nerves would have thrilled, as one who from a height beholds just ahead of the thirst-stricken caravan the living gleam of rustling woods and the glint of laughing waters. Plainly, in the sight of the imagination, he would have beheld these new forces elevating society from its very foundations, lifting the very poorest above the possibility of want, exempting the very lowest from anxiety for the material needs of life; he would have seen these slaves of the lamp of knowledge taking on themselves the traditional curse, these muscles of iron and sinews of steel making the poorest laborer's life a holiday, in which every high quality and noble impulse could have scope to grow.

And out of these bounteous material conditions he would have seen arising, as necessary sequences, moral conditions realizing the golden age of which mankind have always dreamed. Youth no longer stunted and starved; age no longer harried by avarice; the child at play with the tiger; the man with the muckrake drinking in the glory of the stars. Foul things fled, fierce things tame; discord turned to harmony! For how could there be greed where all had enough? How could the vice, the crime, the ignorance, the brutality, that spring from poverty and the fear of poverty, exist where poverty had vanished? Who should crouch where all were freemen; who oppress where all were peers?

More or less vague or clear, these have been the hopes, these the dreams born of the improvements which give this wonderful century its pre-eminence. They have sunk so deeply into the popular mind as radically to change the currents of thought, to recast creeds and displace the most fundamental conceptions. The haunting visions of higher possibilities have not merely gathered splendor and vividness, but their direction has changed—instead of seeing behind the faint tinges of an expiring sunset, all the glory of the daybreak has decked the skies before.

It is true that disappointment has followed disappointment, and that discovery upon discovery, and invention after invention, have neither lessened the toil of those who most need respite, nor brought plenty to the poor. But there have been so many things to which it seemed this failure could be laid, that up to our time the new faith has hardly weakened. We have better appreciated the difficulties to be overcome; but not the less trusted that the tendency of the times was to overcome them.

Now, however, we are coming into collision with facts which there can be no mistaking. From all parts of the civilized world come complaints of industrial depression; of labor condemned to involuntary idleness; of capital massed and wasting; of pecuniary distress among business men;

of want and suffering and anxiety among the working classes. All the dull, deadening pain, all the keen, maddening anguish, that to great masses of men are involved in the words "hard times," afflict the world today. This state of things, common to communities differing so widely in situation, in political institutions, in fiscal and financial systems, in density of population and in social organization, can hardly be accounted for by local causes. There is distress where large standing armies are maintained, but there is also distress where the standing armies are nominal; there is distress where protective tariffs stupidly and wastefully hamper trade, but there is also distress where trade is nearly free; there is distress where autocratic government yet prevails, but there is also distress where political power is wholly in the hands of the people; in countries where paper is money, and in countries where gold and silver are the only currency. Evidently, beneath all such things as these, we must infer a common cause.

That there is a common cause, and that it is either what we call material progress or something closely connected with material progress, becomes more than an inference when it is noted that the phenomena we class together and speak of as industrial depression are but intensifications of phenomena which always accompany material progress, and which show themselves more clearly and strongly as material progress goes on. Where the conditions to which material progress everywhere tends are most fully realized—that is to say, where population is densest, wealth greatest, and the machinery of production and exchange most highly developed —we find the deepest poverty, the sharpest struggle for existence, and the most of enforced idleness.

It is to the newer countries—that is, to the countries where material progress is yet in its earlier stages—that laborers emigrate in search of higher wages, and capital flows in search of higher interest. It is in the older countries—that is to say, the countries where material progress has reached later stages—that widespread destitution is found in the midst of the greatest abundance. Go into one of the new communities where Anglo-Saxon vigor is just beginning the race of progress; where the machinery of production and exchange is yet rude and inefficient; where the increment of wealth is not yet great enough to enable any class to live in ease and luxury; where the best house is but a cabin of logs or a cloth and paper shanty, and the richest man is forced to daily work—and though you will find an absence of wealth and all its concomitants, you will find no beggars. There is no luxury, but there is no destitution. No one makes an easy living, nor a very good living; but every one *can* make a living, and no one able and willing to work is oppressed by the fear of want.

But just as such a community realizes the conditions which all civilized communities are striving for, and advances in the scale of material progress—just as closer settlement and a more intimate connection with the rest of the world, and greater utilization of labor-saving machinery, make possible greater economies in production and exchange, and wealth in consequence increases, not merely in the aggregate, but in proportion to population—so does poverty take a darker aspect. Some get an infinitely better and easier living, but others find it hard to get a living at all. The "tramp" comes with the locomotive, and almshouses and prisons are as surely the marks of "material progress" as are costly dwellings, rich warehouses, and magnificent churches. Upon streets lighted with gas and patrolled by uniformed policemen, beggars wait for the passer-by, and in the shadow of college, and library, and museum, are gathering the more hideous Huns and fiercer Vandals of whom Macaulay prophesied.

This fact—the great fact that poverty and all its concomitants show themselves in communities just as they develop into the conditions toward which material progress tends—proves that the social difficulties existing wherever a certain stage of progress has been reached, do not arise from local circumstances, but are, in some way or another, engendered by progress itself.

And, unpleasant as it may be to admit it, it is at last becoming evident that the enormous increase in productive power which has marked the present century and is still going on with accelerating ratio, has no tendency to extirpate poverty or to lighten the burdens of those compelled to toil. It simply widens the gulf between Dives and Lazarus, and makes the struggle for existence more intense. The march of invention has clothed mankind with powers of which a century ago the boldest imagination could not have dreamed. But in factories where labor-saving machinery has reached its most wonderful development, little children are at work; wherever the new forces are anything like fully utilized, large classes are maintained by charity or live on the verge of recourse to it; amid the greatest accumulations of wealth, men die of starvation, and puny infants suckle dry breasts; while everywhere the greed of gain, the worship of wealth, shows the force of the fear of want. The promised land flies before us like the mirage. The fruits of the tree of knowledge turn as we grasp them to apples of Sodom that crumble at the touch.

It is true that wealth has been greatly increased, and that the average of comfort, leisure, and refinement has been raised; but these gains are not general. In them the lowest class do not share. I do not mean that the condition of the lowest class has nowhere nor in anything been improved; but that there is nowhere any improvement which can be credited to increased productive power. I mean that the tendency of what we call material progress is in nowise to improve the condition of the lowest class in the essentials of healthy, happy human life. Nay, more, that it is still further to depress the condition of the lowest class. The new forces, elevating in their nature though they be, do not act upon the social fabric from underneath, as was for a long time hoped and believed, but strike it at a point intermediate between top and bottom. It is as though an immense wedge were being forced, not underneath society, but through society. Those who are above the point of separation are elevated, but those who are below are crushed down.

This depressing effect is not generally realized, for it is not apparent where there has long existed a class just able to live. Where the lowest class barely lives, as has been the case for a long time in many parts of Europe, it is impossible for it to get any lower, for the next lowest step is out of existence, and no tendency to further depression can readily show itself. But in the progress of new settlements to the conditions of older communities it may clearly be seen that material progress does not merely fail to relieve poverty—it actually produces it. In the United States it is clear that squalor and misery, and the vices and crimes that spring from them, everywhere increase as the village grows to the city, and the march of development brings the advantages of the improved methods of production and exchange. It is in the older and richer sections of the Union that pauperism and distress among the working classes are becoming most painfully apparent. If there is less deep poverty in San Francisco than in New York, is it not because San Francisco is yet behind New York in all that both cities are striving for? When San Francisco reaches the point where New York now is, who can doubt that there will also be ragged and barefooted children on her streets?

This association of poverty with progress is the great enigma of our times. It is the central fact from which spring industrial, social, and political difficulties that perplex the world, and with which statesmanship and philanthropy and education grapple in vain. From it come the clouds that overhang the future of the most progressive and self-reliant nations. It is the riddle which the Sphinx of Fate puts to our civilization, and which not to answer is to be destroyed. So long as all the increased wealth which modern progress brings goes but to build up great fortunes, to increase luxury and make sharper the contrast between the House of Have and the House of Want, progress is not real and cannot be permanent. The reaction must come. The tower leans from its foundations, and every new story but hastens the final catastrophe. To educate men who must be condemned to poverty, is but to make them restive; to base on a state of most glaring social inequality political institutions under which men are theoretically equal, is to stand a pyramid on its apex.

All-important as this question is, pressing itself from every quarter painfully upon attention, it has not yet received a solution which accounts for all the facts and points to any clear and simple remedy. This is shown by the widely varying attempts to account for the prevailing depression. They exhibit not merely a divergence between vulgar notions and scientific theories, but also show that the concurrence which should exist between those who avow the same general theories breaks up upon practical questions into an anarchy of opinion. Upon high economic authority we have been told that the prevailing depression is due to overconsumption; upon equally high authority, that it is due to overproduction; while the wastes of war, the extension of railroads, the attempts of workmen to keep up wages, the demonetization of silver, the issues of paper money, the increase of labor-saving machinery, the opening of shorter avenues to trade, etc., are separately pointed out as the cause, by writers of reputation.

And while professors thus disagree, the ideas that there is a necessary conflict between capital and labor, that machinery is an evil, that competition must be restrained and interest abolished, that wealth may be created by the issue of money, that it is the duty of government to furnish capital or to furnish work, are rapidly making way among the great body of the people, who keenly feel a hurt and are sharply conscious of a wrong. Such ideas, which bring great masses of men, the repositories of ultimate political power, under the leadership of charlatans and demagogues, are fraught with danger; but they cannot be successfully combated until political economy shall give some answer to the great question which shall be consistent with all her teachings, and which shall commend itself to the perceptions of the great masses of men.

It must be within the province of political economy to give such an answer. For political economy is not a set of dogmas. It is the explanation of a certain set of facts. It is the science which, in the sequence of certain phenomena, seeks to trace mutual relations and to identify cause and effect, just as the physical sciences seek to do in other sets of phenomena. It lays its foundations upon firm ground. The premises from which it makes its deductions are truths which have the highest sanction; axioms which we all recognize; upon which we safely base the reasoning and actions of everyday life, and which may be reduced to the metaphysical expression of the physical law that motion seeks the line of least resistance—viz., that men seek to gratify their desires with the least exertion. Proceeding from a basis thus assured, its processes, which consist simply in identification and separation, have the same certainty. In this sense it is as exact a science as geometry, which, from similar truths relative to space, obtains its conclusions by similar means, and its conclusions when valid should be as self-apparent. And although in the domain of political economy we cannot test our theories by artificially produced combinations or conditions, as may be done in some of the other sciences, yet we can apply tests no less conclusive, by comparing societies in which different conditions exist, or by, in imagination, separating, combining, adding or eliminating forces or factors of known direction.

I propose in the following pages to attempt to solve by the methods of political economy the great problem I have outlined. I propose to seek the law which associates poverty with progress, and increases want with advancing wealth; and I believe that in the explanation of this paradox we shall find the explanation of those recurring seasons of industrial and commercial paralysis which, viewed independently of their relations to more general phenomena, seem so inexplicable. Properly commenced and carefully pursued, such an investigation must yield a conclusion that will stand every test, and as truth, will correlate with all other truth. For in the sequence of phenomena there is no accident. Every effect has a cause, and every fact implies a preceding fact.

That political economy, as at present taught, does not explain the persistence of poverty amid advancing wealth in a manner which accords with the deep-seated perceptions of men; that the unquestionable truths which it does teach are unrelated and disjointed; that it has failed to make the progress in popular thought that truth, even when unpleasant, must make; that, on the contrary, after a century of cultivation, during which it has engrossed the attention of some of the most subtle and powerful intellects, it should be spurned by the statesman, scouted by the masses, and relegated in the opinion of many educated and thinking men to the rank of a pseudo-science in which nothing is fixed or can be fixed—must, it seems to me, be due not to any inability of the science when properly pursued, but to some false step in its premises, or overlooked factor in its estimates. And as such mistakes are generally concealed by the respect paid to authority, I propose in this inquiry to take nothing for granted, but to bring even accepted theories to the test of first principles, and should they not stand the test, freshly to interrogate facts in the endeavor to discover their law.

I propose to beg no question, to shrink from no conclusion, but to follow truth wherever it may lead. Upon us is the responsibility of seeking the law, for in the very heart of our civilization today women faint and little children moan. But what that law may prove to be is not our affair. If the conclusions that we reach run counter to our prejudices, let us not flinch; if they challenge institutions that have long been deemed wise and natural, let us not turn back.

PART ONE

I. THE CURRENT DOCTRINE OF WAGES—ITS INSUFFICIENCY

Reducing to its most compact form the problem we have set out to investigate, let us examine, step by step, the explanation which political economy, as now accepted by the best authority, gives of it.

The cause which produces poverty in the midst of advancing wealth is evidently the cause which exhibits itself in the tendency, everywhere recognized, of wages to a minimum. Let us, therefore, put our inquiry into this compact form:

Why, in spite of increase in productive power, do wages tend to a minimum which will give but a bare living?

The answer of the current political economy is, that wages are fixed by the ratio between the number of laborers and the amount of capital devoted to the employment of labor, and constantly tend to the lowest amount on which laborers will consent to live and reproduce, because the increase in the number of laborers tends naturally to follow and overtake any increase in capital. The increase of the divisor being thus held in check only by the possibilities of the quotient, the dividend may be increased to infinity without greater result.

In current thought this doctrine holds all but undisputed sway. It bears the indorsement of the very highest names among the cultivators of political economy, and though there have been attacks upon it, they are generally more formal than real. It is assumed by Buckle as the basis of his generalizations of universal history. It is taught in all, or nearly all, the great English and American universities, and is laid down in textbooks which aim at leading the masses to reason correctly upon practical affairs, while it seems to harmonize with the new philosophy, which, having in a few years all but conquered the scientific world, is now rapidly permeating the general mind.

Thus entrenched in the upper regions of thought, it is in cruder form even more firmly rooted in what may be styled the lower. What gives to the fallacies of protection such a tenacious hold, in spite of their evident inconsistencies and absurdities, is the idea that the sum to be distributed in wages is in each community a fixed one, which the competition of "foreign labor" must still further subdivide. The same idea underlies most of the theories which aim at the abolition of interest and the restriction of competition, as the means whereby the share of the laborer in the general wealth can be increased; and it crops out in every direction among those who are not thoughtful enough to have any theories, as may be seen in the columns of newspapers and the debates of legislative bodies.

And yet, widely accepted and deeply rooted as it is, it seems to me that this theory does not tally with obvious facts. For, if wages depend upon the ratio between the amount of labor seeking employment and the amount of capital devoted to its employment, the relative scarcity or abundance of one factor must mean the relative abundance or scarcity of the other. Thus, capital must be relatively abundant where wages are high, and relatively scarce where wages are low. Now, as the capital used in paying wages must largely consist of the capital constantly seeking investment, the current rate of interest must be the measure of its relative abundance or scarcity. So, if it be true that wages depend upon the ratio between the amount of labor seeking employment and the capital devoted to its employment, then high wages, the mark of the relative scarcity of labor, must be accompanied by low interest, the mark of the relative abundance of capital, and reversely, low wages must be accompanied by high interest.

This is not the fact, but the contrary. Eliminating from interest the element of insurance, and regarding only interest proper, or the return for the use of capital, is it not a general truth that interest is high where and when wages are high, and low where and when wages are low? Both wages and interest have been higher in the United States than in England, in the Pacific than in the Atlantic States. Is it not a notorious fact that where labor flows for higher wages, capital also flows for higher interest? Is it not true that wherever there has been a general rise or fall in wages, there has been at the same time a similar rise or fall in interest? In California, for instance, when wages were higher than anywhere else in the world, so also was interest higher. Wages and interest have in California gone down together. When common wages were $5 a day, the ordinary bank rate of interest was twenty-four per cent. per annum. Now that common wages are $2 or $2.50 a day, the ordinary bank rate is from ten to twelve per cent.

Now, this broad, general fact, that wages are higher in new countries, where capital is relatively scarce, than in old countries, where capital is relatively abundant, is too glaring to be ignored. And although very lightly touched upon, it is noticed by the expounders of the current political economy. The manner in which it is noticed proves what I say, that it is utterly inconsistent with the accepted theory of wages. For in explaining it such writers as Mill, Fawcett, and Price virtually give up the theory of wages upon which, in the same treatises, they formally insist. Though they declare that wages are fixed by the ratio between capital and laborers, they explain the higher wages and interest of new countries by the greater relative production of wealth. I shall hereafter show that this is not the fact, but that, on the contrary, the production of wealth is relatively larger in old and densely populated countries than in new and sparsely populated countries.

The proposition I shall endeavor to prove, is:

That wages, instead of being drawn from capital, are in reality drawn from the product of the labor for which they are paid.

Now, inasmuch as the current theory that wages are drawn from capital also holds that capital is reimbursed from production, this at first glance may seem a distinction without a difference—a mere change in terminology, to discuss which would be but to add to those unprofitable disputes that render so much that has been written upon politico-economic subjects as barren and worthless as the controversies of the various learned societies about the true reading of the inscription on the stone that Mr. Pickwick found. But that it is much more than a formal distinction will be apparent when it is considered that upon the difference between the two propositions are built up all the current theories as to the relations of capital and labor; that from it are deduced doctrines that, themselves regarded as axiomatic, bound, direct, and govern the ablest minds in the discussion of the most momentous questions. For, upon the assumption that wages are drawn directly from capital, and not from the product of the labor, is based, not only the doctrine that wages depend upon the ratio between capital and labor, but the doctrine that industry is limited by capital—that capital must be accumulated before labor is employed, and labor cannot be employed except as capital is accumulated; the doctrine that every increase of capital gives or is capable of giving additional employment to industry; the doctrine that the conversion of circulating capital into fixed capital lessens the fund applicable to the maintenance of labor; the doctrine that more laborers can be employed at low than at high wages; the doctrine that capital applied to agriculture will maintain more laborers than if applied to manufactures; the doctrine that profits are high or low as wages are low or high, or that they depend upon the cost of the subsistence of laborers; together with such paradoxes as that a demand for commodities is not a demand for labor, or that certain commodities may be increased in cost by a reduction in wages or diminished in cost by an increase in wages.

In short, all the teachings of the current political economy, in the widest and most important part of its domain, are based more or less directly upon the assumption that labor is maintained and paid out of existing capital before the product which constitutes the ultimate object is secured. If it be shown that this is an error, and that on the contrary the maintenance and payment of labor do not even temporarily trench on capital, but are directly drawn from the product of the labor, then all this vast superstructure is left without support and must fall. And so likewise must fall the vulgar theories which also have their base in the belief that the sum to be distributed in wages is a fixed one, the individual shares in which must necessarily be decreased by an increase in the number of laborers.

The difference between the current theory and the one I advance is, in fact, similar to that between the mercantile theory of international exchanges and that with which Adam Smith supplanted it. Between the theory that commerce is the exchange of commodities for money, and the theory that it is the exchange of commodities for commodities, there may seem no real difference when it is remembered that the adherents of the mercantile theory did not assume that money had any other use than as it could be exchanged for commodities. Yet, in the practical application of these two theories, there arises all the difference between rigid governmental protection and free trade.

The fundamental truth, that in all economic reasoning must be firmly grasped, and never let go, is that society in its most highly developed form is but an elaboration of society in its rudest beginnings, and that principles obvious in the simpler relations of men are merely disguised and not abrogated or reversed by the more intricate relations that result from the division of labor and the use of complex tools and methods. The steam grist mill, with its complicated machinery exhibiting every diversity of motion, is simply what the rude stone mortar dug up from an ancient river bed was in its day—an instrument for grinding corn. And every man engaged in it, whether tossing wood into the furnace, running the engine, dressing stones, printing sacks, or keeping books, is really devoting his labor to the same purpose that the prehistoric savage did when he used his mortar—the preparation of grain for human food.

And so, if we reduce to their lowest terms all the complex operations of modern production, we see that each individual who takes part in this infinitely subdivided and intricate network of production and exchange is really doing what the primeval man did when he climbed the trees for fruit or followed the receding tide for shellfish—endeavoring to obtain from nature by the exertion of his powers the satisfaction of his desires. If we keep this firmly in mind, if we look upon production as a whole —as the co-operation of all embraced in any of its great groups to satisfy the various desires of each, we plainly see that the reward each obtains for his exertions comes as truly and as directly from nature as the result of that exertion, as did that of the first man.

II. THE MEANING OF THE TERMS

BEFORE proceeding further in our inquiry, let us make sure of the meaning of our terms, for indistinctness in their use must inevitably produce ambiguity and indeterminateness in reasoning. Not only is it requisite in economic reasoning to give to such words as "wealth," "capital," "rent," "wages," and the like, a much more definite sense than they bear in common discourse, but, unfortunately, even in political economy there is, as to some of these terms, no certain meaning assigned by common consent, different writers giving to the same term different meanings, and the same writers often using a term in different senses. Nothing can add to the force of what has been said by so many eminent authors as to the importance of clear and precise definitions, save the example, not an infrequent one, of the same authors falling into grave errors from the very cause they warned against. And nothing so shows the importance of language in thought as the spectacle of even acute thinkers basing important conclusions upon the use of the same word in varying senses. I shall endeavor to avoid these dangers. It will be my effort throughout, as any term becomes of importance, to state clearly what I mean by it, and to use it in that sense and in no other. Let me ask the reader to note and to bear in mind the definitions thus given, as otherwise I cannot hope to make myself properly understood. I shall not attempt to attach arbitrary meanings to words, or to coin terms, even when it would be convenient to do so, but shall conform to usage as closely as is possible, only endeavoring so to fix the meaning of words that they may clearly express thought.

What we have now on hand is to discover whether, as a matter of fact, wages are drawn from capital. As a preliminary, let us settle what we mean by wages and what we mean by capital. To the former word a sufficiently definite meaning has been given by economic writers, but the ambiguities which have attached to the use of the latter in political economy will require a detailed examination.

As used in common discourse "wages" means a compensation paid to a hired person for his services; and we speak of one man "working for wages," in contradistinction to another who is "working for himself." The use of the term is still further narrowed by the habit of applying it solely to compensation paid for manual labor. We do not speak of the wages of professional men, managers or clerks, but of their fees, commissions, or salaries. Thus the common meaning of the word wages is the compensation paid to a hired person for manual labor. But in political economy the word wages has a much wider meaning, and includes all returns for exertion. For, as political economists explain, the three agents or factors in production are land, labor, and capital, and that part of the produce which goes to the second of these factors is by them styled wages.

Thus the term labor includes all human exertion in the production of wealth, and wages, being that part of the produce which goes to labor, includes all reward for such exertion. There is, therefore, in the politico-economic sense of the term wages no distinction as to the kind of labor, or as to whether its reward is received through an employer or not, but wages means the return received for the exertion of labor, as distinguished from the return received for the use of capital, and the return received by the landholder for the use of land. The man who cultivates the soil for himself receives his wages in its produce, just as, if he uses his own capital and owns his own land, he may also receive interest and rent; the hunter's wages are the game he kills; the fisherman's wages are the fish he takes. The gold washed out by the self-employing gold digger is as much his wages as the money paid to the hired coal miner by the purchaser of his labor, and, as Adam Smith shows, the high profits of retail storekeepers are in large part wages, being the recompense of their labor and not of their capital. In short, whatever is received as the result or reward of exertion is "wages."

This is all it is now necessary to note as to "wages," but it is important to keep this in mind. For in the standard economic works this sense of the term wages is recognized with greater or less clearness only to be subsequently ignored.

But it is more difficult to clear away from the idea of capital the ambiguities that beset it, and to fix the scientific use of the term. In general discourse, all sorts of things that have a value or will yield a return are vaguely spoken of as capital, while economic writers vary so widely that the term can hardly be said to have a fixed meaning. Let us compare with each other the definitions of a few representative writers:

"That part of a man's stock," says Adam Smith, "which he expects to afford him a revenue, is called his capital," and the capital of a country or society, he goes on to say, consists of (1) machines and instruments of trade which facilitate and abridge labor; (2) buildings, not mere dwellings, but which may be considered instruments of trade—such as shops, farmhouses, etc.; (3) improvements of land which better fit it for tillage or culture; (4) the acquired and useful abilities of all the inhabitants; (5) money; (6) provisions in the hands of producers and dealers, from the sale of which they expect to derive a profit; (7) the material of, or partially completed, manufactured articles still in the hands of producers or dealers; (8) completed articles still in the hands of producers or dealers. The first four of these he styles fixed capital, and the last four circulating capital, a distinction of which it is not necessary to our purpose to take any note.

Ricardo's definition is:

> Capital is that part of the wealth of a country which is employed in production, and consists of food, clothing, tools, raw materials, machinery, etc., necessary to give effect to labor.—*Principles of Political Economy, Chapter V.*

This definition, it will be seen, is very different from that of Adam Smith, as it excludes many of the things which he includes—as acquired talents, articles of mere taste or luxury in the possession of producers or dealers; and includes some things he excludes—such as food, clothing, etc., in the possession of the consumer.

McCulloch's definition is:

> The capital of a nation really comprises all those portions of the produce of industry existing in it that *may be* directly employed either to support human existence or to facilitate production.—*Notes on Wealth of Nations, Book II, Chapter I.*

This definition follows the line of Ricardo's, but is wider. While it excludes everything that is not capable of aiding production, it includes everything that is so capable, without reference to actual use or necessity for use—the horse drawing a pleasure carriage being, according to McCulloch's view, as he expressly states, as much capital as the horse drawing a plow, because he may, if need arises, be used to draw a plow.

John Stuart Mill, following the same general line as Ricardo and McCulloch, makes neither the use nor the capability of use, but the determination to use, the test of capital. He says:

> Whatever things are destined to supply productive labor with the shelter, protection, tools and materials which the work requires, and to feed and otherwise maintain the laborer during the process, are capital.—*Principles of Political Economy, Book I, Chapter IV.*

These quotations sufficiently illustrate the divergence of the masters. Among minor authors the variance is still greater, as a few examples will suffice to show.

Professor Wayland, whose *Elements of Political Economy* has long been a favorite textbook in American educational institutions, where there has been any pretense of teaching political economy, gives this lucid definition:

> The word capital is used in two senses. In relation to product it means any substance on which industry is to be exerted. In relation to industry, the material on which industry is about to confer value, that on which it has conferred value; the instruments which are used for the conferring of value, as well as the means of sustenance by which the being is supported while he is engaged in performing the operation.—*Elements of Political Economy, Book I, Chapter I.*

Henry C. Carey, the American apostle of protectionism, defines capital as "the instrument by which man obtains mastery over nature, including in it the physical and mental powers of man himself." Professor Perry, a Massachusetts free trader, very properly objects to this that it hopelessly confuses the boundaries between capital and labor, and then himself hopelessly confuses the boundaries between capital and land by defining capital as "any valuable thing outside of man himself from whose use springs a pecuniary increase or profit." An English economic writer of high standing, Mr. William Thornton, begins an elaborate examination of the relations of labor and capital (*On Labor*) by stating that he will include land with capital, which is very much as if one who proposed to teach algebra should begin with the declaration that he would consider the signs plus and minus as meaning the same thing and having the same value. An American writer, also of high standing, Professor Francis A. Walker, makes the same declaration in his elaborate book on *The Wages Question*. Another English writer, N. A. Nicholson (*The Science of*

Exchanges, London, 1873), seems to cap the climax of absurdity by declaring in one paragraph that "capital must of course be accumulated by saving," and in the very next paragraph stating that "the land which produces a crop, the plow which turns the soil, the labor which secures the produce, and the produce itself, if a material profit is to be derived from its employment, are all alike capital." But how land and labor are to be accumulated by saving them he nowhere condescends to explain. In the same way a standard American writer, Professor Amasa Walker (*Science of Wealth*), first declares that capital arises from the net savings of labor and then immediately afterward declares that land is capital.

I might go on for pages, citing contradictory and self-contradictory definitions. But it would only weary the reader. It is unnecessary to multiply quotations. Those already given are sufficient to show how wide a difference exists as to the comprehension of the term capital.

The difficulties which beset the use of the word capital, as an exact term, and which are even more strikingly exemplified in current political and social discussions than in the definitions of economic writers, arise from two facts—first, that certain classes of things, the possession of which to the individual is precisely equivalent to the possession of capital, are not part of the capital of the community; and, second, that things of the same kind may or may not be capital, according to the purpose to which they are devoted.

With a little care as to these points, there should be no difficulty in obtaining a sufficiently clear and fixed idea of what the term capital as generally used properly includes; such an idea as will enable us to say what things are capital and what are not, and to use the word without ambiguity or slip.

Land, labor, and capital are the three factors of production. If we remember that capital is thus a term used in contradistinction to land and labor, we at once see that nothing properly included under either one of these terms can be properly classed as capital. The term land necessarily includes, not merely the surface of the earth as distinguished from the water and the air, but the whole material universe outside of man himself, for it is only by having access to land, from which his very body is drawn, that man can come in contact with or use nature. The term land embraces, in short, all natural materials, forces, and opportunities, and, therefore, nothing that is freely supplied by nature can be properly classed as capital. A fertile field, a rich vein of ore, a falling stream which supplies power, may give to the possessor advantages equivalent to the possession of capital, but to class such things as capital would be to put an end to the distinction between land and capital, and, so far as they relate to each other, to make the two terms meaningless. The term labor, in like manner, includes all human exertion, and hence human powers whether natural or acquired can never properly be classed as capital. In common parlance we often speak of a man's knowledge, skill, or industry as constituting his capital; but this is evidently a metaphorical use of language that must be eschewed in reasoning that aims at exactness. Superiority in such qualities may augment the income of an individual just as capital would, and an increase in the knowledge, skill, or industry of a community may have the same effect in increasing its production as would an increase of capital; but this effect is due to the increased power of labor and not to capital. Increased velocity may give to the impact of a cannon ball the same effect as increased weight, yet, nevertheless, weight is one thing and velocity another.

Thus we must exclude from the category of capital everything that may be included either as land or labor. Doing so, there remain only things which are neither land nor labor, but which have resulted from the union of these two original factors of production. Nothing can be properly capital that does not consist of these—that is to say, nothing can be capital that is not wealth.

III. WAGES NOT DRAWN FROM CAPITAL, BUT PRODUCED BY THE LABOR

THE IMPORTANCE of this digression will, I think, become more and more apparent as we proceed in our inquiry, but its pertinency to the branch we are now engaged in may at once be seen.

It is at first glance evident that the economic meaning of the term wages is lost sight of, and attention is concentrated upon the common and narrow meaning of the word, when it is affirmed that wages are drawn from capital. For, in all those cases in which the laborer is his own employer and takes directly the produce of his labor as its reward, it is plain enough that wages are not drawn from capital, but result directly as the product of the labor. If, for instance, I devote my labor to gathering birds' eggs or picking wild berries, the eggs or berries I thus get are my wages. Surely no one will contend that in such a case wages are drawn from capital. There is no capital in the case. An absolutely naked man, thrown on an island where no human being has before trod, may gather birds' eggs or pick berries.

Or if I take a piece of leather and work it up into a pair of shoes, the shoes are my wages—the reward of my exertion. Surely they are not drawn from capital—either my capital or any one else's capital—but are brought into existence by the labor of which they become the wages; and in obtaining this pair of shoes as the wages of my labor, capital is not even momentarily lessened one iota. For, if we call in the idea of capital, my capital at the beginning consists of the piece of leather, the thread, etc. As my labor goes on, value is steadily added, until, when my labor results in the finished shoes, I have my capital plus the difference in value between the material and the shoes. In obtaining this additional value—my wages—how is capital at any time drawn upon?

Adam Smith, who gave the direction to economic thought that has resulted in the current elaborate theories of the relation between wages and capital, recognized the fact that in such simple cases as I have instanced, wages are the produce of labor, and thus begins his chapter upon the wages of labor:

> *The produce of labor constitutes the natural recompense or wages of labor.* In that original state of things which precedes both the appropriation of land and the accumulation of stock, the whole produce of labor belongs to the laborer. He has neither landlord nor master to share with him.

Had the great Scotchman taken this as the initial point of his reasoning, and continued to regard the produce of labor as the natural wages of labor, and the landlord and master but as sharers, his conclusions would have been very different, and political economy today would not embrace such a mass of contradictions and absurdities; but instead of following the truth obvious in the simple modes of production as a clew through the perplexities of the more complicated forms, he momentarily recognizes it, only immediately to abandon it, and stating that "in every part of Europe twenty workmen serve under a master for one that is independent," he recommences the inquiry from a point of view in which the master is considered as providing from his capital the wages of his workmen.

It is evident that in thus placing the proportion of self-employing workmen as but one in twenty, Adam Smith had in mind but the mechanic arts, and that, including all laborers, the proportion who take their earnings directly, without the intervention of an employer, must, even in Europe a hundred years ago, have been much greater than this. For, besides the independent laborers who in every community exist in considerable numbers, the agriculture of large districts of Europe has, since the time of the Roman Empire, been carried on by the métayer system, under which the capitalist receives his return from the laborer instead of the laborer from the capitalist. At any rate, in the United States, where any general law of wages must apply as fully as in Europe, and where in spite of the advance of manufactures a very large part of the people are yet self-employing farmers, the proportion of laborers who get their wages through an employer must be comparatively small.

But it is not necessary to discuss the ratio in which self-employing laborers anywhere stand to hired laborers, nor is it necessary to multiply illustrations of the truism that where the laborer takes directly his wages they are the product of his labor, for as soon as it is realized that the term wages includes all the earnings of labor, as well when taken directly by the laborer in the results of his labor as when received from an employer, it is evident that the assumption that wages are drawn from capital, on which as a universal truth such a vast superstructure is in standard politico-economic treatises so unhesitatingly built, is at least in large part untrue, and the utmost that can with any plausibility be affirmed is that some wages (i.e., wages received by the laborer from an employer) are drawn from capital. This restriction of the major premise at once invalidates all the deductions that are made from it; but without resting here, let us see whether even in this restricted sense it accords with the facts. Let us pick up the clew where Adam Smith dropped it, and advancing step by step, see whether the relation of facts which is obvious in the simplest forms of production does not run through the most complex.

Next in simplicity to "that original state of things," of which many examples may yet be found, where the whole produce of labor belongs to the laborer, is the arrangement in which the laborer, though working for another person, or with the capital of another person, receives his wages in kind—that is to say, in the things his labor produces. In this case it is as clear as in the case of the self-employing laborer that the wages are really drawn from the product of the labor, and not at all from capital. If I hire a man to gather eggs, to pick berries, or to make shoes, paying him from the eggs, the berries, or the shoes that his labor secures, there can be no question that the source of the wages is the labour for which they are paid. Of this form of hiring is the saer-and-daer stock tenancy, treated of with such perspicuity by Sir Henry Maine in his *Early History of Institutions,* and which so clearly involved the relation of employer and employed as to render the acceptor of cattle the man or vassal of the capitalist who thus employed him. It was on such terms as these that Jacob worked for Laban, and to this day, even in civilized countries, it is not an infrequent mode of employing labor. The farming of land on shares, which prevails to a considerable extent in the Southern States of the Union and in California, the métayer system of Europe, as well as the many cases in which superintendents, salesmen, etc., are paid by a percentage of profits, what are they but the employment of labor for wages which consist of part of its produce?

The next step in the advance from simplicity to complexity is where the wages, though estimated in kind, are paid in an equivalent of something else. For instance, on American whaling ships the custom is not to pay fixed wages, but a "lay," or proportion of the catch, which varies from a sixteenth to a twelfth to the captain down to a three hundredth to the cabin boy. Thus, when a whaleship comes into New Bedford or San

Francisco after a successful cruise, she carries in her hold the wages of her crew, as well as the profits of her owners, and an equivalent which will reimburse them for all the stores used up during the voyage. Can anything be clearer than that these wages—this oil and bone which the crew of the whaler have taken—have not been drawn from capital, but are really a part of the produce of their labor? Nor is this fact changed or obscured in the slightest degree where, as a matter of convenience, instead of dividing up between the crew their proportion of the oil and bone, the value of each man's share is estimated at the market price, and he is paid for it in money. The money is but the equivalent of the real wages, the oil and bone. In no way is there any advance of capital in this payment. The obligation to pay wages does not accrue until the value from which they are to be paid is brought into port. At the moment when the owner takes from his capital money to pay the crew he adds to his capital oil and bone.

IV. THE MAINTENANCE OF LABORERS NOT DRAWN FROM CAPITAL

But a stumbling block may yet remain, or may recur, in the mind of the reader.

As the plowman cannot eat the furrow, nor a partially completed steam engine aid in any way in producing the clothes the machinist wears, have I not, in the words of John Stuart Mill, "forgotten that the people of a country are maintained and have their wants supplied, not by the produce of present labor, but of past?" Or, to use the language of a popular elementary work—that of Mrs. [Millicent Garrett] Fawcett—have I not "forgotten that many months must elapse between the sowing of the seed and the time when the produce of that seed is converted into a loaf of bread," and that "it is, therefore, evident that laborers cannot live upon that which their labor is assisting to produce, but are maintained by that wealth which their labor, or the labor of others, has previously produced, which wealth is capital?"

The assumption made in these passages—the assumption that it is so self-evident that labor must be subsisted from capital that the proposition has but to be stated to compel recognition—runs through the whole fabric of current political economy. And so confidently is it held that the maintenance of labor is drawn from capital that the proposition that "population regulates itself by the funds which are to employ it, and, therefore, always increases or diminishes with the increase or diminution of capital" [Ricardo], is regarded as equally axiomatic, and in its turn made the basis of important reasoning.

Yet being resolved, these propositions are seen to be, not self-evident, but absurd; for they involve the idea that labor cannot be exerted until the products of labor are saved—thus putting the product before the producer.

And being examined, they will be seen to derive their apparent plausibility from a confusion of thought.

I have already pointed out the fallacy, concealed by an erroneous definition, which underlies the proposition that because food, raiment and shelter are necessary to productive labor, therefore industry is limited by capital. To say that a man must have his breakfast before going to work is not to say that he cannot go to work unless a capitalist furnishes him with a breakfast, for his breakfast may, and in point of fact in any country where there is not actual famine will, come not from wealth set apart for the assistance of production, but from wealth set apart for subsistence. And, as has been previously shown, food, clothing, etc.—in short, all articles of wealth—are only capital so long as they remain in the possession of those who propose, not to consume, but to exchange them for other commodities or for productive services, and cease to be capital when they pass into the possession of those who will consume them; for in that transaction they pass from the stock of wealth held for the purpose of procuring other wealth, and pass into the stock of wealth held for purposes of gratification, irrespective of whether their consumption will aid in the production of wealth or not. Unless this distinction is preserved it is impossible to draw the line between the wealth that is capital and the wealth that is not capital, even by remitting the distinction to the "mind of the possessor," as does John Stuart Mill. For men do not eat or abstain, wear clothes or go naked, as they propose to engage in productive labor or not. They eat because they are hungry, and wear clothes because they would be uncomfortable without them. Take the food on the breakfast table of a laborer who will work or not that day as he gets the opportunity. If the distinction between capital and non-capital be the support of productive labor, is this food capital or not? It is as impossible for the laborer himself as for any philosopher of the Ricardo-Mill school to tell. Nor yet can it be told when it gets into his stomach; nor, supposing that he does not get work at first, but continues the search, can it be told until it has passed into the blood and tissues. Yet the man will eat his breakfast all the same.

The fifty square miles of London undoubtedly contain more wealth than within the same space anywhere else exists. Yet were productive labor in London absolutely to cease, within a few hours people would begin to die like rotten sheep, and within a few weeks, or at most a few months, hardly one would be left alive. For an entire suspension of productive labor would be a disaster more dreadful than ever yet befell a beleaguered city. It would not be a mere external wall of circumvallation, such as Titus drew around Jerusalem, which would prevent the constant incoming of the supplies on which a great city lives, but it would be the drawing of a similar wall around each household. Imagine such a suspension of labor in any community, and you will see how true it is that mankind really live from hand to mouth; that it is the daily labor of the community that supplies the community with its daily bread.

Just as the subsistence of the laborers who built the Pyramids was drawn not from a previously hoarded stock, but from the constantly recurring crops of the Nile Valley; just as a modern government when it undertakes a great work of years does not appropriate to it wealth already produced, but wealth yet to be produced, which is taken from producers in taxes as the work progresses; so it is that the subsistence of the laborers engaged in production which does not directly yield subsistence comes from the production of subsistence in which others are simultaneously engaged.

If we trace the circle of exchange by which work done in the production of a great steam engine secures to the worker bread, meat, clothes, and shelter, we shall find that though between the laborer on the engine and the producers of the bread, meat, etc., there may be a thousand intermediate exchanges, the transaction, when reduced to its lowest terms, really amounts to an exchange of labor between him and them. Now the cause which induces the expenditure of the labor on the engine is evidently that some one who has power to give what is desired by the laborer on the engine wants in exchange an engine—that is to say, there exists a demand for an engine on the part of those producing bread, meat, etc., or on the part of those who are producing what the producers of the bread, meat, etc., desire. It is this demand which directs the labor of the machinist to the production of the engine, and hence, reversely, the demand of the machinist for bread, meat, etc., really directs an equivalent amount of labor to the production of these things, and thus his labor, actually exerted in the production of the engine, virtually produces the things in which he expends his wages.

Or, to formularize this principle:

The demand for consumption determines the direction in which labor will be expended in production.

V. THE REAL FUNCTIONS OF CAPITAL

It may now be asked, If capital is not required for the payment of wages or the support of labor during production, what, then, are its functions?

The previous examination has made the answer clear. Capital, as we have seen, consists of wealth used for the procurement of more wealth, as distinguished from wealth used for the direct satisfaction of desire; or, as I think it may be defined, of wealth in the course of exchange.

Capital, therefore, increases the power of labor to produce wealth: (1) By enabling labor to apply itself in more effective ways, as by digging up clams with a spade instead of the hand, or moving a vessel by shoveling coal into a furnace, instead of tugging at an oar. (2) By enabling labor to avail itself of the reproductive forces of nature, as to obtain corn by sowing it, or animals by breeding them. (3) By permitting the division of labor, and thus, on the one hand, increasing the efficiency of the human factor of wealth, by the utilization of special capabilities, the acquisition of skill, and the reduction of waste; and, on the other, calling in the powers of the natural factor at their highest, by taking advantage of the diversities of soil, climate, and situation, so as to obtain each particular species of wealth where nature is most favorable to its production.

Capital does not supply the materials which labor works up into wealth, as is erroneously taught; the materials of wealth are supplied by nature. But such materials partially worked up and in the course of exchange are capital.

Capital does not supply or advance wages, as is erroneously taught. Wages are that part of the produce of his labor obtained by the laborer.

Capital does not maintain laborers during the progress of their work, as is erroneously taught. Laborers are maintained by their labor, the man who produces, in whole or in part, anything that will exchange for articles of maintenance, virtually producing that maintenance.

Capital, therefore, does not limit industry, as is erroneously taught, the only limit to industry being the access to natural material. But capital may limit the form of industry and the productiveness of industry, by limiting the use of tools and the division of labor.

PART TWO

I. THE MALTHUSIAN THEORY, ITS GENESIS AND SUPPORT

Behind the theory we have been considering lies a theory we have yet to consider. The current doctrine as to the derivation and law of wages finds its strongest support in a doctrine as generally accepted—the doctrine to which Malthus has given his name—that population naturally tends to increase faster than subsistence. These two doctrines, fitting in with each other, frame the answer which the current political economy gives to the great problem we are endeavoring to solve.

In what has preceded, the current doctrine that wages are determined by the ratio between capital and laborers has, I think, been shown to be so utterly baseless as to excite surprise as to how it could so generally and so long obtain. It is not to be wondered at that such a theory should have arisen in a state of society where the great body of laborers seem to depend for employment and wages upon a separate class of capitalists, nor yet that under these conditions it should have maintained itself among the masses of men, who rarely take the trouble to separate the real from the apparent. But it is surprising that a theory which on examination appears to be so groundless could have been successively accepted by so many acute thinkers as have during the present century devoted their powers to the elucidation and development of the science of political economy.

The explanation of this otherwise unaccountable fact is to be found in the general acceptance of the Malthusian theory. The current theory of wages has never been fairly put upon its trial, because, backed by the Malthusian theory, it has seemed in the minds of political economists a self-evident truth. These two theories mutually blend with, strengthen, and defend each other, while they both derive additional support from a principle brought prominently forward in the discussions of the theory of rent—viz., that past a certain point the application of capital and labor to land yields a diminishing return. Together they give such an explanation of the phenomena presented in a highly organized and advancing society as seems to fit all the facts, and which has thus prevented closer investigation.

Which of these two theories is entitled to historical precedence it is hard to say. The theory of population was not formulated in such a way as to give it the standing of a scientific dogma until after that had been done for the theory of wages. But they naturally spring up and grow with each other, and were both held in a form more or less crude long prior to any attempt to construct a system of political economy. It is evident, from several passages, that though he never fully developed it, the Malthusian theory was in rudimentary form present in the mind of Adam Smith, and to this, it seems to me, must be largely due the misdirection which on the subject of wages his speculations took. But, however this may be, so closely are the two theories connected, so completely do they complement each other, that Buckle, reviewing the history of the development of political economy in his *Examination of the Scotch Intellect during the Eighteenth Century,* attributes mainly to Malthus the honor of "decisively proving" the current theory of wages by advancing the current theory of the pressure of population upon subsistence. He says in his *History of Civilization in England:*

Scarcely had the Eighteenth Century passed away when it was decisively proved that the reward of labor depends solely on two things; namely, the magnitude of that national fund out of which all labor is paid, and the number of laborers among whom the fund is to be divided. This vast step in our knowledge is due, mainly, though not entirely, to Malthus, whose work on population, besides marking an epoch in the history of speculative thought, has already produced considerable practical results, and will probably give rise to others more considerable still. It was published in 1798; so that Adam Smith, who died in 1790, missed what to him would have been the intense pleasure of seeing how, in it, his own views were expanded rather than corrected. Indeed, it is certain that without Smith there would have been no Malthus; that is, unless Smith had laid the foundation, Malthus could not have raised the superstructure.

The essence of the Malthusian doctrine is, that population tends to increase faster than the power of providing food, and whether this difference be stated as a geometrical ratio for population and an arithmetical ratio for subsistence, as by Malthus; or as a constant ratio for population and a diminishing ratio for subsistence, as by Mill, is only a matter of statement. The vital point, on which both agree, is, to use the words of Malthus, "that there is a natural tendency and constant effort in population to increase beyond the means of subsistence."

The Malthusian doctrine, as at present held, may be thus stated in its strongest and least objectionable form:

That population, constantly tending to increase, must, when unrestrained, ultimately press against the limits of subsistence, not as against a fixed, but as against an elastic barrier, which makes the procurement of subsistence progressively more and more difficult. And thus, wherever reproduction has had time to assert its power, and is unchecked by prudence, there must exist that degree of want which will keep population within the bounds of subsistence.

Although in reality not more repugnant to the sense of harmonious adaptation by creative beneficence and wisdom than the complacent no-theory which throws the responsibility for poverty and its concomitants upon the inscrutable decrees of Providence, without attempting to trace them, this theory, in avowedly making vice and suffering the necessary results of a natural instinct with which are linked the purest and sweetest affections, comes rudely in collision with ideas deeply rooted in the human mind, and it was, as soon as formally promulgated, fought with a bitterness in which zeal was often more manifest than logic. But it has triumphantly withstood the ordeal, and in spite of the refutations of the Godwins, the denunciations of the Cobbetts, and all the shafts that argument, sarcasm, ridicule, and sentiment could direct against it, today it stands in the world of thought as an accepted truth, which compels the recognition even of those who would fain disbelieve it.

The causes of its triumph, the sources of its strength, are not obscure. Seemingly backed by an indisputable arithmetical truth—that a continuously increasing population must eventually exceed the capacity of the earth to furnish food or even standing room, the Malthusian theory is supported by analogies in the animal and vegetable kingdoms, where life everywhere beats wastefully against the barriers that hold its different species in check—analogies to which the course of modern thought, in leveling distinctions between different forms of life, has given a greater and greater weight; and it is apparently corroborated by many obvious facts, such as the prevalence of poverty, vice, and misery amid dense populations; the general effect of material progress in increasing population without relieving pauperism; the rapid growth of numbers in newly settled countries and the evident retardation of increase in more densely settled countries by the mortality among the class condemned to want.

The Malthusian theory furnishes a general principle which accounts for these and similar facts, and accounts for them in a way which harmonizes with the doctrine that wages are drawn from capital, and with all the principles that are deduced from it. According to the current doctrine of wages, wages fall as increase in the number of laborers necessitates a more minute division of capital; according to the Malthusian theory, poverty appears as increase in population necessitates the more minute division of subsistence. It requires but the identification of capital with subsistence, and number of laborers with population, an identification made in the current treatises on political economy, where the terms are often converted, to make the two propositions as identical formally as they are substantially. And thus it is, as stated by Buckle in the passage previously quoted, that the theory of population advanced by Malthus has appeared to prove decisively the theory of wages advanced by Smith.

II. INFERENCES FROM FACTS

The general acceptance of the Malthusian theory and the high authority by which it is indorsed have seemed to me to make it expedient to review its grounds and the causes which have conspired to give it such a dominating influence in the discussion of social questions.

But when we subject the theory itself to the test of straightforward analysis, it will, I think, be found as utterly untenable as the current theory of wages.

In the first place, the facts which are marshaled in support of this theory do not prove it, and the analogies do not countenance it.

And in the second place, there are facts which conclusively disprove it.

I go to the heart of the matter in saying that there is no warrant, either in experience or analogy, for the assumption that there is any tendency in population to increase faster than subsistence. The facts cited to show this simply show that where, owing to the sparseness of population, as in new countries, or where, owing to the unequal distribution of wealth, as among the poorer classes in old countries, human life is occupied with the physical necessities of existence, the tendency to reproduce is at a rate which would, were it to go on unchecked, some time exceed subsistence. But it is not a legitimate inference from this that the tendency to reproduce would show itself in the same force where population was sufficiently dense and wealth distributed with sufficient evenness to lift a whole community above the necessity of devoting their energies to a struggle for mere existence. Nor can it be assumed that the tendency to reproduce, by causing poverty, must prevent the existence of such a community; for this, manifestly, would be assuming the very point at issue, and reasoning in a circle. And even if it be admitted that the tendency to multiply must ultimately produce poverty, it cannot from this alone be predicated of existing poverty that it is due to this cause, until it be shown that there are no other causes which can account for it—a thing in the present state of government, laws, and customs, manifestly impossible.

The globe may be surveyed and history may be reviewed in vain for any instance of a considerable country in which poverty and want can be fairly attributed to the pressure of an increasing population. Whatever be the possible dangers involved in the power of human increase, they have never yet appeared. Whatever may some time be, this never yet has been the evil that has afflicted mankind. Population always tending to overpass the limit of subsistence! How is it, then, that this globe of ours, after all the thousands, and it is now thought millions, of years that man has been upon the earth, is yet so thinly populated? How is it, then, that so many of the hives of human life are now deserted—that once cultivated fields are rank with jungle, and the wild beast licks her cubs where once were busy haunts of men?

It is a fact, that, as we count our increasing millions, we are apt to lose sight of—nevertheless it is a fact—that in what we know of the world's history decadence of population is as common as increase. Whether the aggregate population of the earth is now greater than at any previous epoch is a speculation which can deal only with guesses. Since Montesquieu, in the early part of the last century, asserted, what was then probably the prevailing impression, that the population of the earth had, since the Christian era, greatly declined, opinion has run the other way. But the tendency of recent investigation and exploration has been to give greater credit to what have been deemed the exaggerated accounts of ancient historians and travelers, and to reveal indications of denser populations and more advanced civilizations than had before been suspected, as well as of a higher antiquity in the human race. And in basing our estimates of population upon the development of trade, the advance of the arts, and the size of cities, we are apt to underrate the density of population which the intensive cultivations, characteristic of the earlier civilizations, are capable of maintaining—especially where irrigation is resorted to. As we may see from the closely cultivated districts of China and Europe a very great population of simple habits can readily exist with very little commerce and a much lower stage of those arts in which modern progress has been most marked, and without that tendency to concentrate in cities which modern populations show.

Be this as it may, the only continent which we can be sure now contains a larger population than ever before is Europe. But this is not true of all parts of Europe. Certainly Greece, the Mediterranean Islands, and Turkey in Europe, probably Italy, and possibly Spain, have contained larger populations than now, and this may be likewise true of Northwestern and parts of Central and Eastern Europe.

America also has increased in population during the time we know of it; but this increase is not so great as is popularly supposed, some estimates giving to Peru alone at the time of the discovery a greater population than now exists on the whole continent of South America. And all the indications are that previous to the discovery the population of America had been declining. What great nations have run their course, what empires have arisen and fallen in "that new world which is the old," we can only imagine. But fragments of massive ruins yet attest a grander pre-Incan civilization; amid the tropical forests of Yucatan and Central America are the remains of great cities forgotten ere the Spanish conquest; Mexico, as Cortez found it, showed the superimposition of barbarism upon a higher social development, while through a great part of what is now the United States are scattered mounds which prove a once relatively dense population, and here and there, as in the Lake Superior copper mines, are traces of higher arts than were known to the Indians with whom the whites came in contact.

As to Africa there can be no question. Northern Africa can contain but a fraction of the population that it had in ancient times; the Nile Valley once held an enormously greater population than now, while south of the Sahara there is nothing to show increase within historic times, and widespread depopulation was certainly caused by the slave trade.

As for Asia, which even now contains more than half the human race, though it is not much more than half as densely populated as Europe, there are indications that both India and China once contained larger populations than now, while that great breeding ground of men from which issued swarms that overran both countries and sent great waves of people rolling upon Europe, must have been once far more populous. But the most marked change is in Asia Minor, Syria, Babylonia, Persia, and in short that vast district which yielded to the conquering arms of Alexander. Where were once great cities and teeming populations are now squalid villages and barren wastes.

There is another broad, general fact which cannot fail to strike any one who, thinking of this subject, extends his view beyond modern society. Malthusianism predicates a universal law—that the natural tendency of population is to outrun subsistence. If there be such a law, it must, wherever population has attained a certain density, become as obvious as any of the great natural laws which have been everywhere recognized. How is it, then, that neither in classical creeds and codes, nor in those of the Jews, Egyptians, the Hindus, the Chinese, nor any of the peoples who have lived in close association and have built up creeds and codes, do we find any injunctions to the practice of the prudential restraints of Malthus; but that, on the contrary, the wisdom of the centuries, the religions of the world, have always inculcated ideas of civic and religious duty the very reverse of those which the current political economy enjoins?

III. INFERENCES FROM ANALOGY

If we turn from an examination of the facts brought forward in illustration of the Malthusian theory to consider the analogies by which it is supported, we shall find the same inconclusiveness.

The strength of the reproductive force in the animal and vegetable kingdoms—such facts as that a single pair of salmon might, if preserved from their natural enemies for a few years, fill the ocean; that a pair of rabbits would, under the same circumstances, soon overrun a continent; that many plants scatter their seeds by the hundred fold, and some insects deposit thousands of eggs; and that everywhere through these kingdoms each species constantly tends to press, and when not limited by the number of its enemies, evidently does press, against the limits of subsistence—is constantly cited, from Malthus down to the textbooks of the present day, as showing that population likewise tends to press against subsistence, and, when unrestrained by other means, its natural increase must necessarily result in such low wages and want, or, if that will not suffice, and the increase still goes on, in such actual starvation, as will keep it within the limits of subsistence.

But is this analogy valid? It is from the vegetable and animal kingdoms that man's food is drawn, and hence the greater strength of the reproductive force in the vegetable and animal kingdoms than in man simply proves the power of subsistence to increase faster than population. Does not the fact that all of the things which furnish man's subsistence have the power to multiply many fold—some of them many thousand fold, and some of them many million or even billion fold—while he is only doubling his numbers, show that, let human beings increase to the full extent of their reproductive power, the increase of population can never exceed subsistence? This is clear when it is remembered that though in the vegetable and animal kingdoms each species, by virtue of its reproductive power, naturally and necessarily presses against the conditions which limit its further increase, yet these conditions are nowhere fixed and final. No species reaches the ultimate limit of soil, water, air, and sunshine; but the actual limit of each is in the existence of other species, its rivals, its enemies, or its food. Thus the conditions which limit the existence of such of these species as afford him subsistence man can extend (in some cases his mere appearance will extend them), and thus the reproductive forces of the species which supply his wants, instead of wasting themselves against their former limit, start forward in his service at a pace which his powers of increase cannot rival. If he but shoot hawks, food birds will increase; if he but trap foxes the wild rabbits will multiply; the honey bee moves with the pioneer, and on the organic matter with which man's presence fills the rivers, fishes feed.

Here is a difference between the animal and the man. Both the jayhawk and the man eat chickens, but the more jayhawks the fewer chickens, while the more men the more chickens. Both the seal and the man eat salmon, but when a seal takes a salmon there is a salmon the less, and were seals to increase past a certain point salmon must diminish; while by placing the spawn of the salmon under favorable conditions man can so increase the number of salmon as more than to make up for all he may take, and thus, no matter how much men may increase, their increase need never outrun the supply of salmon.

Granted that man is only a more highly developed animal; that the ring-tailed monkey is a distant relative who has gradually developed acrobatic tendencies, and the humpbacked whale a far-off connection who in early life took to the sea—granted that back of these he is kin to the vegetable, and is still subject to the same laws as plants, fishes, birds, and beasts. Yet there is still this difference between man and all other animals—he is the only animal whose desires increase as they are fed; the only animal that is never satisfied. The wants of every other living thing are uniform and fixed. The ox of today aspires to no more than did the ox when man first yoked him. The sea gull of the English Channel, who poises himself above the swift steamer, wants no better food or lodging than the gulls who circled round as the keels of Cæsar's galleys first grated on a British beach. Of all that nature offers them, be it ever so abundant, all living things save man can take, and care for, only enough to supply wants which are definite and fixed. The only use they can make of additional supplies or additional opportunities is to multiply.

But not so with man. No sooner are his animal wants satisfied than new wants arise. Food he wants first, as does the beast; shelter next, as does the beast; and these given, his reproductive instincts assert their sway, as do those of the beast. But here man and beast part company. The beast never goes further; the man has but set his feet on the first step of an infinite progression—a progression upon which the beast never enters; a progression away from and above the beast.

The demand for quantity once satisfied, he seeks quality. The very desires that he has in common with the beast become extended, refined, exalted. It is not merely hunger, but taste, that seeks gratification in food; in clothes, he seeks not merely comfort, but adornment; the rude shelter becomes a house; the undiscriminating sexual attraction begins to transmute itself into subtile influences, and the hard and common stock of animal life to blossom and to bloom into shapes of delicate beauty. As power to gratify his wants increases, so does aspiration grow. Held down to lower levels of desire, Lucullus will sup with Lucullus; twelve boars turn on spits that Antony's mouthful of meat may be done to a turn; every kingdom of Nature be ransacked to add to Cleopatra's charms, and marble colonnades and hanging gardens and pyramids that rival the hills arise. Passing into higher forms of desire, that which slumbered in the plant and fitfully stirred in the beast, awakes in the man. The eyes of the mind are opened, and he longs to know. He braves the scorching heat of the desert and the icy blasts of the polar sea, but not for food; he watches all night, but it is to trace the circling of the eternal stars. He adds toil to toil, to gratify a hunger no animal has felt; to assuage a thirst no beast can know.

Out upon nature, in upon himself, back through the mists that shroud the past, forward into the darkness that overhangs the future, turns the restless desire that arises when the animal wants slumber in satisfaction. Beneath things, he seeks the law; he would know how the globe was forged and the stars were hung, and trace to their origins the springs of life. And, then, as the man develops his nobler nature, there arises the desire higher yet—the passion of passions, the hope of hopes—the desire that he, even he, may somehow aid in making life better and brighter, in destroying want and sin, sorrow and shame. He masters and curbs the animal; he turns his back upon the feast and renounces the place of power; he leaves it to others to accumulate wealth, to gratify pleasant tastes, to bask themselves in the warm sunshine of the brief day. He works for those he never saw and never can see;

for a fame, or maybe but for a scant justice, that can only come long after the clods have rattled upon his coffin lid. He toils in the advance, where it is cold, and there is little cheer from men, and the stones are sharp and the brambles thick. Amid the scoffs of the present and the sneers that stab like knives, he builds for the future; he cuts the trail that progressive humanity may hereafter broaden into a highroad. Into higher, grander spheres desire mounts and beckons, and a star that rises in the east leads him on. Lo! the pulses of the man throb with the yearnings of the god—he would aid in the process of the suns!

IV. DISPROOF OF THE MALTHUSIAN THEORY

So DEEPLY ROOTED and thoroughly entwined with the reasonings of the current political economy is this doctrine that increase of population tends to reduce wages and produce poverty, so completely does it harmonize with many popular notions, and so liable is it to recur in different shapes, that I have thought it necessary to meet and show in some detail the insufficiency of the arguments by which it is supported, before bringing it to the test of facts; for the general acceptance of this theory adds a most striking instance to the many which the history of thought affords of how easily men ignore facts when blindfolded by a preaccepted theory.

To the supreme and final test of facts we can easily bring this theory. Manifestly the question whether increase of population necessarily tends to reduce wages and cause want, is simply the question whether it tends to reduce the amount of wealth that can be produced by a given amount of labor.

This is what the current doctrine holds. The accepted theory is, that the more that is required from nature the less generously does she respond, so that doubling the application of labor will not double the product; and hence, increase of population must tend to reduce wages and deepen poverty, or, in the phrase of Malthus, must result in vice and misery. To quote the language of John Stuart Mill:

> A greater number of people cannot, in any given state of civilization, be collectively so well provided for as a smaller. The niggardliness of nature, not the injustice of society, is the cause of the penalty attached to overpopulation. An unjust distribution of wealth does not aggravate the evil, but, at most, causes it to be somewhat earlier felt. It is in vain to say that all mouths which the increase of mankind calls into existence bring with them hands. The new mouths require as much food as the old ones, and the hands do not produce as much. If all instruments of production were held in joint property by the whole people, and the produce divided with perfect equality among them, and if in a society thus constituted, industry were as energetic and the

produce as ample as at the present time, there would be enough to make all the existing population extremely comfortable; but when that population had doubled itself, as, with existing habits of the people, under such an encouragement, it undoubtedly would in little more than twenty years, what would then be their condition? Unless the arts of production were in the same time improved in an almost unexampled degree, the inferior soils which must be resorted to, and the more laborious and scantily remunerative cultivation which must be employed on the superior soils, to procure food for so much larger a population, would, by an insuperable necessity, render every individual in the community poorer than before. If the population continued to increase at the same rate, a time would soon arrive when no one would have more than mere necessaries, and, soon after, a time when no one would have a sufficiency of those, and the further increase of population would be arrested by death. (*Principles of Political Economy.*)

All this I deny. I assert that the very reverse of these propositions is true. I assert that in any given state of civilization a greater number of people can collectively be better provided for than a smaller. I assert that the injustice of society, not the niggardliness of nature, is the cause of the want and misery which the current theory attributes to over-population. I assert that the new mouths which an increasing population calls into existence require no more food than the old ones, while the hands they bring with them can in the natural order of things produce more. I assert that, other things being equal, the greater the population, the greater the comfort which an equitable distribution of wealth would give to each individual. I assert that in a state of equality the natural increase of population would constantly tend to make every individual richer instead of poorer.

I thus distinctly join issue, and submit the question to the test of facts.

But observe (for even at the risk of repetition I wish to warn the reader against a confusion of thought that is observable even in writers of great reputation), that the question of fact into which this issue resolves itself is not in what stage of population is most subsistence produced? but in what stage of population is there exhibited the greatest power of producing wealth? For the power of producing wealth in any form is the power of producing subsistence—and the consumption of wealth in any form, or of wealth-producing power, is equivalent to the consumption of subsistence. I have, for instance, some money in my pocket. With it I may buy either food or cigars or jewelry or theater tickets, and just as I expend my money do I determine labor to the production of food, of cigars, of jewelry, or of theatrical representations. A set of diamonds has a value equal to so many barrels of flour—that is to say, it takes on the average as much labor to produce the diamonds as it would to produce so much flour. If I load my wife with diamonds, it is as much an exertion of subsistence-producing power as though I had devoted so much food to purposes of ostentation. If I keep a footman,

I take a possible plowman from the plow. The breeding and maintenance of a race horse require care and labor which would suffice for the breeding and maintenance of many work horses. The destruction of wealth involved in a general illumination or the firing of a salute is equivalent to the burning up of so much food; the keeping of a regiment of soldiers, or of a warship and her crew, is the diversion to unproductive uses of labor that could produce subsistence for many thousands of people. Thus the power of any population to produce the necessaries of life is not to be measured by the necessaries of life actually produced, but by the expenditure of power in all modes.

There is no necessity for abstract reasoning. The question is one of simple fact. Does the relative power of producing wealth decrease with the increase of population?

The facts are so patent that it is only necessary to call attention to them. We have, in modern times, seen many communities advance in population. Have they not at the same time advanced even more rapidly in wealth? We see many communities still increasing in population. Are they not also increasing their wealth still faster? Is there any doubt that while England has been increasing her population at the rate of two per cent. per annum, her wealth has been growing in still greater proportion? Is it not true that while the population of the United States has been doubling every twenty-nine years her wealth has been doubling at much shorter intervals? Is it not true that under similar conditions—that is to say, among communities of similar people in a similar stage of civilization—the most densely populated community is also the richest? Are not the more densely populated Eastern States richer in proportion to population than the more sparsely populated Western or Southern States? Is not England, where population is even denser than in the Eastern States of the Union, also richer in proportion? Where will you find wealth devoted with the most lavishness to non-productive use—costly buildings, fine furniture, luxurious equipages, statues, pictures, pleasure gardens, and yachts? Is it not where population is densest rather than where it is sparsest? Where will you find in largest proportion those whom the general production suffices to keep without productive labor on their part—men of income and of elegant leisure, thieves, policemen, menial servants, lawyers, men of letters, and the like? Is it not where population is dense rather than where it is sparse? Whence is it that capital overflows for remunerative investment? Is it not from densely populated countries to sparsely populated countries? These things conclusively show that wealth is greatest where population is densest; that the production of wealth to a given amount of labor increases as population increases. These things are apparent wherever we turn our eyes. On the same level of civilization, the same stage of the productive arts, government, etc., the most populous countries are always the most wealthy.

Let us take a particular case, and that a case which of all that can be cited seems at first blush best to support the theory we are considering—the case of a community where, while population has largely increased, wages have greatly decreased, and it is not a matter of dubious inference but of obvious fact that the generosity of nature has lessened. That community is California. When upon the discovery of gold the first wave of immigration poured into California it found a country in which nature was in the most generous mood. From the river banks and bars the glittering deposits of thousands of years could be taken by the most primitive appliances, in amounts which made an ounce ($16) per day only ordinary wages. The plains, covered with nutritious grasses, were alive with countless herds of horses and cattle, so plenty that any traveler was at liberty to shift his saddle to a fresh steed, or to kill a bullock if he needed a steak, leaving the hide, its only valuable part, for the owner. From the rich soil which came first under cultivation, the mere plowing and sowing brought crops that in older countries, if procured at all, can only be procured by the most thorough manuring and cultivation. In early California, amid this profusion of nature, wages and interest were higher than anywhere else in the world.

This virgin profusion of nature has been steadily giving way before the greater and greater demands which an increasing population has made upon it. Poorer and poorer diggings have been worked, until now no diggings worth speaking of can be found, and gold mining requires much capital, large skill, and elaborate machinery, and involves great risks. "Horses cost money," and cattle bred on the sagebrush plains of Nevada are brought by railroad across the mountains and killed in San Francisco shambles, while farmers are beginning to save their straw and look for manure, and land is in cultivation which will hardly yield a crop three years out of four without irrigation. At the same time wages and interest have steadily gone down. Many men are now glad to work for a week for less than they once demanded for the day, and money is loaned by the year for a rate which once would hardly have been thought extortionate by the month. Is the connection between the reduced productiveness of nature and the reduced rate of wages that of cause and effect? Is it true that wages are lower because labor yields less wealth? On the contrary! Instead of the wealth-producing power of labor being less in California in 1879 than in 1849, I am convinced that it is greater. And, it seems to me, that no one who considers how enormously during these years the efficiency of labor in California has been increased by roads, wharves, flumes, railroads, steamboats, telegraphs, and machinery of all kinds; by a closer connection with the rest of the world; and by the numberless economies resulting from a larger population, can doubt that the return which labor receives from nature in California is on the whole much greater now than it was in the days of unexhausted placers and virgin soil—the increase in the power of the human factor having more than compensated for the decline in the power of the natural factor. That this conclusion is the correct one is proved by many facts which show that the consumption of wealth is now much greater, as compared with the number of laborers, than it was then. Instead of a population composed almost exclusively of men in the prime of life, a large proportion of women and children are now supported, and other non-producers have increased in much greater ratio than the population; luxury has grown far more than wages have fallen; where the best houses were cloth and paper shanties, are now mansions whose magnificence rivals European palaces; there are liveried carriages on the streets of San Francisco and pleasure yachts on her bay; the class who can live sumptuously on their incomes has steadily grown; there are rich men beside whom the richest of the earlier years would seem little better than paupers—in short, there are on every hand the most striking and conclusive evidences that the production and consumption of wealth have increased with even greater rapidity than the increase of population, and that if any class obtains less it is solely because of the greater inequality of distribution.

What is obvious in this particular instance is obvious where the survey is extended. The richest countries are not those where nature is most prolific; but those where labor is most efficient—not Mexico, but Massachusetts; not Brazil, but England. The countries where population is densest and presses hardest upon the capabilities of nature, are, other things being equal, the countries where the largest proportion of the produce can be devoted to luxury and the support of non-producers, the countries where capital overflows, the countries that upon exigency, such as war, can stand the greatest drain. That the production of wealth must, in proportion to the labor employed, be greater in a densely populated country like England than in new countries where wages and interest are higher, is evident from the fact that, though a much smaller proportion of the population is engaged in productive labor, a much larger surplus is available for other purposes than that of supplying physical needs. In a new country the whole available force of the community is devoted to production—there is no well man who does not do productive work of some kind, no well woman exempt from household tasks. There are no paupers or beggars, no idle rich, no class whose labor is devoted to ministering to the convenience or caprice of the rich, no purely literary or scientific class, no criminal class who live by preying upon society, no large class maintained to guard society against them. Yet with the whole force of the community thus devoted to production, no such consumption of wealth in proportion to the whole population takes place, or can be afforded, as goes on in the old country; for, though the condition of the lowest class is better, and there is no one who cannot get a living, there is no one who gets much more—few or none who can live in anything like what would be called luxury, or even comfort, in the older country. That is to say, that in the older country the consumption of wealth in proportion to population is greater, although the proportion of labor devoted to the production of wealth is less—or that fewer laborers produce more wealth; for wealth must be produced before it can be consumed.

It may, however, be said, that the superior wealth of older countries is due not to superior productive power, but to the accumulations of wealth which the new country has not yet had time to make.

It will be well for a moment to consider this idea of accumulated wealth. The truth is, that wealth can be accumulated but to a slight degree, and that communities really live, as the vast majority of individuals live, from hand to mouth. Wealth will not bear much accumulation; except in a few unimportant forms it will not keep. The matter of the universe, which, when worked up by labor into desirable forms, constitutes wealth, is constantly tending back to its original state. Some forms of wealth will last for a few hours, some for a few days, some for a few months, some for a few years; and there are very few forms of wealth that can be passed from one generation to another. Take wealth in some of its most useful and permanent forms—ships, houses, railways, machinery. Unless labor is constantly exerted in preserving and renewing them, they will almost immediately become useless. Stop labor in any community, and wealth would vanish almost as the jet of a fountain vanishes when the flow of water is shut off. Let labor again exert itself, and wealth will almost as immediately reappear. This has been long noticed where war or other calamity has swept away wealth, leaving population unimpaired. There is not less wealth in London today because of the great fire of 1666; nor yet is there less wealth in Chicago because of the great fire in 1870. On those fire-swept acres have arisen, under the hand of labor, more magnificent buildings, filled with greater stocks of goods; and the stranger, who, ignorant of the history of the city, passes along those stately avenues would not dream that a few years ago all lay so black and bare. The same principle—that wealth is constantly re-created—is obvious in every new city. Given the same population and the same efficiency of labor, and the town of yesterday will possess and enjoy as much as the town founded by the Romans. No one who has seen Melbourne or San Francisco can doubt that if the population of England were transported to New Zealand, leaving all accumulated wealth behind, New Zealand would soon be as rich as England is now; or, conversely, that if the population of England were reduced to the sparseness of the present population of New Zealand, in spite of accumulated wealth, they would soon be as poor. Accumulated wealth seems to play just about such a part in relation to the social organism as accumulated nutriment does to the physical organism. Some accumulated wealth is necessary, and to a certain extent it may be drawn upon in exigencies; but the wealth produced by past generations can no more account for the consumption of the present than the dinners he ate last year can supply a man with present strength.

But without these considerations, which I allude to more for their general than for their special bearing, it is evident that superior accumulations of wealth can account for greater consumption of wealth only in cases where accumulated wealth is decreasing, and that wherever the volume of accumulated wealth is maintained, and even more obviously where it is increasing, a greater consumption of wealth must imply a greater production of wealth. Now, whether we compare different communities with each other, or the same community at different times, it is obvious that the progressive state, which is marked by increase of population, is also marked by an increased consumption and an increased accumulation of wealth, not merely in the aggregate, but per capita. And hence, increase of population, so far as it has yet anywhere gone, does not mean a reduction, but an increase in the average production of wealth.

And the reason of this is obvious. For, even if the increase of population does reduce the power of the natural factor of wealth, by compelling a resort to poorer soils, etc., it yet so vastly increases the power of the human factor as more than to compensate. Twenty men working together will, where nature is niggardly, produce more than twenty times the wealth that one man can produce where nature is most bountiful. The denser the population the more minute becomes the subdivision of labor, the greater the economies of production and distribution, and, hence, the very reverse of the Malthusian doctrine is true; and, within the limits in which we have reason to suppose increase would still go on, in any given state of civilization a greater number of people can produce a larger proportionate amount of wealth, and more fully supply their wants, than can a smaller number.

Look simply at the facts. Can anything be clearer than that the cause of the poverty which festers in the centers of civilization is not in the weakness of the productive forces? In countries where poverty is deepest, the forces of production are evidently strong enough, if fully employed, to provide for the lowest not merely comfort but luxury. The industrial paralysis, the commercial depression which curses the civilized world today, evidently springs from no lack of productive power. Whatever be the trouble, it is clearly not in the want of ability to produce wealth.

It is this very fact—that want appears where productive power is greatest and the production of wealth is largest—that constitutes the enigma which perplexes the civilized world, and which we are trying to unravel. Evidently the Malthusian theory, which attributes want to the decrease of productive power, will not explain it. That theory is utterly inconsistent with all the facts. It is really a gratuitous attribution to the laws of God of results which, even from this examination, we may infer really spring from the maladjustments of men—an inference which, as we proceed, will become a demonstration. For we have yet to find what *does* produce poverty amid advancing wealth.

PART THREE

I. THE INQUIRY NARROWED TO THE LAWS OF DISTRIBUTION—THE NECESSARY RELATION OF THESE LAWS

THE PRECEDING EXAMINATION has, I think, conclusively shown that the explanation currently given, in the name of political economy, of the problem we are attempting to solve, is no explanation at all.

That with material progress wages fail to increase, but rather tend to decrease, cannot be explained by the theory that the increase of laborers constantly tends to divide into smaller portions the capital sum from which wages are paid. For, as we have seen, wages do not come from capital, but are the direct produce of labor. Each productive laborer, as he works, creates his wages, and with every additional laborer there is an addition to the true wages fund—an addition to the common stock of wealth, which, generally speaking, is considerably greater than the amount he draws in wages.

Nor, yet, can it be explained by the theory that nature yields less to the increasing drafts which an increasing population make upon her; for the increased efficiency of labor makes the progressive state a state of continually increasing production per capita, and the countries of densest population, other things being equal, are always the countries of greatest wealth.

So far, we have only increased the perplexities of the problem. We have overthrown a theory which did, in some sort of fashion, explain existing facts; but in doing so have only made existing facts seem more inexplicable. It is as though, while the Ptolemaic theory was yet in its strength, it had been proved simply that the sun and stars do not revolve about the earth. The phenomena of day and night, and of the apparent motion of the celestial bodies, would yet remain unexplained, inevitably to reinstate the old theory unless a better one took its place. Our reasoning has led us to the conclusion that each productive laborer produces his own wages, and that increase in the number of laborers should increase the wages of each; whereas, the apparent facts are that there are many laborers who cannot obtain remunerative employment, and that increase in the number of laborers brings diminution of wages. We have, in short, proved that wages ought to be highest where in reality they are lowest.

Nevertheless, even in doing this we have made some progress. Next to finding what we look for, is to discover where it is useless to look. We have at least narrowed the field of inquiry. For this, at least, is now clear—that the cause which, in spite of the enormous increase of productive power, confines the great body of producers to the least share of the product upon which they will consent to live, is not the limitation of capital, nor yet the limitation of the powers of nature which respond to labor. As it is not, therefore, to be found in the laws which bound the production of wealth, it must be sought in the laws which govern distribution. To them let us turn.

It will be necessary to review in its main branches the whole subject of the distribution of wealth. To discover the cause which, as population increases and the productive arts advance, deepens the poverty of the lowest class, we must find the law which determines what part of the produce is distributed to labor as wages. To find the law of wages, or at least to make sure when we have found it, we must also determine the laws which fix the part of the produce which goes to capital and the part which goes to land owners, for as land, labor, and capital join in producing wealth, it is between these three that the produce must be divided. What is meant by the produce or production of a community is the sum of the wealth produced by that community—the general fund from which, as long as previously existing stock is not lessened, all consumption must be met and all revenues drawn. As I have already explained, production does not merely mean the making of things, but includes the increase of value gained by transporting or exchanging things. There is a produce of wealth in a purely commercial community, as there is in a purely agricultural or manufacturing community; and in the one case, as in the others, some part of this produce will go to capital, some part to labor, and some part, if land have any value, to the owners of land. As a matter of fact, a portion of the wealth produced is constantly going to the replacement of capital, which is constantly consumed and constantly replaced. But it is not necessary to take this into account, as it is eliminated by considering capital as continuous, which, in speaking or thinking of it, we habitually do. When we speak of the produce, we mean, therefore, that part of the wealth produced above what is necessary to replace the capital consumed in production; and when we speak of interest, or the return to capital, we mean what goes to capital after its replacement or maintenance.

It is, further, a matter of fact, that in every community which has passed the most primitive stage some portion of the producc is taken in taxation and consumed by government. But it is not necessary, in seeking the laws of distribution, to take this into consideration. We may consider taxation either as not existing, or as by so much reducing the produce. And so, too, of what is taken from the produce by certain forms of monopoly. After we have discovered the laws of distribution we can then see what bearing, if any, taxation has upon them.

We must discover these laws of distribution for ourselves—or, at least, two out of the three. For, that they are not, at least as a whole, correctly apprehended by the current political economy, may be seen, irrespective of our preceding examination of one of them, in any of the standard treatises.

This is evident, in the first place, from the terminology employed

In all politico-economic works we are told that the three factors in production are land, labor, and capital, and that the whole produce is primarily distributed into three corresponding parts. Three terms, therefore, are needed, each of which shall clearly express one of these parts to the exclusion of the others. Rent, as defined, clearly enough expresses the first of these parts—that which goes to the owners of land. Wages, as defined, clearly enough expresses the second—that part which constitutes the return to labor. But as to the third term—that which should express the return to capital—there is in the standard works a most puzzling ambiguity and confusion.

Of words in common use, that which comes nearest to exclusively expressing the idea of return for the use of capital, is interest, which, as commonly used, implies the return for the use of capital, exclusive of any labor in its use or management, and exclusive of any risk, except such as may be involved in the security. The word profits, as commonly used, is almost synonymous with revenue; it means a gain, an amount received in excess of an amount expended, and frequently includes receipts that are properly rent; while it nearly always includes receipts which are properly wages, as well as compensations for the risk peculiar to the various uses of capital. Unless extreme violence is done to the meaning of the word, it cannot, therefore, be used in political economy to signify that share of the produce which goes to capital, in contradistinction to those parts which go to labor and to land owners.

Now, all this is recognized in the standard works on political economy. Adam Smith well illustrates how wages and compensation for risk largely enter into profits, pointing out how the large profits of apothecaries and small retail dealers are in reality wages for their labor, and not interest on their capital; and how the great profits sometimes made in risky businesses, such as smuggling and the lumber trade, are really but compensations for risk, which, in the long run, reduce the returns to capital so used to the ordinary, or below the ordinary, rate. Similar illustrations are given in most of the subsequent works, where profit is formally defined in its common sense, with, perhaps, the exclusion of rent. In all these works, the reader is told that profits are made up of three elements—wages of superintendence, compensation for risk, and *interest,* or the return for the use of capital.

Thus, neither in its common meaning nor in the meaning expressly assigned to it in the current political economy, can profits have any place in the discussion of the distribution of wealth between the three factors of production. Either in its common meaning or in the meaning expressly assigned to it, to talk about the distribution of wealth into rent, wages, and profits is like talking of the division of mankind into men, women, and human beings.

Yet this, to the utter bewilderment of the reader, is what is done in all the standard works. After formally decomposing profits into wages of superintendence, compensation for risk, and interest—the net return for the use of capital—they proceed to treat of the distribution of wealth between the rent of land, the wages of labor, and the PROFITS of capital.

I doubt not that there are thousands of men who have vainly puzzled their brains over this confusion of terms, and abandoned the effort in despair, thinking that as the fault could not be in such great thinkers, it must be in their own stupidity. If it is any consolation to such men they may turn to Buckle's *History of Civilization,* and see how a man who certainly got a marvelously clear idea of what he read, and who had read carefully the principal economists from Smith down, was inextricably confused by this jumble of profits and interest. For Buckle persistently speaks of the distribution of wealth into rent, wages, interest, *and* profits.

And this is not to be wondered at. For, after formally decomposing profits into wages of superintendence, insurance, and interest, these economists, in assigning causes which fix the general rate of profit, speak of things which evidently affect only that part of profits which they have denominated interest; and then, in speaking of the rate of interest, either give the meaningless formula of supply and demand, or speak of causes which affect the compensation for risk; evidently using the word in its common sense, and not in the economic sense they have assigned to it, from which compensation for risk is eliminated. If the reader will take up John Stuart Mill's *Principles of Political Economy,* and compare the chapter on Profits with the chapter on Interest, he will see the confusion thus arising exemplified in the case of the most logical of English economists, in a more striking manner than I would like to characterize.

Now, such men have not been led into such confusion of thought without a cause. If they, one after another, have followed Dr. Adam Smith, as boys play "follow my leader," jumping where he jumped, and falling where he fell, it has been that there was a fence where he jumped and a hole where he fell.

The difficulty from which this confusion has sprung is in the pre-accepted theory of wages. For reasons which I have before assigned, it has seemed to them a self-evident truth that the wages of certain classes of laborers depended upon the ratio between capital and the number of laborers. But there are certain kinds of reward for exertion to which this theory evidently will not apply, so the term wages has in use been contracted to include only wages in the narrow common sense. This being the case, if the term interest were used, as consistently with their definitions it should have been used, to represent the third part of the division of the produce, all rewards of personal exertion, save those of what are commonly called wageworkers, would clearly have been left out. But by treating the division of wealth as between rent, wages, and profits, instead of between rent, wages, and interest, this difficulty is glossed over, all wages which will not fall under the preaccepted law of wages being vaguely grouped under profits, as wages of superintendence.

To read carefully what economists say about the distribution of wealth is to see that, though they correctly define it, wages, as they use it in this connection, is what logicians would call an undistributed term—it does not mean all wages, but only some wages—viz., the wages of manual labor paid by an employer. So other wages are thrown over with the return to capital, and included under the term profits, and any clear distinction between the returns to capital and the returns to human exertion thus avoided. The fact is that the current political economy fails to give any clear and consistent account of the distribution of wealth. The law of rent *is* clearly stated, but it stands unrelated. The rest is a confused and incoherent jumble.

The very arrangement of these works shows this confusion and inconclusiveness of thought. In no politico-economic treatise that I know of are these laws of distribution brought together, so that the reader can take them in at a glance and recognize their relation to each other; but what is said about each one is enveloped in a mass of political and moral reflections and dissertations. And the reason is not far to seek. To bring together the three laws of distribution as they are now taught, is to show at a glance that they lack necessary relation.

The laws of the distribution of wealth are obviously laws of proportion, and must be so related to each other that any two being given the third may be inferred. For to say that one of the three parts of a whole is increased or decreased, is to say that one or both of the other parts is, reversely, decreased or increased. If Tom, Dick, and Harry are partners in business, the agreement which fixes the share of one in the profits must at the same time fix either the separate or the joint shares of the other two. To fix Tom's share at forty per cent. is to leave but sixty per cent. to be divided between Dick and Harry. To fix Dick's share at forty per cent. and Harry's share at thirty-five per cent. is to fix Tom's share at twenty-five per cent.

But between the laws of the distribution of wealth, as laid down in the standard works, there is no such relation. If we fish them out and bring them together, we find them to be as follows:

Wages are determined by the ratio between the amount of capital devoted to the payment and subsistence of labor and the number of laborers seeking employment.

Rent is determined by the margin of cultivation; all lands yielding as rent that part of their produce which exceeds what an equal application of labor and capital could procure from the poorest land in use.

Interest is determined by the equation between the demands of borrowers and the supply of capital offered by lenders. Or, if we take what is given as the law of profits, it is determined by wages, falling as wages rise and rising as wages fall—or, to use the phrase of Mill, by the cost of labor to the capitalist.

The bringing together of these current statements of the laws of the distribution of wealth shows at a glance that they lack the relation to each other which the true laws of distribution must have. They do not correlate and co-ordinate. Hence, at least two of these three laws are either wrongly apprehended or wrongly stated. This tallies with what we have already seen, that the current apprehension of the law of wages, and, inferentially, of the law of interest, will not bear examination. Let us, then, seek the true laws of the distribution of the produce of labor into wages, rent, and interest. The proof that we have found them will be in their correlation—that they meet, and relate, and mutually bound each other.

With profits this inquiry has manifestly nothing to do. We want to find what it is that determines the division of their joint produce between land, labor, and capital; and profits is not a term that refers exclusively to any one of these three divisions. Of the three parts into which profits are divided by political economists—namely, compensation for risk, wages of superintendence, and return for the use of capital—the latter falls under the term interest, which includes all the returns for the use of capital, and excludes everything else; wages of superintendence falls under the term wages, which includes all returns for human exertion, and excludes everything else; and compensation for risk has no place whatever, as risk is eliminated when all the transactions of a community are taken together. I shall, therefore, consistently with the definitions of political economists, use the term interest as signifying that part of the produce which goes to capital.

To recapitulate:

Land, labor, and capital are the factors of production. The term land includes all natural opportunities or forces; the term labor, all human exertion; and the term capital, all wealth used to produce more wealth. In returns to these three factors is the whole produce distributed. That part which goes to land owners as payment for the use of natural opportunities is called rent; that part which constitutes the reward of human exertion is called wages; and that part which constitutes the return for the use of capital is called interest. These terms mutually exclude each other. The income of any individual may be made up from any one, two, or all three of these sources; but in the effort to discover the laws of distribution we must keep them separate.

Let me premise the inquiry which we are about to undertake by saying that the miscarriage of political economy, which I think has now been abundantly shown, can, it seems to me, be traced to the adoption of an erroneous standpoint. Living and making their observations in a state of society in which a capitalist generally rents land and hires labor, and thus seems to be the undertaker or first mover in production, the great cultivators of the science have been led to look upon capital as the prime factor in production, land as its instrument, and labor as its agent or tool. This is apparent on every page—in the form and course of their reasoning, in the character of their illustrations, and even in their choice of terms. Everywhere capital is the starting point, the capitalist the central figure. So far does this go that both Smith and Ricardo use the term natural wages to express the minimum upon which laborers can live; whereas, unless injustice is natural, all that the laborer produces should rather be held as his natural wages. This habit of looking upon capital as the employer of labor has led both to the theory that wages depend upon the relative abundance of capital, and to the theory that interest varies inversely with wages, while it has led away from truths that but for this habit would have been apparent. In short, the misstep which, so far as the great laws of distribution are concerned, has led political economy into the jungles, instead of upon the mountain tops, was taken when Adam Smith, in his first book, left the standpoint indicated in the sentence, "The produce of labor constitutes the natural recompense of wages of labor," to take that in which capital is considered as employing labor and paying wages.

But when we consider the origin and natural sequence of things, this order is reversed; and capital instead of first is last; instead of being the employer of labor, it is in reality employed by labor. There must be land before labor can be exerted, and labor must be exerted before capital can be produced. Capital is a result of labor, and is used by labor to assist it in further production. Labor is the active and initial force, and labor is therefore the employer of capital. Labor can be exerted only upon land, and it is from land that the matter which it transmutes into wealth must be drawn. Land therefore is the condition precedent, the field and material of labor. The natural order is land, labor, capital; and, instead of starting from capital as our initial point, we should start from land.

There is another thing to be observed. Capital is not a necessary factor in production. Labor exerted upon land can produce wealth without the aid of capital, and in the necessary genesis of things must so produce wealth before capital can exist. Therefore the law of rent and the law of wages must correlate each other and form a perfect whole without reference to the law of capital, as otherwise these laws would not fit the cases which can readily be imagined, and which to some degree actually exist, in which capital takes no part in production. And as capital is, as is often said, but stored-up labor, it is but a form of labor, a subdivision of the general term labor; and its law must be subordinate to, and independently correlate with, the law of wages, so as to fit cases in which the whole produce is divided between labor and capital, without any deduction for rent. To resort to the illustration before used: The division of the produce between land, labor and capital must be as it would be between Tom, Dick, and Harry, if Tom and Dick were the original partners, and Harry came in but as an assistant to and sharer with Dick.

II. RENT AND THE LAW OF RENT

The term rent, in its economic sense—that is, when used, as I am using it, to distinguish that part of the produce which accrues to the owners of land or other natural capabilities by virtue of their ownership—differs in meaning from the word rent as commonly used. In some respects this economic meaning is narrower than the common meaning; in other respects it is wider.

It is narrower in this: In common speech, we apply the word rent to payments for the use of buildings, machinery, fixtures, etc., as well as to payments for the use of land or other natural capabilities; and in speaking of the rent of a house or the rent of a farm, we do not separate the price for the use of the improvements from the price for the use of the bare land. But in the economic meaning of rent, payments for the use of any of the products of human exertion are excluded, and of the lumped payments for the use of houses, farms, etc., only that part is rent which constitutes the consideration for the use of the land—that part paid for the use of buildings or other improvements being properly interest, as it is a consideration for the use of capital.

It is wider in this: In common speech we speak of rent only when owner and user are distinct persons. But in the economic sense there is also rent where the same person is both owner and user. Where owner and user are thus the same person, whatever part of his income he might obtain by letting the land to another is rent, while the return for his labor and capital are that part of his income which they would yield him did he hire instead of owning the land. Rent is also expressed in a selling price. When land is purchased, the payment which is made for the ownership, or right to perpetual use, is rent commuted or capitalized. If I buy land for a small price and hold it until I can sell it for a large price, I have become rich, not by wages for my labor or by interest upon my capital, but by the increase of rent. Rent, in short, is the share in the wealth produced which the exclusive right to the use of natural capabilities gives to the owner. Wherever land has an exchange value there is rent in the economic meaning of the term. Wherever land having a value is used, either by owner or hirer, there is rent actual; wherever it is not used, but still has a value, there is rent potential. It is this capacity of yielding rent which gives value to land. Until its ownership will confer some advantage, land has no value.

Thus rent or land value does not arise from the productiveness or utility of land. It in no wise represents any help or advantage given to production, but simply the power of securing a part of the results of production. No matter what are its capabilities, land can yield no rent and have no value until some one is willing to give labor or the results of labor for the privilege of using it; and what any one will thus give depends not upon the capacity of the land, but upon its capacity as compared with that of land that can be had for nothing. I may have very rich land, but it will yield no rent and have no value so long as there is other land as good to be had without cost. But when this other land is appropriated, and the best land to be had for nothing is inferior, either in fertility, situation, or other quality, my land will begin to have a value and yield rent. And though the productiveness of my land may decrease, yet if the productiveness of the land to be had without charge decreases in greater proportion, the rent I can get, and consequently the value of my land, will steadily increase. Rent, in short, is the price of monopoly, arising from the reduction to individual ownership of natural elements which human exertion can neither produce nor increase.

If one man owned all the land accessible to any community, he could, of course, demand any price or condition for its use that he saw fit; and, as long as his ownership was acknowledged, the other members of the community would have but death or emigration as the alternative to submission to his terms. This has been the case in many communities; but in the modern form of society, the land, though generally reduced to individual ownership, is in the hands of too many different persons to permit the price which can be obtained for its use to be fixed by mere caprice or desire. While each individual owner tries to get all he can, there is a limit to what he can get, which constitutes the market price or market rent of the land, and which varies with different lands and at different times. The law, or relation, which, under these circumstances of free competition among all parties (the condition which in tracing out the principles of political economy is always to be assumed), determines what rent or price can be got by the owner, is styled the law of rent. This fixed with certainty, we have more than a starting point from which the laws which regulate wages and interest may be traced. For, as the distribution of wealth is a division, in ascertaining what fixes the share of the produce which goes as rent, we also ascertain what fixes the share which is left for wages, where there is no co-operation of capital; and what fixes the joint share left for wages and interest, where capital does co-operate in production.

Fortunately, as to the law of rent there is no necessity for discussion. Authority here coincides with common sense, and the accepted dictum of the current political economy has the self-evident character of a geometric axiom. This accepted law of rent, which John Stuart Mill denominates the *pons asinorum* of political economy, is sometimes styled "Ricardo's law of rent," from the fact that, although not the first to announce it, he first brought it prominently into notice. It is:

The rent of land is determined by the excess of its produce over that which the same application can secure from the least productive land in use.

This law, which of course applies to land used for other purposes than agriculture, and to all natural agencies, such as mines, fisheries, etc., has been exhaustively explained and illustrated by all the leading economists since Ricardo. But its mere statement has all the force of a self-evident proposition, for it is clear that the effect of competition is to make the lowest reward for which labor and capital will engage in production, the highest that they can claim; and hence to enable the owner of more productive land to appropriate in rent all the return above that required to recompense labor and capital at the ordinary rate—that is to say, what they can obtain upon the least productive land in use, or at the least productive point, where, of course, no rent is paid.

Perhaps it may conduce to a fuller understanding of the law of rent to put it in this form: The ownership of a natural agent of production will give the power of appropriating so much of the wealth produced by the exertion of labor and capital upon it as exceeds the return which the same application of labor and capital could secure in the least productive occupation in which they freely engage.

This, however, amounts to precisely the same thing, for there is no occupation in which labor and capital can engage which does not require the use of land; and, furthermore, the cultivation or other use of land will always be carried to as low a point of remuneration, all things considered, as is freely accepted in any other pursuit. Suppose, for instance, a community in which part of the labor and capital is devoted to agriculture and part to manufactures. The poorest land cultivated yields an average return which we will call 20, and 20 therefore will be the average return to labor and capital, as well in manufactures as in agriculture. Suppose that from some permanent cause the return in manufactures is now reduced to 15. Clearly, the labor and capital engaged in manufactures will turn to agriculture; and the process will not stop until, either by the extension of cultivation to inferior lands or to inferior points on the same land, or by an increase in the relative value of manufactured products, owing to the diminution of production—or, as a matter of fact, by both processes—the yield to labor and capital in both pursuits has, all things considered, been brought again to the same level, so that whatever be the final point of productiveness at which manufactures are still carried on, whether it be 18 or 17 or 16, cultivation will also be extended to that point. And, thus, to say that rent will be the excess in productiveness over the yield at the margin, or lowest point of cultivation, is the same thing as to say that it will be the excess of produce over what the same amount of labor and capital obtains in the least remunerative occupation.

The law of rent is, in fact, but a deduction from the law of competition, and amounts simply to the assertion that as wages and interest tend to a common level, all that part of the general production of wealth which exceeds what the labor and capital employed could have secured for themselves, if applied to the poorest natural agent in use, will go to land owners in the shape of rent. It rests, in the last analysis, upon the fundamental principle, which is to political economy what the attraction of gravitation is to physics—that men will seek to gratify their desires with the least exertion.

This, then, is the law of rent. Although many standard treatises follow too much the example of Ricardo, who seems to view it merely in its relation to agriculture, and in several places speaks of manufactures yielding no rent (when, in truth, manufactures and exchange yield the highest rents, as is evinced by the greater value of land in manufacturing and commercial cities), thus hiding the full importance of the law, yet, ever since the time of Ricardo, the law itself has been clearly apprehended and fully recognized. But not so its corollaries. Plain as they are, the accepted doctrine of wages (backed and fortified not only as has been hitherto explained, but by considerations whose enormous weight will be seen when the logical conclusion toward which we are tending is reached) has hitherto prevented their recognition. Yet, is it not as plain as the simplest geometrical demonstration, that the corollary of the law of rent is the law of wages, where the division of the produce is simply between rent and wages; or the law of wages and interest taken together, where the division is into rent, wages, and interest? Stated reversely, the law of rent is necessarily the law of wages and interest taken together, for it is the assertion, that no matter what the production which results from the application of labor and capital, these two factors will receive in wages and interest only such part of the produce as they could have produced on land free to them without the payment of rent—that is, the least productive land or point in use. For, if, of the produce, all over the amount which labor and capital could secure from land for which no rent is paid must go to land owners as rent, then all that can be claimed by labor and capital as wages and interest is the amount which they could have secured from land yielding no rent.

Or to put it in algebraic form:

As Produce=Rent+Wages+Interest,
Therefore, Produce—Rent=Wages+Interest.

Thus wages and interest do not depend upon the produce of labor and capital, but upon what is left after rent is taken out; or, upon the produce which they could obtain without paying rent—that is, from the poorest land in use. And hence, no matter what be the increase in productive power, if the increase in rent keeps pace with it, neither wages nor interest can increase.

The moment this simple relation is recognized, a flood of light streams in upon what was before inexplicable, and seemingly discordant facts range themselves under an obvious law. The increase of rent which goes on in progressive countries is at once seen to be the key which explains why wages and interest fail to increase with increase of productive power. For the wealth produced in every community is divided into two parts by what may be called the rent line, which is fixed by the margin of cultivation, or the return which labour and capital could obtain from such natural opportunities as are free to them without the payment of rent.

From the part of the produce below this line wages and interest must be paid. All that is above goes to the owners of land. Thus, where the value of land is low, there may be a small production of wealth, and yet a high rate of wages and interest, as we see in new countries. And, where the value of land is high, there may be a very large production of wealth, and yet a low rate of wages and interest, as we see in old countries. And, where productive power increases, as it is increasing in all progressive countries, wages and interest will be affected, not by the increase, but by the manner in which rent is affected. If the value of land increases proportionately, all the increased production will be swallowed up by rent, and wages and interest will remain as before. If the value of land increases in greater ratio than productive power, rent will swallow up even more than the increase; and while the produce of labor and capital will be much larger, wages and interest will fall. It is only when the value of land fails to increase as rapidly as productive power, that wages and interest can increase with the increase of productive power. All this is exemplified in actual fact.

PART FOUR

THE EFFECT OF INCREASE OF POPULATION UPON THE DISTRIBUTION OF WEALTH

THE MANNER in which increasing population advances rent, as explained and illustrated in current treatises, is that the increased demand for subsistence forces production to inferior soil or to inferior productive points. Thus, if, with a given population, the margin of cultivation is at 30, all lands of productive power over 30 will pay rent. If the population be doubled, an additional supply is required, which cannot be obtained without an extension of cultivation that will cause lands to yield rent that before yielded none. If the extension be to 20, then all the land between 20 and 30 will yield rent and have a value, and all land over 30 will yield increased rent and have increased value.

It is here that the Malthusian doctrine receives from the current elucidations of the theory of rent the support of which I spoke when enumerating the causes that have combined to give that doctrine an almost undisputed sway in current thought. According to the Malthusian theory, the pressure of population against subsistence becomes progressively harder as population increases, and although two hands come into the world with every new mouth, it becomes, to use the language of John Stuart Mill, harder and harder for the new hands to supply the new mouths. According to Ricardo's theory of rent, rent arises from the difference in productiveness of the lands in use, and as explained by Ricardo and the economists who have followed him, the advance in rents which, experience shows, accompanies increasing population, is caused by the inability of procuring more food except at a greater cost, which thus forces the margin of population to lower and lower points of production, commensurately increasing rent. Thus the two theories, as I have before explained, are made to harmonize and blend, the law of rent becoming but a special application of the more general law propounded by Malthus, and the advance of rents with increasing population a demonstration of its resistless operation. I refer to this incidentally, because it now lies in our way to see the misapprehension which has enlisted the doctrine of rent in the support of a theory to which it in reality gives no countenance. The Malthusian theory has been already disposed of, and the cumulative disproof which will prevent the recurrence of a lingering doubt will be given when it is shown, further on, that the phenomena attributed to the pressure of population against subsistence would, under existing conditions, manifest themselves were population to remain stationary.

The misapprehension to which I now refer, and which, to a proper understanding of the effect of increase of population upon the distribution of wealth, it is necessary to clear up, is the presumption, expressed or implied in all the current reasoning upon the subject of rent in connection with population, that the recourse to lower points of production involves a smaller aggregate produce in proportion to the labor expended; though that this is not always the case is clearly recognized in connection with agricultural improvements, which, to use the words of Mill, are considered "as a partial relaxation of the bonds which confine the increase of population." But it is not involved even where there is no advance in the arts, and the recourse to lower points of production is clearly the result of the increased demand of an increased population. For increased population, of itself, and without any advance in the arts, implies an increase in the productive power of labor. The labor of 100 men, other things being equal, will produce much more than one hundred times as much as the labor of one man, and the labor of 1,000 men much more than ten times as much as the labor of 100 men; and, so, with every additional pair of hands which increasing population brings, there is a more than proportionate addition to the productive power of labor. Thus, with an increasing population, there may be a recourse to lower natural powers of production, not only without any diminution in the average production of wealth as compared to labor, but without any diminution at the lowest point. If population be doubled, land of but 20 productiveness may yield to the same amount of labor as much as land of 30 productiveness could before yield. For it must not be forgotten (what often *is* forgotten) that the productiveness either of land or labor is not to be measured in any one thing, but in all desired things. A settler and his family may raise as much corn on land a hundred miles away from the nearest habitation as they could raise were their land in the center of a populous district. But in the populous district they could obtain with the same labor as good a living from much poorer land, or from land of equal quality could make as good a living after paying a high rent, because in the midst of a large population their labor would have become more effective; not, perhaps, in the production of corn, but in the production of wealth generally—or the obtaining of all the commodities and services which are the real object of their labor.

But even where there is a diminution in the productiveness of labor at the lowest point—that is to say, where the increasing demand for wealth has driven production to a lower point of natural productiveness than the addition to the power of labor from increasing population suffices to make up for—it does not follow that the aggregate production, as compared with the aggregate labor, has been lessened.

Let us suppose land of diminishing qualities. The best would naturally be settled first, and as population increased production would take in the next lower quality, and so on. But, as the increase of population, by permitting greater economies, adds to the effectiveness of labor, the cause which brought each quality of land successively into cultivation would at the same time increase the amount of wealth that the same quantity of labor could produce from it. But it would also do more than this—it would increase the power of producing wealth on all the superior lands already in cultivation. If the relations of quantity and quality were such that increasing population added to the effectiveness of labor faster than it compelled a resort to less productive qualities of land, though the margin of cultivation would fall and rent would rise, the minimum return to labor would increase. That is to say, though wages as a proportion would fall, wages as a quantity would rise. The average production of wealth would increase. If the relations were such that the increasing effectiveness of labor just compensated for the diminishing productiveness of the land as it was called into use, the effect of increasing population would be to increase rent by lowering the margin of cultivation without reducing wages as a quantity, and to increase the average production. If we now suppose population still increasing, but, between the poorest quality of land in use and the next lower quality, to be a difference so great that the increased power of labor which comes with the increased population that brings it into cultivation cannot compensate for it—the minimum return to labor will be reduced, and with the rise of rents, wages will fall, not only as a proportion, but as a quantity. But unless the descent in the quality of land is far more precipitous than we can well imagine, or than, I think, ever exists, the average production will still be increased, for the increased effectiveness which comes by reason of the increased population that compels resort to the inferior quality of land attaches to all labor, and the gain on the superior qualities of land will more than compensate for the diminished production on the quality last brought in. The aggregate wealth production, as compared with the aggregate expenditure of labor, will be greater, though its distribution will be more unequal.

Thus, increase of population, as it operates to extend production to lower natural levels, operates to increase rent and reduce wages as a proportion, and may or may not reduce wages as a quantity; while it seldom can, and probably never does, reduce the aggregate production of wealth as compared with the aggregate expenditure of labor, but on the contrary increases, and frequently largely increases it.

But while the increase of population thus increases rent by lowering the margin of cultivation, it is a mistake to look upon this as the only mode by which rent advances as population grows. Increasing population increases rent, without reducing the margin of cultivation; and notwithstanding the dicta of such writers as McCulloch, who assert that rent would not arise were there an unbounded extent of equally good land, increases it without reference to the natural qualities of land, for the increased powers of co-operation and exchange which come with increased population are equivalent to—nay, I think we can say without metaphor, that they give—an increased capacity to land.

I do not mean to say merely that, like an improvement in the methods or tools of production, the increased power which comes with increased population gives to the same labor an increased result, which is equivalent to an increase in the natural powers of land; but that it brings out a superior power in labor, which is localized on land—which attaches not to labor generally, but only to labor exerted on particular land; and which thus inheres in the land as much as any qualities of soil, climate, mineral deposit, or natural situation, and passes, as they do, with the possession of the land.

An improvement in the method of cultivation which, with the same outlay, will give two crops a year in place of one, or an improvement in tools and machinery which will double the result of labor, will manifestly, on a particular piece of ground, have the same effect on the produce as a doubling of the fertility of the land. But the difference is in this respect—the improvement in method or in tools can be utilized on any land; but the improvement in fertility can be utilized only on the particular land to which it applies. Now, in large part, the increased productiveness of labor which arises from increased population can be utilized only on particular land, and on particular land in greatly varying degrees.

Here, let us imagine, is an unbounded savannah, stretching off in unbroken sameness of grass and flower, tree and rill, till the traveler tires of the monotony. Along comes the wagon of the first immigrant. Where to settle he cannot tell—every acre seems as good as every other acre. As to wood, as to water, as to fertility, as to situation, there is absolutely no choice, and he is perplexed by the embarrassment of richness. Tired out with the search for one place that is better than another, he stops—somewhere, anywhere—and starts to make himself a home. The soil is virgin and rich, game is abundant, the streams flash with the finest trout. Nature is at her very best. He has what, were he in a populous district, would make him rich; but he is very poor. To say nothing of the mental craving, which would lead him to welcome the sorriest stranger, he labors under all the material disadvantages of solitude. He can get no temporary assistance for any work that requires a greater union of strength than that afforded by his own family, or by such help as he can permanently keep. Though he has cattle, he cannot often have fresh meat, for to get a beefsteak he must kill a bullock. He must be his own blacksmith, wagonmaker, carpenter, and cobbler—in short, a "jack of all trades and master of none." He cannot have his children schooled, for, to do so, he must himself pay and maintain a teacher. Such things as he cannot produce himself, he must buy in quantities and keep on hand, or else go without, for he cannot be constantly leaving his work and making a long journey to the verge of civilization; and when forced to do so, the getting of a vial of medicine or the replacement of a broken auger may cost him the labor of himself and horses for days. Under such circumstances, though nature is prolific, the man is poor. It is an easy matter for him to get enough to eat; but beyond this, his labor will suffice to satisfy only the simplest wants in the rudest way.

Soon there comes another immigrant. Although every quarter section of the boundless plain is as good as every other quarter section, he is not beset by any embarrassment as to where to settle. Though the land is the same, there is one place that is clearly better for him than any other place, and that is where there is already a settler and he may have a neighbor. He settles by the side of the first comer, whose condition is at once greatly improved, and to whom many things are now possible that were before impossible, for two men may help each other to do things that one man could never do.

Another immigrant comes, and, guided by the same attraction, settles where there are already two. Another, and another, until around our first comer there are a score of neighbors. Labor has now an effectiveness which, in the solitary state, it could not approach. If heavy work is to be done, the settlers have a log-rolling, and together accomplish in a day what singly would require years. When one kills a bullock, the others take part of it, returning when they kill, and thus they have fresh meat all the time. Together they hire a schoolmaster, and the children of each are taught for a fractional part of what similar teaching would have cost the first settler. It becomes a comparatively easy matter to send to the nearest town, for some one is always going. But there is less need for such journeys. A blacksmith and a wheelwright soon set up shops, and our settler can have his tools repaired for a small part of the labor it formerly cost him. A store is opened and he can get what he wants as he wants it; a post-office, soon added, gives him regular communication with the rest of the world. Then come a cobbler, a carpenter, a harness maker, a doctor; and a little church soon arises. Satisfactions become possible that in the solitary state were impossible. There are gratifications for the social and the intellectual nature—for that part of the man that rises above the animal. The power of sympathy, the sense of companionship, the emulation of comparison and contrast, open a wider, and fuller, and more varied life. In rejoicing, there are others to rejoice; in sorrow, the mourners do not mourn alone. There are husking bees, and apple parings, and quilting parties. Though the ballroom be unplastered and the orchestra but a fiddle, the notes of the magician are yet in the strain, and Cupid dances with the dancers. At the wedding, there are others to admire and enjoy; in the house of death, there are watchers; by the open grave, stands human sympathy to sustain the mourners. Occasionally, comes a straggling lecturer to open up glimpses of the world of science, of literature, or of art; in election times, come stump speakers, and the citizen rises to a sense of dignity and power, as the cause of empires is tried before him in the struggle of John Doe and Richard Roe for his support and vote. And, by and by, comes the circus, talked of months before, and opening to children whose horizon has been the prairie, all the realms of the imagination—princes and princesses of fairy tale, mail-clad crusaders and turbaned Moors, Cinderella's fairy coach, and the giants of nursery lore; lions such as crouched before Daniel, or in circling Roman amphitheater tore the saints of God; ostriches who recall the sandy deserts; camels such as stood around when the wicked brethren raised Joseph from the well and sold him into bondage; elephants such as crossed the Alps with Hannibal, or felt the sword of the Maccabees; and glorious music that thrills and builds in the chambers of the mind as rose the sunny dome of Kubla Khan.

Go to our settler now, and say to him: "You have so many fruit trees which you planted; so much fencing, such a well, a barn, a house—in short, you have by your labor added so much value to this farm. Your land itself is not quite so good. You have been cropping it, and by and by it will need manure. I will give you the full value of all your improvements if you will give it to me, and go again with your family beyond the verge of settlement." He would laugh at you. His land yields no more wheat or potatoes than before, but it does yield far more of all the necessaries and comforts of life. His labor upon it will bring no heavier crops, and, we will suppose, no more valuable crops, but it will bring far more of all the other things for which men work. The presence of other settlers—the increase of population—has added to the productiveness, in these things, of labor bestowed upon it, and this added productiveness gives it a superiority over land of equal natural quality where there are as yet no settlers. If no land remains to be taken up, except such as is as far removed from population as was our settler's land when he first went upon it, the value or rent of this land will be measured by the whole of this added capability. If, however, as we have supposed, there is a continuous stretch of equal land, over which population is now spreading, it will not be necessary for the new settler to go into the wilderness, as did the first. He will settle just beyond the other settlers, and will get the advantage of proximity to them. The value or rent of our settler's land will thus depend on the advantage which it has, from being at the center of population, over that on the verge. In the one case, the margin of production will remain as before; in the other, the margin of production will be raised.

Population still continues to increase, and as it increases so do the economies which its increase permits, and which in effect add to the productiveness of the land. Our first settler's land, being the center of population, the store, the blacksmith's forge, the wheelwright's shop, are set up on it, or on its margin, where soon arises a village, which rapidly grows into a town, the center of exchanges for the people of the whole district. With no greater agricultural productiveness than it had at first, this land now begins to develop a productiveness of a higher kind. To labor expended in raising corn, or wheat, or potatoes, it will yield no more of those things than at first; but to labor expended in the subdivided branches of production which require proximity to other producers, and, especially, to labor expended in that final part of production, which consists in distribution, it will yield much larger returns. The wheatgrower may go further on, and find land on which his labor will produce as much wheat, and nearly as much wealth; but the artisan, the manufacturer, the storekeeper, the professional man, find that their labor expended here, at the center of exchanges, will yield them much more than if expended even at a little distance away from it; and this excess of productiveness for such purposes the land owner can claim just as he could an excess in its wheat-producing power. And so our settler is able to sell in building lots a few of his acres for prices which it would not bring for wheat-growing if its fertility had been multiplied many times. With the proceeds, he builds himself a fine house, and furnishes it handsomely. That is to say, to reduce the transaction to its lowest terms, the people who wish to use the land build and furnish the house for him, on condition that he will let them avail themselves of the superior productiveness which the increase of population has given the land.

Population still keeps on increasing, giving greater and greater utility to the land, and more and more wealth to its owner. The town has grown into a city—a St. Louis, a Chicago, or a San Francisco—and still it grows. Production is here carried on upon a great scale, with the best machinery and the most favorable facilities; the division of labor becomes extremely minute, wonderfully multiplying efficiency; exchanges are of such volume and rapidity that they are made with the minimum of friction and loss. Here is the heart, the brain, of the vast social organism that has grown up from the germ of the first settlement; here has developed one of the great ganglions of the human world. Hither run all roads, hither set all currents, through all the vast regions round about. Here, if you have anything to sell, is the market; here, if you have anything to buy, is the largest and the choicest stock. Here intellectual activity is gathered into a focus, and here springs that stimulus which is born of the collision of mind with mind. Here are the great libraries, the storehouses and granaries of knowledge, the learned professors, the famous specialists. Here are museums and art galleries, collections of philosophical apparatus, and all things rare, and valuable, and best of their kind. Here come great actors, and orators, and singers, from all over the world. Here, in short, is a center of human life, in all its varied manifestations.

So enormous are the advantages which this land now offers for the application of labor, that instead of one man with a span of horses scratching over acres, you may count in places thousands of workers to the acre, working tier on tier, on floors raised one above the other, five, six, seven, and eight stories from the ground, while underneath the surface of the earth engines are throbbing with pulsations that exert the force of thousands of horses.

All these advantages attach to the land; it is on this land and no other that they can be utilized, for here is the center of population—the focus of exchanges, the market place and workshop of the highest forms of industry. The productive powers which density of population has attached to this land are equivalent to the multiplication of its original fertility by the hundred fold and the thousand fold. And rent, which measures the difference between this added productiveness and that of the least productive land in use, has increased accordingly. Our settler, or whoever has succeeded to his right to the land, is now a millionaire. Like another Rip Van Winkle, he may have lain down and slept; still he is rich—not from anything he has done, but from the increase of population. There are lots from which for every foot of frontage the owner may draw more than an average mechanic can earn; there are lots that will sell for more than would suffice to pave them with gold coin. In the principal streets are towering buildings, of granite, marble, iron, and plate glass, finished in the most expensive style, replete with every convenience. Yet they are not worth as much as the land upon which they rest—the same land, in nothing changed, which when our first settler came upon it had no value at all.

That this is the way in which the increase of population powerfully acts in increasing rent, whoever, in a progressive country, will look around him, may see for himself. The process is going on under his eyes. The increasing difference in the productiveness of the land in use, which causes an increasing rise in rent, results not so much from the necessities of increased population compelling the resort to inferior land, as from the increased productiveness which increased population gives to the lands already in use. The most valuable lands on the globe, the lands which yield the highest rent, are not lands of surpassing natural fertility, but lands to which a surpassing utility has been given by the increase of population.

The increase of productiveness or utility which increase of population gives to certain lands, in the way to which I have been calling attention, attaches, as it were, to the mere quality of extension. The valuable quality of land that has become a center of population is its superficial capacity—it makes no difference whether it is fertile, alluvial soil like that of Philadelphia; rich bottom land like that of New Orleans; a filled-in marsh like that of St. Petersburg, or a sandy waste like the greater part of San Francisco.

And where value seems to arise from superior natural qualities, such as deep water and good anchorage, rich deposits of coal and iron, or heavy timber, observation also shows that these superior qualities are brought out, rendered tangible, by population. The coal and iron fields of Pennsylvania, that today are worth enormous sums, were fifty years ago valueless. What is the efficient cause of the difference? Simply the difference in population. The coal and iron beds of Wyoming and Montana, which today are valueless, will, in fifty years from now, be worth millions on millions, simply because, in the meantime, population will have greatly increased.

It is a well-provisioned ship, this on which we sail through space. If the bread and beef above decks seem to grow scarce, we but open a hatch and there is a new supply, of which before we never dreamed. And very great command over the services of others comes to those who as the hatches are opened are permitted to say, "This is mine!"

To recapitulate: The effect of increasing population upon the distribution of wealth is to increase rent, and consequently to diminish the proportion of the produce which goes to capital and labor, in two ways: First, By lowering the margin of cultivation. Second, By bringing out in land special capabilities otherwise latent, and by attaching special capabilities to particular lands.

I am disposed to think that the latter mode, to which little attention has been given by political economists, is really the more important.

PART FIVE

THE PERSISTENCE OF POVERTY AMID ADVANCING WEALTH

THE GREAT PROBLEM, of which recurring seasons of industrial depression are but peculiar manifestations, is now, I think, fully solved, and the social phenomena which all over the civilized world appall the philanthropist and perplex the statesman, which hang with clouds the future of the most advanced races, and suggest doubts of the reality and ultimate goal of what we have fondly called progress, are now explained.

The reason why, in spite of the increase of productive power, wages constantly tend to a minimum which will give but a bare living, is that, with increase in productive power, rent tends to even greater increase, thus producing a constant tendency to the forcing down of wages.

In every direction, the direct tendency of advancing civilization is to increase the power of human labor to satisfy human desires—to extirpate poverty, and to banish want and the fear of want. All the things in which progress consists, all the conditions which progressive communities are striving for, have for their direct and natural result the improvement of the material (and consequently the intellectual and moral) condition of all within their influence. The growth of population, the increase and extension of exchanges, the discoveries of science, the march of invention, the spread of education, the improvement of government, and the amelioration of manners, considered as material forces, have all a direct tendency to increase the productive power of labor—not of some labor, but of all labor; not in some departments of industry, but in all departments of industry; for the law of the production of wealth in society is the law of "each for all, and all for each."

But labor cannot reap the benefits which advancing civilization thus brings, because they are intercepted. Land being necessary to labor, and being reduced to private ownership, every increase in the productive power of labor but increases rent—the price that labor must pay for the opportunity to utilize its powers; and thus all the advantages gained by the march of progress go to the owners of land, and wages do not increase. Wages cannot increase; for the greater the earnings of labor the greater the price that labor must pay out of its earnings for the opportunity to make any earnings at all. The mere laborer has thus no more interest in the general advance of productive power than the Cuban slave has in advance in the price of sugar. And just as an advance in the price of sugar may make the condition of the slave worse, by inducing the master to drive him harder, so may the condition of the free laborer be positively, as well as relatively, changed for the worse by the increase in the productive power of his labor. For, begotten of the continuous advance of rents, arises a speculative tendency which discounts the effect of future improvements by a still further advance of rent, and thus tends, where this has not occurred from the normal advance of rent, to drive wages down to the slave point—the point at which the laborer can just live.

And thus robbed of all the benefits of the increase in productive power, labor is exposed to certain effects of advancing civilization which, without the advantages that naturally accompany them, are positive evils, and of themselves tend to reduce the free laborer to the helpless and degraded condition of the slave.

For all improvements which add to productive power as civilization advances consist in, or necessitate, a still further subdivision of labor, and the efficiency of the whole body of laborers is increased at the expense of the independence of the constituents. The individual laborer acquires knowledge of and skill in but an infinitesimal part of the varied processes which are required to supply even the commonest wants. The aggregate produce of the labor of a savage tribe is small, but each member is capable of an independent life. He can build his own habitation, hew out or stitch together his own canoe, make his own clothing, manufacture his own weapons, snares, tools, and ornaments. He has all the knowledge of nature possessed by his tribe—knows what vegetable productions are fit for food, and where they may be found; knows the habits and resorts of beasts, birds, fishes, and insects; can pilot himself by the sun or the stars, by the turning of blossoms or the mosses on the trees; is, in short, capable of supplying all his wants. He may be cut off from his fellows and still live; and thus possesses an independent power which makes him a free contracting party in his relations to the community of which he is a member.

Compare with this savage the laborer in the lowest ranks of civilized society, whose life is spent in producing but one thing, or oftener but the infinitesimal part of one thing, out of the multiplicity of things that constitute the wealth of society and go to supply even the most primitive wants; who not only cannot make even the tools required for his work, but often works with tools that he does not own, and can never hope to own. Compelled to even closer and more continuous labor than the savage, and gaining by it no more than the savage gets—the mere necessaries of life—he loses the independence of the savage. He is not only unable to apply his own powers to the direct satisfaction of his own wants, but, without the concurrence of many others, he is unable to apply them indirectly to the satisfaction of his wants. He is a mere link in an enormous chain of producers and consumers, helpless to separate himself, and helpless to move, except as they move. The worse his position in society, the more dependent is he on society; the more utterly unable does he become to do anything for himself. The very power of exerting his labor for the satisfaction of his wants passes from his own control, and may be taken away or restored by the actions of others, or by general causes over which he has no more influence than he has over the motions of the solar system. The primeval curse comes to be looked upon as a boon, and men think, and talk, and clamor, and legislate as though monotonous manual labor in itself were a good and not an evil, an end and not a means. Under such circumstances, the man loses the essential quality of manhood—the godlike power of modifying and controlling conditions. He becomes a slave, a machine, a commodity—a thing, in some respects, lower than the animal.

I am no sentimental admirer of the savage state. I do not get my ideas of the untutored children of nature from Rousseau, or Chateaubriand, or Cooper. I am conscious of its material and mental poverty, and its low and narrow range. I believe that civilization is not only the natural destiny of man, but the enfranchisement, elevation, and refinement of all his powers, and think that it is only in such moods as may lead him to envy the cud-chewing cattle, that a man who is free to the advantages of civilization could look with regret upon the savage state. But, nevertheless, I think no one who will open his eyes to the facts can resist the conclusion that there are in the heart of our civilization large classes with whom the veriest savage could not afford to exchange. It is my deliberate opinion that if, standing on the threshold of being, one were given the choice of entering life as a Tierra del Fuegan, a black fellow of Australia, an Esquimaux in the Arctic Circle, or among the lowest classes in such a highly civilized country as Great Britain, he would make infinitely the better choice in selecting the lot of the savage. For those classes who in the midst of wealth are condemned to want suffer all the privations of the savage, without his sense of personal freedom; they are condemned to more than his narrowness and littleness, without opportunity for the growth of his rude virtues; if their horizon is wider, it is but to reveal blessings that they cannot enjoy.

There are some to whom this may seem like exaggeration, but it is only because they have never suffered themselves to realize the true condition of those classes upon whom the iron heel of modern civilization presses with full force. As De Tocqueville observes, in one of his letters to Mme. Swetchine, "we so soon become used to the thought of want that we do not feel that an evil which grows greater to the sufferer the longer it lasts becomes less to the observer by the very fact of its duration;"

and perhaps the best proof of the justice of this observation is that in cities where there exists a pauper class and a criminal class, where young girls shiver as they sew for bread, and tattered and barefooted children make a home in the streets, money is regularly raised to send missionaries to the heathen! Send missionaries to the heathen! It would be laughable if it were not so sad. Baal no longer stretches forth his hideous, sloping arms; but in Christian lands mothers slay their infants for a burial fee! And I challenge the production from any authentic accounts of savage life of such descriptions of degradation as are to be found in official documents of highly civilized countries—in reports of Sanitary Commissioners and of inquiries into the condition of the laboring poor.

The simple theory which I have outlined (if indeed it can be called a theory which is but the recognition of the most obvious relations) explains this conjunction of poverty with wealth, of low wages with high productive power, of degradation amid enlightenment, of virtual slavery in political liberty. It harmonizes, as results flowing from a general and inexorable law, facts otherwise most perplexing, and exhibits the sequence and relation between phenomena that without reference to it are diverse and contradictory. It explains why interest and wages are higher in new than in older communities, though the average, as well as the aggregate, production of wealth is less. It explains why improvements which increase the productive power of labor and capital increase the reward of neither. It explains what is commonly called the conflict between labor and capital, while proving the real harmony of interest between them. It cuts the last inch of ground from under the fallacies of protection, while showing why free trade fails to benefit permanently the working classes. It explains why want increases with abundance, and wealth tends to greater and greater aggregations. It explains the periodically recurring depressions of industry without recourse either to the absurdity of "overproduction" or the absurdity of "overconsumption." It explains the enforced idleness of large numbers of would-be producers, which wastes the productive force of advanced communities, without the absurd assumption that there is too little work to do or that there are too many to do it. It explains the ill effects upon the laboring classes which often follow the introduction of machinery, without denying the natural advantages which the use of machinery gives. It explains the vice and misery which show themselves amid dense population, without attributing to the laws of the All-Wise and All-Beneficent defects which belong only to the short-sighted and selfish enactments of men.

This explanation is in accordance with all the facts.

Look over the world today. In countries the most widely differing—under conditions the most diverse as to government, as to industries, as to tariffs, as to currency—you will find distress among the working classes;

but everywhere that you thus find distress and destitution in the midst of wealth you will find that the land is monopolized; that instead of being treated as the common property of the whole people, it is treated as the private property of individuals; that, for its use by labor, large revenues are extorted from the earnings of labor. Look over the world today, comparing different countries with each other, and you will see that it is not the abundance of capital or the productiveness of labor that makes wages high or low; but the extent to which the monopolizers of land can, in rent, levy tribute upon the earnings of labor. Is it not a notorious fact, known to the most ignorant, that new countries, where the aggregate wealth is small, but where land is cheap, are always better countries for the laboring classes than the rich countries, where land is dear? Wherever you find land relatively low, will you not find wages relatively high? And wherever land is high, will you not find wages low? As land increases in value, poverty deepens and pauperism appears. In the new settlements, where land is cheap, you will find no beggars, and the inequalities in condition are very slight. In the great cities, where land is so valuable that it is measured by the foot, you will find the extremes of poverty and of luxury. And this disparity in condition between the two extremes of the social scale may always be measured by the price of land. Land in New York is more valuable than in San Francisco; and in New York, the San Franciscan may see squalor and misery that will make him stand aghast. Land is more valuable in London than in New York; and in London, there is squalor and destitution worse than that of New York.

Compare the same country in different times, and the same relation is obvious. As the result of much investigation, Hallam says he is convinced that the wages of manual labor were greater in amount in England during the middle ages than they are now. Whether this is so or not, it is evident that they could not have been much, if any, less. The enormous increase in the efficiency of labor, which even in agriculture is estimated at seven or eight hundred per cent., and in many branches of industry is almost incalculable, has only added to rent. The rent of agricultural land in England is now, according to Professor Rogers, 120 times as great, measured in money, as it was five hundred years ago, and 14 times as great, measured in wheat; while in the rent of building land, and mineral land, the advance has been enormously greater. According to the estimate of Professor Fawcett, the capitalized rental value of the land of England now amounts to £4,500,000,000, or $21,870,000,000—that is to say, a few thousand of the people of England hold a lien upon the labor of the rest, the capitalized value of which is more than twice as great as, at the average price of Southern negroes in 1860, would be the value of her whole population were they slaves.

In Belgium and Flanders, in France and Germany, the rent and selling price of agricultural land have doubled within the last thirty years. In short, increased power of production has everywhere added to the value of land; nowhere has it added to the value of labor; for though actual wages may in some places have somewhat risen, the rise is clearly attributable to other causes. In more places they have fallen—that is, where it has been possible for them to fall—for there is a minimum below which laborers cannot keep up their numbers. And, everywhere, wages, as a proportion of the produce, have decreased.

How the Black Death brought about the great rise of wages in England in the Fourteenth Century is clearly discernible, in the efforts of the land holders to regulate wages by statute. That that awful reduction in population, instead of increasing, really reduced the effective power of labor, there can be no doubt; but the lessening of competition for land still more greatly reduced rent, and wages advanced so largely that force and penal laws were called in to keep them down. The reverse effect followed the monopolization of land that went on in England during the reign of Henry VIII, in the inclosure of commons and the division of the church lands between the panders and parasites who were thus enabled to found noble families. The result was the same as that to which a speculative increase in land values tends. According to Malthus (who, in his *Principles of Political Economy,* mentions the fact without connecting it with land tenures), in the reign of Henry VII, half a bushel of wheat would purchase but little more than a day's common labor, but in the latter part of the reign of Elizabeth, half a bushel of wheat would purchase three days' common labor. I can hardly believe that the reduction in wages could have been so great as this comparison would indicate; but that there was a reduction in common wages, and great distress among the laboring classes, is evident from the complaints of "sturdy vagrants" and the statutes made to suppress them. The rapid monopolization of the land, the carrying of the speculative rent line beyond the normal rent line, produced tramps and paupers, just as like effects from like causes have lately been evident in the United States.

"Land which went heretofore for twenty or forty pounds a year," said Hugh Latimer, "now is let for fifty or a hundred. My father was a yeoman, and had no lands of his own; only he had a farm at a rent of three or four pounds by the year at the uttermost, and thereupon he tilled so much as kept half a dozen men. He had walk for a hundred sheep, and my mother milked thirty kine; he was able and did find the King a harness with himself and his horse when he came to the place that he should receive the King's wages. I can remember that I buckled his harness when he went to Blackheath Field. He kept me to school; he married my sisters with five pounds apiece, so that he brought them up in godliness and fear of God. He kept hospitality for his neighbors and some alms he gave to the poor. And all this he did of the same farm, where he that now hath it payeth sixteen pounds rent or more by year, and is not able to do anything for his Prince, for himself, nor his children, nor to give a cup of drink to the poor."

"In this way," said Sir Thomas More, referring to the ejectment of small farmers which characterized this advance of rent, "it comes to pass that these poor wretches, men, women, husbands, orphans, widows, parents with little children, householders greater in number than in wealth, all of these emigrate from their native fields, without knowing where to go."

And so from the stuff of the Latimers and Mores—from the sturdy spirit that amid the flames of the Oxford stake cried, "Play the man, Master Ridley!" and the mingled strength and sweetness that neither prosperity could taint nor the ax of the executioner abash—were evolved thieves and vagrants, the mass of criminality and pauperism that still blights the innermost petals and preys a gnawing worm at the root of England's rose.

But it were as well to cite historical illustrations of the attraction of gravitation. The principle is as universal and as obvious. That rent *must* reduce wages, is as clear as that the greater the subtractor the less the remainder. That rent *does* reduce wages, any one, wherever situated, can see by merely looking around him.

There is no mystery as to the cause which so suddenly and so largely raised wages in California in 1849, and in Australia in 1852. It was the discovery of the placer mines in unappropriated land to which labor was free that raised the wages of cooks in San Francisco restaurants to $500 a month, and left ships to rot in the harbor without officers or crew until their owners would consent to pay rates that in any other part of the globe seemed fabulous. Had these mines been on appropriated land, or had they been immediately monopolized so that rent could have arisen, it would have been land values that would have leaped upward, not wages. The Comstock lode has been richer than the placers, but the Comstock lode was readily monopolized, and it is only by virtue of the strong organization of the Miners' Association and the fears of the damage which it might do, that enables men to get $4 a day for parboiling themselves two thousand feet underground, where the air that they breathe must be pumped down to them. The wealth of the Comstock lode has added to rent. The selling price of these mines runs up into hundreds of millions, and it has produced individual fortunes whose monthly returns can be estimated only in hundreds of thousands, if not in millions. Nor is there any mystery about the cause which has operated to reduce wages in California from the maximum of the early days to very nearly a level with wages in the Eastern States, and that is still operating to reduce them. The productiveness of labor has not decreased, on the contrary it has increased, as I have before shown; but, out of what it produces labor has now to pay rent. As the placer deposits were exhausted, labor had to resort to the deeper mines and to agricultural land, but monopolization of these being permitted, men now walk the streets of San Francisco ready to go to work for almost anything—for natural opportunities are now no longer free to labor.

The truth is self-evident. Put to any one capable of consecutive thought this question:

"Suppose there should arise from the English Channel or the German Ocean a No-man's land on which common labor to an unlimited amount should be able to make ten shillings a day and which should remain unappropriated and of free access, like the commons which once comprised so large a part of English soil. What would be the effect upon wages in England?"

He would at once tell you that common wages throughout England must soon increase to ten shillings a day.

And in response to another question, "What would be the effect on rents?" he would at a moment's reflection say that rents must necessarily fall; and if he thought out the next step he would tell you that all this would happen without any very large part of English labor being diverted to the new natural opportunities, or the forms and direction of industry being much changed; only that kind of production being abandoned which now yields to labor and to landlord together less than labor could secure on the new opportunities. The great rise in wages would be at the expense of rent.

Take now the same man or another—some hard-headed business man, who has no theories, but knows how to make money. Say to him: "Here is a little village; in ten years it will be a great city—in ten years the railroad will have taken the place of the stage coach, the electric light of the candle; it will abound with all the machinery and improvements that so enormously multiply the effective power of labor. Will, in ten years, interest be any higher?"

He will tell you, "No!"

"Will the wages of common labor be any higher; will it be easier for a man who has nothing but his labor to make an independent living?"

He will tell you, "No; the wages of common labor will not be any higher; on the contrary, all the chances are that they will be lower; it will not be easier for the mere laborer to make an independent living; the chances are that it will be harder."

"What, then, will be higher?"

"Rent; the value of land. Go, get yourself a piece of ground, and hold possession."

And if, under such circumstances, you take his advice, you need do nothing more. You may sit down and smoke your pipe; you may lie around like the lazzaroni of Naples or the leperos of Mexico; you may go up in a balloon, or down a hole in the ground; and without doing one stroke of work, without adding one iota to the wealth of the community, in ten years you will be rich! In the new city you may have a luxurious mansion; but among its public buildings will be an almshouse.

In all our long investigation we have been advancing to this simple truth: That as land is necessary to the exertion of labor in the production of wealth, to command the land which is necessary to labor, is to command all the fruits of labor save enough to enable labor to exist. We have been advancing as through an enemy's country, in which every step must be secured, every position fortified, and every by-path explored; for this simple truth, in its application to social and political problems, is hid from the great masses of men partly by its very simplicity, and in greater part by widespread fallacies and erroneous habits of thought which lead them to look in every direction but the right one for an explanation of the evils which oppress and threaten the civilized world. And back of these elaborate fallacies and misleading theories is an active, energetic power, a power that in every country, be its political forms what they may, writes laws and molds thought—the power of a vast and dominant pecuniary interest.

But so simple and so clear is this truth, that to see it fully once is always to recognize it. There are pictures which, though looked at again and again, present only a confused labyrinth of lines or scroll work—a landscape, trees, or something of the kind—until once the attention is called to the fact that these things make up a face or a figure. This relation, once recognized, is always afterward clear. It is so in this case. In the light of this truth all social facts group themselves in an orderly relation, and the most diverse phenomena are seen to spring from one great principle. It is not in the relations of capital and labor; it is not in the pressure of population against subsistence, that an explanation of the unequal development of our civilization is to be found. The great cause of inequality in the distribution of wealth is inequality in the ownership of land. The ownership of land is the great fundamental fact which ultimately determines the social, the political, and consequently the intellectual and moral condition of a people. And it must be so. For land is the habitation of man, the storehouse upon which he must draw for all his needs, the material to which his labor must be applied for the supply of all his desires; for even the products of the sea cannot be taken, the light of the sun enjoyed, or any of the forces of nature utilized, without the use of land or its products. On the land we are born, from it we live, to it we return again—children of the soil as truly as is the blade of grass or the flower of the field. Take away from man all that belongs to land, and he is but a disembodied spirit. Material progress cannot rid us of our dependence upon land; it can but add to the power of producing wealth from land; and hence, when land is monopolized, it might go on to infinity without increasing wages or improving the condition of those who have but their labor. It can but add to the value of land and the power which its possession gives. Everywhere, in all times, among all peoples, the possession of land is the base of aristocracy, the foundation of great fortunes, the source of power. As said the Brahmins, ages ago—

To whomsoever the soil at any time belongs, to him belong the fruits of it. White parasols and elephants mad with pride are the flowers of a grant of land.

PART SIX

THE TRUE REMEDY

WE HAVE TRACED the unequal distribution of wealth which is the curse and menace of modern civilization to the institution of private property in land. We have seen that so long as this institution exists no increase in productive power can permanently benefit the masses; but, on the contrary, must tend still further to depress their condition. We have examined all the remedies, short of the abolition of private property in land, which are currently relied on or proposed for the relief of poverty and the better distribution of wealth, and have found them all inefficacious or impracticable.

There is but one way to remove an evil—and that is, to remove its cause. Poverty deepens as wealth increases, and wages are forced down while productive power grows, because land, which is the source of all wealth and the field of all labor, is monopolized. To extirpate poverty, to make wages what justice commands they should be, the full earnings of the laborer, we must therefore substitute for the individual ownership of land a common ownership. Nothing else will go to the cause of the evil—in nothing else is there the slightest hope.

This, then, is the remedy for the unjust and unequal distribution of wealth apparent in modern civilization, and for all the evils which flow from it:

We must make land common property.

But a question of method remains. How shall we do it?

We should satisfy the law of justice, we should meet all economic requirements, by at one stroke abolishing all private titles, declaring all land public property, and letting it out to the highest bidders in lots to suit, under such conditions as would sacredly guard the private right to improvements.

Thus we should secure, in a more complex state of society, the same equality of rights that in a ruder state were secured by equal partitions of the soil, and by giving the use of the land to whoever could procure the most from it, we should secure the greatest production.

Such a plan, instead of being a wild, impracticable vagary, has (with the exception that he suggests compensation to the present holders of land—undoubtedly a careless concession which he upon reflection would reconsider) been indorsed by no less eminent a thinker than Herbert Spencer, who (*Social Statics*) says of it:

> Such a doctrine is consistent with the highest state of civilization; may be carried out without involving a community of goods, and need cause no very serious revolution in existing arrangements. The change required would simply be a change of landlords. Separate ownership would merge into the joint-stock ownership of the public. Instead of being in the possession of individuals, the country would be held by the great corporate body—society. Instead of leasing his acres from an isolated proprietor, the farmer would lease them from the nation. Instead of paying his rent to the agent of Sir John or his Grace, he would pay it to an agent or deputy agent of the community. Stewards would be public officials instead of private ones, and tenancy the only land tenure. A state of things so ordered would be in perfect harmony with the moral law. Under it all men would be equally landlords, all men would be alike free to become tenants. . . . Clearly, therefore, on such a system, the earth might be enclosed, occupied and cultivated, in entire subordination to the law of equal freedom.

But such a plan, though perfectly feasible, does not seem to me the best. Or rather I propose to accomplish the same thing in a simpler, easier, and quieter way, than that of formally confiscating all the land and formally letting it out to the highest bidders.

To do that would involve a needless shock to present customs and habits of thought—which is to be avoided.

To do that would involve a needless extension of governmental machinery—which is to be avoided.

It is an axiom of statesmanship, which the successful founders of tyranny have understood and acted upon—that great changes can best be brought about under old forms. We, who would free men, should heed the same truth. It is the natural method. When Nature would make a higher type, she takes a lower one and develops it. This, also, is the law of social growth. Let us work by it. With the current we may glide fast and far. Against it, it is hard pulling and slow progress.

I do not propose either to purchase or to confiscate private property in land. The first would be unjust; the second, needless. Let the individuals who now hold it still retain, if they want to, possession of what they are pleased to call *their* land. Let them continue to call it *their* land. Let them buy and sell, and bequeath and devise it. We may safely leave them the shell, if we take the kernel. *It is not necessary to confiscate land; it is only necessary to confiscate rent.*

Nor to take rent for public uses is it necessary that the state should bother with the letting of lands, and assume the chances of the favoritism, collusion, and corruption this might involve. It is not necessary that any new machinery should be created. The machinery already exists. Instead of extending it, all we have to do is to simplify and reduce it. By leaving to land owners a percentage of rent which would probably be much less than the cost and loss involved in attempting to rent lands through state agency, and by making use of this existing machinery, we may, without jar or shock, assert the common right to land by taking rent for public uses.

We already take some rent in taxation. We have only to make some changes in our modes of taxation to take it all.

What I, therefore, propose, as the simple yet sovereign remedy, which will raise wages, increase the earnings of capital, extirpate pauperism, abolish poverty, give remunerative employment to whoever wishes it, afford free scope to human powers, lessen crime, elevate morals, and taste, and intelligence, purify government and carry civilization to yet nobler heights, is—*to appropriate rent by taxation.*

In this way the state may become the universal landlord without calling herself so, and without assuming a single new function. In form, the ownership of land would remain just as now. No owner of land need be dispossessed, and no restriction need be placed upon the amount of land any one could hold. For, rent being taken by the state in taxes, land, no matter in whose name it stood, or in what parcels it was held, would be really common property, and every member of the community would participate in the advantages of its ownership.

Now, insomuch as the taxation of rent, or land values, must necessarily be increased just as we abolish other taxes, we may put the proposition into practical form by proposing—

To abolish all taxation save that upon land values.

As we have seen, the value of land is at the beginning of society nothing, but as society develops by the increase of population and the advance of the arts, it becomes greater and greater. In every civilized country, even the newest, the value of the land taken as a whole is sufficient to bear the entire expenses of government. In the better developed countries it is much more than sufficient. Hence it will not be enough merely to place all taxes upon the value of land. It will be necessary, where rent exceeds the present governmental revenues, commensurately to increase the amount demanded in taxation, and to continue this increase as society progresses and rent advances. But this is so natural and easy a matter, that it may be considered as involved, or at least understood, in the proposition to put all taxes on the value of land. That is the first step, upon which the practical struggle must be made. When the hare is once caught and killed, cooking him will follow as a matter of course. When the common right to land is so far appreciated that all taxes are abolished save those which fall upon rent, there is no danger of much more than is necessary to induce them to collect the public revenues being left to individual landholders.

PART SEVEN

I. *OF THE EFFECT UPON THE PRODUCTION OF WEALTH*

THE elder Mirabeau, we are told, ranked the proposition of Quesnay, to substitute one single tax on rent (the *impôt unique*) for all other taxes, as a discovery equal in utility to the invention of writing or the substitution of the use of money for barter.

To whomsoever will think over the matter, this saying will appear an evidence of penetration rather than of extravagance. The advantages which would be gained by substituting for the numerous taxes by which the public revenues are now raised, a single tax levied upon the value of land, will appear more and more important the more they are considered. This is the secret which would transform the little village into the great city. With all the burdens removed which now oppress industry and hamper exchange, the production of wealth would go on with a rapidity now undreamed of. This, in its turn, would lead to an increase in the value of land—a new surplus which society might take for general purposes. And released from the difficulties which attend the collection of revenue in a way that begets corruption and renders legislation the tool of special interests, society could assume functions which the increasing complexity of life makes it desirable to assume, but which the prospect of political demoralization under the present system now leads thoughtful men to shrink from.

Consider the effect upon the production of wealth.

To abolish the taxation which, acting and reacting, now hampers every wheel of exchange and presses upon every form of industry, would be like removing an immense weight from a powerful spring. Imbued with fresh energy, production would start into new life, and trade would receive a stimulus which would be felt to the remotest arteries. The present method of taxation operates upon exchange like artificial deserts and mountains; it costs more to get goods through a custom house than it does to carry them around the world. It operates upon energy, and industry, and skill, and thrift, like a fine upon those qualities. If I have worked harder and built myself a good house while you have been contented to live in a hovel, the taxgatherer now comes annually to make me pay a penalty for my energy and industry, by taxing me more than you. If I have saved while you wasted, I am mulct, while you are exempt. If a man build a ship we make him pay for his temerity, as though he had done an injury to the state; if a railroad be opened, down comes the tax collector upon it, as though it were a public nuisance; if a manufactory be erected we levy upon it an annual sum which would go far toward making a handsome profit. We say we want capital, but if any one accumulate it, or bring it among us, we charge him for it as though we were giving him a privilege. We punish with a tax the man who covers barren fields with ripening grain, we fine him who puts up machinery, and him who drains a swamp. How heavily these taxes burden production only those realize who have attempted to follow our system of taxation through its ramifications, for, as I have before said, the heaviest part of taxation is that which falls in increased prices. But manifestly these taxes are in their nature akin to the Egyptian Pasha's tax upon date trees. If they do not cause the trees to be cut down, they at least discourage the planting.

To abolish these taxes would be to lift the whole enormous weight of taxation from productive industry. The needle of the seamstress and the great manufactory; the cart horse and the locomotive; the fishing boat and the steamship; the farmer's plow and the merchant's stock, would be alike untaxed. All would be free to make or to save, to buy or to sell, unfined by taxes, unannoyed by the taxgatherer. Instead of saying to the producer, as it does now, "The more you add to the general wealth the more shall you be taxed!" the state would say to the producer, "Be as industrious, as thrifty, as enterprising as you choose, you shall have your full reward! You shall not be fined for making two blades of grass grow where one grew before; you shall not be taxed for adding to the aggregate wealth."

And will not the community gain by thus refusing to kill the goose that lays the golden eggs; by thus refraining from muzzling the ox that treadeth out the corn; by thus leaving to industry, and thrift, and skill, their natural reward, full and unimpaired? For there is to the community also a natural reward. The law of society is, each for all, as well as all for each. No one can keep to himself the good he may do, any more than he can keep the bad. Every productive enterprise, besides its return to those who undertake it, yields collateral advantages to others. If a man plant a fruit-tree, his gain is that he gathers the fruit in its time and season. But in addition to his gain, there is a gain to the whole community. Others than the owner are benefited by the increased supply of fruit; the birds which it shelters fly far and wide; the rain which it helps to attract falls not alone on his field; and, even to the eye which rests upon it from a distance, it brings a sense of beauty. And so with everything else. The building of a house, a factory, a ship, or a railroad, benefits others besides those who get the direct profits. Nature laughs at a miser. He is like the squirrel who buries his nuts and refrains from digging them up again. Lo! they sprout and grow into trees. In fine linen, steeped in costly spices, the mummy is laid away. Thousands and thousands of years thereafter, the Bedouin cooks his food by a fire of its encasings, it generates the steam by which the traveler is whirled on his way, or it passes into far-off lands to gratify the curiosity of another race. The bee fills the hollow tree with honey, and along comes the bear or the man.

Well may the community leave to the individual producer all that prompts him to exertion; well may it let the laborer have the full reward of his labor, and the capitalist the full return of his capital. For the more that labor and capital produce, the greater grows the common wealth in which all may share. And in the value or rent of land is this general gain expressed in a definite and concrete form. Here is a fund which the state may take while leaving to labor and capital their full reward. With increased activity of production this would commensurately increase.

And to shift the burden of taxation from production and exchange to the value or rent of land woud not merely be to give new stimulus to the production of wealth; it would be to open new opportunities. For under this system no one would care to hold land unless to use it, and land now withheld from use would everywhere be thrown open to improvement.

The selling price of land would fall; land speculation would receive its death blow; land monopolization would no longer pay. Millions and millions of acres from which settlers are now shut out by high prices would be abandoned by their present owners or sold to settlers upon nominal terms. And this not merely on the frontiers, but within what are now considered well-settled districts. Within a hundred miles of San Francisco would be thus thrown open land enough to support, even with present modes of cultivation, an agricultural population equal to that now scattered from the Oregon boundary to the Mexican line—a distance of 800 miles. In the same degree would this be true of most of the Western States, and in a great degree of the older Eastern States, for even in New York and Pennsylvania is population yet sparse as compared with the capacity of the land. And even in densely populated England would such a policy throw open to cultivation many hundreds of thousands of acres now held as private parks, deer preserves, and shooting grounds.

For this simple device of placing all taxes on the value of land would be in effect putting up the land at auction to whomsoever would pay the highest rent to the state. The demand for land fixes its value, and hence, if taxes were placed so as very nearly to consume that value, the man who wished to hold land without using it would have to pay very nearly what it would be worth to any one who wanted to use it.

And it must be remembered that this would apply, not merely to agricultural land, but to all land. Mineral land would be thrown open to use, just as agricultural land; and in the heart of a city no one could afford to keep land from its most profitable use, or on the outskirts to demand more for it than the use to which it could at the time be put would warrant. Everywhere that land had attained a value, taxation, instead of operating, as now, as a fine upon improvement, would operate to force improvement. Whoever planted an orchard, or sowed a field, or built a house, or erected a manufactory, no matter how costly, would have no more to pay in taxes than if he kept so much land idle. The monopolist of agricultural land would be taxed as much as though his land were covered with houses and barns, with crops and with stock. The owner of a vacant city lot would have to pay as much for the privilege of keeping other people off of it until he wanted to use it, as his neighbor who has a fine house upon his lot. It would cost as much to keep a row of tumble-down shanties upon valuable land as though it were covered with a grand hotel or a pile of great warehouses filled with costly goods.

Thus, the bonus that wherever labor is most productive must now be paid before labor can be exerted would disappear. The farmer would not have to pay out half his means, or mortgage his labor for years, in order to obtain land to cultivate; the builder of a city homestead would not have to lay out as much for a small lot as for the house he puts upon it; the company that proposed to erect a manufactory would not have to expend a great part of their capital for a site. And what would be paid from year to year to the state would be in lieu of all the taxes now levied upon improvements, machinery, and stock.

Consider the effect of such a change upon the labor market. Competition would no longer be one-sided, as now. Instead of laborers competing with each other for employment, and in their competition cutting down wages to the point of bare subsistence, employers would everywhere be competing for laborers, and wages would rise to the fair earnings of labor. For into the labor market would have entered the greatest of all competitors for the employment of labor, a competitor whose demand cannot be satisfied until want is satisfied—the demand of labor itself. The employers of labor would not have merely to bid against other employers, all feeling the stimulus of greater trade and increased profits, but against the ability of laborers to become their own employers upon the natural opportunities freely opened to them by the tax which prevented monopolization.

With natural opportunities thus free to labor; with capital and improvements exempt from tax, and exchange released from restrictions, the spectacle of willing men unable to turn their labor into the things they are suffering for would become impossible; the recurring paroxysms which paralyze industry would cease; every wheel of production would be set in motion; demand would keep pace with supply, and supply with demand; trade would increase in every direction, and wealth augment on every hand.

II. OF THE EFFECT UPON DISTRIBUTION AND THENCE UPON PRODUCTION

But great as they thus appear, the advantages of a transference of all public burdens to a tax upon the value of land cannot be fully appreciated until we consider the effect upon the distribution of wealth.

Tracing out the cause of the unequal distribution of wealth which appears in all civilized countries, with a constant tendency to greater and greater inequality as material progress goes on, we have found it in the fact that, as civilization advances, the ownership of land, now in private hands, gives a greater and greater power of appropriating the wealth produced by labor and capital.

Thus, to relieve labor and capital from all taxation, direct and indirect, and to throw the burden upon rent, would be, as far as it went, to counteract this tendency to inequality, and, if it went so far as to take in taxation the whole of rent, the cause of inequality would be totally destroyed. Rent, instead of causing inequality, as now, would then promote equality. Labor and capital would then receive the whole produce, minus that portion taken by the state in the taxation of land values, which, being applied to public purposes, would be equally distributed in public benefits.

That is to say, the wealth produced in every community would be divided into two portions. One part would be distributed in wages and interest between individual producers, according to the part each had taken in the work of production; the other part would go to the community as a whole, to be distributed in public benefits to all its members. In this all would share equally—the weak with the strong, young children and decrepit old men, the maimed, the halt, and the blind, as well as the vigorous. And justly so—for while one part represents the result of individual effort in production, the other represents the increased power with which the community as a whole aids the individual.

Thus, as material progress tends to increase rent, were rent taken by the community for common purposes the very cause which now tends to produce inequality as material progress goes on would then tend to produce greater and greater equality. Fully to understand this effect, let us revert to principles previously worked out.

We have seen that wages and interest must everywhere be fixed by the rent line or margin of cultivation—that is to say, by the reward which labor and capital can secure on land for which no rent is paid; that the aggregate amount of wealth, which the aggregate of labor and capital employed in production will receive, will be the amount of wealth produced (or rather, when we consider taxes, the net amount), minus what is taken as rent.

We have seen that with material progress, as it is at present going on, there is a twofold tendency to the advance of rent. Both are to the increase of the proportion of the wealth produced which goes as rent, and to the decrease of the proportion which goes as wages and interest. But the first, or natural tendency, which results from the laws of social development, is to the increase of rent as a quantity, without the reduction of wages and interest as quantities, or even with their quantitative increase. The other tendency, which results from the unnatural appropriation of land to private ownership, is to the increase of rent as a quantity by the reduction of wages and interest as quantities.

Now, it is evident that to take rent in taxation for public purposes, which virtually abolishes private ownership in land, would be to destroy the tendency to an absolute decrease in wages and interest, by destroying the speculative monopolization of land and the speculative increase in rent. It would be very largely to increase wages and interest, by throwing open natural opportunities now monopolized and reducing the price of land. Labor and capital would thus not merely gain what is now taken from them in taxation, but would gain by the positive decline in rent caused by the decrease in speculative land values. A new equilibrium would be established, at which the common rate of wages and interest would be much higher than now.

But this new equilibrium established, further advances in productive power, and the tendency in this direction would be greatly accelerated, would result in still increasing rent, not at the expense of wages and interest, but by new gains in production, which, as rent would be taken by the community for public uses, would accrue to the advantage of every member of the community. Thus, as material progress went on, the condition of the masses would constantly improve. Not merely one class would become richer, but all would become richer; not merely one class would have more of the necessaries, conveniences, and elegancies of life, but all would have more. For, the increasing power of production, which comes with increasing population, with every new discovery in the productive arts, with every labor-saving invention, with every extension and facilitation of exchanges, could be monopolized by none. That part of the benefit which did not go directly to increase the reward of labor and capital would go to the state—that is to say, to the whole community.

With all the enormous advantages, material and mental, of a dense population, would be united the freedom and equality that can now be found only in new and sparsely settled districts.

And, then, consider how equalization in the distribution of wealth would react upon production, everywhere preventing waste, everywhere increasing power.

If it were possible to express in figures the direct pecuniary loss which society suffers from the social maladjustments which condemn large classes to poverty and vice, the estimate would be appalling. England maintains over a million paupers on official charity; the city of New York alone spends over seven million dollars a year in a similar way. But what is spent from public funds, what is spent by charitable societies, and what is spent in individual charity, would, if aggregated, be but the first and smallest item in the account. The potential earnings of the labor thus going to waste, the cost of the reckless, improvident, and idle habits thus generated; the pecuniary loss, to consider nothing more, suggested by the appalling statistics of mortality, and especially infant mortality, among the poorer classes; the waste indicated by the gin palaces or low groggeries which increase as poverty deepens; the damage done by the vermin of society that are bred of poverty and destitution—the thieves, prostitutes, beggars, and tramps; the cost of guarding society against them, are all items in the sum which the present unjust and unequal distribution of wealth takes from the aggregate which, with present means of production, society might enjoy. Nor yet shall we have completed the account. The ignorance and vice, the recklessness and immorality engendered by the inequality in the distribution of wealth show themselves in the imbecility and corruption of government; and the waste of public revenues, and the still greater waste involved in the ignorant and corrupt abuse of public powers and functions, are their legitimate consequences.

But the increase in wages, and the opening of new avenues of employment which would result from the appropriation of rent to public purposes, would not merely stop these wastes and relieve society of these enormous losses; new power would be added to labor. It is but a truism that labor is most productive where its wages are largest. Poorly paid labor is inefficient labor, the world over.

What is remarked between the efficiency of labor in the agricultural districts of England where different rates of wages prevail; what Brassey noticed as between the work done by his better paid English navvies and that done by the worse paid labor of the continent; what was evident in the United States as between slave labor and free labor; what is seen by the astonishing number of mechanics or servants required in India or China to get anything done, is universally true. The efficiency of labor always increases with the habitual wages of labor—for high wages mean increased self-respect, intelligence, hope, and energy. Man is not a machine, that will do so much and no more; he is not an animal, whose powers may reach thus far and no further. It is mind, not muscle, which is the great agent of production. The physical power evolved in the human frame is one of the weakest of forces, but for the human intelligence the resistless currents of nature flow, and matter becomes plastic to the human will. To increase the comforts, and leisure, and independence of the masses is to increase their intelligence; it is to bring the brain to the aid of the hand; it is to engage in the common work of life the faculty which measures the animalcule and traces the orbits of the stars!

Who can say to what infinite powers the wealth-producing capacity of labor may not be raised by social adjustments which will give to the producers of wealth their fair proportion of its advantages and enjoyments! With present processes the gain would be simply incalculable, but just as wages are high, so do the invention and utilization of improved processes and machinery go on with greater rapidity and ease. That the wheat crops of Southern Russia are still reaped with the scythe and beaten out with the flail is simply because wages are there so low. American invention, American aptitude for labor-saving processes and machinery are the result of the comparatively high wages that have prevailed in the United States. Had our producers been condemned to the low reward of the Egyptian fellah or Chinese coolie, we would be drawing water by hand and transporting goods on the shoulders of men. The increase in the reward of labor and capital would still further stimulate invention and hasten the adoption of improved processes, and these would truly appear, what in themselves they really are—an unmixed good. The injurious effects of labor-saving machinery upon the working classes, that are now so often apparent, and that, in spite of all argument, make so many people regard machinery as an evil instead of a blessing, would disappear. Every new power engaged in the service of man would improve the condition of all. And from the general intelligence and mental activity springing from this general improvement of condition would come new developments of power of which we as yet cannot dream.

But I shall not deny, and do not wish to lose sight of the fact, that while thus preventing waste and thus adding to the efficiency of labor, the equalization in the distribution of wealth that would result from the simple plan of taxation that I propose, must lessen the intensity with which wealth is pursued. It seems to me that in a condition of society in which no one need fear poverty, no one would desire great wealth—at least, no one would take the trouble to strive and to strain for it as men do now. For, certainly, the spectacle of men who have only a few years to live, slaving away their time for the sake of dying rich, is in itself so unnatural and absurd, that in a state of society where the abolition of the fear of want had dissipated the envious admiration with which the masses of men now regard the possession of great riches, whoever would toil to acquire more than he cared to use would be looked upon as we would now look on a man who would thatch his head with half a dozen hats, or walk around in the hot sun with an overcoat on. When every one is sure of being able to get enough, no one will care to make a packhorse of himself.

And though this incentive to production be withdrawn, can we not spare it? Whatever may have been its office in an earlier stage of development, it is not needed now. The dangers that menace our civilization do not come from the weakness of the springs of production. What it suffers from, and what, if a remedy be not applied, it must die from, is unequal distribution!

Nor would the removal of this incentive, regarded only from the standpoint of production, be an unmixed loss. For, that the aggregate of production is greatly reduced by the greed with which riches are pursued, is one of the most obtrusive facts of modern society. While, were this insane desire to get rich at any cost lessened, mental activities now devoted to scraping together riches would be translated into far higher spheres of usefulness.

III. OF THE EFFECT UPON INDIVIDUALS AND CLASSES

When it is first proposed to put all taxes upon the value of land, and thus confiscate rent, all landholders are likely to take the alarm, and there will not be wanting appeals to the fears of small farm and homestead owners, who will be told that this is a proposition to rob them of their hard-earned property. But a moment's reflection will show that this proposition should commend itself to all whose interests as land holders do not largely exceed their interests as laborers or capitalists, or both. And further consideration will show that though the large land holders may lose relatively, yet even in their case there will be an absolute gain. For, the increase in production will be so great that labor and capital will gain very much more than will be lost to private land ownership, while in these gains, and in the greater ones involved in a more healthy social condition, the whole community, including the land owners themselves, will share.

It is manifest, of course, that the change I propose will greatly benefit all those who live by wages, whether of hand or of head—laborers, operatives, mechanics, clerks, professional men of all sorts. It is manifest, also, that it will benefit all those who live partly by wages and partly by the earnings of their capital—storekeepers, merchants, manufacturers, employing or undertaking producers and exchangers of all sorts—from the peddler or drayman to the railroad or steamship owner—and it is likewise manifest that it will increase the incomes of those whose incomes are drawn from the earnings of capital, or from investments other than in lands, save perhaps the holders of government bonds or other securities bearing fixed rates of interest, which will probably depreciate in selling value, owing to the rise in the general rate of interest, though the income from them will remain the same.

Take, now, the case of the homestead owner—the mechanic, storekeeper, or professional man who has secured himself a house and lot, where he lives, and which he contemplates with satisfaction as a place from which his family cannot be ejected in case of his death. He will not be injured; on the contrary, he will be the gainer. The selling value of his lot will diminish—theoretically it will entirely disappear. But its usefulness to him will not disappear. It will serve his purpose as well as ever. While, as the value of all other lots will diminish or disappear in the same ratio, he retains the same security of always having a lot that he had before. That is to say, he is a loser only as the man who has bought himself a pair of boots may be said to be a loser by a subsequent fall in the price of boots. His boots will be just as useful to him, and the next pair of boots he can get cheaper. So, to the homestead owner, his lot will be as useful, and should he look forward to getting a larger lot, or having his children, as they grow up, get homesteads of their own, he will, even in the matter of lots, be the gainer. And in the present, other things considered, he will be much the gainer. For though he will have more taxes to pay upon his land, he will be released from taxes upon his house and improvements, upon his furniture and personal property, upon all that he and his family eat, drink, and wear, while his earnings will be largely increased by the rise of wages, the constant employment, and the increased briskness of trade. His only loss will be, if he wants to sell his lot without getting another, and this will be a small loss compared with the great gain.

And so with the farmer. I speak not now of the farmers who never touch the handles of a plow, who cultivate thousands of acres and enjoy incomes like those of the rich Southern planters before the war; but of the working farmers who constitute such a large class in the United States—men who own small farms, which they cultivate with the aid of their boys, and perhaps some hired help, and who in Europe would be called peasant proprietors. Paradoxical as it may appear to these men until they understand the full bearings of the proposition, of all classes above that of the mere laborer they have most to gain by placing all taxes upon the value of land. That they do not now get as good a living as their hard work ought to give them, they generally feel, though they may not be able to trace the cause. The fact is that taxation, as now levied, falls on them with peculiar severity. They are taxed on all their improvements—houses, barns, fences, crops, stock. The personal property which they have cannot be as readily concealed or undervalued as can the more valuable kinds which are concentrated in the cities. They are not only taxed on personal property and improvements, which the owners of unused land escape, but their land is generally taxed at a higher rate than land held on speculation, simply because it is improved. But further than this, all taxes imposed on commodities, and especially the taxes which, like our protective duties, are imposed with a view of raising the prices of commodities, fall on the farmer without mitigation. For in a country like the United States, which exports agricultural produce, the farmer cannot be protected. Whoever gains, he must lose. Some years ago the Free Trade League of New York published a broadside containing cuts of various articles of necessity marked with the duties imposed by the tariff, and which read something in this wise: "The farmer rises in the morning and draws on his pantaloons taxed forty per cent. and his boots taxed thirty per cent., striking a light with a match taxed two hundred per cent.," and so on, following him through the day and through life, until, killed by taxation, he is lowered into the grave with a rope taxed forty-five per cent. This is but a graphic illustration of the manner in which such taxes ultimately fall. The farmer would be a great gainer by the substitution of a single tax upon the value of land for all these taxes, for the taxation of land values would fall with greatest weight, not upon the agricultural districts, where land values are comparatively small, but upon the towns and cities where land values are high; whereas taxes upon personal property and improvements fall as heavily in the country as in the city. And in sparsely settled districts there would be hardly any taxes at all for the farmer to pay. For taxes, being levied upon the value of the bare land, would fall as heavily upon unimproved as upon improved land. Acre for acre, the improved and cultivated farm, with its buildings, fences, orchard, crops, and stock, could be taxed no more than unused land of equal quality. The result would be that speculative values would be kept down, and that cultivated and improved farms would have no taxes to pay until the country around them had been well settled. In fact, paradoxical as it may at first seem to them, the effect of putting all taxation upon the value of land would be to relieve the harder working farmers of all taxation.

But the great gain of the working farmer can be seen only when the effect upon the distribution of population is considered. The destruction of speculative land values would tend to diffuse population where it is too dense and to concentrate it where it is too sparse; to substitute for the tenement house, homes surrounded by gardens, and fully to settle agricultural districts before people were driven far from neighbors to look for land. The people of the cities would thus get more of the pure air and sunshine of the country, the people of the country more of the economies and social life of the city. If, as is doubtless the case, the application of machinery tends to large fields, agricultural population will assume the primitive form and cluster in villages. The life of the average farmer is now unnecessarily dreary. He is not only compelled to work early and late, but he is cut off by the sparseness of population from the conveniences, and amusements, the educational facilities, and the social and intellectual opportunities that come with the closer contact of man with man. He would be far better off in all these respects, and his labor would be far more productive, if he and those around him held no more land than they wanted to use. While his children, as they grew up, would neither be so impelled to seek the excitement of a city nor would they be driven so far away to seek farms of their own. Their means of living would be in their own hands, and at home.

In short, the working farmer is both a laborer and a capitalist, as well as a landowner, and it is by his labor and capital that his living is made. His loss would be nominal; his gain would be real and great.

In varying degrees is this true of all landholders. Many landholders are laborers of one sort or another. And it would be hard to find a landowner not a laborer, who is not also a capitalist—while the general rule is, that the larger the landowner the greater the capitalist. So true is this that in common thought the characters are confounded. Thus to put all taxes on the value of land, while it would be largely to reduce all great fortunes, would in no case leave the rich man penniless. The Duke of Westminster, who owns a considerable part of the site of London, is probably the richest land owner in the world. To take all his ground rents by taxation would largely reduce his enormous income, but would still leave him his buildings and all the income from them, and doubtless much personal property in various other shapes. He would still have all he could by any possibility enjoy, and a much better state of society in which to enjoy it.

So would the Astors of New York remain very rich. And so, I think, it will be seen throughout—this measure would make no one poorer but such as could be made a great deal poorer without being really hurt. It would cut down great fortunes, but it would impoverish no one.

Wealth would not only be enormously increased; it would be equally distributed. I do not mean that each individual would get the same amount of wealth. That would not be equal distribution, so long as different individuals have different powers and different desires. But I mean that wealth would be distributed in accordance with the degree in which the industry, skill, knowledge, or prudence of each contributed to the common stock. The great cause which concentrates wealth in the hands of those who do not produce, and takes it from the hands of those who do, would be gone. The inequalities that continued to exist would be those of nature, not the artificial inequalities produced by the denial of natural law. The non-producer would no longer roll in luxury while the producer got but the barest necessities of animal existence.

The monopoly of the land gone, there need be no fear of large fortunes. For then the riches of any individual must consist of wealth, properly so-called—of wealth, which is the product of labor, and which constantly tends to dissipation, for national debts, I imagine, would not long survive the abolition of the system from which they spring. All fear of great fortunes might be dismissed, for when everyone gets what he fairly earns, no one can get more than he fairly earns. How many men are there who fairly earn a million dollars?

IV. OF THE CHANGES THAT WOULD BE WROUGHT IN SOCIAL ORGANIZATION AND SOCIAL LIFE

We are dealing only with general principles. There are some matters of detail—such as those arising from the division of revenues between local and general governments—which upon application of these principles would come up, but these it is not necessary here to discuss. When once principles are settled, details will be readily adjusted.

Nor without too much elaboration is it possible to notice all the changes which would be wrought, or would become possible, by a change which would readjust the very foundation of society, but to some main features let me call attention.

Noticeable among these is the great simplicity which would become possible in government. To collect taxes, to prevent and punish evasions, to check and counter-check revenues drawn from so many distinct sources, now make up probably three fourths, perhaps seven-eighths of the business of government, outside of the preservation of order, the maintenance of the military arm, and the administration of justice. An immense and complicated network of governmental machinery would thus be dispensed with.

In the administration of justice there would be a like saving of strain. Much of the civil business of our courts arises from disputes as to ownership of land. These would cease when the state was virtually acknowledged as the sole owner of land, and all occupiers became practically rent-paying tenants. The growth of morality consequent upon the cessation of want would tend to a like diminution in other civil business of the courts, which could be hastened by the adoption of the common-sense proposition of Bentham to abolish all laws for the collection of debts and the enforcement of private contracts. The rise of wages, the opening of opportunities for all to make an easy and comfortable living, would at once lessen and would soon eliminate from society the thieves, swindlers, and other classes of criminals who spring from the unequal distribution of wealth. Thus the administration of the criminal law, with all its paraphernalia of policemen, detectives, prisons, and penitentiaries, would, like the administration of the civil law, cease to make such a drain upon the vital force and attention of society. We should get rid not only of many judges, bailiffs, clerks, and prison keepers, but of the great host of lawyers who are now maintained at the expense of producers; and talent now wasted in legal subtleties would be turned to higher pursuits.

The legislative, judicial, and executive functions of government would in this way be vastly simplified. Nor can I think that the public debts and the standing armies, which are historically the outgrowth of the change from feudal to allodial tenures, would long remain after the reversion to the old idea that the land of a country is the common right of the people of the country. The former could readily be paid off by a tax that would not lessen the wages of labor nor check production, and the latter the growth of intelligence and independence among the masses, aided, perhaps, by the progress of invention, which is revolutionizing the military art, must soon cause to disappear.

Society would thus approach the ideal of Jeffersonian democracy, the promised land of Herbert Spencer, the abolition of government. But of government only as a directing and repressive power. It would at the same time, and in the same degree, become possible for it to realize the dream of socialism. All this simplification and abrogation of the present functions of government would make possible the assumption of certain other functions which are now pressing for recognition. Government could take upon itself the transmission of messages by telegraph, as well as by mail; of building and operating railroads, as well as of opening and maintaining common roads. With present functions so simplified and reduced, functions such as these could be assumed without danger or strain, and would be under the supervision of public attention, which is now distracted. There would be a great and increasing surplus revenue from the taxation of land values, for material progress, which would go on with greatly accelerated rapidity, would tend constantly to increase rent. This revenue arising from the common property could be applied to the common benefit, as were the revenues of Sparta. We might not establish public tables—they would be unnecessary; but we could establish public baths, museums, libraries, gardens, lecture rooms, music and dancing halls, theaters, universities, technical schools, shooting galleries, play grounds, gymnasiums, etc. Heat, light, and motive power, as well as water, might be conducted through our streets at public expense; our roads be lined with fruit trees; discoverers and inventors rewarded, scientific investigations supported; and in a thousand ways the public revenues made to foster efforts for the public benefit. We should reach the ideal of the socialist, but not through government repression. Government would change its character, and would become the administration of a great co-operative society. It would become merely the agency by which the common property was administered for the common benefit.

Does this seem impracticable? Consider for a moment the vast changes that would be wrought in social life by a change which would assure to labor its full reward; which would banish want and the fear of want; and give to the humblest freedom to develop in natural symmetry.

In thinking of the possibilities of social organization, we are apt to assume that greed is the strongest of human motives, and that systems of administration can be safely based only upon the idea that the fear of punishment is necessary to keep men honest—that selfish interests are always stronger than general interests. Nothing could be further from the truth.

From whence springs this lust for gain, to gratify which men tread everything pure and noble under their feet; to which they sacrifice all the higher possibilities of life; which converts civility into a hollow pretense, patriotism into a sham, and religion into hypocrisy; which makes so much of civilized existence an Ishmaelitish warfare of which the weapons are cunning and fraud?

Does it not spring from the existence of want? Carlyle somewhere says that poverty is the hell of which the modern Englishman is most afraid. And he is right. Poverty is the openmouthed, relentless hell which yawns beneath civilized society. And it is hell enough. The Vedas declare no truer thing than when the wise crow Bushanda tells the eagle-bearer of Vishnu that the keenest pain is in poverty. For poverty is not merely deprivation; it means shame, degradation; the searing of the most sensitive parts of our moral and mental nature as with hot irons; the denial of the strongest impulses and the sweetest affections; the wrenching of the most vital nerves. You love your wife, you love your children; but would it not be easier to see them die than to see them reduced to the pinch of want in which large classes in every highly civilized community live? The strongest of animal passions is that with which we cling to life, but it is an everyday occurrence in civilized societies for men to put poison to their mouths or pistols to their heads from fear of poverty, and for one who does this there are probably a hundred who have the desire, but are restrained by instinctive shrinking, by religious considerations, or by family ties.

From this hell of poverty, it is but natural that men should make every effort to escape. With the impulse to self-preservation and self-gratification combine nobler feelings, and love as well as fear urges in the struggle. Many a man does a mean thing, a dishonest thing, a greedy and grasping and unjust thing, in the effort to place above want, or the fear of want, mother or wife or children.

And out of this condition of things arises a public opinion which enlists, as an impelling power in the struggle to grasp and to keep, one of the strongest—perhaps with many men the very strongest—springs of human action. The desire for approbation, the feeling that urges us to win the respect, admiration, or sympathy of our fellows, is instinctive and universal. Distorted sometimes into the most abnormal manifestations, it may yet be everywhere perceived. It is potent with the veriest savage, as with the most highly cultivated member of the most polished society; it shows itself with the first gleam of intelligence, and persists to the last breath. It triumphs over the love of ease, over the sense of pain, over the dread of death. It dictates the most trivial and the most important actions.

The child just beginning to toddle or to talk will make new efforts as its cunning little tricks excite attention and laughter; the dying master of the world gathers his robes around him, that he may pass away as becomes a king; Chinese mothers will deform their daughters' feet by cruel stocks, European women will sacrifice their own comfort and the comfort of their families to similar dictates of fashion; the Polynesian, that he may excite admiration by his beautiful tattoo, will hold himself still while his flesh is torn by sharks' teeth; the North American Indian, tied to the stake, will bear the most fiendish tortures without a moan, and, that he may be respected and admired as a great brave, will taunt his tormentors to new cruelties. It is this that leads the forlorn hope; it is this that trims the lamp of the pale student; it is this that impels men to strive, to strain, to toil, and to die. It is this that raised the pyramids and that fired the Ephesian dome.

Now, men admire what they desire. How sweet to the storm-stricken seems the safe harbor; food to the hungry, drink to the thirsty, warmth to the shivering, rest to the weary, power to the weak, knowledge to him in whom the intellectual yearnings of the soul have been aroused. And thus the sting of want and the fear of want make men admire above all things the possession of riches, and to become wealthy is to become respected, and admired, and influential. Get money—honestly, if you can, but at any rate get money! This is the lesson that society is daily and hourly dinning in the ears of its members. Men instinctively admire virtue and truth, but the sting of want and the fear of want make them even more strongly admire the rich and sympathize with the fortunate. It is well to be honest and just, and men will commend it; but he who by fraud and injustice gets him a million dollars will have more respect, and admiration, and influence, more eye service and lip service, if not heart service, than he who refuses it. The one may have his reward in the future; he may know that his name is writ in the Book of Life, and that for him is the white robe and the palm branch of the victor against temptation; but the other has his reward in the present. His name is writ in the list of "our substantial citizens;" he has the courtship of men and the flattery of women; the best pew in the church and the personal regard of the eloquent clergyman who in the name of Christ preaches the Gospel of Dives, and tones down into a meaningless flower of Eastern speech the stern metaphor of the camel and the needle's eye. He may be a patron of arts, a Mæcenas to men of letters; may profit by the converse of the intelligent, and be polished by the attrition of the refined. His alms may feed the poor, and help the struggling, and bring sunshine into desolate places; and noble public institutions commemorate, after he is gone, his name and his fame. It is not in the guise of a hideous monster, with horns and tail, that Satan tempts the children of men, but as an angel of light. His promises are not alone of the kingdoms of the world, but of mental and moral principalities and powers. He appeals not only to the animal appetites, but to the cravings that stir in man because he is more than an animal.

Take the case of those miserable "men with muckrakes," who are to be seen in every community as plainly as Bunyan saw their type in his vision—who, long after they have accumulated wealth enough to satisfy every desire, go on working, scheming, striving to add riches to riches. It was the desire "to be something;" nay, in many cases, the desire to do noble and generous deeds, that started them on a career of money getting. And what compels them to it long after every possible need is satisfied, what urges them still with unsatisfied and ravenous greed, is not merely the force of tyrannous habit, but the subtler gratifications which the possession of riches gives—the sense of power and influence, the sense of being looked up to and respected, the sense that their wealth not merely raises them above want, but makes them men of mark in the community in which they live. It is this that makes the rich man so loath to part with his money, so anxious to get more.

Against temptations that thus appeal to the strongest impulses of our nature, the sanctions of law and the precepts of religion can effect but little; and the wonder is, not that men are so self-seeking, but that they are not much more so. That under present circumstances men are not more grasping, more unfaithful, more selfish than they are, proves the goodness and fruitfulness of human nature, the ceaseless flow of the perennial fountains from which its moral qualities are fed. All of us have mothers; most of us have children, and so faith, and purity, and unselfishness can never be utterly banished from the world, howsoever bad be social adjustments.

But whatever is potent for evil may be made potent for good. The change I have proposed would destroy the conditions that distort impulses in themselves beneficent, and would transmute the forces which now tend to disintegrate society into forces which would tend to unite and purify it.

Give labor a free field and its full earnings; take for the benefit of the whole community that fund which the growth of the community creates, and want and the fear of want would be gone. The springs of production would be set free, and the enormous increase of wealth would give the poorest ample comfort. Men would no more worry about finding employment than they worry about finding air to breathe; they need have no more care about physical necessities than do the lilies of the field. The progress of science, the march of invention, the diffusion of knowledge, would bring their benefits to all.

With this abolition of want and the fear of want, the admiration of riches would decay, and men would seek the respect and approbation of their fellows in other modes than by the acquisition and display of wealth. In this way there would be brought to the management of public affairs, and the administration of common funds, the skill, the attention, the fidelity, and integrity that can now be secured only for private interests, and a railroad or gas works might be operated on public account, not only more economically and efficiently than as at present, under joint-stock management, but as economically and efficiently as would be possible under a single ownership. The prize of the Olympian games, that called forth the most strenuous exertions of all Greece, was but a wreath of wild olive; for a bit of ribbon men have over and over again performed services no money could have bought.

Shortsighted is the philosophy which counts on selfishness as the master motive of human action. It is blind to facts of which the world is full. It sees not the present, and reads not the past aright. If you would move men to action, to what shall you appeal? Not to their pockets, but to their patriotism; not to selfishness, but to sympathy. Self-interest is, as it were, a mechanical force—potent, it is true; capable of large and wide results. But there is in human nature what may be likened to a chemical force; which melts and fuses and overwhelms; to which nothing seems impossible. "All that a man hath will he give for his life"—that is self-interest. But in loyalty to higher impulses men will give even life.

It is not selfishness that enriches the annals of every people with heroes and saints. It is not selfishness that on every page of the world's history bursts out in sudden splendor of noble deeds or sheds the soft radiance of benignant lives. It was not selfishness that turned Gautama's back to his royal home or bade the Maid of Orleans lift the sword from the altar; that held the Three Hundred in the Pass of Thermopylæ, or gathered into Winkelried's bosom the sheaf of spears; that chained Vincent de Paul to the bench of the galley, or brought little starving children, during the Indian famine, tottering to the relief stations with yet weaker starvelings in their arms. Call it religion, patriotism, sympathy, the enthusiasm for humanity, or the love of God—give it what name you will; there is yet a force which overcomes and drives out selfishness; a force which is the electricity of the moral universe; a force beside which all others are weak. Everywhere that men have lived it has shown its power, and today, as ever, the world is full of it. To be pitied is the man who has never seen and never felt it. Look around! among common men and women, amid the care and the struggle of daily life, in the jar of the noisy street and amid the squalor where want hides—every here and there is the darkness lighted with the tremulous play of its lambent flames. He who has not seen it has walked with shut eyes. He who looks may see, as says Plutarch, that "the soul has a principle of kindness in itself, and is born to love, as well as to perceive, think, or remember."

And this force of forces—that now goes to waste or assumes perverted forms—we may use for the strengthening, and building up, and ennobling of society, if we but will, just as we now use physical forces that once seemed but powers of destruction. All we have to do is but to give it freedom and scope. The wrong that produces inequality; the wrong that in the midst of abundance tortures men with want or harries them with the fear of want; that stunts them physically, degrades them intellectually, and distorts them morally, is what alone prevents harmonious social development. For, as Marcus Aurelius says, "all that is from the gods is full of providence. We are made for co-operation—like feet, like hands, like eyelids, like the rows of the upper and lower teeth."

THE THEORY OF THE LEISURE CLASS

by

THORSTEIN VEBLEN

CONTENTS

The Theory of the Leisure Class

THORSTEIN VEBLEN

1857–1929

THORSTEIN VEBLEN, iconoclastic American economist and social philosopher, was born of Norwegian parentage on a Wisconsin farm in 1857. He was the sixth of twelve children, and his early years were beset by hardship. When Veblen was eight, the family moved to a farm in Minnesota. At the age of seventeen he became a student in Carleton College, Northfield, Minnesota, and among his teachers in this Congregational institution was John Bates Clark, outstanding economist. It may have been Clark who first aroused his serious interest in economics, though late in life Veblen directed some of his sharpest shafts at certain of Clark's economic theories.

Young Veblen's hunger for knowledge was insatiable, and he studied minerals, plants, and animals, as well as languages and the arts and religions of mankind. For a while he taught at Madison, Wisconsin. Then he left for the Johns Hopkins University in Baltimore. A few years later he received his Ph.D. degree from Yale, and later still he was studying at Cornell. In 1892, on the invitation of Professor J. Laurence Laughlin, he became a teacher in the newly established University of Chicago. During this period he edited the *Journal of Political Economy* and came in contact with a number of distinguished American scholars, among them John Dewey, Franz Boas, Jacques Loeb, and Lester F. Ward. His next teaching position was under President David Starr Jordan at Stanford. From there he went to the University of Missouri. Towards the end of his life he wrote for the *Dial* and lectured at the New School for Social Research in New York City.

The record of Veblen is that of an innovator and nonconformist. By some he has been hailed as a genius; by others derided as an eccentric. Whatever the ultimate verdict on his doctrines may prove to be, it is clear that from the beginning until the end of his career he never lacked disciples. He has been called the father of "institutional" economics. He has also been called a "functionalist." He opposed the existing business system, with its vested interests and its absentee ownership, because, in his view, it was incompatible with a sound industrialism. The flare-up of the so-called Technocratic movement in the early 1930s was partly due to his influence. His literary style is highly individualized, and some of his phrases, such as "conspicuous waste" and "conspicuous consumption," have passed into the currency of the language. He never wrote a systematic treatise on economics. Instead he published nine monographs and many essays.

One of his earliest essays expressed his admiration for David Hume, skeptical Scottish historian, economist, and moral philosopher. He was strongly influenced by Charles Darwin and Herbert Spencer, and in an essay on "Some Neglected Points in the Theory of Socialism," published in 1892, he described himself as a disciple of Spencer. In two later essays, dealing with the economics of Karl Marx, he endeavored to apply the logic of Darwinism to the socialist philosophy. It was Veblen's contention that Marx had been misled by the superficial psychology of the "natural rights" school and by a romantic metaphysics derived from Hegel. The capitalistic order of society might, or might not, develop into a socialistic order. So vast a change would depend on problems of constructive social engineering. Where Marx had stumbled, in Veblen's opinion, was in making the theory of social evolution an intellectual sequence that tends to a goal, "the classless economic structure of the socialistic final term," whereas the Darwinian doctrine envisages a "blindly cumulative causation, in which there is no trend, no final term, no consummation."

The first of Veblen's books was *The Theory of the Leisure Class,* published in 1899 and reprinted in several editions. Its argument is simple. As society advances beyond its primitive stages and men begin to accumulate a surplus beyond their immediate needs, they tend to use this surplus not so much in wise and intelligent living as in efforts to impress their neighbors with the fact that they have a surplus. In every country is a "kept class," a leisure class, in contrast with the "underlying population" which works hard to produce the necessities of life. The leisure class is distinguished by its "pecuniary emulation," its "pecuniary canons of taste," its "conspicuous waste," and its "conspicuous consumption." The workers at the base of the social structure only too often envy the leisure class and strive to imitate its habits. *The Theory of the Leisure Class* is unique in economic literature in its combination of stinging irony and prodigious learning.

Eight more books of economic theory were to follow *The Theory of the Leisure Class.* They are: *The Theory of Business Enterprise* (1904); *The Instinct of Workmanship and the State of the Industrial Arts* (1914); *Imperial Germany and the Industrial Revolution* (1915); *An Inquiry into the Nature of Peace* (1917); *The Higher Learning in America* (1919); *The Vested Interests and the State of the Industrial Arts* (1919); *The Engineers and the Price System* (1921); *Absentee Ownership and Business Enterprise in Recent Times, the Case of America* (1923).

In *The Engineers and the Price System,* consisting of essays contributed to the *Dial,* we come perhaps nearer to the core of Veblen's doctrine than in his longer and more closely reasoned writings. He tells us here that the setting of prices in the contemporary economic world is not a matter of the free play of market forces, but is the result of innumerable controls exercised over the factors of production and distribution. These controls must be changed, and we get a glimpse of a possible alternative to the existing social order. Veblen speaks of a "soviet of technicians," and he says that elimination of the present commercial controls of industry "will call for diligent teamwork on the part of a suitable group of economists and engineers, who will have to be drawn together by self-selection on the basis of a common interest in productive efficiency, economical use of resources, and an equitable distribution of the consumable output."

It was Veblen's distinction that he created an original set of economic categories based on changing industrial conditions rather than on an inflexible system formulated from so-called eternal principles. In his view the basic instincts of human nature are constantly being modified by institutions. The business of the economist is to examine and estimate these institutions. Veblen talked of "cumulative change" rather than of progress. He offered, like Darwin, an evolutionary philosophy which, in the long run, must be validated by patient inquiries. His speculations have proved extraordinarily stimulating not only to experts in the economic field but also to laymen.

THE THEORY OF THE LEISURE CLASS

I. PECUNIARY EMULATION

In the sequence of cultural evolution the emergence of a leisure class coincides with the beginning of ownership. This is necessarily the case, for these two institutions result from the same set of economic forces. In the inchoate phase of their development they are but different aspects of the same general facts of social structure.

It is as elements of social structure—conventional facts—that leisure and ownership are matters of interest for the purpose in hand. An habitual neglect of work does not constitute a leisure class; neither does the mechanical fact of use and consumption constitute ownership. The present inquiry, therefore, is not concerned with the beginning of indolence, nor with the beginning of the appropriation of useful articles to individual consumption. The point in question is the origin and nature of a conventional leisure class on the one hand and the beginnings of individual ownership as a conventional right or equitable claim on the other hand.

The early differentiation out of which the distinction between a leisure and a working class arises is a division maintained between men's and women's work in the lower stages of barbarism. Likewise the earliest form of ownership is an ownership of the women by the able-bodied men of the community. The facts may be expressed in more general terms, and truer to the import of the barbarian theory of life, by saying that it is an ownership of the woman by the man.

There was undoubtedly some appropriation of useful articles before the custom of appropriating women arose. The usages of existing archaic communities in which there is no ownership of women is warrant for such a view. In all communities the members, both male and female, habitually appropriate to their individual use a variety of useful things; but these useful things are not thought of as owned by the person who appropriates and consumes them. The habitual appropriation and consumption of certain slight personal effects goes on without raising the question of ownership; that is to say, the question of a conventional, equitable claim to extraneous things.

The ownership of women begins in the lower barbarian stages of culture, apparently with the seizure of female captives. The original reason for the seizure and appropriation of women seems to have been their usefulness as trophies. The practice of seizing women from the enemy as trophies, gave rise to a form of ownership-marriage, resulting in a household with a male head. This was followed by an extension of slavery to other captives and inferiors, besides women, and by an extension of ownership-marriage to other women than those seized from the enemy. The outcome of emulation under the circumstances of a predatory life, therefore, has been on the one hand a form of marriage resting on coercion, and on the other hand the custom of ownership. The two institutions are not distinguishable in the initial phase of their development; both arise from the desire of the successful men to put their prowess in evidence by exhibiting some durable result of their exploits. Both also minister to that propensity for mastery which pervades all predatory communities. From the ownership of women the concept of ownership extends itself to include the products of their industry, and so there arises the ownership of things as well as of persons.

In this way a consistent system of property in goods is gradually installed. And although in the latest stages of the development, the serviceability of goods for consumption has come to be the most obtrusive element of their value, still, wealth has by no means yet lost its utility as an honorific evidence of the owner's prepotence.

Wherever the institution of private property is found, even in a slightly developed form, the economic process bears the character of a struggle between men for the possession of goods. It has been customary in economic theory, and especially among those economists who adhere with least faltering to the body of modernised classical doctrines, to construe this struggle for wealth as being substantially a struggle for subsistence. Such is, no doubt, its character in large part during the earlier and less efficient phases of industry. Such is also its character in all cases where the "niggardliness of nature" is so strict as to afford but a scanty livelihood to the community in return for strenuous and unremitting application to the business of getting the means of subsistence. But in all progressing communities an advance is presently made beyond this early stage of technological development. Industrial efficiency is presently carried to such a pitch as to afford something appreciably more than a bare livelihood to those engaged in the industrial process. It has not been unusual for economic theory to speak of the further struggle for wealth on this new industrial basis as a competition for an increase of the comforts of life,—primarily for an increase of the physical comforts which the consumption of goods affords.

The end of acquisition and accumulation is conventionally held to be the consumption of the goods accumulated—whether it is consumption directly by the owner of the goods or by the household attached to him and for this purpose identified with him in theory. This is at least felt to be the economically legitimate end of acquisition, which alone it is incumbent on the theory to take account of. Such consumption may of course be conceived to serve the consumer's physical wants—his physical comfort—or his so-called higher wants—spiritual, æsthetic, intellectual, or what not; the latter class of wants being served indirectly by an expenditure of goods, after the fashion familiar to all economic readers.

But it is only when taken in a sense far removed from its naïve meaning that consumption of goods can be said to afford the incentive from which accumulation invariably proceeds. The motive that lies at the root of ownership is emulation; and the same motive of emulation continues active in the further development of the institution to which it has given rise and in the development of all those features of the social structure which this institution of ownership touches. The possession of wealth confers honour; it is an invidious distinction. Nothing equally cogent can be said for the consumption of goods, nor for any other conceivable incentive to acquisition, and especially not for any incentive to the accumulation of wealth.

It is of course not to be overlooked that in a community where nearly all goods are private property the necessity of earning a livelihood is a powerful and ever-present incentive for the poorer members of the community. The need of subsistence and of an increase of physical comfort may for a time be the dominant motive of acquisition for those classes who are habitually employed at manual labour, whose subsistence is on a precarious footing, who possess little and ordinarily accumulate little; but it will appear in the course of the discussion that even in the case of these impecunious classes the predominance of the motive of physical want is not so decided as has sometimes been assumed. On the other hand, so far as regards those members and classes of the community who are chiefly concerned in the accumulation of wealth, the incentive of subsistence or of physical comfort never plays a considerable part. Ownership began and grew into a human institution on grounds unrelated to the subsistence minimum. The dominant incentive was from the outset the invidious distinction attaching to wealth, and, save temporarily and by exception, no other motive has usurped the primacy at any later stage of the development.

Property set out with being booty held as trophies of the successful raid. So long as the group had departed but little from the primitive communal organisation, and so long as it still stood in close contact with other hostile groups, the utility of things or persons owned lay chiefly in an invidious comparison between their possessor and the enemy from whom they were taken. The habit of distinguishing between the interests of the individual and those of the group to which he belongs is apparently a later growth. Invidious comparison between the possessor of the honorific booty and his less successful neighbours within the group was no doubt present early as an element of the utility of the things possessed, though this was not at the outset the chief element of their value. The man's prowess was still primarily the group's prowess, and the possessor of the booty felt himself to be primarily the keeper of the honour of his group. This appreciation of exploit from the communal point of view is met with also at later stages of social growth, especially as regards the laurels of war.

But so soon as the custom of individual ownership begins to gain consistency, the point of view taken in making the invidious comparison on which private property rests will begin to change. Indeed, the one change is but the reflex of the other. The initial phase of ownership, the phase of acquisition by naïve seizure and conversion, begins to pass into the subsequent stage of an incipient organisation of industry on the basis of private property (in slaves); the horde develops into a more or less self-sufficing industrial community; possessions then come to be valued not so much as evidence of successful foray, but rather as evidence of the prepotence of the possessor of these goods over other individuals within the community. The invidious comparison now becomes primarily a comparison of the owner with the other members of the group. Property is still of the nature of trophy, but, with the cultural advance, it becomes more and more a trophy of successes scored in the game of ownership carried on between the members of the group under the quasi-peaceable methods of nomadic life.

Gradually, as industrial activity further displaces predatory activity in the community's everyday life and in men's habits of thought, accumulated property more and more replaces trophies of predatory exploit as the conventional exponent of prepotence and success. With the growth of settled industry, therefore, the possession of wealth gains in relative importance and effectiveness as a customary basis of repute and esteem. Not that esteem ceases to be awarded on the basis of other, more direct evidence of prowess; not that successful predatory aggression or warlike exploit ceases to call out the approval and admiration of the crowd, or to stir the envy of the less successful competitors; but the opportunities for gaining distinction by means of this direct manifestation of superior force grow less available both in scope and frequency. At the same time opportunities for industrial aggression, and for the accumulation of property by the quasi-peaceable methods of nomadic industry, increase in scope and availability. And it is even more to the point that property now becomes the most easily recognised evidence of a reputable degree of success as distinguished from heroic or signal achievement. It therefore becomes the conventional basis of esteem. Its possession in some amount becomes necessary in order to [achieve] any reputable standing in the community. It becomes indispensable to accumulate property, in order to retain one's good name. When accumulated goods have in this way once become the accepted badge of efficiency, the possession of wealth presently assumes the character of an independent and definitive basis of esteem. The possession of goods, whether acquired aggressively by one's own exertion or passively by transmission through inheritance from others, becomes a conventional basis of reputability. The possession of wealth, which was at the outset valued simply as an evidence of efficiency, becomes, in popular apprehension, itself a meritorious act. Wealth is now itself intrinsically honourable and confers honour on its possessor. By a further refinement, wealth acquired passively by transmission from ancestors or other antecedents presently becomes even more honorific than wealth acquired by the possessor's own effort; but this distinction belongs at a later stage in the evolution of the pecuniary culture and will be spoken of in its place.

Prowess and exploit may still remain the basis of award of the highest popular esteem, although the possession of wealth has become the basis of commonplace reputability and of a blameless social standing. The predatory instinct and the consequent approbation of predatory efficiency are deeply ingrained in the habits of thought of those peoples who have passed under the discipline of a protracted predatory culture. According to popular award, the highest honours within human reach may, even yet, be those gained by an unfolding of extraordinary predatory efficiency in war, or by a quasi-predatory efficiency in statecraft; but for the purposes of a commonplace decent standing in the community these means of repute have been replaced by the acquisition and accumulation of goods. In order to stand well in the eyes of the community, it is necessary to come up to a certain, somewhat indefinite, conventional standard of wealth; just as in the earlier predatory stage it is necessary for the barbarian man to come up to the tribe's standard of physical endurance, cunning, and skill at arms. A certain standard of wealth in the one case, and of prowess in the other, is a necessary condition of reputability, and anything in excess of this normal amount is meritorious.

Those members of the community who fall short of this, somewhat indefinite, normal degree of prowess or of property suffer in the esteem of their fellow-men; and consequently they suffer also in their own esteem, since the usual basis of self-respect is the respect accorded by one's neighbours. Only individuals with an aberrant temperament can in the long run retain their self-esteem in the face of the disesteem of their fellows. Apparent exceptions to the rule are met with, especially among people with strong religious convictions. But these apparent exceptions are scarcely real exceptions, since such persons commonly fall back on the putative approbation of some supernatural witness of their deeds.

So soon as the possession of property becomes the basis of popular esteem, therefore, it becomes also a requisite to that complacency which we call self-respect. In any community where goods are held in severalty it is necessary, in order to his own peace of mind, that an individual should possess as large a portion of goods as others with whom he is accustomed to class himself; and it is extremely gratifying to possess something more than others. But as fast as a person makes new acquisitions, and becomes accustomed to the resulting new standard of wealth, the new standard forthwith ceases to afford appreciably greater satisfaction than the earlier standard did. The tendency in any case is constantly to make the present pecuniary standard the point of departure for a fresh increase of wealth; and this in turn gives rise to a new standard of sufficiency and a new pecuniary classification of one's self as compared with one's neighbours. So far as concerns the present question, the end sought by accumulation is to rank high in comparison with the rest of the community in point of pecuniary strength. So long as the comparison is distinctly unfavourable to himself, the normal, average individual will live in chronic dissatisfaction with his present lot; and when he has reached what may be called the normal pecuniary standard of the community, or of his class in the community, this chronic dissatisfaction will give place to a restless straining to place a wider and ever-widening pecuniary interval between himself and this average standard. The invidious comparison can never become so favourable to the individual making it that he would not gladly rate himself still higher relatively to his competitors in the struggle for pecuniary reputability.

In the nature of the case, the desire for wealth can scarcely be satiated in any individual instance, and evidently a satiation of the average or general desire for wealth is out of the question. However widely, or equally, or "fairly," it may be distributed, no general increase of the community's wealth can make any approach to satiating this need, the ground of which is the desire of every one to excel every one else in the accumulation of goods. If, as is sometimes assumed, the incentive to accumulation were the want of subsistence or of physical comfort, then the aggregate economic wants of a community might conceivably be satisfied at some point in the advance of industrial efficiency; but since the struggle is substantially a race for reputability on the basis of an invidious comparison, no approach to a definitive attainment is possible.

What has just been said must not be taken to mean that there are no other incentives to acquisition and accumulation than this desire to excel in pecuniary standing and so gain the esteem and envy of one's fellow-men. The desire for added comfort and security from want is present as a motive at every stage of the process of accumulation in a modern industrial community; although the standard of sufficiency in these respects is in turn greatly affected by the habit of pecuniary emulation. To a great extent this emulation shapes the methods and selects the objects of expenditure for personal comfort and decent livelihood.

Besides this, the power conferred by wealth also affords a motive to accumulation. That propensity for purposeful activity and that repugnance to all futility of effort which belong to man by virtue of his character as an agent do not desert him when he emerges from the naïve communal culture where the dominant note of life is the unanalysed and undifferentiated solidarity of the individual with the group with which his life is bound up. When he enters upon the predatory stage, where self-seeking in the narrower sense becomes the dominant note, this propensity goes with him still, as the pervasive trait that shapes his scheme of life. The propensity for achievement and the repugnance to futility remain the underlying economic motive. The propensity changes only in the form of its expression and in the proximate objects to which it directs the man's activity. Under the regime of individual ownership the most available means of visibly achieving a purpose is that afforded by the acquisition and accumulation of goods; and as the self-regarding antithesis between man and man reaches fuller consciousness, the propensity for achievement—the instinct of workmanship—tends more and more to shape itself into a straining to excel others in pecuniary achievement. Relative success, tested by an invidious pecuniary comparison with other men, becomes the conventional end of action. The currently accepted legitimate end of effort becomes the achievement of a favourable comparison with other men; and therefore the repugnance to futility to a good extent coalesces with the incentive of emulation. It acts to accentuate the struggle for pecuniary reputability by visiting with a sharper disapproval all shortcoming and all evidence of shortcoming in point of pecuniary success. Purposeful effort comes to mean, primarily, effort directed to or resulting in a more creditable showing of accumulated wealth. Among the motives which lead men to accumulate wealth, the primacy, both in scope and intensity, therefore, continues to belong to this motive of pecuniary emulation.

In making use of the term "invidious," it may perhaps be unnecessary to remark, there is no intention to extol or depreciate, or to commend or deplore any of the phenomena which the word is used to characterise.

The term is used in a technical sense as describing a comparison of persons with a view to rating and grading them in respect of relative worth or value—in an æsthetic or moral sense—and so awarding and defining the relative degrees of complacency with which they may legitimately be contemplated by themselves and by others. An invidious comparison is a process of valuation of persons in respect of worth.

II. CONSPICUOUS LEISURE

If its working were not disturbed by other economic forces or other features of the emulative process, the immediate effect of such a pecuniary struggle as has just been described in outline would be to make men industrious and frugal. This result actually follows, in some measure, so far as regards the lower classes, whose ordinary means of acquiring goods is productive labour. This is more especially true of the labouring classes in a sedentary community which is at an agricultural stage of industry, in which there is a considerable subdivision of property, and whose laws and customs secure to these classes a more or less definite share of the product of their industry. These lower classes can in any case not avoid labour, and the imputation of labour is therefore not greatly derogatory to them, at least not within their class. Rather, since labour is their recognised and accepted mode of life, they take some emulative pride in a reputation for efficiency in their work, this being often the only line of emulation that is open to them. For those for whom acquisition and emulation is possible only within the field of productive efficiency and thrift, the struggle for pecuniary reputability will in some measure work out in an increase of diligence and parsimony. But certain secondary features of the emulative process, yet to be spoken of, come in to very materially circumscribe and modify emulation in these directions among the pecuniarily inferior classes as well as among the superior class.

But it is otherwise with the superior pecuniary class, with which we are here immediately concerned. For this class also the incentive to diligence and thrift is not absent; but its action is so greatly qualified by the secondary demands of pecuniary emulation, that any inclination in this direction is practically overborne and any incentive to diligence tends to be of no effect. The most imperative of these secondary demands of emulation, as well as the one of widest scope, is the requirement of abstention from productive work. This is true in an especial degree for the barbarian stage of culture. During the predatory culture labour comes to be associated in men's habits of thought with weakness and subjection to a master. It is therefore a mark of inferiority, and therefore comes to be accounted unworthy of man in his best estate. By virtue of this tradition labour is felt to be debasing, and this tradition has never died out. On the contrary, with the advance of social differentiation it has acquired the axiomatic force due to ancient and unquestioned prescription.

In order to gain and to hold the esteem of men it is not sufficient merely to possess wealth or power. The wealth or power must be put in evidence, for esteem is awarded only on evidence. And not only does the evidence of wealth serve to impress one's importance on others and to keep their sense of his importance alive and alert, but it is of scarcely less use in building up and preserving one's self-complacency. In all but the lowest stages of culture the normally constituted man is comforted and upheld in his self-respect by "decent surroundings" and by exemption from "menial offices." Enforced departure from his habitual standard of decency, either in the paraphernalia of life or in the kind and amount of his everyday activity, is felt to be a slight upon his human dignity, even apart from all conscious consideration of the approval or disapproval of his fellows.

The archaic theoretical distinction between the base and the honourable in the manner of a man's life retains very much of its ancient force even to-day. So much so that there are few of the better class who are not possessed of an instinctive repugnance for the vulgar forms of labour. We have a realising sense of ceremonial uncleanness attaching in an especial degree to the occupations which are associated in our habits of thought with menial service. It is felt by all persons of refined taste that a spiritual contamination is inseparable from certain offices that are conventionally required of servants. Vulgar surroundings, mean (that is to say, inexpensive) habitations, and vulgarly productive occupations are unhesitatingly condemned and avoided. They are incompatible with life on a satisfactory spiritual plane—with "high thinking." From the days of the Greek philosophers to the present, a degree of leisure and of exemption from contact with such industrial processes as serve the immediate everyday purposes of human life has ever been recognised by thoughtful men as a prerequisite to a worthy or beautiful, or even a blameless, human life. In itself and in its consequences the life of leisure is beautiful and ennobling in all civilised men's eyes.

This direct, subjective value of leisure and of other evidences of wealth is no doubt in great part secondary and derivative. It is in part a reflex of the utility of leisure as a means of gaining the respect of others, and in part it is the result of a mental substitution. The performance of labour has been accepted as a conventional evidence of inferior force; therefore it comes itself, by a mental short-cut, to be regarded as intrinsically base.

During the predatory stage proper, and especially during the earlier stages of the quasi-peaceable development of industry that follows the predatory stage, a life of leisure is the readiest and most conclusive evidence of pecuniary strength, and therefore of superior force; provided always that the gentleman of leisure can live in manifest ease and comfort. At this stage wealth consists chiefly of slaves, and the benefits accruing from the possession of riches and power take the form chiefly of personal service and the immediate products of personal service. Conspicuous abstention from labour therefore becomes the conventional mark of superior pecuniary achievement and the conventional index of reputability; and conversely, since application to productive labour is a mark of poverty and subjection, it becomes inconsistent with a reputable standing in the community. Habits of industry and thrift, therefore, are not uniformly furthered by a prevailing pecuniary emulation. On the contrary, this kind of emulation indirectly discountenances participation in productive labour. Labour would unavoidably become dishonourable, as being an evidence of poverty, even if it were not already accounted indecorous under the ancient tradition handed down from an earlier cultural stage. The ancient tradition of the predatory culture is that productive effort is to be shunned as being unworthy of able-bodied men, and this tradition is reinforced rather than set aside in the passage from the predatory to the quasi-peaceable manner of life.

Even if the institution of a leisure class had not come in with the first emergence of individual ownership, by force of the dishonour attaching to productive employment, it would in any case have come in as one of the early consequences of ownership. And it is to be remarked that while the leisure class existed in theory from the beginning of predatory culture, the institution takes on a new and fuller meaning with the transition from the predatory to the next succeeding pecuniary stage of culture. It is from this time forth a "leisure class" in fact as well as in theory. From this point dates the institution of the leisure class in its consummate form.

During the predatory stage proper the distinction between the leisure and the labouring class is in some degree a ceremonial distinction only. The able-bodied men jealously stand aloof from whatever is, in their apprehension, menial drudgery; but their activity in fact contributes appreciably to the sustenance of the group. The subsequent stage of quasi-peaceable industry is usually characterised by an established chattel slavery, herds of cattle, and a servile class of herdsmen and shepherds; industry has advanced so far that the community is no longer dependent for its livelihood on the chase or on any other form of activity that can fairly be classed as exploit. From this point on, the characteristic feature of leisure-class life is a conspicuous exemption from all useful employment.

The normal and characteristic occupations of the class in this mature phase of its life history are in form very much the same as in its earlier days. These occupations are government, war, sports, and devout observances. Persons unduly given to difficult theoretical niceties may hold that these occupations are still incidentally and indirectly "productive"; but it is to be noted as decisive of the question in hand that the ordinary and ostensible motive of the leisure class in engaging in these occupations is assuredly not an increase of wealth by productive effort. At this as at any other cultural stage, government and war are, at least in part, carried on for the pecuniary gain of those who engage in them; but it is gain obtained by the honourable method of seizure and conversion. These occupations are of the nature of predatory, not of productive, employment. Something similar may be said of the chase, but with a difference. As the community passes out of the hunting stage proper, hunting gradually becomes differentiated into two distinct employments. On the one hand it is a trade, carried on chiefly for gain; and from this the element of exploit is virtually absent, or it is at any rate not present in a sufficient degree to clear the pursuit of the imputation of gainful industry. On the other hand, the chase is also a sport—an exercise of the predatory impulse simply. As such it does not afford any appreciable pecuniary incentive, but it contains a more or less obvious element of exploit. It is this latter development of the chase—purged of all imputation of handicraft—that alone is meritorious and fairly belongs in the scheme of life of the developed leisure class.

Abstention from labour is not only an honorific or meritorious act, but it presently comes to be a requisite of decency. The insistence on property as the basis of reputability is very naïve and very imperious during the early stages of the accumulation of wealth. Abstention from labour is the conventional evidence of wealth and is therefore the conventional mark of social standing; and this insistence on the meritoriousness of wealth leads to a more strenuous insistence on leisure. *Nota notæ est nota rei ipsius.* According to well-established laws of human nature, prescription presently seizes upon this conventional evidence of wealth and fixes it in men's habits of thought as something that is in itself substantially meritorious and ennobling; while productive labour at the same time and by a like process becomes in a double sense intrinsically unworthy. Prescription ends by making labour not only disreputable in the eyes of the community, but morally impossible to the noble, freeborn man, and incompatible with a worthy life.

This tabu on labour has a further consequence in the industrial differentiation of classes. As the population increases in density and the predatory group grows into a settled industrial community, the constituted authorities and the customs governing ownership gain in scope and consistency. It then presently becomes impracticable to accumulate wealth by simple seizure, and, in logical consistency, acquisition by industry is equally impossible for high-minded and impecunious men. The alternative open to them is beggary or privation. Wherever the canon of conspicuous leisure has a chance undisturbed to work out its tendency, there will therefore emerge a secondary, and in a sense spurious, leisure class —abjectly poor and living a precarious life of want and discomfort, but morally unable to stoop to gainful pursuits. The decayed gentleman and the lady who has seen better days are by no means unfamiliar phenomena even now. This pervading sense of the indignity of the slightest manual labour is familiar to all civilised peoples, as well as to peoples of a less advanced pecuniary culture. In persons of delicate sensibility, who have long been habituated to gentle manners, the sense of the shamefulness of manual labour may become so strong that, at a critical juncture, it will even set aside the instinct of self-preservation. So, for instance, we are told of certain Polynesian chiefs, who, under the stress of good form, preferred to starve rather than carry their food to their mouths with their own hands. It is true, this conduct may have been due, at least in part, to an excessive sanctity or tabu attaching to the chief's person. The tabu would have been communicated by the contact of his hands, and so would have made anything touched by him unfit for human food. But the tabu is itself a derivative of the unworthiness or moral incompatibility of labour; so that even when construed in this sense the conduct of the Polynesian chiefs is truer to the canon of honorific leisure than would at first appear. A better illustration, or at least a more unmistakable one, is afforded by a certain king of France, who is said to have lost his life through an excess of moral stamina in the observance of good form. In the absence of the functionary whose office it was to shift his master's seat, the king sat uncomplaining before the fire and suffered his royal person to be toasted beyond recovery. But in so doing he saved his Most Christian Majesty from menial contamination.

Summum crede nefas animam præferre pudori,
Et propter vitam vivendi perdere causas.

It has already been remarked that the term "leisure," as here used, does not connote indolence or quiescence. What it connotes is non-productive consumption of time. Time is consumed non-productively (1) from a sense of the unworthiness of productive work, and (2) as an evidence of pecuniary ability to afford a life of idleness. But the whole of the life of the gentleman of leisure is not spent before the eyes of the spectators who are to be impressed with that spectacle of honorific leisure which in the ideal scheme makes up his life. For some part of the time his life is perforce withdrawn from the public eye, and of this portion which is spent in private the gentleman of leisure should, for the sake of his good name, be able to give a convincing account. He should find some means of putting in evidence the leisure that is not spent in the sight of the spectators. This can be done only indirectly, through the exhibition of some tangible, lasting results of the leisure so spent—in a manner analogous to the familiar exhibition of tangible, lasting products of the labour performed for the gentleman of leisure by handicraftsmen and servants in his employ.

The lasting evidence of productive labour is its material product—commonly some article of consumption. In the case of exploit it is similarly possible and usual to procure some tangible result that may serve for exhibition in the way of trophy or booty. At a later phase of the development it is customary to assume some badge or insignia of honour that will serve as a conventionally accepted mark of exploit, and which at the same time indicates the quantity or degree of exploit of which it is the symbol. As the population increases in densit[illegible] relations grow more complex and numerous, all the det[illegible] a process of elaboration and selection; and in this process of elabor[illegible] the use of trophies develops into a system of rank, titles, degrees, and insignia, typical examples of which are heraldic devices, medals, and honorary decorations.

As seen from the economic point of view, leisure, considered as an employment, is closely allied in kind with the life of exploit; and the achievements which characterise a life of leisure, and which remain as its decorous criteria, have much in common with the trophies of exploit. But leisure in the narrower sense, as distinct from exploit and from any ostensibly productive employment of effort on objects which are of no intrinsic use, does not commonly leave a material product. The criteria of a past performance of leisure therefore commonly take the form of "immaterial" goods. Such immaterial evidences of past leisure are quasi-scholarly or quasi-artistic accomplishments and a knowledge of processes and incidents which do not conduce directly to the furtherance of human life. So, for instance, in our time there is the knowledge of the dead languages and the occult sciences; of correct spelling; of syntax and prosody; of the various forms of domestic music and other household art; of the latest proprieties of dress, furniture, and equipage; of games, sports, and fancy-bred animals, such as dogs and race-horses. In all these branches of knowledge the initial motive from which their acquisition proceeded at the outset, and through which they first came into vogue, may have been something quite different from the wish to show that one's time had not been spent in industrial employment; but unless these accomplishments had approved themselves as serviceable evidence of an unproductive expenditure of time, they would not have survived and held their place as conventional accomplishments of the leisure class.

These accomplishments may, in some sense, be classed as branches of learning. Beside and beyond these there is a further range of social facts which shade off from the region of learning into that of physical habit and dexterity.

Decorum set out with being symbol and pantomime and with having utility only as an exponent of the facts and qualities symbolised; but it presently suffered the transmutation which commonly passes over symbolical facts in human intercourse. Manners presently came, in popular apprehension, to be possessed of a substantial utility in themselves; they acquired a sacramental character, in great measure independent of the facts which they originally prefigured. Deviations from the code of decorum have become intrinsically odious to all men, and good breeding is, in everyday apprehension, not simply an adventitious mark of human excellence, but an integral feature of the worthy human soul. There are [illegible] touch us with instinctive revulsion as a breach of [illegible] ave we progressed in the direction of imputing [illegible] to the ceremonial observances of etiquette that few of us, if any, can dissociate an offence against etiquette from a sense of the substantial unworthiness of the offender. A breach of faith may be condoned, but a breach of decorum can not. "Manners maketh man."

In this connection it is worthy of notice that the possibility of producing pathological and other idiosyncrasies of person and manner by shrewd mimicry and a systematic drill have been turned to account in the deliberate production of a cultured class—often with a very happy effect. In this way, by the process vulgarly known as snobbery, a syncopated evolution of gentle birth and breeding is achieved in the case of a goodly number of families and lines of descent. This syncopated gentle birth gives results which, in point of serviceability as a leisure-class factor in the population, are in no wise substantially inferior to others who may have had a longer but less arduous training in the pecuniary proprieties.

There are, moreover, measureable degrees of conformity to the latest accredited code of the punctilios as regards decorous means and methods of consumption. Differences between one person and another in the degree of conformity to the ideal in these respects can be compared, and persons may be graded and scheduled with some accuracy and effect according to a progressive scale of manners and breeding. The award of reputability in this regard is commonly made in good faith, on the ground of conformity to accepted canons of taste in the matters concerned, and without conscious regard to the pecuniary standing or the degree of leisure practised by any given candidate for reputability; but the canons of taste according to which the award is made are constantly under the surveillance of the law of conspicuous leisure, and are indeed constantly undergoing change and revision to bring them into closer conformity with its requirements. So that while the proximate ground of discrimination may be of another kind, still the pervading principle and abiding test of good breeding is the requirement of a substantial and patent waste of time. There may be some considerable range of variation in detail within the scope of this principle, but they are variations of form and expression, not of substance.

Much of the courtesy of everyday intercourse is of course a direct expression of consideration and kindly good-will, and this element of conduct has for the most part no need of being traced back to any underlying ground of reputability to explain either its presence or the approval with which it is regarded; but the same is not true of the code of proprieties. These latter are expressions of status. It is of course sufficiently plain, to any one who cares to see, that our bearing towards menials and other pecuniarily dependent inferiors is the bearing of the superior member in a relation of status, though its manifestation is often greatly modified and softened from the original expression of crude dominance. Similarly, our bearing towards superiors, and in great measure towards equals, expresses a more or less conventionalised attitude of subservience. Witness the masterful presence of the high-minded gentleman or lady, which testifies to so much of dominance and independence of economic circumstances, and which at the same time appeals with such convincing force to our sense of what is right and gracious. It is among this highest leisure class, who have no superiors and few peers, that decorum finds its fullest and maturest expression; and it is this highest class also that gives decorum that definitive formulation which serves as a canon of conduct for the classes beneath. And here also the code is most obviously a code of status and shows most plainly its incompatibility with all vulgarly productive work. A divine assurance and an imperious complaisance, as of one habituated to require subservience and to take no thought for the morrow, is the birthright and the criterion of the gentleman at his best; and it is in popular apprehension even more than that, for this demeanour is accepted as an intrinsic attribute of superior worth, before which the base-born commoner delights to stoop and yield.

III. CONSPICUOUS CONSUMPTION

Already at a point in economic evolution far antedating the emergence of the lady, specialised consumption of goods as an evidence of pecuniary strength had begun to work out in a more or less elaborate system. The beginning of a differentiation in consumption even antedates the appearance of anything that can fairly be called pecuniary strength. It is traceable back to the initial phase of predatory culture, and there is even a suggestion that an incipient differentiation in this respect lies back of the beginnings of the predatory life. This most primitive differentiation in the consumption of goods is like the later differentiation with which we are all so intimately familiar, in that it is largely of a ceremonial character, but unlike the latter it does not rest on a difference in accumulated wealth. The utility of consumption as an evidence of wealth is to be classed as a derivative growth. It is an adaptation to a new end, by a selective process, of a distinction previously existing and well established in men's habits of thought.

In the earlier phases of the predatory culture the only economic differentiation is a broad distinction between an honourable superior class made up of the able-bodied men on the one side, and a base inferior class of labouring women on the other. According to the ideal scheme of life in force at that time it is the office of the men to consume what the women produce. Such consumption as falls to the women is merely incidental to their work; it is a means to their continued labour, and not a consumption directed to their own comfort and fulness of life. Unproductive consumption of goods is honourable, primarily as a mark of prowess and a perquisite of human dignity; secondarily it becomes substantially honourable in itself, especially the consumption of the more desirable things. The consumption of choice articles of food, and frequently also of rare articles of adornment, becomes tabu to the women and children; and if there is a base (servile) class of men, the tabu holds also for them. With a further advance in culture this tabu may change into simple custom of a more or less rigorous character; but whatever be the theoretical basis of the distinction which is maintained, whether it be a tabu or a larger conventionality, the features of the conventional scheme of consumption do not change easily. When the quasi-peaceable stage of industry is reached, with its fundamental institution of chattel slavery, the general principle, more or less rigorously applied, is that the base, industrious class should consume only what may be necessary to their subsistence. In the nature of things, luxuries and the comforts of life belong to the leisure class. Under the tabu, certain victuals, and more particularly certain beverages, are strictly reserved for the use of the superior class.

The ceremonial differentiation of the dietary is best seen in the use of intoxicating beverages and narcotics. If these articles of consumption are costly, they are felt to be noble and honorific. Therefore the base classes, primarily the women, practise an enforced continence with respect to these stimulants, except in countries where they are obtainable at a very low cost. From archaic times down through all the length of the patriarchal régime it has been the office of the women to prepare and administer these luxuries, and it has been the perquisite of the men of gentle birth and breeding to consume them. Drunkenness and the other pathological consequences of the free use of stimulants therefore tend in their turn to become honorific, as being a mark, at the second remove, of the superior status of those who are able to afford the indulgence. Infirmities induced by over-indulgence are among some peoples freely recognised as manly attributes. It has even happened that the name for certain diseased conditions of the body arising from such an origin has passed into everyday speech as a synonym for "noble" or "gentle." It is only at a relatively early stage of culture that the symptoms of expensive vice are conventionally accepted as marks of a superior status, and so tend to become virtues and command the deference of the community; but the reputability that attaches to certain expensive vices long retains so much of its force as to appreciably lessen the disapprobation visited [illegible] upon the men of the wealthy or noble class for an [illegible] ex[illegible] The same invidious distinction adds force to the [illegible] few things that so[illegible] any indulgence of this kind on the part of women, [illegible] decorum; and so[illegible] This invidious traditional distinction has not lost [illegible] intrinsic utility [illegible] the more advanced peoples of to-day. Where the example set by the leisure class retains its imperative force in the regulation of the conventionalities, it is observable that the women still in great measure practise the same traditional continence with regard to stimulants.

This characterisation of the greater continence in the use of stimulants practised by the women of the reputable classes may seem an excessive refinement of logic at the expense of common sense. But facts within easy reach of any one who cares to know them go to say that the greater abstinence of women is in some part due to an imperative conventionality; and this conventionality is, in a general way, strongest where the patriarchal tradition—the tradition that the woman is a chattel—has retained its hold in greatest vigour. In a sense which has been greatly qualified in scope and rigour, but which has by no means lost its meaning even yet, this tradition says that the woman, being a chattel, should consume only what is necessary to her sustenance,—except so far as her further consumption contributes to the comfort or the good repute of her master. The consumption of luxuries, in the true sense, is a consumption directed to the comfort of the consumer himself, and is, therefore, a mark of the master. Any such consumption by others can take place only on a basis of sufferance. In communities where the popular habits of thought have been profoundly shaped by the patriarchal tradition we may accordingly look for survivals of the tabu on luxuries at least to the extent of a conventional deprecation of their use by the unfree and dependent class. This is more particularly true as regards certain luxuries, the use of which by the dependent class would detract sensibly from the comfort or pleasure of their masters, or which are held to be of doubtful legitimacy on other grounds. In the apprehension of the great conservative middle class of Western civilisation the use of these various stimulants is obnoxious to at least one, if not both, of these objections; and it is a fact too significant to be passed over that it is precisely among these middle classes of the Germanic culture, with their strong surviving sense of the patriarchal proprieties, that the women are to the greatest extent subject to a qualified tabu on narcotics and alcoholic beverages. With many qualifications—with more qualifications as the patriarchal tradition has gradually weakened—the general rule is felt to be right and binding that women should consume only for the benefit of their masters. The objection of course presents itself that expenditure on women's dress and household paraphernalia is an obvious exception to this rule; but it will [illegible] sequel that this exception is much more obvious than [illegible]

[illegible]y, and as human [illegible]ages of economic development, consumption of [illegible]ails of life [illegible] stint, especially consumption of the better grades of goods, —ideally all consumption in excess of the subsistence minimum,—pertains normally to the leisure class. This restriction tends to disappear, at least formally, after the later peaceable stage has been reached, with private ownership of goods and an industrial system based on wage labour or on the petty household economy. But during the earlier quasi-peaceable stage, when so many of the traditions through which the institution of a leisure class has affected the economic life of later times were taking form and consistency, this principle has had the force of a conventional law. It has served as the norm to which consumption has tended to conform, and any appreciable departure from it is to be regarded as an aberrant form, sure to be eliminated sooner or later in the further course of development.

The quasi-peaceable gentleman of leisure, then, not only consumes of the staff of life beyond the minimum required for subsistence and physical efficiency, but his consumption also undergoes a specialisation as regards the quality of the goods consumed. He consumes freely and of the best, in food, drink, narcotics, shelter, services, ornaments, apparel, weapons and accoutrements, amusements, amulets, and idols or divinities. In the process of gradual amelioration which takes place in the articles of his consumption, the motive principle and the proximate aim of innovation is no doubt the higher efficiency of the improved and more elaborate products for personal comfort and well-being. But that does not remain the sole purpose of their consumption. The canon of reputability is at hand and seizes upon such innovations as are, according to its standard, fit to survive. Since the consumption of these more excellent goods is an evidence of wealth, it becomes honorific; and conversely, the failure to consume in due quantity and quality becomes a mark of inferiority and demerit.

This growth of punctilious discrimination as to qualitative excellence in eating, drinking, etc., presently affects not only the manner of life, but also the training and intellectual activity of the gentleman of leisure. He is no longer simply the successful, aggressive male,—the man of strength, resource, and intrepidity. In order to avoid stultification he must also cultivate his tastes, for it now becomes incumbent on him to discriminate with some nicety between the noble and the ignoble in consumable goods. He becomes a connoisseur in creditable viands of various degrees of merit, in manly beverages and trinkets, in seemly apparel and architecture, in weapons, games, dancers, and the narcotics. This cultivation of the æsthetic faculty requires time and application, and the demands made upon the gentleman in this direction therefore tend to change his life of leisure into a more or less arduous application to the business of learning how to live a life of ostensible leisure in a becoming way. Closely related to the requirement that the gentleman must consume freely and of the right kind of goods, there is the requirement that he must know how to consume them in a seemly manner. His life of leisure must be conducted in due form. Hence arise good manners in the way pointed out in an earlier chapter. High-bred manners and ways of living are items of conformity to the norm of conspicuous leisure and conspicuous consumption.

Conspicuous consumption of valuable goods is a means of reputability to the gentleman of leisure. As wealth accumulates on his hands, his own unaided effort will not avail to sufficiently put his opulence in evidence by this method. The aid of friends and competitors is therefore brought in by resorting to the giving of valuable presents and expensive feasts and entertainments. Presents and feasts had probably another origin than that of naïve ostentation, but they acquired their utility for this purpose very early, and they have retained that character to the present; so that their utility in this respect has now long been the substantial ground on which these usages rest. Costly entertainments, such as the potlatch or the ball, are peculiarly adapted to serve this end. The competitor with whom the entertainer wishes to institute a comparison is, by this method, made to serve as a means to the end. He consumes vicariously for his host at the same time that he is a witness to the consumption of that excess of good things which his host is unable to dispose of single-handed, and he is also made to witness his host's facility in etiquette.

From the foregoing survey of the growth of conspicuous leisure and consumption, it appears that the utility of both alike for the purposes of reputability lies in the element of waste that is common to both. In the one case it is a waste of time and effort, in the other it is a waste of goods. Both are methods of demonstrating the possession of wealth, and the two are conventionally accepted as equivalents. The choice between them is a question of advertising expediency simply, except so far as it may be affected by other standards of propriety, springing from a different source. On grounds of expediency the preference may be given to the one or the other at different stages of the economic development. The question is, which of the two methods will most effectively reach the persons whose convictions it is desired to affect. Usage has answered this question in different ways under different circumstances.

So long as the community or social group is small enough and compact enough to be effectually reached by common notoriety alone,—that is to say, so long as the human environment to which the individual is required to adapt himself in respect of reputability is comprised within his sphere of personal acquaintance and neighbourhood gossip,—so long the one method is about as effective as the other. Each will therefore serve about equally well during the earlier stages of social growth. But when the differentiation has gone farther and it becomes necessary to reach a wider human environment, consumption begins to hold over leisure as an ordinary means of decency. This is especially true during the later, peaceable economic stage. The means of communication and the mobility of the population now expose the individual to the observation of many persons who have no other means of judging of his reputability than the display of goods (and perhaps of breeding) which he is able to make while he is under their direct observation.

The modern organisation of industry works in the same direction also by another line. The exigencies of the modern industrial system frequently place individuals and households in juxtaposition between whom there is little contact in any other sense than that of juxtaposition. One's neighbours, mechanically speaking, often are socially not one's neighbours, or even acquaintances; and still their transient good opinion has a high degree of utility. The only practicable means of impressing one's pecuniary ability on these unsympathetic observers of one's everyday life is an unremitting demonstration of ability to pay. In the modern community there is also a more frequent attendance at large gatherings of people to whom one's everyday life is unknown; in such places as churches, theatres, ballrooms, hotels, parks, shops, and the like. In order to impress these transient observers, and to retain one's self-complacency under their observation, the signature of one's pecuniary strength should be written in characters which he who runs may read. It is evident, therefore, that the present trend of the development is in the direction of heightening the utility of conspicuous consumption as compared with leisure.

It is also noticeable that the serviceability of consumption as a means of repute, as well as the insistence on it as an element of decency, is at its best in those portions of the community where the human contact of the individual is widest and the mobility of the population is greatest. Conspicuous consumption claims a relatively larger portion of the income of the urban than of the rural population, and the claim is also more imperative. The result is that, in order to keep up a decent appearance, the former habitually live hand-to-mouth to a greater extent than the latter. So it comes, for instance, that the American farmer and his wife and daughters are notoriously less modish in their dress, as well as less urbane in their manners, than the city artisan's family with an equal income. It is not that the city population is by nature much more eager for the peculiar complacency that comes of a conspicuous consumption, nor has the rural population less regard for pecuniary decency. But the provocation to this line of evidence, as well as its transient effectiveness, are more decided in the city. This method is therefore more readily resorted to, and in the struggle to outdo one another the city population push their normal standard of conspicuous consumption to a higher point, with the result that a relatively greater expenditure in this direction is required to indicate a given degree of pecuniary decency in the city. The requirement of conformity to this higher conventional standard becomes mandatory. The standard of decency is higher, class for class, and this requirement of decent appearance must be lived up to on pain of losing caste.

Consumption becomes a larger element in the standard of living in the city than in the country. Among the country population its place is to some extent taken by savings and home comforts known through the medium of neighbourhood gossip sufficiently to serve the like general purpose of pecuniary repute. These home comforts and the leisure indulged in—where the indulgence is found—are of course also in great part to be classed as items of conspicuous consumption; and much the same is to be said of the savings. The smaller amount of the savings laid by by the artisan class is no doubt due, in some measure, to the fact that in the case of the artisan the savings are a less effective means of advertisement, relative to the environment in which he is placed, than are the savings of the people living on farms and in the small villages. Among the latter, everybody's affairs, especially everybody's pecuniary status, are known to everybody else. Considered by itself simply—taken in the first degree—this added provocation to which the artisan and the urban labouring classes are exposed may not very seriously decrease the amount of savings; but in its cumulative action, through raising the standard of decent expenditure, its deterrent effect on the tendency to save cannot but be very great.

A felicitous illustration of the manner in which this canon of reputability works out its results is seen in the practice of dram-drinking, "treating," and smoking in public places, which is customary among the labourers and handicraftsmen of the towns, and among the lower middle class of the urban population generally.

But there are other standards of repute and other, more or less imperative, canons of conduct, besides wealth and its manifestation, and some of these come in to accentuate or to qualify the broad, fundamental canon of conspicuous waste. Under the simple test of effectiveness for advertising, we should expect to find leisure and the conspicuous consumption of goods dividing the field of pecuniary emulation pretty evenly between them at the outset. Leisure might then be expected gradually to yield ground and tend to obsolescence as the economic development goes forward, and the community increases in size; while the conspicuous consumption of goods should gradually gain in importance, both absolutely and relatively, until it had absorbed all the available product, leaving nothing over beyond a bare livelihood. But the actual course of development has been somewhat different from this ideal scheme. Leisure held the first place at the start, and came to hold a rank very much above wasteful consumption of goods, both as a direct exponent of wealth and as an element in the standard of decency, during the quasi-peaceable culture. From that point onward, consumption has gained ground, until, at present, it unquestionably holds the primacy, though it is still far from absorbing the entire margin of production above the subsistence minimum.

The early ascendency of leisure as a means of reputability is traceable to the archaic distinction between noble and ignoble employments. Leisure is honourable and becomes imperative partly because it shows exemption from ignoble labour. The archaic differentiation into noble and ignoble classes is based on an invidious distinction between employments as honorific or debasing; and this traditional distinction grows into an imperative canon of decency during the early quasi-peaceable stage. Its ascendency is furthered by the fact that leisure is still fully as effective an evidence of wealth as consumption. Indeed, so effective is it in the relatively small and stable human environment to which the individual is exposed at that cultural stage, that, with the aid of the archaic tradition which deprecates all productive labour, it gives rise to a large impecunious leisure class, and it even tends to limit the production of the community's industry to the subsistence minimum. This extreme inhibition of industry is avoided because slave labour, working under a compulsion more rigorous than that of reputability, is forced to turn out a product in excess of the subsistence minimum of the working class. The subsequent relative decline in the use of conspicuous leisure as a basis of repute is due partly to an increasing relative effectiveness of consumption as an evidence of wealth; but in part it is traceable to another force, alien, and in some degree antagonistic, to the usage of conspicuous waste.

This alien factor is the instinct of workmanship. Other circumstances permitting, that instinct disposes men to look with favour upon productive efficiency and on whatever is of human use. It disposes them to deprecate waste of substance or effort. The instinct of workmanship is present in all men, and asserts itself even under very adverse circumstances. So that however wasteful a given expenditure may be in reality, it must at least have some colourable excuse in the way of an ostensible purpose. The manner in which, under special circumstances, the instinct eventuates in a taste for exploit and an invidious discrimination between noble and ignoble classes has been indicated in an earlier chapter. In so far as it comes into conflict with the law of conspicuous waste, the instinct of workmanship expresses itself not so much in insistence on substantial usefulness as in an abiding sense of the odiousness and æsthetic impossibility of what is obviously futile. Being of the nature of an instinctive affection, its guidance touches chiefly and immediately the obvious and apparent violations of its requirements. It is only less promptly and with less constraining force that it reaches such substantial violations of its requirements as are appreciated only upon reflection.

So long as all labour continues to be performed exclusively or usually by slaves, the baseness of all productive effort is too constantly and deterrently present in the mind of men to allow the instinct of workmanship seriously to take effect in the direction of industrial usefulness; but when the quasi-peaceable stage (with slavery and status) passes into the peaceable stage of industry (with wage labour and cash payment) the instinct comes more effectively into play. It then begins aggressively to shape men's views of what is meritorious, and asserts itself at least as an auxiliary canon of self-complacency. All extraneous considerations apart, those persons (adults) are but a vanishing minority to-day who harbour no inclination to the accomplishment of some end, or who are not impelled of their own motion to shape some object or fact or relation for human use. The propensity may in large measure be overborne by the more immediately constraining incentive to a reputable leisure and an avoidance of indecorous usefulness, and it may therefore work itself out in make-believe only; as for instance in "social duties," and in quasi-artistic or quasi-scholarly accomplishments, in the care and decoration of the house, in sewing-circle activity or dress reform, in proficiency at dress, cards, yachting, golf, and various sports. But the fact that it may under stress of circumstances eventuate in inanities no more disproves the presence of the instinct than the reality of the brooding instinct is disproved by inducing a hen to sit on a nestful of china eggs.

This latter-day uneasy reaching-out for some form of purposeful activity that shall at the same time not be indecorously productive of either individual or collective gain marks a difference of attitude between the modern leisure class and that of the quasi-peaceable stage. At the earlier stage, as was said above, the all-dominating institution of slavery and status acted resistlessly to discountenance exertion directed to other than naïvely predatory ends. It was still possible to find some habitual employment for the inclination to action in the way of forcible aggression or repression directed against hostile groups or against the subject classes within the group; and this served to relieve the pressure and draw off the energy of the leisure class without a resort to actually useful, or even ostensibly useful employments. The practice of hunting also served the same purpose in some degree. When the community developed into a peaceful industrial organisation, and when fuller occupation of the land had reduced the opportunities for the hunt to an inconsiderable residue, the pressure of energy seeking purposeful employment was left to find an outlet in some other direction. The ignominy which attaches to useful effort also entered upon a less acute phase with the disappearance of compulsory labor; and the instinct of workmanship then came to assert itself with more persistence and consistency.

The line of least resistance has changed in some measure, and the energy which formerly found a vent in predatory activity, now in part takes the direction of some ostensibly useful end. Ostensibly purposeless leisure has come to be deprecated, especially among that large portion of the leisure class whose plebeian origin acts to set them at variance with the tradition of the *otium cum dignitate*. But that canon of reputability which discountenances all employment that is of the nature of productive effort is still at hand, and will permit nothing beyond the most transient vogue to any employment that is substantially useful or productive. The consequence is that a change has been wrought in the conspicuous leisure practised by the leisure class; not so much in substance as in form. A reconciliation between the two conflicting requirements is effected by a resort to make-believe. Many and intricate polite observances and social duties of a ceremonial nature are developed; many organisations are founded, with some specious object of amelioration embodied in their official style and title; there is much coming and going, and a deal of talk, to the end that the talkers may not have occasion to reflect on what is the effectual economic value of their traffic. And along with the make-believe of purposeful employment, and woven inextricably into its texture, there is commonly, if not invariably, a more or less appreciable element of purposeful effort directed to some serious end.

In the narrower sphere of vicarious leisure a similar change has gone forward. Instead of simply passing her time in visible idleness, as in the best days of the patriarchal régime, the housewife of the advanced peaceable stage applies herself assiduously to household cares. The salient features of this development of domestic service have already been indicated.

Throughout the entire evolution of conspicuous expenditure, whether of goods or of services or human life, runs the obvious implication that in order to effectually mend the consumer's good fame it must be an expenditure of superfluities. In order to be reputable it must be wasteful. No merit would accrue from the consumption of the bare necessaries of life, except by comparison with the abjectly poor who fall short even of the subsistence minimum; and no standard of expenditure could result from such a comparison, except the most prosaic and unattractive level of decency. A standard of life would still be possible which should admit of invidious comparison in other respects than that of opulence; as, for instance, a comparison in various directions in the manifestation of moral, physical, intellectual, or æsthetic force. Comparison in all these directions is in vogue to-day; and the comparison made in these respects is commonly so inextricably bound up with the pecuniary comparison as to be scarcely distinguishable from the latter. This is especially true as regards the current rating of expressions of intellectual and æsthetic force or proficiency; so that we frequently interpret as æsthetic or intellectual a difference which in substance is pecuniary only.

The use of the term "waste" is in one respect an unfortunate one. As used in the speech of everyday life the word carries an undertone of deprecation. It is here used for want of a better term that will adequately describe the same range of motives and of phenomena, and it is not to be taken in an odious sense, as implying an illegitimate expenditure of human products or of human life. In the view of economic theory the expenditure in question is no more and no less legitimate than any other expenditure. It is here called "waste" because this expenditure does not serve human life or human well-being on the whole, not because it is waste or misdirection of effort or expenditure as viewed from the standpoint of the individual consumer who chooses it. If he chooses it, that disposes of the question of its relative utility to him, as compared with other forms of consumption that would not be deprecated on account of their wastefulness. Whatever form of expenditure the consumer chooses, or whatever end he seeks in making his choice, has utility to him by virtue of his preference. As seen from the point of view of the individual consumer, the question of wastefulness does not arise within the scope of economic theory proper. The use of the word "waste" as a technical term, therefore, implies no deprecation of the motives or of the ends sought by the consumer under this canon of conspicuous waste.

But it is, on other grounds, worth noting that the term "waste" in the language of everyday life implies deprecation of what is characterised as wasteful. This common-sense implication is itself an outcropping of the instinct of workmanship. The popular reprobation of waste goes to say that in order to be at peace with himself the common man must be able to see in any and all human effort and human enjoyment an enhancement of life and well-being on the whole. In order to meet with unqualified approval, any economic fact must approve itself under the test of impersonal usefulness—usefulness as seen from the point of view of the generically human. Relative or competitive advantage of one individual in comparison with another does not satisfy the economic conscience, and therefore competitive expenditure has not the approval of this conscience.

In strict accuracy nothing should be included under the head of conspicuous waste but such expenditure as is incurred on the ground of an invidious pecuniary comparison. But in order to bring any given item or element in under this head it is not necessary that it should be recognised as waste in this sense by the person incurring the expenditure. It frequently happens that an element of the standard of living which set out with being primarily wasteful, ends with becoming, in the apprehension of the consumer, a necessary of life; and it may in this way become as indispensable as any other item of the consumer's habitual expenditure. As items which sometimes fall under this head, and are therefore available as illustrations of the manner in which this principle applies, may be cited carpets and tapestries, silver table service, waiter's services, silk hats, starched linen, many articles of jewellery and of dress. The indispensability of these things after the habit and the convention have been formed, however, has little to say in the classification of expenditures as waste or not waste in the technical meaning of the word. The test to which all expenditure must be brought in an attempt to decide that point is the question whether it serves directly to enhance human life on the whole—whether it furthers the life process taken impersonally. For this is the basis of award of the instinct of workmanship, and that instinct is the court of final appeal in any question of economic truth or adequacy. It is a question as to the award rendered by a dispassionate common sense. The question is, therefore, not whether, under the existing circumstances of individual habit and social custom, a given expenditure conduces to the particular consumer's gratification or peace of mind; but whether, aside from acquired tastes and from the canons of usage and conventional decency, its result is a net gain in comfort or in the fulness of life. Customary expenditure must be classed under the head of waste in so far as the custom on which it rests is traceable to the habit of making an invidious pecuniary comparison—in so far as it is conceived that it could not have become customary and prescriptive without the backing of this principle of pecuniary reputability or relative economic success.

It is obviously not necessary that a given object of expenditure should be exclusively wasteful in order to come in under the category of conspicuous waste. An article may be useful and wasteful both, and its utility to the consumer may be made up of use and waste in the most varying proportions. Consumable goods, and even productive goods, generally show the two elements in combination, as constituents of their utility; although, in a general way, the element of waste tends to predominate in articles of consumption, while the contrary is true of articles designed for productive use. Even in articles which appear at first glance to serve for pure ostentation only, it is always possible to detect the presence of some, at least ostensible, useful purpose; and on the other hand, even in special machinery and tools contrived for some particular industrial process, as well as in the rudest appliances of human industry, the traces of conspicuous waste, or at least of the habit of ostentation, usually become evident on a close scrutiny. It would be hazardous to assert that a useful purpose is ever absent from the utility of any article or of any service, however obviously its prime purpose and chief element is conspicuous waste; and it would be only less hazardous to assert of any primarily useful product that the element of waste is in no way concerned in its value, immediately or remotely.

IV. PECUNIARY CANONS OF TASTE

It is not only with respect to consumable goods—including domestic animals—that the canons of taste have been coloured by the canons of pecuniary reputability. Something to the like effect is to be said for beauty in persons. In order to avoid whatever may be matter of controversy, no weight will be given in this connection to such popular predilection as there may be for the dignified (leisurely) bearing and portly presence that are by vulgar tradition associated with opulence in mature men. These traits are in some measure accepted as elements of personal beauty. But there are certain elements of feminine beauty, on the other hand, which come in under this head, and which are of so concrete and specific a character as to admit of itemised appreciation. It is more or less a rule that in communities which are at the stage of economic development at which women are valued by the upper class for their service, the ideal of female beauty is a robust, large-limbed woman. The ground of appreciation is the physique, while the conformation of the face is of secondary weight only. A well-known instance of this ideal of the early predatory culture is that of the maidens of the Homeric poems.

This ideal suffers a change in the succeeding development, when, in the conventional scheme, the office of the high-class wife comes to be a vicarious leisure simply. The ideal then includes the characteristics which are supposed to result from or to go with a life of leisure consistently enforced. The ideal accepted under these circumstances may be gathered from descriptions of beautiful women by poets and writers of the chivalric times. In the conventional scheme of those days ladies of high degree were conceived to be in perpetual tutelage, and to be scrupulously exempt from all useful work. The resulting chivalric or romantic ideal of beauty takes cognisance chiefly of the face, and dwells on its delicacy, and on the delicacy of the hands and feet, the slender figure, and especially the slender waist. In the pictured representations of the women of that time, and in modern romantic imitators of the chivalric thought and feeling, the waist is attenuated to a degree that implies extreme debility. The same ideal is still extant among a considerable portion of the population of modern industrial communities; but it is to be said that it has retained its hold most tenaciously in those modern communities which are least advanced in point of economic and civil development, and which show the most considerable survivals of status and of predatory institutions. That is to say, the chivalric ideal is best preserved in those existing communities which are substantially least modern. Survivals of this lackadaisical or romantic ideal occur freely in the tastes of the well-to-do classes of Continental countries.

In modern communities which have reached the higher levels of industrial development, the upper leisure class has accumulated so great a mass of wealth as to place its women above all imputation of vulgarly productive labour. Here the status of women as vicarious consumers is beginning to lose its place in the affections of the body of the people; and as a consequence the ideal of feminine beauty is beginning to change back again from the infirmly delicate, translucent, and hazardously slender, to a woman of the archaic type that does not disown her hands and feet, nor, indeed, the other gross material facts of her person. In the course of economic development the ideal of beauty among the peoples of the Western culture has shifted from the woman of physical presence to the lady, and it is beginning to shift back again to the woman; and all in obedience to the changing conditions of pecuniary emulation. The exigencies of emulation at one time required lusty slaves; at another time they required a conspicuous performance of vicarious leisure and consequently an obvious disability; but the situation is now beginning to outgrow this last requirement, since, under the higher efficiency of modern industry, leisure in women is possible so far down the scale of reputability that it will no longer serve as a definitive mark of the highest pecuniary grade.

Apart from this general control exercised by the norm of conspicuous waste over the ideal of feminine beauty, there are one or two details which merit specific mention as showing how it may exercise an extreme constraint in detail over men's sense of beauty in women. It has already been noticed that at the stages of economic evolution at which conspicuous leisure is much regarded as a means of good repute, the ideal requires delicate and diminutive hands and feet and a slender waist. These features, together with the other, related faults of structure that commonly go with them, go to show that the person so affected is incapable of useful effort and must therefore be supported in idleness by her owner. She is useless and expensive, and she is consequently valuable as evidence of pecuniary strength. It results that at this cultural stage women take thought to alter their persons, so as to conform more nearly to the requirements of the instructed taste of the time; and under the guidance of the canon of pecuniary decency, the men find the resulting artificially induced pathological features attractive. So, for instance, the constricted waist which has had so wide and persistent a vogue in the communities of the Western culture, and so also the deformed foot of the Chinese. Both of these are mutilations of unquestioned repulsiveness to the untrained sense. It requires habituation to become reconciled to them. Yet there is no room to question their attractiveness to men into whose scheme of life they fit as honorific items sanctioned by the requirements of pecuniary reputability. They are items of pecuniary and cultural beauty which have come to do duty as elements of the ideal of womanliness.

The connection here indicated between the æsthetic value and the invidious pecuniary value of things is of course not present in the consciousness of the valuer. So far as a person, in forming a judgment of taste, takes thought and reflects that the object of beauty under consideration is wasteful and reputable, and therefore may legitimately be accounted beautiful; so far the judgment is not a *bona fide* judgment of taste and does not come up for consideration in this connection. The connection which is here insisted on between the reputability and the apprehended beauty of objects lies through the effect which the fact of reputability has upon the valuer's habits of thought. He is in the habit of forming judgments of value of various kinds—economic, moral, æsthetic, or reputable—concerning the objects with which he has to do, and his attitude of commendation towards a given object on any other ground will affect the degree of his appreciation of the object when he comes to value it for the æsthetic purpose. This is more particularly true as regards valuation on grounds so closely related to the æsthetic ground as that of reputability. The valuation for the æsthetic purpose and for the purpose of repute are not held apart as distinctly as might be. Confusion is especially apt to arise between these two kinds of valuation, because the value of objects for repute is not habitually distinguished in speech by the use of a special descriptive term. The result is that the terms in familiar use to designate categories or elements of beauty are applied to cover this unnamed element of pecuniary merit, and the corresponding confusion of ideas follows by easy consequence. The demands of reputability in this way coalesce in the popular apprehension with the demands of the sense of beauty, and beauty which is not accompanied by the accredited marks of good repute is not accepted. But the requirements of pecuniary reputability and those of beauty in the naïve sense do not in any appreciable degree coincide. The elimination from our surroundings of the pecuniarily unfit, therefore, results in a more or less thorough elimination of that considerable range of elements of beauty which do not happen to conform to the pecuniary requirement.

The underlying norms of taste are of very ancient growth, probably far antedating the advent of the pecuniary institutions that are here under discussion. Consequently, by force of the past selective adaptation of men's habits of thought, it happens that the requirements of beauty, simply, are for the most part best satisfied by inexpensive contrivances and structures which in a straightforward manner suggest both the office which they are to perform and the method of serving their end.

It may be in place to recall the modern psychological position. Beauty of form seems to be a question of facility of apperception. The proposition could perhaps safely be made broader than this. If abstraction is made from association, suggestion, and "expression," classed as elements of beauty, then beauty in any perceived object means that the mind readily unfolds its apperceptive activity in the directions which the object in question affords. But the directions in which activity readily unfolds or expresses itself are the directions to which long and close habituation has made the mind prone. So far as concerns the essential elements of beauty, this habituation is an habituation so close and long as to have induced not only a proclivity to the apperceptive form in question, but an adaptation of physiological structure and function as well. So far as the economic interest enters into the constitution of beauty, it enters as a suggestion or expression of adequacy to a purpose, a manifest and readily inferable subservience to the life process. This expression of economic facility or economic serviceability in any object—what may be called the economic beauty of the object—is best served by neat and unambiguous suggestion of its office and its efficiency for the material ends of life.

On this ground, among objects of use the simple and unadorned article is æsthetically the best. But since the pecuniary canon of reputability rejects the inexpensive in articles appropriated to individual consumption, the satisfaction of our craving for beautiful things must be sought by way of compromise. The canons of beauty must be circumvented by some contrivance which will give evidence of a reputably wasteful expenditure, at the same time that it meets the demands of our critical sense of the useful and the beautiful, or at least meets the demand of some habit which has come to do duty in place of that sense. Such an auxiliary sense of taste is the sense of novelty; and this latter is helped out in its surrogateship by the curiosity with which men view ingenious and puzzling contrivances. Hence it comes that most objects alleged to be beautiful, and doing duty as such, show considerable ingenuity of design and are calculated to puzzle the beholder—to bewilder him with irrelevant suggestions and hints of the improbable—at the same time that they give evidence of an expenditure of labour in excess of what would give them their fullest efficiency for their ostensible economic end.

This may be shown by an illustration taken from outside the range of our everyday habits and everyday contact, and so outside the range of our bias. Such are the remarkable feather mantles of Hawaii, or the well-known carved handles of the ceremonial adzes of several Polynesian islands. These are undeniably beautiful, both in the sense that they offer a pleasing composition of form, lines, and colour, and in the sense that they evince great skill and ingenuity in design and construction. At the same time the articles are manifestly ill fitted to serve any other economic purpose. But it is not always that the evolution of ingenious and puzzling contrivances under the guidance of the canon of wasted effort works out so happy a result. The result is quite as often a virtually complete suppression of all elements that would bear scrutiny as expressions of beauty, or of serviceability, and the substitution of evidences of misspent ingenuity and labour, backed by a conspicuous ineptitude; until many of the objects with which we surround ourselves in everyday life, and even many articles of everyday dress and ornament, are such as would not be tolerated except under the stress of prescriptive tradition. Illustrations of this substitution of ingenuity and expense in place of beauty and serviceability are to be seen, for instance, in domestic architecture, in domestic art or fancy work, in various articles of apparel, especially of feminine and priestly apparel.

The canon of beauty requires expression of the generic. The "novelty" due to the demands of conspicuous waste traverses this canon of beauty, in that it results in making the physiognomy of our objects of taste a congeries of idiosyncrasies; and the idiosyncrasies are, moreover, under the selective surveillance of the canon of expensiveness.

This process of selective adaptation of designs to the end of conspicuous waste, and the substitution of pecuniary beauty for æsthetic beauty, has been especially effective in the development of architecture. It would be extremely difficult to find a modern civilised residence or public building which can claim anything better than relative inoffensiveness in the eyes of any one who will dissociate the elements of beauty from those of honorific waste. The endless variety of fronts presented by the better class of tenements and apartment houses in our cities is an endless variety of architectural distress and of suggestions of expensive discomfort. Considered as objects of beauty, the dead walls of the sides and back of these structures, left untouched by the hands of the artist, are commonly the best feature of the building.

What has been said of the influence of the law of conspicuous waste upon the canons of taste will hold true, with but a slight change of terms, of its influence upon our notions of the serviceability of goods for other ends than the æsthetic one. Goods are produced and consumed as a means to the fuller unfolding of human life; and their utility consists, in the first instance, in their efficiency as means to this end. The end is, in the first instance, the fulness of life of the individual, taken in absolute terms. But the human proclivity to emulation has seized upon the consumption of goods as a means to an invidious comparison, and has thereby invested consumable goods with a secondary utility as evidence of relative ability to pay. This indirect or secondary use of consumable goods lends an honorific character to consumption, and presently also to the goods which best serve this emulative end of consumption. The consumption of expensive goods is meritorious, and the goods which contain an appreciable element of cost in excess of what goes to give them serviceability for their ostensible mechanical purpose are honorific. The marks of superfluous costliness in the goods are therefore marks of worth —of high efficiency for the indirect, invidious end to be served by their consumption; and conversely, goods are humilific, and therefore unattractive, if they show too thrifty an adaptation to the mechanical end sought and do not include a margin of expensiveness on which to rest a complacent invidious comparison. This indirect utility gives much of their value to the "better" grades of goods. In order to appeal to the cultivated sense of utility, an article must contain a modicum of this indirect utility.

While men may have set out with disapproving an inexpensive manner of living because it indicated inability to spend much, and so indicated a lack of pecuniary success, they end by falling into the habit of disapproving cheap things as being intrinsically dishonourable or unworthy because they are cheap. As time has gone on, each succeeding generation has received this tradition of meritorious expenditure from the generation before it, and has in its turn further elaborated and fortified the traditional canon of pecuniary reputability in goods consumed; until we have finally reached such a degree of conviction as to the unworthiness of all inexpensive things, that we have no longer any misgivings in formulating the maxim, "Cheap and nasty." So thoroughly has this habit of approving the expensive and disapproving the inexpensive been ingrained into our thinking that we instinctively insist upon at least some measure of wasteful expensiveness in all our consumption, even in the case of goods which are consumed in strict privacy and without the slightest thought of display. We all feel, sincerely and without misgiving, that we are the more lifted up in spirit for having, even in the privacy of our own household, eaten our daily meal by the help of hand-wrought silver utensils, from hand-painted china (often of dubious artistic value) laid on high-priced table linen. Any retrogression from the standard of living which we are accustomed to regard as worthy in this respect is felt to be a grievous violation of our human dignity. So, also, for the last dozen years candles have been a more pleasing source of light at dinner than any other. Candle-light is now softer, less distressing to well-bred eyes, than oil, gas, or electric light. The same could not have been said thirty years ago, when candles were, or recently had been, the cheapest available light for domestic use. Nor are candles even now found to give an acceptable or effective light for any other than a ceremonial illumination.

A political sage still living has summed up the conclusion of this whole matter in the dictum: "A cheap coat makes a cheap man," and there is probably no one who does not feel the convincing force of the maxim.

V. THE HIGHER LEARNING AS AN EXPRESSION OF THE PECUNIARY CULTURE

In the school life of today, learned ritual is in a general way best at home in schools whose chief end is the cultivation of the "humanities." This correlation is shown, perhaps more neatly than anywhere else, in the life-history of the American colleges and universities of recent growth. There may be many exceptions from the rule, especially among those schools which have been founded by the typically reputable and ritualistic churches, and which, therefore, started on the conservative and classical plane or reached the classical position by a short cut; but the general rule as regards the colleges found in the newer American communities during the present century has been that so long as the community has remained poor, and so long as the constituency from which the colleges have drawn their pupils has been dominated by habits of industry and thrift, so long the reminiscences of the medicine-man have found but a scant and precarious acceptance in the scheme of college life. But so soon as wealth begins appreciably to accumulate in the community, and so soon as a given school begins to lean on a leisure-class constituency, there comes also a perceptibly increased insistence on scholastic ritual and on conformity to the ancient forms as regards vestments and social and scholastic solemnities. So, for instance, there has been an approximate coincidence between the growth of wealth among the constituency which supports any given college of the Middle West and the date of acceptance

—first into tolerance and then into imperative vogue—of evening dress for men and of the décolleté for women, as the scholarly vestments proper to occasions of learned solemnity or to the seasons of social amenity within the college circle. Apart from the mechanical difficulty of so large a task, it would scarcely be a difficult matter to trace this correlation. The like is true of the vogue of the cap and gown.

Cap and gown have been adopted as learned insignia by many colleges of this section within the last few years; and it is safe to say that this could scarcely have occurred at a much earlier date, or until there had grown up a leisure-class sentiment of sufficient volume in the community to support a strong movement of reversion towards an archaic view as to the legitimate end of education. This particular item of learned ritual, it may be noted, would not only commend itself to the leisure-class sense of the fitness of things, as appealing to the archaic propensity for spectacular effect and the predilection for antique symbolism; but it at the same time fits into the leisure-class scheme of life as involving a notable element of conspicuous waste. The precise date at which the reversion to cap and gown took place, as well as the fact that it affected so large a number of schools at about the same time, seems to have been due in some measure to a wave of atavistic sense of conformity and reputability that passed over the community at that period.

It may not be entirely beside the point to note that in point of time this curious reversion seems to coincide with the culmination of a certain vogue of atavistic sentiment and tradition in other directions also. The wave of reversion seems to have received its initial impulse in the psychologically disintegrating effects of the Civil War. Habituation to war entails a body of predatory habits of thought, whereby clannishness in some measure replaces the sense of solidarity, and a sense of invidious distinction supplants the impulse to equitable, everyday serviceability. As an outcome of the cumulative action of these factors, the generation which follows a season of war is apt to witness a rehabilitation of the element of status, both in its social life and in its scheme of devout observances and other symbolic or ceremonial forms. Throughout the eighties, and less plainly traceable through the seventies also, there was perceptible a gradually advancing wave of sentiment favouring quasi-predatory business habits, insistence on status, anthropomorphism, and conservatism generally. The more direct and unmediated of these expressions of the barbarian temperament, such as the recrudescence of outlawry and the spectacular quasi-predatory careers of fraud run by certain "captains of industry," came to a head earlier and were appreciably on the decline by the close of the seventies. The recrudescence of anthropomorphic sentiment also seems to have passed its most acute stage before the close of the eighties. But the learned ritual and paraphernalia here spoken of are a still remoter and more recondite expression of the barbarian animistic sense; and these, therefore, gained vogue and elaboration more slowly and reached their most effective development at a still later date. There is reason to believe that the culmination is now already past. Except for the new impetus given by a new war experience, and except for the support which the growth of a wealthy class affords to all ritual, and especially to whatever ceremonial is wasteful and pointedly suggests gradations of status, it is probable that the late improvements and augmentation of scholastic insignia and ceremonial would gradually decline. But while it may be true that the cap and gown, and the more strenuous observance of scholastic proprieties which came with them, were floated in on this post-bellum tidal wave of reversion to barbarism, it is also no doubt true that such a ritualistic reversion could not have been effected in the college scheme of life until the accumulation of wealth in the hands of a propertied class had gone far enough to afford the requisite pecuniary ground for a movement which should bring the colleges of the country up to the leisure-class requirements in the higher learning. The adoption of the cap and gown is one of the striking atavistic features of modern college life, and at the same time it marks the fact that these colleges have definitely become leisure-class establishments, either in actual achievement or in aspiration.

As further evidence of the close relation between the educational system and the cultural standards of the community, it may be remarked that there is some tendency latterly to substitute the captain of industry in place of the priest, as the head of seminaries of the higher learning. The substitution is by no means complete or unequivocal. Those heads of institutions are best accepted who combine the sacerdotal office with a high degree of pecuniary efficiency. There is a similar but less pronounced tendency to intrust the work of instruction in the higher learning to men of some pecuniary qualification. Administrative ability and skill in advertising the enterprise count for rather more than they once did, as qualifications for the work of teaching. This applies especially in those sciences that have most to do with the everyday facts of life, and it is particularly true of schools in the economically single-minded communities. This partial substitution of pecuniary for sacerdotal efficiency is a concomitant of the modern transition from conspicuous leisure to conspicuous consumption, as the chief means of reputability. The correlation of the two facts is probably clear without further elaboration.

The attitude of the schools and of the learned class towards the education of women serves to show in what manner and to what extent learning has departed from its ancient station of priestly and leisure-class prerogative, and it indicates also what approach has been made by the truly learned to the modern, economic or industrial, matter-of-fact standpoint. The higher schools and the learned professions were until recently tabu to the women. These establishments were from the outset, and have in great measure continued to be, devoted to the education of the priestly and leisure classes.

The women, as has been shown elsewhere, were the original subservient class, and to some extent, especially so far as regards their nominal or ceremonial position, they have remained in that relation down to the present. There has prevailed a strong sense that the admission of women to the privileges of the higher learning (as to the Eleusinian mysteries) would be derogatory to the dignity of the learned craft. It is therefore only very recently, and almost solely in the industrially most advanced communities, that the higher grades of schools have been freely opened to women. And even under the urgent circumstances prevailing in the modern industrial communities, the highest and most reputable universities show an extreme reluctance in making the move. The sense of class worthiness, that is to say of status, of an honorific differentiation of the sexes according to a distinction between superior and inferior intellectual dignity, survives in a vigorous form in these corporations of the aristocracy of learning. It is felt that the women should, in all propriety, acquire only such knowledge as may be classed under one or the other of two heads: (1) such knowledge as conduces immediately to a better performance of domestic service—the domestic sphere; (2) such accomplishments and dexterity, quasi-scholarly and quasi-artistic, as plainly come in under the head of a performance of vicarious leisure. Knowledge is felt to be unfeminine if it is knowledge which expresses the unfolding of the learner's own life, the acquisition of which proceeds on the learner's own cognitive interest, without prompting from the canons of propriety, and without reference back to a master whose comfort or good repute is to be enhanced by the employment or the exhibition of it. So, also, all knowledge which is useful as evidence of leisure, other than vicarious leisure, is scarcely feminine.

For an appreciation of the relation which these higher seminaries of learning bear to the economic life of the community, the phenomena which have been reviewed are of importance rather as indications of a general attitude than as being in themselves facts of first-rate economic consequence. They go to show what is the instinctive attitude and animus of the learned class towards the life process of an industrial community. They serve as an exponent of the stage of development, for the industrial purpose, attained by the higher learning and by the learned class, and so they afford an indication as to what may fairly be looked for from this class at points where the learning and the life of the class bear more immediately upon the economic life and efficiency of the community, and upon the adjustment of its scheme of life to the requirements of the time. What these ritualistic survivals go to indicate is a prevalence of conservatism, if not of reactionary sentiment, especially among the higher schools where the conventional learning is cultivated.

To these indications of a conservative attitude is to be added another characteristic which goes in the same direction, but which is a symptom of graver consequence than this playful inclination to trivialities of form and ritual. By far the greater number of American colleges and universities, for instance, are affiliated to some religious denomination and are somewhat given to devout observances. Their putative familiarity with scientific methods and the scientific point of view should presumably exempt the faculties of these schools from animistic habits of thought; but there is still a considerable proportion of them who profess an attachment to the anthropomorphic beliefs and observances of an earlier culture. These professions of devotional zeal are, no doubt, to a good extent expedient and perfunctory, both on the part of the schools in their corporate capacity, and on the part of the individual members of the corps of instructors; but it can not be doubted that there is after all a very appreciable element of anthropomorphic sentiment present in the higher schools. So far as this is the case it must be set down as the expression of an archaic, animistic habit of mind. This habit of mind must necessarily assert itself to some extent in the instruction offered, and to this extent its influence in shaping the habits of thought of the student makes for conservatism and reversion; it acts to hinder his development in the direction of matter-of-fact knowledge, such as best serves the ends of industry.

The college sports, which have so great a vogue in the reputable seminaries of learning today, tend in a similar direction; and, indeed, sports have much in common with the devout attitude of the colleges, both as regards their psychological basis and as regards their disciplinary effect. But this expression of the barbarian temperament is to be credited primarily to the body of students, rather than to the temper of the schools as such; except in so far as the colleges or the college officials—as sometimes happens—actively countenance and foster the growth of sports. The like is true of college fraternities as of college sports, but with a difference. The latter are chiefly an expression of the predatory impulse simply; the former are more specifically an expression of that heritage of clannishness which is so large a feature in the temperament of the predatory barbarian. It is also noticeable that a close relation subsists between the fraternities and the sporting activity of the schools.

But all these features of the scheme of life of the learned class, and of the establishments dedicated to the conservation of the higher learning, are in a great measure incidental only. They are scarcely to be accounted organic elements of the professed work of research and instruction for the ostensible pursuit of which the schools exist. But these symptomatic indications go to establish a presumption as to the character of the work performed—as seen from the economic point of view—and as to the bent which the serious work carried on under their auspices gives to the youth who resort to the schools. The presumption raised by the considerations already offered is that in their work also, as well as in their ceremonial, the higher schools may be expected to take a conservative position; but this presumption must be checked by a comparison of the economic character of the work actually performed, and by something of a survey of the learning whose conservation is intrusted to the higher schools. On this head, it is well known that the accredited seminaries of learning have, until a recent date, held a conservative position. They have taken an attitude of deprecation towards all innovations. As a general rule a new point of view or a new formulation of knowledge have been countenanced and taken up within the schools only after these new things have made their way outside of the schools. As exceptions from this rule are chiefly to be mentioned innovations of an inconspicuous kind and departures which do not bear in any tangible way upon the conventional point of view or upon the conventional scheme of life; as, for instance, details of fact in the mathematico-physical sciences, and new readings and interpretations of the classics, especially such as have a philological or literary bearing only. Except within the domain of the "humanities," in the narrow sense, and except so far as the traditional point of view of the humanities has been left intact by the innovators, it has generally held true that the accredited learned class and the seminaries of the higher learning have looked askance at all innovation. New views, new departures in scientific theory, especially new departures which touch the theory of human relations at any point, have found a place in the scheme of the university tardily and by a reluctant tolerance, rather than by a cordial welcome; and the men who have occupied themselves with such efforts to widen the scope of human knowledge have not commonly been well received by their learned contemporaries. The higher schools have not commonly given their countenance to a serious advance in the methods or the content of knowledge until the innovations have outlived their youth and much of their usefulness—after they have become commonplaces of the intellectual furniture of a new generation which has grown up under, and has had its habits of thought shaped by, the new, extra-scholastic body of knowledge and the new standpoint. This is true of the recent past. How far it may be true of the immediate present it would be hazardous to say, for it is impossible to see present-day facts in such perspective as to get a fair conception of their relative proportions.

So far, nothing has been said of the Mæcenas function of the well-to-do, which is habitually dwelt on at some length by writers and speakers who treat of the development of culture and of social structure. This leisure-class function is not without an important bearing on the higher learning and on the spread of knowledge and culture. The manner and the degree in which the class furthers learning through patronage of this kind is sufficiently familiar. It has been frequently presented in affectionate and effective terms by spokesmen whose familiarity with the topic fits them to bring home to their hearers the profound significance of this cultural factor. These spokesmen, however, have presented the matter from the point of view of the cultural interest, or of the interest of reputability, rather than from that of the economic interest. As apprehended from the economic point of view, and valued for the purpose of industrial serviceability, this function of the well-to-do, as well as the intellectual attitude of members of the well-to-do class, merits some attention and will bear illustration.

By way of characterisation of the Mæcenas relation, it is to be noted that, considered externally, as an economic or industrial relation simply, it is a relation of status. The scholar under patronage performs the duties of a learned life vicariously for his patron, to whom a certain repute inures after the manner of the good repute imputed to a master for whom any form of vicarious leisure is performed. It is also to be noted that, in point of historical fact, the furtherance of learning or the maintenance of scholarly activity through the Mæcenas relation has most commonly been a furtherance of proficiency in classical lore or in the humanities. This knowledge tends to lower rather than to heighten the industrial efficiency of the community.

Further, as regards the direct participation of the members of the leisure class in the furtherance of knowledge. The canons of reputable living act to throw such intellectual interest as seeks expression among the class on the side of classical and formal erudition, rather than on the side of the sciences that bear some relation to the community's industrial life. The most frequent excursions into other than classical fields of knowledge on the part of members of the leisure class are made into the discipline of law and of the political, and more especially the administrative, sciences. These so-called sciences are substantially bodies of maxims of expediency for guidance in the leisure-class office of government, as conducted on a proprietary basis. The interest with which this discipline is approached is therefore not commonly the intellectual or cognitive interest simply. It is largely the practical interest of the exigencies of that relation of mastery in which the members of the class are placed. In point of derivation, the office of government is a predatory function, pertaining integrally to the archaic leisure-class scheme of life. It is an exercise of control and coercion over the population from which the class draws its sustenance. This discipline, as well as the incidents of practice which give it its content, therefore has some attraction for the class apart from all questions of cognition.

All this holds true wherever and so long as the governmental office continues, in form or in substance, to be a proprietary office; and it holds true beyond that limit, in so far as the tradition of the more archaic phase of governmental evolution has lasted on into the later life of those modern communities for whom proprietary government by a leisure class is now beginning to pass away.

For that field of learning within which the cognitive or intellectual interest is dominant—the sciences properly so called—the case is somewhat different, not only as regards the attitude of the leisure class, but as regards the whole drift of the pecuniary culture. Knowledge for its own sake, the exercise of the faculty of comprehension without ulterior purpose, should, it might be expected, be sought by men whom no urgent material interest diverts from such a quest. The sheltered industrial position of the leisure class should give free play to the cognitive interest in members of this class, and we should consequently have, as many writers confidently find that we do have, a very large proportion of scholars, scientists, savants derived from this class and deriving their incentive to scientific investigation and speculation from the discipline of a life of leisure. Some such result is to be looked for, but there are features of the leisure-class scheme of life, already sufficiently dwelt upon, which go to divert the intellectual interest of this class to other subjects than that causal sequence in phenomena which makes the content of the sciences. The habits of thought which characterise the life of the class run on the personal relation of dominance, and on the derivative, invidious concepts of honour, worth, merit, character, and the like. The causal sequence which makes up the subject matter of science is not visible from this point of view. Neither does good repute attach to knowledge of facts that are vulgarly useful. Hence it should appear probable that the interest of the invidious comparison with respect to pecuniary or other honorific merit should occupy the attention of the leisure class, to the neglect of the cognitive interest. Where this latter interest asserts itself it should commonly be diverted to fields of speculation or investigation which are reputable and futile, rather than to the quest of scientific knowledge. Such indeed has been the history of priestly and leisure-class learning so long as no considerable body of systematised knowledge had been intruded into the scholastic discipline from an extra-scholastic source. But since the relation of mastery and subservience is ceasing to be the dominant and formative factor in the community's life process, other features of the life process and other points of view are forcing themselves upon the scholars.